AUSPICIOUS VISION

EDWARD WALES ROOT AND AMERICAN MODERNISM

Edward Wales Root
Ca. 1940
Photograph by Richard Carver Wood (1902–89)
Collection of John B. Root

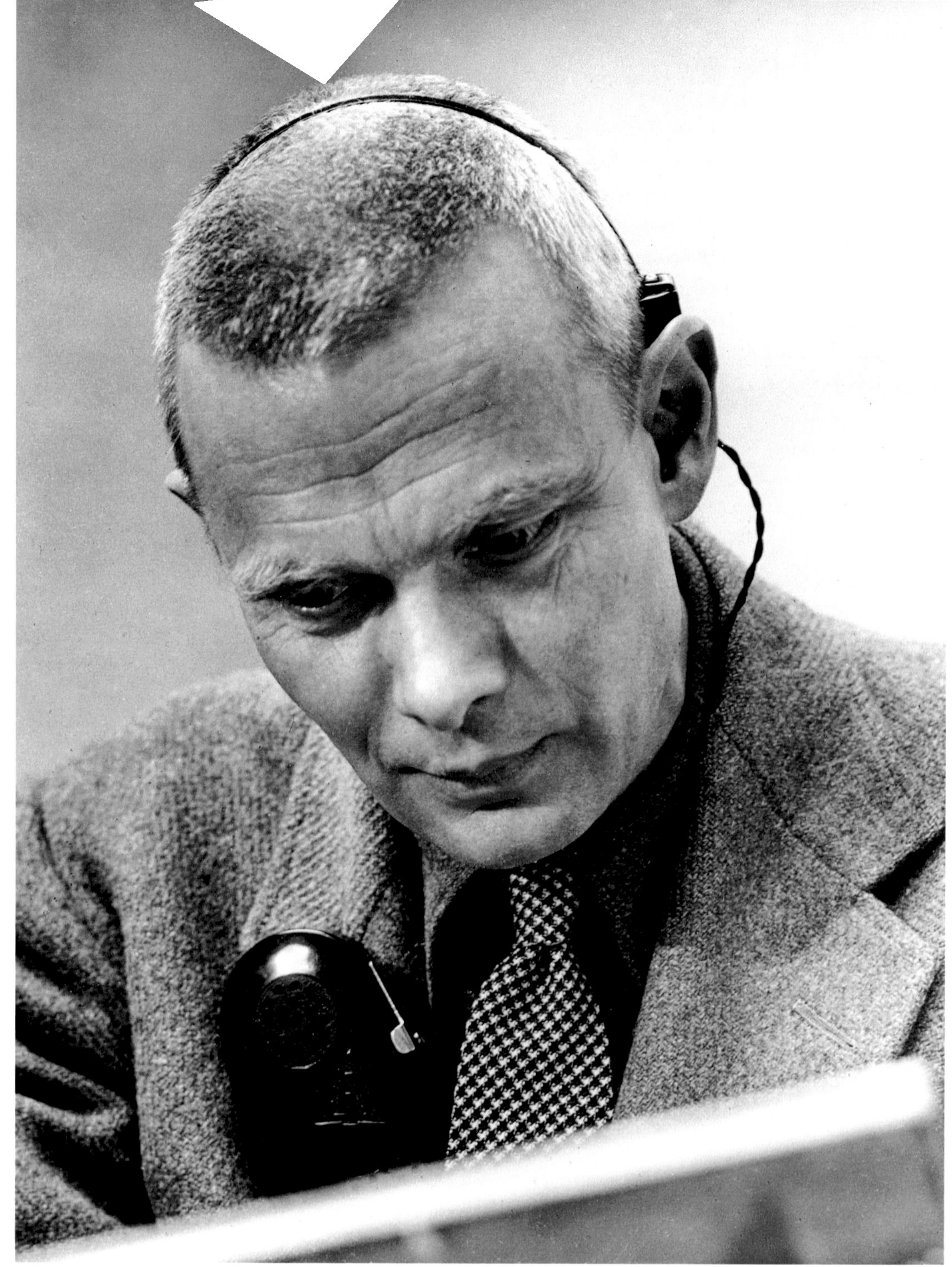

"He was essentially a shy man. This may be due, in part, to his disability. And certainly he was not one to show his accomplishments or erudition, of which he had a great deal. He was a bit of a—I don't want to say Renaissance man—but he did all sorts of things and did them well. He played golf, he knew good wines from bad ones, he had an interest in sports, and he was a good fly fisherman. He did a lot of different things and whatever he did he did well. I think he hid his light under a bushel; he tended to do that. And I think that permeated, to a certain extent, his collecting. He didn't make a big fuss out of it, what he acquired, or what he intended to do with what he had acquired."

—John B. Root, 2007

33 West

Dear Mr. Root

Your favor was

this morning. If you will

make the check payable to

Rockwell Kent - 16 E. 33

I am very glad you like the

and hope you may get a co

renewing pleasure from it.

Faithfully

Arthur B.

Mch. 29th 1911

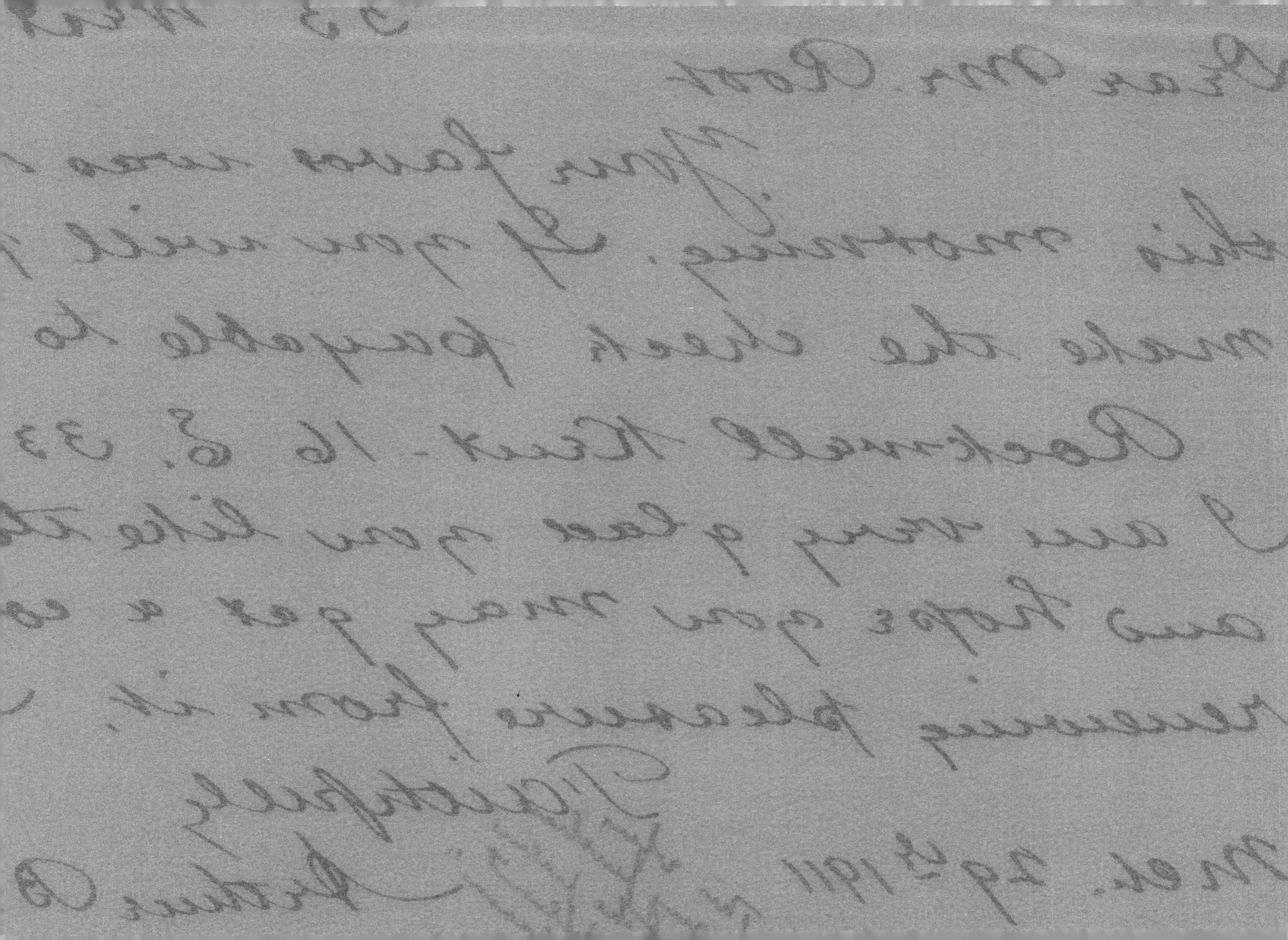

33 W[...]

Dear Mr. Root

Your favor was r[...]
this morning. If you will [...]
make the check payable to
Rockwell Kent - 16 E. 33
I am very glad you like th[...]
and hope you may get a [...]
[...]ing pleasure from it.

Faithfully
Arthur [...]

Mch. 29th 1911

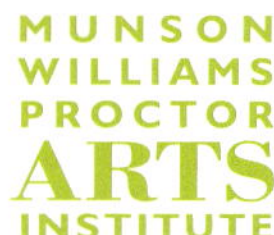

AUSPICIOUS VISION

EDWARD WALES ROOT AND AMERICAN MODERNISM

Mary E. Murray
Curator of Modern and Contemporary Art
Paul D. Schweizer
Director and Chief Curator
Michael D. Somple
Curatorial Research Assistant

With a contribution by Suzanne Smeaton *and* Lisa Koenigsberg

John Bigelow Taylor and Dianne Dubler
Principal Photographers

Auspicious Vision: Edward Wales Root and American Modernism is published in conjunction with the exhibition of the same title, held in Utica, N.Y., from October 14, 2007 through February 24, 2008, to honor the fiftieth anniversary of Edward Wales Root's (1884–1956) bequest of 227 modern American paintings and drawings to the Munson-Williams-Proctor Arts Institute.

The lead corporate sponsor for the exhibition, its accompanying catalog, and related educational programs is M&T Bank. Financial support was also provided by The Community Foundation of Herkimer and Oneida Counties, Inc.; the New York State Council on the Arts; the New York Council for the Humanities, a state affiliate of the National Endowment for the Humanities; the F. X. Matt II Memorial Fund, a donor advised fund of The Community Foundation of Herkimer and Oneida Counties, Inc.; The Observer-Dispatch; and Brodock Press. Additional financial support was provided by an endowment established at the Munson-Williams-Proctor Arts Institute by David E. and Jane B. Sayre Bryant.

The Henry Luce Foundation provided funding for the conservation of artworks in the Root bequest.

General program support for the Museum of Art is made possible by public funds from the New York State Council on the Arts, a state agency.

National Tour Sponsor **MetLife Foundation**

Murray, Mary E.
Auspicious Vision: Edward Wales Root and American Modernism /
Mary E.Murray, Paul D. Schweizer, Michael D. Somple;
with a contribution by Suzanne Smeaton and Lisa Koenigsberg;
John Bigelow Taylor and Dianne Dubler, principal photographers.
p. cm.
Published in conjunction with an exhibition held at the
Munson-Williams-Proctor Arts Institute, Utica, N.Y., Oct. 14, 2007–Feb. 24, 2008.
Includes bibliographical references and index.
Summary: "50th-anniversary commemoration of Edward Wales Root's bequest in late 1956 of 227 modern American paintings and drawings to the Munson-Williams-Proctor Arts Institute's Museum of Art"—Provided by publisher.

ISBN 978-0-915895-34-2 (softcover: alk. paper)

1. Art, American—20th century—Exhibitions.
2. Root, Edward Wales, d. 1956—Art collections—Exhibitions.
3. Art—New York (State)—Utica—Exhibitions.
4. Munson-Williams-Proctor Arts Institute. Museum of Art—Exhibitions.
I. Schweizer, Paul D. II. Somple, Michael D., 1975–
III. Munson-Williams-Proctor Arts Institute. IV. Title.

N6512.M7857 2008
709.7309'04–dc22

2008028800

Munson-Williams-Proctor Arts Institute
310 Genesee Street
Utica, NY 13502
315-797-0000
www.mwpai.org

Printed in the United States of America.

Design: Marty Blake Graphic Design, Jamesville, New York
Production: Michele Murphy, MWPAI Publications Manager
Printing: Brodock Press, Utica, New York
Editor: Ellen B. Damsky

TABLE OF CONTENTS

DEDICATED TO THE MEMORY OF

Edward Wales Root

(1884–1956)

Collector, Benefactor, Educator, and

Friend of American Artists

Consultant in Art, 1949–56

Munson-Williams-Proctor Institute

DIRECTOR'S FOREWORD

Twenty years ago the Museum began an ambitious plan to generate knowledge about its renowned permanent collection, and to make that information available to a wide audience by publishing scholarly catalogs of its American and European paintings, drawings, furniture, timepieces, and ceramics. This volume, the eighth in that ongoing series, accompanied the exhibition, *Auspicious Vision: Edward Wales Root and American Modernism*, a 50th-anniversary commemoration of Edward Wales Root's bequest in late 1956 of 227 modern American paintings and drawings to the Munson-Williams-Proctor Arts Institute's Museum of Art.

Root, a pioneering collector of American modernism, is one of the Institute's greatest benefactors. During the first five decades of the twentieth century he assembled a large collection of works by American artists who were his contemporaries. In 1953, The Metropolitan Museum of Art in New York City honored him with an exhibition, the first time a private collection of modern American art was ever shown at that institution. "For the successful creation of a contemporary art collection," the Metropolitan's curator, Robert B. Hale, wrote, "the stars must be most auspicious."

Although Root was enthusiastic about what he described as the "rather strange developments" of European vanguard art, and even advised the Museum when it assembled a collection of modern European paintings and sculpture in the 1950s, he believed it was his patriotic duty to collect the works of American artists. Root did so with great insight for nearly fifty years. The quality, chronological scope, and number of different artists whose works he collected is impressive: beautiful and historically important works by the progressive and avant-garde painters who embraced modernist tendencies in the first decades of the twentieth century, key pictures by a number of the most prominent "American scene" artists of the 1930s, and a canonical group of works by the abstract artists who emerged in the 1940s and early 1950s.

Root's 1956 bequest was, in its time, one of the most important donations of modern American art to a public institution. It was described in the *New York Times* as "one of the largest treasure-troves of American paintings in private hands." His gift helped forge the identity of the Museum, then only beginning its third decade as a public institution. It also influenced its subsequent collecting activity and exhibition program. The expectation that Root would donate most of his American modernist pictures to the Museum also influenced the decision the Institute's Board of Trustees made before Root died to commission Philip Johnson to design his first art museum building, which opened to international acclaim in 1960.

It is fitting that *Auspicious Vision* opened to the public on the same mid-October weekend that, in 1960, marked the Institute's dedication of Johnson's building, which provided sufficient gallery space to show Root's entire bequest. When the collection was exhibited for the first time in the winter of 1961–62, the Museum published a checklist of all the pictures in the bequest. Around that time, the Museum's staff began a scholarly catalog of Root's collection. This project doubled in size and complexity in the early 1970s after Root's widow donated her husband's large trove of personal papers to the Museum. This led to a decision that the catalog the Museum was planning to publish would be paired with a biography that treated Root in more detail than the nine-page profile Aline B. Saarinen published in *The Proud Possessors* in 1958 which, though brief, has the merits of being written by someone who knew Root personally. Both the catalog and biography languished until 2001 when, with the 50th anniversary of Root's bequest approaching, the Institute's Board of Trustees endorsed my recommendation to exhibit Root's entire bequest a second time for a new generation of museumgoers. It was also decided that the publication accompanying this exhibition would include the long-awaited catalogue raisonné of Root's bequest, and an art-historical assessment of Root's role as a pioneering collector of modern American art.

The massive amount of research needed to compile definitive catalog entries for the 227 pictures in Root's bequest was facilitated by the information that was gathered, beginning in the mid 1960s, by the Museum's de facto first curator of modern art, Joseph S. Trovato, and his wife, Ruth Osgood Trovato. Their long acquaintance with Root gave them insights and information that otherwise might have been lost. Although Joe and Ruth Trovato are now deceased, it is gratifying to imagine how pleased they would be to know their groundbreaking effort has finally seen the light of day in this catalog.

Shortly after the Museum recommitted itself to this project, Mary E. Murray, Curator of Modern and Contemporary Art, and the team of assistants she supervised, undertook the Herculean task of researching and compiling all the relevant bibliographic and exhibition citations that accumulated over the past several decades about the works by the eighty artists in the bequest, which range in date from a 1896–97 watercolor by Louis M. Eilshemius to a ca. 1955 drawing by Saul Steinberg. The length of many of these citations is eloquent proof of the continued relevance of Root's pictures for generations of scholars and museumgoers.

Even the most cursory review of the information that Ms. Murray and her team of assistants assembled in the pages of this catalog reveals insights about Root's aesthetic preferences, his picture-buying habits, and the pioneering role he played as a patron of American modernism. For example, sixty percent of the works are figurative images, the rest are abstractions. Root was very active as a collector in the late 1920s and early 1930s and then, again, during the period of the Second World War. He purchased nearly half of the 227 pictures within one or two years of being made, a practice that reveals how confident he was acquiring the newest American art. More than fifty percent of the pictures in his bequest were executed within a fifteen-year period of time between 1940 and 1955. About half the pictures are drawings and watercolors. However, he did not spend as much money on art as two other collectors with whom he is often compared, his friend, Duncan Phillips of Washington, D.C., and Ferdinand Howald of Columbus, Ohio. Did Root's more limited financial resources, and the domestic setting in Clinton, N.Y., where he housed and displayed his collection, predispose him to collect small and medium sized works on paper or, as some of his writings suggest, did he have a special fondness for drawings because of the insights they provide about the creative process?

The catalog also shows that, although Root purchased works from many of New York City's leading commercial art galleries, fully twenty percent of his bequest was acquired from the Frank K. M. Rehn Galleries over a period of slightly more than two decades. He purchased nearly all twenty-one of his watercolors by Charles E. Burchfield from this gallery. This beautiful group of pictures—the largest number of works by any artist in the bequest—combined with the sixteen pictures by Theodoros Stamos, and the fifteen by George B. Luks, represent nearly one-quarter of Root's entire gift and gives the collection much of its distinct character. However, it also contains pictures by other artists who were popular during Root's lifetime, such as John Wesley Carroll, Peppino Mangravite, and Henry Varnum Poor, but who are largely forgotten today. Who can say whether they will return to favor in the future? In a similar vein, one cannot help but wonder what prevented Root from acquiring works by other artists who were critically acclaimed during his lifetime, such as, for example, William Glackens, Georgia O'Keeffe, Jacob Lawrence, or Hans Hofmann. Is it fair to assume that artists who are not represented in Root's bequest did not conform to his modernist agenda, or were there personal or commercial reasons why he did not collect their works? At the time of Root's death late in 1956 the Abstract Expressionist artists whose works he collected had achieved international fame. If he had lived several years longer, would his enthusiasm for the latest developments in contemporary American art have led him to collect the work of, say, Jasper Johns or Andy Warhol?

All museum projects of this size and complexity depend for their success on the vision and dedication of talented colleagues. In this instance, the Institute is deeply indebted to Mary E. Murray, whose enthusiasm for Edward Root has influenced every aspect of this project: the comprehensiveness and accuracy of the catalogue raisonné, her brilliantly conceived thematic installation of Root's pictures, and her articulate advocacy of Root's role as an important patron of modern American art.

Another member of the Museum's "Root group" who made a substantial contribution to this project was Michael D. Somple, Curatorial Research Assistant. His unflagging energy and rapidly acquired knowledge of Root's extensive archive of unpublished and published materials at the Museum and Hamilton College made him an indispensable part of the research effort leading to this publication. Mr. Somple also organized the related exhibition, *Branches of Root's Bequest:*

Edward Wales Root's Other Gifts, which featured additional American and European artworks Root donated to the Museum during his lifetime, or were given by or purchased from Root's wife after his death.

It was a collaborator's dream for me to work with Mary Murray and Michael Somple on the introductory essay in this catalog, which draws liberally on Root's archival resources and examines, in detail for the first time, Root's fifty-year involvement with contemporary American art. The essay also discusses Root's aesthetic point of view, and the impact he had on the Museum during its first twenty years as a public institution, a seminal period about which first-hand recollections are no longer available. The essay that guest authors Suzanne Smeaton and Lisa Koenigsberg wrote about the frames in Root's bequest provides groundbreaking insights about modern American framing practice. Because the pictures in his bequest were never reframed by the Museum, Root's collection reflects the constellation of framing options that were in force when he assembled it.

Our institutional collaborator in this 50th-anniversary tribute to Root was the Emerson Gallery at Hamilton College, where he taught art appreciation from 1920 until 1940. Root's object-based approach to art education, his efforts to promote American art, and his activities as a naturalist were the focus of the collateral exhibition, *The Best Kind of Life: Edward W. Root as Teacher, Collector, and Naturalist*, which was organized by Susanna White of Hamilton College's Emerson Gallery. Nine of the artworks Root bequeathed to the Museum were included in the Emerson Gallery's exhibition.

Despite the significance of Root's achievement as a pioneering patron of early American modernism, his name is inexplicably missing from several important recent studies of modern American patronage. I anticipate that this catalog and its accompanying exhibition will help restore Root to his rightful place in this history by putting into intellectual circulation a wealth of information about his achievement as one of the most important collectors of early American modernism. I hope, as well, that it will encourage other scholars to undertake research on Root and his collection, using the archival resources cited throughout this catalog.

In 2001, to commemorate Root's generosity and service to the Munson-Williams-Proctor Arts Institute, the Board of Trustees designated the Museum's largest and most elegant gallery the Edward Wales Root Sculpture Court. With this landmark exhibition and catalog, the happy result of countless hours of dedicated work by numerous individuals, the Museum again honors, with gratitude and pride, the memory of this extraordinary individual who, for nearly fifty years, supported the newest trends in American art.

I would like to express in closing my profound gratitude to the corporate, public, and private sponsors who provided the unprecedented level of financial assistance that enabled the Museum to celebrate and document the taste and generosity of a man whose collection, the tangible record of a keen and inquisitive mind, vividly demonstrates Root's lifelong belief in the life-affirming power of an original work of art which, as he noted, expresses visual facts that have emotional significance. This is Root's greatest gift to the central New York State community where he lived, collected, and championed the cause of modern American art, and the message his collection will bring to other communities when a group of his pictures are exhibited during the next several years at other museums in the United States.

—Paul D. Schweizer, Ph.D.
Director and Chief Curator

ACKNOWLEDGMENTS

Mary E. Murray, Paul D. Schweizer, and Michael D. Somple would like thank the following persons for their generous contributions to *Auspicious Vision: Edward Wales Root and American Modernism*: John B. Root, for his unfailing grace in sharing recollections about his father and mother and their art collecting; Milton Bloch, Munson-Williams-Proctor Arts Institute President; Rayna Schneider, Administrative Assistant to the Director, Museum of Art; Marty Blake, designer; Michele Murphy, Publications Manager; editor Ellen B. Damsky; guest authors Suzanne Smeaton and Lisa Konigsberg; and Susanna White, Associate Director, Emerson Gallery, Hamilton College, who has created the complementary exhibition and catalog, *The Best Kind of Life: Edward W. Root as Teacher, Collector, and Naturalist*.

At the Munson-Williams-Proctor Arts Institute we have been supported by numerous colleagues: Tara Avella, Museum Preparator; John Bach, Director of Communications and Development; Lance Bennett, Head of Engineering; Bonnie Conway, former Museum Preparator; Kathryn Corcoran, Director of Library Services; Anna T. D'Ambrosio, Museum of Art Assistant Director and Curator of Decorative Arts; Bill Doherty, Information Technology Manager and superman; Lorelei Eurto, Assistant Registrar; Meg Giannetti, School Programs and Museum Events Coordinator; Timothy Hickey, Library Assistant; Barbara Kane, Museum Educator for Public Programs; Elena Lochmatow, Exhibition Coordinator; Maggie Mazzullo, Museum Registrar; David McHarg, Publications and Website Manager; Jason Nickel, former Museum Technician; April Oswald, Director of Museum Education; Jim Quinn, Painter; Debora Ryan, former Registrar; Dariusz Sady, Museum Technician; Kathleen Salsbury, Assistant Librarian; Joe Schmidt, Public Relations Manager; Michael Schuyler, Assistant Librarian and Archivist; Tony Spiridigloizzi, Vice President and Treasurer; and Rainer Maria Werner, Museum Technician.

Thanks to Museum of Art interns and work-study students: Katerina Adair, Hamilton College intern; Samantha Beachell, Pratt at MWP work-study student; Hannah Marie Brewer, Pratt at MWP intern; Christine Caruana, University of Rochester intern; Anna Kreeger, intern; Arielle Schraeter, Hamilton College intern; and Carolyn Strobel, Mount Holyoke College intern.

We are also indebted to the staff at the Williamstown Art Conservation Center for their care of the Root collection: Thomas J. Branchick, Director and Head of Paintings Conservation; Rob Conzett, Office Manager; Michael Heslip, Conservator of Paintings; Rebecca Johnston, Conservator of Paper; Leslie Paisley, Head of Paper Conservation; Sandra L. Webber, Conservator of Paintings; and Xian Zhang, Analytical Scientist. Additional conservation services were provided by Susan S. Blakney, Conservator, and Diane Falvey, Associate Conservator, West Lake Conservators, Ltd., Skaneateles, N.Y.

We thank these colleagues for their generous assistance with this project: Nikki Barbano, Senior Assistant, Alumni Relations, Hamilton College; X. Theodore Barber, Archivist, University Library, The New School; Joel Beck, Estate of Williams Baziotes; Barbara Bertucio, Registrar, Albany Institute of History and Art; Marisa Bourgoin, Richard Manoogian Chief of Reference Services, Archives of American Art; Erin Breslin, Director of Marketing and Communications, Schenectady Museum & Suits-Bueche Planetarium; William Brice, Los Angeles; Sarah Cash, Bechhoefer Curator of American Art, Corcoran Gallery of Art; Thérèse Chen, Director of Registration, Fine Arts Museums of San Francisco; Katherine Collett, Assistant Archivist, Hamilton College; Matt Conway, Registrar, Herbert F. Johnson Museum of Art; Paul S. D'Ambrosio, Vice President and Chief Curator, New York State Historical Association and Farmers' Museum; Nora Donnelly, Senior Registrar, The Institute of Contemporary Art, Boston; Heather Farley, Collections Assistant, Everson Museum of Art; Susan C. Faxon, Associate Director and Curator, Addison Gallery of American Art; Michael Flanagan, former Registrar, Everson Museum of Art; Frances Francis, High Museum of Art; Paula Beversdorf Gabbard, Fine Arts Librarian, Avery Library, Columbia University; John Gilmore; Jane Glover, Coordinator, American Art Study Center, Legion of Honor, Fine Arts Museums of San Francisco; Larry Goodsight, Vice President, Business Media Solutions, WCNY, Syracuse; Judy Gould, Fine Arts Museums of San Francisco; Nina Gray, Independent Scholar, New York; Stamatina Gregory, Dedalus Foundation, Inc.; Jeffrey Guerrier, Manager of Library Services, Montclair Art Museum; Jayna Hanson, Intern, Archives of American Art; Lucy Harper, Librarian, Memorial Art Gallery of the University of Rochester; Carmen Hendershott, Archival Reference, The New School; Mark Henderson, Reference Librarian, The Getty Research Institute; Kathleen Heyworth, Burchfield-Penney Art Center; D. Roger Howlett, Childs Gallery, Boston; Chris Hunter, Director of Archives and Collections, Schenectady Museum & Suits-Beuche Planetarium; Jonathan Jackson, Reference Assistant, Syracuse University Library; Nicole Johnson, Woodruff Center, High Museum of Art; Tullis Johnson, Research Assistant, Burchfield-Penney Art Center; Insley Julier, Harvard Art Museum Archives; William Keeler, Librarian Archivist, Rochester Historical Society; Pam Kennedy, Sales Supervisor, WCNY, Syracuse; Marie Kroeger, Archives Volunteer, Art Institute of Chicago; Ann Kuebel, Assistant Registrar, Memorial Art Gallery of the University of Rochester; Danielle Labbate, Curatorial Assistant, Montclair Art Museum; Reid Larson, Hamilton College Library; Touran K. Latham; Margaret M. Leahy, Registration Assistant, Addison Gallery of American Art; Cheryl Leibold, Archivist, Pennsylvania Academy of the Fine Arts; Leah Levy, Trustee, Estate of Jay DeFeo; Marina Libel, Registration Department, The Metropolitan Museum of Art; Peter Macara, Assistant Director / Registrar, Provincetown Art Association and Museum; Ted Mann, Assistant Curator of American Art, Solomon R. Guggenheim Museum of Art; Juliann McDonough, Curatorial Associate, Addison Gallery of American Art; Marjorie McNinch, Reference Archivist, Manuscripts & Archives, Hagley Museum and Library; David A. Miller, Senior Conservator of Paintings, Indianapolis Museum of Art; Cathy Moras, Archivist, Cranbrook Archives; Laura Nadeau, Brodock Press; David Nathans, former Acting Director, Emerson Gallery, Hamilton College; Robin O'Dell, Curatorial Assistant, Museum of Fine Arts, St. Petersburg, Fla.; Darlene Oden, Registration Department, Whitney Museum of American Art; Kate Nearpass Ogden, Associate Professor of Art History, The Richard Stockton College of New Jersey; Angela O'Neal, Digital Projects Manager, Ohio Historical Society; Richard Porter, Wally Findlay Galleries; Michelle Povilaitis, Associate Registrar, The Metropolitan Museum of Art; Scott Propeack, Collections Manager, Burchfield-Penney Art Center; Justin Rabideau, Collections Assistant, Everson Museum of Art; Meghan McQuaide Reiff, Registrar, Arnot Art Museum, Elmira N.Y.; Kimberly Richards, Archivist, Booth Library, Chemung County Historical Society; Jacqueline Rogers, Reference Associate, Frick Art Reference Library; Vincent Rossi, Jr.; William Salzillo, Professor of Art, Hamilton College; Jennifer L. Schauer, Department Assistant, Collection Management and Exhibition Registration, The Museum of Modern Art; Nicolette A. Schneider, Reference and Access Services Librarian, Special Collections Research Center, Syracuse University Library; Marjorie B. Searl, Chief Curator, Memorial Art Gallery of the University of Rochester; Charles and Lenore Seliger; Lou Siegel; Tomm F. Sprick, Director, Union Carbide Information Center; Sandy Stein, Assistant to Reba White Williams, New York; the Estate of Saul Steinberg; Jonathan Stuhlman, Curator of American Art, Mint Museum of Art; June Tablak; Susanne Trierenberg, Galerie Nierendorf, Berlin; Elizabeth Tufts-Brown, Associate Registrar, Carnegie Museum of Art; John Vernon, Archivist, Modern Civilian Records, Textual Archives Services Division, National Archives and Records Administration; John Warren, Warren Art Books, Merchantville, N.J.; Nancy Weekly, Head of Collections and the Charles Cary Rumsey Curator, Burchfield-Penney Art Center; Deborah Kiley Weyhe, Weyhe Gallery; Reba White Williams, Independent Scholar, New York; and Paul Worman, Paul Worman Fine Art, New York.

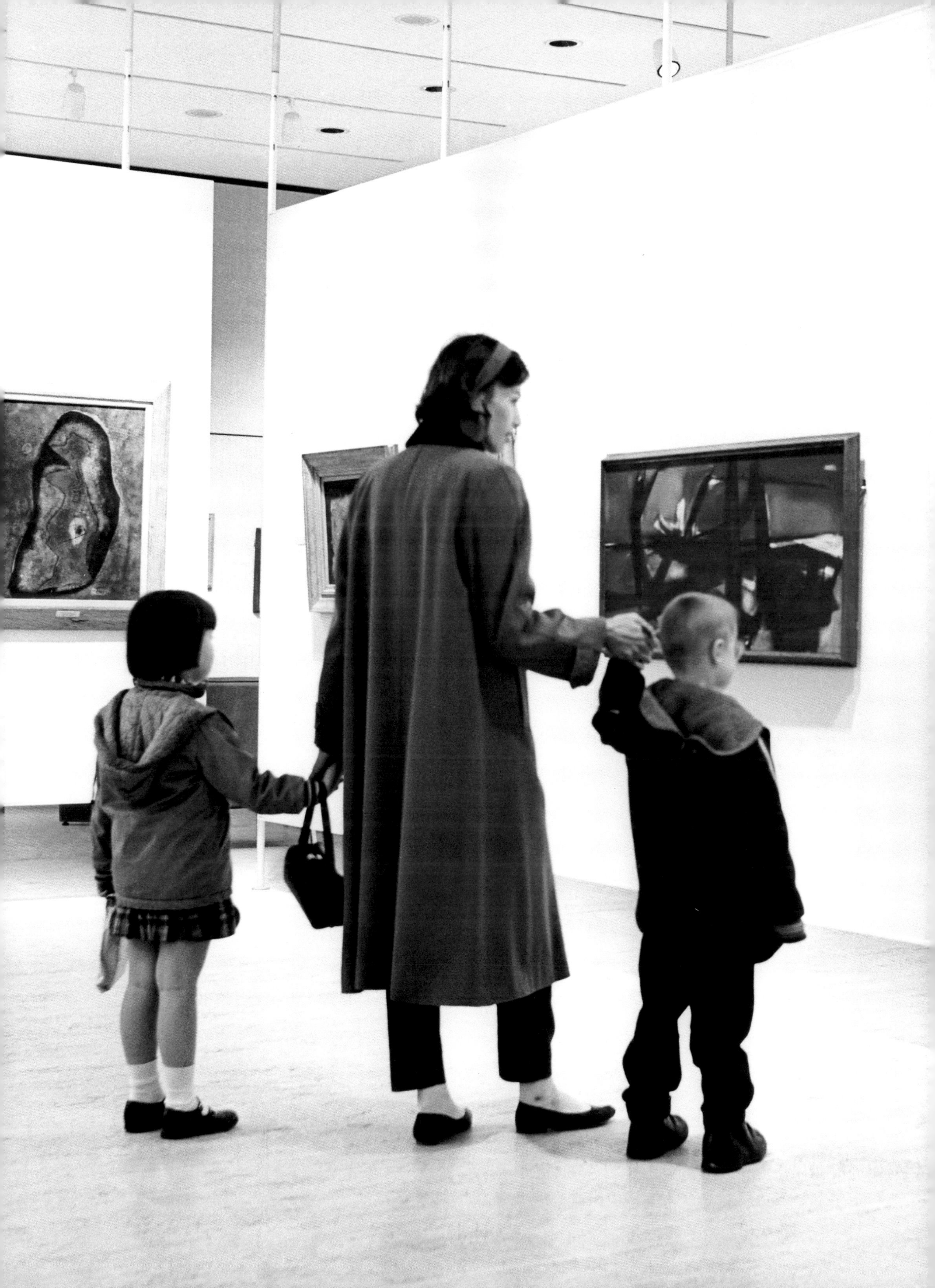

AUSPICIOUS VISION

EDWARD WALES ROOT AND AMERICAN MODERNISM

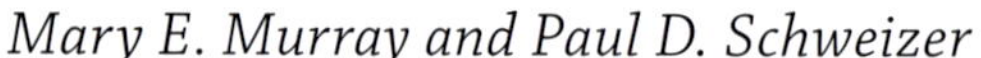

Mary E. Murray and Paul D. Schweizer

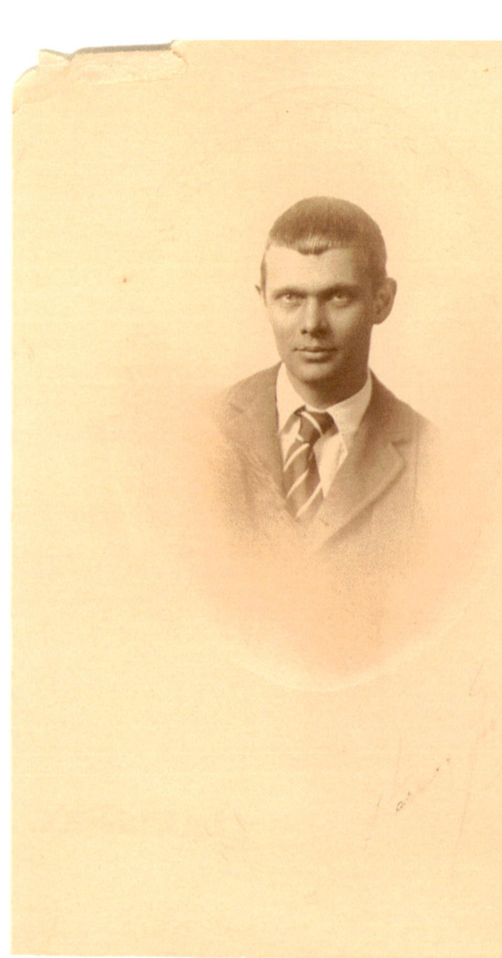

FIG. 1
Edward Wales Root, ca. 1930

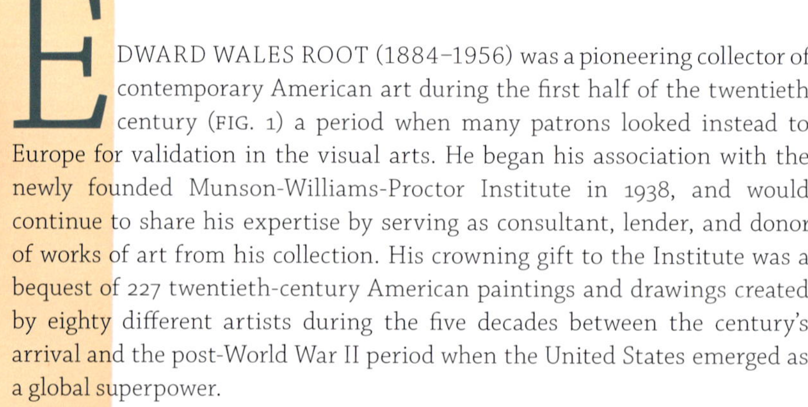

EDWARD WALES ROOT (1884–1956) was a pioneering collector of contemporary American art during the first half of the twentieth century (FIG. 1) a period when many patrons looked instead to Europe for validation in the visual arts. He began his association with the newly founded Munson-Williams-Proctor Institute in 1938, and would continue to share his expertise by serving as consultant, lender, and donor of works of art from his collection. His crowning gift to the Institute was a bequest of 227 twentieth-century American paintings and drawings created by eighty different artists during the five decades between the century's arrival and the post-World War II period when the United States emerged as a global superpower.

In February 1953, when The Metropolitan Museum of Art opened an exhibition of 132 paintings, watercolors, and drawings from Root's holdings, Robert Beverly Hale (1901–85), curator of American Painting and Sculpture at the Metropolitan, noted the adventurous spirit, acuity, serious scholarship and, perhaps, good fortune the collector of contemporary material must possess: "Indeed, for the successful creation of a collection of contemporary art the stars must be most auspicious."[1] *Auspicious Vision: Edward Wales Root and American Modernism* documents the fiftieth anniversary of Edward Root's generous bequest, pays homage to one of the Institute's great patrons, and celebrates the vital legacy of his advocacy for new art.

Although he was enthusiastic about what he called the "rather strange developments" of European avant-garde art, Root believed it was his duty to collect works by American artists.[2] He purchased nearly half of the works in the bequest within two years of their creation and, because Root consistently patronized the galleries that featured contemporary art, his collection is a cross section of the major movements in American art during the first half of the twentieth century. He acquired signature pieces by many of the artists whose achievements helped to define the history of this era.

Root's aesthetic taste is characterized by a respect for formal properties, humanistic themes, and a special appreciation for nature-based subjects. In the first decades of the twentieth century he bought paintings and drawings from a group of progressive and avant-garde American artists whose works reflected the dynamic vitality of modern urban American life or the more radical European styles of Post-Impressionism, Fauvism, and Cubism. In the

1930s, with money inherited from his parents, Root could afford to collect more ambitiously. During this decade he acquired major paintings by a number of American Scene artists who exploited native subjects during the country's darkest periods of the Depression and early years of World War II. In the post-War era, as American artists explored abstract and non-objective art, Root primarily acquired paintings and drawings by artists of the New York School and those who worked in the Pacific Northwest.

The style and subject matter of many of the works that Root bequeathed to the Museum reflect the artistic self-inquiry of an exciting, if unsettled era. And though much of the art work that Root collected was untested at the time of purchase, he remained steadfast in his patronage through several artistic generations. When he was a professor of art appreciation at Hamilton College, Root explained in a paper he delivered to his fellow teachers why knowledge and a belief in contemporary art was an intellectual imperative. "To show youth only what the past has discovered," he noted, "is to suggest that emotional and mental growth are over, that we of today have become spiritually unproductive, capable only of receiving from the past, incapable of giving to the future."[3]

THE ROOT FAMILY

Edward Root was the youngest child of Clara Wales (1853–1928) and Elihu Root, Sr. (1845–1937), who distinguished himself as a New York City lawyer before President William McKinley (1843–1901) appointed him Secretary of War in 1899. Elihu later served as Secretary of State for Theodore Roosevelt (1858–1919), was United States Senator representing New York and received the Nobel Peace Prize in 1912. In 1909 he was, moreover, a founder of the American Federation of Arts, an agency that he believed—through national tours of original works of art—would promote a cultivated and educated populace. In addition to a term as President of the American Federation of Arts, Elihu introduced legislation in the Senate in 1910 that led to the creation of the U.S. Fine Arts Commission.[4] Elihu's aesthetic sensibility is revealed in his description of the landscape surrounding what the Root family called the Homestead (FIG. 2) in Clinton, New York, now on the campus of Hamilton College:

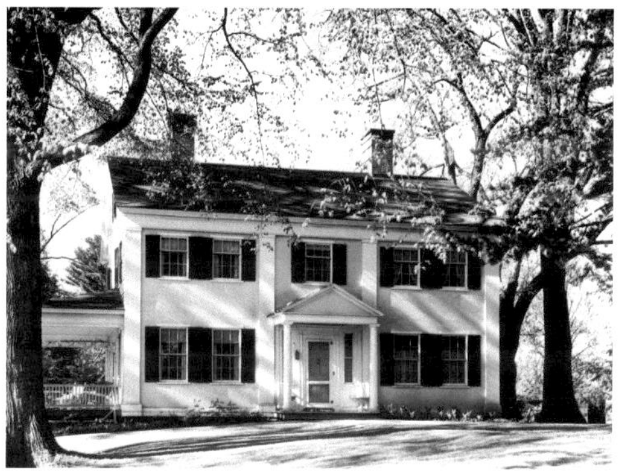

FIG. 2
The Homestead, Clinton, New York
Richard Carver Wood (1902–89), photographer

> In planting a picture of trees, there are two things to look out for—contrasting shades of green alongside each other, and variety of outline. We say there are colors in autumn, but look at that gingko, the hemlock and the butternut together now. What variety there is.... One of the most beautiful sights I ever saw was on a winter's day over in the pasture. I came upon a group of witch hazel with the sun shining full on their golden bloom as it stood out against the white of the snow and the blue of the sky.[5]

"Much has been written, and more will be written in the future, of the importance of Edward Root as a patron of American art, and particularly of his encouragement and support of younger artists before they had achieved much of a reputation."

—*Charles E. Burchfield, 1957*

Elihu attributed this aspect of his personality to his own father, Oren Root (1803–85), whom he described as having "a Renaissance of culture."[6] Elihu's sensitivity to the visual pleasures of the natural world was an important model for his younger son, Edward, who similarly developed profound feeling for beauty in art and nature.

As a child, Edward lived in New York City and Washington, D. C. He (FIG. 3) spent summers at the Homestead in Clinton, which is eight miles southeast of Utica. (As an adult, he and his wife, Grace Cogswell Root [1891–1975] lived seasonally at the Homestead and in New York City.) After graduating from Hamilton College in 1905, Edward searched for his calling in life but, because he was deaf from early childhood, he did not cultivate a career in law and public service like his father and elder brother, Elihu Root, Jr. (1881–1967). After testing his mettle as a cowboy in Texas, Edward turned to journalism in New York. It was as a newspaperman that he became acquainted with contemporary painting, which intrigued the young Root, who began to visit galleries, meet artists, and generally find his path in life.[7] Root taught art appreciation at Hamilton College between 1920–40, which helped focus the direction of his life's work. His self-image during his twenty-year tenure evolved from a 1928 description as a teacher and son of Elihu to a 1947 statement in which he called himself a "collector of modern pictures... not a writer or lecturer."[8] Perhaps because he was deaf, Edward developed a more acute visual compass than a hearing person might have; Grace (FIG. 4) once noted that her husband had been frustrated by his deafness and, as a result, turned his "emotional life into eyes as the one way out."[9]

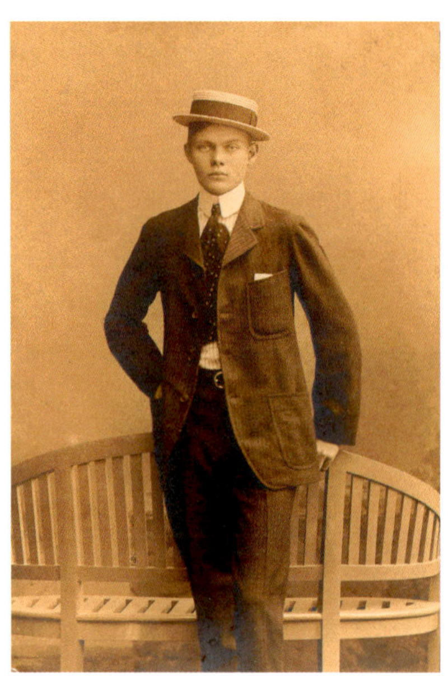

FIG. 3
Edward Wales Root, ca. 1900

Root's biographer, Aline B. Saarinen (1914–72), considered Root's condition a significant enough factor of his life to make it a central thesis around which she wove her 1958 biography of him and, as early as a 1953 *New York Times* review of the exhibition of his collection at the Metropolitan Museum, she made the connection between Root's deafness and his involvement with the visual arts.[10] Certainly Grace was sympathetic with Edward's condition because one of her ancestors also had been deaf, a circumstance that may have been one of the factors that led him to feel a special kinship for her when they met in 1916.[11] Two years before this, Root ruminated about the valuable lessons he learned from his deafness:

> [People] who from infancy have been damaged... have... been able to learn the supreme lesson of life. While still children we have been privileged... to discover that the ultimate glory of the individual must inevitably consist in the pride of indifference to individual defeat.... To die on the high tide of vigorous and fair seeming youth without yet experienced the limitation of mortality... is to graduate from existence without yet having acquired that tragic nobility of patience which is, in my estimation, the most distinguishing characteristic of the gods themselves.[12]

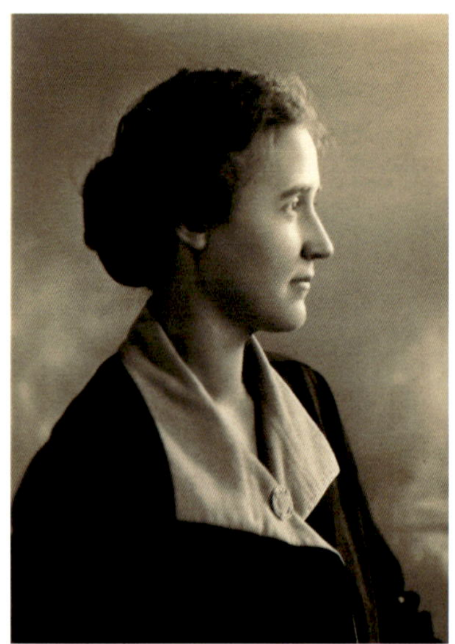

FIG. 4
Grace Cogswell Root, ca. 1920

Root's comments in a 1922 article, "Pictures and the College"—on teaching art appreciation to college students—about Laura Bridgman (1829–89), the first deaf-mute and blind woman to be educated in the United States, are equally significant in a number of ways to his deafness.[13] Most importantly, Charles Dickens's (1812–70) description in *American Notes* (1842) of how Bridgman transcended her handicap was a story with which Root doubtless personally identified. Additionally, Dickens's description of how Bridgman's innate intelligence was exposed to the facts and experiences of the world may have confirmed or clarified some of Root's own thoughts about the meaning and nature of culture. It is also easy to imagine that Root identified with Bridgman's teachers who, as Dickens noted, in approximate terms, helped the blind to see; Root alluded to such an idea in his 1922 article. It probably reflected, as well, Root's feelings about his own teachers and the view he had of what he hoped to achieve as an instructor of art appreciation at Hamilton College. Dickens's remarks about Bridgman's growing awareness of the world might also have resonated with Root. His successful college career, capped by the academic honor of graduating Phi Beta Kappa was, like Bridgman's, achieved in spite of his deafness.[14]

FRIEND OF CONTEMPORARY AMERICAN ARTISTS

In her book, *The Proud Possessors: The Lives, Times and Tastes of Some Adventurous American Art Collectors* (1958), Saarinen included Root with more legendary American collectors like J. Pierpont Morgan (1837–1913), Isabella Stewart Gardner (1840–1924), John Quinn (1870–1924), and Peggy Guggenheim (1898–1974). In an insightful comment about Root's self-effacing ways and studious nature, she noted that he, by contrast, had "very little pride in possession. He was always, even in his personal relationships, the observer. He collected things in order to observe them intimately, study them, analyze them, understand them."[15]

Root began collecting art in the first decade of the twentieth century. He was living in New York City and working in the editorial office of the New York *Evening Sun* where he witnessed heated arguments about modern art between the critics in his office, Charles FitzGerald and Frederick James Gregg (d. 1928).[16] This was a life-altering experience for Root, then in his early twenties. Edward soon gravitated to a circle of artists known as The Eight, whose artistic ambitions and bohemian lifestyles challenged the genteel values of the waning Gilded Age.

Root met one of the artists of this group, Ernest Lawson (1873–1939) late in 1909 after learning that the artist was destitute. In her chapter on Root, Saarinen described this now legendary encounter, an event that established Root's modus operandi as an art collector and friend of contemporary American artists.[17] Motivated by intellectual curiosity and a concern for Lawson's welfare, rather than by any ambition on his part to begin building an art collection, Root gave Lawson $250 for his landscape painting, *Winter, Spuyten Duyvil* (FIG. 5), a work that was included in the notorious exhibition of The Eight that took place at the Macbeth Galleries nearly two years earlier.[18] This was a watershed experience for Root and an important milestone in the story of American art patronage. Additionally, for Root personally, as he remarked later in life, this picture taught him that art was something that "appealed primarily to the emotions."[19]

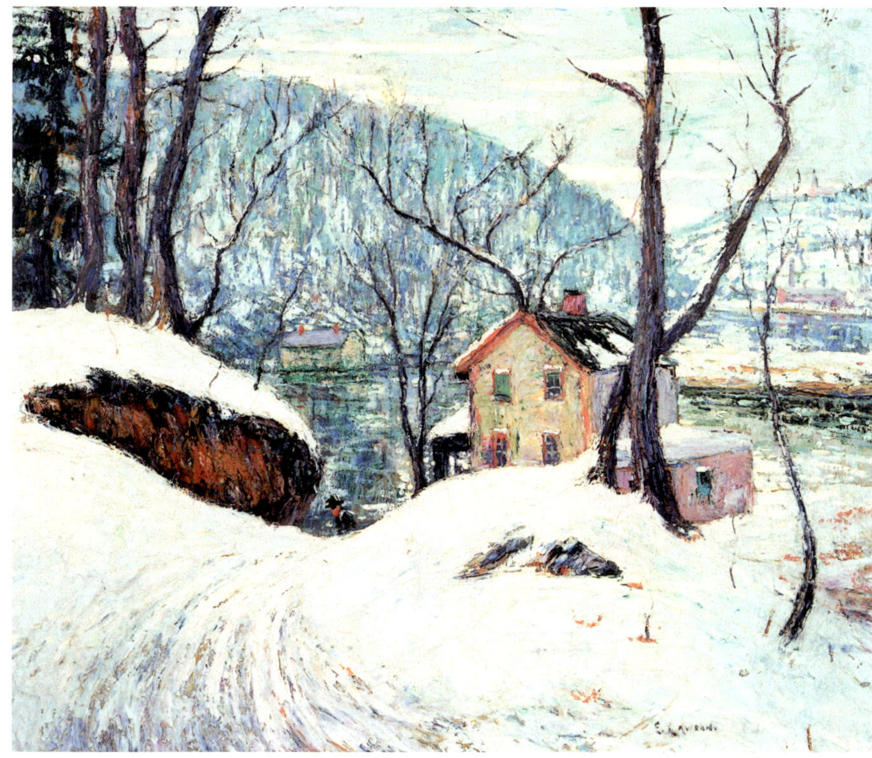

FIG. 5
Ernest Lawson
Winter, Spuyten Duyvil, ca. 1908
Oil on canvas, 25 ⅛ x 30 in.
Museum purchase, 58.41

Root's best friend among The Eight was George B. Luks (1866–1933), who was as ebullient as Root was reserved. A close camaraderie developed between the two when Root studied painting and drawing with the artist. Together they tramped around New York, from the zoo to vaudeville shows, to sketch everything they saw, and Root became a steady patron of Luks's work. Around 1909–10 the artist painted Root's portrait (coll. John B. Root) and in 1917, when Edward and Grace were married, Luks gave them his watercolor, *Dyckman Street Church* (FIG. 6), which Root described as the first picture of the couple's "mutual collection."[20] Although Edward later tried to sell this watercolor to purchase something else, this remark suggests that he considered Grace a collaborator in the contemporary American collection they assembled over the next nearly forty years.[21] Luks, Edward, and Grace traveled together for fishing trips and, from time to time, Luks visited the Roots in Clinton. The artist gave spirited painting demonstrations to the students enrolled in the art appreciation course Root taught at Hamilton College, and he also had "drying out" sessions at the Homestead to palliate bouts of hard drinking.[22] Until Luks's death in 1933, he and Edward exchanged witty letters on a variety of topics including the development of a "new hearing instrument."[23] There is a letter from the artist dated Sunday, June 8, 1924, on which Luks sketched a charming drawing of God blessing Edward and Grace.[24] Root was very cognizant of the life-enhancing pleasures that someone like himself, a "would-be student of pictures," derived from the "friendship and companionship of an artist of the better sort." He probably had Luks in mind when he wrote in 1922:

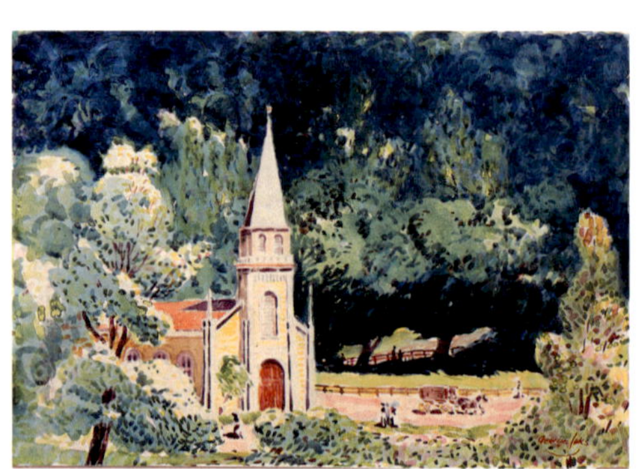

FIG. 6
George B. Luks
Dyckman Street Church, ca. 1915
Watercolor and graphite on wove paper, 15 ⅛ x 22 5⁄16 in.
Museum purchase, 58.293

> To share one's experience with such a man, even occasionally; to have him observe what you only see and to be… conducted through the living world by a living being, vital, observant, reflective, sympathetic, expressive—is in itself a liberal education.[25]

It is probable that Luks' opinions helped to shape the younger Root's attitude about supporting American contemporary artists. Luks's feeling about this matter is reflected in a 1923 interview with the *New York Tribune*, where he was quoted as saying, "Americans should patronize their own artists. Why should an American home be full of English portraits… we should encourage contemporary American art. When you have done that, then you are building a country."[26]

Root's assistance to artists included the generous loan of works from his collection to public exhibitions. He has the distinction of being one of a very small group of individuals who both loaned to and purchased from the landmark 1913 Armory Show (International Exhibition of Modern Art). He lent ten Luks drawings depicting animals in the Bronx Zoo.[27] Although Root was attracted to the work of some of the European modernists in the exhibition—especially the expressive Fauve paintings of Henri Matisse (1869–1954) and Marcel Duchamp's (1887–1968) notorious Cubist figure composition, *Nude Descending a Staircase, No. 2* (1912, Philadelphia Museum of Art)—Root felt a patriotic responsibility to support American artists. This led him to purchase for $800 the most expensive of the three paintings that Maurice B. Prendergast (1858–1924) included in the exhibition, the festive, multi-figured composition, *Landscape with Figures* (FIG. 7). In buying this work, Root joined an elite group of adventurous collectors like Arthur Jerome Eddy (1859–1920), Lillie P. Bliss (1864–1931), John Quinn, and Walter C. Arensberg (1878–1954), who also patronized this show. Although the amount that Root paid for this work was less than what some of Prendergast's colleagues, like George Bellows (1882–1925), Arthur B. Davies (1862–1928), Robert Henri (1865–1929), and Luks asked for their paintings at the Armory Show, it was comparable to what other artists, like William J. Glackens (1870–1938), Marsden Hartley

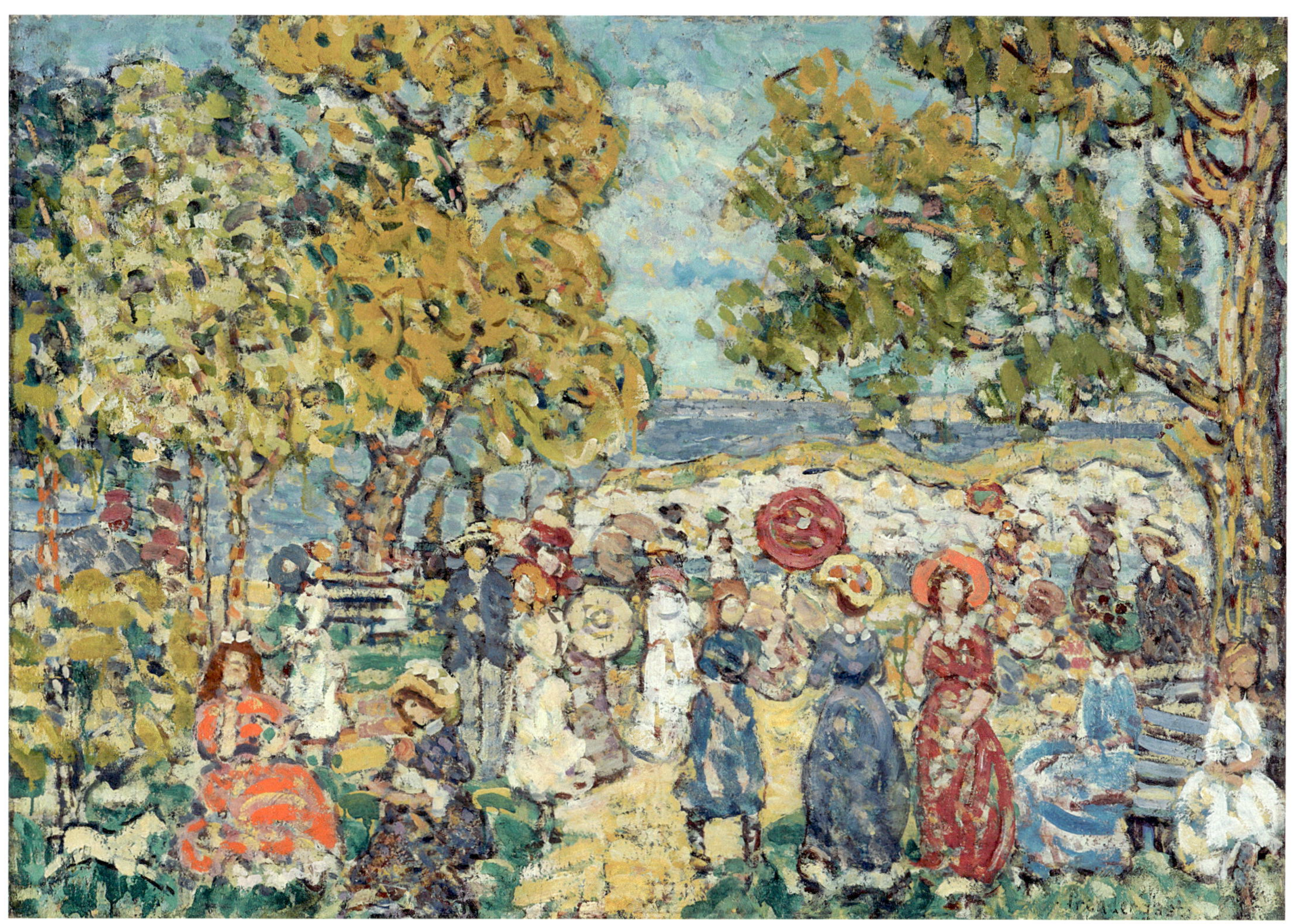

FIG. 7
Maurice B. Prendergast
Landscape with Figures
Ca. 1912
Oil on canvas
29 ⅝ x 42 ⅞ in.
Cat. no. 159

(1877–1943), Lawson, and John Sloan (1871–1951) were asking.[28] A year earlier, with Luks's encouragement, Root had purchased Prendergast's Venetian watercolor, *Canal* (cat. no. 158) from the 1912 American Watercolor Society exhibition. Prendergast (who, like Root, suffered from deafness) was the most radical member of The Eight.[29] The decorative shapes and jewel-like colors he used in his pictures are stylistically related to progressive tendencies in European Post-Impressionist painting.

Luks's riotous lifestyle and bumptious personality seem far removed from the patrician environment in which Edward was raised. On the other hand, one does not get the impression that Edward was slumming with his artist-colleagues. Root consistently befriended painters of immigrant and blue-collar backgrounds, many of whom held leftist or Socialist political views, because he always connected with them through their art. When he had his name removed from the Social Register Root quipped that it was because he had more friends in the telephone directory.[30] This anecdote presents Edward as an interesting character, someone who was, perhaps, quietly rebellious. The Root and Wales families were long-established members of New York City's cultural elite, and Edward's commitment to the art of his time occasionally put him at odds with established institutions.[31]

Another member of The Eight whom Root held in high regard but did not know very well because of his reserved demeanor was Davies. He was a principal organizer of the Armory Show and for several years thereafter experimented in his own art with faceted geometric forms that were based, however naively, on the Cubism of Pablo Picasso (1881–1973) and others. His true genius, however, was his pastoral sensibility, which, as Root noted, was shaped by the formative years he spent in the Mohawk Valley of central New York State, a region to which Root himself was passionately attracted and described in the following terms: "It is a country to be born in," Root noted, "to live in; to die in; to arouse indeterminable desires and bestow sensuous delights—a proper nursery for the poet, the artist and the man of thought."[32] Two years after the Armory Show, in 1915, Root purchased for $2,000 Davies's landscape, *Refluent Season* (before 1911, Munson-Williams-Proctor Arts Institute). Root's willingness to pay such a large amount for this work was grounded in his conviction that Davies was the "most comprehensive artistic intelligence that has as yet, in America, attempted to express itself in paint."[33] Despite the high opinion Root had for Davies, he nevertheless, assessed the artist's oeuvre with cool discernment. In the margin of his copy of the Armory Show catalog, Root had nothing good to say about the three oil paintings that Davies displayed in the exhibition. He remarked that *Hill Wind* (not dated, ex. coll. Duncan Phillips) was a "failure," that *A Line of Mountains* (ca. 1911, Virginia Museum of Fine Arts) was "too contrasted," and that *Seadrift* (date and whereabouts unknown) was "too subjective."[34]

facing page
FIG. 8
Edward Hopper
The Camel's Hump, 1931
Oil on canvas
32 ¼ x 50 ⅛ in.
Cat. no. 105

FIG. 9
Jo Hopper
Map of South Truro, Cape Cod
Ca. 1936
Graphite and colored pencil on wove paper
5 ¼ x 16 ⅛ in.
R.G. 13, F. 29, Edward Wales Root Papers, Munson-Williams-Proctor Arts Institute Archives

After receiving an inheritance from his mother, who died in 1928, Root was able to collect art on a more ambitious scale as well as build a private art gallery adjacent to the Homestead in Clinton to display and store his growing collection.[35] A number of the most important pictures that Root acquired during the 1930s came from Frank K. M. Rehn (1886–1956), who was a leading art dealer in New York during these years. Rehn's eponymous gallery played a key role promoting the work of several artists who shaped the history of early twentieth-century art in the United States, a group that was critically acclaimed in the *Brooklyn Daily Eagle* as a "choice little symposium of contemporary American painting."[36]

One of the greatest purchases Root made at the Rehn Galleries during this decade—and one of the most important works in his entire bequest to the Munson-Williams-Proctor Institute—is Edward Hopper's *The Camel's Hump* (FIG. 8). The picture depicts the grass-covered dunes on Cape Cod where Hopper (1882–1967) and his wife, Jo (1883–1968), spent their summers for nearly forty years (FIG. 9). In a manner typical of his relationship with many other artists, Root became an early supporter of Hopper; his patronage provided moral support at a time when Hopper was receiving little critical recognition and had to make a living as a commercial artist. Root's enthusiasm for Hopper's work predates by nearly a decade his purchase of *The Camel's Hump*. In 1927 he bought Hopper's watercolor, *Skyline Near Washington Square (Self Portrait)* (cat. no. 106) and then, the same year it was painted, his oil painting, *Freight Cars, Gloucester* (1928, Addison Gallery of American Art).[37] In May 1928 Root also published a complimentary review of an exhibition of Hopper's watercolors and etchings that was organized by the Utica Art Society. Root remarked, "painting of this kind is something of which one never grows tired," and added that it was a sign of "the renaissance of American taste" that some of the watercolors in the exhibition were already owned by America's great museums.[38]

While Root did not acquire as many works by Hopper as he did by other artists, Root praised what he described as Hopper's classicism, identifying

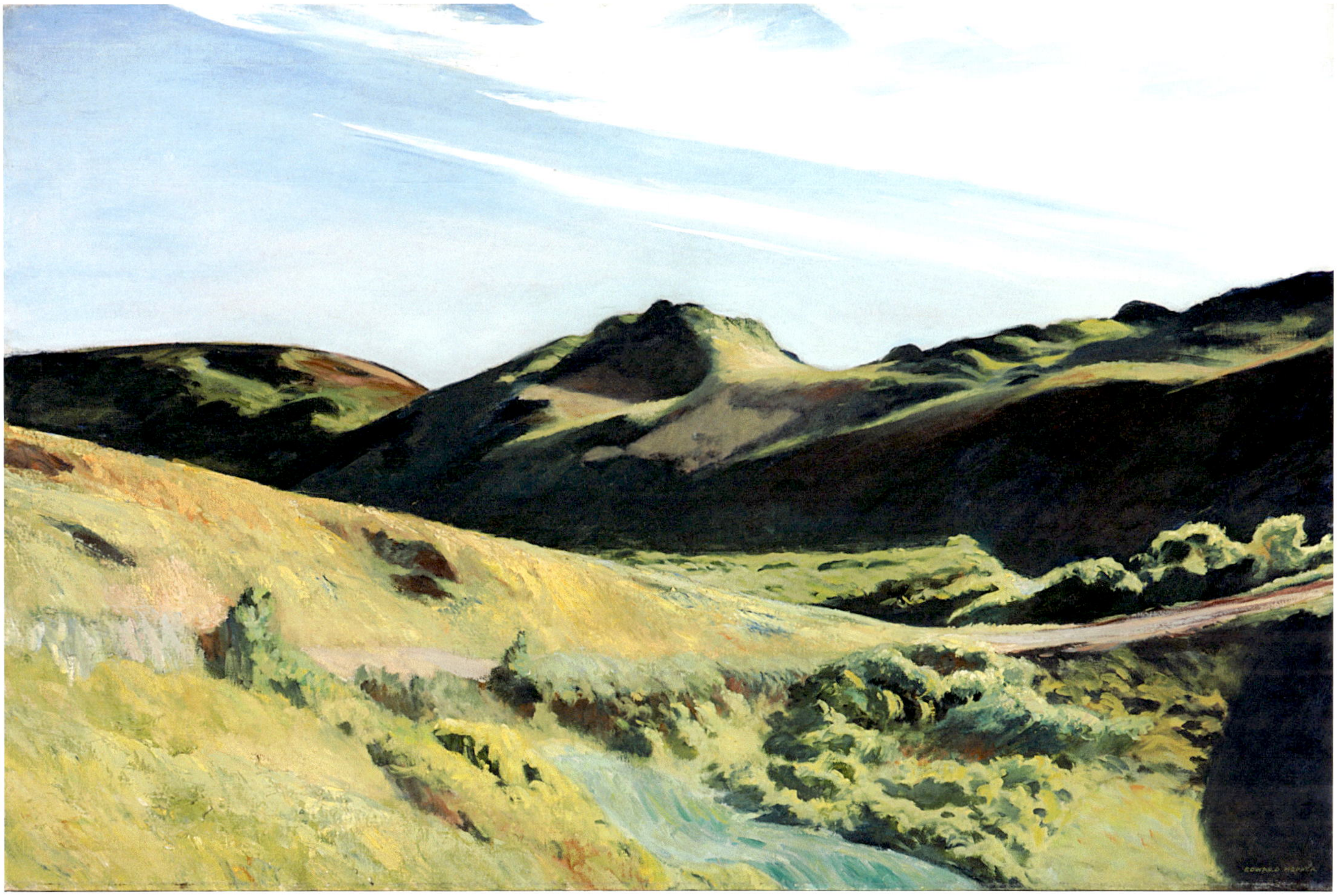

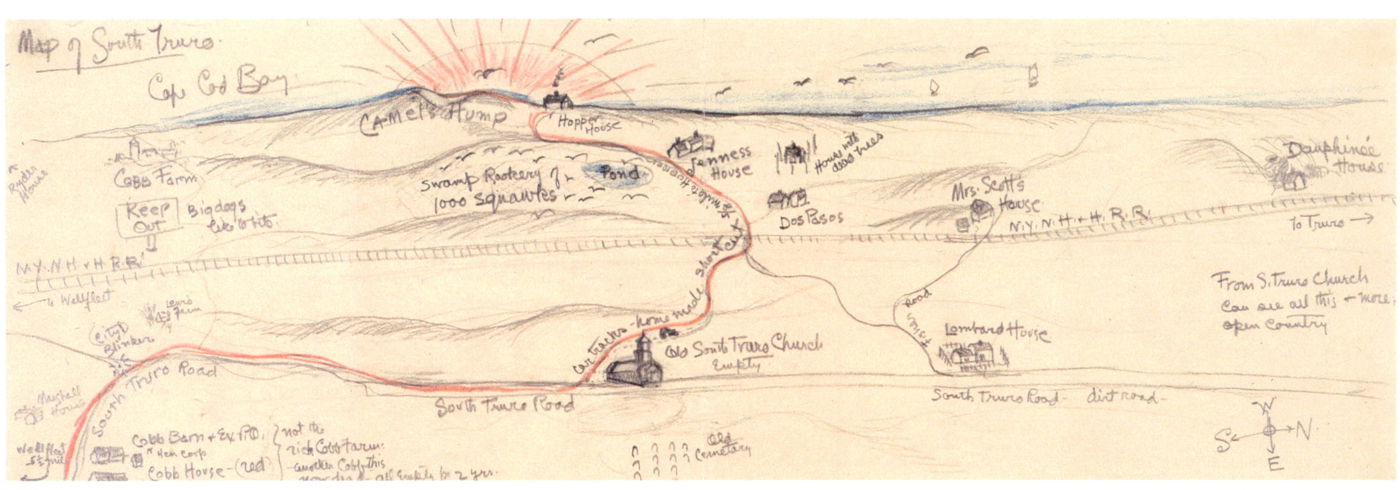
Map of South Truro.
Cape Cod Bay
Camel's Hump
Hopper House
Jenness House
House with dead trees
Dauphinée House
Cobb Farm
Ryder House
Swamp Rookery of 1000 squawkes
Pond
Keep Out
Big dogs like to bite
Dos Pasos
Mrs. Scott's House
N.Y. N.H. & H. R.R.
To Truro
to Wellfleet
Lewis Farm
(City) Blinker
From S. Truro Church Can see all this + more, open country
Lombard House
Old South Truro Church Empty
car tracks - home made short cut
South Truro Road
South Truro Road - dirt road -
Marshall House
Wellfleet 5½ miles
Cobb Barn & Ex P.O.
Cobb House - (red)
not the rich Cobb farm
Old Cemetery
W
S
N
E

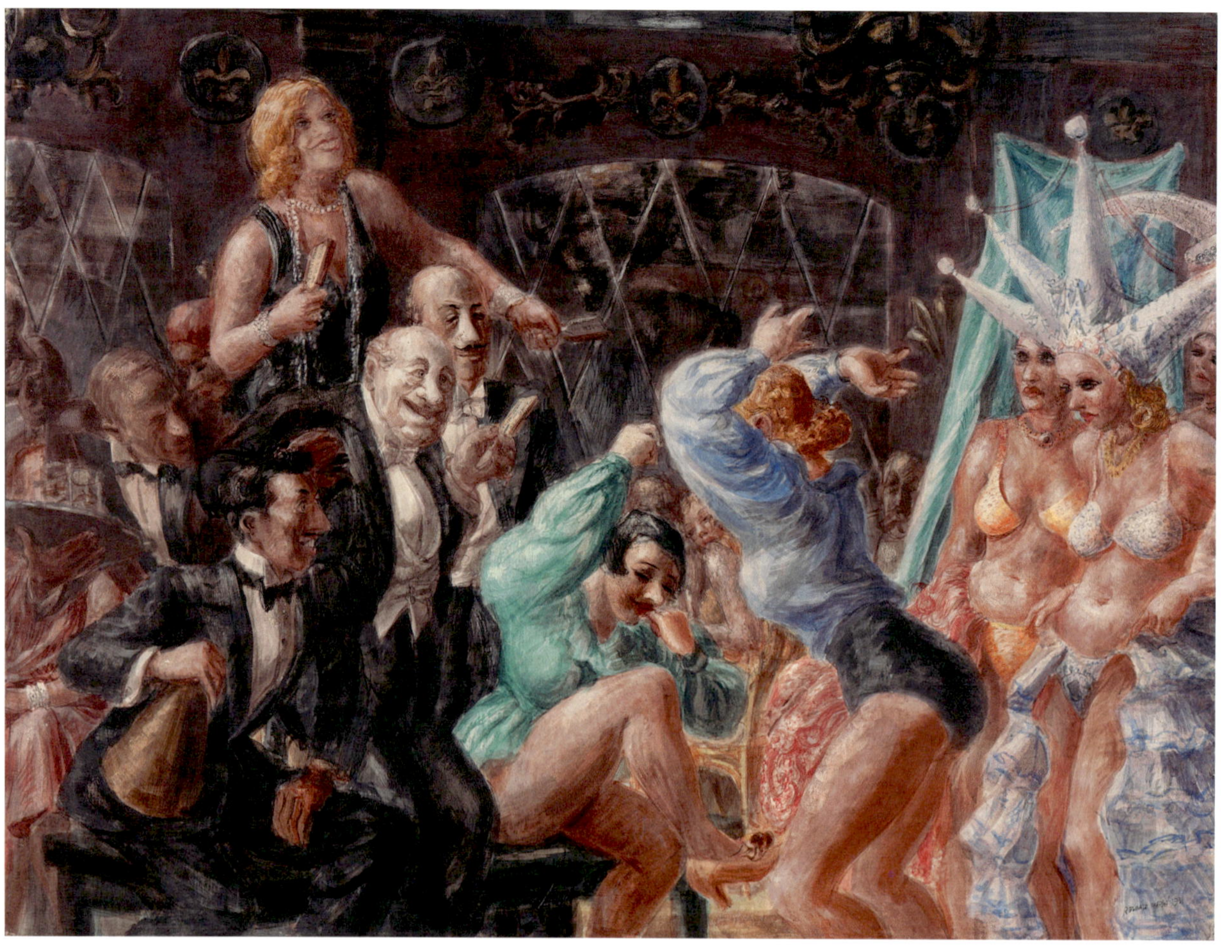

FIG. 10
Reginald Marsh
Texas Guinan and Her Gang, 1931
Tempera on linen
36 ¼ x 48 ¼ in.
Cat. no. 140

"three purely formal motives... sparkling color, mass, and space: three of the most everlasting and potent motives known to art." Root noted, too, the profundity of feeling in Hopper's paintings, an "almost agonizing sense of loneliness or even a kind of romantic feeling for the remote and strange."[39] And, when Thomas Brown Rudd (1898–1955), an administrator at Hamilton College (as well as a Munson-Williams-Proctor Institute trustee and senior executive during its formative years), asked Root around 1948 to which American artist the college might consider awarding an honorary degree, Root confidently replied: "If I were giving a degree to the man whom I thought posterity would acclaim as the greatest American painter of my generation I should give it to Edward Hopper. But I doubt if Hopper would accept a degree and if he did it would be a social agony for him to appear and receive it."[40]

Rehn's gallery also represented Reginald Marsh (1898–1954), an artist whose paintings have the opposite emotional tenor of those by Hopper. Like George Luks in an earlier era, Marsh celebrated New York at its most colorful. He trekked all over to capture the city's vitality because it had everything he liked to paint: "girls, bums, athletes, muscles, tugs and ocean liners, clouds, and movement, all in one."[41] At this stage in Root's life, twenty years after he had befriended Luks and with whom he had roamed around town, Root was a husband, father, and college professor, so he did not join the younger Marsh on his excursions, but nevertheless vicariously enjoyed the artist's urban adventures: over a three-year period in the early 1930s Root acquired from Rehn in quick succession Marsh's *Lower Manhattan (New York Skyline)* (cat.

no. 139), and then two humorous figure paintings: *Zeke Youngblood's Dance Marathon* (cat. no. 141), followed by *Texas Guinan and Her Gang* (FIG. 10).[42]

Rehn also played a key role in promoting the work of Charles E. Burchfield (1893–1967), the artist with whom Root is most closely associated. In 1928, the year that Root convinced the Metropolitan Museum to purchase one of Burchfield's watercolors, he acquired for himself *Country Blacksmith Shop (Blacksmith Shop)* (cat. no. 28), from the Montross Gallery.[43] This was Root's first purchase for what would ultimately be a significant collection of Burchfield watercolors, twenty-one of which he gave to the Museum, the largest group of works by any artist in the bequest.

Edward and Grace met Burchfield for the first time in late January 1929, on a visit to their friend Harry D. Yates (1903–96), who lived in Buffalo. In his studio, Burchfield showed them watercolor sketches he had made as a young artist in 1916–18. Root described them as "joyful and unpremeditated" and was so impressed with their vivid colors and decorative forms that he urged Rehn to show them at his gallery.[44] He even purchased ten of these early watercolors at this time for himself (cat. nos. 29–32, 34, 39, 40, 43, 44, 46). Such was the affinity between artist and patron that Root continued to acquire Burchfield's work for the next two decades (cat. nos. 26, 27, 33, 35–38, 41, 42, 45), which was somewhat unusual for him—more typically Root supported an artist at the beginning of his or her career. His gift to the Museum, therefore, includes important examples of Burchfield's early, middle, and later stylistic phases.

Because Root endorsed Burchfield so avidly, he readily forgave any artistic lapses as "almost proofs of his great gifts. Is it much to be wondered at that anyone who... is so interested in so many things should sometimes use too many points of emphasis, that anyone who is so sensitive to both the pathos and magnificence of life should sometimes become sentimental or rhetorical?"[45] Root's unreserved admiration for Burchfield was based on his acute understanding of the artist's subject matter, as well as his extremely close observation of his paintings, as revealed in this statement:

> The number and range of his emotional reactions to luminous effects is prodigious. He reacts equally to the light of winter and summer, of autumn and spring, of days that are overcast and days that are bright, of rain storms and snow storms, of night and evening, of morning and noon. He is moved by and impelled to record the subtlest and most unusual effects of illumination, natural and unnatural—the color of the air before a storm, the white flash of lightning beyond the trees, the glow of flames, the play of electric radiance on pavements and walls, the sheen on stagnant pools and wet asphalt (FIG. 11).[46]

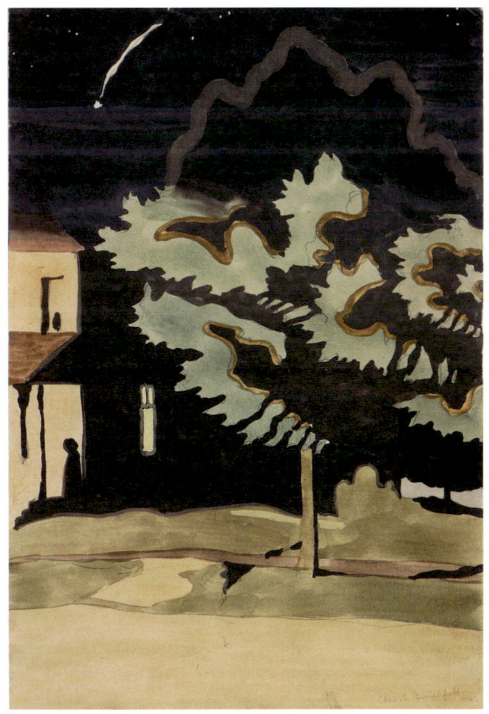

FIG. 11
Charles E. Burchfield
House and Tree by Arc Light (Shooting Star; House At Night; House and Tree)
July 28, 1916
Transparent watercolor and graphite on white watercolor paper
19 ⅞ x 13 ⅞ in.
Cat. no. 34

The kinship that Root and Burchfield had for each other also produced an exchange of letters that went on for twenty years, documenting one of the great artist-patron relationships in American art. Their early, more formal correspondence quickly gave way to letters that are heartfelt, trusting, gracious, and respectful. In April 1932, for example, Burchfield wrote to Root expressing discomfort at being classified as an American Scene artist:

> What do you think of the so-called American wave? People like yourselves who have always believed in American painting, must feel like chuckling over the sudden discovery that there are artists in America,

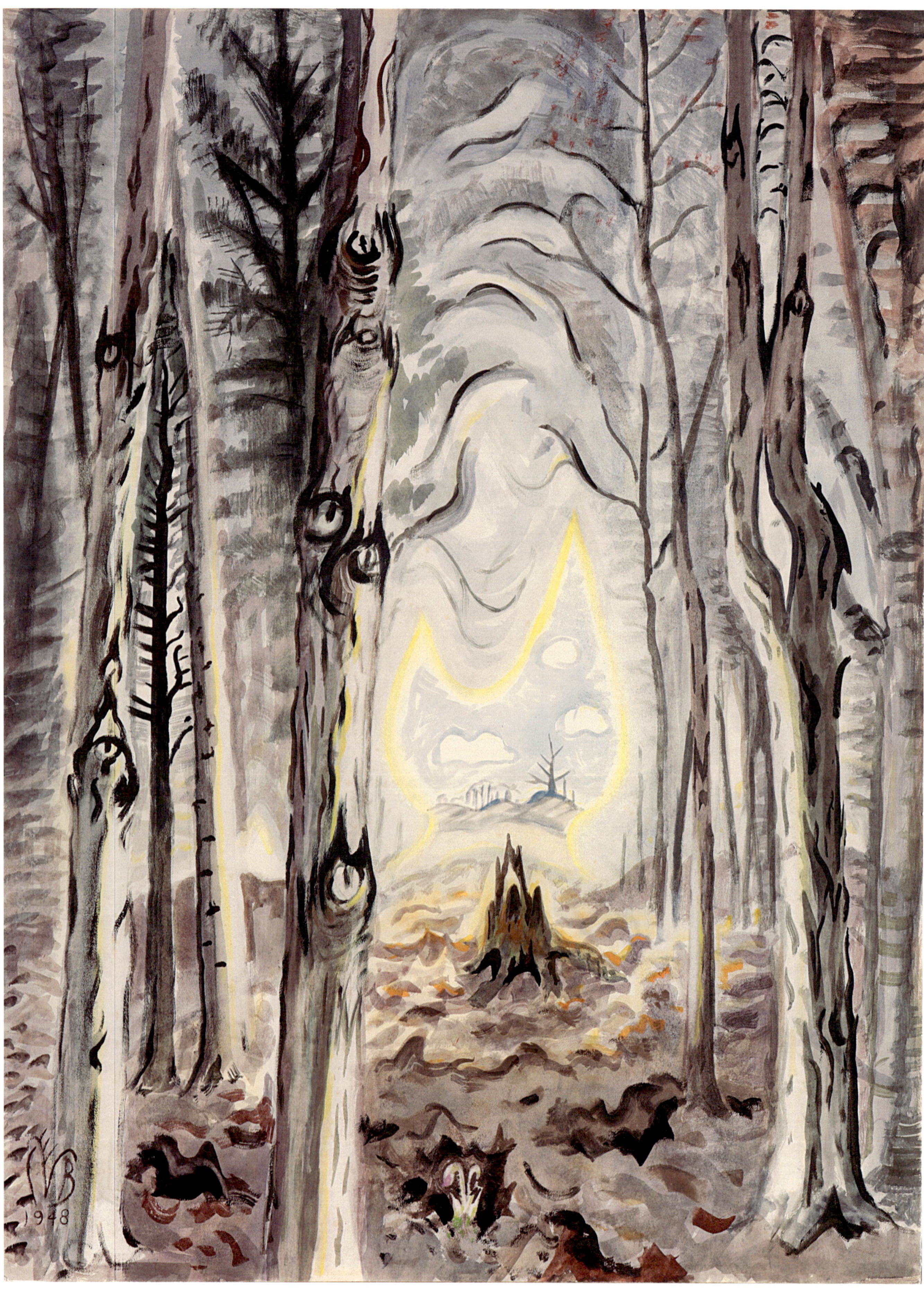
1948

> a little patronage wouldn't come amiss to many worthwhile artists... I wish they would quit talking about the American Scene. The American Scene is no better or worse than any other scene, and the worthwhile artist doesn't care about a subject for its national character. I have been spoken of a one of the exponents of "American Scenism" [sic], which I consider a libel. The scene itself has never been [the] main motive that impelled me to paint.[47]

facing page
FIG. 12
Charles E. Burchfield
Flame of Spring, 1948
Transparent watercolor on watercolor paper, two sheets vertically joined on the left side
40 x 29 ¾ in.
Cat. no. 33

Root's letter in reply to Burchfield's question about the American Scene has not survived but the artist's feeling about this matter can be discerned in a thoughtful article Root published about Burchfield several years later, in which he introduced the artist to his readers with the statement:

> It is of little importance if any particular American artist sometimes depicts objects of unmistakably American appearance; it is of much greater importance if his interpretation of these objects endows them with some sort of general significance. If, then, we are to do justice to Charles Burchfield as an artist we must avoid supposing that he paints America because it is American. He would be the first to deny having any such intention. He paints because he likes to paint and because through painting he can express a philosophy based on nature.[48]

Both Burchfield's philosophy of nature—his abiding subject that surpasses restricting nationalistic characterizations—and Root's appreciation of landscape imagery are evoked in the last Burchfield that the Roots bought, *Flame of Spring* (FIG. 12). The artist wrote that he was so pleased the work had found the right home, "I have a special fondness for this picture for in it I seemed to find the means to express something for which I had been searching for years... something elemental, expressive of the immanence of spring."[49] When Burchfield received an honorary degree from Hamilton College, Edward wrote, "This college admires... your incomparable feeling for the floral and faunal aspects of our landscapes.... No other American artist has done more to remind men of their fundamental and inescapable relation to nature."[50]

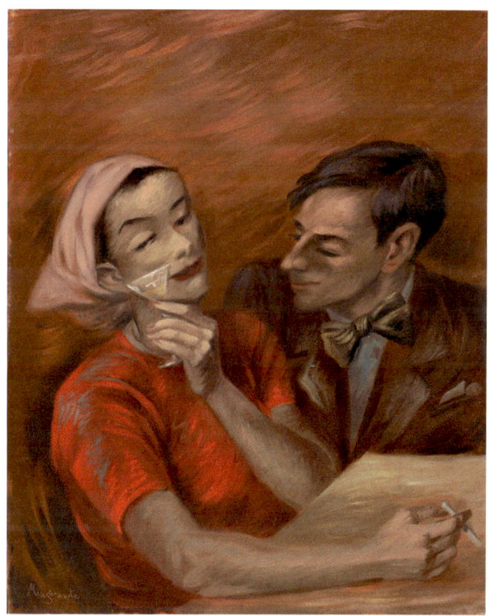

FIG. 13
Peppino Mangravite
Young Couple Drinking, 1937
Oil on linen
24 x 20 in.
Cat. no. 136

Root also befriended Peppino ("Gino") Mangravite (1896–1978), another artist represented by Rehn with whom he corresponded for twenty years.[51] Root and Mangravite discussed subjects as wide-ranging as creating a college-level curriculum for studio art, the question of limiting civil liberties during wartime, and the role of the government in arts funding. On a personal level, Root offered encouragement for the Mangravite family's health and well-being, financial assistance, and moral support for Peppino's balancing act of teaching and painting full time. And, not surprisingly, he writes sensitively and with praise about Mangravite's paintings, commenting in particular on *Young Couple Drinking* (FIG. 13):

> I have a sentimental weakness for the girl and note with approval her classical pallor as compared with the attenuated flush of the young gent in the background. I wish you were not almost the only living American painter who can handle such a subject with a little human tenderness but that's the fact.[52]

The representational painting style of Hopper, Marsh, Mangravite, and

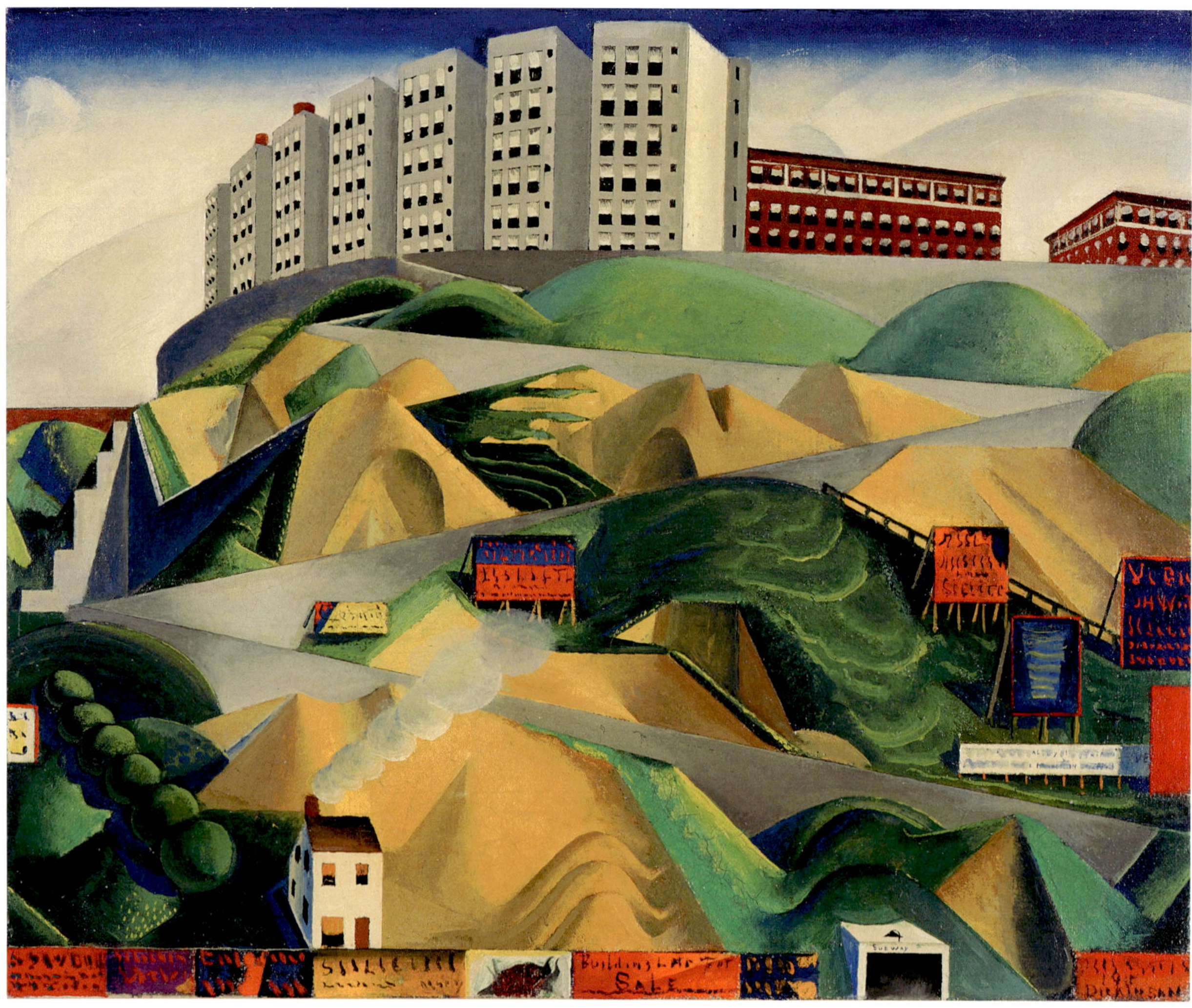

FIG. 14
Preston Dickinson
Fort George Hill, 1915
Oil on linen
14 x 17 in.
Cat. no. 71

facing page
FIG. 15
Charles Sheeler
Siphon, 1923
Charcoal and watercolor on white paper
16 7/16 x 12 ½ in.
Cat. no. 181

the other artists Rehn represented—which bears no trace of what some conservative critics at the time believed was the corrupting influence of European modernist art—is the hallmark of Root's taste from the time of his early his association with The Eight until the 1940s. A notable exception to this tendency in Root's collection, however, is Preston Dickinson's (1891–1930) *Fort George Hill* (FIG. 14), a work Root purchased from the Charles Daniel Gallery the same year Dickinson painted it. The artist made this picture shortly after a sojourn in Paris, where he saw radical paintings by artists such as Picasso and Matisse. The rich, expressive colors and geometric forms of *Fort George Hill* easily make this the most stylistically advanced picture Root owned at that time. During the 1920s Root also purchased from the Daniel Gallery works by three other progressive young American artists, Charles Demuth (1883–1935, cat. nos. 68–70), Elsie Driggs (1898–1992, cat. nos. 76–77), and Charles Sheeler (1883–1965, cat. nos. 180–81), who similarly combined recognizable subject matter with a modernist sensibility (FIG. 15).

The story of Root 's first Demuth watercolor purchase is an especially poignant example of how his concern for an artist's welfare motivated him to buy. In the spring of 1923, more than a decade after easing Lawson's difficult financial circumstances by purchasing one of his paintings, Root received a letter from Charles Daniel (1878–1971) asking if he would be willing to pur-

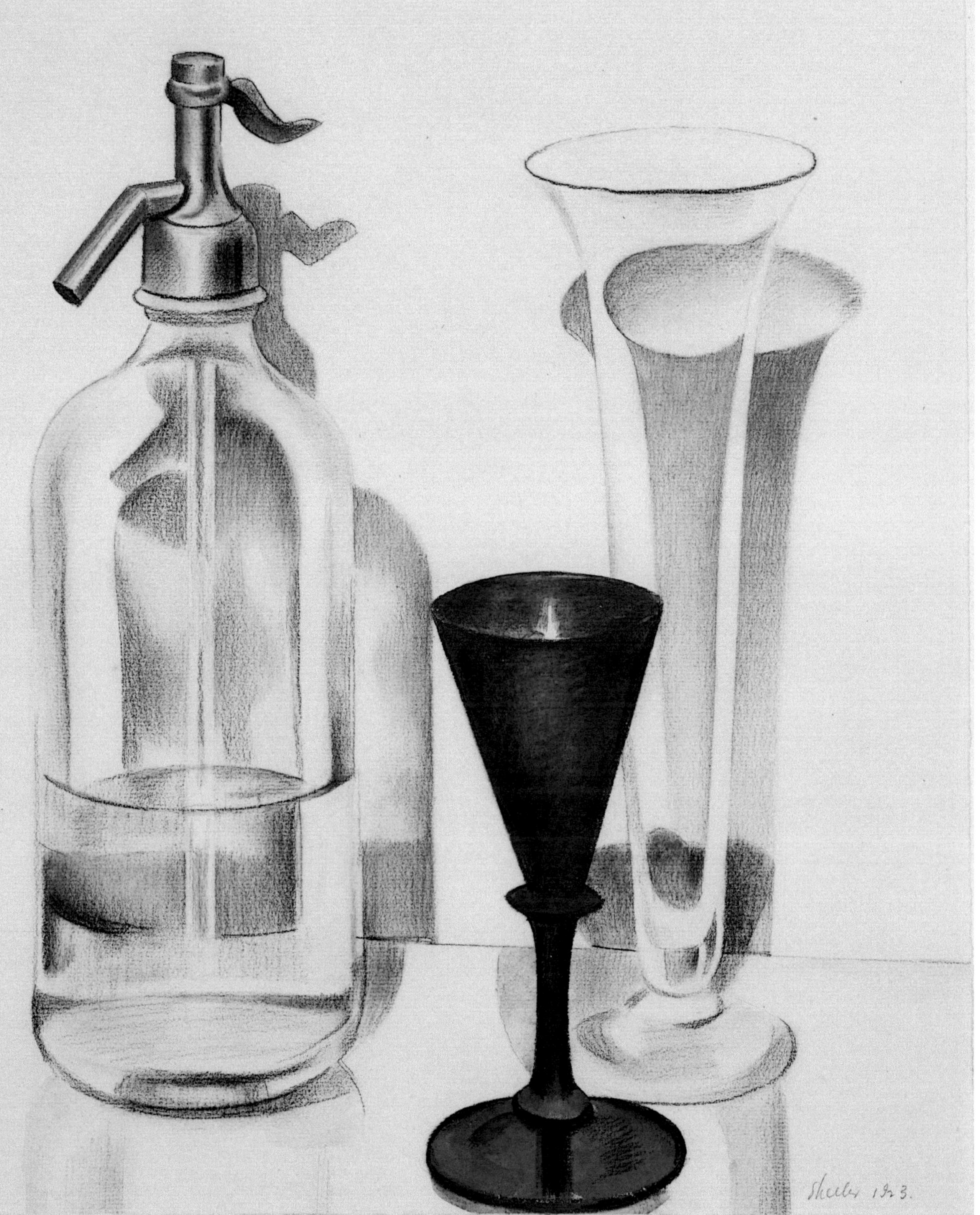
Sheeler 1923.

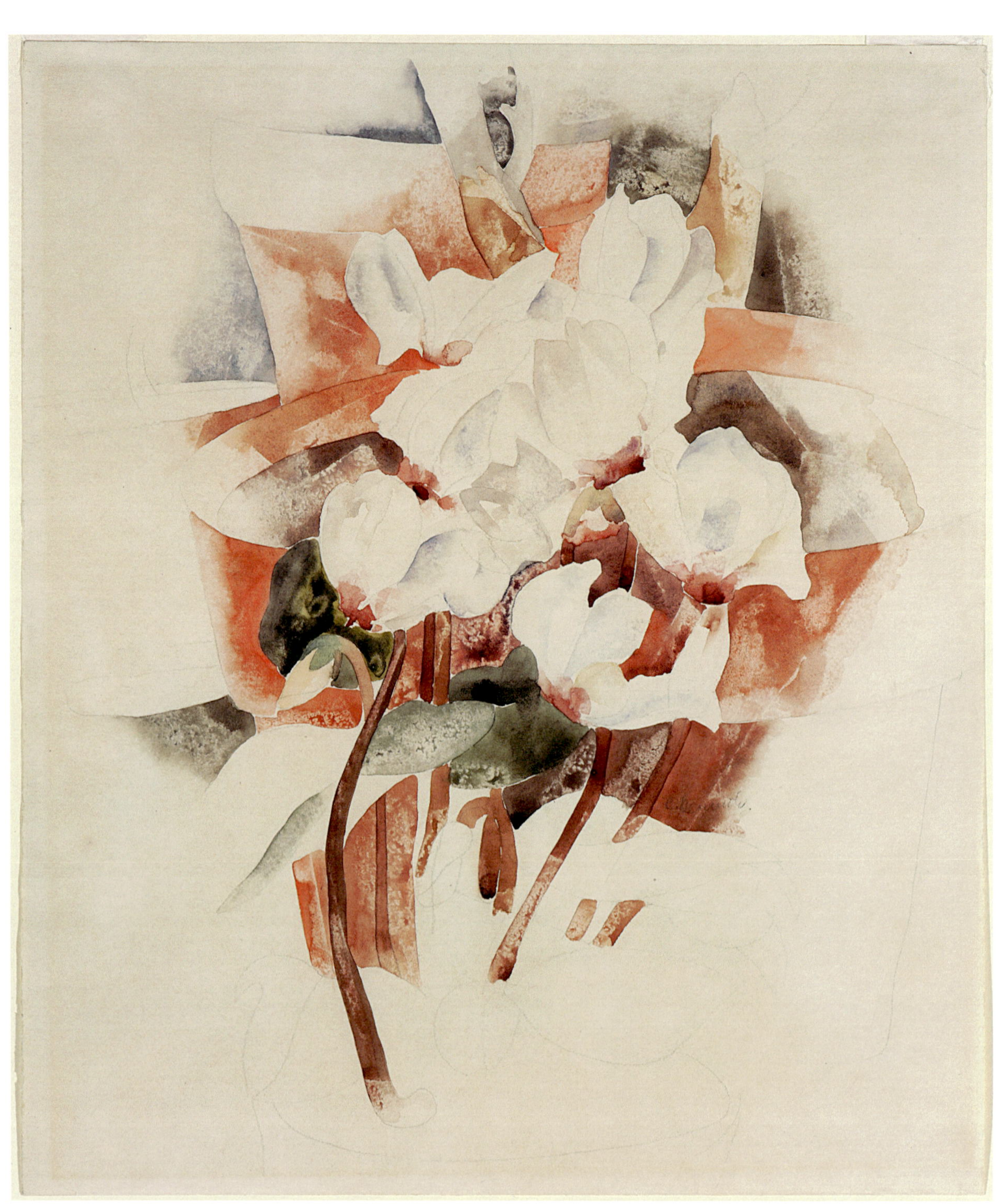

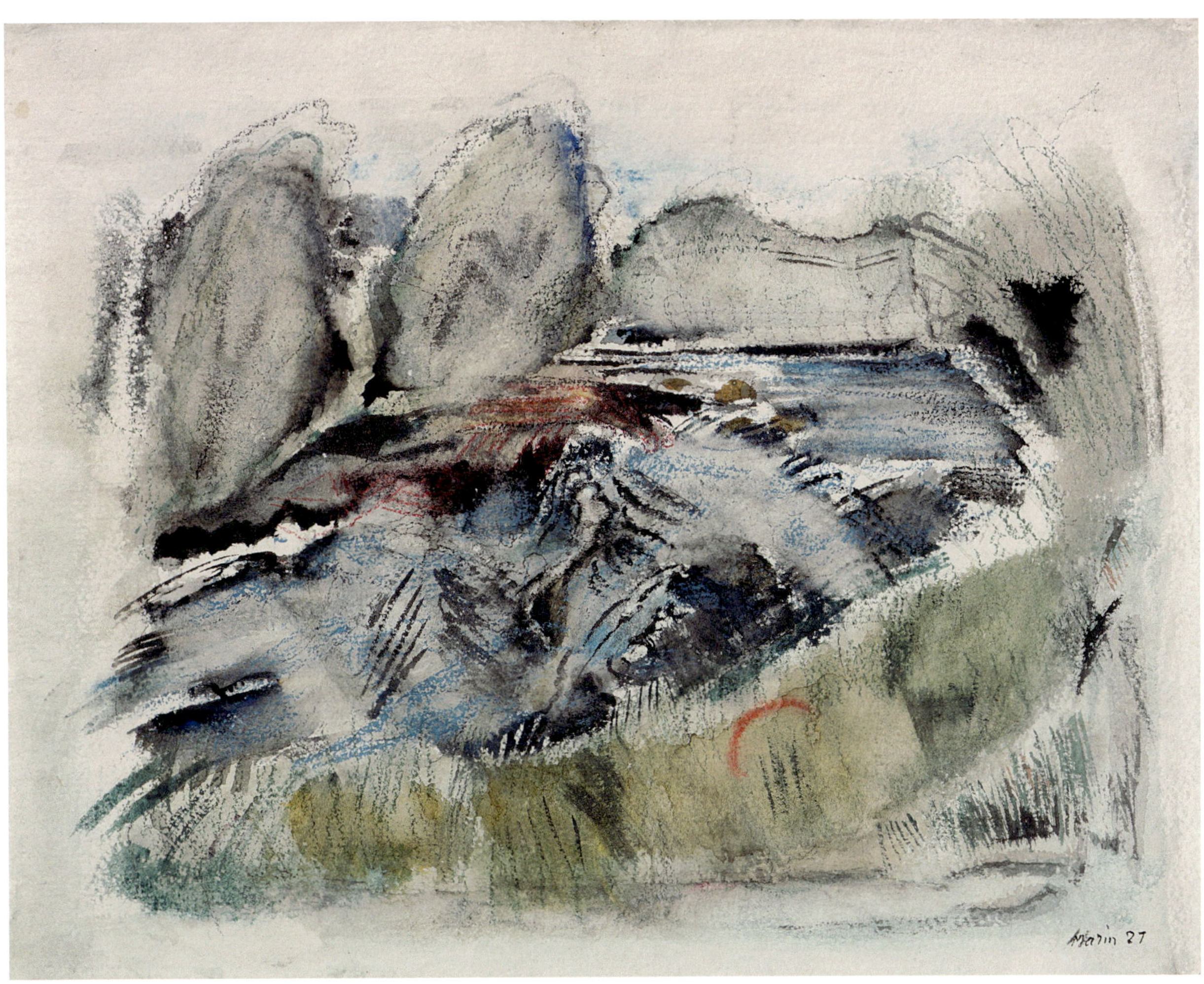

chase one of the artist's pictures because Demuth, "whose exquisite watercolors you have admired… is seriously ill with diabetes." Root responded shortly thereafter by sending Daniel two checks totaling $175. Root gave Daniel an additional $75 check in the fall of 1926 and received, in exchange, Demuth's watercolor, *Cyclamen (Flower Study)* (FIG. 16).[53]

During the 1930s, in addition to his extensive patronage of the Rehn Gallery, Root also frequented Edith G. Halpert's (1900–70) legendary Downtown Gallery. Early in 1931 Root acquired from her Demuth's *Purple Iris* (cat. no. 70). Several months later he remarked to his wife Grace that Demuth's watercolor reminded him "of a Chinese poem, unfinished, yet complete."[54] In 1937 he also acquired from Halpert a watercolor by John Marin (1870–1953), despite his reservations that Marin was "deeply moving but does not satisfy."[55] Years later Halpert recounted to Saarinen that she finally succeeded in selling Marin's watercolor, *White Mountain Country, The Rapids (The Rapids, New Hampshire)* (FIG. 17) to Root, after sending him to examine the watercolors in the *Winslow Homer Centenary Exhibition*, on view at the Whitney Museum of American Art.[56] After seeing the show, Root returned to the Downtown Gallery and said to Halpert, "All right, how much is this Marin, I know what you [now] mean—the continuity."[57]

Early in 1946 Root purchased another painting from Halpert, *Colors of Spring in the Harbor*, by Stuart Davis (1894–1964, FIG. 18). In this work Davis's semi-abstract imagery floats in a cubist grid of flat, overlapping, boldly colored

facing page
FIG. 16
Charles Demuth
Cyclamen (Flower Study)
Ca. 1921
Watercolor and graphite on white laid watercolor paper
13 7/8 x 11 7/8 in.
Cat. no. 68

above
FIG. 17
John Marin
White Mountain Country, The Rapids (The Rapids, New Hampshire), 1927
Watercolor, graphite, crayon and colored pencil on heavy watercolor paper
13 7/16 x 17 1/8 in.
Cat. no. 138

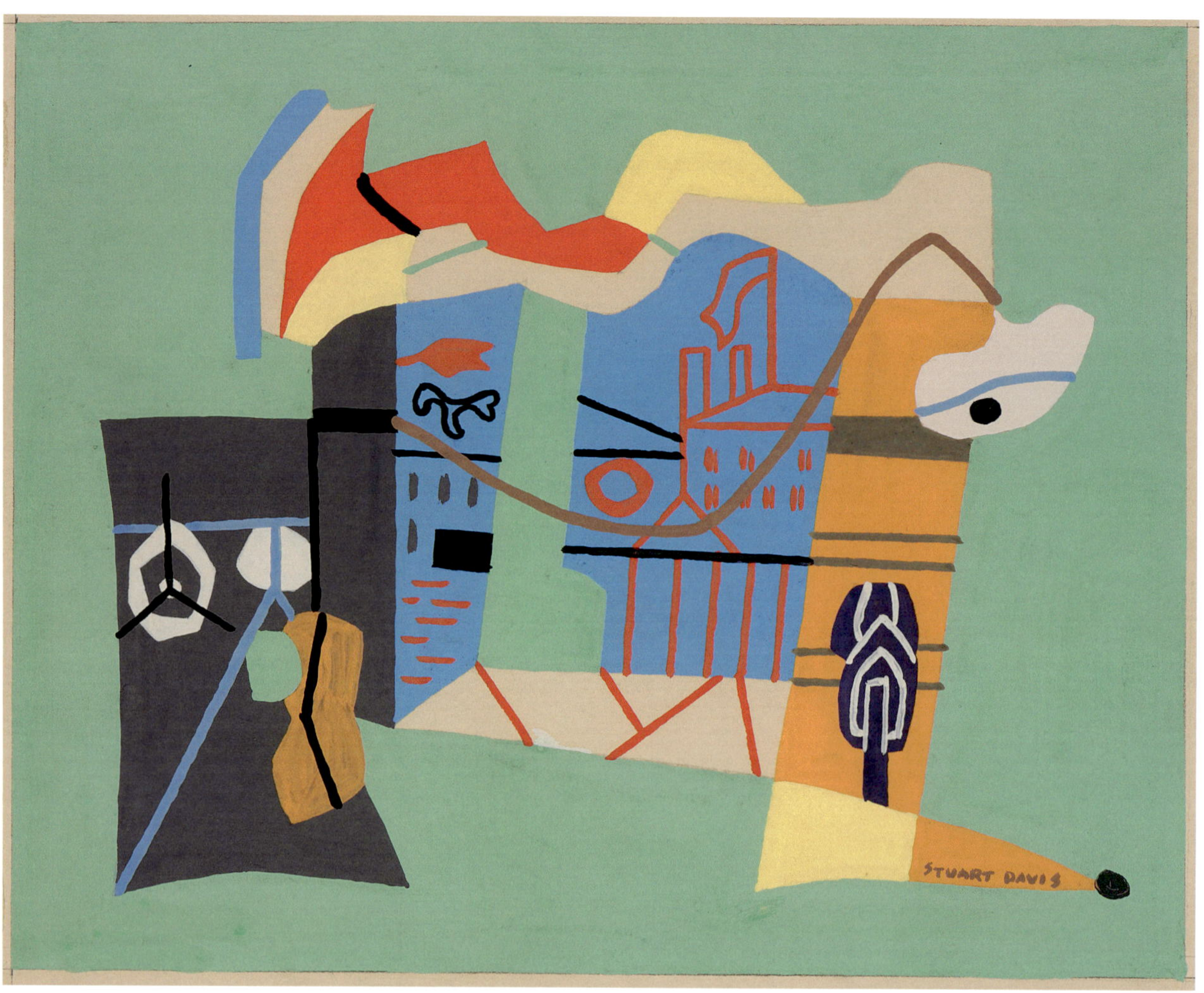

FIG. 18
Stuart Davis
Colors of Spring in the Harbor, 1939
Gouache on watercolor board
12 x 16 in.
Cat. no. 65

planes. In a lecture on modern art at the Munson-Williams-Proctor Institute in April 1947, Root noted that Davis composed pictures in the "abstract Cubist tradition," and that he was "not greatly concerned to associate these sensations and ideas with their natural source."[58]

A month before this lecture Root purchased from Halpert *No Feather Pillow* (FIG. 19), one of the four paintings by Arthur G. Dove (1880–1946) that Root bequeathed to the Institute. A true pioneer of modernism, Dove was one of the very first artists in Europe or the United States to paint abstract imagery at the beginning of the twentieth century.[59] It is unclear how much contact Root had with Dove's long-time dealer, the sometimes-acerbic photographer Alfred Stieglitz (1864–1946). Halpert knew that Root resented strong-arm salesmanship and that he probably was not comfortable with Stieglitz's hectoring manner.[60] She succeeded in selling *No Feather Pillow* to him because of her skills as a dealer, of course, but also because Root was deeply moved by Dove's pictures. He noted that Dove's imagery was based on a "feeling for nature" but that he transformed it into "something rich and strange."[61] This idea is a central tenet of Root's worldview. The ameliorating benefit of a picture that used nature as its source of inspiration was articulated by Root in 1920 when, at thirty-six years of age, he noted that nature "was not merely a heartless, terrifying mystery" but, instead, served as a bond between mankind and the "source of our origin."[62]

Root's four Dove paintings can be seen as a bridge linking his acquisitions of early American modernists and the group of younger artists he collected during the last decade of his life. Artist and Munson-Williams-Proctor

Institute School of Art director William C. Palmer (1906–87) remembered that Root told him in the mid-1940s "new things are happening. I don't know that I understand them or that I like them. But I must find out. I must buy them and try to find out."[63] Root reflected on this watershed period in his career as a collector:

> When I went back to New York to live during the winter of 1944–45 the production of abstractions by American artists was just beginning to be general. During that winter I became acquainted with the work of Tobey, Gatch, Baziotes, Stamos and Bertoia. These artists, several of them very young, seemed to me to have a special feeling for their medium and to be making a serious effort to develop new modes of expression. Therefore I have their pictures, and the pictures of certain other modern American artists, sympathetic attention.[64]

In the 1940s, Root had less money with which to purchase art so he began, as he had earlier in life, to collect the work of emerging artists. At this time, because of their mutual interest in art and nature, he developed a close friendship with Theodoros Stamos (1922–97), who started exhibiting in the early 1940s at commercial galleries and in 1946 at the Whitney Museum of American Art. Stamos vividly recalled that

> Edward Root and I met many years ago during my first showing at the old Whitney Museum. He liked that painting and purchased it.

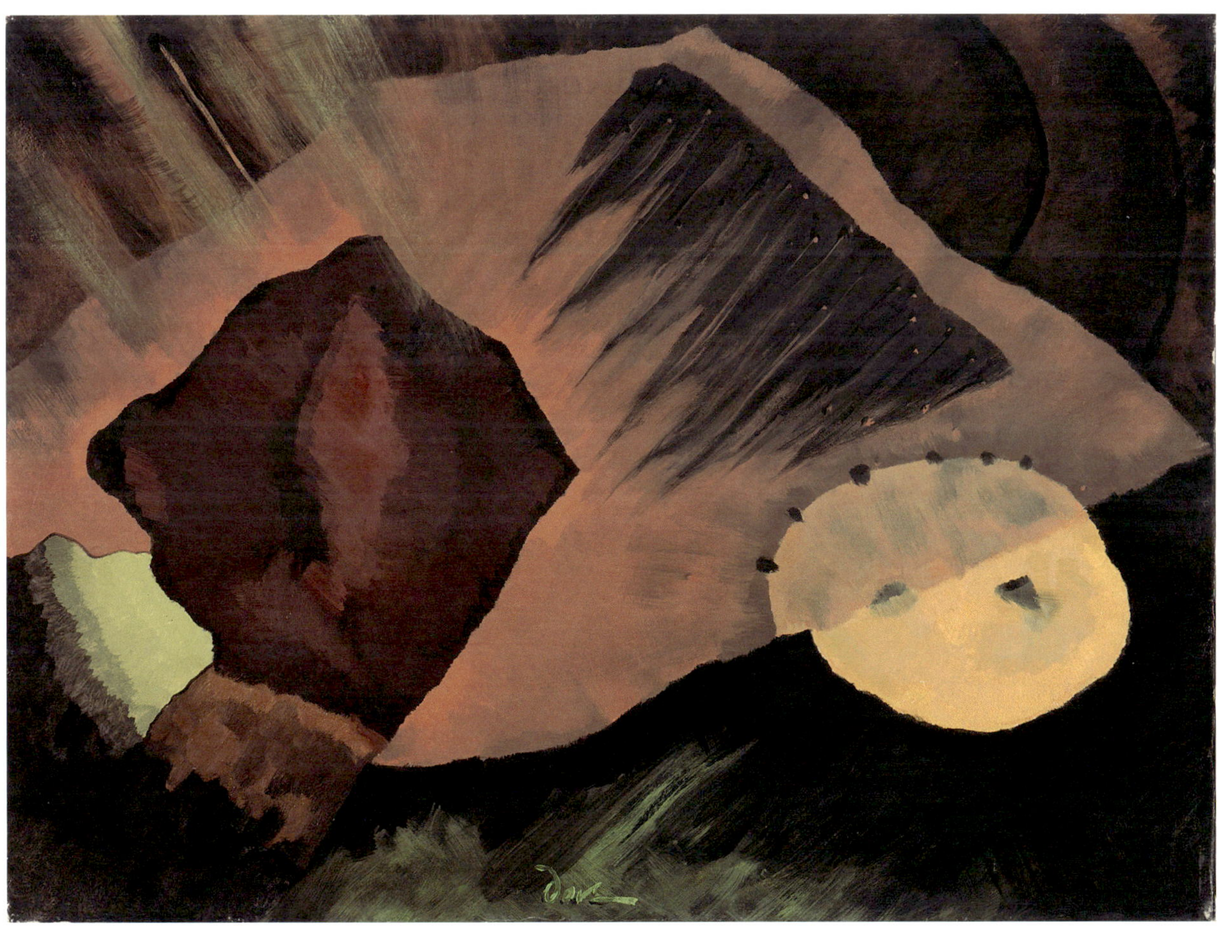

FIG. 19
Arthur G. Dove
No Feather Pillow, 1940
Oil and wax emulsion on linen
16 x 22 in.
Cat. no. 73

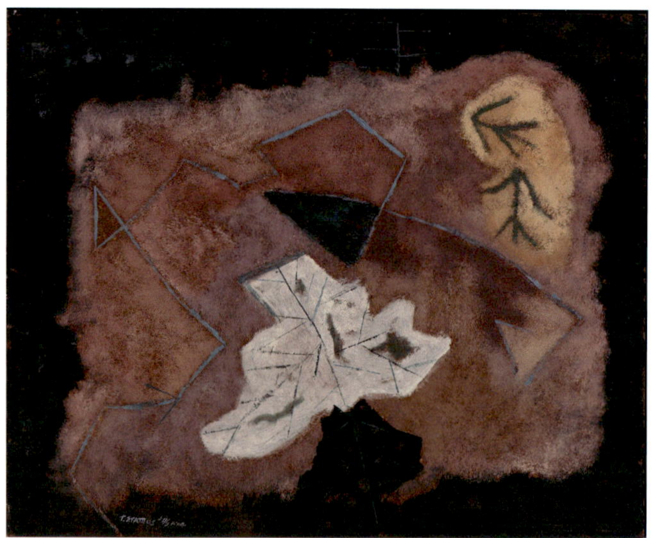

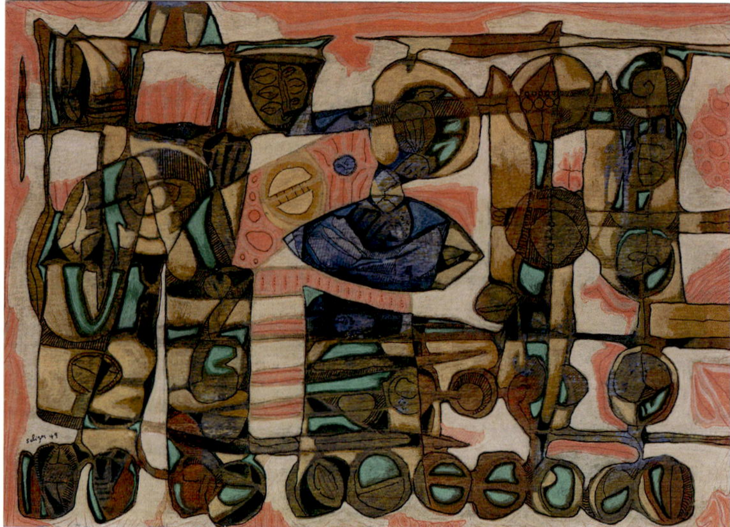

above
FIG. 20
Theodoros Stamos
Movement of Plants, 1945
Oil on Masonite
16 x 20 in.
Cat. no. 199

above right
FIG. 21
Charles Seliger
Cross-Section: Plant Life, 1949
Oil, tempera, and ink on thin cardboard
7 ⅞ x 11 ¼ in.
Cat. no. 174

> He came to the gallery that handles my work, saw several more, and bought three of them—it was that day that I met Edward. He liked the paintings because… they had roots in Nature, about which I think Edward was one of the most learned of men.[65]

The paintings to which Stamos refers are *Movement of Plants* (FIG. 20), *Blue Fish, Bone,* and *Cosmological Battle (Formlings)* (cat. nos. 190, 191, 193). Root in fact was one of Stamos's first patrons, acquiring numerous paintings between 1945 and 1953. Stamos later recollected, "Edward visited me in my studio quite often, where I left him to go through the paintings which were stacked along the walls. He would sit by himself, going through them and… arriving at three or four which he would buy at once, outright."[66] The sixteen Stamos paintings that Root bequeathed to the Museum follow only the larger group of watercolors by Burchfield that Root donated.

The earliest works by Stamos in Root's bequest, such as the charming *Blue Fish*, 1944, are representational, but by the next year, he began painting more abstractly, so that in *Seedling (The Embryo; Vortex and Spiral)* (cat. no. 201), *Movement of Plants*, and *Cosmological Battle (Formlings)*, all painted in 1945, Stamos used earth-toned colors as well as forms resembling leaves, pine cones, or similar organic material that float in an undefined space. The compositions suggest pulsating cycles of seasonal change at an essential level. In the mid-1940s Stamos also created paintings with a predominately blue-green palette, as if he were evoking oceanic realms.

At several venues during the 1950s, Stamos presented a lecture entitled "Why Nature in Art," in which he outlined his influences, of which Arthur Dove is noteworthy for this essay:

> For me Dove is one of our most original painters whether he worked in a semi-abstract or totally abstract vein… in the 1930s Dove's forms loosened and became more organic with color patterns related to flames and amorphous growths of woods of which he was so fond. But his canvases always built into beautiful compositions that at times resemble the expressive glory of Chinese calligraphic characters while never deviating from their base in a physical world. He responded openly to farmlands, the wind, the rain and the sea.[76]

Stamos also lauded "Oriental" picture making and recommended it as a model of understanding contemporary abstraction. He noted that Pacific

Northwest artists Mark Tobey (1890–1976) and Morris Graves (1910–2001) openly subscribed to Asian philosophy while the paintings of Mark Rothko (1903–1970) and Jackson Pollock (1912–56) emulated Eastern sources in their evocation of the infinite. All of these artists are represented in Root's collection.

Root was similarly attracted to nature-based imagery by Charles Seliger (b. 1926), who was an adolescent when he showed at Peggy Guggenheim's (1898–1979) Art of This Century, a showcase for artists of the emerging New York School. Seliger's paintings of organic form reflected the artist's belief that life was a renewing, organic process, in which "things were always becoming... developing [into] the mysterious and beautiful."[68] By 1948, after the Carlebach Gallery in New York began representing the artist, Root acquired eight of his recent paintings and drawings (cat. nos. 172–79), which he subsequently bequeathed to the Museum. In contrast to Stamos's vision of nature, Seliger's compositions are tiny, jewel-toned obsessive renderings of plants and insects (FIGS. 20, 21). But like Stamos, Seliger was fascinated by natural history. The small fanciful insect pictures he made at this time were based on the artist's readings of books by entomologist Jean-Henri Fabre (1823–1915). Seliger recalled that Root liked these paintings very much and called them "my little beasties."[69] Indeed, Seliger's recollections of Root are very warm: "Edward Root was probably one of the most superior art collectors. I mean just a remarkable, sensitive man. He followed your work with such devotion it was unbelievable."[70]

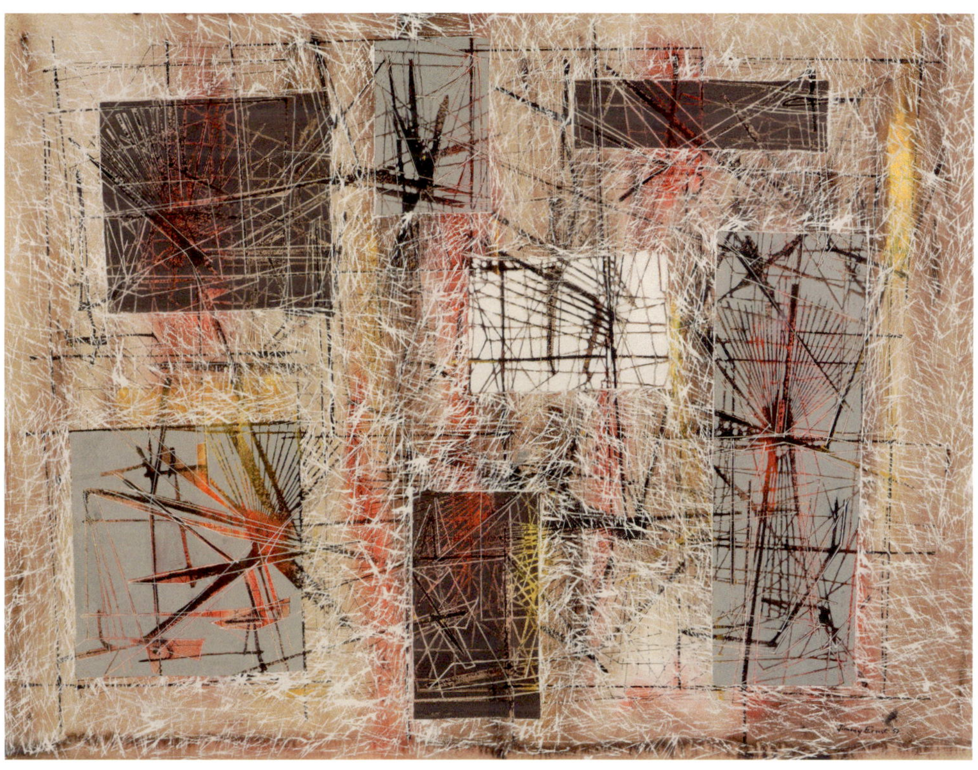

FIG. 22
Jimmy Ernst
Honky Tonk, 1951
Gouache on heavy white paper
22 3/8 x 30 in.
Cat. no. 80

Jimmy Ernst (1920–84), son of artist Max Ernst (1891–1976), emigrated to the United States in 1938 and worked briefly at Art of This Century. When the young Ernst launched himself as a professional artist, showing with increasing success at the Norlyst, Laurel, and Grace Borgenicht Galleries, Root bought five of his works on paper (FIG. 22). It should be noted, however, that when Root purchased three of these works from Ernst's 1950 Laurel Gallery show he wasn't exactly a voice crying in the wilderness; other buyers included The Museum of Modern Art, Nelson Rockefeller (1908–79), and the Toledo Museum of Art.[71]

The Ernsts that Root purchased were among the scores of drawings he acquired by New York's young, emerging artists. His friend Bartlett H. Hayes, Jr. (1904–88), Director of the Addison Gallery of American Art, recalled Root's opinions about drawings:

It was he who one time called my attention to the fact that a draw-

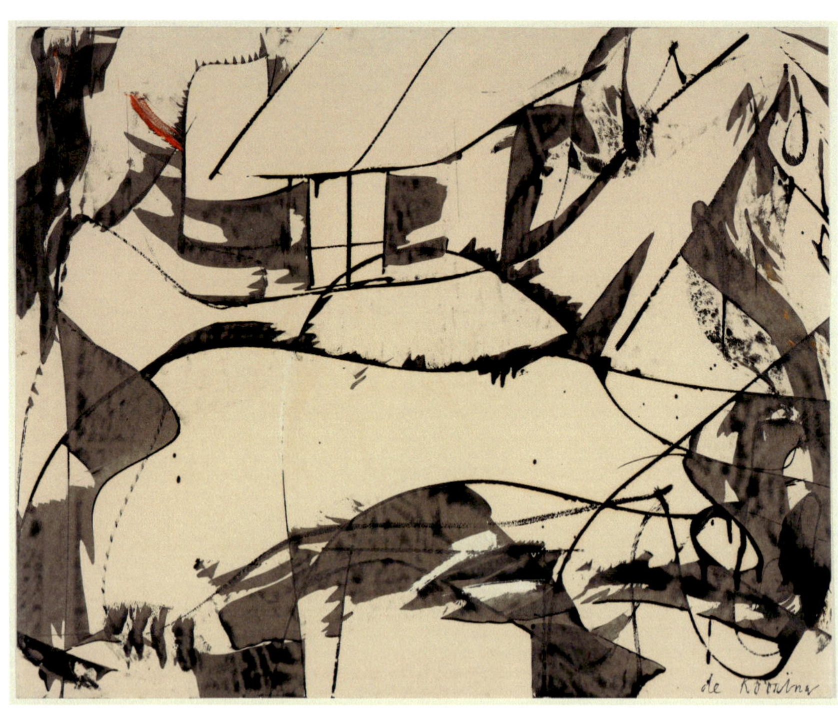

> ing is no more than the trace left by the hand, the record of a gesture, and that the human quality in the drawing arises from the relation between the emotional and rational guidance of the muscles and the changes in them of which the drawing is the brief historical chart.[72]

FIG. 23
Boardman Robinson
Bathers Wrestling, before 1928
Ink and wash with crayon on white paper
19 x 13 in., irregular
Cat. no. 161

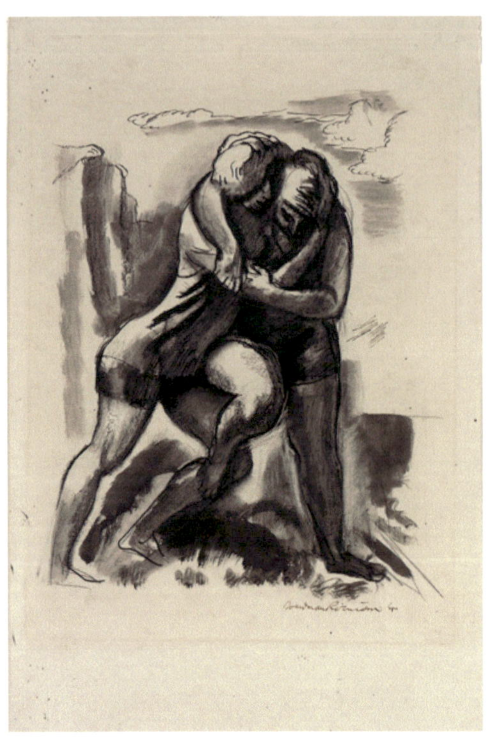

Root collected works on paper by two artists, William Harris (active 1940s), and Don Manfredi (b. 1930) who are ciphers because so little information can be found about them sixty years after they exhibited in New York galleries (cat. nos. 103, 134). Others, however, enjoyed renown. Federico Castellón (1914–71) was championed by both the Mexican muralist Diego Rivera (1886–1957) and the Weyhe Gallery, where Root purchased graphic arts for many years. Root bought twelve Castellón works on paper that depict the young man's Dalíesque dreamscapes. He donated five of his works to the Institute in the early 1950s and included the remaining seven in his bequest (cat. nos. 52–58). From Weyhe Root also bought decoratively patterned images by Edward J. Stevens, Jr. (1923–88, cat. no. 210), whose photograph graced the cover of a 1950 *Life* magazine article entitled "Nineteen Young American Artists."[73] The *Life* article also featured Stephen Greene (1918–99, cat. no. 101), a Prix de Rome recipient whose sensitively wrought vegetable still life Root acquired in 1949.

Root's eclectic taste at this unsettled artistic moment is demonstrated by other acquisitions of the period. His friendships with writers included contributors to *The New Yorker*, and his art collection had ink drawings by cartoonists William Steig (1907–2003, cat. nos. 204–06)—selections of whose series "Small Fry," "Lonely Ones," "All Embarrassed," and "About People" were shown at Munson-Williams-Proctor Institute in February 1947—and Saul Steinberg (1914–99, cat. nos. 207–08).[74] Root had, in fact, a long-standing appreciation for cartooning. On January 21, 1928 he wrote to the editors of the *Utica Daily Press* praising the "powerful, living line-draftsmanship" of Boardman Robinson's (1876–1952) youthful drawings; the letter was occasioned by a

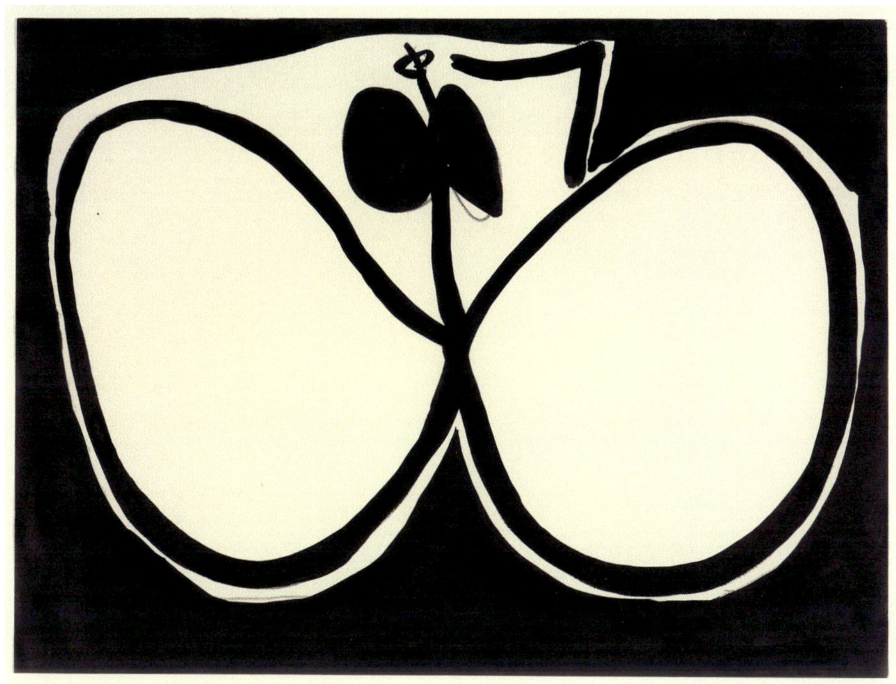

Robinson exhibition at the Utica Art Society, from which Root purchased the drawing, *Bathers Wrestling* (FIG. 23). Root recollected that, as a young newspaperman at the New York *Evening Sun*, he was "deeply impressed by the series of cartoons by... [Robinson] which appeared on the editorial page of the *Tribune* about 1910 or, perhaps, a little earlier.... Their wit and the breadth and ease with which they were drawn gave them...the unique distinction of being executed by a man who was not only a journalist but an artist."[75] Root's admiration for Robinson's drawings coincided with his friendships with members of The Eight who began their careers as artist-reporters and whose training demanded the telling narrative gesture by minimal drawing means.

facing page
FIG. 24
Willem de Kooning
Abstract Drawing, 1951
Oil and enamel on heavy wove paper
24 5/16 x 30 ½ in.
Cat. no. 67

above
FIG. 25
Robert Motherwell
Nude, 1952
Brush-applied black ink over graphite on wove paper, mounted on illustration board
21 ⅞ x 29 ¾ in.
Cat. no. 147

Root collected works on paper created with a wide variety of materials and an equally wide range of emotional content. The polar opposite of cartoons are the expressionist, semi-figurative pieces by John Edward Heliker (1909–2000, cat. no. 104), and Joseph Glasco (1925–96, cat. nos. 93–95). These complement the drawings and small paintings that Root was simultaneously buying from older or better-known artists such as William A. Baziotes (1912–63, cat. nos. 2–6), Willem de Kooning (1904–97), Arshile Gorky (1904–48, cat. no. 96), Robert Motherwell (1915–91), Jackson Pollock (1912–56, cat. nos. 151–52), and Mark Rothko (1903–70, cat. no. 162). Root's drawings by de Kooning and Motherwell make an interesting comparison in that they are both figurative studies in the tradition of nude studio models, and tradition in contemporary art was a quality Root admired (FIG. 24, 25).[76] Beyond the drawings' subjects, though, they are poles apart in tone: the former is all scraped pigment (or flesh) while the other is sensual.[77]

The expressionist style of this era was initially difficult to comprehend, even by artworld insiders such as critics, gallery owners, and museum trustees, who struggled to find meaning in and give explanations for abstractions' seemingly random marks of paint. Root was a true leader among collectors because, even with reservations, he had faith in artists' sincerity. He patronized galleries run by Betty Parsons (1900–82)—The Wakefield Bookshop,

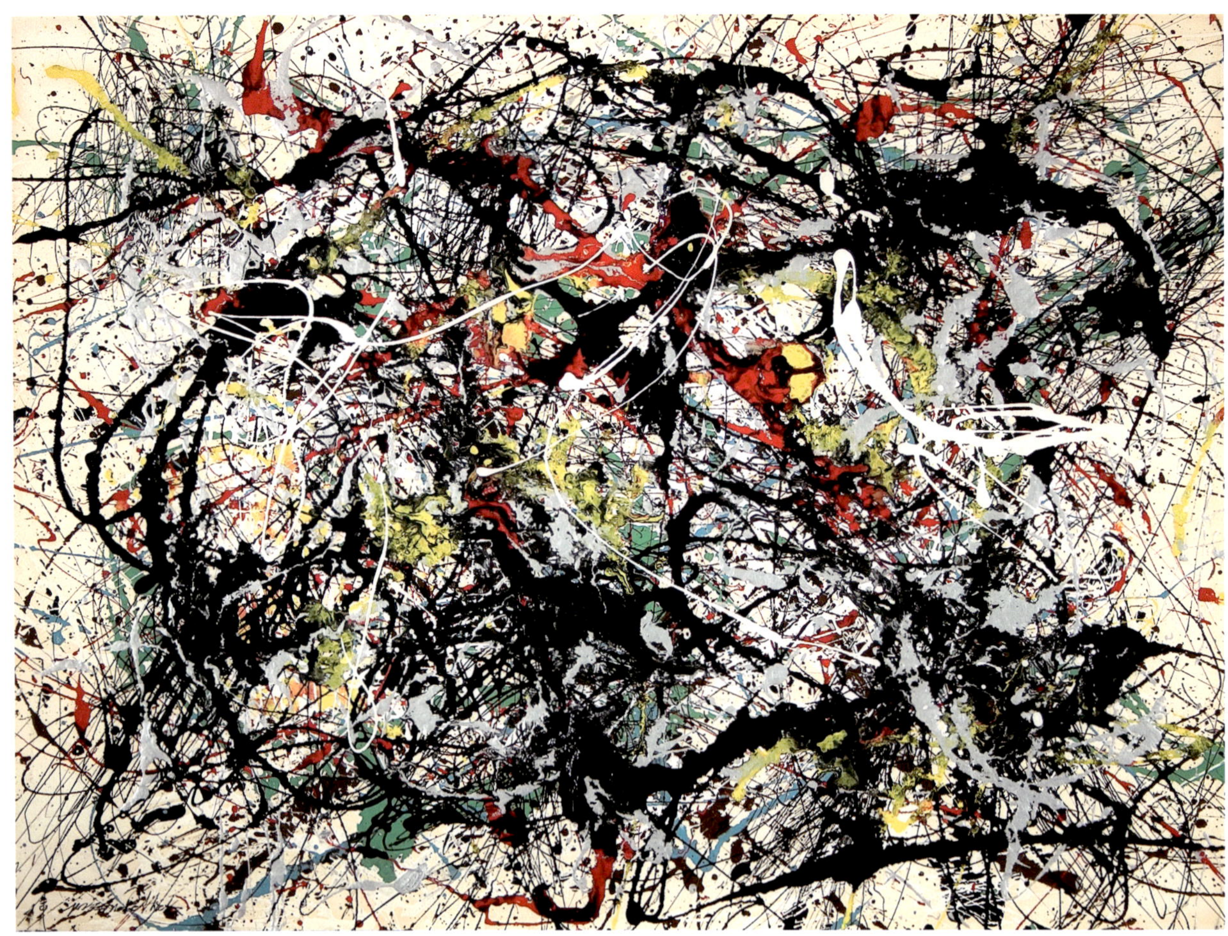

FIG. 26
Jackson Pollock
Number 34, 1949, 1949
Oil and enamel paint on white paperboard mounted on Masonite
22 x 30 ½ in.
Cat. no. 152

facing page
FIG. 27
Mark Rothko
Number 11 (Untitled: Abstraction), 1947
Oil on linen
39 ⅜ x 38 ⅝ in.
Cat. no. 162

Mortimer Brandt, and finally, the Betty Parsons Gallery. He also bought Abstract Expressionist paintings and drawings from New York dealers such as the Willard, Kootz, and Egan Galleries. It is surmised that he first encountered the work of Pollock at Art of This Century, but waited until the artist broke through to his pour paintings before acquiring anything by him. In January 1949 Root bought Pollock's dense and discretely colored *Number 20, 1948* (cat. no. 151) from Parsons. Root purchased a more baroque, colorful, and slightly larger picture, *Number 34, 1949* from a second exhibition that Parsons held for Pollock in 1949 (FIG. 26). A week after that show closed, Root wrote in a letter to the Munson-Williams-Proctor Institute's Community Arts Program Director, Harris K. Prior (1911–75), about "the small under glass Pollock which you liked when you saw it in the [Parsons] exhibition." Root marveled that "the more I look at … [it] the more it seems to me to be extraordinary as an example of almost explosive vitality kept within the bounds of a complex and orderly form."[78]

Root bought Rothko's *Omens of Gods and Birds* (1944–45, coll. Christopher Rothko), but in the months between his two Pollock purchases he traded it for Rothko's *Number 11 (Untitled Abstraction)* (FIG. 27).[79] This painterly abstraction reveals the artist at an interesting moment, when he abandoned representational, symbolic imagery in search of a more universal visual communication that would convey the most profound human emotional content. As with his Marin purchase from Halpert in 1937, Root equivocated about the works he had bought from Parsons. In a May 12, 1949 letter to his friend Bartlett Hayes,

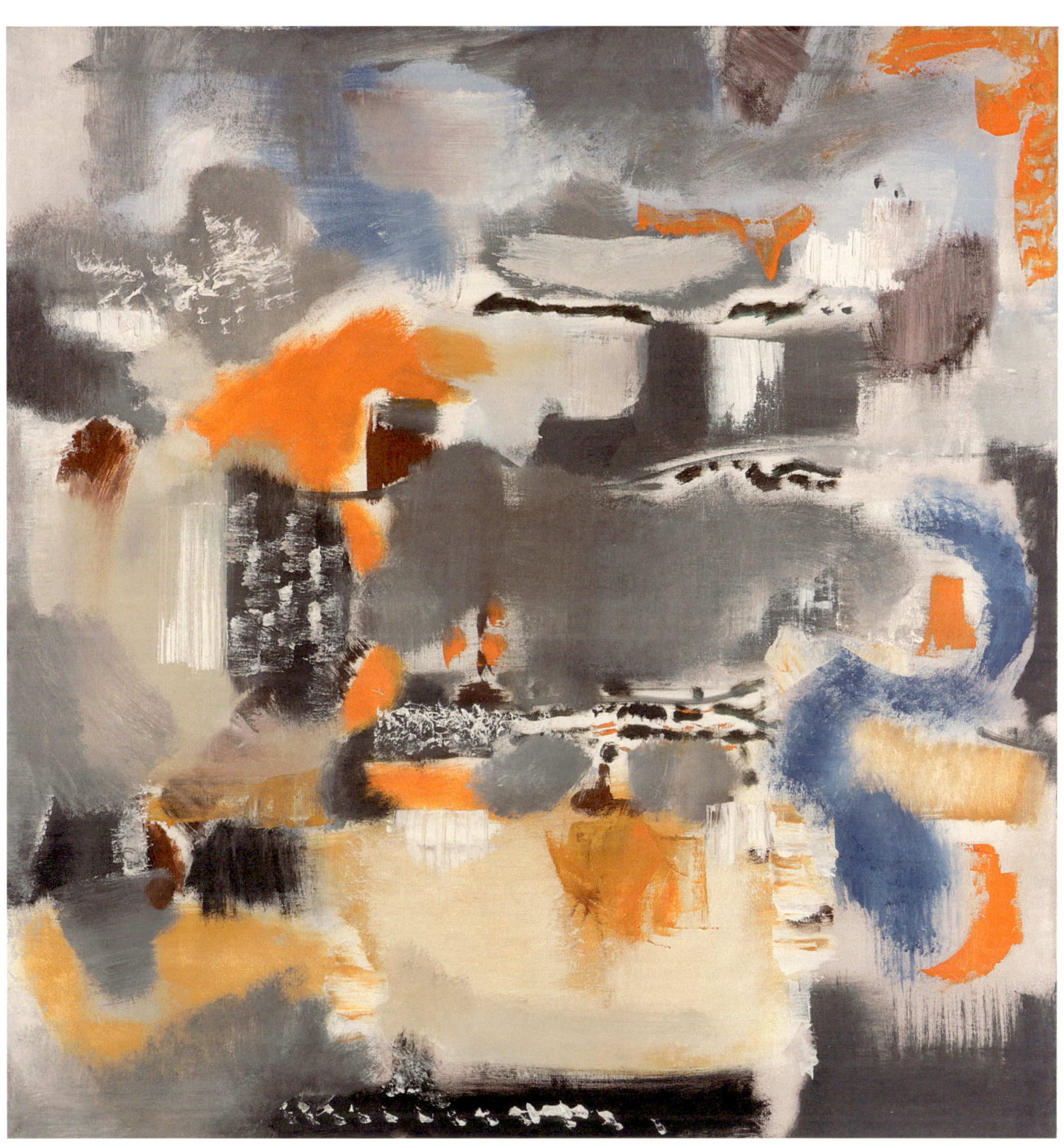

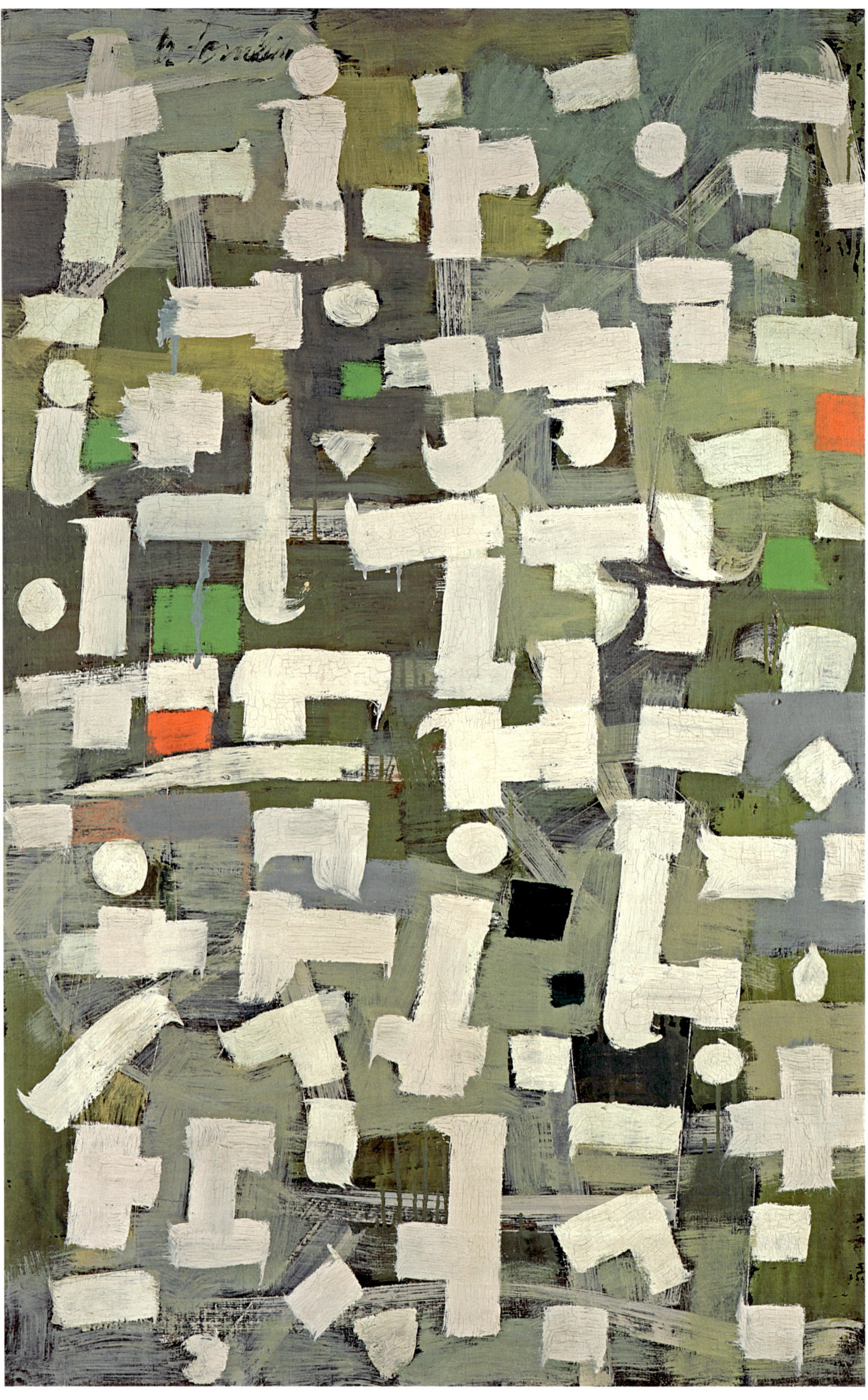

he confessed, "Pollock and Rothko still seem to me to be brilliant executants, but unsatisfying companions."[80] Root nevertheless acquired the paintings the better to understand them.

Two years after buying the Rothko, Root also purchased from the Betty Parsons Gallery two of Bradley Walker Tomlin's (1899–1953) "calligraphic"-style pictures, *Number 11* (FIG. 28), and the largest picture among the works he bequeathed to the Museum, Tomlin's *Number 1*, 1951 (cat. no. 220). In the mid-1940s when the Rehn Gallery represented Tomlin, Root bought the artist's Synthetic Cubist-inspired composition, *Watermelon* (FIG. 29). After meeting a number of the young Abstract Expressionists, however, Tomlin's style underwent a radical transformation and, in 1950, he began exhibiting with Parsons. Two years later, when Tomlin was included The Museum of Modern Art's epochal *15 Americans* exhibition, Root wrote a short statement about the artist for the catalog. For those "who enjoy sensitively manipulated pigment and linear suggestions of movement," Root remarked about Tomlin's pictures, the "complex arrangements of bands, pot-hooks, boomerangs, letters, dots, rectangles, zigzags and so forth [are] a sort of pictorial equivalent of ballet, in which the many figures shimmy, gyrate, contort or drift at two or more levels with stimulating spontaneity and with an over-all coordination which is as satisfying as it is unobtrusive."[81] Root's colorful description of Tomlin's marks, which he insightfully compared to a dance, was published several months before the art critic Harold Rosenberg (1906–78) used a similar kinetic trope in his famous article, "American Action Painting," to describe the art of the Abstract Expressionists. Rosenberg wrote

> At a certain moment the canvas began to appear to one painter after another as an arena in which to act—rather than as a space in which to reproduce, re-design, analyze, or "express" an object, actual or imagined. What was to go on the canvas was not a picture but an event.[82]

facing page
FIG. 28
Bradley Walker Tomlin
Number 11, ca. 1949
Oil on linen
44 ⅛ x 29 in.
Cat. no. 221

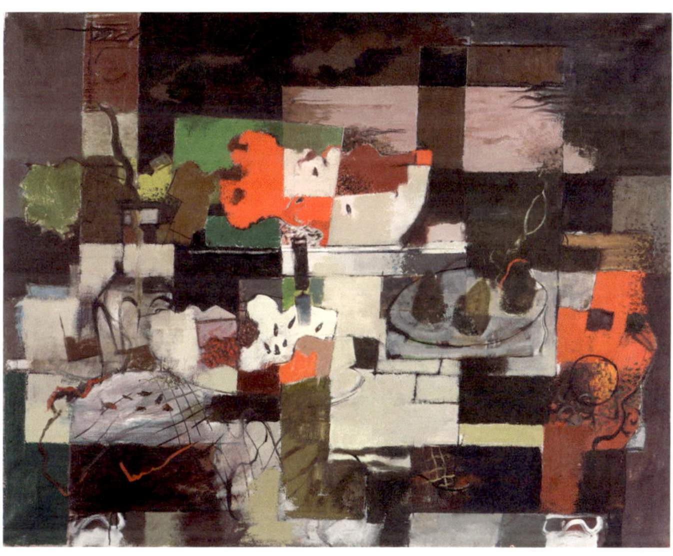

FIG. 29
Bradley Walker Tomlin
Watermelon, 1942
Oil on linen
37 x 48 ⅛ in.
Cat. no. 222

Root's comments about dance may also be an extension of his growing interest in music during the later years of his life, as improvements in hearing aid technology made it possible for him to overcome the deafness that handicapped his younger years. In his struggle to formulate critical standards by which he could understand and judge thoroughly abstract compositions such as those by Tomlin, Root thought that their appeal lay in their ability to evoke a feeling for "organized sensations" while, simultaneously conveying—like the music he was discovering—"spiritual overtones." The boundary between these two realms perplexed him. Echoing the European abstract painter, Wassily Kandinsky (1866–1944), Root noted: "I think that perhaps Kandinsky was right. Where does sensation end and spirituality begin? Who can say?"[83]

Root could ponder this question as he reflected on the work of Pacific Northwest artists, Graves and Tobey. Graves, who was inspired by Zen Buddhism, sought to be in the moment when he painted. He believed that "painting is a way of knowledge" that might reveal a reality beyond the material world. The works by Graves that Root bequeathed to the Museum can be described as meditations in which the artist made simple but mindful brushstrokes for a flower, a bird, or water (cat. nos. 97–100, FIG. 30).

Tobey similarly was inspired by spiritual impulses based on his Bahá'í faith, as signaled in a work such as *Vita Nova* (cat. no. 218) or *Voyage of the Saints* (cat. no. 219), a later picture in which Tobey's modulated line creates a unified composition reflecting the artist's beliefs that "our minds and hearts must be unlocked [to a] vision of unity between all persons." Many of Tobey's paintings in the Root collection, however, are animated with a dazzling line that depicts in abstract terms the vitality of New York City. *Partitions of the City* (FIG. 31)—which Root purchased directly from the artist in 1951—and *Awakening Night* (cat. no. 214), are cityscapes abstracted into overall patterns of pulsating figures, traffic, electric signs, and buildings. In *New York Tablet* (FIG. 38), Tobey formed a monolith that suggests the glass façade of a skyscraper; critic Robert M. Coates (1897–1973) described the painting as suggesting "a window view over a multitude of glittering buildings."[84]

Root believed that Tobey was the "most original of all American painters, but his pictures are so different in every respect from our accepted ideas of what a picture should be."[85] The difference in Root's mind may have been Tobey's calligraphic painting style, called "white writing," that was consonant with similar experiments by other artists of the Abstract Expressionist era. Root studied his Tobeys carefully, as demonstrated by some notes he made on scrap paper remarking that "each picture is built up out of lines of a certain type" and with diagrams of the paintings' basic linear structure.[86]

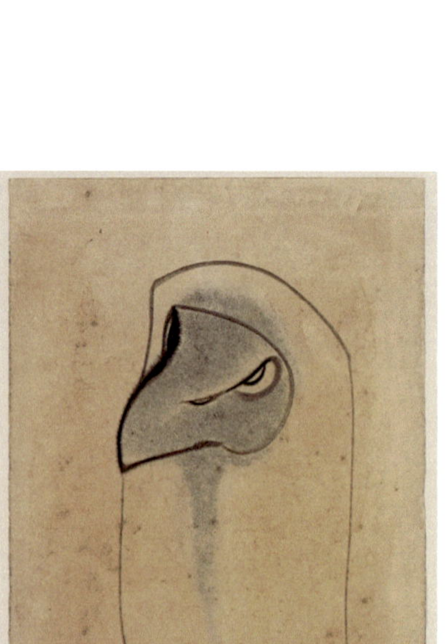

FIG. 30
Morris Graves
Nestling (Fledgling), 1950
Watercolor and pastel on laid watercolor paper
18 ⅞ x 12 ½ in.
Cat. no. 99

facing page
FIG. 31
Mark Tobey
Partitions of the City, 1945
Tempera and opaque watercolor on Masonite
30 ½ x 23 ⅞ in.
Cat. no. 216

When Graves and Tobey began exhibiting their work at commercial galleries and museums in New York City, Root was an early patron. Art dealer Marian Willard Johnson (1904–85), who was instrumental in promoting them on the East Coast, recollected that Edward began visiting her New York gallery around 1941 or 1942. Later, in 1950, Root and Willard traveled together to the West Coast.[88] Root's interest in the contemporary artists of this region may have been encouraged by Harris Prior who, when he assumed the directorship of the Munson-Williams-Proctor Institute's Community Arts Program (the forerunner of today's Museum of Art) in 1947, was an authority on painting in the Pacific Northwest and, less than a year after his arrival in Utica, organized the traveling exhibition, *Ten Painters of the Pacific Northwest*.[89] It should be noted, though, that Root had acquired his first Graves drawing in 1945, before he met Prior. Nevertheless, between 1945 and 1951, Root confidently purchased from Willard four more Graves drawings, three of which within a year of their creation. Between 1946 and 1953 Root also bought from the Willard Gallery five of the six Tobeys he gave the Museum. As with Graves, Root acquired each of them within a year of their being made.

Root's loyalty to his artist-friends was reciprocated. When he died in December 1956, the Munson-Williams-Proctor Institute quickly organized an exhibition to honor him the following spring.[90] One painting each by thirty-six artists whom Root had supported was included.[91] While fourteen had predeceased Root, many of the others personally selected their work for the show. Several artists wrote glowing testimonies to Root for the exhibition catalog. Charles Burchfield admired Root's "complete independence and his uncompromising honesty." Morris Kantor (1896–1974) "was impressed with Root's sincere devotion to American art and his understanding and kindness to artists." William Palmer noted that Root "believed in the growth and development of art and its contribution to life," while Mark Tobey found Root, "never preaching but showing in his choice of paintings a discrimination without pretense of any kind."[92] A few years later, Harris Prior authored the article, "Edward Root: Talent Scout," in which he noted significant purchases Root made by artists

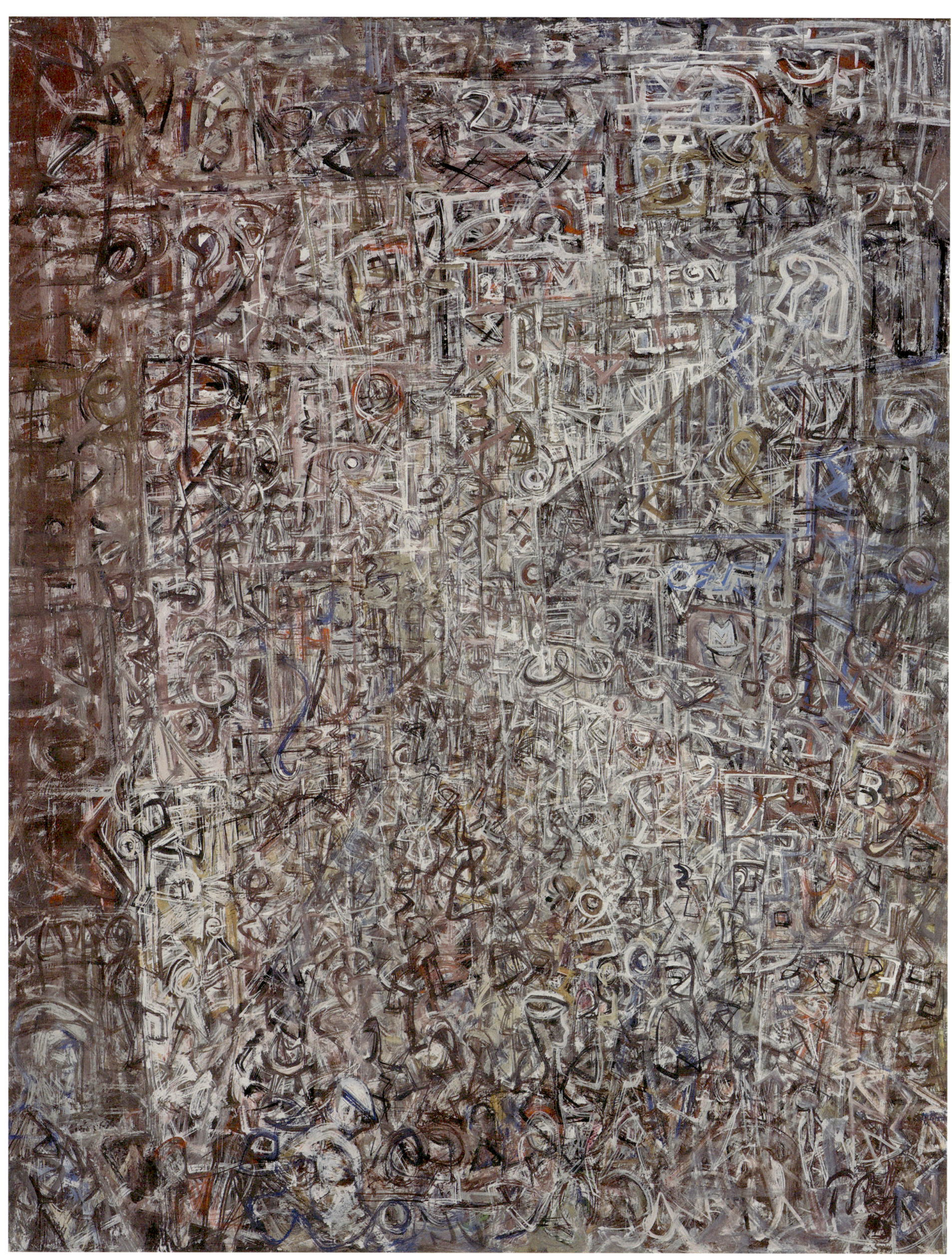

when they still qualified as emerging.[93] Prior believed that Root's promotion of new talent in his lifetime held up well because Root acquired art "with love, humility and perceptiveness... not in order to carry out any museum concept of general completeness or even of individual importance, but simply to provide visual nourishment for an acquisitive eye and mind, and occasionally to help an artist over a difficult period in his life."[94]

MODERNISM AT THE METROPOLITAN MUSEUM OF ART

In the spring of 1953, The Metropolitan Museum of Art in New York presented a large exhibition of 132 of Root's paintings, watercolors, and drawings (FIG. 32).[95] The show featured the work of sixty-seven American and six British artists. Only nine of these artists were deceased when it took place. Among those who did not have the satisfaction of seeing their pictures included in the exhibition were some of Root's oldest and closest friends: Luks, Prendergast, Davies, and Demuth. Chronologically, the works in the show spanned the first six decades of the twentieth century, and ranged in date from Louis M. Eilshemius' (1864–1941) watercolor, *Black Hills, Delaware Water Gap*, 1896–97 (cat no. 78), to Glasco's *Boy* (cat. no. 93), and Motherwell's *Nude* (cat. no. 147), both executed in 1952 and, as such, the most contemporary pieces in the show. Root acquired more than half of the works in the exhibition during the fertile period that began in New York in the winter of 1944–45 when he became aware of the young American artists who, as he noted, were "making a serious effort to develop new modes of expression."[96] Root subsequently bequeathed ninety of the American pictures in the Metropolitan Museum's exhibition to the Munson-Williams-Proctor Institute. The sixteen English and Irish pictures in the show, all from the 1940s and early 1950s, reflect the interest Edward and his wife Grace developed for contemporary British art in the post-War years.[97]

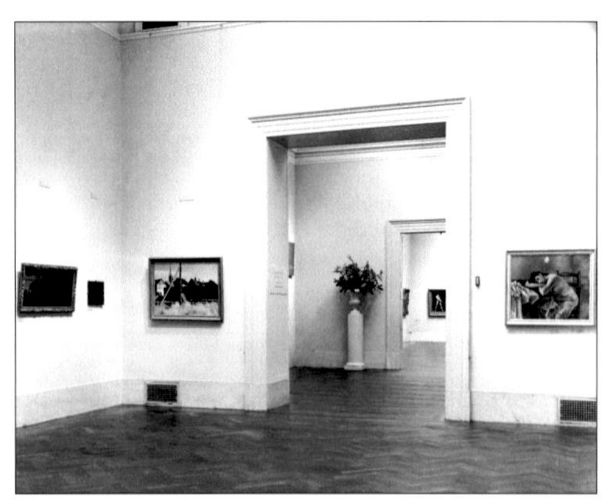

FIG. 32
Edward W. Root collection installed in The Metropolitan Museum of Art, 1953

This exhibition marked the first time a private collection of contemporary art was ever shown at the Metropolitan Museum.[98] It came into being, frankly, because of nepotism. Edward's family had long-standing ties to the museum. His maternal grandfather, Salem H. Wales (1825–1902) helped found the museum in 1870 and for many years was a trustee.[99] Edward's father, Elihu, also served as a trustee, and eventually was First Vice President. He stepped down from the board on May 11, 1931, six years before his death.[100] Edward's older brother, Elihu Jr. (1881–1967) served on the board with his father for many years, and was Vice President at the time of his brother's exhibition.[101]

At the same time, however, showcasing Root's collection was a public relations boon for the Metropolitan, which had come under fire from American artists for the institution's resistance to avant-garde art. In 1950 twenty-eight artists signed an open letter to Director Francis Henry Taylor (1903–57), protesting the reactionary tastes of the jurors who had selected a recent exhibition for the museum that did not include Abstract Expressionist paintings. The Metropolitan in fact was long-resistant to new art but this incident accrued more notoriety than others when *Life* magazine published a story, "The Metropolitan and Modernism," that featured photographer Nina Leen's (1909–95) portrait of fourteen of the signatories who were dubbed "The Irascibles."[102] Nine of the pictured artists had work in Root's collection—Baziotes, de Kooning, Ernst, Motherwell, Pollock, Richard Pousette-Dart (1916–92), Rothko, Stamos, Tomlin—and all but Pousette-Dart were featured in the 1953 Root show.

The 1953 exhibition was not, in fact, the first time Root had lent works to the Metropolitan. In 1920 he placed on long-term loan three paintings from his collection, Davies's *Refluent Season* (before 1911, Munson-Williams-Proctor Arts Institute), Luks's *The Pawnbroker's Daughter* (1905, Munson-Williams-Proctor Arts Institute), and Prendergast's *Landscape with Figures* (FIG. 7).[103] A January 15, 1920 letter from Metropolitan Museum Director, Edward Robinson (1858–1931), to Root thanking him for the loan of the Prendergast and the two other pictures is revealing inasmuch as Robinson gets two of the three names wrong: "I have the honor to inform you that your offer to lend to the Museum three paintings: *The Park*, by W. B. Prendergast; *The Pawnbroker's Daughter*, by George Luks; and *Refluent Season*, by Albert B. Davies has been accepted."[104] It would appear, however, that Root's generosity, at least with respect to the Prendergast painting, created a certain amount of controversy at the museum. He confided years later to Hermon More (1887–1968), Curator at the Whitney Museum of Art, that the Metropolitan's curator, Bryson Burroughs (1869–1934) simply did not like the Prendergast and, therefore, while it was on loan "skied it over the doorway of the long American School gallery."[105] Resentment among some individuals at the museum about Prendergast's painting—presumably because its bright colors and painterly *facture* challenged conventional notions of artistic propriety and craftsmanship—may have been even stronger than Root realized. Walter Pach (1883–1958), the well-connected chronicler of early twentieth-century American art world politics, shed some light on this matter in his gossipy retelling of Burroughs's behind-the-scenes explanation about why the Metropolitan Museum would not undertake Pach's suggestion to organize a retrospective exhibition of Prendergast's work. "It's no use for you to try any more," Burroughs explained to Pach," there is still too much bitterness here about that work of his hanging out in the gallery."[106]

Root's family connections at the Metropolitan Museum gave him access and social standing among the museum's elite. He used these connections on occasion to forward the careers of artists in whom he had faith. He sent a letter dated February 14, 1928 to President Robert W. de Forest (1848–1931) urging him to allow curator Burroughs to buy several modern American paintings.[107] The eighty-one year old de Forest was a socially prominent New Yorker who was also President of the American Federation of Arts—the organization Edward's father helped to found.[108] Root's letter to de Forest is lost, but the reply he received two days later invited Root to recommend "whatever he liked," and that "any pictures you send to the Museum for inspection will be addressed" to Bryson Burroughs.[109] Despite whatever lingering resentment there might still have been at the museum about Root's Prendergast loan, he played an instrumental role in the Metropolitan Museum's purchase, that spring, of Burchfield's 1927 watercolor, *August Afternoon*.[110] Root was not successful the following year when he suggested to de Forest that the museum should purchase Hopper's recently completed oil painting, *Blackwell's Island* (1928, collection Robert and Soledad Hurst). In a letter dated January 30, 1929, de Forest's assistant asked Root to have the Rehn Galleries send *Blackwell's Island* "to the Museum for consideration."[111] Ultimately, however, Root's effort to encourage the Metropolitan to buy this work was unsuccessful. Grace Root recollected that her husband visited de Forest at his home on Washington Square to advocate for the Hopper purchase. According to Grace's notes, "Mr. de Forest told answer by showing him his Impressionists."[112] The museum's unwillingness to buy *Blackwell's Island* still vexed Root two decades later. Reminiscing in the early 1950s about this, Root sardonically commented that "the average age of the [museum's acquisition] committee was seventy-two . . . and none of them like liked anything more modern than the Barbizon School. . . they'd never seen a Hopper before."[113]

By 1953, with Root's own good provenance, the Metropolitan could afford to be somewhat more daring. Curator Robert Beverly Hale, writing in the February 1953 issue of *The Metropolitan Museum of Art Bulletin*, applauded the adventurous spirit that the collector of contemporary material must possess, because "values are uncrystallized and the books have not been written."[114] According to Hale, the collector must have a "wide acquaintance with artists" who can be good judges of others' work; have an understanding of art of the past, but not be bound by that; have "sympathy with the experiments and aspirations of youth," and delight in the contemporary moment. Hale wrote nearly in wonder (if not skepticism) about the ascendancy of non-objective painting and the temerity that a collector of such art must exhibit: "It takes an extraordinary flair to move surely in this unsettled phase of contemporary art.... Edward Root is one of the few American collectors who has had the courage to enter this field."[115]

Root's exhibition elicited generally favorable critical response from the New York press, national art journals, and Utica's daily newspaper, which noted: "In a reversal of a time-honored policy, The Metropolitan Museum of Art... is for the first time offering a public exhibition of a private collection of modern art—that of Root."[116]

Venerable art critic Henry McBride (1867–1962) described the collection as "all of one piece," noting that it demonstrated

> honesty of judgment, the complete absence of anything resembling snobbism, the intelligent comprehension of what painting is and a sympathy with the problems of the artist, and finally, an effect of patriotism build upon the belief that art is at the base of culture and that it is a good citizen's duty to patronize it to the best of his ability.[117]

And while McBride found some infelicitous pieces, he applauded works by Davies, Burchfield, Prendergast, Hopper, Luks, Kantor, Eilshemius and John Piper (1903–92), as well as the younger generation painters, Tobey, Ernst, Stamos, Pollock, Motherwell, and Norman Lewis (1909–79) as "represented by their very best" or "discerningly represented."

Aline B. Louchheim (later Saarinen) wrote two pieces about the show for the *New York Times*. In the first she was complimentary: "Collected over the last fifty years, the works illuminate the taste and courage of a collector who moved with his times—understanding, enjoying, and buying the advanced art of each period." But, like McBride, Louchheim described the collection as "unpretentious," so much so that it sometimes struggled to hold the spaces of the Metropolitan's galleries. She diplomatically noted that "in so personal a collection and one for which expenditures were of necessity never astronomic, not all the artists are represented at their best....But the astonishing thing is that quality does remain high throughout the long panorama of years and through so many different visions and styles."[118]

In her second piece, published three days later, Louchheim offered an opinion about the special significance of Prendergast's *Landscape with Figures*:

> This Prendergast is, in a way, a key to Mr. Root's taste and a clue to the reason he has been able to accept the advanced art of each decade. He is far more interested in a sense of creativity, in design and formal quali-

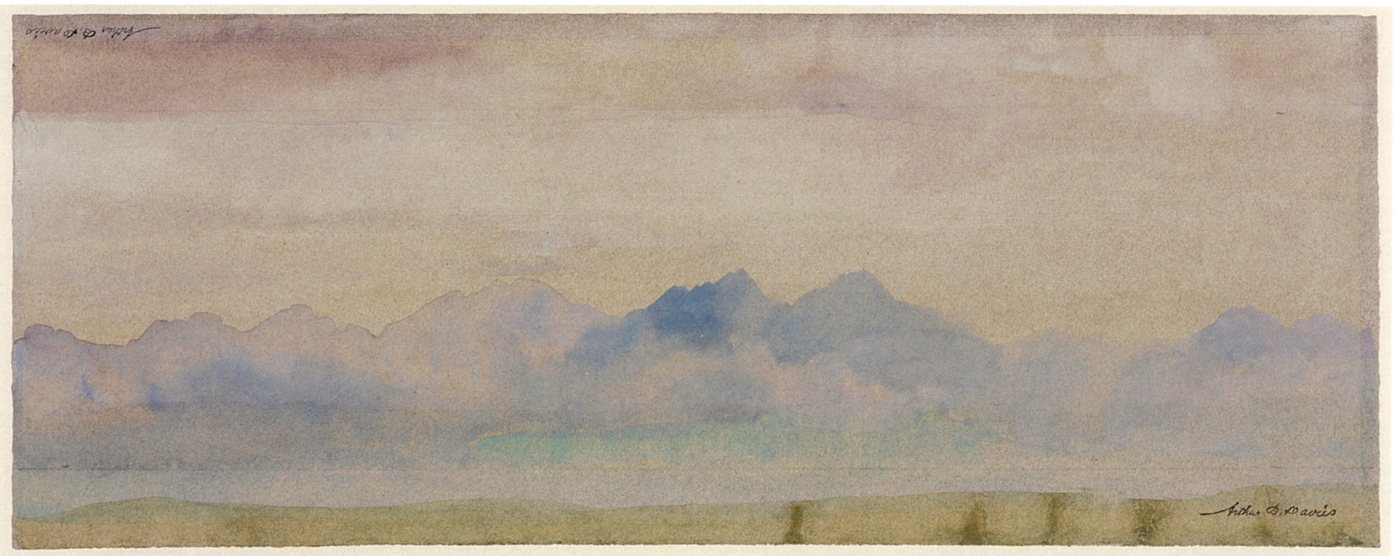

FIG. 33
Arthur B. Davies
La Bella Range, ca. 1928
Watercolor on gray-toned laid paper
9 ½ x 24 ¾ in.
Cat. no. 63

ties and in expression of emotion than in subject matter. He recognizes how in harsh visual terms Hopper makes his statement about loneliness; but he also sees how Tobey's threading line creates a cosmos.[119]

Louchheim characterized Root's collection as intimate, personal, and consistent from start to finish, noting connections in the bravura, painterly style of Luks with the new abstraction, as well as the continuum of nature-based subjects from Demuth, Burchfield, and Stamos. In Root's collection, she found "no abrupt shock."[120]

The critic at the *New York Herald Tribune* praised Root's distinguished taste and inquiring mind but ultimately determined that Root's collection was overly refined and emotionally aloof, lacking in its detachment the expressive fire found in works by Abraham Rattner (1893–1978), Rico Lebrun (1900–64), or Jack Levine (b. 1915).[121] And he was further disappointed in the works by artists such as Luks and Stuart Davis, who "do stand for dynamism" because the Root collection harbored "uniquely placid examples... [and] the tortured Gorky is here actually elegant."[122]

Sidney Geist (1914–2005), whose review appeared in *Art Digest*, more favorably described Root's collection as "distinguished, catholic, and, in view of the changes that a half century have brought to American art, amazingly elastic."[123] About individual works, Geist commented respectfully on Prendergast's Armory Show painting but noted insightfully that, while "it is easy to be impressed by large works, Root's perceptiveness is evident in his happy choices of small pieces." In particular he praised Davies's *La Bella Range* (FIG. 33), Luks's *Closing the Café* (FIG. 34), and "two excellent flower pieces by Demuth" (FIG. 16, and cat. no. 69). Geist further praised Root's mid-century holdings by Gorky (cat. no. 96), Pollock (FIG. 26, and cat. no. 151), and Rothko (FIG. 27), making special mention of de Kooning's *Abstract Drawing* (FIG. 24) as "one of the very best things in the show."[124] In closing, Geist commended Root for trusting his own taste in buying contemporary art, before artists' reputations were established and when artists most needed patronage. This remark echoes Root's perception of himself as a collector; he preferred to cultivate younger talents rather than assemble a collection of known, and therefore safe, artworks that flattered him.

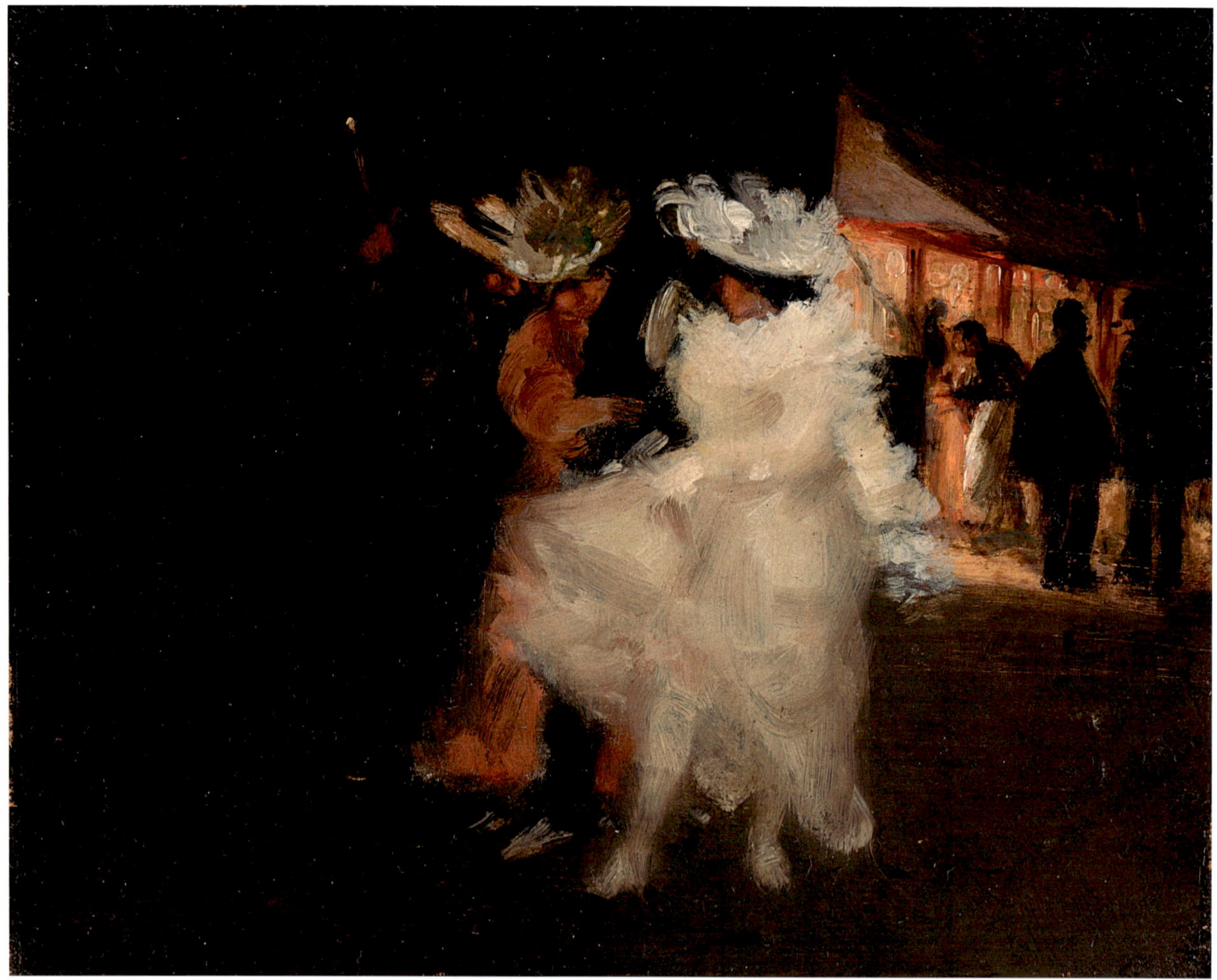

FIG. 34
George B. Luks
Closing the Café, 1904
Oil on hardwood panel
8 ½ x 10 ⅝ in.
Cat. no. 129

In the twenty-five or so years that elapsed between the late 1920s when Root tried to persuade the Metropolitan Museum to purchase modern American paintings and the early 1950s when he was invited to exhibit his collection there, Root's stature as a advocate and collector of modern art had grown. His collection had expanded, augmented by the adventurous American and British pictures he acquired after World War II. He enjoyed the respect and collegiality of a distinguished group of artists, educators, and museum professionals who shared his views about the need to incorporate studio-based courses in college art classes so students could learn the "fundamental motives of art," and the "thought and feeling of particular artists."[125] In 1944 he began serving as a respected and valued member of the Addison Gallery of American Art's art committee.[126] In 1948 Root had the satisfaction of seeing that he owned works by seven of the eleven artists *Look* magazine declared were America's best contemporary painters.[127] The same year The Museum of Modern Art borrowed seven pictures from him for a summer exhibition, *New York Private Collections*.[128] A year later the trustees of the Munson-Williams-Proctor Institute invited him to become the Museum's Consultant in Art, a position he retained for the remainder of his life.[129] Shortly thereafter the Museum of Modern Art's brilliant and influential curator, Dorothy C. Miller (1904–2003), invited Root to write about Tomlin for the landmark exhibition, *15 Americans*, a show to which Root also lent Baziotes' *Mummy*.[130]

The attention and esteem that Root received in the late 1940s from his artist friends and museum colleagues nevertheless were tempered by the coronary artery disease that he developed at this time, an event that led him to begin thinking about the ultimate disposition of his collections.[131] His brother's position at this time as a trustee of the Metropolitan Museum doubtless contributed in some important but possibly intangible way to the exhibition of his collection there, an event that cast him more prominently in the public eye than he otherwise would have allowed himself to be.[132]

ROOT'S AESTHETIC POINTS OF VIEW

The paintings and drawings Root purchased over five decades are the most important measure of his taste, but valuable insights about his modernist aesthetic also can be gleaned from his writings and lectures. The articles and catalog forewords he published about nine contemporary artists, and his lectures and more personal musings represent an effort similar to that achieved by other early twentieth-century American collectors who wrote about American modernism such as Arthur Jerome Eddy (1859–1920), Albert C. Barnes (1872–1951), Katherine S. Dreier (1877–1952), and Duncan Phillips (1886–1966).[133] Additionally, however, Root wrote and lectured thoughtfully about teaching art appreciation to college students, a discipline that emerged during his adult life, and about which there was considerable discussion about its methodologies, not to mention its very legitimacy in the college curriculum.

Many of Root's thoughts on these two subjects exist in his extensive archive of unpublished notes, memoranda, and letters. This unpublished material survived because Root was fastidious by nature, as Saarinen noted, but also because he may have harbored a closely guarded view of its importance.[134] Additional insights can be gathered from the notations and comments he wrote in the margins of some of his books, which are now in the Institute's Art Reference Library. All of this unpublished material provides a more textured picture of Root's aesthetic taste and his ideas about art education, than his published writings otherwise would provide.

The following summary of some of the leading aspects of Root's modernist aesthetic, drawn from his published and unpublished sources dating from 1913 to 1955, includes an examination of Root's definition of art, a discussion of his interest in formalism, and a review of the evolution of his taste from figurative to abstract art. Among the sources under consideration here are Root's 1922 article, "Pictures and the College," his review of the book *The American Renaissance* (1928), by R. L. Duffus (1888–1972), Root's 1936 essay titled "Charles E. Burchfield," and several drafts he prepared for the talk, "Some Characteristics of Modern Art," he presented at the opening of an American Federation of Arts touring show, *Pioneers of Modern Art in America*, which was on view at the Munson-Williams-Proctor Institute April 13–30, 1947. Root speaks for himself as much as possible in this summary. Even though his language is sometimes obscure, his writing reveals the workings of a keenly analytical mind, one that struggled to understand the art of his time. Collectively, Root's papers reveal a carefully reasoned, highly personal, and unmistakably original point of view.

Root's Definition of Art

An early indication of what Root considered art to be appeared in an article that announced the special course he began teaching at Hamilton College in the fall of 1920. Presumably written by him, the article lists the course's aims and methods. Students would learn about "interpretative" pictures as well as "decorative pictures, pure design, household furnishings and objects d'art [sic] of all kinds." What is significant about this description is the implication that certain works of art would be considered to contain meaning while other, decorative, artworks presumably would not. This suggests that Root defined art at this time as something that could be interpreted.[135] He had more to say about this matter several years later in his review of R. L. Duffus' 1928 book, *The American Renaissance*. The focus of Root's comments was the author's prediction that the dominant art form in America would be industrial design, not "interpretative" art. Root argued that even if this transpired, the industrial objects that would be produced did not have to be devoid of interpretive possibilities. He cited Henry Varnum Poor's (1888–1970) pottery, Rockwell Kent's (1882–1971) commercial advertisements, and Burchfield's watercolors as examples of the kind of art that could "vitalize the standards of our designing profession."[136]

The Human Element

In 1922, two years after he started teaching at Hamilton College, Root published his thoughtful article, "Pictures and the College." This essay, which addressed some of the pedagogical challenges that teaching art appreciation to college students presented, is an important, early expression of Root's aesthetic thinking and contains a number of comments that reveal his thoughts about the role of art in the larger public sphere. He proposed that art was something that satisfies a person's spiritual need to feel connected to the world. Such a need is prompted by "profound sensations of loneliness, incompleteness and mental and emotional sterility." A work of art can ameliorate these feelings of alienation when it enables the viewer "to apprehend the significance of visible phenomena connected with his own experience."[137] These sentiments reveal a lot about the melancholic side of Root's personality. Wouldn't another type of person interpret art more joyously?

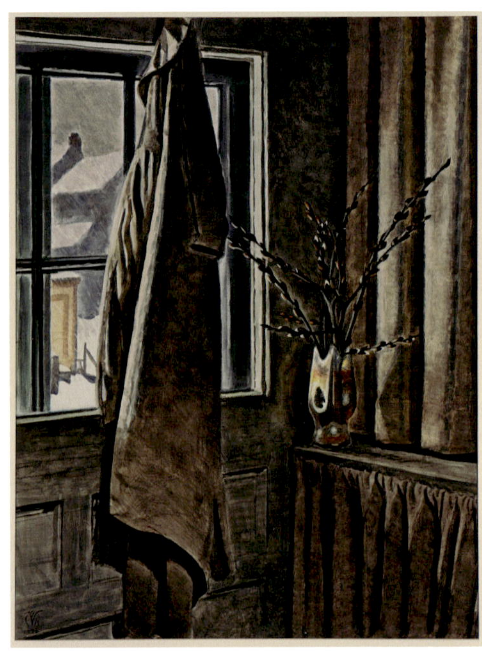

FIG. 35
Charles E. Burchfield
Pussy Willows, 1936
Watercolor on paper
32 15/16 x 25 ¼ in.
Cat. no. 41

This connection between art and human feeling appeared in several writings by Root, the earliest of which dates to February 16, 1913, when he commented in a notebook that certain works of art in the Armory Show were failures because their forms were empty and lifeless, devoid of human meaning. He believed the artists who created such works tried to express themselves in (abstract?) forms that were "beyond their capacities to fill with significant thought."[138] Six years later, in a letter expressing concern that architect Philip Hooker's (1766–1836) Second Presbyterian Church in Albany, New York, was threatened with partial demolition, Root further noted that buildings manifest "the divine sense of order which lived in the hearts and minds of those that designed them."[139] In his review of *The American Renaissance*, Root argued that art schools could help to humanize industrial design by teaching students about the "emotional quality of style."[140] And, in a 1930 Hamilton College lecture on Italian Renaissance art, he suggested that artists were not concerned with "visual facts as such, but only with those visual facts that have emotional significance."[141] He reiterated these beliefs in notes for a ca. 1935 lecture: "Art is the communicating agent of emotions more or less agreeable in that they have resulted from the artist's perception of his actual or possible accordance with life."[142] In other words, art conveys to the viewer the pleasant sensations an artist experiences when his spirit is in harmony with nature, or when he perceives the possibility that it can be so. Root included similar sentiments in an inspired essay he published in 1936 about Burchfield. In this case, however, Root acknowledged the possibility that the definition of art might change sometime in the future because of the increasing amount of non-representational art being created. He made a distinction in this article between two kinds of paintings, a Burchfield (FIG. 35), that demonstrates "the legitimacy of the connection between art and experience," and an "abstraction" by Picasso. Root marveled that the latter picture had "so sensitive and vital a feeling for design," but cautioned that the "message of this Picasso is not one to be easily associated with the fundamental experiences of life." The formal qualities of this artwork are "an experience by itself. Perhaps only this sort of experience will in the future be called art."[143] In the text for his April 1947 lecture at the Munson-Williams-Proctor Institute, Root made a similar assessment of Stuart Davis's "abstract Cubist" forms in *Colors of Spring in the Harbor* (FIG. 18), deeming them "less applicable to everyday life."[144] In this lecture, Root nevertheless favorably commented on the effect that the abstract pictorial elements in Baziotes' *Three Forms* (1946, Addison Gallery of American Art) had on him. The picture's "varied surface, subdued color, subtle balance, simplicity and horizontal drift," Root noted, "have a remarkably tranquilizing effect."[145] He similarly admired paintings by André Masson (1896–1987) and Louis Schanker (1903–81, cat. no. 168), finding them "moving in both form and content."[146]

Several years later Root recollected that when, as a young man, he purchased Lawson's painting, *Winter, Spuyten Duyvil* (FIG. 5), he learned "that art was something which appealed primarily to the emotions."[147] Therefore, for Root, British critic Clive Bell's (1881–1964) assertion that in order "to appreciate a work of art we need bring with us nothing but a sense of form and colour [sic] and a knowledge of three-dimensional space" was too radical and impersonal a separation between art and life.[149] Bell's opinion that the contemplation of a work of art was "unrelated to the significance of life" ran counter to Root's belief that an innate connection existed between art and life. Root may have had Bell in mind when he remarked in his 1930 Hamilton College lecture on Italian art, "there is a school of modern criticism which deplores this [humanistic?] contribution in so far as it affected Renaissance painting. In the opinion of this school, painting should be divorced in so far as possible from association with the real and should therefore employ an abstract symbolism."[150] Root countered Bell in a December 27, 1940 letter to Hamilton College President William H. Cowley (1899–1978), in which Root eloquently articulated his humanistic definition of art in his report about fine arts educational practices at several New England colleges: "Art, as I understand it, is essentially the expression of various attitudes toward life." As World War II raged in Europe, Root stated that art could serve as a barometer of larger cultural forces because it "records the development—or decline—of the human understanding and is in part to be explained by and in part explanatory of the conditions amidst which it is created."[151]

Root and Formalism

While Root sought a connection to the human experience in the visual arts, he also had gained a firsthand knowledge of the formal elements—lines, shapes, forms, space, texture, light, and color—that contribute to the style and visual impact of a work of art when he began taking private art classes with Luks around 1909–10. There are numerous instances in Root's writings in which he addressed these formal properties.[152] Root's sensitivity to them mirrors, surprisingly, perhaps, an approach to art appreciation advocated by Bell and his fellow British critic Roger Fry (1866–1934). Marginal notes that appear throughout Root's personal copy of Fry's *Vision and Design* (1920) suggest that he read the twenty-five essays in this important book very carefully, and that he had what might be described as a personal dialogue with the author. Root even prepared summaries of some of the key points Fry discussed in the book's first two essays, "Art and Life," and "An Essay in Aesthetics."[153]

In "Art and Life" Fry presented a telescopic view of art and history and then asserted from this evidence that the "usual assumption of a direct and decisive connection between life and art is by no means correct." Root's checkmark in the margin adjacent to the next sentence, where Fry noted that art is sometimes influenced by life, but "much more by its own internal forces,"[154] indicates that this idea attracted his attention. Several paragraphs later, after noting how Impressionism marked the climax of a kind of representational art that had evolved since the thirteenth century, Fry observed, and Root emphasized with another checkmark, that "once representation had been pushed to this point where further development was impossible, it was inevitable that artists should... question the validity of the fundamental assumption that art aimed at representation."[155] Root also marked Fry's statement that the "new movement" led to the "re-establishment of purely aesthetic criteria in place of the criterion of conformity to appearance," and that the emergence of these new aesthetic criteria paved the way for an appreciation of "a great deal of barbaric and primitive art the very meaning of which escaped the understanding of those who demanded a certain standard of skill in representation before they could give serious consideration to a work of art."[156] Another comment by Fry that similarly caught Root's attention is that modern art "appeals only to the aesthetic sensibility, and that in most men it is comparatively weak." In the margin next to this sentence Root wrote, "or undeveloped."[157] The idea that the general public had little knowledge or appreciation of art is a subject Root wrote thoughtfully about several times.

The second chapter of *Vision and Design*, "An Essay in Aesthetics," is Fry's most important theoretical expression that the merits of a work of art should be based on a consideration of its formal elements, not on its ability to reproduce natural appearances. Fry's ideas here prompted Root to make numerous marginal comments. When, for example, Fry argued that art, being an expression of the "imaginative life," does not require the same kind of morally "responsive action" that a similar event in real life would require, Root, instead of commenting on the distinction Fry made here between art and morality, focused instead on the reflexive aspect of Fry's sentence and countered that "the creation of a work of art in itself is a responsive action."[158]

Later, when Fry commented that the "average business man" would be more "admirable" and "respectable" if his "imaginative life were not so squalid and incoherent," Root wrote sarcastically, "I suppose the Rotary Club is looking after his morals."[159] When Fry remarked that the "imaginative life," no matter how interesting, would not be of "profound importance to mankind" without an "emotional aspect," Root wrote, "apparently the author, unlike Clive Bell, is willing to consider the emotions of life, as proper to artistic expression."

When Fry sought to make a distinction between two kinds of artistic beauty—one being "sensuous charm" and the other in which objects have "extreme ugliness"—Root, slightly annoyed with the opacity of Fry's language, wrote at the bottom of the page:

> a design—an arrangement of different reflections of light. If it expresses no idea must be beautiful of itself; but if it expresses an idea it may have to be comparatively ugly in order to express the idea. In that case

> the beauty of the design derives from its likeness to or harmony with the idea. Isn't this what Fry is trying to say?[160]

Near the end of his essay Fry identified the various methods an artist has at his disposal, what he called "the emotional elements of design," to arouse the viewer. The first of these, according to Fry, is "the rhythm of the line." In the margin Root wrote his own term, "movement," to describe this formal element of a work of art. Next to Fry's following sentence, "the second element is mass," Root wrote, "substance." Root wrote "space" next to Fry's next statement, "the third element is space." Adjacent to Fry's sentence, "the fourth element is that of light and shade," Root wrote, "illumination." He took exception to Fry's fifth and final design element, "colour [sic]," writing, "color is merely illumination and ought not to be separately listed." Therefore, with Fry as his guide but in three cases using different words, Root listed four formal elements in a work of art: movement, substance, space, and illumination.[161] When Fry noted shortly thereafter, "these emotional elements of design are connected with essential conditions of our physical existence," Root wrote approvingly in the margin, "they are the genetic motives."[162] What this final comment by Root suggests is that he and Fry held similar beliefs about humankind's innate ability to empathize with the formal elements of a work of art. The formal analysis of art was not, therefore, merely one of a several different methodologies that could be used to analyze and discuss a work of art. It was, instead, the *sine qua non* of art appreciation.

Considered in this light, Root's comments—that artists are concerned with visual facts that have emotional significance; that certain works in his collection were "moving in both form and content"; or that his Lawson painting taught him "that art was something which appealed primarily to the emotions"—take on added significance. His ruminations about the nature of art and about man's aptitude to appreciate art were not based on an impersonal, intellectual construct but, instead, on his belief in a hereditary link between art and humankind.

The Evolution of Root's Taste from Figurative to Abstract Art

The paintings that Root purchased at the advent of his collecting career by Lawson, Luks, Prendergast, Dickinson, and Davies fairly represent his liberal but nevertheless conventional taste for figurative imagery. Despite Louchheim's belief that Root was not interested in subject matter per se, it was not until around 1944–45 with the acquisition of monotypes by Harry Bertoia (1915–78, FIG. 36) that Root bought his first abstract or non-representational picture.[163] Although Root's burgeoning interest in abstract art in the mid-1940s parallels the historical record, it was not inevitable that he would follow this trend. A more conservative collector might have shunned these works because the relatively radical set of principles that abstract American art embodied represented a repudiation of the figurative works he collected up to this point. Root's embrace of abstract art at this time is all the more striking when one considers that he was approaching sixty, his health was declining, and the artists who created these works were considerably younger than he.

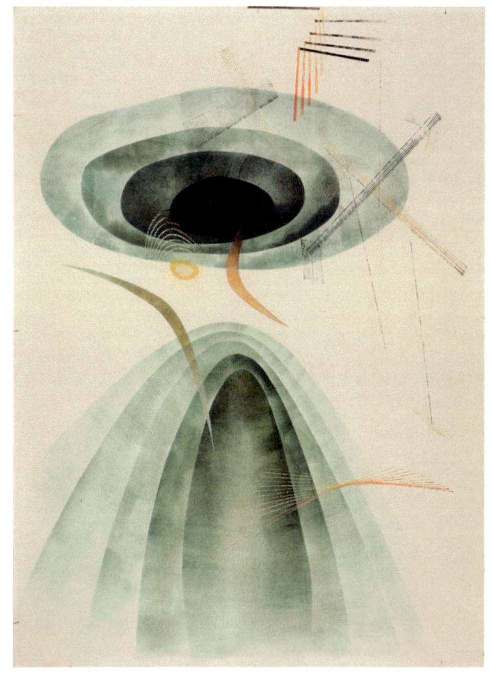

FIG. 36
Harry Bertoia
Descending Force, 1944
Ink on white paper-faced board
41 ¼ x 30 ⅝ in.
Cat. no. 11

Several of Root's writings show the evolution of his thinking about figurative and abstract art. In his 1930 Hamilton College lecture, for example, Root mentioned the bias he then had for figurative imagery. Framing his remarks in terms reminiscent of the Renaissance era's *Paragone*, or debate about the

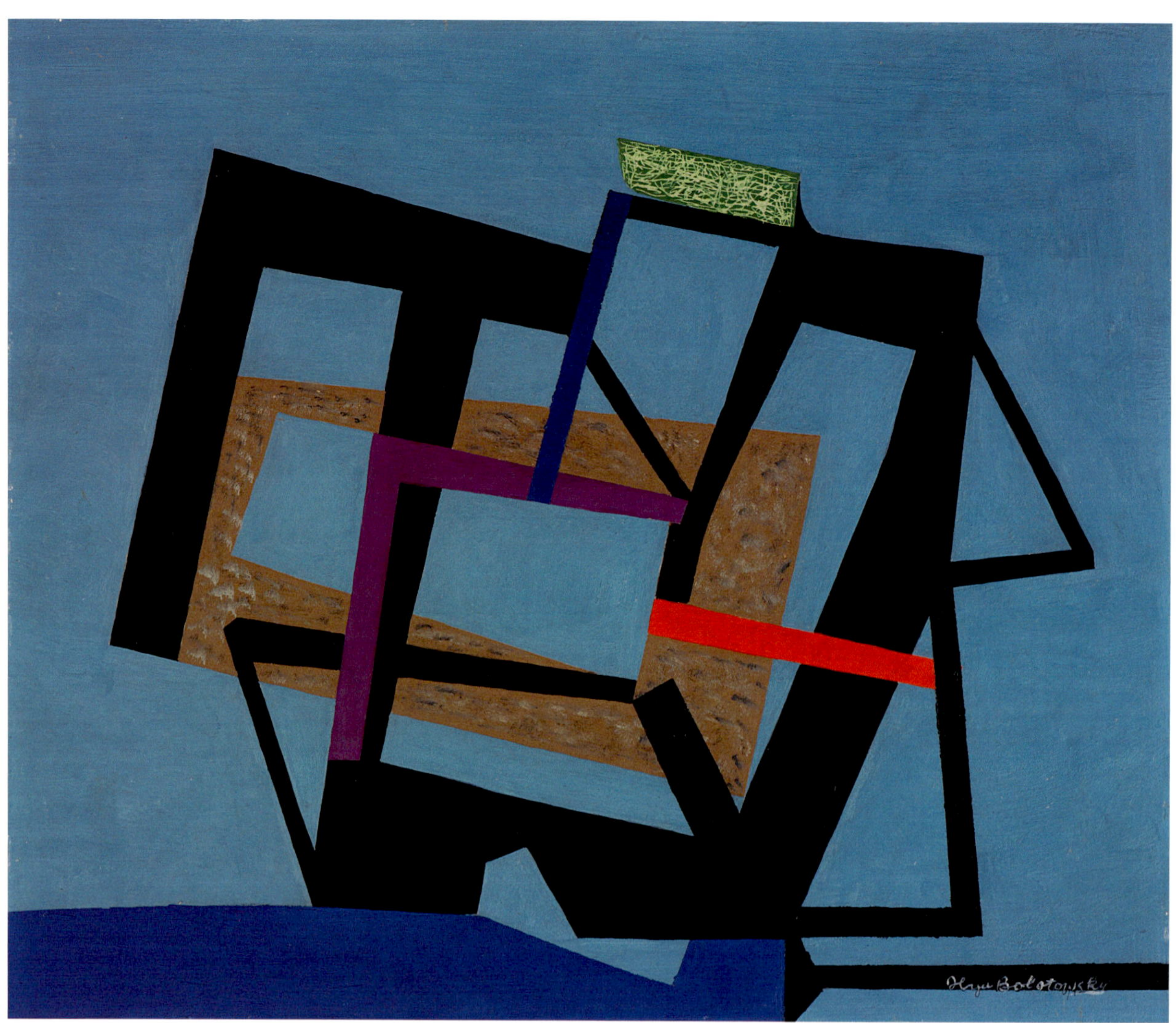

FIG. 37
Ilya Bolotowsky
Marine Variation No. 2
Ca. 1940-42
Oil on Masonite
11 x 13 ¼ in.
Cat. no. 18

relative merits of painting, sculpture, and architecture, Root described what he believed was the appropriate form of expression for music, architecture, and painting. "I am content," he noted, "to leave music and architecture their traditional function of moving mankind by abstract means, and to ask of painting no more than that it shall continue to communicate as heretofore the poignancy and beauty of the world we see." He had a sympathetic interest in abstract art and believed it to be as equally grounded in humanistic values as was figurative art and, therefore, not necessary. "Personally I enjoy abstract painting, but I cannot help suspecting that its motives derive largely from life."[164] Root also worried that modern artists sought to eliminate "the dramatic, psychological, and characteristic, and even the realistically formal from art," and that they take "liberties with natural appearance to a degree undreamed of during the High Renaissance."[165]

Root's first, significant exposure to the work of America's younger generation of abstract artists took place fifteen years later. His lexicographic mind led him to organize and classify the various kinds of abstract art that he encountered during these years. The script for his April 1947 Munson-Williams-Proctor Institute lecture (for which he prepared more conscientiously than his audience had a right to expect, given that the Institute's *Bulletin* noted that Root would "speak informally"[166]) is an articulate and carefully reasoned explanation of what he believed certain modern artists were trying to achieve in their works. He noted that the European avant-garde artists who exhibited at the 1913 Armory Show planted the seed of the abstract tendencies found in the works of the young American artists he was beginning to collect.[167] Looking back from a nearly thirty-five year perspective, Root declared that Odilon Redon (1840–1916) and Wassily Kandinsky (1866–1944) were the "precursors of the two modern schools of painting which have flowered [in the United States] since." He described Redon as the forerunner of the European Surrealists as well as those American artists who displayed surrealist tendencies in their pictures. Kandinsky influenced the work of those modern artists who "show an increasing tendency to use a non-objective symbolism to express subject states." Root illustrated this latter point by showing his audience Ilya Bolotowsky's (1907–81) *Marine Variation No. 2* (FIG. 37), a small painting he acquired about a year earlier. In an effort to describe Bolotowsky's intentions, Root insightfully noted that the picture represents the effort of an artist "who responds emotionally to sensations and ideas which originate within himself and which he does not wish to associate with natural objects. He has not made a picture of something outside himself which he finds agreeable; he has made a picture of something inside himself which he finds agreeable."[168] Root also discussed in this lecture a class of modern American pictures that reflect in varying degrees the influence of Paul Klee (1879–1940). "If you visit the New York galleries this spring or next winter," Root observed, "you will notice quite often non-objective paintings which are not primarily concerned with sensations but which try to present symbols which are the equivalent of general ideas." He illustrated this trend with three artworks in his collection: Bertoia's *Quadrilaterals* (cat. no. 13) and two paintings he purchased several months earlier, Tobey's *New York Tablet* (FIG. 38), and Stamos's *Ancestral Construction* (FIG. 39). On the thorny question about the meaning and legitimacy of an abstract picture, Root remarked about the Stamos, "metamorphic pictures of this sort invariably arouse speculation as to what they

below left
FIG. 38
Mark Tobey
New York Tablet, 1946
Tempera and chalk on laid paper mounted on wood panel
24 ⅞ x 19 in.
Cat. no. 215

below
FIG. 39
Theodoros Stamos
Ancestral Construction, 1946
Oil on Masonite
30 x 24 in.
Cat. no. 188

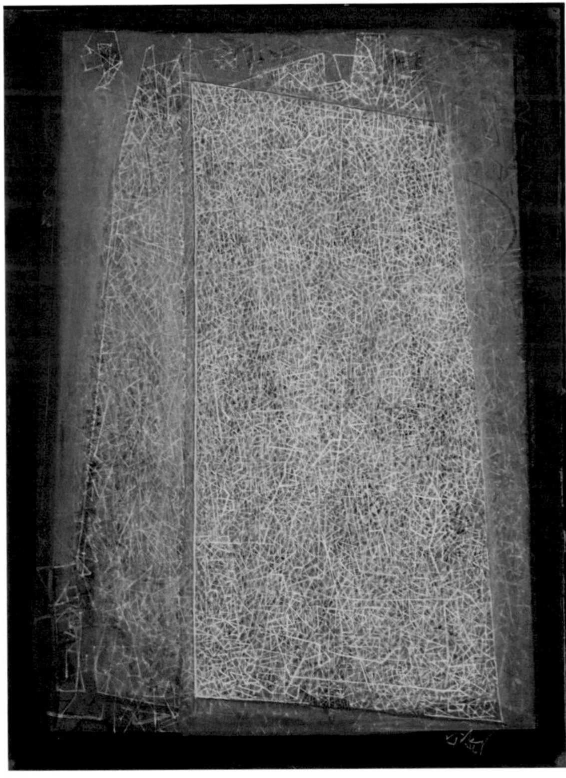

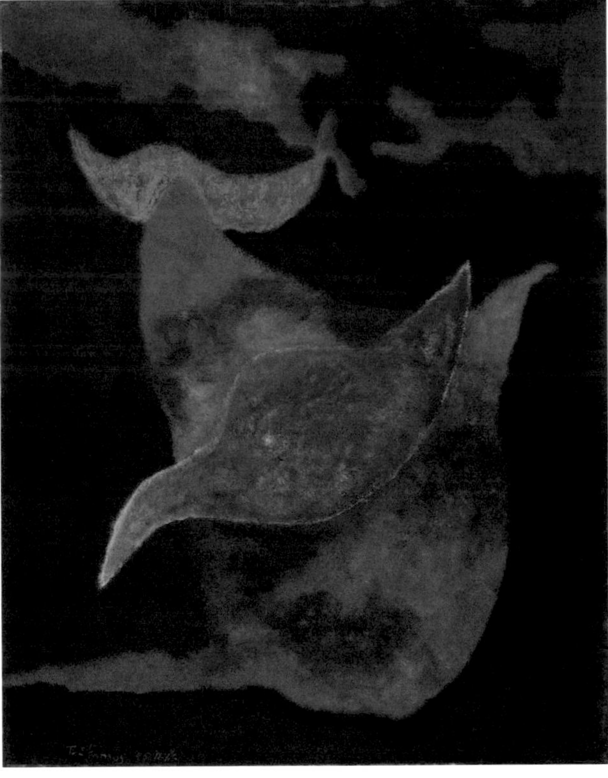

represent, and I think that because of this they have a value which we are apt to overlook." In his opinion, the meaning of Stamos's picture derived from its generalized forms, which "summon up in the observer's mind a number of images." Root's use of the word "metamorphic" to describe the picture's nature-based imagery is noteworthy. This type of picture's ability to represent a "class of things," and to "arouse speculation" helps to explain his interpretation of Stamos's pictures, as well as why he bought so many of them.[169]

Another, even more methodical effort by Root to classify various kinds of mid-century American abstraction, appeared in the Institute's 1950 exhibition brochure, *Current Trends in British and American Painting from the Collection of Mr. Edward W. Root.* In his introductory notes about abstract pictures in the exhibition that he had acquired over the past five or so years, Root commented:

> In some of the paintings abstraction seems to be used as a means of expressing the artist's feelings for organization (Nicholson) or construction (Ernst, Tobey); in other paintings, as a means of expressing the artist's feeling for nature (Sutherland, Stamos); in yet other paintings, as a means of expressing the artist's feeling for ideas (Gorky, Tobey, Matta). Finally, there are some pictures in which the abstraction combines very noticeably the expression of a feeling for organization with the expression of a feeling for either nature or ideas (Dove, Gatch, Conolly, Heliker).[170]

What is most significant about this scheme is Root's struggle to create some kind of intellectual framework and therefore, achieve a better understanding of the most recent contemporary art.[171]

Root's Search for Critical Standards to Judge Art

One of Root's earliest official associations with the Munson-Williams-Proctor Institute was a series of "picture criticism" classes he conducted for three small groups of adult students in 1944 and 1945.[172] Root adapted the methodology described by the English literary critic I. A. Richards (1893–1979) in his influential book *Practical Criticism: A Study of Literary Judgment* (1929), which was notorious because it outlined an experiment Richards conducted with students who criticized unattributed poems by the likes of John Donne (1572–1631), Christina Rossetti (1830–1894), Gerald Manley Hopkins (1844–1889), and Edna St. Vincent Millay (1892–1950).[173] At this pivotal moment in American art history, when mimesis as a critical standard could not be used to judge the abstract pictorial language emerging at mid-century, it comes as no surprise that Root would be drawn to the ideas in Richards' text, which provided an example for developing critical language to organize, as Richards noted, the world "of abstract opinion and disputation about matters of feeling."[174] Richards outlined his aims:

> First, to introduce a new kind of documentation to those who are interested in the contemporary state of culture.... Secondly, to provide a new technique for those who wish to discover for themselves what they think and feel about poetry (and cognate matters) and why they should like or dislike it. Thirdly, to prepare the way for educational methods more efficient than those we use now in developing discrimination and the power to understand what we hear and read.[175]

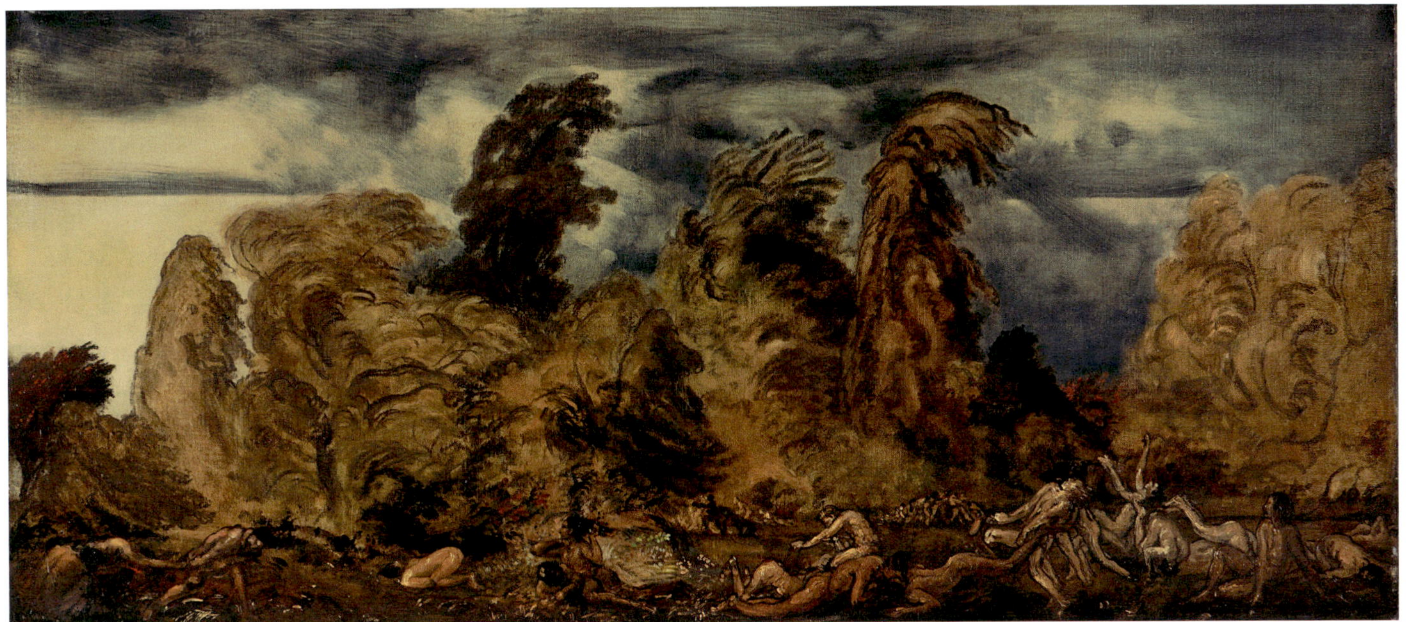

FIG. 40
Arthur B. Davies
Inland Tempest (Inland Storm)
Not dated
Oil on linen
18 x 40 in.
Cat. no. 62

Root modified Richards' method for his visual analysis class, stating that the purpose "is to give participants a definite and objective approach to pictorial art and afford them the opportunity of enjoying the use of their own minds." He installed four artworks for his students to examine in terms of the following elements:

(a) Its subject (i.e. what it represents).
(b) Its motive (i.e. the aspect of the subject which has moved the artist and been emphasized in the work).
(c) Its expressiveness (i.e. the suitability of its medium, execution and composition to the expression of motive).
(d) Its special appeal (i.e. the particular kind of people, if any, for whom it has been made. Children? Other artists? etc.).
(e) Its non-artistic intention (i.e. does it seek to achieve anything beyond the expression of the motive? Does it consciously seek to achieve social or political reform, etc.?).
(f) Its value (i.e. potential value to others besides the artist).[176]

Root asked his students to apply this methodology to works of art in his collection including graphic arts by Francisco de Goya y Lucientes (1746–1828), Rembrandt van Rijn (1606–69), and George Grosz (1893–1959) and paintings by Davies, *Inland Tempest* (FIG. 40), and Tomlin, *Watermelon* (FIG. 29).

The strength of Root's method is that it encouraged careful looking. For example, in Root's reading of Goya, *And There Is No Remedy*, from the series, *The Disasters of War*, he described the print's motive as "the horror and inhuman cruelty of war;"[177] its forms: "its rough execution, unmitigated realism, perfect legibility, and strongly contrasted values, all seem to help the expression of the violent theme;" and its value as "[causing] an intelligent sensitive person to have a revulsion against war." About Grosz's lithograph, *Street Scene*, from his *Ecce Homo* portfolio, Root described the form as well-suited to the subject matter: "The lack of perspective, the lack of horizontality and verticality in the architecture and the lack of balance in the composition suggest an unfamiliar, unnatural, unstable world and by so doing enhance the suggestion of moral disorganization." Root believed that the audience for this work was limited to viewers "who are used to modern methods of pictorial expression" which would be, unfortunately, too small to "induce repulsion in other individuals who would impel them to seek reform and regeneration."[178]

If his descriptions are careful and his appreciation for form relative to expression apt, Root occasionally wrote the odd or incomprehensible interpretation, as, for example, the "associated ideas" of Tomlin's *Watermelon*: "I should say that this picture unlike most School of Paris cubist pictures showed a feeling for the mystery of the universe."[179]

One must ask what Root's effort to systematize visual analysis tells us about his cast of mind, even as it appears Root was keenly aware of the *limitations* a systematized method of visual analysis had on the interpretation of a work of art—as revealed in the statement he wrote about Tomlin in which Root stated unequivocally that pictorial meaning derived from a human quality that transcended any kind of rigid methodology.[180]

Why Abstraction?

In response to the question he posed to himself, "Why Abstraction," Root compiled a list on the back of a calendar page dated "July 4, 1946":

> The urge to be original.
> Desire to avoid competition with camera.
> Reaction against the formlessness of Impressionism.
> Desire to approximate musical form.
> Discovery of art forms (say African or Polynesian) which do not stress likeness (also El Greco, Byzantines, Blake).
> Reaction against scientific materialism. Fear of life. The Eastern spirit. Hatred of mankind. Liking for machine.[181]

Shortly thereafter, in a four-page outline of notes for his 1947 lecture at the Institute, Root struggled to understand why so many contemporary artists were exploring this new idiom:

> Why has this tendency persisted and increased? Is it merely because abstraction satisfies our desire for change? The answer to that is that it has been going on for nearly forty years. Its novelty value disappeared years ago. Is it because it is easier to do? Even the more traditional artists admit that it is harder to do good abstractions than good figurative works. Why then do so many artists tend to abstraction?
> A. Some paint abstractions because other artists do, just as some paint realistically for the same reason.
> B. Some use an abstract method to communicate genuinely felt motives that might be as well or better communicated by more concrete traditional means.
> C. Finally some by means of abstraction achieve a stronger suggestion of the motives which appeal to them than they could by the accepted figurative method.[182]

In the final draft for the lecture, Root invoked the authority of the Greek philosopher Plato as justification for the rise of abstraction. Pointing out that Plato spoke about the absolute beauty of simple geometric shapes, Root speculated that the philosopher would be interested in modern art because the "drift of modern art is away from imitation and toward geometry." Root saw a certain philosophical inevitability in the emergence of abstraction, even though, if his words are narrowly interpreted, this development would only take place in the realm of "geometric" pictures.[183] At the conclusion of this lecture, Root asked his audience why they thought so many contemporary artists "use a non-objective symbolism and paint what they imagine rather than what they see." He considered the answer to this question a key to understanding the momentous cultural changes that were taking place in America in the post-World War II era. "If you can answer this question," Root noted, "you will be in a fair way to explain the change that is coming over western thought." This statement is significant because it suggests that Root considered art to be a part of larger cultural or societal tendencies. "Art is only one straw in the wind," Root added, "no queerer than politics, economics or sociology."[184]

While Root believed that abstract painting was flourishing in the United States, he wisely refrained from commenting on the significance of its popularity. In the penultimate draft he prepared for his 1947 lecture at the Institute, Root noted that

> the practice of non-objective painting by men of talent seems to be growing. It is particularly favored at present by delvers into the subconscious. What this portends I do not know. Leonardo da Vinci would certainly consider non-objective painting to be the final descent into decadence; many objective [representational] painters living today consider it to be so. Whether they are right or wrong only the future can determine.[185]

Some of Root's last thoughts about the idea of pictorial abstraction appeared in the Munson-William-Proctor Institute's 1950 exhibition brochure, *Current Trends in British and American Painting From the Collection of Mr. Edward W. Root*. At this moment of his life, as his health was beginning to deteriorate, Root waxed nostalgically about one of the most influential artistic experiences of his youth, and how the seeds that were planted by that event had, nearly four decades later, come full circle. "As far back as 1913… [at] the celebrated Armory Show… I became convinced at that time that representation was not an inevitable or even desirable concomitant of every kind of painting." Root added, almost apologetically, that if he "collected representational painting between the wars it was because that was the kind of painting which I saw in the galleries devoted to the exhibition of American pictures." This is not an entirely accurate representation of the American art scene between the wars, of course, considering that he could have purchased abstract pictures in the 1930s by, among others, Arthur Dove, who was desperate for enlightened patronage during these years.

EDWARD WALES ROOT AND MUNSON-WILLIAMS-PROCTOR ARTS INSTITUTE

Munson-Williams-Proctor Institute was founded in 1935 by members of the last generation of the family whose names it bears. The family left a substantial endowment to create and maintain the arts institution, but its personal collections of fine and decorative arts had not been developed methodically, so it is a felicitous coincidence of timing that Root—with his knowledge of art, museums, and collecting practices—was approaching retirement from Hamilton College at approximately the same time. Unlike some of his contemporaries such as Duncan Phillips, John Ringling (1866–1936), Ralph Hubbard Norton (1875–1953), Marion Koogler McNay (1883–1950) or Sterling Clark (1877–1956), Root was not a wealthy industrialist or financier, and he seems never to have aspired to establish a museum bearing his name, as these other collectors had. The origins, therefore, of the Munson-Williams-Proctor Institute present the more unusual union of financing from one party and expertise from another.[186]

In the first decade of his relationship with the new Institute, and particularly after his 1940 retirement from teaching at Hamilton College, Root's participation grew incrementally but steadily.[187] From as early as 1938, the Institute benefited from Root's attention; in the fall of that year, it hosted "Exhibition of Watercolors and Pastels by Eleven American Moderns from a Distinguished Private Collection." Eight years later, from September 29 to October 19, 1946, the Community Arts Program (precursor to the Museum of Art) featured "Paintings from the Collection of Edward W. Root," with thirty-two pieces presented in the Main Gallery. In the intervening eight years, Root's profile had risen considerably and he was no longer anonymous. In addition to lending art, Root taught his art appreciation seminar for adults and was an occasional guest speaker.

The year 1949 was red-letter in the Root and Munson-Williams-Proctor Institute association. On November 2, 1949 the Board of Trustees invited Root to serve as an advisor to the Community Arts program, specifically to assist Harris K. Prior, its Director from 1947 to late 1956, as an advisor on acquisitions. It was also in 1949 that Root began thinking about donating the major portion of his collection to the Institute.[188] Perhaps because of this commitment, Root made his first gift of artwork, the first of hundreds, to the Institute also in 1949. It was an anonymous donation of an oil painting by Luigi Lucioni (1900–88), *Vermont Landscape*, dated ca. 1944.[189] Root made a public donation of fourteen paintings and drawings by American artists the following year. In 1953 he gave 167 Old Master prints, dating from the fifteenth to the twentieth centuries, and twenty-two drawings and small paintings, as well as 154 prints by American artists.[190] The following year, he donated fifty-eight eighteenth- and nineteenth-century Japanese woodcuts.[191] When he passed away in late 1956, Root bequeathed 227 paintings and drawings, the material of *Auspicious Vision*, to the Museum of Art.

Root's gifts of art were an important consideration when Prior and Root drafted the Museum's first acquisition policy in early 1950. The two men created lists of artists whom they believed would form the best representation of American art. Root's list of artists' names included his annotations such as "adequately represented in the Root Collection"—meaning that that artist was not given priority on the acquisition list—or "represented by a minor work in the Root Collection." Root understood that his own collection was personal and domestically scaled, so even though he owned a small Rothko from 1947 (cat. no. 162), in 1953 the Museum acquired *No. 18, 1951*, which represents the artist in his most glorious signature style. And, in 1954, the Museum purchased the monumental frieze, *Number 2, 1949*, by Jackson Pollock.[192] Root also supported the acquisition of work by painters on Prior's list, artists not represented in the Root collection, whose work may not have matched his personal taste—Isabel Bishop (1902–88) and Georgia O'Keeffe (1887–1986), for example.[193] Prior sought to expand the collection historically by including artists such as John Singleton Copley (1738–1815), William S. Mount (1807–68), Winslow Homer (1836–1910), Thomas Eakins (1844–1916), Albert Pinkham Ryder (1847–1917), and Hudson River School painters, but the acquisition policy itself states: "Except for unusually advantageous opportunities, collecting in this area should be postponed for the time being."[194] Interestingly, Root recommended no sculpture, though Prior listed thirteen names, several of which are now represented in the collection, including Alexander Calder (1898–1976), José de Creeft (1884–1982), Gaston Lachaise (1882–1935), and David Smith (1906–65). Between 1952 and 1956, Root and Prior also actively acquired European twentieth-century paintings and sculptures, so that the Institute's twentieth-century American holdings would have stylistic context.[195]

Root and Prior collaborated successfully, with the full support of the Institute's Board of Trustees, until 1955 when illness prevented Root from touring New York City galleries as frequently as he once had.[196] In late 1956 Harris Prior departed Utica for the directorship of the American Federation of Arts and Root passed away.

Edward Root's contribution to Munson-Williams-Proctor Institute was instrumental in establishing the organization as a professional entity. This was achieved because Root's relationship with the administration of the Institute was one of mutual high regard: it trusted his taste to form the collection and he entrusted to it the perpetual care of his lifetime's work. Therefore, while his name does not grace the institution, Root's vision infuses Munson-Williams-Proctor Arts Institute and his legacy has permeated considerations both pragmatic and philosophical.

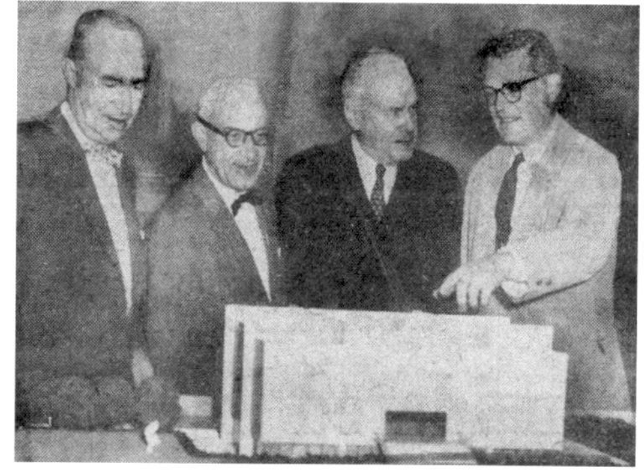

FIG. 41
Philip Johnson's model for the Museum of Art, examined by William C. Murray, President; William C. Palmer, Director of the School of Art; Clement R. Newkirk, consultant; and Richard B. McLanathan, Director of the Community Arts Program. Reproduced from the *Syracuse Herald-Journal*, October 31, 1957.

After the Museum's collections, the most tangible manifestation of the Root-Munson-Williams-Proctor Institute partnership was the building campaign the Board of Trustees undertook in 1954. This venture was based in some measure on Root's intention to bequeath his holdings to the Institute. The exhibition program during Root's lifetime was limited to renovated spaces in Fountain Elms, the 1850 Italianate mansion that was the founders' home, and it was not, understandably, ideal for the display of contemporary art. When Harris Prior saw Root's collection installed at the Metropolitan Museum, he commented, "I realized how inadequate our Institute lighting is when I saw colors I never knew were present in the works I had seen before."[197]

In the spring of 1954 Prior and the Institute Trustees contacted architectural historian Henry Russell Hitchcock (1903–87) for advice about selecting an architect for the new Museum building. That summer and autumn, candidates visited Utica: Pietro Belluschi (1899–1994), Philip Johnson (1906–2005), Eero Saarinen (1910–61), and Edward Durrell Stone (1902–78). In a May 23, 1955 memorandum to the Board, Prior expressed doubt about Belluschi's busy schedule but otherwise emphasized that "any one… would give us a good design… it is very difficult to choose among them."[198] In spite of his declining health, Root participated in the search. He and Grace hosted visiting architects Belluschi, Johnson, and Saarinen at the Homestead and met Stone in

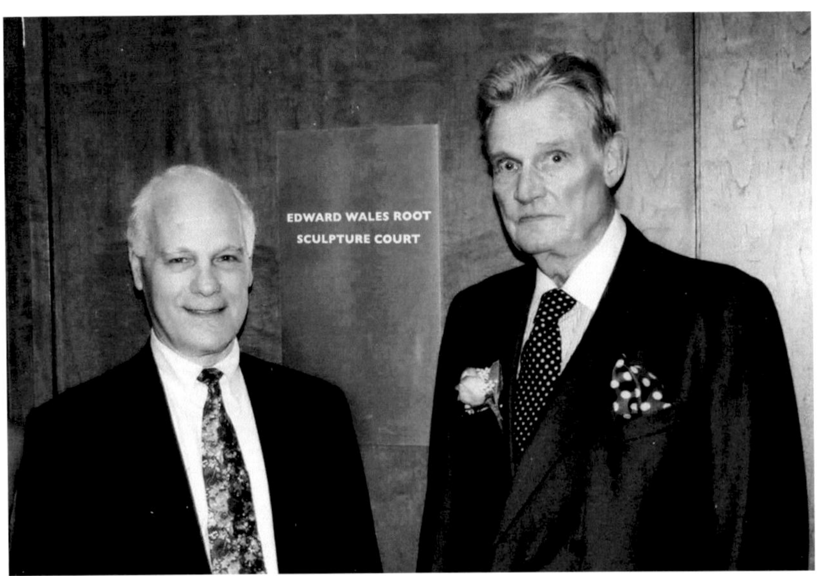

FIG. 42
Milton J. Bloch, Munson-Williams-Proctor Arts Institute President, and John B. Root at the dedication of the Edward Wales Root Sculpture Court, May 3, 2001

New York.[199] By fall 1955 the Institute awarded the commission to Johnson (FIG. 41) and his simple, elegant structure was inaugurated to critical acclaim in October 1960.[200]

After the Johnson building opened, the Institute organized the exhibition *Edward Wales Root Bequest*, on view from November 5, 1961 to February 24, 1962, in a fitting tribute to a great benefactor. Before *Auspicious Vision*, this was the only instance that the entire bequest has been exhibited in toto. And forty years later, another generation at Munson-Williams-Proctor Arts Institute sought to pay homage to Root when, on May 3, 2001, it dedicated the Museum of Art's grandest gallery as the Edward Wales Root Sculpture Court (FIG. 42). This dedication clearly demonstrates that Root's multivalent contributions to the Munson-Williams-Proctor Institute continue to benefit staff, scholars, students and other patrons fifty years hence. One means to measure the extent of Root's importance is the long list of exhibitions to which his pictures have been included; during his lifetime and later, with Institute loans, paintings and drawings from the Root collection have been available to venues as diverse as Venice *Biennales* and small university galleries.

The Museum runs the risk, however, of institutionalizing and historicizing Root's vision. For Root, his collection was not so precious (though the artists who created the work were). Root did not expect the Institute to be compelled to keep everything he had donated, but should monitor the collection to see how artworks age: "The small part that doesn't date should be held and the remainder sold. I should add that it might be as well not to be in too great a hurry to make up one's mind about what is valid and what is not."[201] Root's mission, from his first art purchase, was to encourage contemporary artists in their work, but his opinion expressed here indicates that he envisioned a museum of contemporary art as a living entity. As it happens, the Munson-Williams-Proctor Arts Institute Museum of Art has retained all of Root's pieces, but his model has enabled subsequent generations of Museum personnel to collect with a similar conviction in support of contemporary art, and that may be his most important gift of all.

ENDNOTES

1. Robert B. Hale, "The Growth of a Collection," *The Metropolitan Museum of Art Bulletin* 11, no. 6 (February 1953): 153–55.

2. In an April 1952 letter from Root to the Munson-Williams-Proctor Institute's President Thomas Brown Rudd (1898–1955), Root used the expression "rather strange developments." Record Group 4.21, Folder 139, Joseph S. Trovato Papers, Munson-Williams-Proctor Arts Institute Archives. (Subsequent references to documents in the Institute's archives are abbreviated: R[ecord] G[roup] [number], F[older] [number].)

3. Edward W. Root, "College Teaching and Contemporary Pictures," College Art Association Conference, March 30, 1932, unpublished paper, 3–4. R. G. 13, F. 260, Edward Wales Root Papers, Munson-Williams-Proctor Arts Institute Archives. (Subsequent references to documents in the Institute's Root archives are abbreviated: "Root Papers, MWPAI Archives.")

4. Royal Cortissoz, "Address by Royal Cortissoz," *Elihu Root: President of the Century Association, 1918–1927* (New York: The Century Association, 1937), 11–18.

5. Philip C. Jessup, *Elihu Root*, vol. 2 (New York: Dodd, Mead, 1938), 501.

6. Ibid., vol. 1, 3. See also, Aline B. Saarinen, "The Quiet World: Edward Wales Root," *The Proud Possessors: The Lives, Times and Tastes of Some Adventurous American Art Collectors* (New York: Random House, 1958), 261. For Edward Root's comment to Saarinen about his father's "latent taste," see her February 8, 1956 interview with Root, 4, in the Aline Saarinen Professional Papers, 1906–1969, 2.2: Research Material for *The Proud Possessors*, Box 6, Folders 48–51, Archives of American Art, Smithsonian Institution. (Subsequent references to documents in Saarinen's research material for *The Proud Possessors* are abbreviated, "Aline Saarinen Papers, AAA-SI.")

7. In an October 9, 1938 letter to Hamilton College's President, William H. Cowley (1899–1978), Root explained that his acquaintance with The Eight, from 1909, taught him that the study of art should begin with art and not with books or photographs. R. G. 13, F. 156, Root Papers, MWPAI Archives.

8. For the 1928 description of Root as a lecturer and son of Elihu Root, see "Who's Who in the December Bulletin," *Association of American Colleges Bulletin* 14, no. 6 (December 1928): 547. For Root's remark in 1947 that he was a collector, see Edward W. Root, "Some Characteristics of Modern Art," 1, R. G. 13, F. 242, Root Papers, MWPAI Archives.

9. Grace Root to Saarinen, ca. 1957, frame 886, microfilm reel 2070, Aline Saarinen Papers, AAA-SI.

10. Saarinen, *The Proud Possessors*, 251–52, 260; and Aline B. Louchheim (later, Saarinen), "A Collector with Personal Vision," *New York Times*, February 15, 1953, 12.

11. For Grace Root's family's experience with deafness, see Susanna White, "The Best Kind of Life: Edward W. Root as Teacher, Collector, and Naturalist," in *The Best Kind of Life: Edward W. Root as Teacher, Collector, and Naturalist* (Clinton, N.Y.: Emerson Gallery, Hamilton College, 2007), 8–9, 16n18. Grace's correspondence with Louis M. Balfour (1908–2007), an authority on the history of deaf education, is in the Gallaudet University Archives.

12. Edward W. Root, "If I Had My Life to Live Over Again," November 25, 1914, 1–2, R. G. 13, F. 255, Root Papers, MWPAI Archives.

13. Edward W. Root, "Pictures and the College," *American Magazine of Art* 13, no. 5 (May 1922): 144.

14. Charles Dickens, *American Notes and Pictures from Italy* (Oxford: Oxford University Press, 1989), 29–45.

15. Saarinen, *The Proud Possessors*, 261.

16. John Loughery, "The *New York Sun* and Modern Art in America: Charles FitzGerald, Frederick James Gregg, James Gibbons Huneker, Henry McBride," *Arts Magazine* 59, no. 4 (December 1984): 77–82.

17. Saarinen, *The Proud Possessors*, 255. Saarinen does not indicate when Root first met Lawson but this probably occurred in early December 1909, several weeks after he received a letter from Lawson indicating that he was "trying to sell a picture or two for 'half price' as I am hard up." Root wrote across the top of Lawson's at some later date: "I think this was the letter which made me buy Spuyten Duyvil for $250." Lawson to Root, November 30, 1909, Aline Saarinen Papers, AAA-SI.

18. Root's personal copy of the catalog the Macbeth Galleries published for this February 1908 exhibition is filed in R. G. 13, F. 73, Root Papers, MWPAI Archives. Root's picture is reproduced opposite four Lawson titles, none of which is *Winter, Spuyten Duyvil*.

19. Edward W. Root, "I Remember Quite Clearly How I Came to Buy My First Painting," ca. 1950, 5, R. G. 13, F. 255, Root Papers, MWPAI Archives.

20. Luks's portrait of Edward Root, ca. 1909–10, is illustrated in White, *The Best Kind of Life: Edward W. Root as Teacher, Collector, and Naturalist*, 23. For Edward's comment to Saarinen that the Luks watercolor was the first picture in his and his wife's collection, see her February 8, 1956 interview with Root, 3, Aline Saarinen Papers, AAA-SI.

21. For *Dyckman Street Church* see Mary E. Murray, *American 20th-Century Watercolors from the Munson-Williams-Proctor Arts Institute* (Utica, N.Y.: Munson-Williams-Proctor Arts Institute, 2000), 28–29, cat. no. 6.

22. John Buttrick Root (b. 1922), Edward's son, to Mary E. Murray, April 2002, characterized Luks's visits to Clinton as drying out.

23. Luks to Root, April 30, 1933, Aline Saarinen Papers, AAA-SI.

24. Luks to Root, June 8, 1924, R. G. 13, F. 33, Root Papers, MWPAI Archives.

25. Root, "Pictures and the College," 148.

26. "Young Boswell Interviews George Luks," *New York Tribune*, February 16, 1923.

27. See Milton W. Brown, *The Story of the Armory Show* (New York: Abbeville Press, 1988), 89 (illus.), 287, cat. no. 917. See also, George B. Luks, *Bronx Park, May 8, 1904: Thirty-three Drawings of Animals in the Bronx Zoo* (Andover, Mass.: Addison Gallery of American Art, 1990).

28. For the Prendergast painting that Root purchased at the Armory Show, see Brown, *Story of the Armory Show*, 303, cat. no. 895. For Root's recollections about the appearance of the picture's paint surface when he purchased it, the frame he commissioned for it, and how the work was displayed when he loaned it during the 1920s to The Metropolitan Museum of Art, see his ca. 1933 letter to the Whitney Museum of American Art's curator, Hermon More (1887–1968) in R. G. 13, F. 48A, Root Papers, MWPAI Archives. For the prices of the works by the other American artists who exhibited at the Armory Show, see Brown, *Story of the Armory Show*, 244–327.

29. For Edward's comment to Saarinen about Prendergast's deafness, see her February 8, 1956 interview with Root, 2, in the Aline Saarinen Papers, AAA-SI.

30. Saarinen, *The Proud Possessors*, 264.

31. Saarinen, in *The Proud Possessors*, 259, remarked that Root "felt protective and grateful to the struggling American artists who had released him into the visual world and to men like Luks who had introduced him to a boisterous Bohemia so unlike the polished world in which he grew up."

32. Edward W. Root, "An Appreciation," in Duncan Phillips, *Arthur B. Davies: Essays on the Man and His Art* (Cambridge, Mass.: Riverside, 1924), 61.

33. Ibid., 65. See also *Edward W. Root: Collector and Teacher*, introductory essay by Joseph S. Trovato (Clinton, N.Y.: Fred L. Emerson Gallery, Hamilton College, 1982), 42, for the following undated comment by Root about Davies: "Perhaps some future generation will agree with the writer's opinion that Arthur B. Davies is the greatest master of the landscape with figure that the occident has yet produced."

34. Root's annotated Armory Show catalog is filed in R. G. 13, F. 72, Root Papers, MWPAI Archives. For the three paintings that Davies exhibited at the Armory Show, see Bennard B. Perlman, *The Lives, Loves and Art of Arthur B. Davies* (Albany, N.Y.: State University of New York, 1998), 223–26.

35. For about a ten-year period between 1915 and the mid-1920s Root purchased very few works of art. In a 1924 letter to the Macbeth Galleries, regarding the possible purchase of a Davies canvas, *Flood* (location unknown), Root explained: "I would buy the picture gladly, but I have no more loose money to invest in paintings and have not had for a number of years. All my buying was done while I was a young man without a family to support." R. G. 13, F. 17, Root Papers, MWPAI Archives.

36. Helen Appleton Read, untitled article, *Brooklyn Daily Eagle*, May 5, 1935, quoted in Edna M. Lindemann, *The Art Triangle: Artist, Dealer, Collector* (Buffalo, N.Y.: Burchfield Art Center, 1989), 32n70.

37. Root donated Hopper's *Freight Cars, Gloucester* to the Addison Gallery of American Art in 1956 in honor of the gallery's 25th anniversary. See Susan C. Faxon et al., *Addison Gallery of American Art, 65 Years: A Selective Catalogue* (Andover, Mass.: Addison Gallery of American Art, 1996), 403, cat. no. 146.

38. Edward W. Root, "Hopper's Works Now on Exhibition Here," *Utica Daily Press*, March 3, 1928, 9.

39. Edward W. Root, untitled comments on Hopper, in Joseph S. Trovato, ed., *Learning About Pictures from Mr. Root* (Clinton, N.Y.: The Edward W. Root Art Center, Hamilton College, 1965), unpaginated.

40. Additional research in Rudd's papers at the Munson-Williams-Proctor Arts Institute and at Hamilton College may shed light on how Rudd's positions at both institutions contributed to Root's decision to give his collection to the Institute. Rudd, apparently, was persuaded by Root's comments that Hopper would be unwilling to accept an honorary degree; so, instead, the college awarded one to Burchfield. For Root's comments to Rudd about Hopper, see the research notes, 3, Saarinen compiled during her May 1957 visit to Root's home in Clinton, N.Y., in the Aline Saarinen Papers, AAA-SI.

41. Marsh to the Buffalo Fine Arts Academy (Albright-Knox Art Gallery), ca. 1944, quoted in Steven A. Nash et al., *Albright-Knox Art Gallery: Painting and Sculpture from Antiquity to 1942* (New York: Rizzoli, 1979), 560.

42. Prior to his bequest, Root donated to Munson-Williams-Proctor Institute two conté crayon drawings, a gouache, an etching, and a lithograph by Marsh.

43. The dates of the Montross show were March 26 to April 7, 1928; see Joseph S. Trovato, *Charles Burchfield: Catalogue of Paintings in Public and Private Collections* (Utica, N.Y.: Munson-Williams-Proctor Institute, 1970), 321. Marina Libel of The Metropolitan Museum of Art, in an August 8, 2007 email message to Michael D. Somple of the Munson-Williams-Proctor Arts Institute, noted that the accession card for the watercolor in the Montross show that the Metropolitan Museum acquired at this time, *August Afternoon*, 1927, indicates that the museum purchased it "from Edward W. Root in April of 1928."

44. Edward W. Root, "Charles E. Burchfield," *American Art Portfolios (Series One)* (New York: Raymond and Raymond, 1936), 65. Slightly different accounts of how Burchfield and Rehn became associated were published, successively, by Hale, "The Growth of a Collection," 154; Burchfield in *Edward Wales Root, 1884–1956: An American Collector*, prologue by Aline B. Saarinen (Utica, N.Y.: Munson-Williams-Proctor Institute, 1957), unpaginated; Saarinen, *The Proud Possessors*, 262; Grace Root in Trovato, *Charles Burchfield*, 345; and Harry Yates, as recounted in Lindemann, *The Art Triangle*, 36. An alternative interpretation of the significance of the role Root played in bringing the artist and dealer together was proposed by M. Sue Kendall, "Serendipity at the Sunwise Turn: Mary Mowbray-Clark and the Early Patronage of Charles Burchfield," in Nannette V. Maciejunes and Michael D. Hall et al., *The Paintings of Charles Burchfield: North by Midwest* (New York: Harry N. Abrams, 1997), 89–90.

45. Root, "Charles E. Burchfield," 67.

46. Root, untitled comments on Burchfield, *Learning about Pictures from Mr. Root*, unpaginated.

47. Burchfield to "Friends" (Edward and Grace Root), April 25, 1932, R. G. 13, F. 8, Root Papers, MWPAI Archives

48. Root, "Charles E. Burchfield," 65.

49. Burchfield to Root, May 22, 1950 letter, R. G. 13, F. 8, Root Papers, MWPAI Archives.

50. For the statement Root wrote about Burchfield for the Doctor of Fine Arts degree Hamilton College awarded him in 1948, see the research notes, 3 (verso), Saarinen compiled during her May 1957 visit to Root's home in Clinton, N.Y., in the Aline Saarinen Papers, AAA-SI.

51. See R. G. 13, F. 38, Root Papers, MWPAI Archives. Thanks to Mangravite's generosity, the Institute owns copies of Root's letters to the artist, which is not typical—Root's papers in the Institute's archives generally only include artists' responses to him.

52. Root to Mangravite, July 7, 1938, R. G. 13, F. 38, Root Papers, MWPAI Archives.

53. Charles Daniel to Root, May 8, 1923, quoted in *Edward W. Root: Collector and Teacher*, 26.

54. Grace Root, "Perceptions of Edward Wales Root: May 1931 through October 1949," Aline Saarinen Papers, AAA-SI.

55. Duncan Phillips to Root, April 15, 1927, frame 938, microfilm reel 2070, Aline Saarinen Papers, AAA-SI. Grace Root revealed what Edward thought of Marin in a letter she wrote to her close friend, Louise S. B. Saunders (1870–1961): "Edward doesn't like Marin as much as Demuth but saw one recently of distant water at Weyhe's which he liked immensely" (Grace Root to Louise Saunders [July 1925], Saunders Family Papers [0000.61], Hamilton College Library Archives, Clinton, N.Y.).

56. *Winslow Homer Centenary Exhibition* (New York: Whitney Museum of American Art, 1936), 23–28. The exhibition was held from December 15, 1936 to January 15, 1937. In the exhibition catalog's introductory essay, 11, Lloyd Goodrich (1897–1987) remarked, in terms that might have influenced Root's thinking about Marin, "Homer was a master of the watercolor medium. His characteristic boldness and swiftness were the very qualities required for it."

57. Halpert, in an October 1956 interview with Saarinen, Aline Saarinen Papers, AAA-SI. Halpert mentioned the respect she had for Root four years later when she told Joseph S. Trovato (1912–83), the Munson-Williams-Proctor Institute's Assistant to the Museum Director: "I would be delighted to have a part of any plans relating to Edward Root. As you know, I had great respect for him." Joseph S. Trovato, "Foreword," *Selections from the Edith Gregor Halpert Collection* (Clinton, N.Y.: The Edward W. Root Art Center, Hamilton College, 1960), unpaginated.

58. Root, "Some Characteristics of Modern Art," 5, R. G. 13, F. 242, Root Papers, MWPAI Archives.

59. Root's interest in Dove dates back to at least 1930–31. In his personal copy of the checklist for The Museum of Modern Art's exhibition, *Painting and Sculpture by Living Americans: Ninth Loan Exhibition*, December 2, 1930 to January 20, 1931, Root wrote next to the three Dove entries that the artist was an "interesting disciple of Kandinskyism." Root's copy of this checklist is filed in R. G. 13, F. 74, Root Papers, MWPAI Archives.

60. Halpert, in an October 1956 interview with Saarinen, noted that Root "resented if he thought 'You want to sell me that picture;'" see Aline Saarinen Papers, AAA-SI. For Root's relationship with art dealers, see also White, "The Best Kind of Life: Edward W. Root as Teacher, Collector, and Naturalist," in *The Best Kind of Life: Edward W. Root as Teacher, Collector, and Naturalist*, 11.

61. Edward W. Root, "Foreword," *Current Trends in British and American Painting from the Collection of Mr. Edward W. Root, Clinton, New York* (Utica, N.Y.: Munson-Williams-Proctor Institute, 1950), unpaginated.

62. See Grace Root's ca. 1957 transcription of part of Edward's 1920–21 lecture on the "The Italian School," 1, Aline Saarinen Papers, AAA-SI.

63. For Root's remark to Palmer about his interest in the new art that was emerging in the mid-1940s, see research notes, 8, Saarinen compiled during her May 1957 visit to Root's home in Clinton, N.Y., Aline Saarinen Papers, AAA-SI.

64. Root, "Foreword," *Current Trends in British and American Painting*, unpaginated.

65. Theodoros Stamos, in *Edward Wales Root, 1884–1956: An American Collector*, unpaginated.

66. Ibid.

67. Stamos, "Why Nature In Art," in *Theodoros Stamos, 1922–1997: A Retrospective* (Athens, Greece: National Gallery and Alexander Soutzos Museum, 1997), 462.

68. Paul Cummings' May 14, 1968 interview with Charles Seliger, transcript, 88, AAA-SI.

69. Ibid., 55. Root's whimsical use of this term "beasties" is of a kind with his ca. 1950 recollection, "I Remember Quite Clearly How I Came to Buy My First Painting," 3, about the fateful day late in 1909 when he visited Lawson's studio for the first time. There he found Lawson's friend, artist Walt Kuhn (1877–1949) busying himself "making drawings ... of ladybugs and other insects wearing large boots and carrying umbrellas ... Kuhn's little bugs dressed in the garments of humanity have always seemed to me to be the heralds of the great anthropomorphic menagerie of Walt Disney."

70. Cummings' May 14, 1968 interview with Seliger, transcript, 53, AAA-SI.

71. See microfilm reel 2423, frame 315, Laurel Gallery Papers, AAA-SI.

72. See Bartlett H. Hayes, Jr., "Address at Opening of Exhibition to Honor the Memory of Edward Wales Root," Munson-Williams-Proctor Institute, April 28, 1957, 8, R. G. 4.21, F. 164, Trovato Papers, MWPAI Archives. See also, Hayes's "The Root of American Painting," *ARTnews* 56, no. 9 (January 1958): 29. Root's remark that a drawing is the "record of a gesture" echoes the English art critic Roger Fry's (1866–1934) statement: "The drawn line is the record of a gesture, and that gesture is modified by the artist's feeling which is thus communicated to us directly," in Roger Fry, *Vision and Design* (New York: Brentano's, 1924), 22. Root owned a copy of *Vision and Design* (see Appendix 4) and made extensive marginal notations on the page of Fry's book where this statement appears. Also, in 1922, Root wrote ("Pictures and the College," 148) that drawings were very useful for the professor of art appreciation because "they offer a wealth of illustration for the lecturer—movement, construction, design, composition, the poetry of light and shade, the dramatic, the psychological, the fantastic, the humorous, the satiric—almost every kind of pictorial motive is to be discovered in them."

73. "Nineteen Young American Artists," *Life* (March 20, 1950): 82–93.

74. See "Community Arts: Print Room," MWPI *Bulletin* (February 1947): unpaginated. The subject of Root and his associations with literati has yet to be explored. Alexander H. Woollcott (1887–1943) was a fellow Hamilton College graduate, Class of 1909, and the Roots were frequent hosts to visiting writers, including E. M. Forster (1879–1970), whom Root mentioned to artist Peppino Mangravite in an April 27, 1947 letter. See R. G. 13, F. 38, Root Papers, MWPAI Archives. Edmund Wilson (1895–1972) also mentions visiting with the Roots in *Upstate* (New York: Farrar, Straus and Giroux, 1971), 121–22.

75. Edward W. Root, "Clinton Man Comments on Art Exhibit," *Utica Daily Press*, January 21, 1928, 9.

76. A theme that consistently appears in Root's writings is the link between modern art and the pictorial traditions of the past. This might seem, on the surface, to contradict Root's aversion to "book learning" and his often-professed allegiance to the "artists' point of view" but, in fact, as his published and unpublished writings indicate, Root was extraordinarily well read in a variety of subjects including art history (see Appendix 4). This served him well when he discussed the similarities between the work of a certain modern artist and a specific art-historical tradition. He wisely recognized, however, that it would defeat the goals he was attempting to achieve with his undergraduate students if he flaunted this kind of knowledge in a classroom setting. Nevertheless, the connections Root made between modern and historical art—an effort he shared with many of his contemporaries—seems like an attempt to soften the doctrinaire radicalism of some of the avant-garde's ideology. Moreover, for people who wrote about, collected, or sold modern art, the effort they made to discuss this material in terms similar to those used by the dealer Edith Halpert when she described to Root the "continuity" between the work of Marin and Winslow Homer (see note 57), represented an earnest attempt to blunt the vitriolic criticism leveled at modernism, and to reassure its advocates that modern art had lasting aesthetic merits.

77. For the de Kooning, see Judith Wolfe, in Paul D. Schweizer et al., *Masterworks of American Art from the Munson-Williams-Proctor Institute* (New York: Harry N. Abrams, 1989), 190–91, cat. no. 87; for the Motherwell, see Mary E. Murray, in Mary E. Murray and Paul D. Schweizer, *Life Lines: American Master Drawings, 1788–1963, from the Munson-Williams-Proctor Institute* (Utica, N.Y.: Munson-Williams-Proctor Institute, 1994), 130–31, cat. no. 57.

78. Edward W. Root to Harris K. Prior, December 17, 1949, quoted in *Edward W. Root: Collector and Teacher*, 56.

79. For an illustration of Rothko's *Omens of Gods and Birds*, see David Anfam, *Mark Rothko, The Works on Canvas: Catalogue Raisonné* (New Haven: Yale University Press, 1998), 226.

80. Faxon, "Portraits of Patronage: The History of the Addison Gallery's Collection and Its Donors," 58.

81. Edward W. Root, "Bradley Walker Tomlin," in Dorothy C. Miller, ed., *15 Americans* (New York: The Museum of Modern Art, 1952), 24.

82. Harold Rosenberg, "The American Action Painters," *ARTnews* 51, no. 8 (December 1952): 22.

83. Root, "Some Characteristics of Modern Art," 7, R. G. 13, F. 242, Root Papers, MWPAI Archives.

84. Robert M. Coates, "The Art Galleries, Mazes and Planes," *The New Yorker* (October 13, 1951): 98.

85. Root to Thomas B. Rudd, ca. 1948, 3 (recto and verso), research notes Saarinen compiled during her May 1957 visit to Root's home in Clinton, N.Y., in the Aline Saarinen Papers, AAA-SI.

86. R. G. 13, F. 66, Edward W. Root Papers, MWPAI Archives.

87. Grace Root to Saarinen, ca. 1957, Aline Saarinen Papers, AAA-SI.

88. Grace Root to Saarinen, December 4, 1957, 2, Aline Saarinen Papers, AAA-SI.

89. Harris K. Prior, "Ten Painters of the Pacific Northwest," in *Ten Painters of the Pacific Northwest* (Utica, N.Y.: Munson-Williams-Proctor Institute, October 1947–March 1948), 3–6. See also, Harris K. Prior, "The Pacific Northwest," *The League Quarterly* 21, no. 2 (Winter 1949): 18–23. At the time of his appointment Prior was also named director of the Institute's Cultural Program, the forerunner of what is now the Institute's separately directed Performing Arts Division. See "Trustees Appoint Harris K. Prior Director of Community Arts Program," MWPI *Year Book* (1945–46): 10; and "Harris K. Prior," MWPI *Bulletin* (January 1947): unpaginated.

90. *Edward Wales Root, 1884–1956: An American Collector.* The exhibition took place from April 28 through May 26, 1957.

91. Only two works in the exhibition were in the Institute's permanent collection: Dove's painting, *The Other Side* (1944), and Everett Shinn's (1876–1953) pastel, *The Docks*, New York City (1901).

92. *Edward Wales Root, 1884–1956: An American Collector*, unpaginated.

93. Harris K. Prior, "Edward Root, Talent Scout," *Art in America* 50, no. 1 (1962): 70–73.

94. Ibid., 71. The significance of Root's achievement as a collector takes on added meaning relative to the argument made by Deirdre Robson ("The Avant-Garde and the On-Guard: Some Influences on the Potential Market for the First Generation Abstract Expressionists in the 1940s and Early 1950s," *Art Journal* 47, no. 3 [Autumn 1988]: 215–21), that the principal early collectors of post-War American modernism were a class of the "newly prosperous," such as Roy R. Neuberger (b. 1903), which Root was not. And even though Robson does not consider Root part of this new class of collector, her remark, 216, that he "began to collect seriously in 1929" (because of the money he inherited at this time when his mother died in June 1928), overlooks the intent with which he collected modern American art during the previous three decades. One-third of the works Root bequeathed to the Munson-Williams-Proctor Institute, for example, were acquired by him before January 1944.

While most of the Root literature written by his peers is complimentary, there is one serious exception, the autobiography of Karl With (1891–1980). In autumn 1941 World War II refugee With was invited by Hamilton College President William H. Cowley to teach art history and to consult at the Institute's fledgling art museum. With's account of his tenure ran toward the histrionic in his description of Root: "a wealthy most influential trustee and frustrated amateur painter; a modest collector of modern Americana paintings, who considered himself a foremost authority on art and art education. He was so convinced of himself and his superiority that he blandly told me that my educational principles and approach would never work." See Roland Jaeger, ed., *Karl With. Autobiography of Ideas: Memoirs of an Extraordinary Art Scholar* (Berlin: Mann, 1997), 231.

95. *The Edward Root Collection: Exhibited at The Metropolitan Museum* (New York: The Metropolitan Museum of Art, February 12–April 12, 1953).

96. Root, "Foreword," *Current Trends in British and American Painting*, unpaginated.

97. Grace Root to Saarinen, December 17, 1956, 3, Aline Saarinen Papers, AAA-SI. Root developed an interest in British art because of one his students. See White, "The Best Kind of Life: Edward W. Root as Teacher, Collector, and Naturalist," in *The Best Kind of Life: Edward W. Root as Teacher, Collector, and Naturalist*, 15.

98. Saarinen, *The Proud Possessors*, 265–66.

99. Wales was also the grandfather of the wife of the great collector, Henry Francis du Pont (1880–1969). Louchheim noted ("A Collector with Personal Vision," *New York Times*, February 15, 1953, 12) that Root's "uncle" appointed him a "Fellow in Perpetuity" of the Metropolitan Museum.

100. "The Board of Trustees," *The Metropolitan Museum of Art Bulletin* 26, no. 6 (June 1931): 138.

101. Louchheim, "A Collector with Personal Vision," 12. See also, Deborah Pokinski, David Nathans et al., "Elihu Root, Jr., Class of 1903: Lawyer-Painter," *Elihu Root Jr., Class of 1903: Lawyer-Painter* (Clinton, N.Y.: Emerson Gallery, Hamilton College, 2004), 7–17. Root was apparently not interested in this kind of public service. Saarinen wrote (*The Proud Possessors*, 260) that he was distressed by the spectacle of people, "diseased by dutifulness."

102. "The Metropolitan and Modernism," *Life* (January 15, 1951): 34.

103. For Root's loan to the Metropolitan of the Luks and Prendergast pictures, see Hale, "The Growth of a Collection," 153–54. In February 1943 Root bought McFee's ca. 1941 oil, *Still Life—Knife* (cat. no. 144), from the Metropolitan's *Artists for Victory* exhibition. In fall 1944, he loaned Kuniyoshi's 1943 oil, *Empty Town in Desert* (cat. no. 114), to another *Artists for Victory* exhibition sponsored by the Metropolitan.

104. Edward Robinson to Root, January 15, 1920, R. G. 13, F. 76, Root Papers, MWPAI Archives.

105. Root to More, ca. 1933, R. G. 13, F. 48A, Root Papers, MWPAI Archives.

106. Walter Pach, *Queer Thing, Painting: Forty Years in the World of Art* (New York and London: Harper and Brothers, 1938), 228.

107. Louchheim, "A Collector with Personal Vision," 12, noted that Root asked de Forest "if the curator might not have two or three thousand dollars to spend independently of the purchasing committee."

108. Robert de Forest's enthusiasm for early American decorative art led him and his wife to donate the funds that enabled the Metropolitan to build the American Wing, which opened in 1924. See Amelia Peck, "Robert de Forest and the Founding of the American Wing," *The Magazine Antiques* 157, no. 1 (January 2000): 176–81. See also, "Robert W. de Forest," *The Metropolitan Museum of Art Bulletin* 26, no. 6 (June 1931): 140.

109. Robert de Forest to Root, February 16, 1928, Aline Saarinen Papers, AAA-SI. See also, Louchheim, "A Collector with Personal Vision," 12.

110. See note 43.

111. Margaret N. Hogan to Root, January 30, 1929, Aline Saarinen Papers, AAA-SI.

112. Grace Root to Saarinen, ca. 1957, Aline Saarinen Papers, AAA-SI.

113. Louchheim, "A Collector with Personal Vision," 12. Five years later Saarinen narrated a slightly more elaborate version of Root's effort to convince the Metropolitan to purchase Hopper's *Blackwell's Island* in *The Proud Possessors*, 265–66.

114. Hale, "The Growth of a Collection," 153.

115. Ibid., 153–54.

116. "Root Collections Feature Utica, New York Exhibits," *Utica Observer-Dispatch* March 1, 1953, 2A. The Munson-Williams-Proctor Institute's Community Arts Program Director, Harris K. Prior, generously commented to Root in a March 3, 1953 letter: "I was amazed by the scope of the collection, for I had not known there were so many good 'realist' works... even the very small paintings all have something very big about them." R. G. 13, F. 76, Root Papers, MWPAI Archives.

117. Henry McBride, "Patriotism and Art," *ARTnews* 52, no. 1 (March 1953): 40.

118. Aline B. Louchheim, "Root's Collection of Art Displayed," 21. Less than a year after Root's death, Grace Root confided to Saarinen that when Edward's collection was exhibited at the Metropolitan, she "neither knew nor cared what the individual pictures had cost." Grace Root to Saarinen, July 8, 1957, 3 (verso), Aline Saarinen Papers, AAA-SI.

119. Louchheim, "A Collector with Personal Vision," *New York Times*, February 15, 1953, 12.

120. Ibid.

121. "Root's U.S. Pictures at the Met," *New York Herald Tribune*, February 15, 1953, 4:7. Saarinen (*Proud Possessors*, 263), underscored this point: "He did not care for expressionist paintings; and the 'social consciousness' canvases of the thirties, which ignited a collector like Joseph Hirshhorn [1899–1981], interested him not at all." Root's friend Bartlett Hayes similarly wrote ("The Root of American Painting," 30) that Root bought "pictures from the modern avant-garde, always preferring a gentle, lyric image to the more violent forms that were emerging."

122. "Root's U.S. Pictures at the Met," *New York Herald Tribune*, February 15, 1953, 4:7.

123. Sidney Geist, "One Man's Collection," *Art Digest* 27, no. 11 (March 1, 1953): 13.

124. Ibid.

125. Committee of the College Art Association, "A Statement on the Practice of Art Courses," *College Art Journal* 4, no. 1 (November 1944): 34.

126. Faxon, "Portraits of Patronage: The History of the Addison Gallery's Collection and Its Donors," 56.

127. "Are These Men The Best Painters in America Today?" *Look*, February 3, 1948, 44–48.

128. The Museum of Modern Art, *New York Private Collections* (New York: The Museum of Modern Art, July 21–September 12, 1948). Root had similarly lent to MoMA's summer 1946 collectors' show, *Paintings from New York Private Collections*, July 2–September 22, 1946.

129. The Minutes of MWPI's Board of Trustees record that on November 1, 1949 "Mr. Rudd reported that he believed it would be of great service to the Institute if Mr. Edward W. Root might be appointed Consultant in Art to the Institute... to advise with the Trustees, Officers and Directors... in regard to various art matters from time to time." See also the correspondence between Root and Rudd, R. G. 4.21, Box 6, F. 139, Trovato Papers, MWPAI Archives.

130. Miller, ed., *15 Americans*, 24, 45.

131. Grace Root to Saarinen, August 30, 1957, 3A, Aline Saarinen Papers, AAA-SI. Faxon has noted ("Portraits of Patronage: The History of the Addison Gallery's Collection and Its Donors," 56) that in 1949 Root had discussions with Bartlett Hayes about the pictures he would bequeath to the Addison Gallery of American Art and the Munson-Williams-Proctor Institute. Lindemann noted (*The Art Triangle*, 40) that in 1951 Root discussed his estate with Harris K. Prior. He began donating large parts of his collection to MWPI in the early 1950s (see Appendix 1).

132. Louchheim (later Saarinen) noted in 1953 ("A Collector with Personal Vision," 12) and again in 1958 (*The Proud Possessors*, 266) that Edward's brother was a trustee at the Metropolitan at the time the exhibition took place. Deirdre Robson wrote more emphatically about this connection when she noted that the "unusual presentation of... [Root's] relatively avant-garde collection at the Metropolitan... was most probably due to the fact that the then Vice President of the Museum, Elihu Root, Jr., was Edward Root's brother." See Robson, "The Avant-Garde and the On-Guard: Some Influences on the Potential Market for the First Generation Abstract Expressionists in the 1940s and Early 1950s," 221n48.

133. Abraham A. Davidson, *Early American Modernist Painting, 1910–1935* (New York: Harper and Row, 1981), 175.

134. Saarinen, *The Proud Possessors*, 262.

135. [Edward W. Root?], "Special Course in Art to be Conducted by Edward W. Root, '05," *Hamilton Life*, November 23, 1920, 8.

136. Edward W. Root, review of *The American Renaissance*, by R. L. Duffus, *Association of American Colleges Bulletin* 14, no. 6 (December 1928): 503.

137. Root, "Pictures and the College," 145.

138. Quoted in *Edward W. Root: Collector and Teacher*, 7.

139. Root to the editor of the *Albany Knickerbocker Press*, August 1, 1919, R. G. 13, F. 261, Root Papers, MWPAI Archives. In the fourth draft for his 1947 MWPI lecture, Root regretted that "Manet, Cézanne and many later artists have ignored again and again the spiritual aspects of life in order to concentrate on the sensuous." See Edward W. Root, "Some of the Characteristics of Contemporary Painting," 16, R. G. 13, F. 242, Root Papers, MWPAI Archives.

140. Root, review of *The American Renaissance*, by R. L. Duffus, 503.

141. Edward W. Root, "Art Club Paper," 7, Edward W. Root '05 Folders. Hamilton College Alumni Biographical Materials (0000.182). Hamilton College Library Archives, Clinton, N.Y.

142. Edward W. Root, "A Statement Introductory to a Course in Appreciation of Painting," ca. 1935, 2, R. G. 13, F. 191, Root Papers, MWPAI Archives.

143. Root, "Charles E. Burchfield," 68. Root expressed similar sentiments to one of his students: "About 'modern' art I remember his saying, in effect, every painting is a fresh experience. We should not quibble over the fact that a Picasso lady does not look quite like a lady. We don't complain that an elm tree is not an oak. A picture is itself." See William G. Roehrick, Jr., "Edward W. Root as a Teacher," MWPI *Bulletin* (March 1957): unpaginated.

144. Root, "Some Characteristics of Modern Art," 6, R. G. 13, F. 242, Root Papers, MWPAI Archives.

145. Root, "Some Characteristics of Modern Art," 7, R. G. 13, F. 242, Root Papers, MWPAI Archives. For an illustration of this painting, see Faxon et al., *Addison Gallery of American Art, 65 Years: A Selective Catalogue*, 322, cat. no. 25.

146. Root, "Some Characteristics of Modern Art," 13, R. G. 13, F. 242, Root Papers, MWPAI Archives.

147. Root, "I Remember Quite Clearly How I Came to Buy My First Painting," ca. 1950, 4–5, R. G. 13, F. 255, Root Papers, MWPAI Archives.

148. Clive Bell, *Art* (New York: Frederick A. Stokes, [1913]), 27.

149. Ibid., 28.

150. Root, "Art Club Paper," 5, Edward W. Root '05 Folders. Hamilton College Alumni Biographical Materials (0000.182). Hamilton College Library Archives, Clinton, N.Y.

151. Root to William H. Cowley, December 27, 1940, 12–13, Edward W. Root '05 Folders. Hamilton College Alumni Biographical Materials (0000.182). Hamilton College Library Archives, Clinton, N.Y.

152. By way of example, see Root's discussion of the "three purely formal motives" in Hopper's watercolor, *Skyline Near Washington Square*, 1925 (cat. no. 106) quoted in Trovato, ed., *Learning About Pictures from Mr. Root*, unpaginated. In the fourth draft for his April 13, 1947 lecture at MWPI, Root described "form" as "organized sensations." See Root, "Some of the Characteristics of Contemporary Painting," 15, R. G. 13, F. 242, Root Papers, MWPAI Archives.

153. The first chapter was prepared from notes for a 1917 lecture; the second was originally published in 1909. Root's summaries of these two chapters are in R. G. 13, F. 249, Root Papers, MWPAI Archives.

154. Fry, "Art and Life," *Vision and Design*, 6.

155. Ibid., 7.

156. Ibid., 8.

157. Ibid., 10.

158. Fry, "An Essay in Aesthetics," *Vision and Design*, 14.

159. Ibid., 15.

160. Ibid., 20.

161. Ibid., 22.

162. Ibid., 23. The word "motive" frequently appears in Root's writings. What he meant by this term appears in his earliest published article, "Pictures and the College" (1922) where, in a discussion of drawings, 148, he remarked about the wealth of information they provide "on the side of motive… movement, construction, design, composition, the poetry of light and shade, the dramatic, the psychological, the fantastic, the humorous, the satiric—almost every kind of pictorial motive is to be discovered in them." He expanded on this definition in a memorandum, "To be Considered by the Critic of Painting," ca. 1944–45, where he noted, 1, that "motives" were "moving experiences which the artist has attempted to communicate by means of his work." See R. G. 13, F. 254, Root Papers, MWPAI Archives.

163. Louchheim, "A Collector with Personal Vision," 12.

164. Root, "Art Club Paper," 5, Edward W. Root '05 Folders. Hamilton College Alumni Biographical Materials (0000.182). Hamilton College Library Archives, Clinton, N.Y.

165. Ibid., 6–7.

166. "Pioneers of Modern Art in America," MWPI *Bulletin* (April 1947): unpaginated.

167. Additional thoughts Root had about the European Expressionists, Fauves, Cubists, and Futurists who exhibited at the Armory Show appear in the four pages of notes he prepared for his April 13, 1947 lecture at MWPI. See, "Modern Art Introduced to America at the Armory Show, N. Y., in 1913," R. G. 13, F. 254, Root Papers, MWPAI Archives.

168. Root, "Some Characteristics of Modern Art," 6, R. G. 13, F. 242, Root Papers, MWPAI Archives.

169. Ibid., 7–8.

170. Root, "Foreword," *Current Trends in British and American Painting*, unpaginated.

171. Another example of Root's effort to categorize the various currents of modern American art can be seen in an untitled and undated memorandum in which he arranged the figurative and abstract works in his collection into five categories: "Objective Realism," "Objective Distortions," "Objective Abstractions," "Non-Objective Compositions," and "Mixed Combinations." He created subsets under each of these categories as well. See R. G. 13, F. 241, Root Papers, MWPAI Archives.

172. For these classes, see Trovato, ed., "Foreword," *Learning About Pictures from Mr. Root*, unpaginated. The November 7, 1944 Minutes of MWPI's Board of Trustees note that "Mr. Root gave an interesting series of five lessons on art in the summer and is giving another series now. When Mr. [Thomas B.] Rudd asked him about remuneration he said he did not wish to be paid. Later he said he would like to make these talks a gift to the Future Development Fund." The trustees therefore allocated $500 to the fund that was used more than a decade later for a new museum building, designed by Philip Johnson (1906–2005).

173. Root co-taught an extracurricular version of this class at Hamilton College in 1940. He described its methods and goals to President William H. Cowley: "In this course groups of poems and groups of pictures are considered alternately for their sense, motive, form, tone, intention and value. The procedure for the course derives largely from I. A. Richards' book, *Practical Criticism*. In this course Mr. [Robert B.] Rudd [1887–1971] and I hope to give the undergraduates a simple critical approach to poetry and pictures, a realization of the extent to which the motives of art and literature are similar or dissimilar, and an informal cooperative method of study with each other and ourselves." Root to William H. Cowley, December 27, 1940, 16, Edward W. Root '05 Folders. Hamilton College Alumni Biographical Materials (0000.182). Hamilton College Library Archives, Clinton, N.Y.

174. I. A. Richards, *Practical Criticism: A Study of Literary Judgment* (New York: Harcourt, Brace and World, n.d.), 5. Root sought to develop critical standards even before the rise of mid-century abstraction. In 1918, when he was thirty-four years old, he noted in a letter to his father that he was using his time to "hunt for social, political and economic principles with a view to getting standards of criticism. I know there are such things and that if you can really arrive at them out of your reading and experience they are of immense help." Root to Elihu Root, Sr., December 30, 1918, Aline Saarinen Papers, AAA-SI.

175. Richards, *Practical Criticism: A Study of Literary Judgment*, 3.

176. Trovato, ed., "Foreword," *Learning About Pictures from Mr. Root*, unpaginated. For Root's handwritten outline of this procedure, see "To be Considered by the Critic of Painting," R. G. 13, F. 254, Root Papers, MWPAI Archives.

177. Edward W. Root, "[Goya] *The Disasters of War (Los Desastres de la Guerra)*," in Trovato, ed., *Learning About Pictures from Mr. Root*, no. 2.

178. Ibid., "[Grosz] *Street Scene* (*Vorstadt*)," no. 4.

179. Ibid., "[Tomlin] *Watermelon*," no. 7.

180. Root, "Bradley Walker Tomlin," in Miller, ed., *15 Americans*, 24.

181. Edward W. Root, "Why Abstraction," R. G. 13, F. 241, Root Papers, MWPAI Archives.

182. Root, "Modern Art Introduced to America at the Armory Show, N. Y., in 1913," 2–3, R. G. 13, F. 254, Root Papers, MWPAI Archives.

183. Root, "Some Characteristics of Modern Art," 1, R. G. 13, F. 242, Root Papers, MWPAI Archives.

184. Ibid., 14.

185. Root, "Some of the Characteristics of Contemporary Painting," 19–20, R. G. 13, F. 242, Root Papers, MWPAI Archives.

186. In this respect, Root is more often compared to Ferdinand Howald (1856–1934), a coal tycoon who sold his business after seventy-one of his miners died in an accident. He largely patronized the Charles Daniel Gallery and in 1931 gave 271 works to the Columbus Museum of Art, Columbus, Ohio and about one hundred more to his family. Because Root continued to collect for twenty more years after Howald died, it is difficult to compare the Howald and Root collections for, as Saarinen pointed out, "Root's more personal collection uniquely spanned the whole period up to the avant-garde present of the fifties," *The Proud Possessors*, 267. See also, Karl J. Bolander, "Ferdinand Howald and His Collection," *Bulletin of the Columbus Gallery of Fine Arts* 1, no. 1 (January 1931): 7–12; Edgar P. Richardson, "The Ferdinand Howald Collection," in Marcia Tucker and Kasha Linville, *American Paintings in the Ferdinand Howald Collection* (Columbus, Ohio: Columbus Gallery of Fine Arts, 1969), 1–6; Mahonri Sharp Young, "Ferdinand Howald and His Artists," *American Art Journal* 1, no. 2 (Autumn 1969): 119–28; Kasha Linville, "Howald's American Line," *ARTnews* 69 (Summer 1970): 52–55 and "The Howald Collection at Wildenstein," *Arts Magazine* 44 (Summer 1970): 16–18.

187. It is possible that the onset of World War II precipitated Root's retirement from Hamilton College, for which "enrollments plummeted, and resources were redirected to support the war effort," according to William Salzillo and Susanna White, in "A Century of Curiosities: The Story of the Hamilton College Collection," in *Hamilton Collects: A Century of Curiosities: The Story of the Hamilton College Collection* (Clinton, N.Y.: Emerson Gallery, Hamilton College, 2005), 24.

188. The December 6, 1949 Minutes of MWPI's Board of Trustees note that "Mr. [Thomas B.] Rudd... conveyed the invitation of the Board to Mr. Root to become Consultant in Art... and that Mr. Root had accepted and was now working with Mr. Prior on various matters in that area." For the acquisition policy that Prior and Root subsequently wrote, see the Minutes of MWPI's Board of Trustees for December 6, 1949, April 4, 1950, and August 3, 1954. For Root's May 12, 1949 letter to Bartlett Hayes about the works he was planning to donate to the Munson-Williams-Proctor Institute and the Addison Gallery of American Art, see Faxon, "Portraits of Patronage: The History of the Addison Gallery's Collection and Its Donors," 56, 58.

189. The Lucioni had played an amusing role for Root; he hung it in his guest room and measured his visitors' sense of aesthetic adventure by their responses to it. See Saarinen, *The Proud Possessors*, 263.

190. See Appendix 1, and "The Edward W. Root Collection of Prints," MWPI *Bulletin* (March 1953): unpaginated, and "Another Root Gift," MWPI *Bulletin* (January 1954): unpaginated.

191. "Root Gift of Japanese Prints," MWPI *Bulletin* (January 1955): unpaginated.

192. See Schweizer et al., *Masterworks of American Art from the Munson-Williams-Proctor Institute*, 178–83, cat. no. 83 (Pollock); 186–87, cat. no. 85 (Rothko).

193. Ibid., 164–65, cat. no. 76 (O'Keeffe); 176–77, cat. no. 82 (Bishop).

194. "Community Arts Program / Munson-Williams-Proctor Institute / Additions to the Collection," R. G. 4.21, Box 6, F. 139, Trovato Papers, MWPAI Archives. See also Root-Prior correspondence, R. G. 13, Box 5, F. 233, Root Papers, MWPAI Archives.

195. See Mary E. Murray, "'Rather Strange Developments': Collecting European Sources for American Painting at the Munson-Williams-Proctor Arts Institute," in Mary E. Murray, ed., *Collecting Modernism: European Masterworks from the Munson-Williams-Proctor Arts Institute* (Utica, N.Y.: Munson-Williams-Proctor Arts Institute, 2005), 6–12.

196. Grace Root to Saarinen, August 8, 1957, 3, Aline Saarinen Papers, AAA-SI. Grace Root noted in this letter, "when his arterial condition worsened sharply in '52 we gave away the fishing rods, [and] golf sticks and settled into living quietly and entirely between Clinton and N.Y."

197. Harris K. Prior to Root, March 3, 1953, R. G. 13, F. 76, Root Papers, MWPAI Archives.

198. R. G. 9.51, F. 44, Physical Plant Papers, Johnson Building, MWPAI Archives.

199. See Rand Carter, *Philip Johnson, Museum of Art Building: An Anniversary Exhibition* (Utica, N.Y.: Munson-Williams-Proctor Institute, 1985) for a review of the commission and construction of the building.

200. See "Art: The Little League," *Time* (October 31, 1960): 64; Richard B. K. McLanathan, "Elegant Practicality in Utica," *Museum News* 39, no. 3 (November 1960): 14–19; "The Perfect, Professional Museum," *Architectural Forum* (December 1960): 91–97; and Nancy Vars, "Utica Museum Receives International Renown," *Syracuse Post-Standard*, May 6, 1962, 19.

201. Lindemann, *The Art Triangle*, 40.

TRENDS IN MODERN AMERICAN FRAMING

THE EDWARD WALES ROOT BEQUEST

A CASE STUDY

Suzanne Smeaton
and Lisa Koenigsberg

"Frames have always been an insoluble problem to me."

—Robert Motherwell

DWARD WALES ROOT (1884–1956) WAS AMONG THE EARLIEST collectors of early twentieth-century American art. In 1909 he purchased his first work of art from the painter Ernest Lawson (1873–1939), one of a progressive group of American artists known as The Eight. This group shared an antipathy for the conservative artistic traditions championed at that time, for example, by New York's National Academy of Design.[1] Root embraced the work of these contemporary American artists. By contrast, his immediate predecessors, the collectors Thomas B. Clarke (1848–1931) and John Gellatly (1852–1931) "stopped short of the new generation of American painters that Edward Root saw confounding the art world at the turn of the century—the realists… and such of the American impressionists as Maurice B. Prendergast (1858–1924). These were the young men who instigated the Armory Show of 1913."[2] The collection Root ultimately assembled, spanning five decades of American art, was unique at the time because of its chronological breadth and the number of artists that it included.[3] In 1953, 132 works from his collection were exhibited at The Metropolitan Museum of Art, the first time a private collection of contemporary art had been exhibited at the Metropolitan.[4]

Frame studies have emerged in the United States since the 1986 exhibition, *The Art of the Edge* at the Art Institute of Chicago. Previous generations of collectors and museums did not devote as much attention to frames as they do now. This essay on American frame taste in the first half of the twentieth century includes new information on the frames of this period, especially those dating from the early 1920s into the 1950s. It is a case study for this relatively new field of scholarly research.[5] The observations and conclusions offered in this essay owe much to Root, and to the Munson-Williams-Proctor Arts Institute Museum of Art's stewardship of his collection, since a vast majority of the frames in the collection were not changed or conserved during Root's lifetime or after he bequeathed it to the Museum in 1956.

Virtually all of Root's purchases were made from the artists' dealers. The frames' broad diversity of styles and lack of cohesive aesthetic suggest that Root was not involved in their selection and did not reframe a work after it entered his collection. This allows historians an undiluted view of the artists' and dealers' choices, rather than those of an individual collector. Root's frames, therefore, are an important resource that can offer valuable insights regarding prevailing modern American frame aesthetics and, in a larger sense, the negotiations and economic dynamics that took place between the artist who made the unframed artwork (and sometimes selected or made the frame that surrounded it), and the dealer who sold the same framed work to Root. This essay recaptures as much of that history as possible.

The frames in the Root collection can be grouped into seven stylistic categories. The first three relate to historical precedent, namely: transitional frames spanning nineteenth- and twentieth-century aesthetics as seen, for example, in the frames with reeded moldings chosen by George B. Luks (1866–1933); frames that reflect a French influence on works by Morris Kantor (1896–1974), Raphael Soyer (1899–1987), Eugene Speicher (1883–1962) and others; and early twentieth-century artist-designed and -crafted frames on paintings by Arthur B. Davies (1862–1928) and Prendergast. The four later frame styles reveal a different set of concerns. The modernist frames on works by Reginald Marsh (1898–1954), Edward Hopper (1882–1967), Arthur G. Dove (1880–1946), Yasuo Kuniyoshi (1889–1953) and others explore surface, texture, and tonality. Later modernist frames on works by Theodoros Stamos (1922–97), William A. Baziotes (1912–63), and some of their contemporaries demonstrate a similar concern for surface, texture, and tonality, as do the mid-century artist-designed frames by Lee Gatch (1902–68), and the mid-century presentations on works, for example, by Ilya Bolotowsky (1907–81), Jackson Pollock (1912–56), Charles Howard (1899–1978), and Mark Tobey (1890–1976).

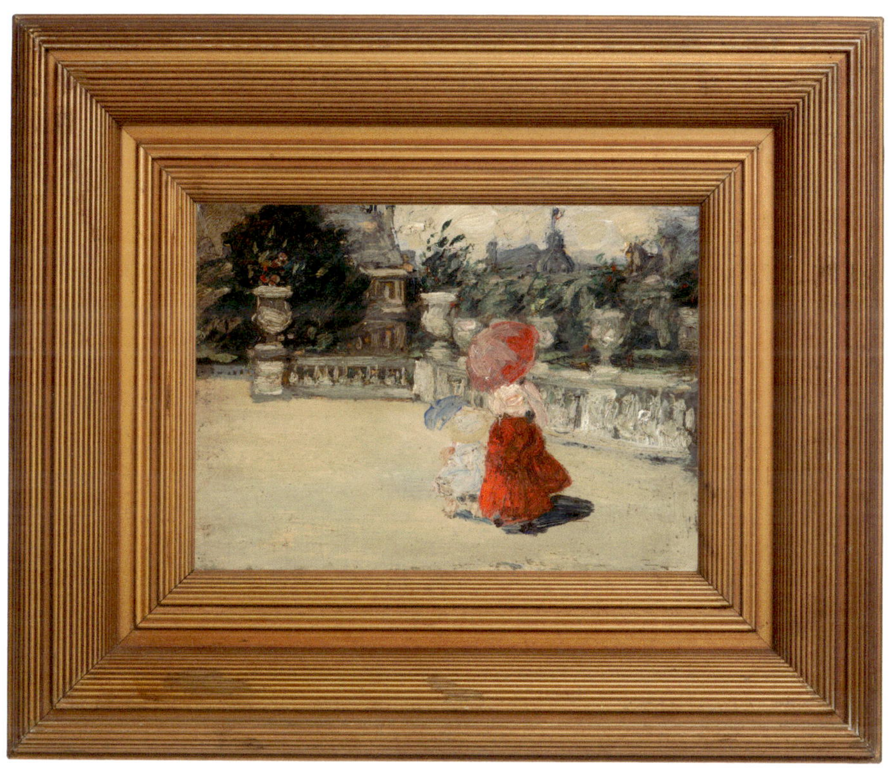

FIG. 1
George B. Luks (1866–1933)
Luxembourg Gardens, Paris, No. 3
1902 (cat. no. 123)
in a reeded, gilded molding, stamped by H. Lieber Company, Indianapolis, ca. 1921

The transitional frames in the Root collection reflect the shift from late nineteenth- to early twentieth-century aesthetics. They demonstrate the stylistic evolution from traditional complex moldings that are ornamented with details made out of composition or "compo," as it is commonly called, to simpler moldings with carved rather than applied ornament.[6] The surface treatment of these frames features a greater use of rubbed and painted surfaces than of traditional gold leaf. The hand-carved, dark walnut Italianate frame with a slim gilded liner on Luks's *Closing the Café,* 1904 (cat. no. 129), is a typical example of the nineteenth century's preference for elaborately ornamented frames.[7] By contrast, the ten oil sketches that Luks painted in 1902 in Paris, of which *Luxembourg Gardens, Paris, No. 3* (FIG. 1) is a typical example, are understated, reeded moldings that were popularized in the nineteenth century by James Abbott McNeill Whistler (1834–1903) and the British Pre-Raphaelites.[8]

The French impulse in this collection is strong. The use of French frames expresses the prevailing thought, originating in the late nineteenth century, that European frames would add an element of cachet to an American pic-

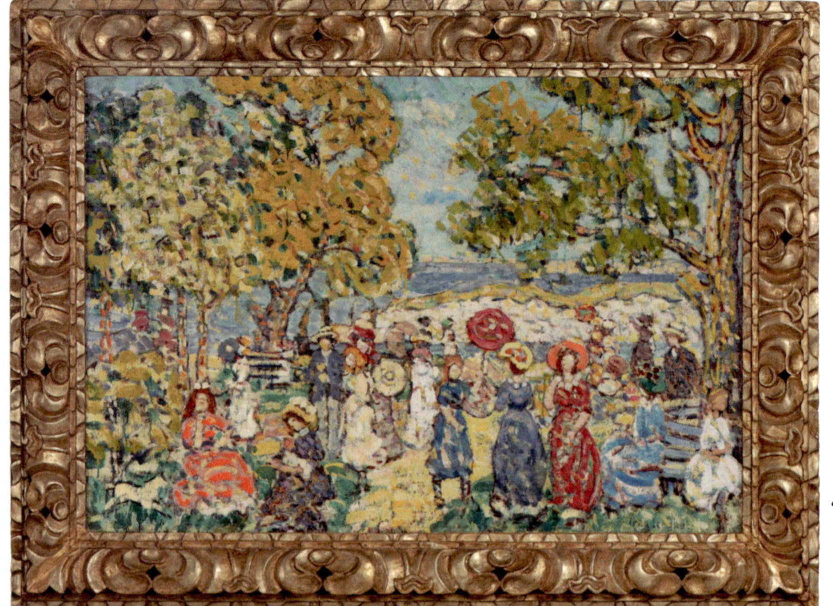

FIG. 3
Maurice B. Prendergast (1858–1924)
Landscape with Figures, ca. 1912
(cat. no. 159), in a gilded and painted frame made by Charles Prendergast (1863-1948) that was inspired by seventeenth-century designs, inscribed "Prendergast" on the back of the top rail, and possibly made between 1913-20

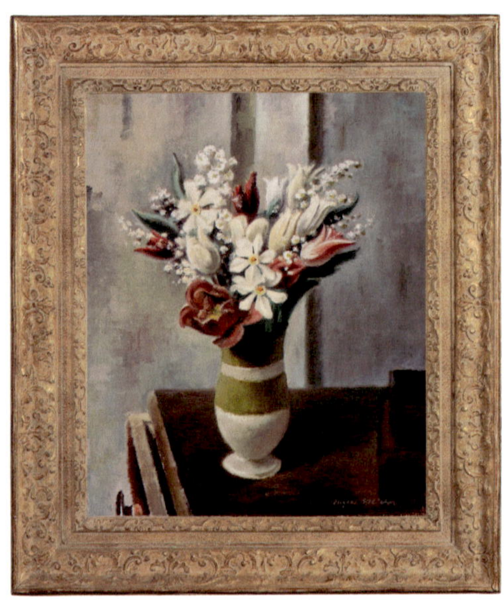

FIG. 2
Eugene Speicher (1883–1962)
Spring Bouquet–Brown Table, 1943
(cat. no. 187), in a machine carved, gilded and distressed frame based on eighteenth-century French designs, by an unknown maker
ca. 1943

ture, which was often considered of lesser stature regardless of the quality of the work. The incorporation of European—largely French—design elements into American frame design validated the artwork and linked it to the more exalted European tradition.[9]

An original Barbizon-style frame surrounds Kantor's *Nocturne, Marblehead*, 1930 (cat. no. 109).[10] However, the frame's surface has been abraded and the original gold has been covered with a gray wash. This raises the question: why was this frame used? It is possible that a canvas was created to fill this frame, as there does not appear to be a relationship, historically or aesthetically, between the frame style and the work. Similarly, a generic mid-twentieth-century French-style frame meant to suggest "art" appears on Soyer's *Study for "Sentimental Girl,"* 1934 (cat. no. 184). A paper label on the back reads, "Louvre Frame Co[mpany]," and the cloth liner is painted with gesso.[11] Greater stylistic dilution is evident in the frame on Speicher's *Spring Bouquet–Brown Table,* 1943 (FIG. 2), which was embellished with machine carving, and its surface both gilded and distressed.[12]

The impulse to follow the French models and frequent departures from faithful replication of French antecedents persisted well into the twentieth century, as evidenced by the frame surrounding Speicher's *Brigham's Yard, Kingston*, 1928 (cat. no. 185). It is similar in intent to the one that surrounds Luks's undated portrait, *Mexican Boy* (cat. no. 131). Less elegant versions of earlier French models also surround two works by John Wesley Carroll (1892–1959): *Little Boy,* before 1936 (cat. no. 50), and *The Blue Feather*, 1937 (cat. no. 49). The gilded and rubbed surfaces on these frames were painted light gray to imply age. Also, the decorative forms were coarsely executed, which sets them apart from their crisply rendered predecessors. Another version of a French revival frame, with carved details, a light gray, natural finish and a cloth liner, surrounds Julian Levi's (1900–82) *Lobsterman*, 1945 (cat. no. 115).

The two frames in the Root collection by Charles Prendergast (1863–1948), Maurice's younger brother, are remarkable examples of early-twentieth-century artist-designed frames. One example surrounds Davies's undated painting, *Inland Tempest (Inland Storm)* (cat. no. 62). The other is on Maurice Prendergast's *Landscape with Figures* (FIG. 3).[13] Both frames illustrate European influences adapted for American taste.[14] The latter is a broad, leafy design inspired by seventeenth-century examples. The most unusual construction

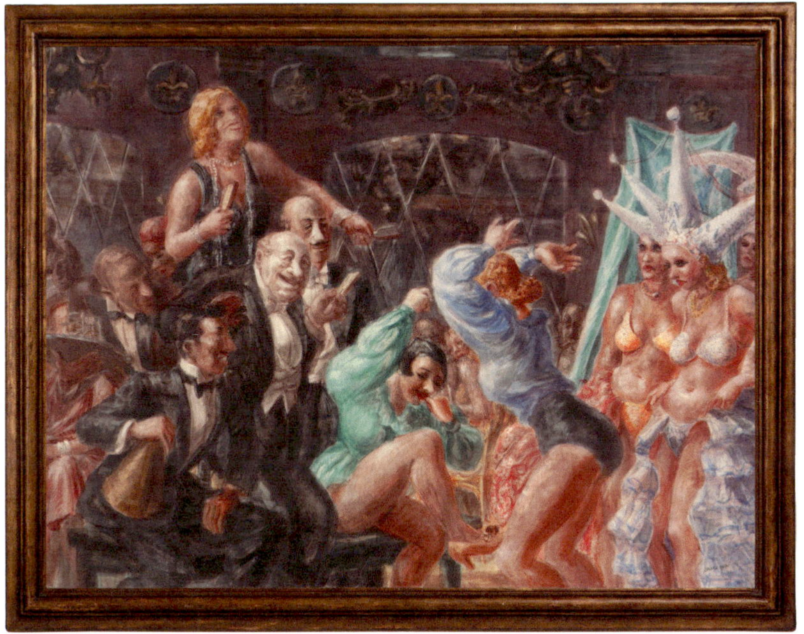

FIG. 4
Reginald Marsh (1898–1954)
Texas Guinan and Her Gang, 1931
(cat. no. 140), in an unornamented, slope away molding that was gilded, rubbed, and burnished, with a Royal Art Framing Company label, ca. 1931

feature of this frame is the dowels that were used to anchor the carved ornament on the front to a supporting understructure.

The Charles Prendergast frame on *Landscape with Figures* is the only known exception to the belief that the frames on Root's works reflect prevailing taste rather than an aesthetic choice on his part. This is evident in the letter Root wrote, probably in late December of 1933, to Hermon More (1887–1968), Curator at the Whitney Museum of American Art, who had requested *Landscape with Figures* for the Whitney's 1934 Maurice Prendergast exhibition.

> The oil which I am sending you I bought out of the Armory Show in March [February] 1913. From 1920 until about 1927 it hung at the Metropolitan Museum, but I don't think Mr. [Bryson] Burroughs liked it very much, because he skied it over the doorway of the long American School gallery.... I have dated the painting 1913 [sic] but it did not have the appearance of a new picture when I bought it. Charles Prendergast made the frame for me later at my request and from an earlier frame of his own make [sic] that I had seen somewhere and admired.[15]

There are two nearly identical Charles Prendergast frames on paintings in the Brooklyn Museum's collection. One surrounds Davies's *Dancing Children*, 1902, and the other Lawson's *Winter Landscape: Washington Bridge*, ca. 1907–10. It is possible either of these frames was the one Root admired.[16]

In the 1930s, frames on American modernist paintings generally exhibited little, if any, decoration and established a new vision for the twentieth century that distanced itself from elaborate patterns and flowery embellishments and, instead, emphasized tonal, coloristic qualities. This new vision is apparent on frames for three Marsh paintings: *Lower Manhattan (New York Skyline)*, 1930 (cat. no. 139); *Texas Guinan and Her Gang* (FIG. 4); and *Zeke Youngblood's Dance Marathon*, 1932 (cat. no. 141).[17] Even though the profile of the latter frame slopes into the painting—in contrast to the profiles on the two other that slope away—all three lack ornament.[18] Gilding was used, but their rubbed and burnished surfaces are decidedly quiet and might be seen as complementary to Marsh's depictions of urban daily life and the immediacy of his realist style. The frames on *Lower Manhattan* and *Texas Guinan and Her*

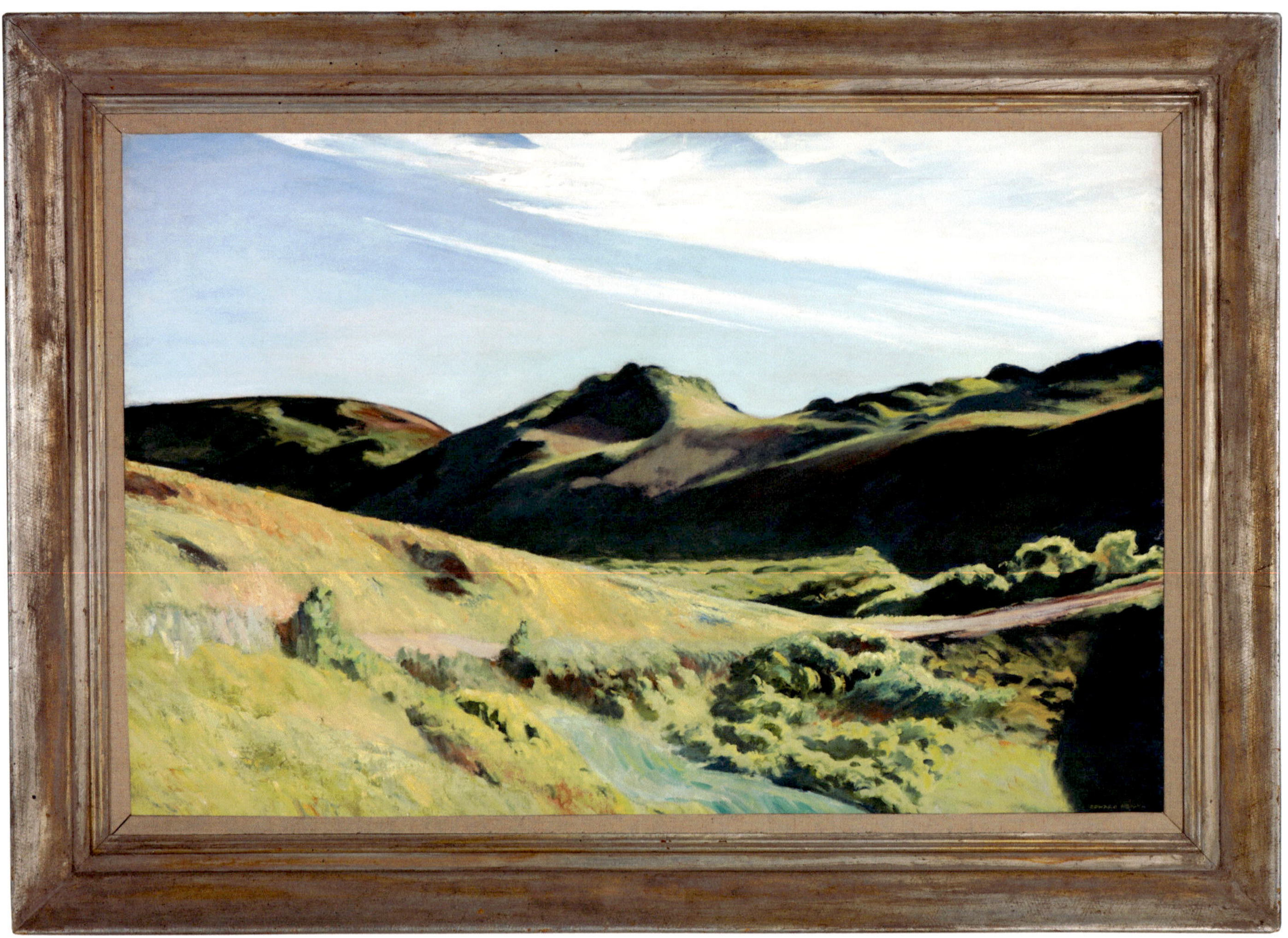

FIG. 5
Edward Hopper (1882–1967)
The Camel's Hump, 1931
(cat. no. 105), in a frame signed by Carl Sandelin (active in New York City, ca. 1931–40), decorated with crosshatching and silver gilt, ca. 1931

Gang bear identical Royal Art Framing Company labels. A different Royal Art Framing Company label identifies the simple, undecorated frames that surround two later paintings by Peppino Mangravite (1896–1978), *Young Couple Drinking*, 1937 (cat. no. 136), and *Young Girl with Yellow Kerchief (Portrait of Frances Mangravite)*, 1941 (cat. no. 137).[19]

Another variation on unornamented 1930s frames is seen on Hopper's *The Camel's Hump* (FIG. 5). The frame was made of length molding to which gesso was applied and scored in a crosshatch pattern for textural effect and subsequently silver-gilded. The following inscription appears on the back in the right-hand corner of the lower horizontal rail: "Frame made for / Hopper painting by / Carl Sandelin 857 Lex[ington] Ave / NYC." Sandelin, who was active in New York City in the 1930s, framed other paintings for Hopper as well.[20]

The frames for Dove's two 1937 works, *Summer Orchard* (cat. no. 74) and *Tree Composition* (FIG. 6), are narrow, gilded in silver and devoid of ornament. Dove made and finished his own frames; brushstrokes are evident in a corner detail of the frame for *Tree Composition* (FIG. 7).[21] There are many references to frames in Dove's correspondence. For example, in a letter he wrote to his dealer, Alfred Stieglitz (1864–1946) on August 9, 1930, Dove expressed concern that some of his frames did not harmonize with the artworks.

> I have an idea . . . about my last show. There was just something in those frames that did not blaze the way it should. . . . [I] should like to take a few of them and redo the frames. They look so much more brilliant.

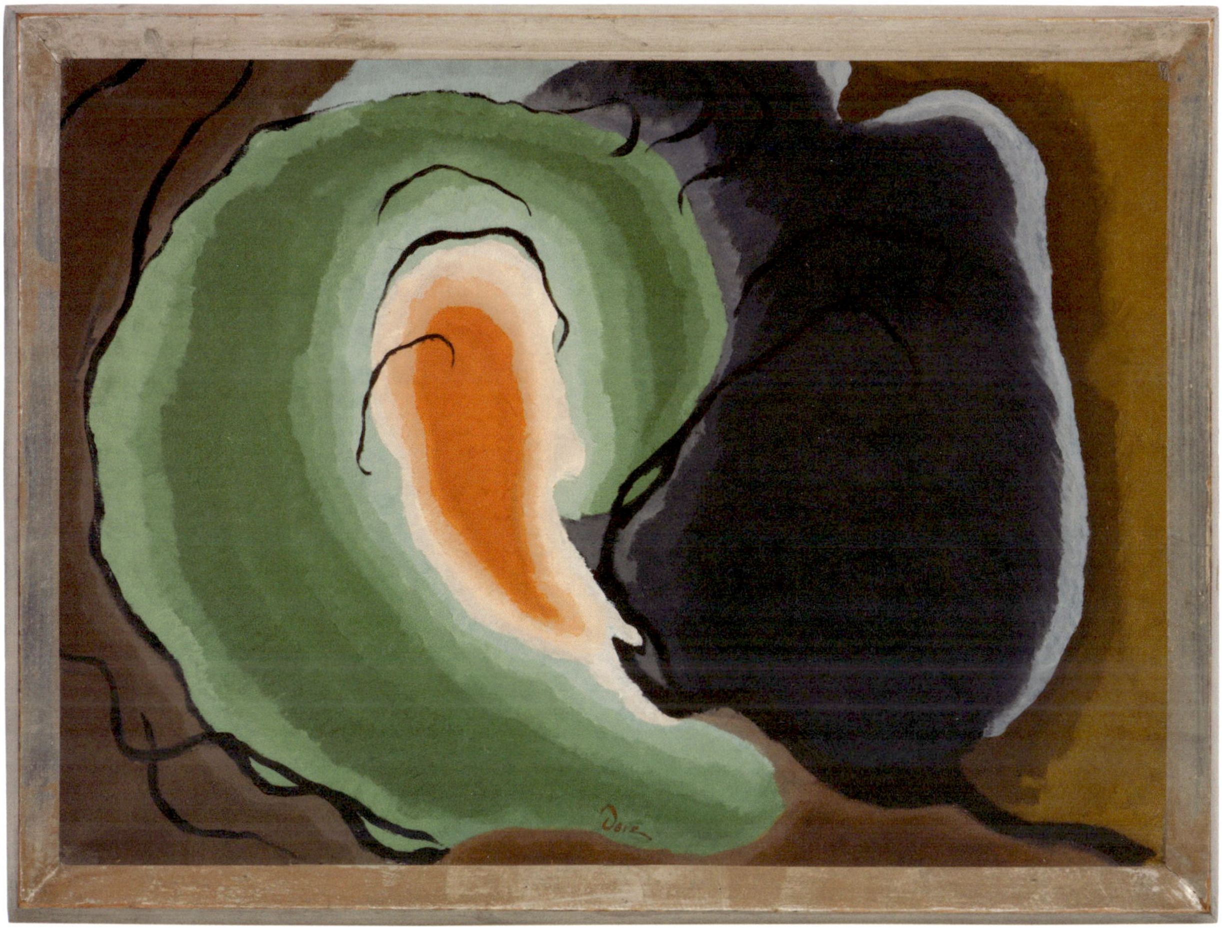

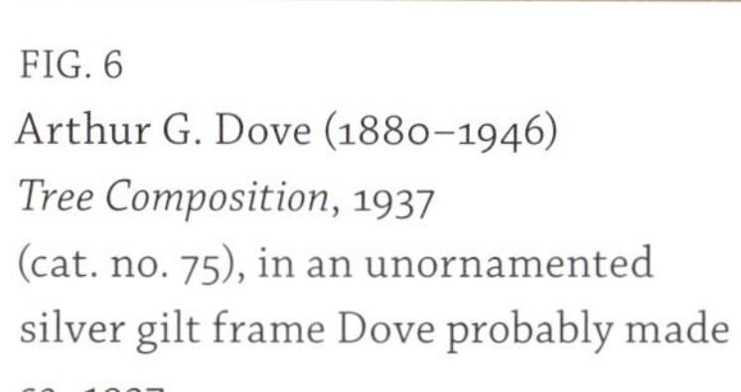

FIG. 6
Arthur G. Dove (1880–1946)
Tree Composition, 1937
(cat. no. 75), in an unornamented silver gilt frame Dove probably made ca. 1937

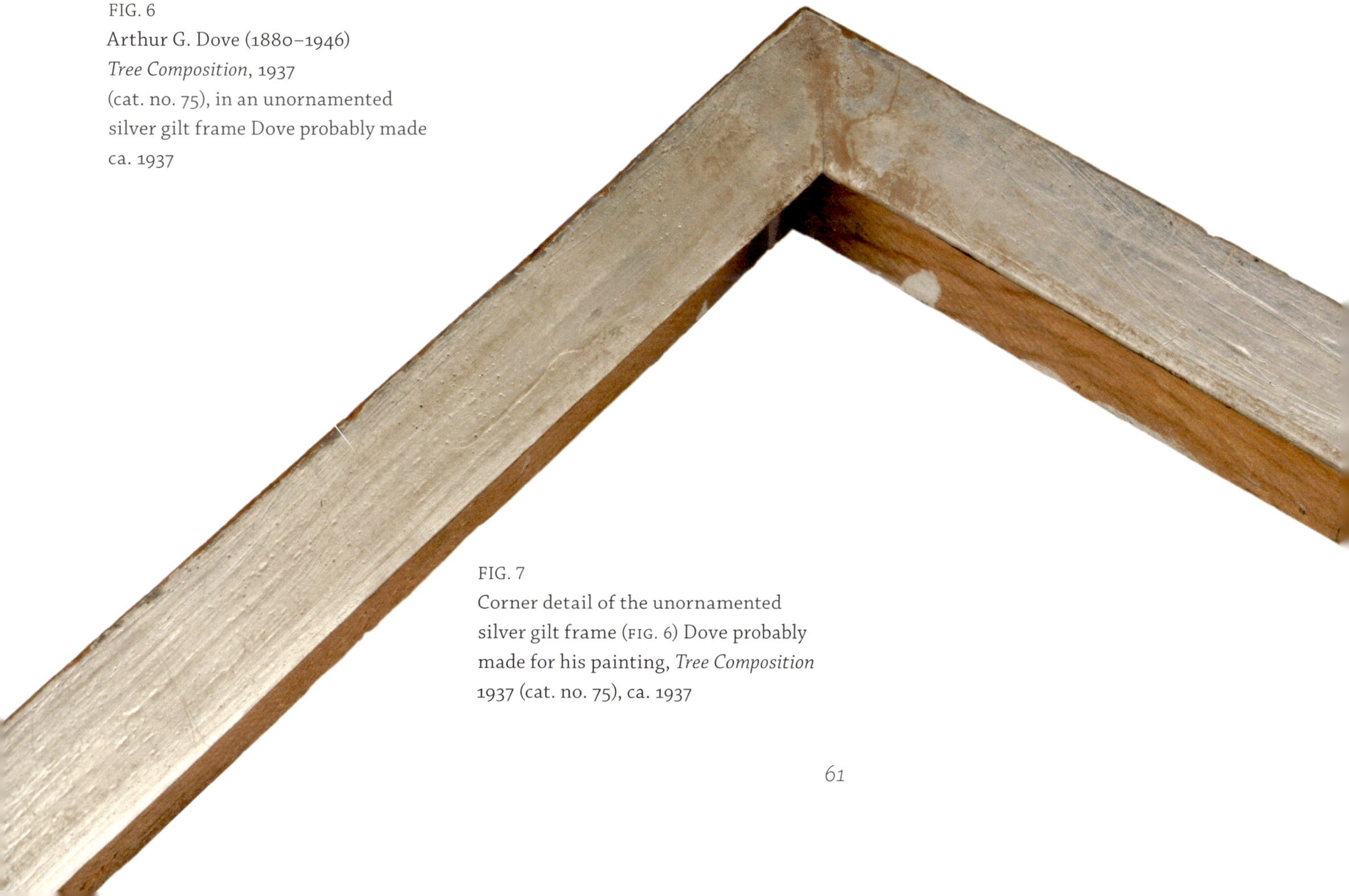

FIG. 7
Corner detail of the unornamented silver gilt frame (FIG. 6) Dove probably made for his painting, *Tree Composition* 1937 (cat. no. 75), ca. 1937

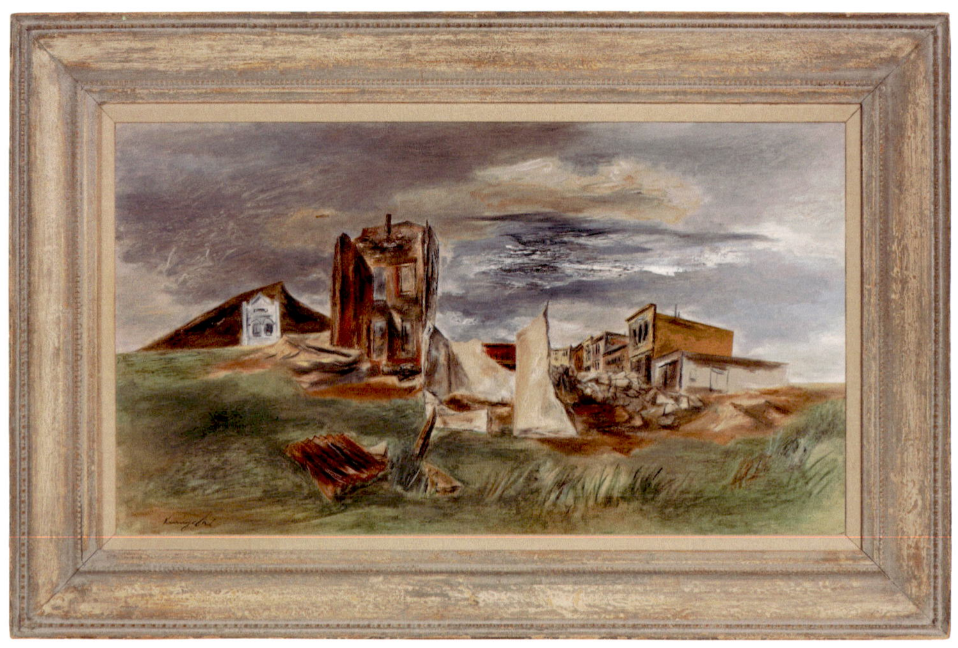

FIG. 8
Yasuo Kuniyoshi (1889–1953)
Empty Town in Desert, 1943 (cat. no. 114)
in a beaded frame with a painted and rubbed gray over white finish, and a cloth liner, by an unknown maker, ca. 1943

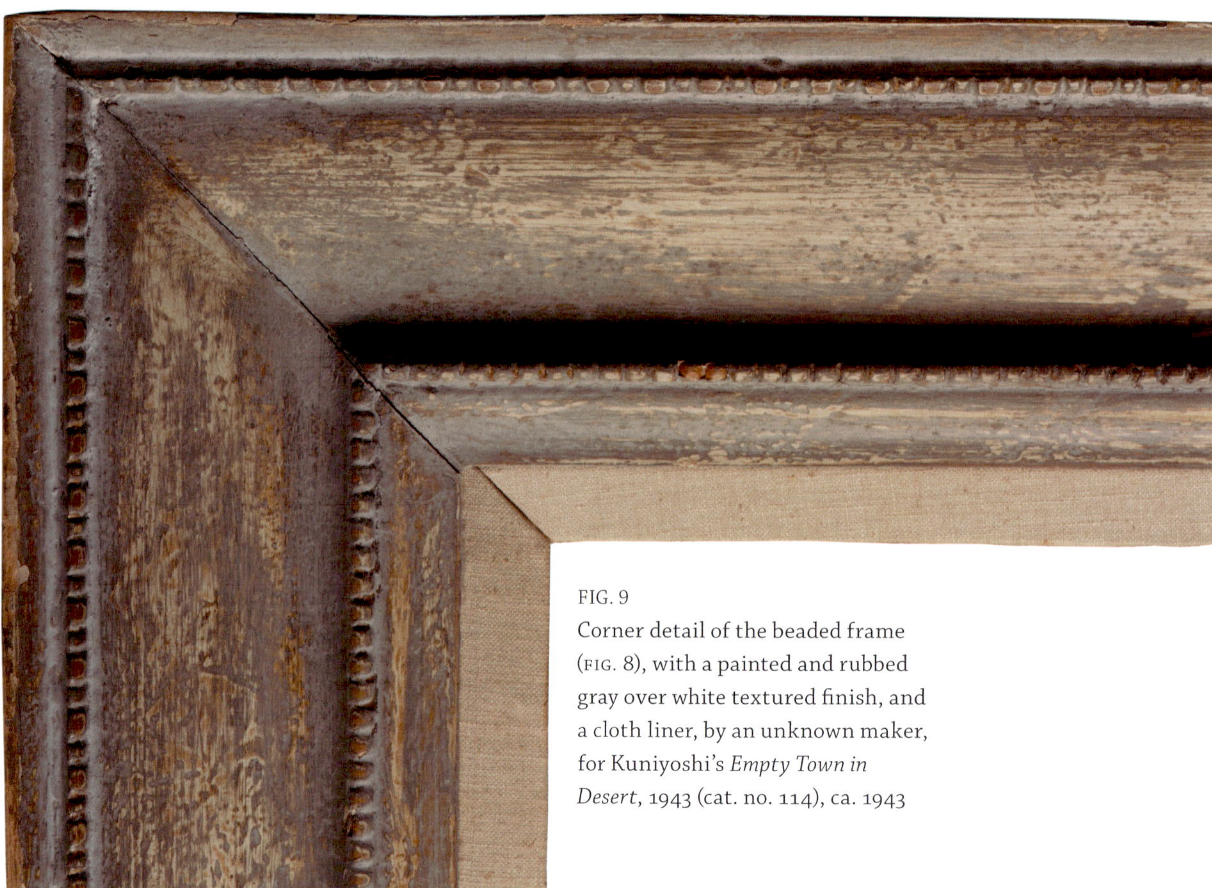

FIG. 9
Corner detail of the beaded frame (FIG. 8), with a painted and rubbed gray over white textured finish, and a cloth liner, by an unknown maker, for Kuniyoshi's *Empty Town in Desert*, 1943 (cat. no. 114), ca. 1943

Dove clearly wished to control the presentation of his work but was constrained by his limited financial resources. "As you say," Dove pointed out to Stieglitz, "it comes to a matter of money and in my case the place of that. Feel quite delighted to be able to make the sort of thing I want to go with the paintings."[22]

Painted and rubbed surfaces became popular in the 1930s and 1940s. When Henry Lee McFee (1886–1953) framed *Boy*, 1932 (cat. no. 143), he used a soft ogee profile that was painted and then perhaps stained.[23] The frame's rubbed and lightly scored surface is compatible with the color and texture of the chair upon which the young boy is seated, creating a subtle link between the painting and its surround.

Yasuo Kuniyoshi created a similar resonance between frame and artwork in two pictures, *By the Sea*, 1942 (cat. no. 113), and *Empty Town in Desert* (FIG. 8). In the latter he used a traditional profile embellished with two rows of beading that border a wide frieze. The frame's rubbed gray over white finish echoes the colors of the picture's clouds, and its textured surface (FIG. 9) is replicated in Kuniyoshi's vigorous brush stokes.[24]

Charles E. Burchfield (1893–1967) employed yet another approach. Seven of Root's Burchfield frames have a light gray finish with even lighter-colored painted wood liners, such as the one on his 1948 watercolor, *Flame of Spring* (FIG. 10).[25] In 1929 Burchfield began a relationship with the dealer Frank K. M. Rehn (1886–1956) which lasted for nearly forty years. The cost of some of Burchfield's frames must have been incurred by Rehn as records indicate that Rehn deducted both his commission and the cost of framing when making disbursements to Burchfield.[26] However, a 1932 letter in the archives of the Burchfield-Penney Art Center, and three letters Burchfield wrote to Edward and Grace Root (1891–1975) between May and October 1937, suggest that at least some of the frames he used in the 1930s were made by a Buffalo frame maker, Carl L. Bredemeier (1892–1946). Burchfield's correspondence with the Roots also indicates that Bredemeier, as well as Burchfield himself, carved ornament on some of his frames but, at some point during that decade, Burchfield stopped doing this. "I have given up carving my frames," he noted in a letter to Edward; "on none of my new ones have I done any carving. I think they are better plain."[27]

Later modernist frames on paintings by Stamos, Baziotes, and their contemporaries often feature simple, angular profiles made of wormy chestnut that often was rubbed or abraded and joined with painted liners. Henry Heydenryk, Jr. (1905–94) pioneered the use of wormy chestnut in 1938. As he explained in *The Art and History of Frames*, the chestnut tree blight in the United States left in its wake dead trees that were infested by worms. This wood, considered undesirable by the lumber industry, was steamed to exterminate the worms and then dried—a process that creates grained and textured wood filled with wormholes, hence the term "wormy chestnut."[28] Wormwood was an inexpensive, understated and nuanced framing material well suited to the psychologically charged and emotionally evocative painting styles emerg-

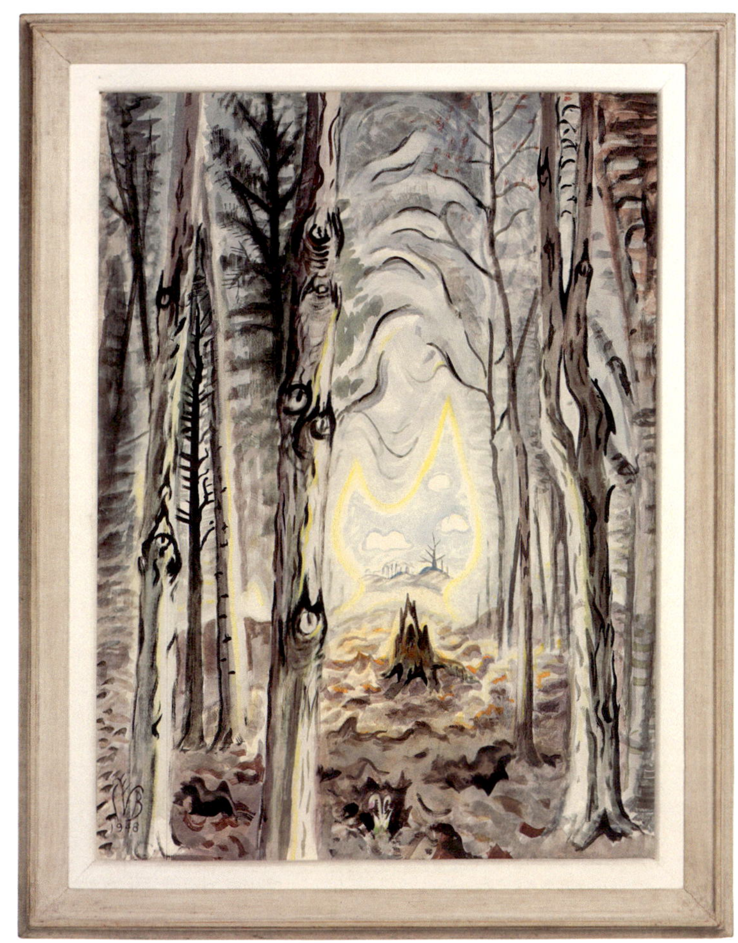

FIG. 10
Charles E. Burchfield (1893–1967)
Flame of Spring, 1948 (cat. no. 33), in a light gray frame with a lighter-colored wooden liner, by an unknown maker, ca. 1948

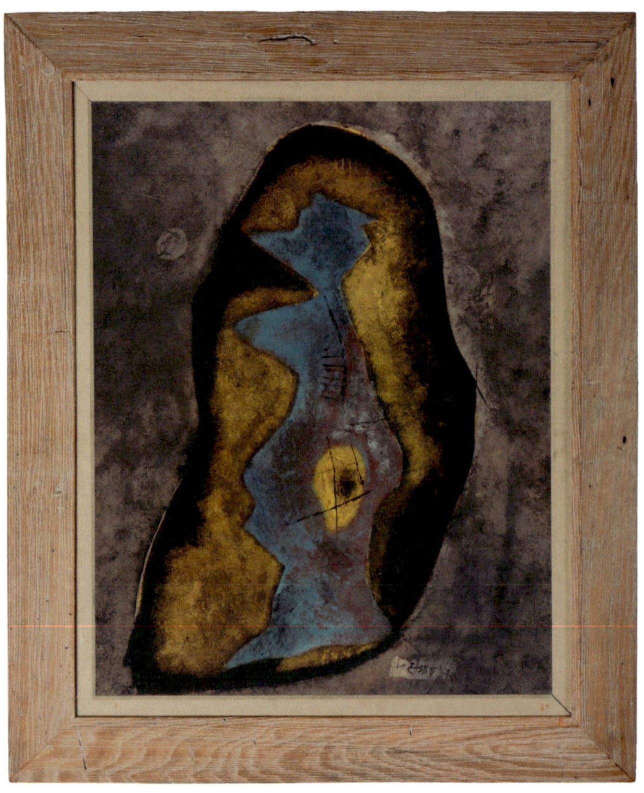

FIG. 11
Theodoros Stamos (1922–97)
Monolith, 1947 (cat. no. 198), in a wormy chestnut frame with a textured surface, natural finish, and painted wooden liner, possibly made by Stamos, ca. 1947

ing in American art in the 1940s. The introduction of wormy chestnut was a transformative moment in modern American frame taste and signaled the ascendancy of natural wood frames. Decorative gilding gave way to painted and manipulated surfaces, and, in time, to natural wood frames. The use of this alternative material mirrors the socio-cultural and aesthetic trends of the post-World War I era and the impact of the Great Depression, historical watersheds that created economic hardships for both artists and dealers who, as has been demonstrated, were largely responsible for the frames on the paintings in the Root collection.

Theodoros Stamos operated a frame shop in New York City from 1941 until 1948.[29] It is highly likely that the wormy chestnut frame on his painting *Monolith* (FIG. 11), was of his own making. A compelling case can be made that Stamos also made frames for Baziotes' works. They had a close relationship. Both men were of Greek descent and were active in the Abstract Expressionist movement. They also exhibited together—in 1948, for example, at The Museum of Modern Art and the Venice Biennale—and, as it has been observed, Stamos's artistic style during the late 1940s was influenced by Baziotes.[30] Frames on two of Root's Baziotes paintings, *Toy*, 1949 (cat. no. 6), and *The Mummy*, 1950 (cat. no. 4), were made of the same material and have the same profile as the frame on Stamos's *Monolith* (FIG. 11).[31] The finish on the two Baziotes frames is also the same, albeit slightly darker in tone.[32]

Another work by Baziotes in the Root bequest, *Black on White* (FIG. 12), was painted during the years Stamos had a frame shop. Although the rounded outer edge of this work's frame distinguishes its profile from the two Baziotes frames mentioned above, the distinctive textured surface of the wood, evident in a corner detail (FIG. 13), creates a sense of integration between the surface texture of the painting and the frame it surrounds. The aged or weathered-looking finish that exists on this frame was described by the painter Robert Motherwell (1915–91) in a 1946 letter to William L. McKim (d. 1977), a trustee of the Society of the Four Arts, Palm Beach, Fla., where Motherwell's 1943 painting, *Personage* (Norton Museum of Art), was exhibited after it was purchased by the collector Ralph Norton (1875–1953). "The kind of frame that seems to go best with present-day pictures," Motherwell wrote, "is wide and plain wood that has been 'pickled.'"[33]

Not all of the wormy chestnut frames made at this time used wood grain as an understated textural complement to the works they surround. For example, the frame on Clayton S. Price's (1874–1950) *Head*, 1949 (cat. no. 160), has an uneven and assertive surface treatment that complements the rawness of Price's paint strokes. Similar wood frames with narrow profiles are on Perle Fine's (1908–88) *Taurus*, 1946 (cat. no. 86), and Charles Seliger's (b. 1926) *Organic Form: Air, Sea, Land Enveloped*, 1948 (cat. no. 177). While these frames are expressive of a mid-twentieth-century aesthetic vision, economic considerations continued to influence the choice of materials and techniques. During this period self-expression remained paramount. One wonders, however, if the manipulation of a profile that is scratched, scrubbed, or scored and given a surface tonality that blends with a prominent color in the painting—as seen, for example, in the frame for Baziotes' 1945 *Black on White* (FIG.

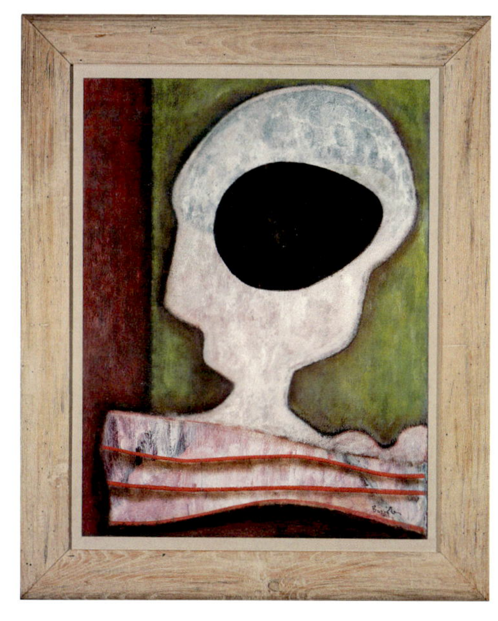

FIG. 12
William A. Baziotes (1912–63), *Black on White*, 1945 (cat. no. 2) in a wormy chestnut frame with a textured surface, semi-opaque white finish and a painted wooden liner, possibly made by Theodoros Stamos (1922–97), ca. 1945

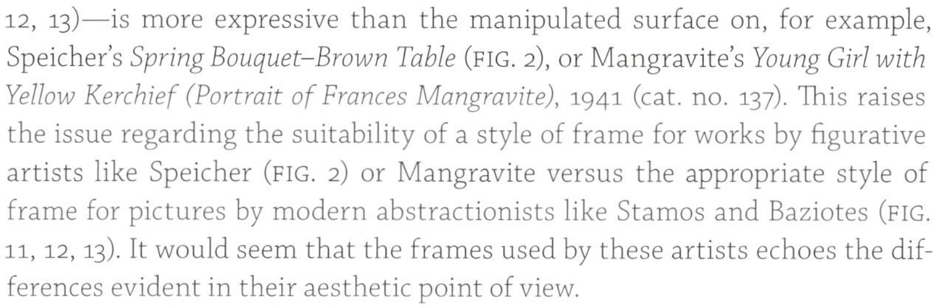

12, 13)—is more expressive than the manipulated surface on, for example, Speicher's *Spring Bouquet–Brown Table* (FIG. 2), or Mangravite's *Young Girl with Yellow Kerchief (Portrait of Frances Mangravite)*, 1941 (cat. no. 137). This raises the issue regarding the suitability of a style of frame for works by figurative artists like Speicher (FIG. 2) or Mangravite versus the appropriate style of frame for pictures by modern abstractionists like Stamos and Baziotes (FIG. 11, 12, 13). It would seem that the frames used by these artists echoes the differences evident in their aesthetic point of view.

A frame feature that the figurative and abstract artists in the Root collection share, however, is the use of a cloth-covered liner. The frames on paintings by figurative artists such as Soyer, Mangravite, Kuniyoshi, McFee, and Levi, as well as those by abstract artists such as Stamos, Baziotes, Gatch, Tobey, and Reuben Tam (1916–91)—many of which date from the 1940s and early 1950s—have cloth-covered liners.[34] It remains a question when this frame detail began appearing on modern American paintings. The paintings in the Root bequest dating from approximately the time of the Second World War that have this feature indicate cloth liners were popular at that time.[35]

Lee Gatch's frames demonstrate the efforts of mid-twentieth-century American artists to create their own frames. In a 1958 article about framing, the artist and author Dorothy Gees Seckler (1910–93) commented on Gatch's sensitivity to frames in her discussion of one of his "mosaic" frames. "Among the very few artists who have successfully designed and made their own frames is Lee Gatch who enhances his delicate paint surfaces with frames of a subtle, angular mosaic." In a caption for a detail of Gatch's painting, *The Thespian* (formerly, World House Galleries, New York), Seckler noted: "This one uses pieces of canvas in slightly varying tones; others utilize the contrasting grains of wood rectangles."[36] Gatch made a variety of designs over the years including, in the 1950s, "drawer front" frames that united in a radical way the canvas and its surround. These frames recall an Italian *cassetta*-style frame with its characteristic wide, flat frieze.[37] Gatch's *cassetta* derivatives include the frames for *The Eye of Silence*, 1951 (cat. no. 89), and *Winter Garden No. 5* (FIG. 14). What appear to be Italian *cassetta*-style frames surrounding both these paintings are, in fact, wooden drawer fronts. By attaching his canvases directly to these drawer fronts, Gatch created the illusion of a separate frame and artwork. Like Dove's frames, they demonstrate that economic con-

FIG. 13
Corner detail of the wormy chestnut frame (FIG. 12), with a textured surface, semi-opaque white finish and a painted wooden liner, possibly made by Stamos for Baziotes' painting, *Black on White*, 1945 (cat. no. 2), ca. 1945

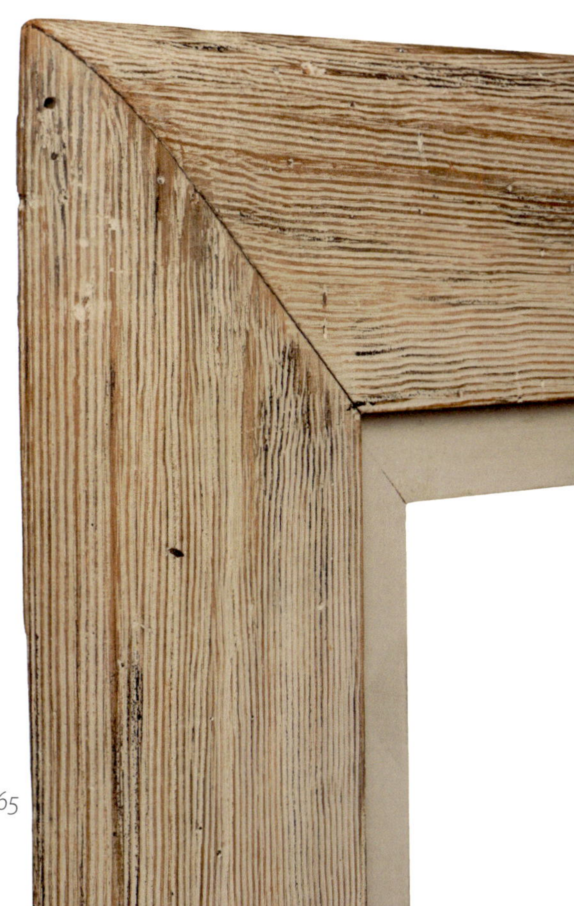

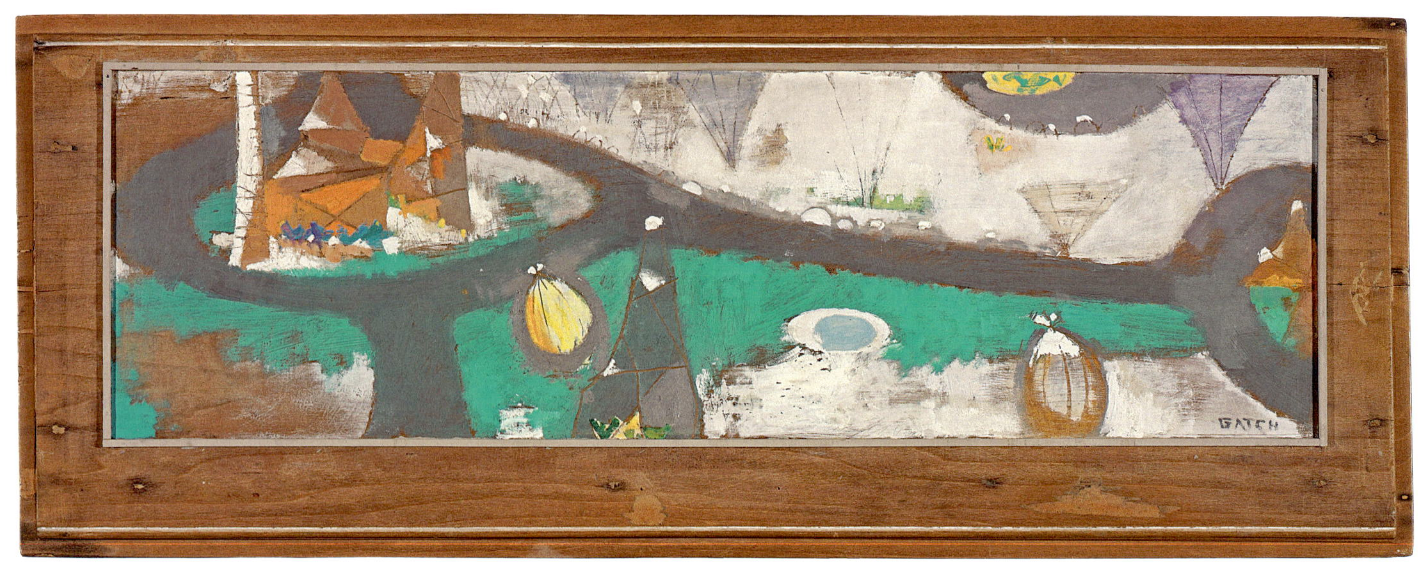

FIG. 14
Lee Gatch (1902–68)
Winter Garden No. 5, 1952
(cat. no. 92), mounted on a wooden "drawer front" frame with a natural finish, made by the artist, ca. 1952

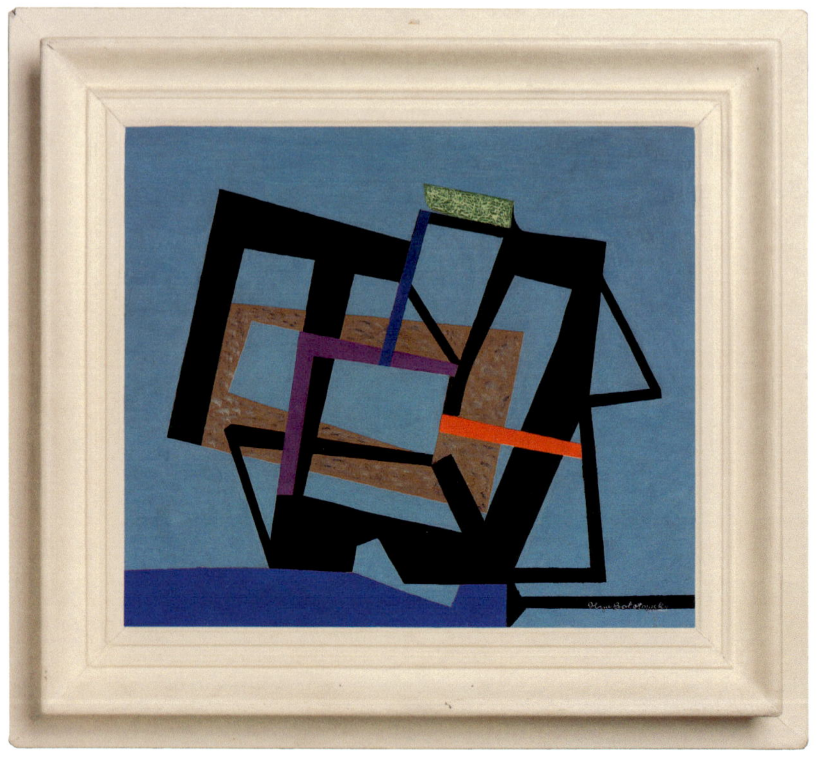

FIG. 15
Ilya Bolotowsky (1907–81)
Marine Variation No. 2, ca. 1940–42
(cat. no. 18), in a white frame by an unknown maker, ca. 1940–42

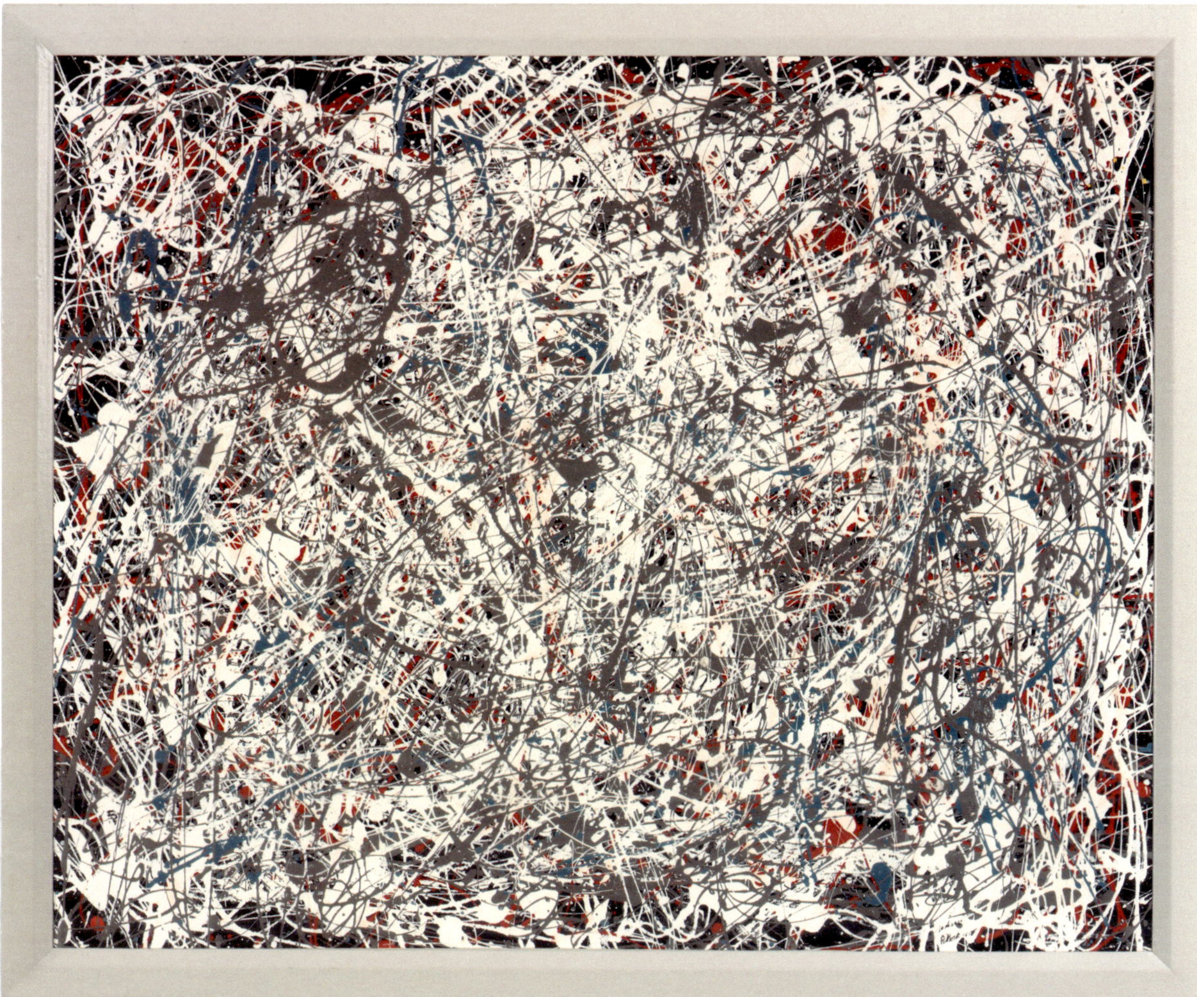

FIG. 16
Jackson Pollock (1912–56)
Number 20, 1948 (cat. no. 151), in a white frame, by an unknown maker after 1948

straints need not prevent a frame design from being complementary to the work and expressive of the artist's aesthetic. Gatch's integration of the frame and painting surface is a further iteration of the trend toward minimal surrounds in mid-twentieth century American framing practice.

The outstanding feature on the frames in the Root collection that surround the works of such mid-century artists as Bolotowsky, Pollock, Howard, Tobey, and Stuart Davis (1894–1964) (cat. no. 65) is the absence of gilding. It is difficult to imagine Pollock or Tobey placing a gilded frame on their works. Despite the stark, minimalist approach to framing that these artists adopted, specific and deliberate complements are still apparent. There is, for example, a sophisticated, all-white profile surrounding Bolotowsky's vigorously colored painting, *Marine Variation No. 2* (FIG. 15). White moldings also complement such abstract works as Tam's *Horizon Conditions*, 1944 (cat. no. 211); Arshile Gorky's (1904–48), *Making the Calendar*, 1947 (cat. no. 96); Stamos's *Bone*, 1945 (cat. no. 191); Harry Bertoia's (1915–78) undated *Mandala* (cat. no. 12); and Pollock's two paintings, *Number 20, 1948* (FIG. 16) and *Number 34, 1949* (cat. no. 152).[38] The use of white moldings may allude to the white frames the French artists, Camille Pissarro (1830–1903) and Edgar Degas (1834–1917), began using as early as 1877.[39] French chemist Michel-Eugène Chevreul (1786–1889), whose color theory was of critical importance to late-nineteenth-century avant-garde European painters, described the visual impact an artist could achieve by using a white frame. "White placed beside a colour heightens its tone," Chevreul wrote; "it is as if we took away from it the white light that had weakened its intensity."[40]

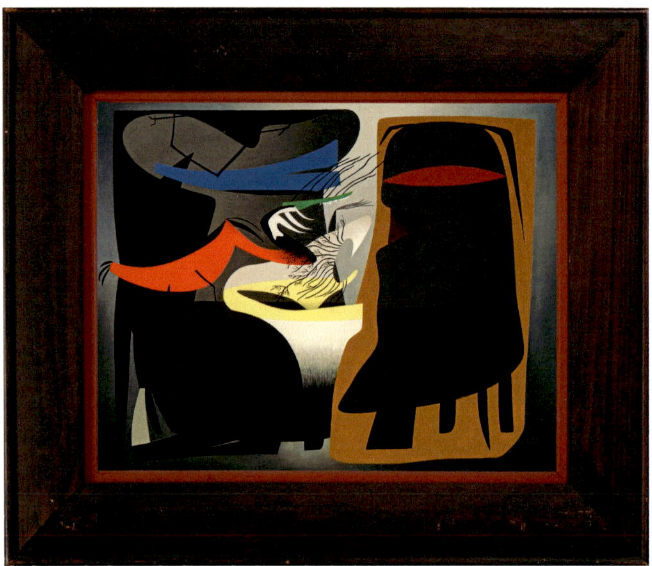

FIG. 17
Charles Howard (1899–1978)
Wild Park, 1944 (cat. no. 108), in a brown frame with a painted wooden liner, by an unknown maker, ca. 1944

In addition to the use of white, Chevreul advocated the use of frame colors that complemented or matched the predominant colors of the painting it surrounded.[41] This idea, which influenced the framing practice of artists such as Degas and French artist, Georges Seurat (1859–1891), is also evident in the austere wood frame that surrounds American artist Charles Howard's *Wild Park* (FIG. 17), which appears to be a purposeful choice by the artist.[42] The frame is separated from the painting by a slim, maroon-colored painted wood liner similar in tone to the elliptical shape in the upper right corner of the composition, but darker than the red form at the left of the design. The dynamic relationship that exists between the painting and its frame is also evident in Tobey's *Awakening Night* (FIG. 18). This work has a wide, unembellished frame that emulates the appearance of a frame and a mat (FIG. 19).[43] This ensemble mirrors the trompe l'oeil tradition of illusionism so prominent in late nineteenth-century American art.[44]

An examination of frames in the Root collection, embracing the period from 1921 to 1952, makes a critical contribution to understanding the history of frames and framing practice in the first half of the twentieth century and, by extension, to the history of taste in America during these dynamic years. Root seems to have accepted the prevailing concepts of modern American framing: gilded moldings surround the earliest works in his collection whereas bolder, simpler and more assertive frames define the borders of the later pictures. In contrast to the personal and deliberate reasoning that guided the pictures he purchased, as discussed in the preceding essay by Mary E. Murray and Paul D. Schweizer, the variety of frame styles that surround the works Root bequeathed to the Munson-Williams-Proctor Arts Institute suggests that he had no conscious approach or consistent guiding aesthetic or philosophy about framing. Most of the frames in his collection were designed, made, or chosen by the artist whose work it surrounds, or added to a work by a dealer. They appear to have been added to the pictures very close in time to when the work itself was made and have not been removed, changed, or modified for more than fifty years. Root's collection, therefore, tells us more about cultural taste with regard to frames than would a collection in which frame selection was a conscious process that was undertaken by a dealer or collector. It is exactly this sort of collection that should be studied to understand prevailing ideas about modern American framing.

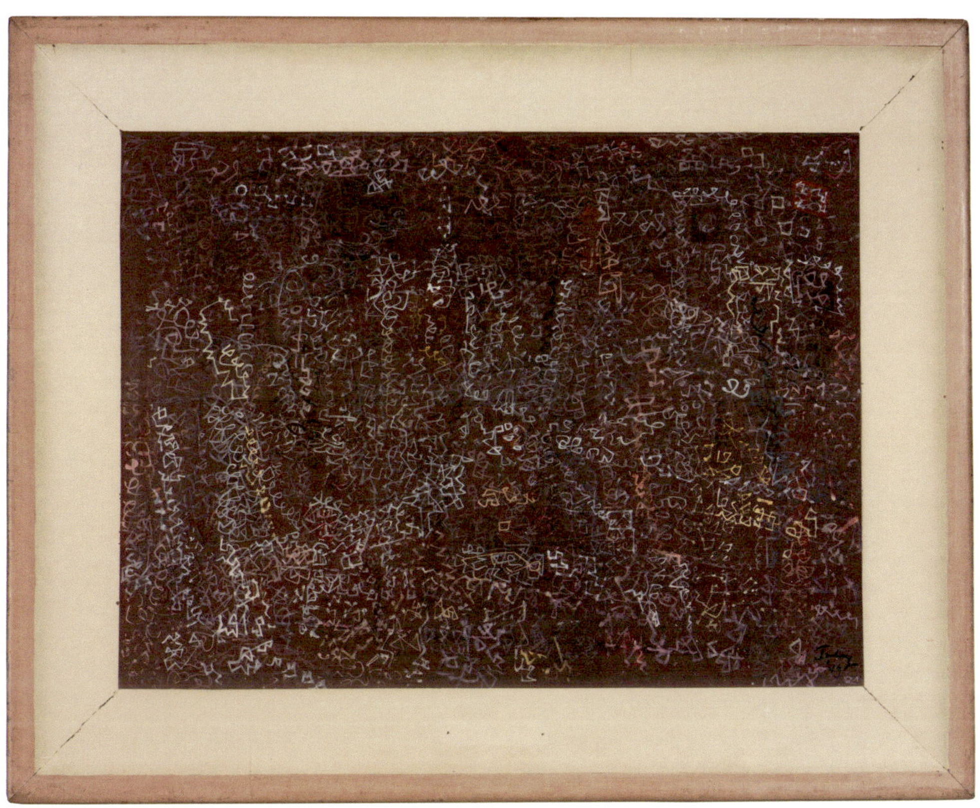

FIG. 18
Mark Tobey (1890–1976), *Awakening Night*, 1949 (cat. no. 214), in a frame with a gray, shallow, inner cove and a narrower, mauve, raised outer edge that creates the appearance of a frame and a mat, by an unknown maker, ca. 1949

FIG. 19
Corner detail of the frame (FIG. 18), with a gray, shallow, inner cove and a narrower, mauve, raised outer edge that creates the appearance of a frame and a mat, by an unknown maker, for Tobey's *Awakening Night*, 1949 (cat. no. 214), ca. 1949

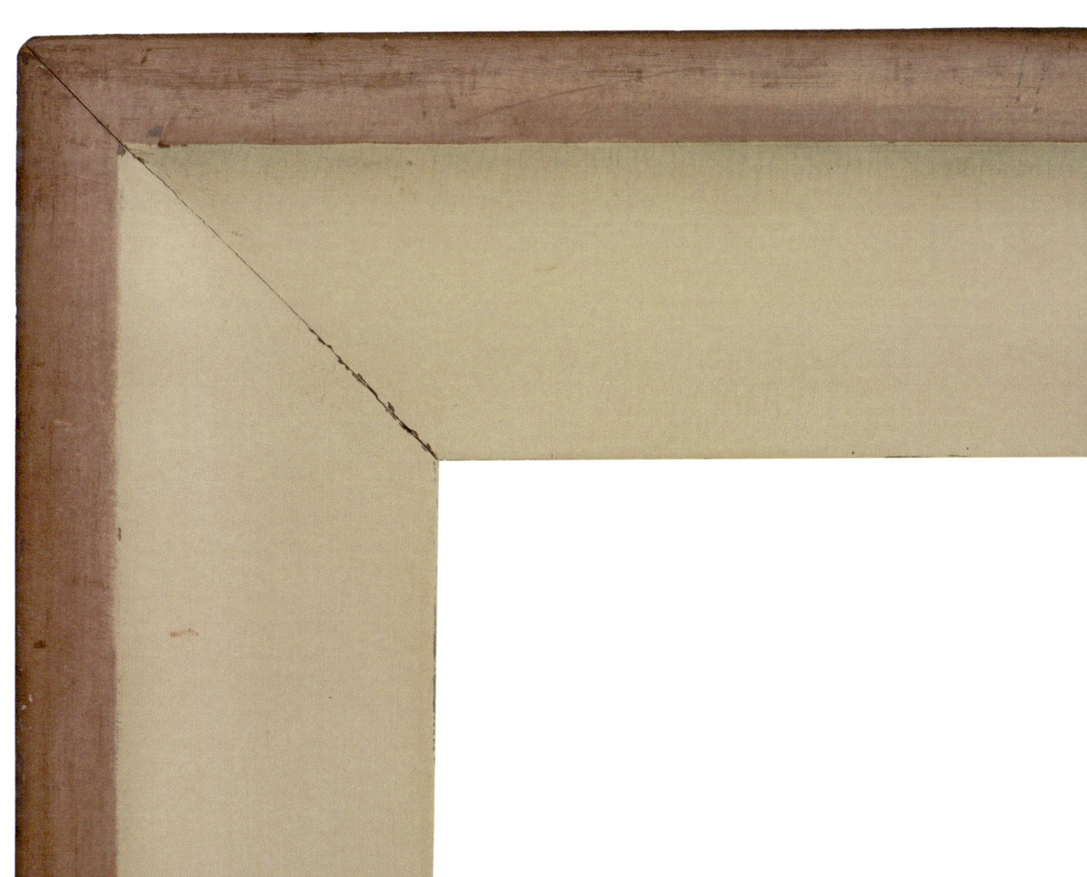

ENDNOTES

1. Mary E. Murray, *American Twentieth-Century Watercolors at the Munson-Williams-Proctor Arts Institute* (Utica, N.Y.: Munson-Williams-Proctor Arts Institute, 2000), 13. Also, Edna M. Lindemann, *The Art Triangle: Artist, Dealer, Collector* (Buffalo, N.Y.: Burchfield Art Center, 1989), 37–38.

2. Aline B. Saarinen, *The Proud Possessors: The Lives, Times and Tastes of Some Adventurous American Art Collectors* (New York: Random House, 1958), 258.

3. Lindemann, *The Art Triangle*, 35. Ferdinand Howald (1856–1934) is the only individual whose collection of modern American art rivaled Root's. He bequeathed 271 works to the Columbus Museum of Art and approximately one hundred more to his family. The American pictures Howald gave to the Columbus Museum were by 36 artists in contrast to the 227 pictures by 80 artists that Root bequeathed to the Munson-Williams-Proctor Arts Institute. Both men collected only thirteen of the same artists' works. For Howald, see Abraham A. Davidson, *Early American Modernist Painting*, 1910–1930 (New York: Harper and Row: 1981), 174–75. Also, see Edgar P. Richardson, "The Ferdinand Howald Collection," in Marcia Tucker and Kasha Linville, *American Paintings in the Ferdinand Howald Collection* (Columbus, Ohio: Columbus Gallery of Fine Arts, 1969), 1–6; and Mahonri Sharp Young, "Ferdinand Howald and His Artists," *American Art Journal* 1, no. 2 (Autumn 1969): 119–28.

4. Saarinen, *The Proud Possessors*, 265. For a contemporary assessment of Root as a collector and the works he exhibited at the Metropolitan Museum in 1953, written by the Associate Curator of American Paintings and Sculpture, see Robert Beverly Hale, "The Growth of a Collection," *The Metropolitan Museum of Art Bulletin* 11 (February 1953): 153–63. A copy of the exhibition's four-page checklist, *The Edward Root Collection Exhibited at The Metropolitan Museum*, February 12–April 12, 1953, is in the Edward Wales Root Papers, Munson-Williams-Proctor Arts Institute Archives, Record Group 13, Folder 76. (Subsequent references to documents in the Institute's Root archives are abbreviated: R[ecord] G[roup] [number], F[older] [number], Root Papers, MWPAI Archives.) For a review of the Metropolitan Museum's exhibition, see Aline B. Louchheim (later, Saarinen), "Root's Collection of Art Displayed," *New York Times*, February 12, 1953, 21.

5. Research on the early twentieth-century American frames in the Howald Collection at the Columbus Museum of Art is in progress by the authors. Brief surveys of modern American frame practice appear in William B. Adair, *The Frame in America, 1860–1960* (Washington, D.C.: Federal Reserve Board, 1995), 8–11; and in Tracy Gill, *The American Frame: From Origin to Originality* (New York: Gill and Lagodich Fine Period Frames, 2003), 44. See also, Suzanne Smeaton, "Embracing Realism: Frames of the Ashcan Painters, 1895–1925," in James W. Tottis et al., *Life's Pleasures: The Ashcan Artists' Brush with Leisure, 1895–1925* (Detroit, Mich.: Detroit Institute of Arts, 2007), 91–105.

6. Composition or "compo," is a moldable putty-like material made of chalk, hide glue, linseed oil, and resin that is pressed into molds. The use of this material eliminates the labor-intensive process of hand carving decorative embellishments.

7. A liner is an undecorated flat section of a frame that creates a visual transition between the perimeter of a painting and the frame's ornamental sections. Liners are typically gilded, painted, or covered with cloth.

8. Reeded molding, fashioned out of parallel convex bands of wood or compo, are so-named because of their resemblance to bundled reeds. Root noted in a hand-written memorandum that Luks framed these ten oil sketches (cat. nos. 119–28) in 1921. This is one of the rare surviving comments Root made about the frames in his collection, which, in this case, were presumably selected by the artist himself. It is noteworthy that Luks chose a style of frame that became popular in Europe decades earlier. All ten frames were stamped on the back with a capital L inside a diamond. This is likely the mark of the Indianapolis art supplier, H. Lieber Company, which sold picture frames and moldings in the United States and Europe. The authors thank David A. Miller, Senior Conservator of Paintings, Indianapolis Museum of Art, for this information.

9. On the dominance of European references and sources for American artists, architects, and patrons during the period from 1885–1920, see Wayne Craven, *American Art: History and Culture* (New York: Harry N. Abrams, 1994), 287. "American millionaires," Craven noted, "wanted their clubs, libraries, train stations and art museums to express a rebirth of the grandeur of European golden ages past."

10. A Barbizon frame features stylized floral elements on a convex molding. It is a nineteenth-century interpretation of a Louis XIVth frame, and is named after the Barbizon school of nineteenth-century landscape painters who worked near the French village of Barbizon, near Fontainebleau Forest. Works with frames of this design became popular in the United States in the post-Civil War era.

11. The term *cloth liner* is used instead of the frequently employed expression, *linen liner*, because technical analysis has not been undertaken on the liners discussed in this essay. That being said, the frame for Baziotes' painting, *Shadow*, 1951 (cat. no. 5), has a graphite inscription, "linen" written on the back the liner's wooden support.

12. A frame that is *distressed* has a surface treatment intended to simulate the appearance of age and wear.

13. Two other paintings in the Museum's collection, formerly owned by Root, also have Charles Prendergast frames. Davies's *Refluent Season*, before 1911 (acc. no. 58.39, see "Appendix 2: Purchases and Gifts of Art from Grace Root between 1956 and 1964") is inscribed "Prendergast 1909" on the back of the top rail. The frame on Maurice Prendergast's *Beach, St. Malo*, ca. 1907 (acc. no. 86.64), has a paper liner that covers the entire back of the frame and obscures whatever signature or inscription Charles Prendergast made. This painting and the front of the frame are illustrated in Carol Clark, Nancy Mowll Mathews, and Gwendolyn Owens, *Maurice Brazil Prendergast, Charles Prendergast: A Catalogue Raisonné* (Williamstown, Mass.: Williams College Museum of Art, 1990), 230.

14. Much has been written about the Italian, French, and Spanish sources for Charles Prendergast's frames. See, for example, Gill, *The American Frame: From Origin to Originality*, 37. Also, Carol Derby, "Charles Prendergast's Frames: Reuniting Design and Craftsmanship," in W. Anthony Gengarelly and Carol Derby, *The Prendergasts and the Arts and Crafts Movement* (Williamstown, Mass.: Williams College Museum of Art, 1989), 29–43.

15. Root to More, ca. 1933, R. G. 13, F. 48A, Root Papers, MWPAI Archives. Bryson Burroughs (1869–1934) was Curator of Paintings at the Metropolitan Museum from 1909 to 1934. According to Carol Clark, Root paid $125 for the frame. See, Paul D. Schweizer et al., *Masterworks of American Art from the Munson-Williams-Proctor Institute* (New York: Harry N. Abrams, 1989), 110, cat. no. 49.

16. The authors do not know of any other frames by Charles Prendergast that have a similar design. The pioneering collector Lillie P. Bliss (1864–1931) bequeathed the Davies painting to the Brooklyn Museum in 1931. Laura Leggett Barnes (1874–1966), widow of the collector Albert C. Barnes (1872–1951), bequeathed the Lawson painting to the Brooklyn Museum in 1967. For the provenances of these paintings, see Teresa A. Carbone, Barbara Dayer Gallati, and Linda S. Ferber, *American Paintings in the Brooklyn Museum: Artists Born by 1876* (Brooklyn, N.Y.: Brooklyn Museum, 2006), 440, 751–52. The Prendergast frame on the Brooklyn Museum's Davies painting is illustrated in Smeaton, "Embracing Realism: Frames of the Ashcan Painters, 1895–1925," in Tottis et al., *Life's Pleasures: The Ashcan Artists' Brush with Leisure, 1895–1925*, 96.

17. The frame on Marsh's 1932 *Zeke Youngblood's Dance Marathon* (cat. no. 141) has a graphite inscription on the back of the top rail that reads: "Made by KONZAL +[?] SOMMERFELD . . . [?] Reginald Marsh." Nothing is presently known about these, presumably, two frame makers.

18. The term *profile* designates the contours of a frame's cross-section. A frame with a slope away profile has its highest point near the picture plane with the majority of the molding receding outwards from this point towards the outer edge of the frame.

19. The Royal Art Framing Company, which was located in New York City, is perhaps best known for making distinctive monogram frames for the painter Childe Hassam (1859–1935). For information about this company, see Susan G. Larkin, "How Hassam Framed Hassams," in H. Barbara Weinberg et al., *Childe Hassam: American Impressionist* (New York: Metropolitan Museum of Art, 2004), 334–35, 342nn44–45.

20. Other Hopper paintings in public collections that have documented Sandelin frames include *Ground Swell*, 1939, Corcoran Gallery of Art, Washington, D.C.. For an illustration of this frame and Hopper's wife's remark about the frame on another work by her husband, see Suzanne Smeaton "On the Edge of Change," in Eli Wilner, ed., *The Gilded Edge: The Art of the Frame* (San Francisco: Chronicle Books, 2000), 73, 80–81. Three paintings in the collection of the Addison Gallery of American Art, Andover, Mass., also have Sandelin frames: Hopper's *Railroad Train*, 1908; Waldo Peirce's (1884–1970) *The Birches*, 1937; and Robert Gwathmey's (1903–88) *Sharecroppers*, ca. 1940. In 1940, for what might be the last time, Sandelin's name appeared in the New York City telephone directory. His address that year was 133 East 60th Street. Nina Gray provided this information to Paul D. Schweizer in a May 4, 2007 email message.

21. For additional comments on Dove's frames, see Smeaton, "On the Edge of Change," in Wilner, ed. *The Gilded Edge*, 73.

22. Dove to Stieglitz, August 9, 1930, Alfred Stieglitz Papers, Beinecke Rare Book and Manuscript Library, Yale University, Box 13, Folder 325.

23. An ogee curve combines convex and concave lines to form an S shape.

24. The two Kuniyoshi frames are stylistically related to the frame on a painting by Marsh, *The Britannic Sails*, 1939 (acc. no. 53.414), that Root gave the Museum in 1953 (see "Appendix 1: Edward W. Root's Gifts to the Munson-Williams-Proctor Institute, 1949 to 1955"). In contrast to the frames on Marsh's 1930 *Lower Manhattan (New York Skyline)* (cat. no. 139) and his 1931 *Texas Guinan and Her Gang* (cat. no. 140), the frame for *The Britannic Sails* shares with the two Kuniyoshi frames a traditional profile ornamented with beaded decoration, a cream-colored finish, and a cloth-covered liner.

25. Six additional Burchfield watercolors in the Root bequest (cat. nos. 26, 28, 37, 41, 42, 45) were originally in frames with similar finishes and painted liners although the profile of each is slightly different. For conservation reasons, the watercolors are no longer exhibited in these frames.

26. For Rehn's business transactions with Burchfield in the early 1930s, see Lindemann, *The Art Triangle*, 25, 33n99.

27. Burchfield to Root, October 6, 1937, R. G. 13, F. 8, Root Papers, MWPAI Archives. Burchfield noted in his May 31 letter to the Roots (R. G. 13, F. 8) that he wanted to reframe four watercolors (cat. nos. 26, 28, 42, 45) they purchased in the late 1920s and early 1930s because he considered the existing frames "terrible." In this letter his use of the phrase "have them made" suggests that someone else would make the new frames. This comment is consistent with archival documentation at the Burchfield-Penney Art Center, which indicates that Bredemeier was designing and hand-carving frames for Burchfield in 1932. (Nancy Weekly, Head of Collections and the Charles Cary Rumsey Curator, Burchfield-Penney Art Center, Buffalo, N.Y., and Tullis Johnson, Research Assistant, provided information about Bredemeier to Paul D. Schweizer in April 5, and August 13, 2007 email messages.) The frames on two other Root watercolors (cat. nos. 37, 41) have similar but not identical decoration that was either carved or shaped with a file on the top edge of the four corners of each frame. Root purchased these works before Burchfield wrote Root on October 6, 1937 saying he then preferred plain frames.

28. Henry Heydenryk Jr., *The Art and History of Frames: An Enquiry into the Enhancement of Paintings* (New York: James H. Heineman, 1963), 108.

29. *Dictionary of Art*, s.v. "Theodoros Stamos."

30. Roberta Smith, "Theodoros Stamos, 74, Abstract Painter Dies," *New York Times*, February 4, 1997.

31. Two other Stamos paintings that Root bequeathed to the Museum, *Conversation Piece* (cat. no. 192), and *The Reward* (cat. no. 200), both 1948, have frames that are similar in material, finish, and profile to the frame on Stamos's *Monolith* (FIG. 11), and the ones on Baziotes' *Toy*, 1949 (cat. no. 6), and *The Mummy*, 1950 (cat. no. 4). The five frames are also similar to the frame on another Baziotes painting, *Three Forms*, 1946, which Root gave the Addison Gallery of American Art. The frame on yet another Stamos painting bequeathed by Root to the Munson-Williams-Proctor Arts Institute, *Seedling (The Embryo; Vortex and Spiral)*, 1945 (cat. no. 201), with carved decoration and a cloth liner, is similar in style and finish to the frame on another Stamos painting, *Hibernation*, 1947, that Root also gave to the Addison (see "Appendix 3: Edward W. Root's Gifts of Art to the Addison Gallery of American Art, Everson Museum of Art, Museum of Modern Art, and Whitney Museum of American Art"). For Root's relationship with the Addison Gallery, see Susan C. Faxon, "Portraits of Patronage: The History of the Addison Gallery's Collection and Its Donors," in *Addison Gallery of American Art: 65 Years* (Andover, Mass.: Addison Gallery of American Art, 1996), 55–56, 58.

32. A crayon inscription on the back of the frame for Baziotes' *The Mummy*, 1950 (cat. no. 4), reads: "Heavy / scratched / dark brown." The frame on another Baziotes painting that Root gave the Museum, *Shadow*, 1951 (cat. no. 5), constructed of wormy chestnut and with an elaborate profile, bears Heydenryk and Kootz Gallery labels.

33. Motherwell to McKim, February 22, 1946, curatorial files, Norton Museum of Art, published, courtesy of the Norton Museum of Art. The authors thank Jonathan Stuhlman, Curator of American Art, Mint Museum of Art, for sharing this letter. For pickled wood finishes, see "Pickling: A Pickled Finish," http://antiquerestorers.com/Articles/SAL/pickle.htm.

34. The following figurative artists in the Root bequest have frames with cloth-covered liners: Maurice Sterne (1878–1957), *Three Figures, Bali*, 1912 (cat. no. 209); Speicher, *Brigham's Yard, Kingston*, 1928 (cat. no. 185); Soyer, *Study for "Sentimental Girl,"* 1934 (cat. no. 184); Mangravite, *Young Couple Drinking*, 1937 (cat. no. 136), and *Young Girl with Yellow Kerchief (Portrait of Frances Mangravite)*, 1941 (cat. no. 137); McFee, *Still Life–Knife*, ca. 1941 (cat. no. 144); Kuniyoshi, *By the Sea*, 1942 (cat. no. 113), and *Empty Town in Desert* (FIG. 8); and Levi, *Lobsterman*, 1945 (cat. no. 115). Abstract artists in the Root bequest that used frames with cloth covered liners include: Stamos, *Seedling (The Embryo; Vortex and Spiral*, 1945 (cat. no. 201); Tam, *Waipahee Mountains*, 1949 (cat. no. 213); Baziotes, *Shadow*, 1951 (cat. no. 5); Gatch, *Winter Garden No. 3 (Winter Garden)*, 1951 (cat. no. 91); and Tobey, *Voyage of the Saints*, 1952 (cat. no. 219).

35. Motherwell wrote in his February 22, 1946 letter to McKim (see n. 33) that a neutral-colored liner would help the appearance of his painting *Personage* if, to make the picture compatible with older works, it was exhibited in an historical frame. "The best way to make the picture go with older pictures is to put an old-style frame on it—I think a neutral grey (natural) linen insert helps almost any picture in such a frame."

36. Dorothy Gees Seckler, "The Art of Framing," *Art in America* 46, no. 1 (Spring 1958): 84.

37. The Italian word *cassetta* means, "little box" and, in this context, refers to a frame with a wide, flat frieze bordered by raised inner and outer moldings and carved corner decorations. This frame style dates from the fifteenth and sixteenth centuries.

38. Pollock's *Number 20, 1948* (cat. no. 151) is no longer exhibited in the frame illustrated in FIG. 16 because its tapered inside edge obscured the outer edges of the composition and its interior dimensions had the potential to abrade the edges of the work's paper support.

39. For Pissarro's and Degas' use of white frames in 1877, see Matthias Waschek, "Camille Pissarro: From Impressionist Frame to Decorative Object," in Eva Mendgen et al., *In Perfect Harmony: Picture + Frame, 1850–1920* (Amsterdam: Van Gogh Museum, 1995), 141–42.

40. Ibid., 142. Michel-Eugène Chevreul published his observations on color theory in *De la loi du contraste simultané des couleurs* (Paris, 1839). This volume became a pivotal work for the Impressionists and Neo-Impressionists. See also *Dictionary of Art*, s.v. "Michel-Eugène Chevreul."

41. For Chevreul's recommendation that a frame's color should be neutral or white, or match the dominant colors of the artwork it surrounds, see Isabelle Cahn, "Edgar Degas: Gold or Color," in Mendgen et al., *Perfect Harmony*, 131–32.

42. For Degas' use of colored frames, see ibid., 132; for Seurat, see Matthias Waschek, "Georges Seurat: The Frame as Boundary and Extension of the Artwork," ibid., 153–62.

43. The term *mat* is used to describe a paper or cardboard border that surrounds a picture. It assures that the picture's glazing does not rest directly on the surface of the artwork, and provide a visual transition or contrast between the picture and its frame.

44. *Trompe l'oeil* ("fool the eye") is a French term that describes a style of painting in which the objects depicted are so naturalistic in appearance that they look real. For a masterful example of this tradition in the Museum's collection, see John F. Peto's (1854–1907) *Fish House Door with Eel Basket*, 1890s (acc. no. 65.15). The painting's original frame, a plain, wide, flat profile that is similar in shape and color to the boards depicted in the painting, expands the composition onto the frame surface.

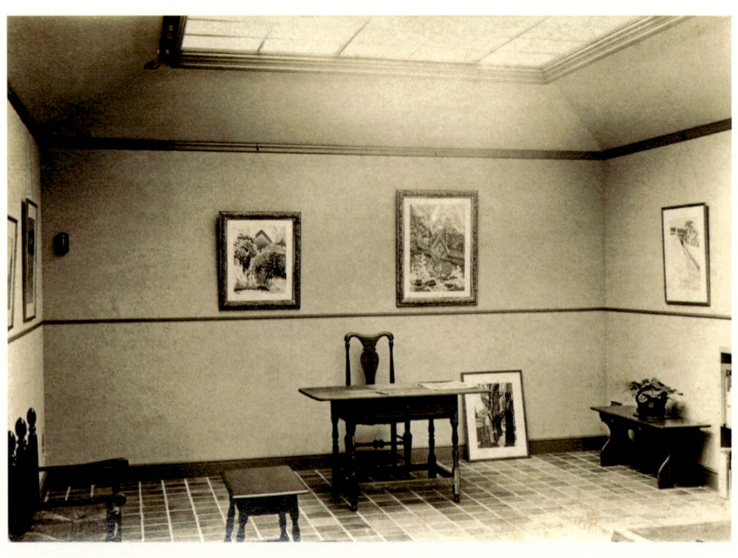

In the early 1930s, Edward W. Root built an addition called the "pocket gallery" to his home. On view are several Charles E. Burchfield watercolors, including *The Insect Chorus*, *Childhood's Garden*, *Poplar Walk*, and *Country Road.*

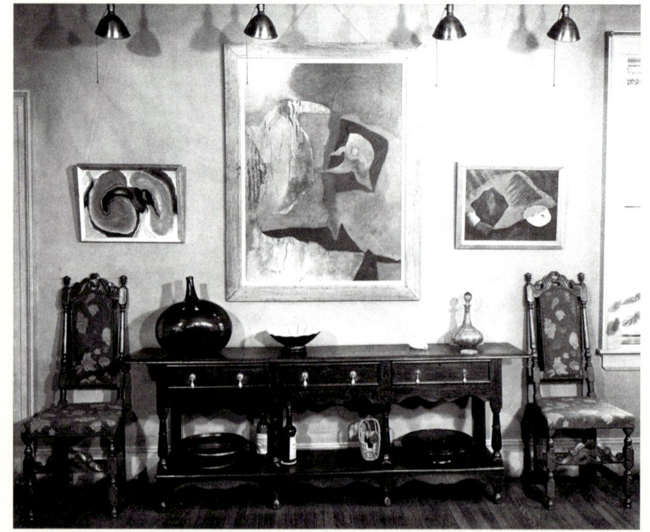

The Root Family Homestead, ca. 1948-49, with Arthur G. Dove, *Summer Orchard*, Theodoros Stamos, *The Reward*, and Dove, *No Feather Pillow.*

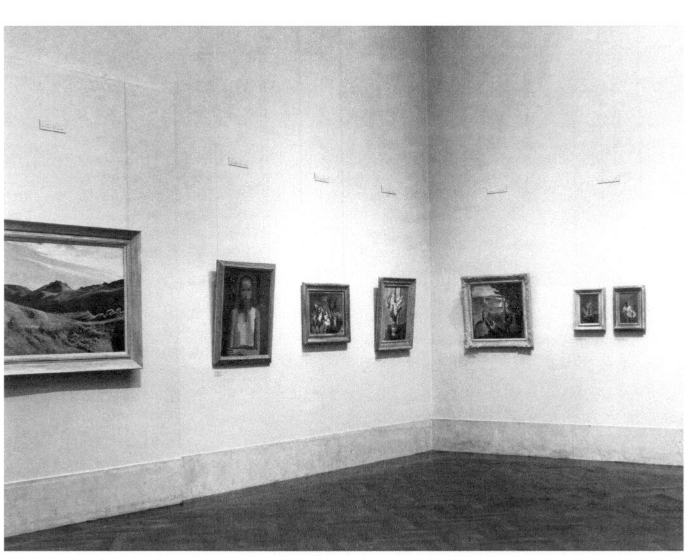

The Edward Root Collection, The Metropolitan Museum of Art, New York, February 12–April 12, 1953, installation photograph with paintings by Edward Hopper, John Wesley Carroll, Raymond Breinin, Eugene Speicher, and Franklin C. Watkins.

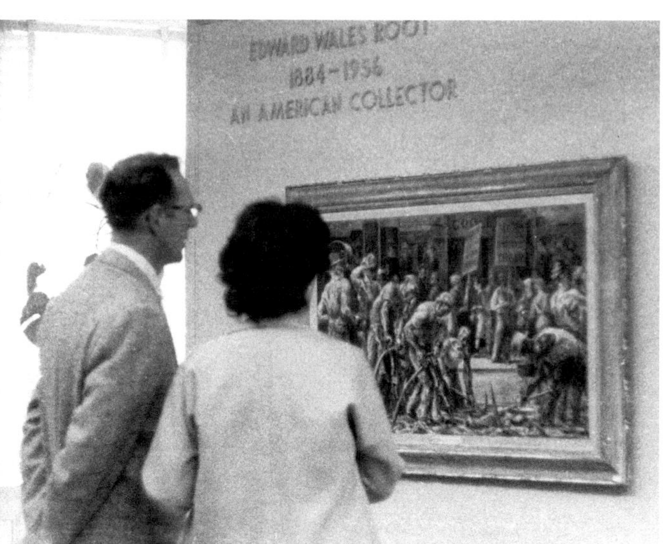

Edward Wales Root, 1884-1956: An American Collector, a memorial exhibition held at Munson-Williams-Proctor Institute from April 28 to May 26, 1957.

CATALOGUE OF THE EDWARD W. ROOT BEQUEST

Joseph Trovato, Mary E. Murray,
Paul D. Schweizer, and Michael D. Somple

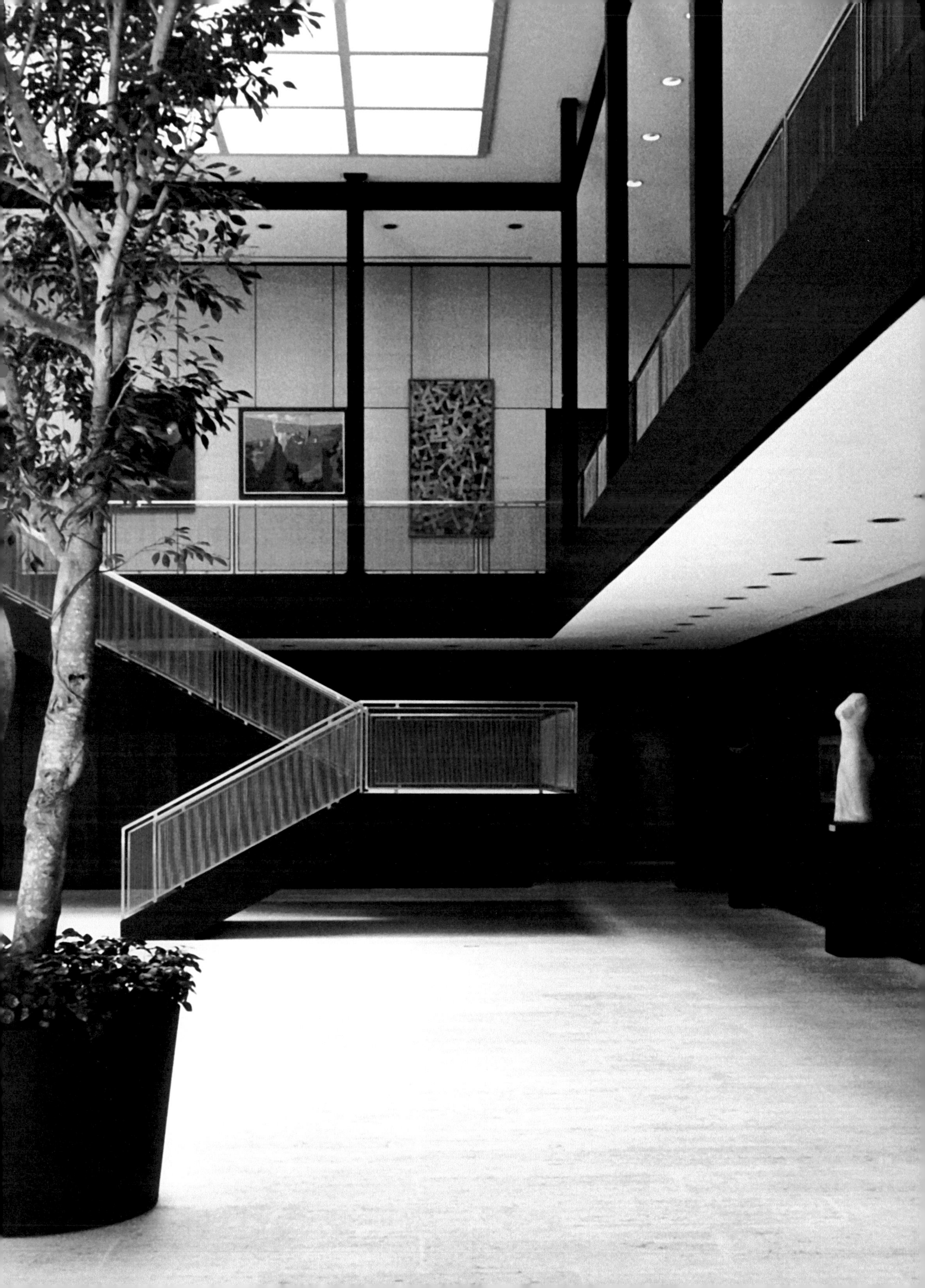

NOTES TO THE CATALOGUE

Each alphabetically arranged entry contains standard catalog information—artist's name, dates, place of birth and death; the art work's title and date; media; measurements; inscriptions; watermark, if applicable; provenance; exhibition and publication histories. The maximum dimensions of each work are given in inches, with height preceding width.

In the EXHIBITIONS section, exhibitions for which a checklist or catalog was published are so noted, and, in the interest of saving space, exhibition publications are not repeated under the PUBLICATIONS section. For exhibition publications that assigned catalog numbers for each work of art, the catalog numbers only are noted. For exhibition publications that are paginated but did not assign catalog numbers, "catalog" is noted, followed by the page number on which the art work is listed. For exhibition publications that are not paginated and for which catalog numbers were not assigned for each work of art, "catalog" is simply noted. Exhibition publications that illustrate the artworks are indicated by "illus." with the page number or figure number of the reproduction. In the interest of saving space, for multi-venue traveling shows, the first or organizing venue is listed only. All second references to the American Federation of the Arts are cited, "AFA."

The PUBLICATIONS section lists books and articles in which the work appears. Reviews of exhibitions that included works from Root's collection, in which his works are not specifically mentioned, are not cited.

In 2000 the Institute changed its name from Munson-Williams-Proctor Institute to Munson-Williams-Proctor Arts Institute. Exhibitions and publications dating before 2000 retain the original name.

The designation "Root Art Center," documents instances when a work of art from the Root Bequest was displayed by itself at the Root Art Center, Hamilton College, and for which no specific exhibition title is known.

Sidebar narratives are included in the catalog for five artists whose reputations and careers are not so well known as they were more than fifty years ago when Root collected their works.

Supplementary documentation or cataloging matters that the authors were not able to resolve prior to the publication of this catalog are designated in brackets.

PEGGY BACON

(Ridgefield, Conn., 1895–Kennebunk, Me., 1987)

1. *The Optimist*, 1938

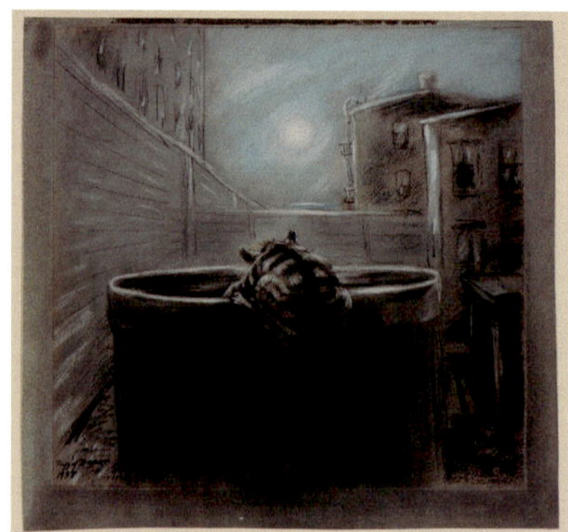

Pastel on deep gray pastel paper
15 3/16 x 16 3/16 in.
57.317
Signed and dated lower left (black crayon): Peggy Bacon / 1938
Purchased from Frank K. M. Rehn Galleries, New York, May 1939

EXHIBITIONS

"Manhattan Cats by Peggy Bacon," Frank K. M. Rehn Galleries, New York, March 27–April 15, 1939 (cat. no. 2). "The Edward Root Collection," The Metropolitan Museum of Art, New York, February 12–April 12, 1953 (catalog, 1). "Edward Wales Root Bequest," Munson-Williams-Proctor Institute, Utica, N.Y., November 5, 1961–February 24, 1962 (catalog). "Prints by American Artists," Root Art Center, Hamilton College, Clinton, N.Y., January 9–February 12, 1967. "Carnival of the Animals," MWPI, December 10–31, 1972. "Peggy Bacon Retrospective," National Collection of Fine Arts, Washington, D.C., December 5, 1975–February 8, 1976. "The Animal Kingdom in American Art," Everson Museum of Art, Syracuse, N.Y., February 3–April 2, 1978 (traveling exhibition, cat. no. 13, illus. no. 7).

PUBLICATIONS

Paintings, Drawings & Sculptures in the Museum of Art (Utica, N.Y.: Munson-Williams-Proctor Institute, 1961), 6. *Peggy Bacon: Personalities and Places* (Washington, D.C.: National Collection of Fine Arts, Smithsonian Institution Press, 1975), cat. no. 35, illus. fig. 39.

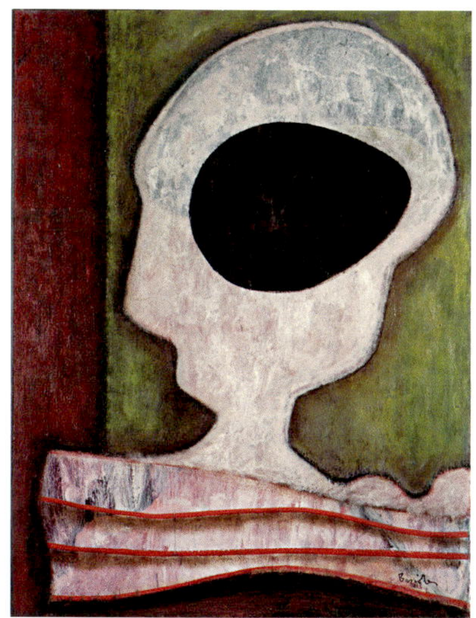

WILLIAM A. BAZIOTES

(Pittsburgh, Pa., 1912–New York, N.Y., 1963)

2. *Black on White*, 1945

Oil on linen
36 ¼ X 28 ⅛ in.
57.69
Signed lower right (black paint): Baziotes
Signed verso: Black On White / W. Baziotes (covered by lining)
Purchased from Kootz Gallery, New York, March 1946

EXHIBITIONS

"William Baziotes: Paintings and Water Colors," Kootz Gallery, New York, February 12–March 2, 1946 (cat. no. 12). "Paintings from the Collection of Edward W. Root," Munson-Williams-Proctor Institute, Utica, N.Y., September 29–October 20, 1946; "Current Trends in British and American Painting from the Collection of Mr. Edward W. Root," MWPI, December 3–31, 1950 (cat. no. 1). "20th-Century American Painting from the Edward W. Root Collection," Smithsonian Institution, Washington, D.C., July 1959–July 1960 (traveling exhibition). "Edward Wales Root Bequest," MWPI, November 5, 1961–February 24, 1962 (catalog, illus.). "European Sources of Contemporary American Art: Kandinsky," Root Art Center, Hamilton College, Clinton, N.Y., September 15–October 6, 1963 (cat. no. 2). "Selections from the Edward W. Root Collection," Root Art Center, February 22–March 21, 1970. "Edward W. Root: Collector and Teacher," Fred L. Emerson Gallery, Hamilton College, October 2–November 14, 1982 (catalog, 49). "Figuratively Speaking," MWPI, April 11–October 22, 1985. "Two Hundred Years of American Art," The Art Museum Association of America, November 15, 1986–May 8, 1988 (traveling exhibition, cat. no. 65, illus., 79).

PUBLICATION

Paintings, Drawings & Sculptures in the Museum of Art (Utica, N.Y.: Munson-Williams-Proctor Institute, 1961), 7.

3. *Glass Form*, ca. 1944

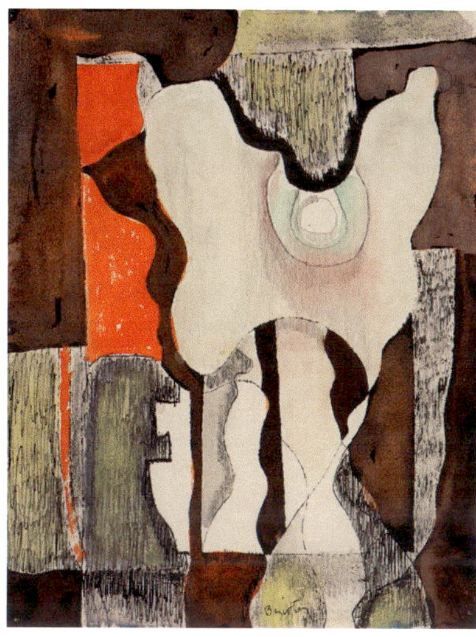

Watercolor on white laid watercolor paper
14 x 11 in.
57.310
Signed lower edge right of center (black ink): Baziotes
Inscribed verso upper left (black ink): glass form 27 [number encircled] / TOP
Purchased from Kootz Gallery, New York

EXHIBITIONS

"William Baziotes: Paintings and Water Colors," Kootz Gallery, New York, February 12–March 12, 1946 (cat. no. 22). "Paintings from the Collection of Edward W. Root," Munson-Williams-Proctor Institute, Utica, N.Y., September 29–October 20, 1946. "20th-Century American Painting from the Edward W. Root Collection," Smithsonian Institution, Washington, D.C., May 1959–May 1960 (traveling exhibition). "Edward Wales Root Bequest," MWPI, November 5, 1961–February 24, 1962 (catalog). "European Sources of Contemporary American Art: Kandinsky," Root Art Center, Hamilton College, Clinton, N.Y., September 15–October 6, 1963 (cat. no. 4). "On Paper," American Federation of Arts, September 1966–September 1967 (traveling exhibition). "American Art in Upstate New York," Albright-Knox Art Gallery, Buffalo, N.Y., July 12, 1974–April 27, 1975 (traveling exhibition, cat. no. 3). Rome Community Art Center, Rome, N.Y., September 14–November 9, 1975. "Watercolors: Historic and Contemporary," Hathorn Gallery, Skidmore College, Saratoga Springs, N.Y., February 4–20, 1977 (cat. no. 1). "Abstract Expressionism," MWPI, July 19–August 18, 1985. "American Twentieth-Century Watercolors at the Munson-Williams-Proctor Arts Institute," MWPAI, April 30–July 10, 2000 (traveling exhibition, cat. no. 38, illus.).

PUBLICATION

Paintings, Drawings & Sculptures in the Museum of Art (Utica, N.Y.: Munson-Williams-Proctor Institute, 1961), 7.

4. *The Mummy*, 1950

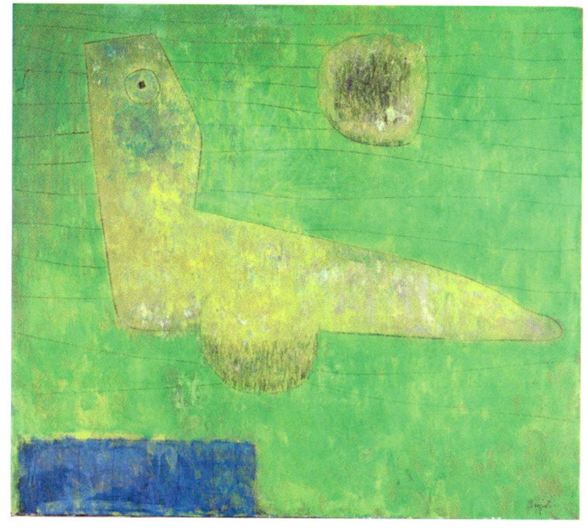

Oil on canvas
36 ¼ x 41 ⅞ in.
57.70
Signed lower right (black paint): Baziotes
Inscribed verso upper left: "The Mummy" / Wm. Baziotes 1950
Purchased from Kootz Gallery, New York

EXHIBITIONS

"New Paintings by Baziotes," Kootz Gallery, New York, February 7–27, 1950 (catalog). "Current Trends in British and American Painting from the Collection of Edward W. Root," Munson-Williams-Proctor Institute, Utica, N.Y., December 3–31, 1950 (cat. no. 4). "15 Americans," The Museum of Modern Art, New York, April 9–July 27, 1952 (catalog, 45). "The Edward Root Collection," The Metropolitan Museum of Art, New York, February 12–April 12, 1953 (catalog, 1). "New Trends in 20th-Century American Painting," Root Art Center, Hamilton College, Clinton, N.Y., October 26–November 30, 1958. "20th-Century American Painting from the Edward W. Root Collection," Smithsonian Institution, Washington, D.C., July 1959–July 1960 (traveling exhibition). "New Trends in 20th-Century American Painting," Union College, Schenectady,

N.Y., March 5–26, 1961. "Edward Wales Root Bequest," MWPI, November 5, 1961–February 24, 1962 (catalog). "European Sources of Contemporary American Art: Kandinsky," Root Art Center, September 15–October 6, 1963 (cat. no. 4). "William Baziotes: A Memorial Exhibition," Solomon R. Guggenheim Museum, New York, February 11–March 1965 (traveling exhibition, cat. no. 16, color pl. 16). "Paintings and Drawings from the Edward Root Bequest," Root Art Center, April 7–May 5, 1968. "The Root Bequest," Root Art Center, May 11–June 8, 1969. Kirkland Art Center, Clinton, N.Y., October 16–November 16, 1974. "Abstract Expressionism," MWPI, July 19–August 18, 1985. "Nature in Art," MWPI, June 2–September 1, 1987.

PUBLICATIONS

Hess, Thomas B. *Abstract Painting: The Background and American Phase* (New York: The Viking Press, 1951), 122, illus. pl. no. 76. *Paintings, Drawings & Sculptures in the Museum of Art* (Utica, N.Y.: Munson-Williams-Proctor Institute, 1961), 7.

5. *Shadow*, 1951

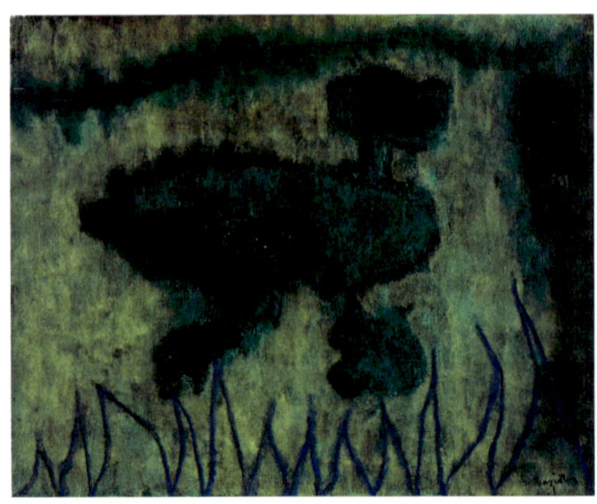

Oil on canvas
24 x 30 ¼ in.
57.71
Signed lower right (black paint): Baziotes
Signed verso top: Shadow / Baziotes, 1951
Purchased from Kootz Gallery, New York

EXHIBITIONS

"The Lyrical New Paintings of Baziotes," Kootz Gallery, New York, February 12–March 5, 1951 (cat. no. 5). "Five Decades of American Painting," Union College, Schenectady, N.Y., September 27–October 23, 1959. "Edward Wales Root Bequest," Munson-Williams-Proctor Institute, Utica, N.Y., November 5, 1961–February 24, 1962 (catalog). "European Sources of Contemporary American Art: Kandinsky," Root Art Center, Hamilton College, Clinton, N.Y., September 15–October 6, 1963 (cat. no. 5). "Abstract Paintings and Drawings from the Root Bequest," Root Art Center, September 11–October 9, 1966. "Selections from the Edward W. Root Collection," Root Art Center, February 22–March 21, 1970. Kirkland Art Center, Clinton, N.Y., October 16–November 16, 1974. "Post-War Modernism," San Jose Museum of Art, November 4–December 31, 1977 (catalog).

PUBLICATION

Paintings, Drawings & Sculptures in the Museum of Art (Utica, N.Y.: Munson-Williams-Proctor Institute, 1961), 7.

6. *Toy*, 1949

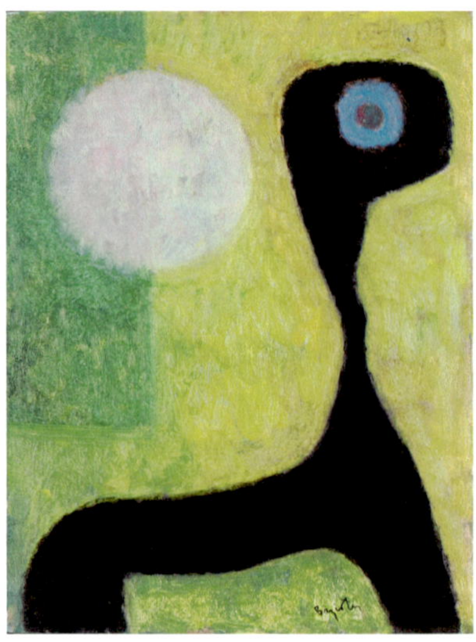

Oil on canvas
18 x 14 $^{3}/_{16}$ in.
57.72
Signed lower edge right of center (black paint): Baziotes; signed verso top: "Toy" / William / Baziotes 1949
Purchased from Kootz Gallery, New York

EXHIBITIONS

"New Paintings by Baziotes," Kootz Gallery, New York, February 7–27, 1950 (catalog). "Current Trends in British and American Painting from the Collection of Edward W. Root," Munson-Williams-Proctor Institute, Utica, N.Y., December 3–31, 1950 (traveling exhibition, cat. no. 3). "20th-Century American Painting from the Edward W. Root Collection," Smithsonian Institution, Washington, D.C., July 1959–July 1960 (traveling exhibition). "Edward Wales Root Bequest," MWPI, November 5, 1961–February 24, 1962 (catalog). "European Sources of Contemporary American Art: Kandinsky," Root Art Center, Hamilton College, Clinton, N.Y., September 15–October 6, 1963 (cat. no. 6). "The New York School: The First Generation, Paintings of the 1940s–1950s," Los Angeles County Museum of Art, June 9–August 8, 1965 (cat. no. 4, illus.). "Selections from the Edward W. Root Collection," Root Art Center, February 22–March 21, 1970. "Post-War Modernism," San Jose Museum of Art, November 4–December 31, 1977 (catalog). "Five Decades of Collecting: Edward W. Root," MWPI, April 2–May 28, 1978. "Masterworks of American Art from the Munson-Williams-Proctor Institute Museum of Art," Knoxville Museum of Art, Knoxville, Tenn., February 26–August 23, 1998. "American Masterworks from the MWPAI, Celebrating an Educational Alliance with Pratt Institute," Hirschl & Adler Galleries, New York, November 16–December 29, 2006 (catalog).

PUBLICATIONS

Prior, Harris K. "Edward Root—Talent Scout," *Art in America* L (1962): 70, illus. no. 3. *Paintings, Drawings & Sculptures in the Museum of Art* (Utica, N.Y.: Munson-Williams-Proctor Institute, 1961), 7. Schweizer, Paul D., et al. *Masterworks of American Art from the Munson-Williams-Proctor Institute* (New York: Harry N. Abrams, Inc., 1989), cat. no. 84, illus., 184.

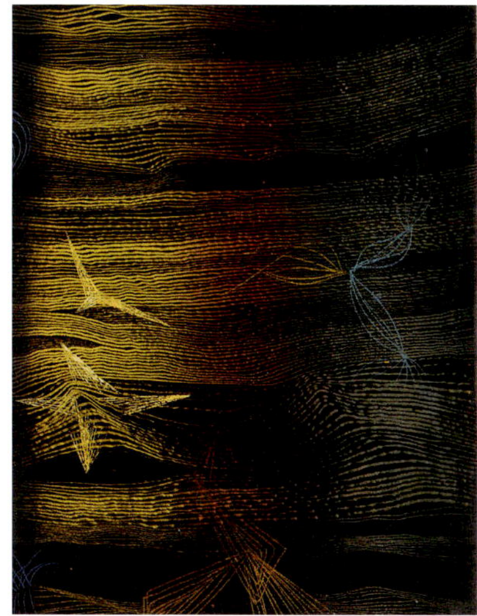

HARRY BERTOIA

(San Lorenzo, Italy, 1915–Barto, Pa., 1978)

7. *Black Ground Composition No. 1*, 1945

Ink on wove paper
16 ¼ x 13 ⅜ in., irregular
57.73
Inscribed verso upper right (red crayon, in artist's hand): Nov. 20, 45
Purchased from Nierendorf Gallery, New York, ca. 1945–46

EXHIBITIONS

"Paintings from the Collection of Edward W. Root," Munson-Williams-Proctor Institute, Utica, N.Y., September 29–October 20, 1946. "Edward Wales Root Bequest," MWPI, November 5, 1961–February 24, 1962 (catalog). "European Sources of Contemporary American Art: Kandinsky," Root Art Center, Hamilton College, Clinton, N.Y., September 15–October 6, 1963 (cat. no. 7).

8. *Black Ground Composition No. 2*, not dated

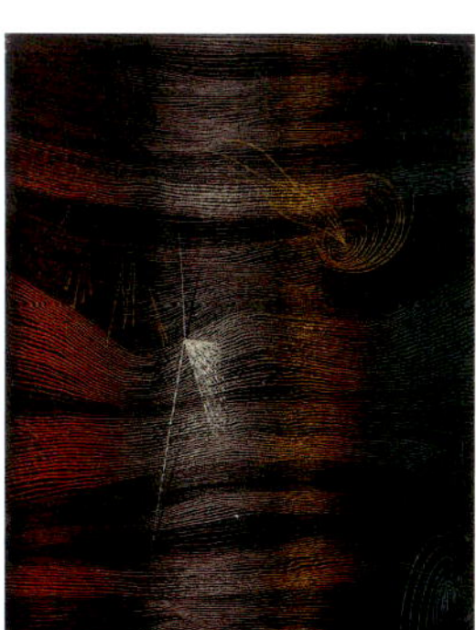

Ink on warm-toned paper mounted on board
12 ¾ x 16 ⅜ in., irregular
57.74
Purchased from Nierendorf Gallery ca. 1944–46

EXHIBITIONS

"The New Landscape in Art and Science," American Federation of Arts, October 1958–May 1960 (traveling exhibition). "Edward Wales Root Bequest," Munson-Williams-Proctor Institute, Utica, N.Y., November 5, 1961–February 24, 1962 (catalog). "On Paper," AFA, September, 1966–September 1967 (traveling exhibition). Rome Art and Community Center, Rome, N.Y., September 14–November 9, 1975.

9. *Coiling Lines*, not dated

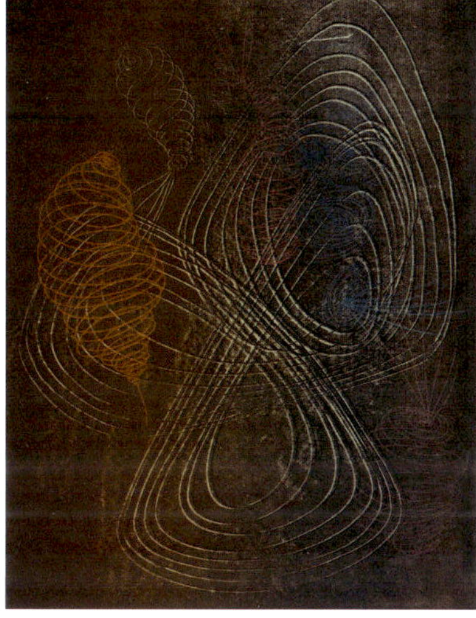

Ink on Japanese paper
17 ⅛ x 13 ⅜ in., irregular
57.75
Signed verso upper right edge (graphite): Harry Bertoia / VII-3
Purchased from Nierendorf Gallery, New York, ca. 1944–46

EXHIBITIONS

"Trends in 20th-Century American Painting," Union College, Schenectady, N.Y., March 5–26, 1961. "Edward Wales Root Bequest," Munson-Williams-Proctor Institute, Utica, N.Y., November 5, 1961–February 24, 1962 (catalog).

10. *Coiling Lines*, ca. 1944

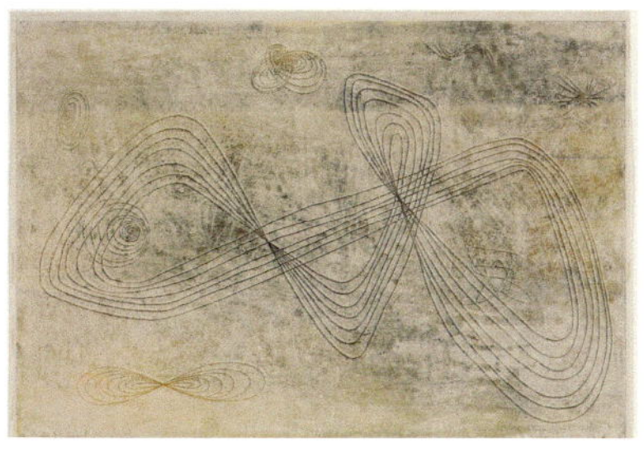

Ink on wove paper
25 ¼ x 36 ¾ in.
57.76
Signed verso upper right (graphite): Harry Bertoia / XIII-2
Purchased from Nierendorf Gallery, New York, ca. 1944–46

EXHIBITIONS

"The Edward Root Collection," The Metropolitan Museum of Art, New York, February 12–April 12, 1953 (catalog, 1). "Trends in the 20th-Century American Painting," Union College, Schenectady, N.Y., March 5–26, 1961. "Edward Wales Root Bequest," Munson-Williams-Proctor Institute, Utica, N.Y., November 5, 1961–February 24, 1962 (catalog).

11. *Descending Force*, 1944

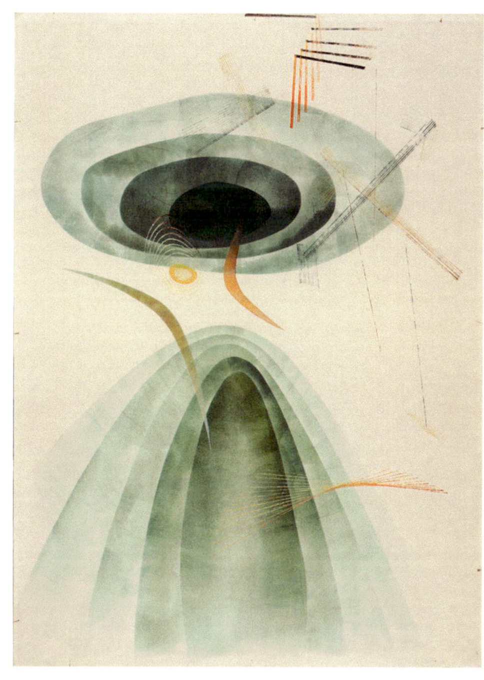

Ink on white paper-faced board
41 ¼ x 30 ⅝ in.
57.77
Inscribed verso top, upside down: 319 / 1944
Purchased from Nierendorf Gallery, New York, ca. 1944–46

EXHIBITIONS

"Paintings from the Collection of Edward W. Root," Munson-Williams-Proctor Institute, Utica, N.Y., September 29–October 20, 1946. "The New Landscape in Art and Science," American Federation of Arts, October 1958–May 1960 (traveling exhibition). "Edward Wales Root Bequest," MWPI, November 5, 1961–February 24, 1962 (catalog). "European Sources of Contemporary American Art: Kandinsky," Root Art Center, Hamilton College, Clinton, N.Y., September 15–

October 6, 1963 (cat. no. 8). "Five Decades of Collecting: Edward W. Root," MWPI, April 2–May 28, 1978.

12. *Mandala*, not dated

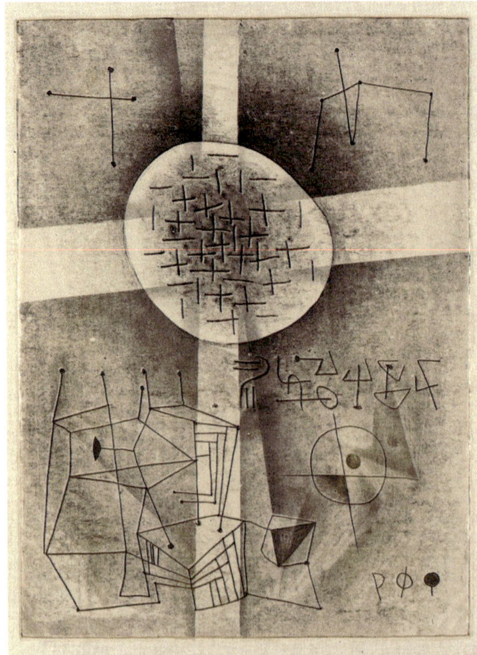

Ink on thin white paper mounted on thin fabric
23 13⁄16 x 18 in.
57.78
Purchased from Nierendorf Gallery, New York, ca. 1944–46

EXHIBITIONS
"20th-Century American Painting from the Edward W. Root Collection," Smithsonian Institution, Washington, D.C., July 1959–July 1960 (traveling exhibition). "Edward Wales Root Bequest," Munson-Williams-Proctor Institute, Utica, N.Y., November 5, 1961–February 24, 1962 (catalog). "Abstract Paintings and Drawings from the Root Bequest," Root Art Center, Hamilton College, Clinton, N.Y., September 11–October 9, 1966. Root Art Center, December 2–18, 1971. "Influences of Klee," MWPI, December 19, 1987–May 12, 1988.

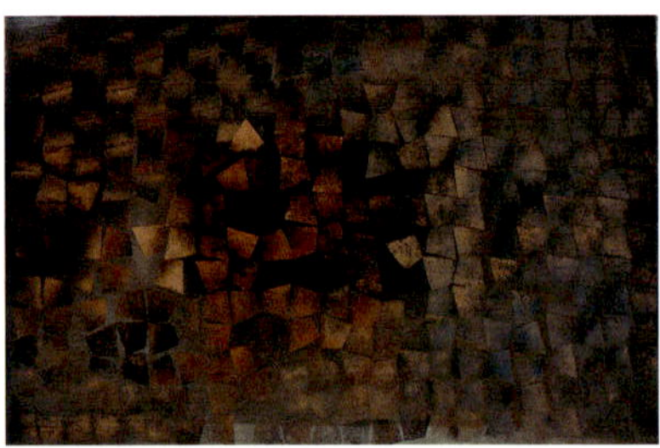

13. *Quadrilaterals*, ca. 1944–45

Ink on wove paper
25 x 38 ¼ in.
57.79
Watermark verso upper right: [N] GELLER ZONEN HOLLAND
Purchased from Nierendorf Gallery, New York, ca. 1944–45

EXHIBITIONS
"Current Trends in British and American Painting from the Collection of Edward W. Root," Munson-Williams-Proctor Institute, Utica, N.Y., December 3–31, 1950, (traveling exhibition, cat. no. 5). "The Edward Root Collection," The Metropolitan Museum of Art, New York, February 12–April 12, 1953 (catalog, 1). "Five Decades of American Painting," Union College, Schenectady, N.Y., September 27–October 23, 1959 (catalog, illus.). "Edward Wales Root Bequest," MWPI, November 5, 1961–February 24, 1962 (catalog, illus.). "European Sources of Contemporary American Art: Kandinsky," Root Art Center, Hamilton College, Clinton, N.Y., September 15–October 6, 1963 (cat. no. 9). "Abstract Paintings and Drawings from the Root Bequest," Root Art Center, September 11–October 9, 1966. "Prints from American Artists," Root Art Center, January 8–February 12, 1967. "The Root Bequest," Root Art Center, May 11–June 8, 1969. Root Art Center, December 2–18, 1971. "Edward W. Root: Collector and Teacher," Fred L. Emerson Gallery, Hamilton College, October 2–November 14, 1982 (catalog, 50).

14. *Small Composition No. 1*

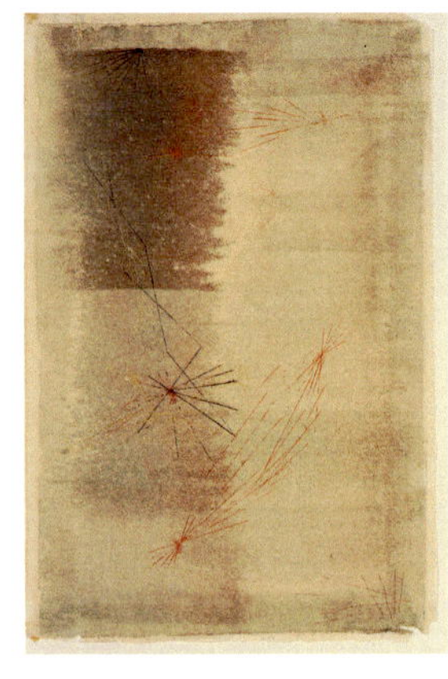

Not dated
Ink on Japanese paper (backed with tissue paper)
15 ⅛ x 10 1⁄16 in.
57.80
Inscribed verso upper right: Group VI-3
Purchased from Nierendorf Gallery, New York, ca. 1944–46

EXHIBITION
"Edward Wales Root Bequest," Munson-Williams-Proctor Institute, Utica, N.Y., November 5, 1961–February 24, 1962 (catalog).

15. *Small Composition No. 2*

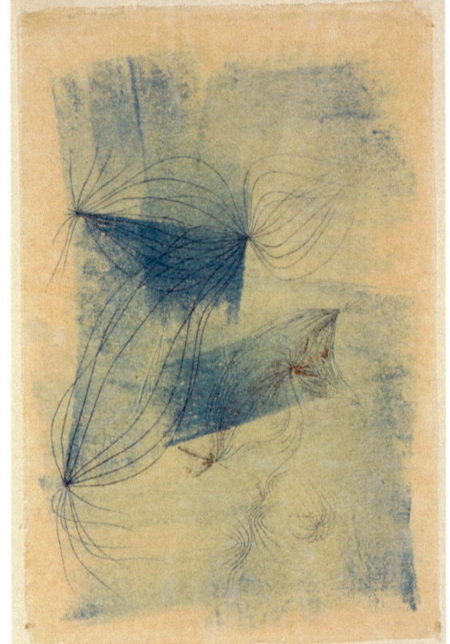

Not dated
Ink on Japanese paper
15 ⅛ x 10 in.
57.81
Inscribed upper right (graphite): Series VI-17/30
Purchased from Nierendorf Gallery, New York, ca. 1944–46

EXHIBITION
"Edward Wales Root Bequest," Munson-Williams-Proctor Institute, Utica, N.Y., November 5, 1961–February 24, 1962 (catalog).

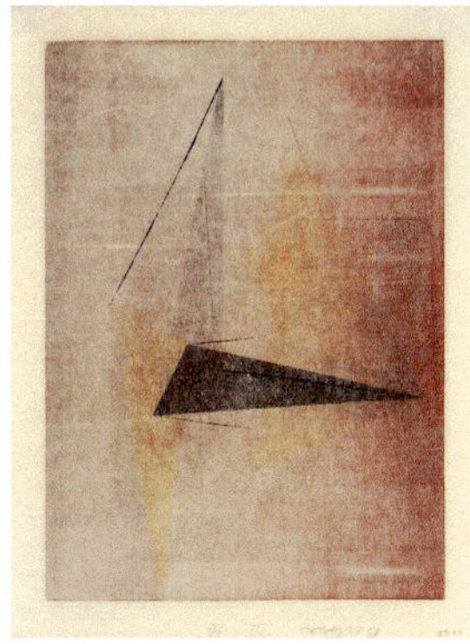

16. *Small Composition No. 3*
Not dated
Ink on Japanese paper
10 ¼ x 7 ¾ in.
57.82
Signed verso lower right (graphite): Bertoia III-16
Purchased from Nierendorf Gallery, New York, ca. 1944–46

EXHIBITION
"Edward Wales Root Bequest," Munson-Williams-Proctor Institute, Utica, N.Y., November 5, 1961–February 24, 1962 (catalog).

17. *Small Composition No. 4*
Not dated

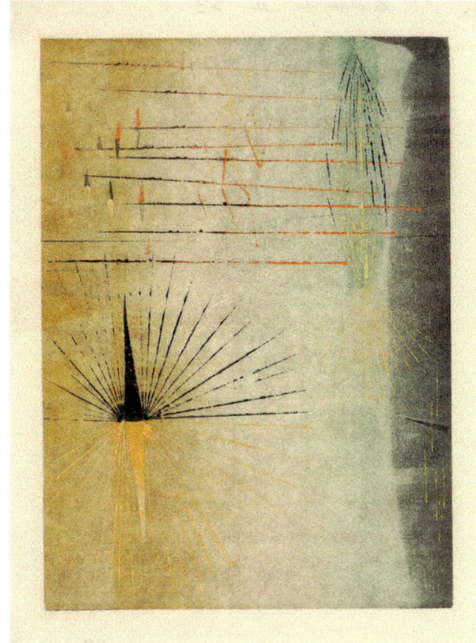

Ink on Japanese paper
10 ⅜ x 7 ⅝ in.
57.83
Signed verso left (graphite): Bertoia III 23
Purchased from Nierendorf Gallery, New York, ca. 1944–46

EXHIBITION
"Edward Wales Root Bequest," Munson-Williams-Proctor Institute, Utica, N.Y., November 5, 1961–February 24, 1962 (catalog).

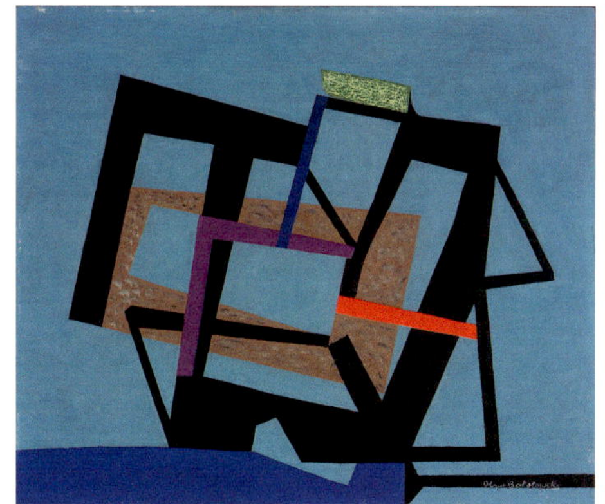

ILYA BOLOTOWSKY

(St. Petersburg, Russia, 1907–New York, N.Y., 1981)

18. *Marine Variation No. 2*
Ca. 1940–42
Oil on Masonite
11 x 13 ¼ in.
57.84
Signed lower right (white paint): Ilya Bolotowsky
Purchased from Nierendorf Gallery, New York, March 1946

EXHIBITIONS
"Artists and Quakers Join in Helping the Hungry in Europe," Nierendorf Gallery, New York, March 25–30, 1946, Auction March 30, 1946 (checklist no. 7). "New Trends in 20th-Century American Painting," Root Art Center, Hamilton College, Clinton, N.Y., October 26–November 31, 1958. "New Trends in 20th-Century American Painting," Union College, Schenectady, N.Y., March 5–26, 1961. "Edward Wales Root Bequest," Munson-Williams-Proctor Institute, Utica, N.Y., November 5, 1961–February 24, 1962 (catalog). "Abstract Painting and Drawing from the Root Bequest," Root Art Center, September 11–October 9, 1966. "Paintings and Drawings from the Edward W. Root Bequest," Root Art Center, April 7–May 5, 1968. "Contemporary Artists: Early and Late Paintings," Root Art Center, April 4–May 2, 1973. "20th-Century American Painting," Executive Mansion, Albany, N.Y., September–November 1974. "Five Decades of Collecting: Edward W. Root," MWPI, April 2–May 28, 1978. "Edward W. Root: Collector and Teacher," Fred L. Emerson Gallery, Hamilton College, October 2–November 14, 1982 (catalog, 50). "Order and Enigma: American Art Between the Wars," MWPI, October 13–December 16, 1984 (traveling exhibition, catalog, illus. fig. 56).

PUBLICATION
Paintings, Drawings & Sculptures in the Museum of Art (Utica, N.Y.: Munson-Williams-Proctor Institute, 1961), 8.

RAYMOND BREININ

(Vitebsk, Russia, 1909–Westchester, N.Y., 2000)

19. *The Winged Guide*, 1943

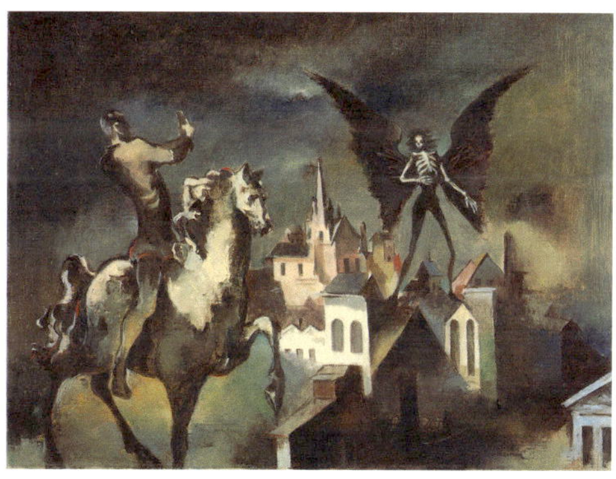

Oil on canvas
16 x 22 in.
57.85
Signed lower right (black paint): Breinin
Inscribed verso: The Winged Guide / Raymond Breinin / 1943

EXHIBITIONS
"The Edward Root Collection," The Metropolitan Museum of Art, New York, N.Y., February 12–April 12, 1953 (catalog, 1). "Edward Wales Root Bequest," Munson-Williams-Proctor Institute, Utica, N.Y., November 5, 1961–February 24, 1962 (catalog).

PUBLICATION
Paintings, Drawings & Sculptures in the Museum of Art (Utica, N.Y.: Munson-Williams-Proctor Institute, 1961), 8.

WILLIAM BRICE

(b. New York, N.Y., 1921, lives Los Angeles, Calif.)

20. *Boys with Dog*, 1949

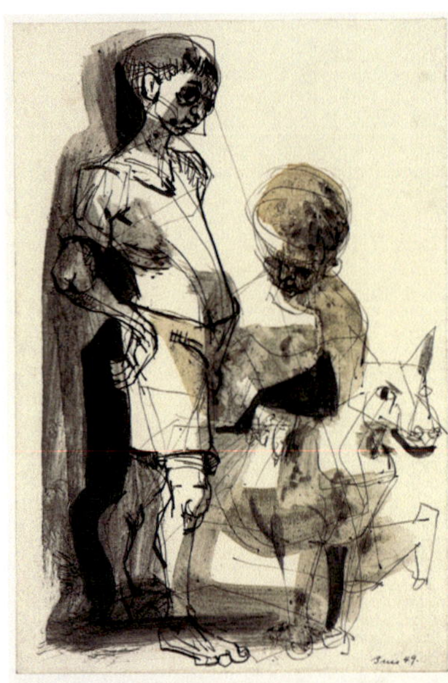

Graphite and ink on paper mounted to board
8 ¾ x 6 in.
57.286
Signed and dated lower right (black ink): Brice '49
Purchased from The Downtown Gallery, New York, ca. 1949

EXHIBITIONS

"Edward Wales Root Bequest," Munson-Williams-Proctor Institute, Utica, N.Y., November 5, 1961–February 24, 1962 (catalog). "The Figure in 20th-Century Paintings and Drawings," Root Art Center, Hamilton College, Clinton, N.Y., April 15–May 6, 1962.
"Five Decades of Collecting: Edward W. Root," MWPI, April 2–May 28, 1978.
"Edward W. Root: Collector and Teacher," Fred L. Emerson Gallery, Hamilton College, October 2–November 14, 1982 (catalog, 54).

PUBLICATION

Paintings, Drawings & Sculptures in the Museum of Art (Utica, N.Y.: Munson-Williams-Proctor Institute, 1961), 8.

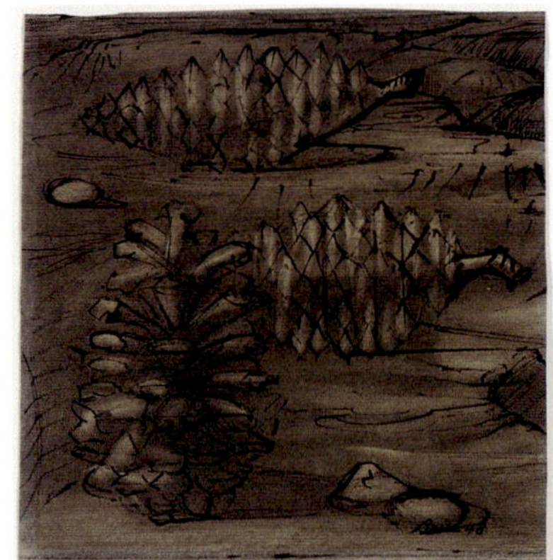

21. *Pine Cones*, 1948

Ink on laid paper
10 x 9 ¾ in.
57.321
Signed and dated lower right (black ink): Brice '48
Purchased from The Downtown Gallery, New York, ca. 1949

EXHIBITIONS

"American Watercolors and Drawings," Root Art Center, Hamilton College, Clinton, N.Y., April 4–May 7, 1961. "Edward Wales Root Bequest," Munson-Williams-Proctor Institute, Utica, N.Y., November 5, 1961–February 24, 1962 (catalog). "Paintings and Drawings from the Edward W. Root Bequest," Root Art Center, April 7–May 5, 1968. "Selections from the Edward W. Root Collection," Root Art Center, February 22–March 21, 1970.

PUBLICATION

Paintings, Drawings & Sculptures in the Museum of Art (Utica, N.Y.: Munson-Williams-Proctor Institute, 1961), 8.

22. *Rosebud*, 1949

Crayon, ink and graphite on paper mounted on board
8 ¾ x 5 ⅜ in.
57.287
Signed lower right (black ink): Brice '49
Purchased from The Downtown Gallery, New York, ca. 1949

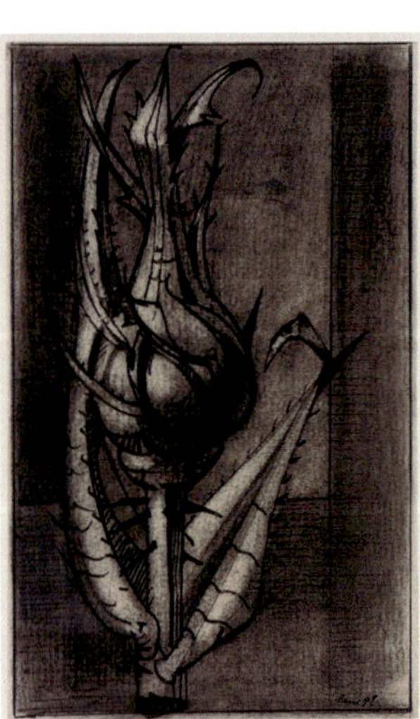

EXHIBITIONS

"Edward Wales Root Bequest," Munson-Williams-Proctor Institute, Utica, N.Y., November 5, 1961–February 24, 1962 (catalog). "American Drawings and Watercolors from the Munson-Williams-Proctor Institute," E. B. Crocker Art Gallery, Sacramento, Calif., October 25–November 24, 1974 (cat. no. 4).

PUBLICATION

Paintings, Drawings & Sculptures in the Museum of Art (Utica, N.Y.: Munson-Williams-Proctor Institute, 1961), 8.

23. *Sea Plant*, 1948

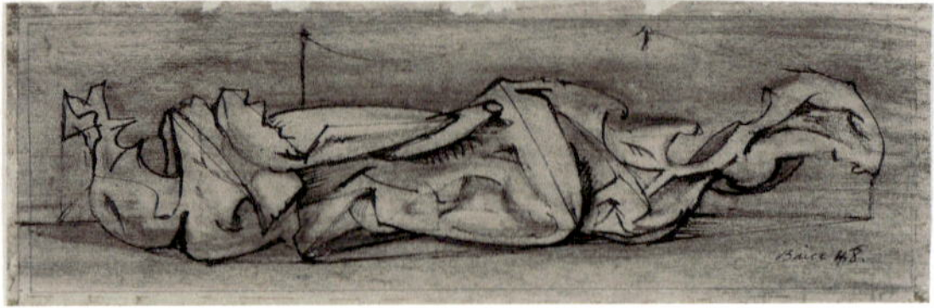

Crayon, ink and graphite on wove paper
5 x 15 ½ in.
57.86
Signed and dated lower right (black ink): Brice 48
Purchased from The Downtown Gallery, New York, ca. 1949

EXHIBITIONS

"American Watercolors and Drawings," Root Art Center, Hamilton College, Clinton, N.Y., April 4–May 7, 1961.
"Edward Wales Root Bequest," Munson-Williams-Proctor Institute, Utica, N.Y., November 5, 1961–February 24, 1962 (catalog). "Selections from the Edward W. Root Collection," Root Art Center, February 22–March 21, 1970.

PUBLICATION

Paintings, Drawings & Sculptures in the Museum of Art (Utica, N.Y.: Munson-Williams-Proctor Institute, 1961), 8.

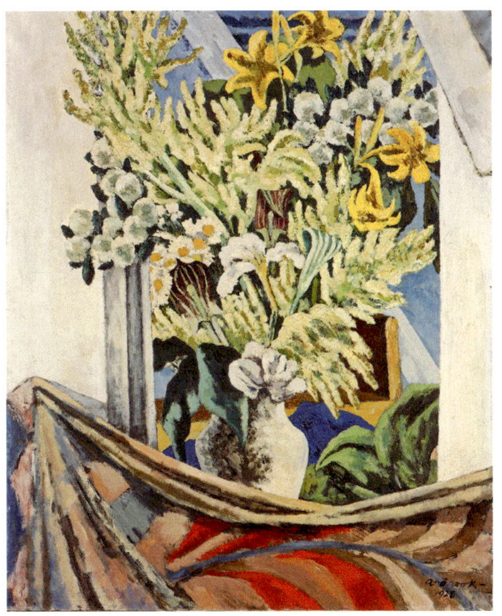

ALEXANDER BROOK

(Brooklyn, N.Y., 1898–Sag Harbor, N.Y., 1980)

24. *Bouquet*, 1928

Oil on linen
36 x 30 in.
57.87
Signed lower right (black paint): A. Brook- / 1928
Purchased from The Downtown Gallery, New York, October 1930

EXHIBITIONS

"Edward Wales Root Bequest," Munson-Williams-Proctor Institute, Utica, N.Y., November 5, 1961–February 24, 1962 (catalog). Root Art Center, Hamilton College, Clinton, N.Y., March 1964. "Nature in Art," MWPI, June 2–September 1, 1987. "The Art Triangle: Artist, Dealer, Collector," Burchfield Art Center, Buffalo, N.Y., May 13–June 25, 1989 (traveling exhibition, cat. no. 1).

PUBLICATION

Paintings, Drawings & Sculptures in the Museum of Art (Utica, N.Y.: Munson-Williams-Proctor Institute, 1961), 8.

25. *The Yellow Fan*, 1930

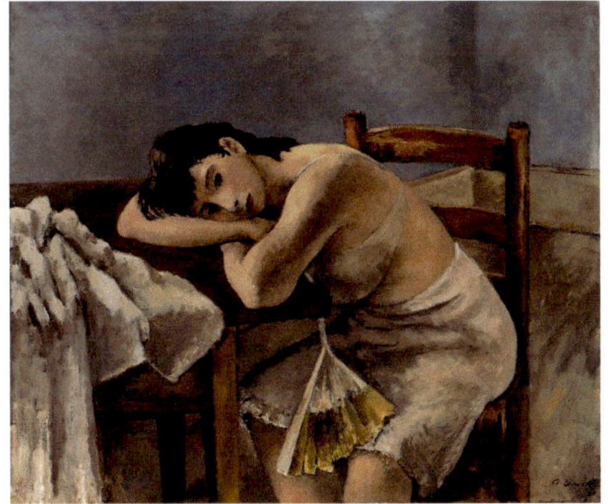

Oil on linen
30 x 36 in.
57.88
Signed and dated lower right (black paint): A. Brook / '30
Purchased from The Downtown Gallery, New York, February 1931

EXHIBITIONS

"Alexander Brook," The Downtown Gallery, New York, January 5–24, 1932 (cat. no. 1).
"American Painting and Sculpture 1862–1932," The Museum of Modern Art, New York, October 31, 1932–January 31, 1933 (cat. no. 9, illus.). "Alexander Brook: Exhibition of Paintings," Department of Fine Arts, Carnegie Institute, Pittsburgh, Pa., April 5–May 17, 1934 (cat. no. 38). "The Edward Root Collection," The Metropolitan Museum of Art, New York, February 12–April 12, 1953 (catalog, 1). "Five Decades of American Painting," Union College, Schenectady, N.Y., September 27–October 23, 1959. Museum of Art building inaugural exhibition, Munson-Williams-Proctor Institute, Utica, N.Y., October 15–December 31, 1960. "Edward Wales Root Bequest," MWPI, November 5, 1961–February 24, 1962 (catalog, illus.). "The Figure in 20th-Century Paintings and Drawings," Root Art Center, Hamilton College, Clinton, N.Y., April 15–May 6, 1962.
"Prints by American Artists," Root Art Center, January 9–February 12, 1967.
"Paintings and Drawings from the Edward Root Bequest," Root Art Center, April 7–May 5, 1968. "The Root Bequest," Root Art Center, May 11–June 8, 1969. "Five Decades of Collecting: Edward W. Root," MWPI, April 2–May 28, 1978. "Edward W. Root: Collector and Teacher," Fred L. Emerson Gallery, Hamilton College, October 2–November 14, 1982 (catalog, 31). "Figuratively Speaking," MWPI, April 11–November 10, 1985. "Two Hundred Years of American Art," The Art Museum Association of America, November 15, 1986–May 8, 1988 (traveling exhibition, cat. no. 48, illus., 42).
"The Art Triangle: Artist, Dealer, Collector," Burchfield Art Center, Buffalo, N.Y., May 13–June 25, 1989 (traveling exhibition, cat. no. 3, illus., 44).

PUBLICATIONS

Jewell, Edward Alden. *Alexander Brook* (New York: Whitney Museum of American Art, 1931), illus., 41. Jewell, Edward Alden.
"Exhibition by Alexander Brook," *New York Times* January 6, 1932, 18. Salinger, Margaretta. "Americans in Two Exhibitions," *Parnassus* IV (November 1932): 5–6, illus., 5. *Alexander Brook* (New York: American Artists Group, Inc., 1945), illus. *Paintings, Drawings & Sculptures in the Museum of Art* (Utica, N.Y.: Munson-Williams-Proctor Institute, 1961), 8. Prior, Harris K. "Edward Root—Talent Scout," *Art in America* L (1962), 70, illus., no. 2. Schweizer, Paul D., et al. *Masterworks of American Art from the Munson-Williams-Proctor Institute* (New York: Harry N. Abrams, Inc., 1989), cat. no. 62, illus., 137.

CHARLES E. BURCHFIELD

(Ashtabula, Ohio, 1893–West Seneca, N.Y., 1967)

26. *Apple Orchard (Orchard in the Spring; Decrepitude in Springtime)*

1920

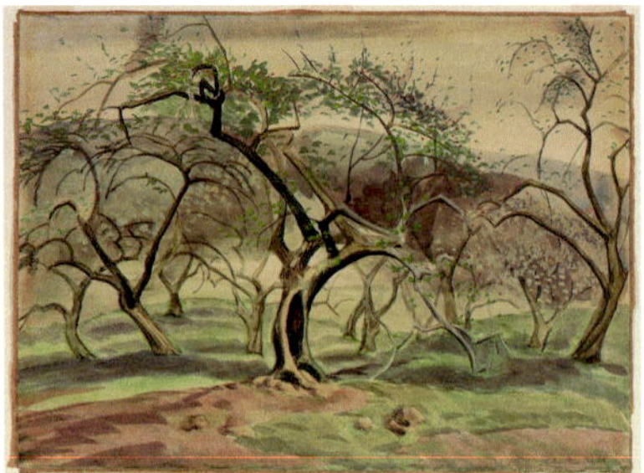

Opaque and transparent watercolor on white paper
19 ¼ x 26 ¾ in.
57.89
Signed and dated lower right (graphite): Chas Burchfield
Purchased from Frank K. M. Rehn Galleries, New York, November 1932

EXHIBITIONS

"Exhibition of Watercolors and Pastels by Eleven American Moderns from a Distinguished Private Collection," Munson-Williams-Proctor Institute, Utica, N.Y., fall 1938. "Paintings by Burchfield from the Collection of Edward W. Root," Fogg Art Museum, Harvard University, Cambridge, Mass., ca. February 6–March 1, 1940.

"Charles Burchfield," Whitney Museum of American Art, New York, January 11–February 26, 1956 (cat. no. 1). "Five American Artists of the 20th Century: Davies, Luks, Burchfield, Tobey, Stamos," Root Art Center, Hamilton College, Clinton, N.Y., December 7, 1958–March 28, 1959. "Edward Wales Root Bequest," MWPI, November 5, 1961–February 24, 1962 (catalog). "Paintings by Charles Burchfield," Root Art Center, May 13–June 10, 1962 (cat. no. 14). "American 20th-Century Watercolors from MWPI," Albany Institute of History and Art, Albany, N.Y., September 10–October 4, 1967.

"Hopper-Burchfield," The Katonah Gallery, Katonah, N.Y., September 7–30, 1969. "The Nature of Charles Burchfield, A Memorial Exhibition," MWPI, April 9–June 14, 1970 (cat. no. 81). "Charles Burchfield," Ohio State Fair, Columbus, August 2–September 3, 1970 (cat. no. 47). "Burchfield Watercolors," MWPI, June 5–August 29, 1982.

PUBLICATIONS

Straus, John W. "Catalogue of Paintings by Charles E. Burchfield," Honors thesis, Harvard College, 1942, cat. no. 450.
Paintings, Drawings & Sculptures in the Museum of Art (Utica, N.Y.: Munson-Williams-Proctor Institute, 1961), 9.
American Art in Upstate New York (Buffalo, N.Y.: Buffalo Fine Arts Academy, 1974), 7.
Trovato, Joseph S. *Charles Burchfield: Catalogue of Paintings in Public and Private Collections* (Utica, N.Y.: MWPI, 1970), cat. no. 600, illus., 450.

27. *Childhood's Garden (A Memory of Childhood)*

August 22, 1917

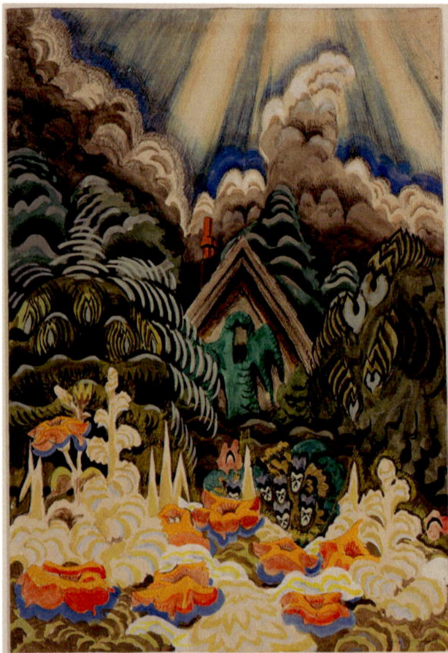

Opaque and transparent watercolor with graphite on slightly textured cream-colored paper
27 x 19 in.
57.90
Signed and dated lower right (graphite): Chas. Burchfield / 1917
Inscribed verso lower right: "Childhood's Garden" / A memory of Childhood / an attempt / to recreate the way a flower garden / looks to a child
Inscribed verso lower left: B-267 / "A memory of childhood"
Inscribed verso lower left upside down (erased but legible): "Conceived" about July 7, 1917 / Completed August 22, 1917
Inscribed verso upper right: (graphite): Root
Purchased from Frank K. M. Rehn Galleries, New York, February 1930

EXHIBITIONS

"Charles Burchfield: Early Watercolors 1916–1918," The Museum of Modern Art, New York, April 11–26, 1930 (cat. no. 19).

"Paintings from the Collection of Edward W. Root," Munson-Williams-Proctor Institute, Utica, N.Y., September 29–October 20, 1946;

"20th-Century American Painting from the Edward W. Root Collection," Smithsonian Institution, Washington, D.C., July 1959–July 1960 (traveling exhibition). "Edward Wales Root Bequest," MWPI, November 5, 1961–February 24, 1962 (catalog). "Paintings by Charles Burchfield," Root Art Center, Hamilton College, Clinton, N.Y., May 13–June 10, 1962 (cat. no. 12). "American Traditionalists of the 20th Century," Columbus Museum of Arts and Crafts, Columbus, Ga., February 16–March 17, 1963 (catalog, 16).

"Yesterday and Today," Oswego Art Gallery, Oswego, N.Y., May 30–June 14, 1964.

"American 20th-Century Watercolors from MWPI," Albany Institute of History and Art, Albany, N.Y., September 10–October 4, 1967.

"Landscapes," MWPI, April 7–May 4, 1969.

"Hopper-Burchfield," The Katonah Gallery, Katonah, N.Y., September 7–30, 1969. "The Nature of Charles Burchfield, A Memorial Exhibition," MWPI, April 9–June 14, 1970 (cat. no. 76). "Charles Burchfield: Hymn to Nature," Burchfield Art Center, Buffalo State College, April 30–June 30, 1972 (cat. no. 13). "American Drawings and Watercolors from the Munson-Williams-Proctor Institute," E. B. Crocker Art Gallery, Sacramento, Calif., October 25–November 24, 1974 (cat. no. 6, illus.). "Watercolors: Historic and Contemporary," Hathorn Gallery, Skidmore College, Saratoga Springs, N.Y., February 4–20, 1977 (cat. no. 4, illus. frontispiece). "Five Decades of Collecting: Edward W. Root," MWPI, April 2–May 28, 1978. "Burchfield Watercolors," MWPI, June 5–August 29, 1982. "Order and Enigma: American Art Between the Wars," MWPI, October 13–December 16, 1984 (traveling exhibition, catalog, illus. fig. 2). "Personal Places: American Landscapes, 1905–1930," Sarah Lawrence College, Bronxville, N.Y., February 16–April 20, 1988. "Charles Burchfield: The Sacred Woods," Burchfield Art Center, June 12, 1993–May 22, 1994 (traveling exhibition, catalog, illus. pl. 31).

"The Paintings of Charles Burchfield: North by Midwest," Columbus Museum of Art, Columbus, Ohio, March 23–May 18, 1997 (traveling exhibition, cat. no. 48, illus.).

PUBLICATIONS

Straus, John W. "Catalogue of Paintings by Charles E. Burchfield," Honors thesis, Harvard College, 1942, cat. no. 238. *Paintings, Drawings & Sculptures in the Museum of Art* (Utica, N.Y.: Munson-Williams-Proctor Institute, 1961), 9. Trovato, Joseph S. *Charles Burchfield: Catalogue of Paintings in Public and Private Collections* (Utica, N.Y.: MWPI, 1970), cat. no. 348. *Hymn to Nature*, WNED-TV, Buffalo, N.Y., 1970. *American Art in Upstate New York* (Buffalo, N.Y.: Buffalo Fine Arts Academy, 1974), 6. Baigell, Matthew. *Charles Burchfield* (New York: Watson-Guptill, 1976), illus., 75. Schweizer, Paul D., et al. *Masterworks of American Art from the Munson-Williams-Proctor Institute* (New York: Harry N. Abrams, Inc., 1989), cat. no. 55, illus. 122. "Charles Burchfield: The Centenary," *American Art Review* V, no. 3 (Spring 1993): 106–07, illus., cover. Townsend, J. Benjamin, ed. *Charles Burchfield's Journals: The Poetry of Place* (Albany, N.Y.: State University of New York Press, 1993), 318 n. 4, illus. fig. 69. Maciejunes, Nanette and Hendricks, Norine. "Charles Burchfield's Painted Memories," *The Magazine Antiques* CLI (March 1997): 458–69, illus. pl. III. Hamm, Patricia D. and Nancy Weekly. "Beyond Imagery: An Overview of Charles Burchfeld's Materials and Techniques," *Watercolor* 3 (Spring 1997): 116–28, illus., 118.

28. *Country Blacksmith Shop (Blacksmith Shop)*, 1928

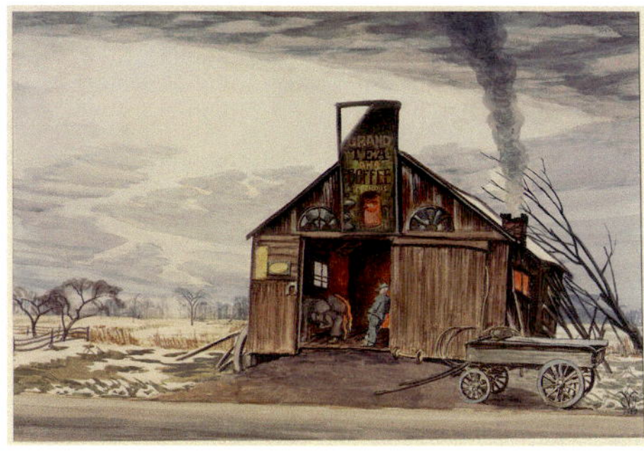

Transparent watercolor on white paper
23 ½ x 36 in.
57.91
Signed and dated lower right (black paint): Monogram / 1929
Purchased from Montross Gallery, New York, March 1928

EXHIBITIONS

"Exhibition of Recent Paintings by Charles Burchfield," Montross Gallery, New York, March 26–April 7, 1928 (cat. no. 9). "Edward W. Root Loan Exhibition," Utica Art Society, Utica, N.Y., May 1928. "Paintings by Nineteen Living Americans," The Museum of Modern Art, New York, December 13, 1929–January 12, 1930 (cat. no. 5). "An Exhibition of Water Colors and Oils by Charles Burchfield," Department of Fine Arts, Carnegie Institute, Pittsburgh, Pa., March 8–April 3, 1938 (cat. no. 19). "Paintings by Burchfield from the Collection of Edward W. Root," Fogg Art Museum, Harvard University, Cambridge, Mass. ca. February 6–March 1, 1940. "Paintings from the Collection of Edward W. Root," Munson-Williams-Proctor Institute, Utica, N.Y., September 29–October 20, 1946. "An Exhibition of Paintings by Charles Burchfield," Buffalo Historical Society, Buffalo, N.Y., October 13–November 16, 1958. "Five American Artists of the 20th Century: Davies, Luks, Burchfield, Tobey, Stamos," Root Art Center, Hamilton College, Clinton, N.Y., December 7, 1958–March 28, 1959. "Edward Wales Root Bequest," MWPI, November 5, 1961–February 24, 1962 (catalog). "Paintings by Charles Burchfield," Root Art Center, May 13–June 10, 1962 (cat. no. 16). "A Tribute to Charles E. Burchfield," New York State Exposition, Syracuse, N.Y., September 1–7, 1964 (checklist no. 7). "American 20th-Century Watercolors from MWPI," Albany Institute of History and Art, Albany, N.Y., September 10–October 4, 1967. "Landscapes," MWPI, April 7–May 4, 1969. "The Nature of Charles Burchfield: A Memorial Exhibition," MWPI, April 9–June 14, 1970 (cat. no. 153). "American Watercolors," Art Gallery, State University College, New Paltz, N.Y., November 17–December 8, 1974. "Five Decades of Collecting: Edward W. Root," MWPI, April 2–May 28, 1978. "Burchfield Watercolors," MWPI, June 5–August 29, 1982. "The Art Triangle: Artist, Dealer, Collector," Burchfield Art Center, Buffalo, N.Y., May 13–June 25, 1989 (traveling exhibition, cat. no. 20, illus., 48).

PUBLICATIONS

Mannes, Marya. "News of the Month," *Creative Arts* II (May 1928): illus., XLIX. Hopper, Edward, "Charles Burchfield–American," *Arts* XIV (July 1928): 5–12. *Chicago Evening Post Magazine* (December 31, 1929), illus. Pemberton, Murdock. *Modern Art Picture Book* (New York: Alfred A. Knopf, 1930), illus. pl. no. 44. O' Connor, John, Jr. "Charles Burchfield: Exhibition of His Paintings at the Carnegie Institute," *Carnegie Magazine* XI (March 1938): 312. "Pittsburgh: A Comprehensive Showing of the Work of Charles Burchfield," *Art News* XXXVI (April 2, 1938): 18. Straus, John W. "Catalogue of Paintings by Charles E. Burchfield," Honors thesis, Harvard College, 1942, cat. no. 563, illus. *Paintings, Drawings & Sculptures in the Museum of Art* (Utica, N.Y.: Munson-Williams-Proctor Institute, 1961), 9. Strongin, Ted. "Artist's Talent, Collector's Wisdom Shown," *Knickerbocker News* (Albany), June 21, 1962, 5c, illus. Trovato, Joseph S. *Charles Burchfield: Catalogue of Paintings in Public and Private Collections* (Utica, N.Y.: MWPI, 1970), cat. no. 730, illus., 345. *American Art in Upstate New York* (Buffalo, N.Y.: Buffalo Fine Arts Academy, 1974), 7. Townsend, J. Benjamin, ed. *Charles Burchfield's Journals: The Poetry of Place* (Albany, N.Y.: State University of New York Press, 1993), 51, illus. fig. 16.

29. *Country Road (The Pink Road; Drawing of Road)*, July 11, 1916

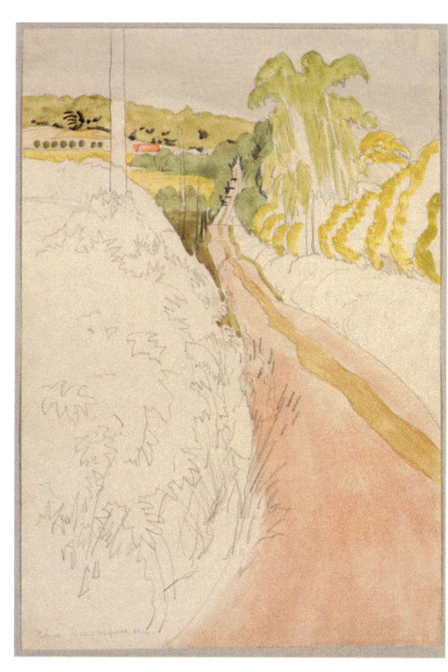

Transparent watercolor and graphite on white wove watercolor paper
20 x 13 ⅞ in.
57.92
Painted: Goshen Road–2 Mile Road, Salem, Ohio
Signed and dated lower left (graphite): Chas. E. Burchfield 1916–
Inscribed verso center: "The Road / July 11, 1916"
Purchased from Frank K. M. Rehn Galleries, New York, February 1929

EXHIBITIONS

"Exhibition of Watercolors and Pastels by Eleven American Moderns from a Distinguished Private Collection," Munson-Williams-Proctor Institute, Utica, N.Y., fall 1938. Museum of Art building inaugural exhibition, MWPI, October 15–December 31, 1960. "Edward Wales Root Bequest," MWPI, November 5, 1961–February 24, 1962 (catalog). "Paintings by Charles Burchfield," Root Art Center, Hamilton College, Clinton, N.Y., May 13–June 10, 1962 (cat. no. 3). "American 20th-Century Watercolors from MWPI," Albany Institute of History and Art, Albany, N.Y., September 10–October 4, 1967. "The Nature of Charles Burchfield, A Memorial

Exhibition," MWPI, April 9–June 14, 1970 (cat. no. 52). "Watercolors: Historic and Contemporary," Hathorn Gallery, Skidmore College, Saratoga Springs, N.Y., February 4–20, 1977 (cat. no. 5). "Burchfield Watercolors," MWPI, June 5–August 29, 1982.

PUBLICATIONS

Straus, John W. "Catalogue of Paintings by Charles E. Burchfield," Honors thesis, Harvard College, 1942, cat. nos. 129 and 153 [repeated in error]. *Paintings, Drawings & Sculptures in the Museum of Art* (Utica, N.Y.: Munson-Williams-Proctor Institute, 1961), 9. Trovato, Joseph S. *Charles Burchfield: Catalogue of Paintings in Public and Private Collections* (Utica, N.Y.: MWPI, 1970), cat. no. 183. *American Art in Upstate New York* (Buffalo, N.Y.: Buffalo Fine Arts Academy, 1974), 5.

30. *Dead Sunflower (Portrait of a Sunflower; Cornfield)* September 9, 1916

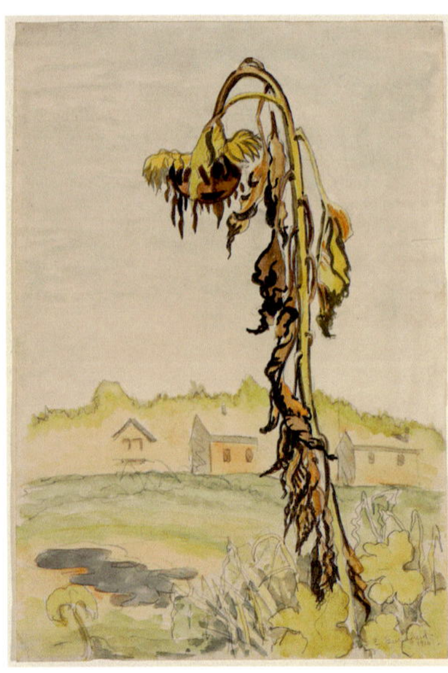

Transparent watercolor on watercolor paper
19 ⅞ x 13 15/16 in.
57.93
Signed and dated lower right (graphite): Chas. E. Burchfield / 1916
Inscribed verso center: "September" / September 9, 1916
Painted: Goshen Road–2 Mile Road, Salem, Ohio
Purchased from Frank K. M. Rehn Galleries, New York, February 1929

EXHIBITIONS

"Early Water Colors by Charles Burchfield," Phillips Memorial Gallery, Washington, D.C., November 5, 1933–February 15, 1934. "Exhibition of Watercolors and Pastels by Eleven American Moderns from a Distinguished Private Collection," Munson-Williams-Proctor Institute, Utica, N.Y., fall 1938. "Paintings by Burchfield from the Collection of Edward W. Root," Fogg Art Museum, Harvard University, Cambridge, Mass., ca. February 6–March 1, 1940. "The Edward Root Collection," The Metropolitan Museum of Art, New York, February 12–April 12, 1953 (catalog, 1). "Five American Artists of the 20th Century: Davies, Luks, Burchfield, Tobey, Stamos," Root Art Center, Hamilton College, Clinton, N.Y., December 7, 1958–March 28, 1959. "Edward Wales Root Bequest," MWPI, November 5, 1961–February 24, 1962 (catalog). "Paintings by Charles Burchfield," Root Art Center, May 13–June 10, 1962 (cat. no. 4). "American 20th-Century Watercolors from MWPI," Albany Institute of History and Art, Albany, N.Y., September 10–October 4, 1967. "The Nature of Charles Burchfield, A Memorial Exhibition," MWPI, April 9–June 14, 1970 (cat. no. 55). "Burchfield Watercolors," MWPI, June 5–August 29, 1982. "American Flower Genre," Whitney Museum of American Art, New York, February 29–May 20, 1984 (cat. no. 135, illus.). "Nature in Art," MWPI, January 17–February 15, 1987. "The Early Works of Charles E. Burchfield, 1915–1921," Columbus Museum of Art, Columbus, Ohio, December 13, 1987–February 7, 1988 (traveling exhibition, cat. no. 22, illus.)

PUBLICATIONS

Straus, John W. "Catalogue of Paintings by Charles E. Burchfield," Honors thesis, Harvard College, 1942, cat. nos. 111 and 151 [repeated in error]. *Paintings, Drawings & Sculptures in the Museum of Art* (Utica, N.Y.: Munson-Williams-Proctor Institute, 1961), 9. Trovato, Joseph S. *Charles Burchfield: Catalogue of Paintings in Public and Private Collections* (Utica, N.Y.: MWPI, 1970), cat. no. 164, illus., 41. *American Art in Upstate New York* (Buffalo, N.Y.: Buffalo Fine Arts Academy, 1974), 5. Townsend, J. Benjamin, ed. *Charles Burchfield's Journals: The Poetry of Place* (Albany, N.Y.: State University of New York Press, 1993), 691 n. 28.

31. *Decorative Landscape, Hot Morning Sunlight*, June 26, 1916

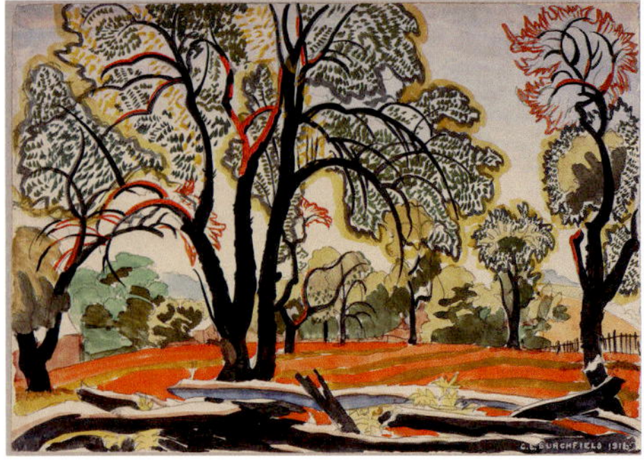

Transparent and opaque watercolor with graphite on white wove paper
13 ⅞ x 19 ⅞ in.
57.94
Signed and dated lower right (white paint): C. E. BURCHFIELD 1916
Painted: Post's Woods, Salem, Ohio
Inscribed verso: "Noon in the Orchard / June 26, 1916"
Purchased from Frank K. M. Rehn Galleries, New York, February 1929

EXHIBITIONS

"Charles Burchfield: Early Water Colors," The Museum of Modern Art, New York, April 11– 26, 1930 (cat. no. 7). "Early Water Colors of Charles Burchfield," Phillips Memorial Gallery, Washington, D.C., November 5, 1933–February 15, 1934. "Exhibition of Watercolors and Pastels by Eleven American Moderns from a Distinguished Private Collection," Munson-Williams-Proctor Institute, Utica, N.Y., fall 1938. "Paintings by Burchfield from the Collection of Edward W. Root," Fogg Art Museum, Harvard University, Cambridge, Mass., ca. February 6–March 1, 1940. "The Edward Root Collection," The Metropolitan Museum of Art, New York, February 12–April 12, 1953 (as *Morning Sunlight*, catalog, 1). "Five American Artists of the 20th Century: Davies, Luks, Burchfield, Tobey, Stamos," Root Art Center, Hamilton College, Clinton, N.Y., December 7, 1958–March 28, 1959. "20th-Century American Painting from the Edward W. Root Collection," Smithsonian Institution, Washington, D.C., July 1959–July 1960 (traveling exhibition). Museum of Art building inaugural exhibition, MWPI, October 15–December 31, 1960. "Edward Wales Root Bequest," MWPI, November 1961–February 24, 1962 (catalog). "Paintings by Charles Burchfield," Root Art Center, May 13–June 10, 1962 (cat. no. 5). "Charles Burchfield Early Watercolors," Albright-Knox Art Gallery, Buffalo, N.Y., April 24–May 19, 1963 (cat. no. 10, illus., 19).

"American 20th-Century Watercolors from MWPI," Albany Institute of History and Art, Albany, N.Y., September 10–October 4, 1967. "The Nature of Charles Burchfield, A Memorial Exhibition," MWPI, April 9–June 14, 1970 (cat. no. 56). "Celebration," Carnegie Institute, Pittsburgh, Pa., October 25, 1974–January 5, 1975 (cat. no. 54, illus.). "Five Decades of Collecting: Edward W. Root," MWPI, April 2–May 28, 1978. "Burchfield Watercolors," MWPI, June 5–August 29, 1982. "Edward W. Root: Collector and Teacher," Fred L. Emerson Gallery, Hamilton College, October 2–November 14, 1982 (catalog, illus., 28). "Nature Framed," MWPI, March 15–May 20, 1985. "Insights," MWPI, January 7–April 13, 1986. "Nature in Art," MWPI, January 17–February 15 and June 2–September 1, 1987. "Extending the Golden Year: Charles Burchfield Centennial," Emerson Gallery, March 6–April 25, 1993 (cat. no. 24, illus., 58).

PUBLICATIONS

Straus, John W. "Catalogue of Paintings by Charles E. Burchfield," Honors thesis, Harvard College, 1942, cat. no. 148. *Paintings, Drawings & Sculptures in the Museum of Art* (Utica, N.Y.: Munson-Williams-Proctor Institute, 1961), 9. Trovato, Joseph S. *Charles Burchfield: Catalogue of Paintings in Public and Private Collections* (Utica, N.Y.: MWPI, 1970), cat. no. 203, color pl., 17. Townsend, J. Benjamin, ed. *Charles Burchfield's Journals: The Poetry of Place* (Albany, N.Y.: State University of New York Press, 1993), 16, illus. fig. 2.

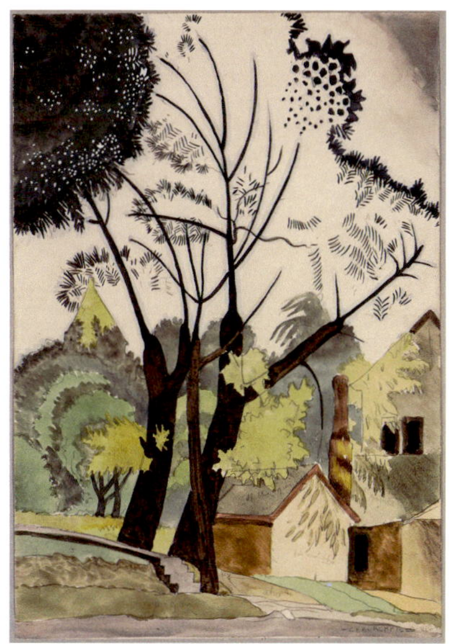

32. *Decorative Landscape, Shadow (Willows on Vine Street; Shadow)* September 23, 1916

Transparent watercolor and graphite on white paper
19 ⅞ x 13 ⅞ in.
57.95
Signed and dated lower right (graphite): C E BURCHFIELD—1916
Inscribed verso: "Cool Day in September / September 23, 1916"
Purchased from Frank K. M. Rehn Galleries, New York, February 1929

EXHIBITIONS

"Charles Burchfield: Early Water Colors 1916–1918," The Museum of Modern Art, New York, April 11–26, 1930 (cat. no. 6). "Early Water Colors By Charles Burchfield," Phillips Memorial Gallery, Washington D.C., November 5, 1933–February 15, 1934. "Exhibition of Watercolors and Pastels by Eleven American Moderns from a Distinguished Private Collection," Munson-Williams-Proctor Insitute, Utica, N.Y., fall 1938. "Paintings by Burchfield from the Collection of Edward W. Root," Fogg Art Museum, Harvard University, Cambridge, Mass., ca. February 6–March 1, 1940. "The Edward Root Collection," The Metropolitan Museum of Art, New York, February 12–April 12, 1953 (as *Shadows*, catalog, 1). "Edward Wales Root Bequest," MWPI, November 5, 1961–February 24, 1962 (catalog). "Paintings by Charles Burchfield," Root Art Center, Hamilton College, Clinton, N.Y., May 13–June 10, 1962 (cat. no. 6). "American 20th-Century Watercolors from MWPI," Albany Institute of History and Art, Albany, N.Y., September 10–October 4, 1967. "The Nature of Charles Burchfield, A Memorial Exhibition," MWPI, April 9–June 14, 1970 (cat. no. 57). "Burchfield Watercolors," MWPI, June 5–August 29, 1982.

PUBLICATIONS

Straus, John W. "Catalogue of Paintings by Charles E. Burchfield," Honors thesis, Harvard College, 1942, cat. nos. 98 and 100 [repeated in error]. *Paintings, Drawings & Sculptures in the Museum of Art* (Utica, N.Y.: Munson-Williams-Proctor Institute, 1961), 9. Trovato, Joseph S. *Charles Burchfield: Catalogue of Paintings in Public and Private Collections* (Utica, N.Y.: MWPI, 1970), cat. no. 152, color pl., 16. *American Art in Upstate New York* (Buffalo, N.Y.: Buffalo Fine Arts Academy, 1974), 5.

33. *Flame of Spring*, 1948

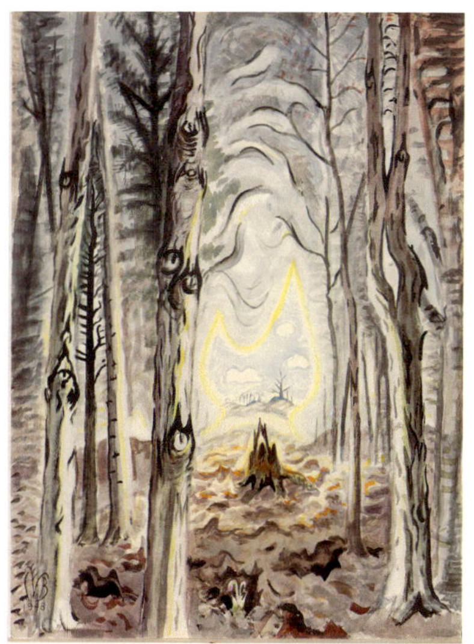

Transparent watercolor on watercolor paper, two sheets vertically joined on the left side
40 x 29 ¾ in.
57.96
Signed and dated lower left (black paint): Monogram / 1948
Inscribed verso on mount: Burchfield / "Flames of Spring" / 40 x 30 / (1948)
Painted: Woods interior, east of Gowanda, N.Y.
Purchased from Frank K. M. Rehn Galleries, New York, May 1950

EXHIBITIONS

"Charles Burchfield," Frank K. M Rehn Galleries, New York, April 10–May 10, 1950 (cat. no. 10). "10th-Anniversary Celebration," Des Moines Art Center, Des Moines, Ia., June 1–July 20, 1958. "An Exhibition of Paintings by Charles Burchfield," Buffalo

Historical Society, Buffalo, N.Y., October 13–November 16, 1958. Museum of Art building inaugural exhibition, Munson-Williams-Proctor Institute, Utica, N.Y., October 15–December 31, 1960. "Edward Wales Root Bequest," MWPI, November 5, 1961–February 24, 1962 (catalog). "Charles Burchfield Recent Paintings," Buffalo State College, Buffalo, N.Y., April 24–May 19, 1963 (cat. no. 4). "Tribute to Charles E. Burchfield," New York State Exposition, Syracuse, N.Y., September 1–7, 1964 (checklist no. 11). "Charles Burchfield, His Golden Year, A Retrospective Exhibition of Watercolors, Oils, and Graphics," The University of Arizona Art Gallery, Tucson, Ariz., November 14, 1965–January 9, 1966 (cat. no. 82, illus., 67). "American 20th-Century Watercolors from MWPI," Albany Institute of History and Art, Albany, N.Y., September 10–October 4, 1967. "The Nature of Charles Burchfield, A Memorial Exhibition," MWPI, April 9–June 14, 1970 (cat. no. 187). "American Watercolors," Art Gallery, State University College, New Paltz, N.Y., November 17–December 8, 1974, (catalog, illus. on cover.) "Through the Looking Glass," Memorial Art Gallery, Rochester, N.Y., December 5, 1980–January 25, 1981. "Burchfield Watercolors," MWPI, June 5– August 29, 1982. "Nature Framed," MWPI, March 15–May 20, 1985. "Nature in Art," MWPI, June 2–September 1, 1987. "The Art Triangle: Artist, Dealer, Collector," Burchfield Art Center, Buffalo, N.Y., May 13– June 25, 1989 (traveling exhibition, cat. no. 30, illus., 14). "Charles Burchfield: The Sacred Woods," Burchfield Art Center, June 12, 1993–May 22, 1994 (traveling exhibition, catalog, illus. fig. 54).

PUBLICATIONS

Paintings, Drawings & Sculptures in the Museum of Art (Utica, N.Y.: Munson-Williams-Proctor Institute, 1961), 9. Strongin, Ted. "Artist's Talent, Collector's Wisdom, Shown," *Knickerbocker News* (Albany), June 21, 1962, 5c, illus. Trovato, Joseph S. *Charles Burchfield: Catalogue of Paintings in Public and Private Collections* (Utica, N.Y.: MWPI, 1970), cat. no. 861, illus., 173. *American Art in Upstate New York* (Buffalo, N.Y.: Buffalo Fine Arts Academy, 1974), 7. Townsend, J. Benjamin, ed. *Charles Burchfield's Journals: The Poetry of Place* (Albany, N.Y.: State University of New York Press, 1993), 676 n. 20, illus. fig. 39.

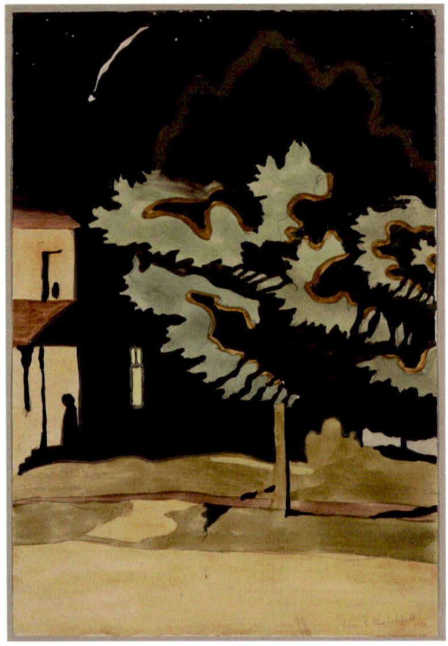

34. *House and Tree by Arc Light (Shooting Star; House At Night; House and Tree)*, July 28, 1916

Transparent watercolor and graphite on white watercolor paper
19 7/8 x 13 7/8 in.
57.97
Signed and dated lower right (graphite): Chas. E. Burchfield / 1916
Inscribed verso center: "Shooting Star" / July 28, 1916
Painted: Carlisle House across from Burchfield's house on 4th Street, Salem, Ohio
Purchased from Frank K. M. Rehn Galleries, New York, February 1929

EXHIBITIONS:

"Early Water Colors by Charles Burchfield," Phillips Memorial Gallery, Washington, D.C., November 5, 1933–February 15, 1934. "Exhibition of Watercolors and Pastels by Eleven American Moderns from a Distinguished Private Collection," Munson-Williams-Proctor Institute, Utica, N.Y., fall 1938. "Paintings by Burchfield from the Collection of Edward W. Root," Fogg Art Museum, Harvard University, Cambridge, Mass., ca. February 6–March 1, 1940. "The Edward Root Collection," The Metropolitan Museum of Art, New York, February 12–April 12, 1953 (catalog, 1). "Five American Artists of the 20th Century: Davies, Luks, Burchfield, Tobey, Stamos," Root Art Center, Hamilton College, Clinton, N.Y., December 7, 1958–March 28, 1959. "Contemporary American Watercolors and Drawings," Smithsonian Institution, Washington, D.C., May 1959–May 1960 (traveling exhibition). "Edward Wales Root Bequest," MWPI, November 5, 1961–February 24, 1962 (catalog). "Paintings by Charles Burchfield," Root Art Center, May 13–June 10, 1962 (cat. no. 7). "20th-Century Watercolors from MWPI," Albany Institute of History and Art, Albany, N.Y., September 10–October 4, 1967. "The Nature of Charles Burchfield, A Memorial Exhibition," MWPI, April 9–June 14, 1970 (cat. no. 60). "The Natural Paradise: Painting in America 1800–1950," The Museum of Modern Art, New York, September 29–November 30, 1976 (catalog, illus., 37). "Burchfield Watercolors," MWPI, June 5–August 29, 1982. "Fire and Ice: A History of Halley's and Other Comets in Art," National Air and Space Museum, Smithsonian Institution, Washington, D.C., October 23, 1985–April 14 1986.

PUBLICATIONS

Straus, John W. "Catalogue of Paintings by Charles E. Burchfield," Honors thesis, Harvard College, 1942, cat. no. 122. *Paintings, Drawings & Sculptures in the Museum of Art* (Utica, N.Y.: Munson-Williams-Proctor Institute, 1961), 9. Prior, Harris K. "Edward Root–Talent Scout," *Art in America* L (1962): 72, illus. fig. 11. Trovato, Joseph S. *Charles Burchfield: Catalogue of Paintings in Public and Private Collections* (Utica, N.Y.: MWPI, 1970), cat. no. 174, illus., 39. *American Art in Upstate New York* (Buffalo, N.Y.: Buffalo Fine Arts Academy, 1974), 6. Townsend, J. Benjamin, ed. *Charles Burchfield's Journals: The Poetry of Place* (Albany, N.Y.: State University of New York Press, 1993), 18, illus. fig. 3.

35. *House by a Railroad*, 1927

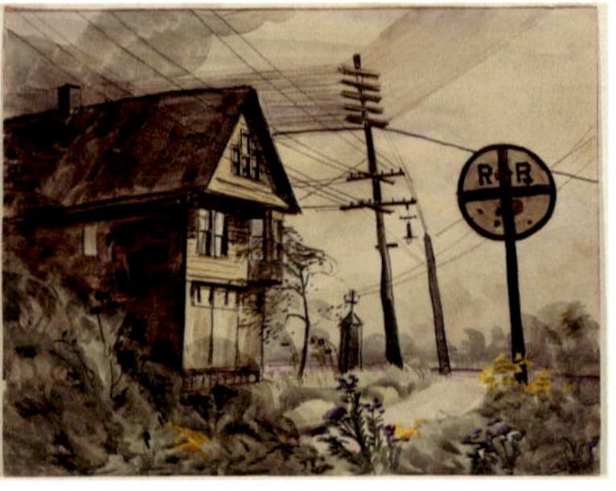

Transparent and opaque watercolor and black crayon on light cream-colored paper mounted on brown paper
16 x 20 ¾ in.
57.98
Signed and dated lower right (black paint): Monogram / 1927
Inscribed verso upper right (graphite): Burchfield / 204 ½ / will bring glass
Painted: South Buffalo, N.Y.
Purchased from Frank K. M. Rehn Galleries, New York, February 1936

EXHIBITIONS

"Exhibition of Recent Paintings by Charles Burchfield," Montross Gallery, New York, March 26–April 7, 1928 (cat. no. 7). "Exhibition of Watercolors and Pastels by Eleven American Moderns from a Distinguished Private Collection," Munson-Williams-Proctor Institute, Utica, N.Y., fall 1938.
"Paintings by Burchfield from the Collection of Edward W. Root," Fogg Art Museum, Harvard University, Cambridge, Mass., ca. February 6–March 1, 1940. "Five American Artists of the 20th Century: Davies, Luks, Burchfield, Tobey, Stamos," Root Art Center, Hamilton College, Clinton, N.Y., December 7, 1958–March 28, 1959. "20th-Century American Painting from the Edward W. Root Collection," Smithsonian Institution, Washington, D.C., July 1959–July 1960 (traveling exhibition). "Edward Wales Root Bequest," MWPI, November 5, 1961–February 24, 1962 (catalog). "Paintings by Charles Burchfield," Root Art Center, May 13–June 10, 1962 (cat. no. 15). "A Tribute to Charles E. Burchfield," New York State Exposition, Syracuse, N.Y., September 1–7, 1964 (checklist no. 6). "On Paper," American Federation of Arts, September 1966–September 1967 (traveling exhibition). "The Nature of Charles Burchfield, A Memorial Exhibition," MWPI, April 9–June 14, 1970 (cat. no. 150). "American Watercolors," Art Gallery, State University College, New Paltz, N.Y., November 17–December 8, 1974. Rome Community Art Center, Rome, N.Y., September 14–November 9, 1975.
"Burchfield Watercolors," MWPI, June 5–August 29, 1982. "The Art Triangle: Artist, Dealer, Collector," Burchfield Art Center, Buffalo, N.Y., May 13–June 25, 1989 (traveling exhibition, cat. no. 19, illus., 69). "The Paintings of Charles Burchfield: North by Midwest," Columbus Museum of Art, Columbus, Ohio, March 23–May 18, 1997 (traveling exhibition, cat. no. 6, illus.).

PUBLICATIONS

Hopper, Edward. "Charles Burchfield–American," *Arts* XIV (July 1928): 6, illus. Rehn Galleries advertisement, *Creative Arts* (April 1930): sup. 78, illus. Straus, John W. "Catalogue of Paintings by Charles E. Burchfield," Honors thesis, Harvard College, 1942, cat. no. 549, illus. Larkin, Oliver W. *Arts and Life in America* (New York: Rinehart and Company, Inc., 1949), 426. *Paintings, Drawings & Sculptures in the Museum of Art* (Utica, N.Y.: Munson-Williams-Proctor Institute, 1961), 9. "Exhibition of Watercolors and Drawings by Leading American Artists at Everson Museum of Art," *Syracuse Herald Journal* January 8, 1967. Trovato, Joseph S. *Charles Burchfield: Catalogue of Paintings in Public and Private Collections* (Utica, N.Y.: MWPI, 1970), cat. no. 713, illus., 18. *American Art in Upstate New York* (Buffalo, N.Y.: Buffalo Fine Arts Academy, 1974), 7. Davenport, Guy. *Charles Burchfield's Seasons* (San Francisco: Pomegranate Books, 1994), color pl. 7. Hamm, Patricia D. and Nancy Weekly. "Beyond Imagery: An Overview of Charles Burchfeld's Materials and Techniques," *Watercolor* 3 (Spring 1997): 116–28, illus., 118.

36. *The Insect Chorus*
September 5, 1917

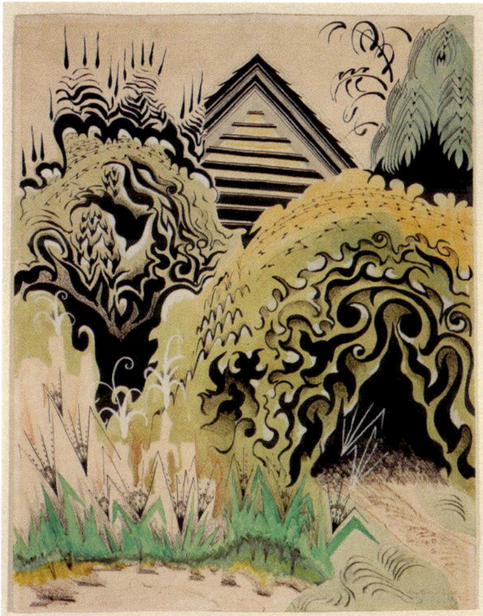

Opaque and transparent watercolor with ink, graphite, and crayon on off-white paper
20 x 15 ⅞ in.
57.99
Signed and dated lower right (graphite): Chas Burchfield / 1917
Inscribed verso upper center (red crayon): The Insect Chorus / September 5, 1917
Inscribed verso lower left (graphite or black crayon): B–274
Inscribed verso right center: Chas–Burchfield / 1917; verso upper left (graphite): 1 [encircled]; upper center (graphite): M.M. Photo; upper right (graphite): Root; center (red pencil, in artist's hand): The Insect Chorus / September 5, 1917; lower right center (graphite, in artist's hand): "The Insect Chorus" / It is late Sunday afternoon in August, / the child stands alone in the garden / listening to the metallic sounds of / insects; they are all his world, / so to his mind all things become / saturated with their presence—crickets / lurk in depth of the grass, the shadows / of the trees conceal fantastic creatures, / and the boy looks with fear at the / black interior of the arbor, not knowing / what terrible thing might be there.; lower left (graphite): B–274; lower right (graphite): Black
Painted: Salem, Ohio (probably backyard of Burchfield's house)
Purchased from Frank K. M. Rehn Galleries, New York, February 1930

EXHIBITIONS

"Charles Burchfield Early Watercolors 1916–1918," The Museum of Modern Art, New York, April 11–26, 1930 (cat. no. 15). "Early Water Colors By Charles Burchfield," Phillips Memorial Gallery, Washington D.C., November 5, 1933–February 15, 1934.
"Exhibition of Watercolors and Pastels by Eleven American Moderns from a Distinguished Private Collection," Munson-Williams-Proctor Institute, Utica, N.Y., fall 1938. "Paintings by Burchfield from the Collection of Edward W. Root," Fogg Art Museum, Harvard University, Cambridge, Mass., ca. February 6–March 1, 1940. "The Edward Root Collection," The Metropolitan Museum of Art, New York, February 12–April 12, 1953 (catalog, 1). Museum of Art building inaugural exhibition, MWPI, October 15–December 31, 1960. "Edward Wales Root Bequest," MWPI, November 5, 1961–February 24, 1962 (catalog). "Paintings by Charles Burchfield," Root Art Center, Hamilton College, Clinton, N.Y., May 13–June 10, 1962 (cat. no. 13). "Charles Burchfield Early Watercolors," Albright-Knox Art Gallery, Buffalo, N.Y., April 24–May 19, 1963 (cat. no. 18). "A Tribute to Charles E. Burchfield," New York State Exposition, Syracuse, N.Y., September 1–7, 1964 (checklist no. 4). "American 20th-Century Watercolors from MWPI," Albany Institute of History and Art, Albany, N.Y., September 10–October 4, 1967. "Eight American Masters of Watercolor," Los Angeles County Museum of Art, Los Angeles, Calif., April 23–June 16, 1968 (cat. no. 87, illus.). "The Root Bequest," Root Art Center, May 11–June 8, 1969. "The Nature of Charles Burchfield, A Memorial Exhibition," MWPI, April 9–June 14, 1970 (cat. no. 81). "Charles Burchfield: Hymn to Nature," Burchfield Art Center, Buffalo, N.Y., April 30–June 30, 1972 (cat. no. 9). "Five Decades of Collecting: Edward W. Root," MWPI, April 2–May 28, 1978. "Burchfield Watercolors," MWPI, June 5–August 29, 1982.
"Charles Burchfield–A Retrospective Exhibition," Metropolitan Museum of Art, January 30–March 25, 1984. "The Early Works of Charles E. Burchfield 1915–1921," Columbus Museum of Art, Columbus, Ohio, December 13, 1987–February 7, 1988 (traveling exhibition, cat. no. 49, illus.). "The Art

CHARLES E. BURCHFIELD

Triangle: Artist, Dealer, Collector," Burchfield Art Center, May 13–June 25, 1989 (traveling exhibition, cat. no. 11). "The Modernist Tradition in American Watercolors: 1919–39," Mary and Leigh Block Gallery, Northwestern University, Evanston, Ill., April 5–June 22, 1991 (catalog, illus., 49). "Charles Burchfield: The Sacred Woods," Burchfield Art Center, June 12, 1993–May 22, 1994 (traveling exhibition, catalog, illus. fig. 9). "The Paintings of Charles Burchfield: North by Midwest," Columbus Museum of Art, March 23–May 18, 1997 (traveling exhibition, cat. no. 47, illus.). "American Twentieth-Century Watercolors at the Munson-Williams-Proctor Arts Institute," MWPAI, April 30–July 10, 2000 (traveling exhibition, cat. no. 8, illus.).

PUBLICATIONS

Straus, John W. "Catalogue of Paintings by Charles E. Burchfield," Honors thesis, Harvard College, 1942, cat. no. 268. *Paintings, Drawings & Sculptures in the Museum of Art* (Utica, N.Y.: Munson-Williams-Proctor Institute, 1961), 9. Trovato, Joseph S. *Charles Burchfield: Catalogue of Paintings in Public and Private Collections* (Utica, N.Y.: MWPI, 1970), no. 382, illus., frontispiece. *Hymn to Nature*, WNED-TV, Buffalo, N.Y., 1970. Soffer, Miriam. "Charles Burchfield, Romantic Realist," *NAHO* 8 (summer 1975): 3–5, illus., 3. "Charles Burchfield: The Centenary," *American Art Review* V, no. 3 (Spring 1993): 106–07, illus., 107. Townsend, J. Benjamin, ed. *Charles Burchfield's Journals: The Poetry of Place* (Albany, N.Y.: State University of New York Press, 1993), 224, 666 n. 27, 691 n. 32, illus. fig. 44. Cotter, Holland. "Back to Innocence in Burchfield's Spiritual Landscapes," *New York Times*, July 9, 1993. Dunning, William. *The Roots of Postmodernism* (Englewood Cliffs, N.J.: Prentice-Hall, 1995), 122, illus. fig. 8-2. May, Stephen, "Charles Burchfield," *ARTnews* (November 1997): 235, illus. Maciejunes, Nanette and Hendricks, Norine. "Charles Burchfield's Painted Memories, " *The Magazine Antiques* CLI (March 1997): 458–69, illus. pl. V.

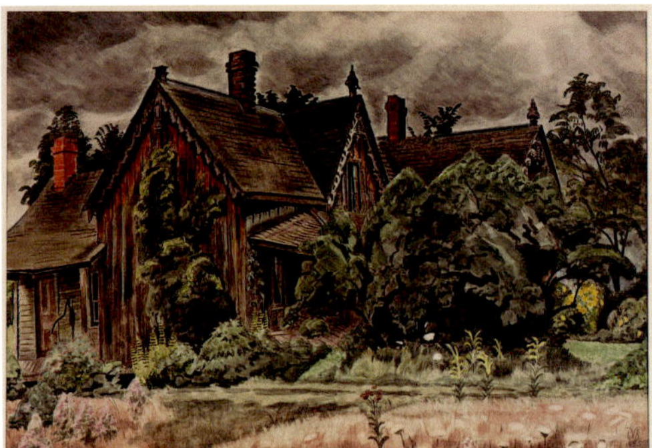

37. *Lace Gables*, 1935

Watercolor on paper
24 x 36 in.
57.100
Signed and dated lower right (brown paint): Monogram / 1935

EXHIBITIONS

"Paintings by Burchfield from the Collection of Edward W. Root," Fogg Art Museum, Harvard University, Cambridge, Mass., ca. February 6–March 1, 1940. "The Edward Root Collection," The Metropolitan Museum of Art, New York, February 12–April 12, 1953 (catalog, 1). "Edward Wales Root Bequest," Munson-Williams-Proctor Institute, November 5, 1961–February 24, 1962 (catalog). "Paintings by Charles Burchfield," Root Art Center, Hamilton College, Clinton, N.Y., May 13– June 10, 1962 (cat. no. 22). "Learning About Pictures from Mr. Root," Root Art Center, January 4–31, 1965 (catalog, illus.). "American Drawings and Watercolors from the Munson-Williams-Proctor Institute," E. B. Crocker Art Gallery, Sacramento, Calif., October 25–November 24, 1974 (cat. no. 7). "The Art Triangle: Artist, Dealer, Collector," Burchfield Art Center, Buffalo, N.Y., May 13–June 25, 1989 (traveling exhibition, cat. no. 25). "American Realism Between the Wars: 1919 to 1941," Nassau County Museum of Art, Roslyn Harbor, N.Y., April 10–June 5, 1994 (catalog, illus. fig. 50, 26).

PUBLICATIONS

Paintings, Drawings & Sculptures in the Museum of Art (Utica, N.Y.: Munson-Williams-Proctor Institute, 1961), 9. Trovato, Joseph S. *Charles Burchfield: Catalogue of Paintings in Public and Private Collections* (Utica, N.Y.: MWPI, 1970), cat. no. 840, illus., 19. *American Art in Upstate New York* (Buffalo, N.Y.: Buffalo Fine Arts Academy, 1974), 7. "Charles Burchfield: The Centenary," *American Art Review* V, no. 3 (Spring 1993): 106–07, illus., 107. Townsend, J. Benjamin, ed. *Charles Burchfield's Journals: The Poetry of Place* (Albany, N.Y.: State University of New York Press, 1993), 689 n. 20, 695 n. 38, illus. fig. 104.

38. *Locomotive Repair Shops*, 1936

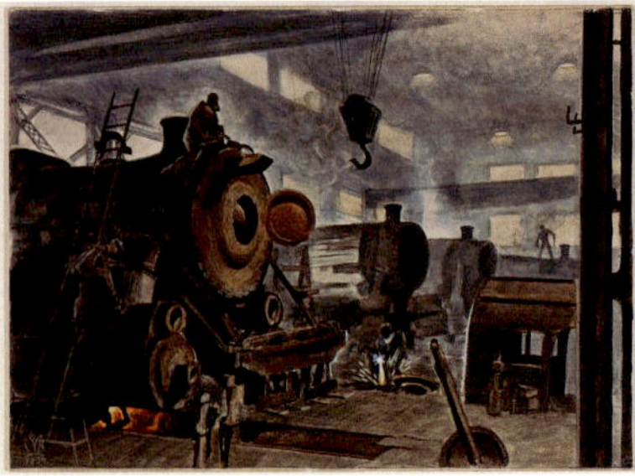

Opaque and transparent watercolor and black crayon on white paper
13 ¹⁄₁₆ x 18 in.
57.101
Signed and dated lower left (white crayon): Monogram / 1936
Painted: Altoona, Pa. One of seven watercolors commissioned by *Fortune* for article on the Pennsylvania Railroad
Purchased from Frank K. M. Rehn Galleries, New York, January 1937

EXHIBITIONS

"Watercolors by Charles Burchfield—Prints by Peggy Bacon," Frank K. M. Rehn Galleries, New York, November 16–December 5, 1936 (cat. no. 12). "An Exhibition of Water Colors and Oils by Charles Burchfield," Department of Fine Arts, Carnegie Institute, Pittsburgh, Pa., March 8–April 3, 1938 (cat. no. 31). "Paintings by Burchfield from the Collection of Edward W. Root," Fogg Art Museum, Harvard University, Cambridge, Mass., ca. February 6–March 1, 1940. "20th-Century American Painting from the Edward W. Root Collection," Smithsonian Institution, Washington, D.C., July 1959–July 1960 (traveling exhibition). "Edward Wales Root Bequest," Munson-Williams-Proctor Institute, Utica, N.Y., November 5, 1961–February 24, 1962 (catalog). "Paintings by Charles Burchfield," Root Art Center, Hamilton College, Clinton, N.Y., May 13–June 10, 1962 (cat. no. 23). "Charles Burchfield, His Golden Year, A Retrospective Exhibition of Watercolors, Oils, and Graphics," The University of Arizona Art Gallery, Tucson, Ariz., November 14, 1965–January 9, 1966 (cat. no. 81, illus., 35). "American 20th-Century Watercolors from MWPI," Albany Institute of History and Art, Albany, N.Y., September 10–October 4, 1967. "The Railroad in American Art," Washington County Museum of Fine Arts, Hagerstown, Md., October 4–November 30, 1968. "American Art of the Depression Era," Amherst College, Amherst, Mass., February 25–March 19, 1969 (catalog, illus.,

8). "Hopper-Burchfield," The Katonah Gallery, Katonah, N.Y., September 7–30, 1969. "The Nature of Charles Burchfield, A Memorial Exhibition," MWPI, April 9–June 14, 1970 (cat. no. 187). "Watercolors: Historic and Contemporary," Hathorn Gallery, Skidmore College, Saratoga Springs, N.Y., February 4–20, 1977 (cat. no. 6). "Burchfield Watercolors," MWPI, June 5–August 29, 1982. "The Machine Image in 20th-Century Art," MWPI, November 5, 1983–February 5, 1984.

PUBLICATIONS

"Pennsylvania Railroad: Paintings by Charles Burchfield," *Fortune* XIII (May 1936): 68, illus. O'Connor, John Jr. "Charles Burchfield: Exhibition of His Paintings at Carnegie Institute," *Carnegie Magazine* XI (March 1938): 312. "Pittsburgh: A Comprehensive Showing of the Work of Burchfield," *Art News* XXXVI (April 2, 1938): 18. Straus, John W. "Catalogue of Paintings by Charles E. Burchfield," Honors thesis, Harvard College, 1942, cat. no. 686, illus. *Paintings, Drawings & Sculptures in the Museum of Art* (Utica, N.Y.: Munson-Williams-Proctor Institute, 1961), 9. *Charles Burchfield: Fifty Years of His Art*, produced by the Radio-TV Bureau, University of Arizona, Tucson, 1965–1966. *American Art in Upstate New York* (Buffalo, N.Y.: Buffalo Fine Arts Academy, 1974), 7. Trovato, Joseph S. *Charles Burchfield: Catalogue of Paintings in Public and Private Collections* (Utica, N.Y.: MWPI, 1970), cat. no. 861, illus., 173. Baur, John. *The Inlander: Life and Work of Charles Burchfield 1893–1967* (Newark, Del.: University of Delaware Press, 1982), 172, illus. fig. 147. Townsend, J. Benjamin, ed. *Charles Burchfield's Journals: The Poetry of Place* (Albany, N.Y.: State University of New York Press, 1993), 472, 693 n. 65.

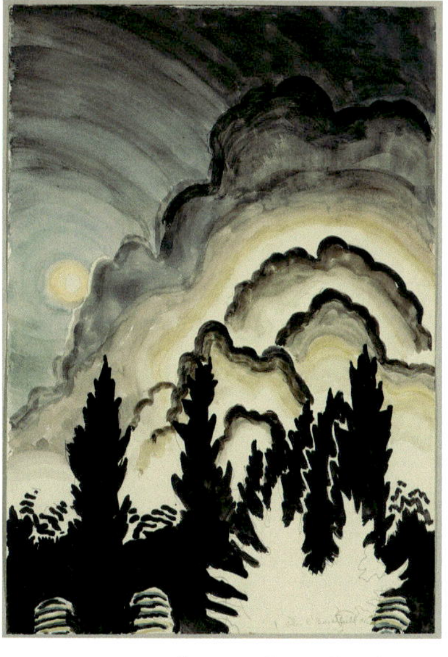

39. *Moon and Cumulus Cloud (Thunder Clouds)*, July 13, 1916

Transparent and opaque watercolor with graphite on white watercolor paper
19 15/16 x 13 7/8 in.
57.102
Signed lower right (graphite): Chas E Burchfield 1916
Inscribed verso center: Lightning and the Moon / July 13, 1916
Purchased from Frank K. M. Rehn Galleries, New York, February 1929

EXHIBITIONS

"Exhibition of Watercolors and Pastels by Eleven American Moderns from a Distinguished Private Collection," Munson-Williams-Proctor Institute, Utica, N.Y., fall 1938. "Five American Artists of the 20th Century: Davies, Luks, Burchfield, Tobey, Stamos," Root Art Center, Hamilton College, Clinton, N.Y., December 7, 1958–March 28, 1959. Gov. Rockefeller's Suite, Hotel Utica, Inaugural Opening, October 13–17, 1960. "Edward Wales Root Bequest," MWPI, November 5, 1961–February 24, 1962 (catalog). "Paintings by Charles Burchfield," Root Art Center, May 13–June 10, 1962 (cat. no. 8). "A Tribute to Charles E. Burchfield," New York State Exposition, Syracuse, N.Y., September 1–7, 1964 (checklist no. 2). "American 20th-Century Watercolors from MWPI," Albany Institute of History and Art, Albany, N.Y., September 10–October 4, 1967. "Paintings and Drawings from the Edward W. Root Bequest," Root Art Center, April 7–May 5, 1968. "The Nature of Charles Burchfield, A Memorial Exhibition," MWPI, April 9–June 14, 1970 (cat.no. 62). "Burchfield Watercolors," MWPI, June 5–August 29, 1982. "Nature Framed," MWPI, July 16–August 15, 1985. "Nature in Art," MWPI, January 17–February 15 and June 2–September 1, 1987.

PUBLICATIONS

Straus, John W. "Catalogue of Paintings by Charles E. Burchfield," Honors thesis, Harvard College, 1942, cat. no. 124. *Paintings, Drawings & Sculptures in the Museum of Art* (Utica, N.Y.: Munson-Williams-Proctor Institute, 1961), 9. Trovato, Joseph S. *Charles Burchfield: Catalogue of Paintings in Public and Private Collections* (Utica, N.Y.: MWPI, 1970), cat. no. 175. *American Art in Upstate New York* (Buffalo, N.Y.: Buffalo Fine Arts Academy, 1974), 6.

40. *Poplar Walk (Three Poplars, Hot Sunlight; Row of Poplars)*, June 7, 1916

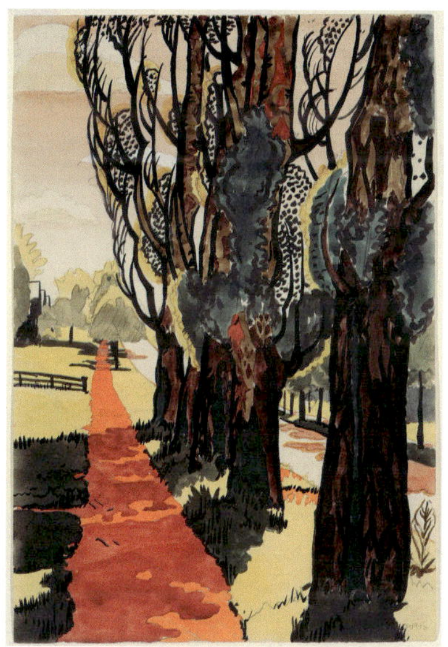

Transparent and opaque watercolor on white paper with color notations in graphite
19 7/8 x 13 15/16 in.
57.103
Signed and dated lower right: C E BURCHFIELD—1916
Inscribed verso lower left (graphite): June 7, 1916–
Painted: Salem, Ohio
Purchased from Frank K. M. Rehn Galleries, New York, February 1929

EXHIBITIONS

"Exhibition of Watercolors and Pastels by Eleven American Moderns from a Distinguished Private Collection," Munson-Williams-Proctor Institute, Utica, N.Y., fall 1938. "Paintings by Burchfield from the Collection of Edward W. Root," Fogg Art Museum, Harvard University, Cambridge, Mass., ca. February 6–March 1, 1940.

CHARLES E. BURCHFIELD

Museum of Art building inaugural exhibition, MWPI, October 15–December 31, 1960. "Edward Wales Root Bequest," MWPI, November 5, 1961–February 24, 1962 (catalog). "Paintings by Charles Burchfield," Root Art Center, Hamilton College, Clinton, N.Y., May 13–June 10, 1962 (cat. no. 9). "American 20th-Century Watercolors from MWPI," Albany Institute of History and Art, Albany, N.Y., September 10–October 4, 1967. "The Nature of Charles Burchfield, A Memorial Exhibition," MWPI, April 9–June 14, 1970 (cat. no. 65). "Burchfield Watercolors," MWPI, June 5–August 29, 1982. "Nature Framed," MWPI, March 15–May 20 and July 16–August 15, 1985. "Nature in Art," MWPI, January 17–February 15 and June 2–September 1, 1987. "American Twentieth-Century Watercolors at the Munson-Williams-Proctor Arts Institute," MWPAI, April 30–July 10, 2000 (traveling exhibition, cat. no. 7, illus.). "American Masterworks from the MWPAI, Celebrating an Educational Alliance with Pratt Institute," Hirschl & Adler Galleries, New York, November 16–December 29, 2006 (catalog).

PUBLICATIONS

Paintings, Drawings & Sculptures in the Museum of Art (Utica, N.Y.: Munson-Williams-Proctor Institute, 1961), 9. Trovato, Joseph S. *Charles Burchfield: Catalogue of Paintings in Public and Private Collections* (Utica, N.Y.: MWPI, 1970), cat. no. 135. *American Art in Upstate New York* (Buffalo, N.Y.: Buffalo Fine Arts Academy, 1974), 6.

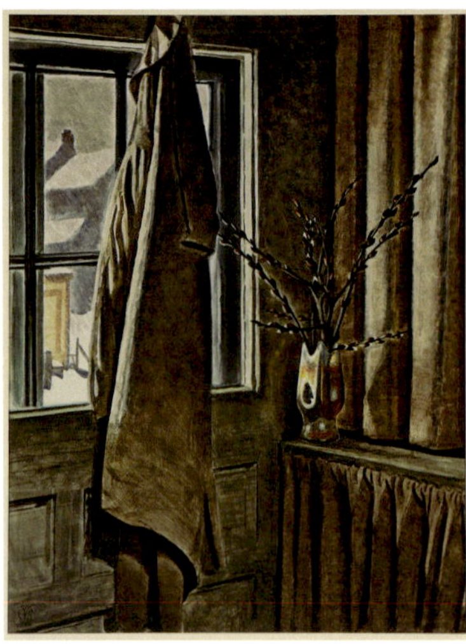

41. *Pussy Willows*, 1936

Watercolor on paper
32 15/16 x 25 ¼ in.
57.104
Signed and dated lower left (black paint): Monogram / 1936
Purchased from Frank K. M. Rehn Galleries, New York

EXHIBITIONS

["Watercolors by Charles Burchfield–Prints by Peggy Bacon," Frank K.M. Rehn Gallery, New York, November 16–December 5, 1936]. "Paintings by Burchfield from the Collection of Edward W. Root," Fogg Art Museum, Harvard University, Cambridge, Mass., ca. February 6–March 1, 1940. "Five American Artists of the 20th Century: Davies, Luks, Burchfield, Tobey, Stamos," Root Art Center, Hamilton College, Clinton, N.Y., December 7, 1958–March 28, 1959. "Edward Wales Root Bequest," Munson-Williams-Proctor Institute, Utica, N.Y., November 5, 1961–February 24, 1962 (catalog). "Paintings by Charles Burchfield," Root Art Center, May 13–June 10, 1962 (cat. no. 25). "American Drawings and Watercolors from the Munson-Williams-Proctor Institute," E. B. Crocker Art Gallery, Sacramento, Calif., October 25–November 24, 1974 (cat. no. 8). "The Artist's Studio in American Painting, 1840–1983," Allentown Art Museum, Allentown, Pa., September 25, 1983–January 8, 1984 (catalog, illus.). "The Paintings of Charles Burchfield: North by Midwest," Columbus Museum of Art, Columbus, Ohio, March 23–May 18, 1997 (traveling exhibition, cat. no. 13, illus.).

PUBLICATIONS

"Burchfield's America," *Life* December 28, 1936, 24–29, illus., 28. *Paintings, Drawings & Sculptures in the Museum of Art* (Utica, N.Y.: Munson-Williams-Proctor Institute, 1961), 10. Trovato, Joseph S. *Charles Burchfield: Catalogue of Paintings in Public and Private Collections* (Utica, N.Y.: MWPI, 1970), cat. no. 853, illus., 20. *American Art in Upstate New York* (Buffalo: Buffalo Fine Arts Academy, 1974), 7. "Charles Burchfield: The Centenary," *American Art Review* V, no. 3 (Spring 1993): 106–07, illus., 106. Townsend, J. Benjamin, ed. *Charles Burchfield's Journals: The Poetry of Place* (Albany, N.Y.: State University of New York Press, 1993), 569, 669 n. 13, 676 n. 21, illus., frontispiece.

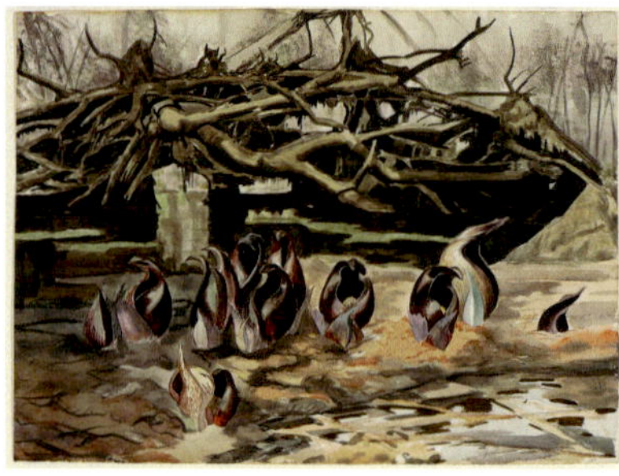

42. *Skunk Cabbage*, 1931

Opaque and transparent watercolor on heavy watercolor paper
21 ⅞ x 29 ⅞ in.
57.105
Signed and dated lower right (black crayon): Monogram / 1931
Inscribed verso upper center (graphite): #233 [obscured]
Painted: East of Jamison Road, Gardenville, New York
Purchased from Frank K. M. Rehn Galleries, New York, October 1931

EXHIBITIONS

"Exhibition of Water Colors by Charles Burchfield," Frank K. M. Rehn Galleries, New York, October 26–November 14, 1931 (cat. no. 13). "Five American Artists of the 20th Century: Davies, Luks, Burchfield, Tobey, Stamos," Root Art Center, Hamilton College, Clinton, N.Y., December 7, 1958–March 28, 1959. Museum of Art building inaugural exhibition, Munson-Williams-Proctor Institute, Utica, N.Y., October 15–December 31, 1960. "Edward Wales Root Bequest," MWPI, November 5, 1961–February 24, 1962 (catalog). "Paintings by Charles Burchfield," Root Art Center, May 13–June 10, 1962 (cat. no. 19). "American 20th-Century Watercolors from MWPI," Albany Institute of History and Art, Albany, N.Y., September 10–October 4, 1967. "The Nature of Charles Burchfield, A Memorial Exhibition," MWPI, April 9–June 14, 1970 (cat. no. 170). "20th-Century American Painting," Executive Mansion, Albany, N.Y., September–November 1974. "Burchfield Watercolors," MWPI, June 5–August 29, 1982. "The Art Triangle: Artist, Dealer, Collector," Burchfield Art Center, Buffalo, N.Y., May 13–June 25, 1989 (traveling exhibition, cat. no. 23). "American Twentieth-Century Watercolors at the Munson-Williams-Proctor Arts Institute," MWPAI, April 30–July 10, 2000 (traveling exhibition, cat. no. 23, illus.).

PUBLICATIONS

"Charles Burchfield-Rehn Galleries," *Art News* XXX (October 31, 1931): 10. Straus, John W. "Catalogue of Paintings by Charles E. Burchfield," Honors thesis, Harvard College, 1942, cat. no. 609, illus. *Paintings, Drawings & Sculptures in the Museum of Art* (Utica, N.Y.: Munson-Williams-Proctor Institute, 1961), 10. Trovato, Joseph S. *Charles Burchfield: Catalogue of Paintings in Public and Private Collections* (Utica, N.Y.: MWPI, 1970), cat. no. 773, illus., 147. *American Art in Upstate New York* (Buffalo, N.Y.: Buffalo Fine Arts Academy, 1974), 7. *Georgia O'Keeffe: Natural Issues 1918–1924* (Williamstown, Mass.: Williams College Museum of Art, 1992), 38, illus. fig. 12. Townsend, J. Benjamin, ed. *Charles Burchfield's Journals: The Poetry of Place* (Albany, N.Y.: State University of New York Press, 1993), 345 n. 33, 483, illus. fig. 74.

43. *Summer Shower and Sunlight (Summer Shower)*, May 1916

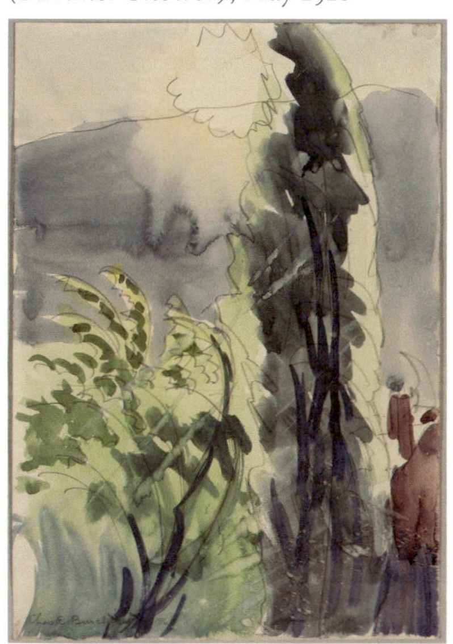

Transparent watercolor and graphite on white watercolor paper
14 x 9 ⅞ in.
57.106
Signed and dated left (graphite): Chas. E. Burchfield 1916
Inscribed verso lower right: May 1916
Purchased from Frank K. M. Rehn Galleries, New York, February 1929

EXHIBITIONS

"Exhibition of Watercolors and Pastels by Eleven American Moderns from a Distinguished Private Collection," Munson-Williams-Proctor Institute, Utica, N.Y., fall 1938. "Five American Artists of the 20th Century: Davies, Luks, Burchfield, Tobey, Stamos," Root Art Center, Hamilton College, Clinton, N.Y., December 7, 1958–March 28, 1959. "Edward Wales Root Bequest," MWPI, November 5, 1961–February 24, 1962 (catalog). "Paintings by Charles Burchfield," Root Art Center, May 13–June 10, 1962 (cat. no. 10). "A Tribute to Charles E. Burchfield," New York State Exposition, Syracuse, N.Y., September 1–7, 1964 (checklist no. 3). "American 20th-Century Watercolors from MWPI," Albany Institute of History and Art, Albany, N.Y., September 10–October 4, 1967. "The Nature of Charles Burchfield, A Memorial Exhibition," MWPI, April 9–June 14, 1970 (cat. no. 69). "Burchfield Watercolors," MWPI, June 5–August 29, 1982.

PUBLICATIONS

Straus, John W. "Catalogue of Paintings by Charles E. Burchfield," Honors thesis, Harvard College, 1942, cat. no. 147. *Paintings, Drawings & Sculptures in the Museum of Art* (Utica, N.Y.: Munson-Williams-Proctor Institute, 1961), 10. Trovato, Joseph S. *Charles Burchfield: Catalogue of Paintings in Public and Private Collections* (Utica, N.Y.: MWPI, 1970), cat. no. 202. *American Art in Upstate New York* (Buffalo, N.Y.: Buffalo Fine Arts Academy, 1974), 6.

44. *Trees and Fields, Noon Sunlight (Orange Trees)*, June 1915

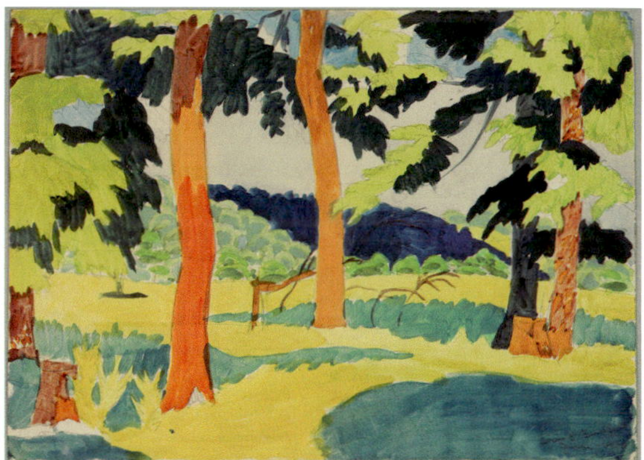

Transparent and opaque watercolor with graphite on white paper
13 ⅞ x 20 in.
57.107
Signed and dated lower right (graphite): Chas E. Burchfield / June–1915
Inscribed verso center: June 1915
Purchased from Frank K. M. Rehn Galleries, New York, February 1929

EXHIBITIONS

"Edward Wales Root Bequest," Munson-Williams-Proctor Institute, Utica, N.Y., November 5, 1961–February 24, 1962 (catalog). "Paintings by Charles Burchfield," Root Art Center, Hamilton College, Clinton, N.Y., May 13–June 10, 1962 (cat. no. 2). "A Tribute to Charles E. Burchfield," New York State Exposition, Syracuse, N.Y., September 1–7, 1964 (checklist no. 1). Root Art Center, September 1964. "Charles Burchfield, His Golden Year, A Retrospective Exhibition of Watercolors, Oils, and Graphics," The University of Arizona Art Gallery, Tucson, Ariz., November 14, 1965–January 9, 1966 (cat. no. 80, illus., 109). "American 20th-Century Watercolors from MWPI," Albany Institute of History and Art, Albany, N.Y., September 10–October 4, 1967. "The Nature of Charles Burchfield, A Memorial Exhibition," MWPI, April 9–June 14, 1970 (cat. no. 50). "American Art in Upstate New York," Albright-Knox Art Gallery, Buffalo, N.Y., July 12, 1974–April 27, 1975 (traveling exhibition, catalog, 5). "Five American Masters of Watercolor," Terra Museum of American Art, Evanston, Ill., May 5–July 12, 1981 (catalog, illus., 28). "Burchfield Watercolors," MWPI, June 5–August 29, 1982. "Charles Burchfield–A Retrospective Exhibition," The Metropolitan Museum of Art, New York, January 30–March 25, 1984. "The Advent of Modernism: Post-Impressionism in North American Art, 1900–1918," High Museum, Atlanta, Ga., March 4, 1986–April 19, 1987 (traveling exhibition, catalog, illus., 72).

PUBLICATIONS

Straus, John W. "Catalogue of Paintings by Charles E. Burchfield," Honors thesis, Harvard College, 1942, cat. no. 15. *Paintings, Drawings & Sculptures in the Museum of Art* (Utica, N.Y.: Munson-Williams-Proctor Institute, 1961), 10. Trovato, Joseph S. *Charles Burchfield: Catalogue of Paintings in Public and Private Collections* (Utica, N.Y.: MWPI, 1970), cat. no. 25, illus. color pl., 14.

CHARLES E. BURCHFIELD

45. *Village in the Swamps*, 1930

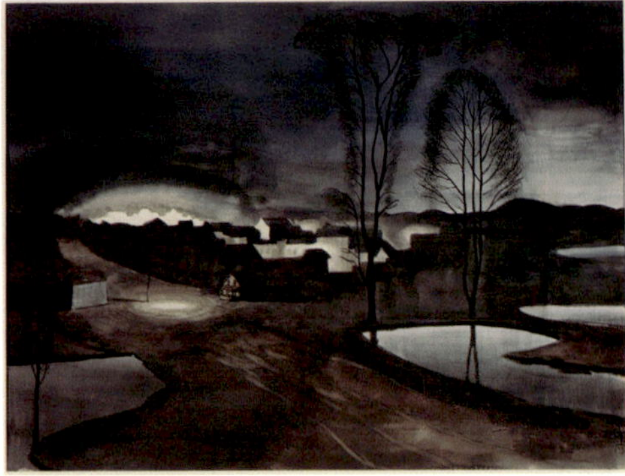

Transparent watercolor with chalk or crayon on heavy watercolor paper
23 7/16 x 30 7/16 in.
57.108
Signed and dated lower right (black paint): Monogram / 1930
Painted: Gowanda, N.Y.
Purchased from Frank K. M. Rehn Galleries, New York, October 1930

EXHIBITIONS

"Paintings by Burchfield from the Collection of Edward W. Root," Fogg Art Museum, Harvard University, Cambridge, Mass., ca. February 6–March 1, 1940. "Paintings from the Collection of Edward W. Root," Munson-Williams-Proctor Institute, Utica, N.Y., September 29–October 20, 1946. "The Edward Root Collection," The Metropolitan Museum of Art, New York, February 12–April 12, 1953 (catalog, 1). "Five Decades of American Painting," Union College, Schenectady, N.Y., September 27–October 23, 1959. "The American Muse," Corcoran Gallery of Art, Washington, D.C., April 4–May 17, 1959 (cat. no. 73). Museum of Art building inaugural exhibition, MWPI, October 15–December 31, 1960. "Edward Wales Root Bequest," MWPI, November 5, 1961–February 24, 1962 (catalog). "Paintings by Charles Burchfield," Root Art Center, Hamilton College, Clinton, N.Y., May 13– June 10, 1962 (cat. no. 18). "Masters of the Landscape: East and West," MWPI, September 15–October 13, 1963 and Memorial Art Gallery, Rochester, N.Y., November 1–December 1, 1963 (cat. no. 71, illus., 75). Root Art Center, March 1964. "The Twenties Revisited," The Gallery of Modern Art, New York, June 29–September 6, 1965. "American 20th-Century Watercolors from MWPI," Albany Institute of History and Art, Albany, N.Y., September 10–October 4, 1967. "The Nature of Charles Burchfield, A Memorial Exhibition," MWPI, April 9–June 14, 1970 (cat. no. 153). "American Art in Upstate New York," Albright-Knox Art Gallery, Buffalo, N.Y., July 12, 1974–April 27, 1975 (traveling exhibition, catalog, 7). "Burchfield Watercolors," MWPI, June 5–August 29, 1982. "Regionalism / American Scenes," MWPI, March 1984. "The Art Triangle: Artist, Dealer, Collector," Burchfield Art Center, Buffalo, N.Y., May 13–June 25, 1989 (traveling exhibition, cat. no. 22, illus., 63).

PUBLICATIONS

Straus, John W. "Catalogue of Paintings by Charles E. Burchfield," Honors thesis, Harvard College, 1942, cat. no. 600, illus. "AFA Golden Anniversary," *Eye on the Arts* (April 1959), illus. *Paintings, Drawings & Sculptures in the Museum of Art* (Utica, N.Y.: Munson-Williams-Proctor Institute, 1961), 10. Harold, Margaret, ed. *Landscape by the Masters* (Fort Lauderdale, Fla.: Allied Publications, Inc., 1964), illus. L–38. Trovato, Joseph S. *Charles Burchfield: Catalogue of Paintings in Public and Private Collections* (Utica, N.Y.: MWPI, 1970), cat. no. 765, illus., 144.

46. *Village Lane, Morning Sunlight (The Garden Poles)* July 22, 1916

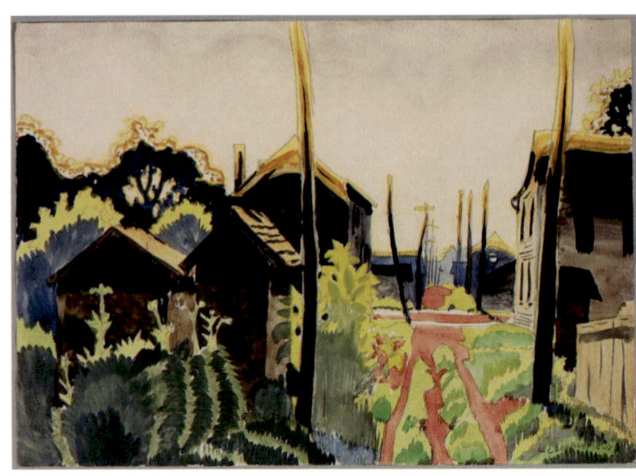

Watercolor and graphite on white wove paper
13 7/8 x 19 7/8 in.
57.109
Signed and dated lower right (graphite): C E BURCHFIELD–1916
Inscribed verso center: Early in the Day / July 22, 1916
Purchased from Frank K. M. Rehn Galleries, New York, February 1929

EXHIBITIONS

"Paintings by Burchfield from the Collection of Edward W. Root," Fogg Art Museum, Harvard University, Cambridge, Mass., ca. February 6–March 1, 1940. "Five American Artists of the 20th Century: Davies, Luks, Burchfield, Tobey, Stamos," Root Art Center, Hamilton College, Clinton, N.Y., December 7, 1958–March 28, 1959. "20th-Century American Painting from the Edward W. Root Collection," Smithsonian Institution, Washington, D.C., July 1959–July 1960 (traveling exhibition). "Edward Wales Root Bequest," Munson-Williams-Proctor Institute, Utica, N.Y., November 5, 1961–February 24, 1962 (catalog). "Paintings by Charles Burchfield," Root Art Center, May 13–June 10, 1962 (cat. no. 11). "American 20th-Century Watercolors from MWPI," Albany Institute of History and Art, Albany, N.Y., September 10–October 4, 1967. "The Nature of Charles Burchfield, A Memorial Exhibition," MWPI, April 9–June 14, 1970 (cat. no. 71). "Burchfield Watercolors," MWPI, June 5–August 29, 1982. "The Art Triangle: Artist, Dealer, Collector," Burchfield Art Center, Buffalo, N.Y., May 13–June 25, 1989 (traveling exhibition, cat. no. 8).

PUBLICATIONS

Straus, John W. "Catalogue of Paintings by Charles E. Burchfield," Honors thesis, Harvard College, 1942, cat. no. 114. *Paintings, Drawings & Sculptures in the Museum of Art* (Utica, N.Y.: Munson-Williams-Proctor Institute, 1961), 10. Trovato, Joseph S. *Charles Burchfield: Catalogue of Paintings in Public and Private Collections* (Utica, N.Y.: MWPI, 1970), cat. no. 167, illus., 15. *American Art in Upstate New York* (Buffalo, N.Y.: Buffalo Fine Arts Academy, 1974), 6.

KENNETH CALLAHAN

(Spokane, Wash., 1905–Seattle, Wash., 1986)

47. *Cascade Mountains, Series II, No. 3*, 1949

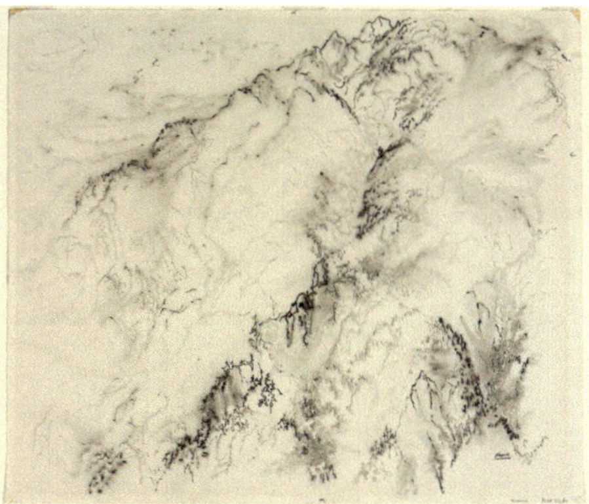

Crayon and ink on smooth wove paper
20 ½ x 24 ¾ in.
57.111
Signed lower right (black ink): Kenneth / Callahan
Inscribed lower right (graphite): Frame 81 xx 3 ½ x 4 3 [in circle]
Purchased from Maynard Walker Gallery, New York

EXHIBITIONS

Maynard Walker Gallery, New York, April 11–30, 1949. "The Edward Root Collection," The Metropolitan Museum of Art, New York, February 12–April 12, 1953 (catalog, 1). "Kenneth Callahan," Maynard Walker Gallery, November 16–December 5, 1953 (catalog, 3). Museum of Art building inaugural exhibition, Munson-Williams-Proctor Institute, Utica, N.Y., October 15–December 31, 1960. "Edward Wales Root Bequest," MWPI, November 5, 1961–February 24, 1962. "On Paper," American Federation of Arts, September 1966–September 1967 (traveling exhibition). "Landscapes," MWPI, April 7–May 4, 1969. Kirkland Art Center, Clinton, N.Y., February 6–March 6, 1972. "American Drawings and Watercolors from the Munson-Williams-Proctor Institute," E. B. Crocker Art Gallery, Sacramento, Calif., October 25–November 24, 1974 (cat. no. 9, illus.).

PUBLICATION

Paintings, Drawings & Sculptures in the Museum of Art (Utica, N.Y.: Munson-Williams-Proctor Institute, 1961), 10.

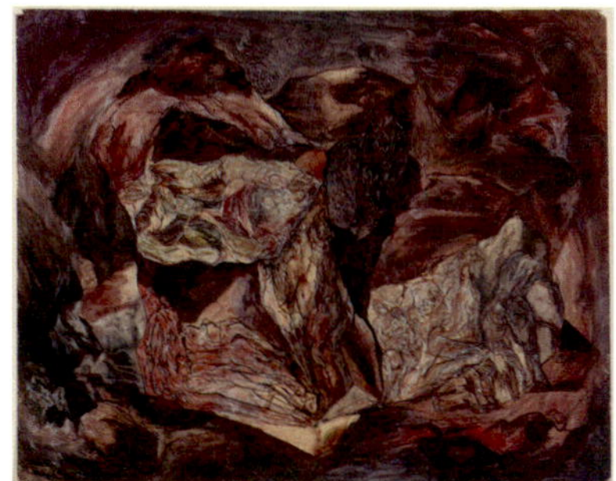

48. *Dwellers in the Cliffs*

Ca. 1943–44
Opaque watercolor and tempera on smooth white paper
16 ¾ x 21 ⅜ in.
57.110.1
Purchased from American British Art Center, New York, February 1946

EXHIBITIONS

"Paintings and Drawings by Kenneth Callahan," American British Center, New York, February 4–23, 1946 (cat. no. 19). "Paintings from the Collection of Edward W. Root," Munson-Williams-Proctor Institute, Utica, N.Y., September 29–October 20, 1946. "Kenneth Callahan," Maynard Walker Gallery, New York, November 16–December 5, 1953 (catalog, 5, as *Cliff Dwellers*). "Trends in 20th-Century American Painting," Union College, Schenectady, N.Y., March 5–26, 1961. "Edward Wales Root Bequest," MWPI, November 5, 1961–February 24, 1962 (catalog). "The Figure in 20th-Century Paintings and Drawings," Root Art Center, Hamilton College, Clinton, N.Y., April 15–May 6, 1962. "On Paper," American Federation of Arts, September 1966–September 1967 (traveling exhibition). Rome Community Art Center, Rome, N.Y., September 14–November 9, 1975. "Watercolors: Historic and Contemporary," Hathorn Gallery, Skidmore College, Saratoga Springs, N.Y., February 4–20, 1977 (cat. no. 8). "Figuratively Speaking," MWPI, April 11–November 10, 1985. "Northwest Mythologies: The Interactions of Mark Tobey, Morris Graves, Kenneth Callahan and Guy Anderson," Tacoma Art Museum, Tacoma, Wash., May 3–August 10, 2003 (catalog, 132, illus., 131).

PUBLICATIONS

Paintings, Drawings & Sculptures in the Museum of Art (Utica, N.Y.: Munson-Williams-Proctor Institute, 1961), 10. Orton, Thomas and Patricia Grieve Watkinson. *Kenneth Callahan* (La Conner, Wash.: Museum of Northwest Art, 2000), illus.

JOHN WESLEY CARROLL

(Wichita, Kans., 1892–Albany, N.Y., 1959)

49. *The Blue Feather*, 1937

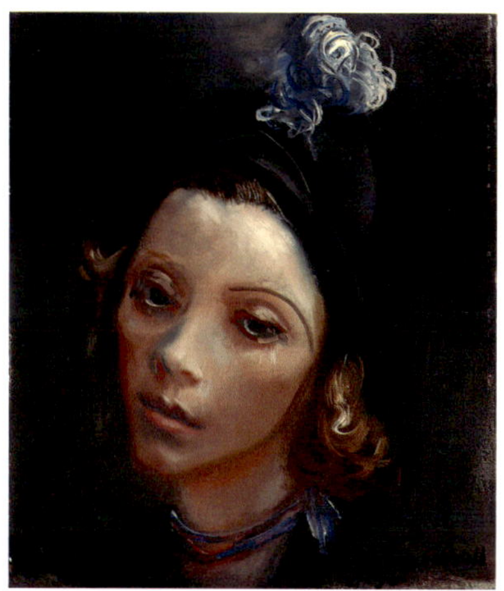

Oil on canvas
16 ⅛ x 14 in.
57.112
Signed and dated lower right (black paint): John Carroll / 37
Purchased from Frank K. M. Rehn Galleries, New York, January 1940

EXHIBITIONS

"Five Decades of American Painting," Union College, Schenectady, N.Y., September 27–October 23, 1959. "Edward Wales Root Bequest," Munson-Williams-Proctor Institute, Utica, N.Y., November 5, 1961–February 24, 1962 (catalog). "The Thirties, Reactions to Crisis," Lowe Art Center, Syracuse University, March 31–April 17, 1974 (catalog). "The Art Triangle: Artist, Dealer, Collector," Burchfield Art Center, Buffalo, N.Y., May 13–June 25, 1989 (traveling exhibition, cat. no. 35).

PUBLICATIONS

Paintings, Drawings & Sculptures in the Museum of Art (Utica, N.Y.: Munson-Williams-Proctor Institute, 1961), 10. "The Central New York Factor: Burchfield exhibit uncovers the pivotal relationship between artist / collector / dealer," *Munson-Williams-Proctor Institute Bulletin* (March 1989), illus.

JOHN WESLEY CARROLL

John Wesley Carroll was born on a moving train as it passed through the Wichita area of Kansas on August 14, 1892. His parents were relocating from West Virginia to California. Carroll was raised in urban San Francisco, but spent many summers on his father's ranch outside of the city. He began to study painting in 1902 through his public school and then more seriously at the Mark Hopkins Institute of Art in San Francisco. After three years at the Institute, he attended the University of California at Berkeley as a student of engineering from 1913 to 1915. During these two years, he also worked as a sketch artist for the *Oakland Tribune* newspaper.

Carroll left the Berkeley engineering program in 1915 to study art under the guidance of Frank Duveneck (1849–1919) at the Art Academy of Cincinnati. Due to personal and artistic conflicts, Duveneck threw Carroll out of his class after only six months. In 1918, Carroll joined the United States Navy. His job was in the dissection room preparing and drawing anatomical parts for study. He was sent to France to make drawings of the United States fleet in action, but was unhappy with these assignments and felt his time in the Navy was wasted. Carroll wanted to fight, not make art. Following his discharge from the Navy, Carroll moved to Macon, Georgia where he took a job at an insane asylum and created sketches of the inmates for the institution's records.

In 1920, Carroll moved to Woodstock, New York, where he held a variety of jobs such as making frames for Eugene Speicher (1883–1962), helping George Bellows (1882–1925) build a house, and designing stained glass windows for Tiffany & Company. It was during these years that Carroll developed his lush figure studies of young, beautiful women in hazy, dreamy poses. He quickly became a respected member of the Woodstock Art Colony and a commercial success.

In 1924, Carroll won a purchase prize from the Pennsylvania Academy of the Fine Arts in Philadelphia. He joined the Frank K. M. Rehn Gallery in 1927 where he exhibited for the next twenty years. His cohorts in the Rehn stable included Charles Burchfield (1893–1967), Edward Hopper (1882–1967), Reginald Marsh (1898–1954), Henry Varnum Poor (1888–1970), and Eugene Speicher (1883–1962). Between 1932 and 1945, Edward Wales Root (1884–1956) purchased five Carroll paintings through the Rehn Gallery.

Carroll enjoyed teaching and his career lasted for thirty-three years. In 1930, he became the head of the painting department at the Detroit Society of Arts and Crafts. Due to his success as a teacher, Carroll bought a large farm in Chatham, New York in 1934. There his hobbies, carried over from his boyhood, included hunting and riding horses—he owned five horses and a dozen hunting dogs. From 1934 to 1942, Carroll made a weekly drive from his home in Chatham to the school in Detroit. In 1936, he married Georgia "Pinky" Finnckel (1905–67). He returned to the United States Navy for another tour of duty during World War II and returned to the United States in 1944 where he resumed teaching painting at the Art Students League in New York until 1955. Carroll maintained a studio in New York City, but split his time between New York and his Chatham farm. He died in Albany, New York on November 7, 1959.

Carroll was described as a tall, rugged man, and many people knew him as a former cowboy, yet the wistful, languid figures in his paintings clash with his persona. Root's picture choices are characteristic examples of Carroll's mature and lyrical style. Carroll's sentimental imagery runs counter to the trends prevailing in mid-century American art. Despite the commercial success Carroll enjoyed during his lifetime, he is largely unknown today.

—Michael D. Somple

50. *Little Boy*, before 1936

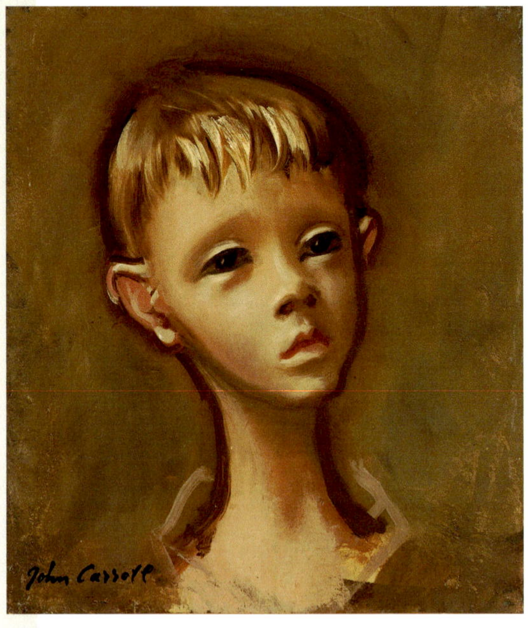

Oil on canvas
16 ⅛ x 14 ⅛ in.
57.113
Signed lower left (black paint): John Carroll
Purchased from Frank K. M. Rehn Galleries, New York, January 1945

EXHIBITIONS

"Paintings by John Carroll," Frank K. M. Rehn Galleries, New York, January 4–31, 1936 (cat. no. 6). "Paintings by John Carroll," Rehn Galleries, January 12–20, 1940 (cat. no. 21). "Paintings from the Collection of Edward W. Root," Munson-Williams-Proctor Institute, Utica, N.Y. September 29–October 20, 1946. "Edward Wales Root Bequest," MWPI, November 5, 1961–February 24, 1962 (catalog). "The Figure in 20th-Century Paintings and Drawings," Root Art Center, Hamilton College, Clinton, N.Y., April 15–May 6, 1962.

PUBLICATION

Paintings, Drawings & Sculptures in the Museum of Art (Utica, N.Y.: Munson-Williams-Proctor Institute, 1961), 10.

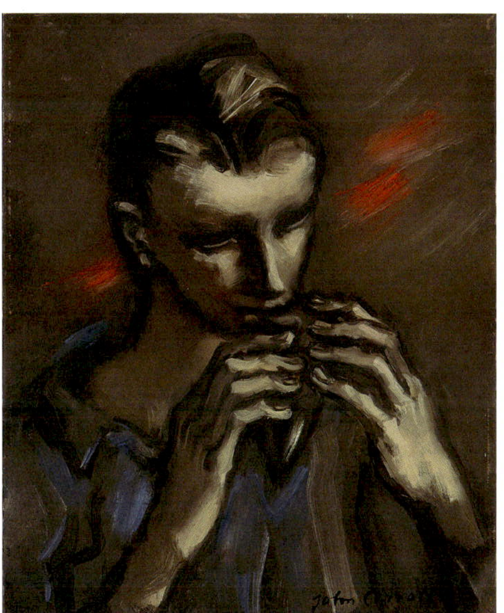

51. *Ocarina*, 1939

Oil on loosely woven coarse fabric
22 ¼ x 18 ¼ in.
57.114
Signed lower right (black paint): John Carroll
Inscribed verso upper right at angle: Pierre
Purchased from Frank K. M. Rehn Galleries, New York, January 1940, in exchange for Carroll's *Lilies of the Valley*

EXHIBITIONS

"Paintings by John Carroll," Frank K. M. Rehn Galleries, New York, January 2–20, 1940 (cat. no. 7). "Edward Wales Root Bequest," Munson-Williams-Proctor Institute, Utica, N.Y., November 5, 1961–February 24, 1962 (catalog). Root Art Center, Hamilton College, Clinton, N.Y., October 1964. "Music," Kirkland Art Center, Clinton, N.Y., October 25–November 30, 1967. "The Art Triangle: Artist, Dealer, Collector," Burchfield Art Center, Buffalo, N.Y., May 13–June 25, 1989 (traveling exhibition, cat. no. 36).

PUBLICATION

Paintings, Drawings & Sculptures in the Museum of Art (Utica, N.Y.: Munson-Williams-Proctor Institute, 1961), 11.

FEDERICO CASTELLÓN

(Almeria, Spain, 1914–New York, N.Y., 1971)

52. *Flaming Feet*, 1938

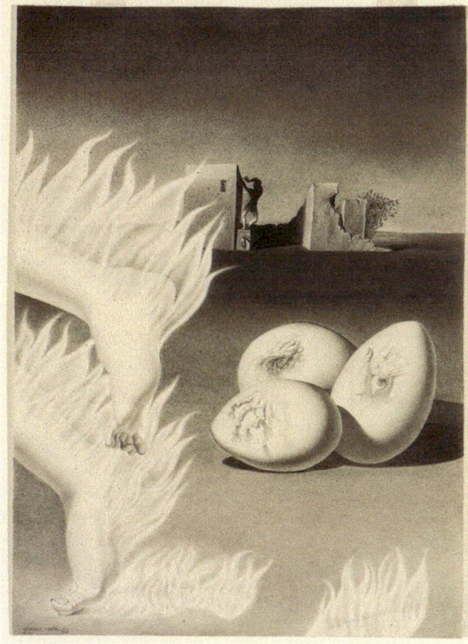

Graphite on smooth white paper spattered with red paint
15 ⅛ x 11 in.
57.115
Signed and dated lower left (graphite): FEDERICO CASTELLÓN NY '38
Inscribed verso lower center (graphite): In the Empty Rooms and Halls of a Deserted House I Follow the / Flaming Feet of an Unperceived Evasive Woman. Very Maddening! / Unsatisfied Hopes Remain Hopelessly Unborn
Purchased from Weyhe Gallery, New York, May 1938

EXHIBITIONS

"Paintings from the Collection of Edward W. Root," Munson-Williams-Proctor Institute, Utica, N.Y., September 29–October 20, 1946. "American Watercolors and Drawings," Root Art Center, Hamilton College, Clinton, N.Y., April 4–May 7, 1961. "Edward Wales Root Bequest," MWPI, November 5, 1961–February 24, 1962 (catalog). "The Figure in 20th-Century Paintings and Drawings," Root Art Center, April 15–May 6, 1962. "Paintings and Drawings from the Edward W. Root Bequest," Root Art Center, April 7–May 5, 1968. "Selections from the Edward W. Root Collection," Root Art Center, February 22–March 21, 1970. "Edward W. Root: Collector and Teacher," Fred L. Emerson Gallery, Hamilton College, October 2–November 14, 1982 (catalog, 38). "European Modernism 1920s–1950s," MWPI, November 11, 1987–March 2, 1988.

PUBLICATION

Paintings, Drawings & Sculptures in the Museum of Art (Utica, N.Y.: Munson-Williams-Proctor Institute, 1961), 11.

53. *Growth Forms*, 1935

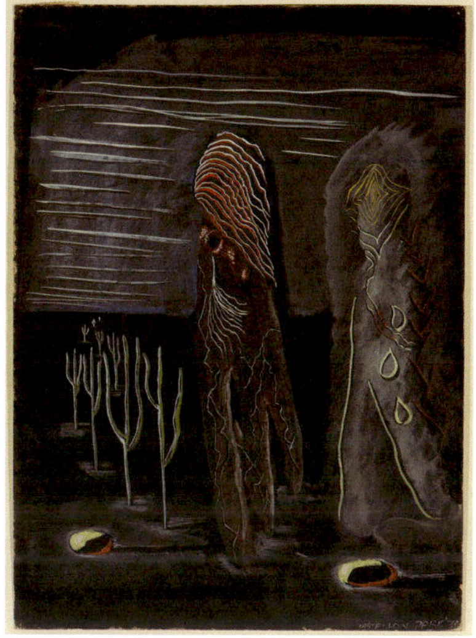

Opaque watercolor on wove paper
15 ⅞ x 11 ¼ in.
57.116
Signed and dated lower right (white paint): Castellon Paris '3 [worn away]
Inscribed verso lower right (graphite): 16 x 22 / [illegible inscription]
Purchased from Weyhe Gallery, New York

EXHIBITIONS

"Edward Wales Root Bequest," Munson-Williams-Proctor Institute, Utica, N.Y., November 5, 1961–February 24, 1962 (catalog). "The Figure in 20th-Century Paintings and Drawings," Root Art Center, Hamilton College, Clinton, N.Y., April 15–May 6, 1962. "American 20th-Century Watercolors from MWPI," Albany Institute of History and Art, Albany, N.Y., September 10–October 4, 1967. "Selections from the Edward W. Root Collection," Root Art Center, February 22–March 21, 1970. "Order and Enigma: American Art Between the Wars," October 14–December 16, 1984, MWPI (traveling exhibition, catalog, illus. color pl. 6).

PUBLICATION

Paintings, Drawings & Sculptures in the Museum of Art (Utica, N.Y.: Munson-Williams-Proctor Institute, 1961), 11.

FEDERICO CASTELLÓN

54. *Keep in the Shadow or You'll Be Trampled on by the Horse!* 1938

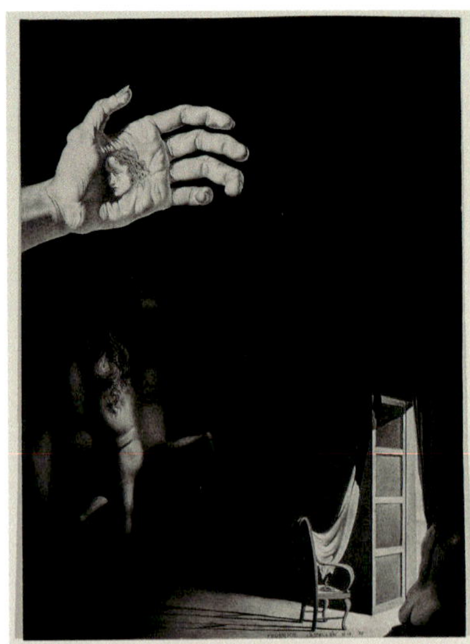

Graphite on heavy wove paper
15 x 11 in.
57.117
Signed and dated lower right (graphite): FEDERICO CASTELLÓN NY '38
Inscribed verso center (graphite): "Keep in the Shadow or You'll Be / Trampled on by the horse!"
Purchased from Weyhe Gallery, New York

EXHIBITIONS

"The Figure in 20th-Century Paintings and Drawings," Root Art Center, Hamilton College, Clinton, N.Y., April 10–May 6, 1962.
"Edward Wales Root Bequest," Munson-Williams-Proctor Institute, Utica, N.Y., November 5, 1961–February 24, 1962 (catalog, as *Keep in the Shadows*). "Selections from the Edward W. Root Collection," Root Art Center, February 22–March 21, 1970.
"Order and Enigma: American Art Between the Wars," October 14–December 16, 1984, MWPI (traveling exhibition, catalog, illus. fig. 49). "Life Lines: American Master Drawings (1788–1962) from the Munson-Williams-Proctor Institute," MWPI, September 17–November 13, 1994 (traveling exhibition, cat. no. 40, illus. color pl. 19).

PUBLICATION

Paintings, Drawings & Sculptures in the Museum of Art (Utica, N.Y.: Munson-Williams-Proctor Institute, 1961), 11.

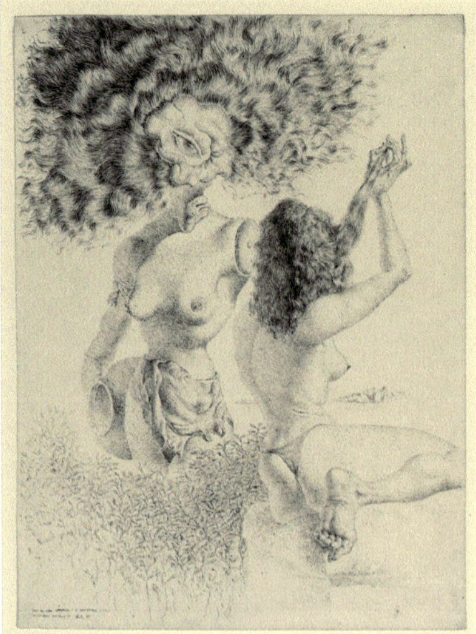

55. *Sight and Sound Embattled in a Half Crazed State*, 1937

Ink on wove paper
15 ⅞ x 11 ⅞ in.
57.118
Signed and dated lower left (ink): SIGHT AND SOUND EMBATTLED IN A HALF CRAZED STATE / FEDERICO CASTELLÓN NY '37
Purchased from Weyhe Gallery, New York

EXHIBITIONS

"Paintings from the Collection of Edward W. Root," Munson-Williams-Proctor Institute, Utica, N.Y., September 29–October 20, 1946.
"Edward Wales Root Bequest," MWPI, November 5, 1961–February 24, 1962 (catalog, as *Sight and Sound Embattled*). "The Figure in 20th-Century Paintings and Drawings," Root Art Center, Hamilton College, Clinton, N.Y., April 15–May 6, 1962.
"Selections from the Edward W. Root Collection," Root Art Center, February 22–March 21, 1970. "American Drawings and Watercolors from the Munson-Williams-Proctor Institute," E. B. Crocker Art Gallery, Sacramento, Calif., October 25–November 24, 1974 (cat. no. 11). "Five Decades of Collecting: Edward W. Root," MWPI, April 2–May 28, 1978. "European Modernism 1920s–1950s," MWPI, November 11, 1987–March 2, 1988.

PUBLICATION

Paintings, Drawings & Sculptures in the Museum of Art (Utica, N.Y.: Munson-Williams-Proctor Institute, 1961), 11.

56. *Three Figures and a Tree*, 1935

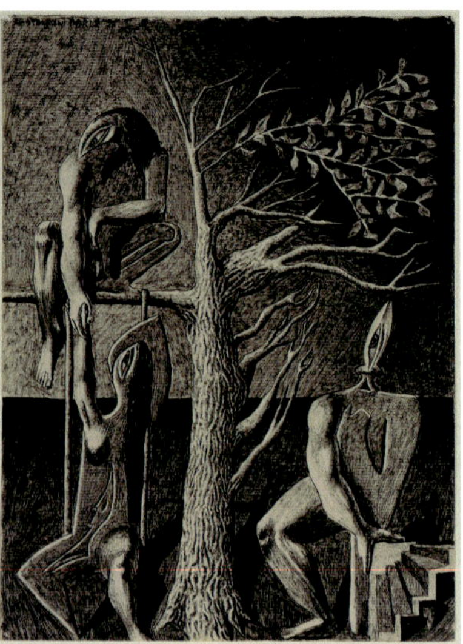

Ink and dry brush on paper
15 ⅞ x 11 ⅞ in.
57.119
Signed and dated upper left: CASTELLON PARIS '35
Purchased from Weyhe Gallery, New York

EXHIBITIONS

"The Edward Root Collection," The Metropolitan Museum of Art, New York, February 12–April 12, 1953 (catalog, 1).
"Edward Wales Root Bequest," Munson-Williams-Proctor Institute, Utica, N.Y., November 5, 1961–February 24, 1962 (catalog). "The Figure in 20th-Century Paintings and Drawings," Root Art Center, Hamilton College, Clinton, N.Y., April 15–May 6, 1962.
"Selections from the Edward W. Root Collection," Root Art Center, February 22–March 21, 1970. Kirkland Art Center, Clinton, N.Y., February 6–March 6, 1972. "European Modernism 1920s–1950s," MWPI, November 11, 1987–March 2, 1988.

PUBLICATION

Paintings, Drawings & Sculptures in the Museum of Art (Utica, N.Y.: Munson-Williams-Proctor Institute, 1961), 11.

57. *The Tree Woman Looking at the Moon*, 1937

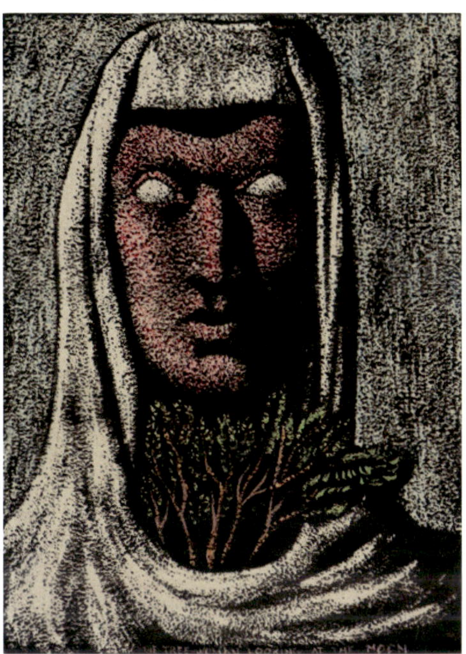

Gouache on board
11 5/16 x 8 ½ in.
57.285
Signed and dated verso: Federico Castellon NY '37
Inscribed bottom center (pink paint): THE TREE WOMAN LOOKING AT THE MOON
Purchased from Weyhe Gallery, New York

EXHIBITIONS

"New Trends in 20th-Century American Painting," Union College, Schenectady, N.Y., March 5–26, 1961. "Edward Wales Root Bequest," Munson-Williams-Proctor Institute, Utica, N.Y., November 5, 1961–February 24, 1962 (catalog). "The Figure in 20th-Century Paintings and Drawings," Root Art Center, Hamilton College, Clinton, N.Y., April 15–May 6, 1962.

PUBLICATION

Paintings, Drawings & Sculptures in the Museum of Art (Utica, N.Y.: Munson-Williams-Proctor Institute, 1961), 11.

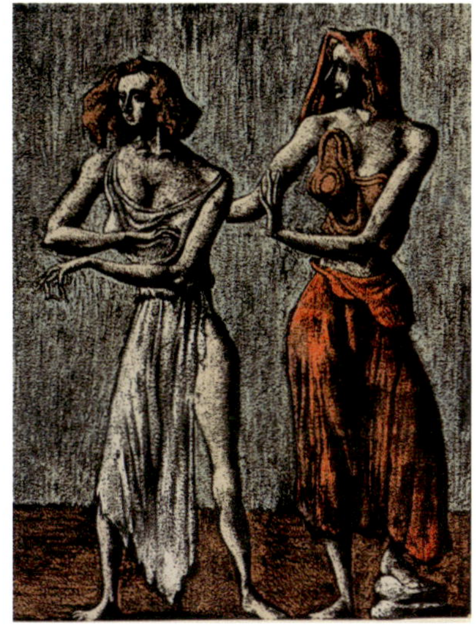

58. *Two Women*, 1937

Gouache on board
12 ⅞ x 10 in.
57.284
Signed and dated verso center on diagonal, upper right to lower left (black paint): Federico Castellón NY '37
Inscribed verso center left (graphite): off white / 14 ½ x 19 ¼
Purchased from Weyhe Gallery, New York

EXHIBITIONS

"Edward Wales Root Bequest," Munson-Williams-Proctor Institute, Utica, N.Y., November 5, 1961–February 24, 1962 (catalog). "The Figure in 20th-Century Paintings and Drawings," Root Art Center, Hamilton College, Clinton, N.Y., April 15–May 6, 1962. "American 20th-Century Watercolors from MWPI," Albany Institute of History and Art, Albany, N.Y., September 10–October 4, 1967.

PUBLICATION

Paintings, Drawings & Sculptures in the Museum of Art (Utica, N.Y.: Munson-Williams-Proctor Institute, 1961), 12.

WILLIAM CONGDON

(Providence, R.I., 1912–Milan, Italy, 1998)

59. *Piazza Navona*, 1950

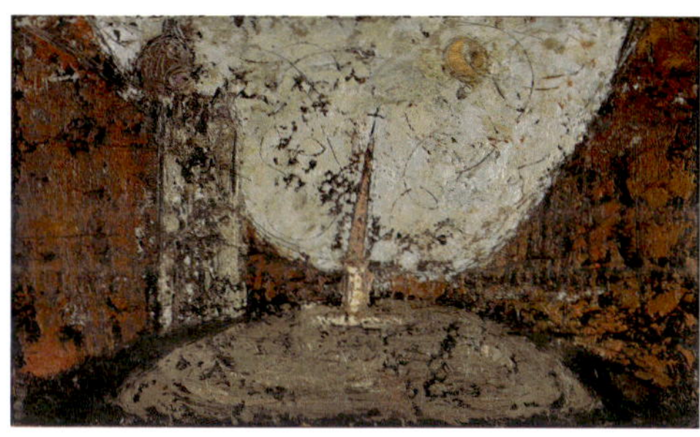

Oil, enamel, metallic, and earth pigments on plywood attached to wooden stretcher
20 ⅜ x 35 ⅜ in.
57.120
Signed and dated lower right: WC / Navona / 50
Inscribed verso upper left: Congdon; verso center: Piazza / Navona / Rome
Purchased from Betty Parsons Gallery, New York, April 1952

EXHIBITIONS

"The Edward Root Collection," The Metropolitan Museum of Art, New York, February 12–April 12, 1953 (catalog, 1). "20th-Century American Paintings from the Edward W. Root Collection," Smithsonian Institution, Washington, D.C., July 1959–July 1960 (traveling exhibition). "Edward Wales Root Bequest," Munson-Williams-Proctor Institute, Utica, N.Y., November 5, 1961–February 24, 1962 (catalog). Root Art Center, Hamilton College, Clinton, N.Y., March 1964. "Paintings and Drawings from the Edward W. Root Bequest," Root Art Center, April 7–May 5, 1968. "Five Decades of Collecting: Edward W. Root," MWPI, April 2–May 28, 1978.

PUBLICATION

Paintings, Drawings & Sculptures in the Museum of Art (Utica, N.Y.: Munson-Williams-Proctor Institute, 1961), 12.

HOWARD NORTON COOK

(Springfield, Mass., 1901–Santa Fe, N.M., 1980)

60. *Group of Kids*, ca. 1934

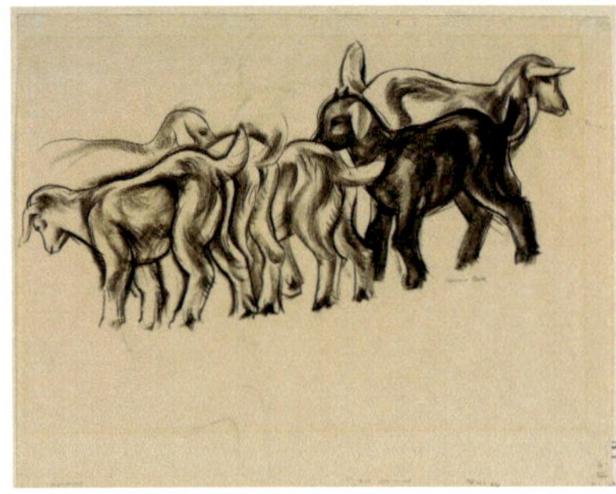

Crayon on wove paper
17 x 22 in.
57.121
Signed center right (graphite): Howard Cook; inscribed lower left (graphite): GROUP OF KIDS; lower center: 2 ½ / 3 off-white ½ flat nat. wood; lower right: 20 ¼ x 26; lower right: #2 / 25
Purchased from Weyhe Gallery, New York, February 1937

EXHIBITIONS

"Prints and Drawings by Howard Cook," Weyhe Gallery, New York, February 8–27, 1937 [possibly included; checklist does not specify individual works]. "Edward Wales Root Bequest," Munson-Williams-Proctor Institute, Utica, N.Y., November 5, 1961–February 24, 1962 (catalog).

PUBLICATION

Paintings, Drawings & Sculptures in the Museum of Art (Utica, N.Y.: Munson-Williams-Proctor Institute, 1961), 12.

61 . *Horses on the La Motta Ranch, La Salle Co., Texas*, ca. 1934

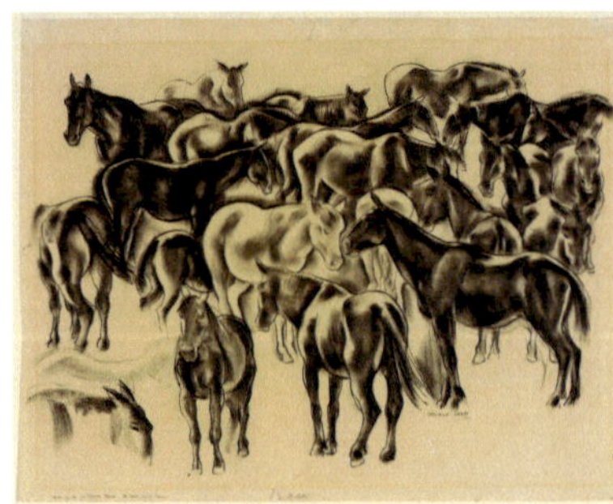

Crayon on wove paper
17 ⅛ x 22 ¹⁄₁₆ in.
57.122
Signed center right (graphite): Howard Cook / Texas; inscribed lower left (graphite): Horses on the LA MOTTA RANCH, LaSalle Co., Texas; left center: 3 / 3 ½ off white; lower right: 75
Purchased from Weyhe Gallery, New York, February 1937

EXHIBITIONS

["Prints and Drawings by Howard Cook," Weyhe Gallery, New York, February 8–27, 1937.] "Edward Wales Root Bequest," Munson-Williams-Proctor Institute, Utica, N.Y., November 5, 1961–February 24, 1962 (catalog). "Carnival of the Animals," MWPI, December 10–31, 1972. "American Drawings and Watercolors from the Munson-Williams-Proctor Institute," E. B. Crocker Art Gallery, Sacramento, Calif., October 25–November 24, 1974 (cat. no. 14). "Five Decades of Collecting: Edward W. Root," MWPI, April 2–May 28, 1978.

PUBLICATION

Paintings, Drawings & Sculptures in the Museum of Art (Utica, N.Y.: Munson-Williams-Proctor Institute, 1961), 14.

ARTHUR B. DAVIES

(Utica, N.Y., 1862–Florence, Italy, 1928)

62. *Inland Tempest (Inland Storm)*, not dated

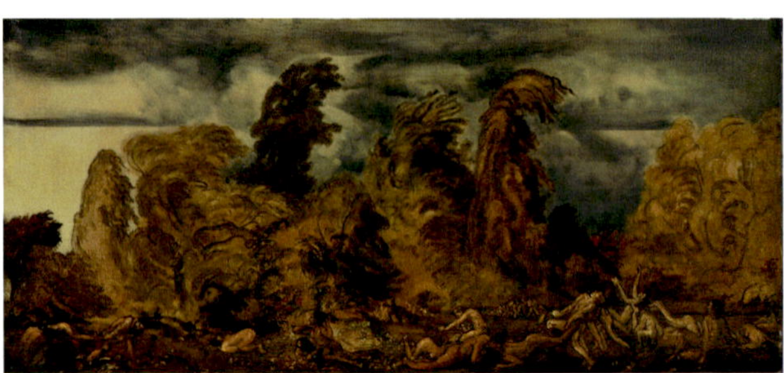

Oil on linen
18 x 40 in.
57.123
Signed lower left (light brown paint): A B Davies
Probably ex collection Wright Ludington, Santa Barbara, Calif.; purchased from Mrs. Cornelius J. Sullivan, New York, March 1939

EXHIBITIONS

"Loan Exhibition of Paintings, Watercolors, Drawings, Etchings, and Sculpture by Arthur B. Davies," Macbeth Galleries, New York, January 2–31, 1918 (catalog). "XVIII Esposizione Biennale Internazionale d'Arte," Venice, Italy, July 6–August 21, 1932. "Exhibition of Early and Middle Periods of the Work of Arthur B. Davies," Gallery of Mrs. Cornelius J. Sullivan, New York, February 7–28, 1939 (cat. no. 38). "Paintings from the Collection of Edward W. Root," Munson-Williams-Proctor Institute, Utica, N.Y., September 29–October 20, 1946. "The Edward Root Collection," The Metropolitan Museum of Art, New York, February 12–April 12, 1953 (catalog, 1). "Five Decades of American Painting," Union College, Schenectady, N.Y., September 27–October 23, 1959. Museum of Art Building inaugural exhibition, MWPI, October 15–December 31, 1960. "Edward Wales Root Bequest," MWPI, November 5, 1961–February 24, 1962 (catalog, illus.). "Arthur B. Davies, 1862–1928: A Centennial Exhibition," MWPI, July 8, 1962–June 23, 1963 (traveling exhibition, cat. no. 28, illus.). "Yesterday and Today," Oswego Art Gallery, Inc., Oswego, N.Y., May 30–June 14, 1964. "American Painting: The Tradition of Realism," Everson Museum of Art, Syracuse, N.Y., October 6–30, 1964. "Learning About Pictures from Mr. Root," Root Art Center, Hamilton College, Clinton, N.Y., January 4–31, 1965 (catalog, illus.). "Prints by American Artists," Root Art Center, January 9–February 12, 1967. "Arthur B. Davies," MWPI, December 15, 1974–January 5, 1975. "Works by Arthur B. Davies," M. Knoedler and Co., New York, March 1–31, 1975 (traveling exhibition, cat. no. 20, illus., 26). "Edward W. Root: Collector and Teacher," Fred L. Emerson Gallery, Hamilton College, October 2–November 14, 1982 (catalog, illus., 42).

PUBLICATIONS

Price, F. Newlin. "Davies The Absolute," *International Studio* LXXV (June 1922): 216, illus., 214 (titled *Inland Storm*).
Paintings, Drawings & Sculptures in the Museum of Art (Utica, N.Y.: Munson-Williams-Proctor Institute, 1961), 14.

63. *La Bella Range*, ca. 1928

Watercolor on gray-toned laid paper
9 ½ x 24 ¾ in.
57.124
Signed lower right (stamped, black ink): Arthur B. Davies
Signed upper left (stamped, upside down, black ink): Arthur B. Davies
Purchased from Ferargil Galleries, New York, December 1931

EXHIBITIONS

"Arthur B. Davies: Water Colors–Bronzes," Ferargil Galleries, New York, March 25–April 8, 1929 (cat. no. 14). "An Exhibition of Watercolors by Arthur B. Davies and Pastels by Dwight Williams (A Teacher of Davies)," Syracuse Museum of Fine Arts, Syracuse, N.Y., October 1931 (cat. no. 11). "Arthur B. Davies: Exhibition of Paintings, Sculpture and Drawings from the Estate," Ferargil Galleries, December 7–25, 1931. "Exhibition of Watercolors and Pastels by Eleven American Moderns from a Distinguished Private Collection," Munson-Williams-Proctor Institute, Utica, N.Y., fall 1938. "The Edward Root Collection," The Metropolitan Museum of Art, New York, February 12–April 12, 1953 (catalog, 1). "Edward Wales Root Bequest," MWPI, November 5, 1961–February 24, 1962 (catalog). "American Drawings and Watercolors from the Munson-Williams-Proctor Institute," E. B. Crocker Art Gallery, Sacramento, Calif., October 25–November 24, 1974 (cat. no. 17, illus.).

PUBLICATIONS

Paintings, Drawings & Sculptures in the Museum of Art (Utica, N.Y.: Munson-Williams-Proctor Institute, 1961), 14. *American Art in Upstate New York* (Buffalo, N.Y.: Buffalo Fine Arts Academy, 1974), 12.

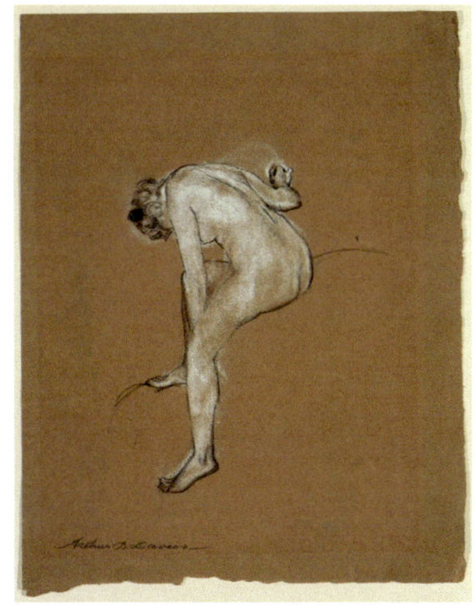

64. *Seated Nude*, not dated

Charcoal and chalk on brown-toned paper
12 ⅝ x 10 in.
57.125
Signed lower right (charcoal): Arthur B. Davies
Inscribed lower left corner: 12
Ex. collection John Quinn; to Edward Root through Weyhe Gallery, New York, February 1923

EXHIBITIONS

"Five American Artists of the 20th Century: Davies, Luks, Burchfield, Tobey, Stamos," Root Art Center, Hamilton College, Clinton, N.Y., December 7, 1958–March 28, 1959. "American Watercolors and Drawings," Root Art Center, April 4–May 7, 1961. "Edward Wales Root Bequest," Munson-Williams-Proctor Institute, Utica, N.Y., November 5, 1961–February 24, 1962 (catalog). "Arthur B. Davies: Paintings, Drawings and Lithographs," Everson Museum of Art, Syracuse, N.Y., October 25, 1966–February 26, 1967. "The Root Bequest," Root Art Center, May 11–June 8, 1969. "Arthur B. Davies," MWPI, December 15, 1974–January 5, 1975. "American Works of Art on Paper, 1850–1925," Schenectady Museum & Planetarium, Schenectady, N.Y., January 11–April 6, 1980 (cat. no. 23).

PUBLICATIONS

John Quinn, 1870–1925, Collection of Paintings, Watercolors, Drawings, and Sculpture (Huntington, N.Y.: Pidgeon Hill Press, 1926), 23, illus. 164. *Paintings, Drawings & Sculptures in the Museum of Art* (Utica, N.Y.: Munson-Williams-Proctor Institute, 1961),14. *American Art in Upstate New York* (Buffalo, N.Y.: Buffalo Fine Arts Academy, 1974), 11.

STUART DAVIS

(Philadelphia, Pa., 1894–New York, N.Y., 1964)

65. *Colors of Spring in the Harbor*

1939

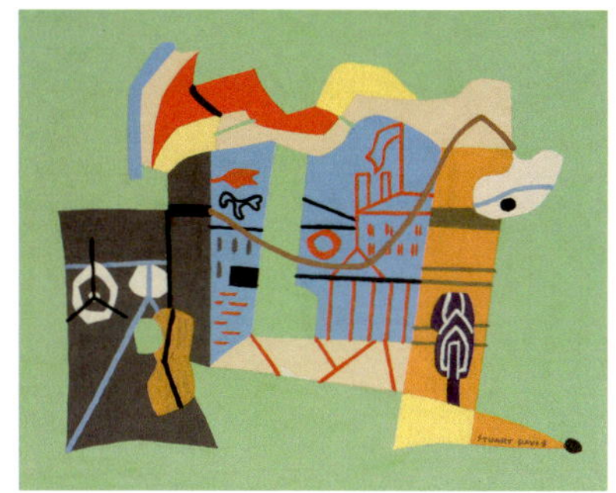

Gouache on watercolor board
12 x 16 in.
57.126
Signed lower right (green paint): STUART DAVIS
Purchased from The Downtown Gallery, New York, February 1946

EXHIBITIONS

"Stuart Davis Retrospective Exhibition: Gouaches, Watercolors, Drawings, 1912 to 1941," The Downtown Gallery, New York, January 29–February 16, 1946 (cat. no. 27). "Paintings from the Collection of Edward W. Root," Munson-Williams-Proctor Institute, Utica, N.Y., September 29–October 20, 1946. "The Edward Root Collection," The Metropolitan Museum of Art, New York, February 12–April 12, 1953 (catalog, 1). "Edward Wales Root Bequest," MWPI, November 5, 1961–February 24, 1962 (catalog). "American Drawings and Watercolors from the Munson-Williams-Proctor Institute," E. B. Crocker Art Gallery, Sacramento, Calif., October 25–November 24, 1974 (cat. no. 20). "Watercolors: Historic and Contemporary," Hathorn Gallery, Skidmore College, Saratoga Springs, N.Y., February 4–20, 1977 (cat. no. 13, illus.). "Edward W. Root: Collector and Teacher," Fred L. Emerson Gallery, Hamilton College, Clinton, N.Y., October 2–November 14, 1982 (catalog, 48).

PUBLICATIONS

"Root's U.S. Pictures at Met," *New York Herald Tribune*, February 15, 1953, section 4, 7. *Paintings, Drawings & Sculptures in the Museum of Art* (Utica, N.Y.: Munson-Williams-Proctor Institute, 1961), 15. *American Art in Upstate New York* (Buffalo, N.Y.: Buffalo Fine Arts Academy, 1974), 15.

ADOLF DEHN

(Waterville, Minn., 1895–New York, N.Y., 1968)

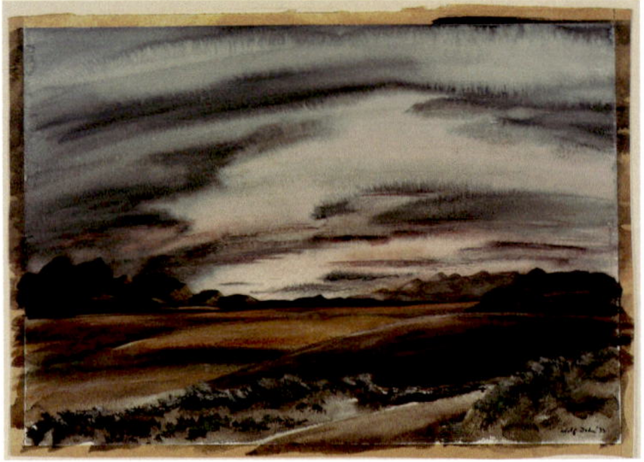

66. *After Sunset*, 1939

Watercolor on white paper
15 9/16 x 22 ½ in., irregular
57.127
Signed and dated lower right (black ink): Adolf Dehn '39
Inscribed verso center (graphite): After Sun Set / $75.00
Purchased from Weyhe Gallery, New York, 1940

EXHIBITIONS

"Paintings from the Collection of Edward W. Root," Munson-Williams-Proctor Institute, Utica, N.Y., September 29–October 20, 1946. "American Watercolors and Drawings," Root Art Center, Hamilton College, Clinton, N.Y., April 4–May 7, 1961. "Edward Wales Root Bequest," MWPI, November 5, 1961–February 24, 1962 (catalog). "Prints by American Artists," Root Art Center, January 9–February 12, 1967. "American 20th-Century Watercolors from MWPI," Albany Institute of History and Art, Albany, N.Y., September 10–October 4, 1967. "Five Decades of Collecting: Edward W. Root," MWPI, April 2–May 28, 1978.

PUBLICATION

Paintings, Drawings & Sculptures in the Museum of Art (Utica, N.Y.: Munson-Williams-Proctor Institute, 1961), 15.

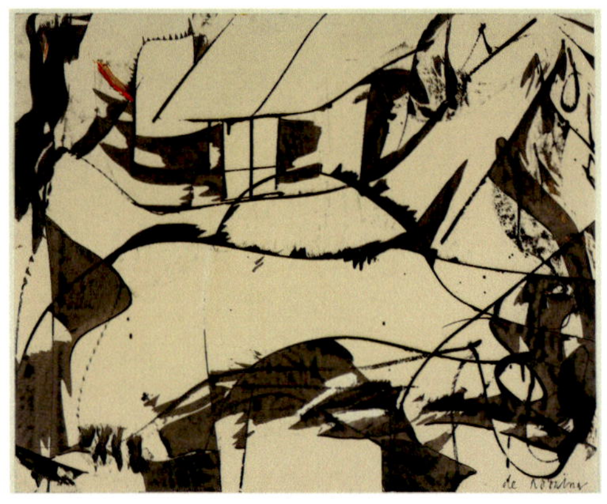

WILLEM DE KOONING

(Rotterdam, Holland, 1904–East Hampton, N.Y., 1997)

67. *Abstract Drawing*, 1951

Oil and enamel on heavy wove paper
24 5/16 x 30 ½ in.
57.128
Signed lower right (black paint): de Kooning
Purchased from Egan Gallery, New York

EXHIBITIONS

"Willem de Kooning," Egan Gallery, New York, April 1951. "The Edward Root Collection," The Metropolitan Museum of Art, New York, February 12–April 12, 1953 (catalog, 1, as *Untitled*). "New Trends in 20th-Century American Painting," Root Art Center, Hamilton College, Clinton, N.Y., October 26, 1958–January 26, 1959. "Contemporary American Watercolors and Drawings from the Edward W. Root Collection," Smithsonian Institution, Washington, D.C., June 1, 1959–May 31, 1960 (traveling exhibition). "Abstract Expressionist Drawings," American Federation of Arts, January 1961–January 1962 (traveling exhibition). "Edward Wales Root Bequest," Munson-Williams-Proctor Institute, Utica, N.Y., November 5, 1961–February 24, 1962 (catalog, as *Untitled: Abstract Drawing*). "European Sources of Contemporary American Art: Kandinsky," Root Art Center, September 15–October 6, 1963 (cat. no. 11). "On Paper," AFA, September 1966–September 1967 (traveling exhibition). "Paintings and Drawings: Selections from the Edward W. Root Bequest," Root Art Center, April 7–May 5, 1968. "Selections from the Edward W. Root Collection," Root Art Center, May 11–June 8, 1969. "20th-Century Prints and Drawings," Schenectady Museum & Planetarium, Schenectady, N.Y., December 15, 1971–January 15, 1972. "Willem de Kooning: Drawings and Sculptures," Walker Art Center, Minneapolis, Minn., February 1, 1974–August 1, 1975 (cat. no. 38). "Watercolors: Historic and Contemporary," Hathorn Gallery, Skidmore College, Saratoga Springs, N.Y., February 4–20, 1977 (cat. no. 14). "Edward W. Root: Collector and Teacher," Fred L. Emerson Gallery, Hamilton College, October 2–November 14, 1982 (catalog, 60, illus., 59). "Life Lines: American Master Drawings (1788-1962) from the Munson-Williams-Proctor Institute," MWPI, September 17–November 13, 1994 (traveling exhibition, cat. no. 55, illus. color pl. 22).

PUBLICATIONS

Geist, Sidney. "One Man's Collection," *Art Digest* XXVII (March 1, 1953): 13, illus. *Paintings, Drawings & Sculptures in the Museum of Art* (Utica, N.Y.: Munson-Williams-Proctor Institute, 1961), 15. Hess, Thomas B. *Willem de Kooning Drawings* (Greenwich, Conn.: New York Graphic Society, 1972), illus. pl. 29. Larson, Philip and Peter Schjeldahl. *De Kooning: drawings / sculptures* (New York: E. P. Dutton and Co., Inc., 1974), cat. no. 38. *American Art in Upstate New York* (Buffalo, N.Y.: Buffalo Fine Arts Academy, 1974), 15. *Willem de Kooning, Pittsburgh International Series* (Pittsburgh: Museum of Art, Carnegie Institute, 1979), cat. no. 79, illus., 109. Schweizer, Paul D., et al. *Masterworks of American Art from the Munson-Williams-Proctor Institute* (New York: Harry N. Abrams, 1989), cat. no. 87, illus., 190.

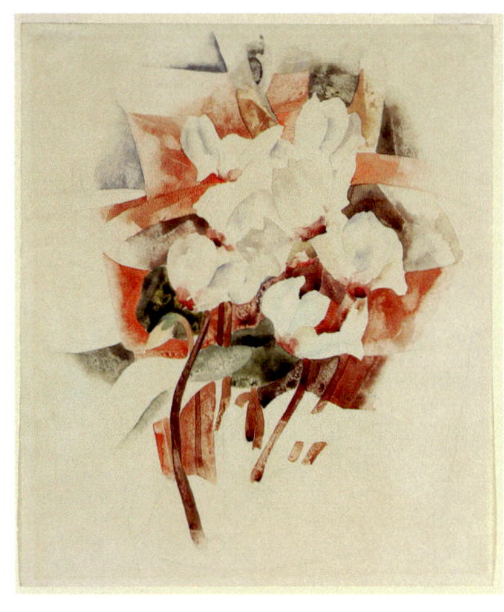

CHARLES DEMUTH

(Lancaster, Pa., 1883–1935)

68. *Cyclamen (Flower Study)*

Ca. 1921

Watercolor and graphite on white laid watercolor paper
13 ⅞ x 11 ⅞ in.
57.129
Signed lower right center (graphite): C. Demuth
Inscribed verso lower center (graphite): [unknown] 43 / ⅝ [unknown] flat / new [unknown] / 3 1 / 3 bottom / mount / 3 x 3 ¼
Purchased from Charles Daniel Gallery, New York [November 1926]

EXHIBITIONS

"Edward W. Root Loan Exhibition," Utica Art Society, Utica, N.Y., May 1928. "Exhibition of Watercolors and Pastels by Eleven American Moderns from a Distinguished Private Collection," Munson-Williams-Proctor Institute, Utica, N.Y., fall 1938.

"Paintings from the Collection of Edward W. Root," MWPI, September 29–October 20, 1946. "The Edward Root Collection," The Metropolitan Museum of Art, New York, February 12–April 12, 1953 (catalog, 1). "American Watercolors and Drawings," Root Art Center, Hamilton College, Clinton, N.Y., April 4–May 7, 1961.

"Edward Wales Root Bequest," MWPI, November 5, 1961–February 24, 1962 (catalog). "Charles Demuth of Lancaster," The Pennsylvania Historical and Museum Commission, William Penn Memorial Museum, Harrisburg, Pa., September 24–November 6, 1966 (cat. no. 85). "American 20th-Century Watercolors from MWPI," Albany Institute of History and Art, Albany, N.Y., September 10–October 4, 1967.

"Paintings by Charles Demuth," Akron Art Institute, Akron, Ohio, April 16–May 12, 1968 (cat. no. 76). "20th-Century American Painting," Executive Mansion, Albany, N.Y., September–November 1974. "Five Decades of Collecting: Edward W. Root," MWPI, April 2–May 28, 1978. "Edward W. Root: Collector and Teacher," Fred L. Emerson Gallery, Hamilton College, October 2–November 14, 1982 (catalog, 25, illus., 26).

"Nature in Art," MWPI, January 17–February 15 and June 2–September 1, 1987.

PUBLICATIONS

Paintings, Drawings & Sculptures in the Museum of Art (Utica, N.Y.: Munson-Williams-Proctor Institute, 1961), 15.
American Art in Upstate New York (Buffalo, N.Y.: Buffalo Fine Arts Academy, 1974), 17.

69. *Poppies*, 1918

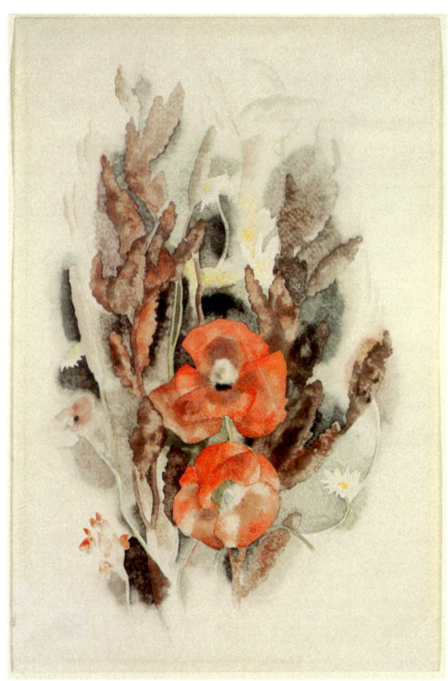

Watercolor and graphite on laid watercolor paper
17 ¹⁵⁄₁₆ x 11 ⅞ in.
57.130
Signed and dated lower edge left of center along stem (graphite): C. Demuth, 1918
Purchased from Mrs. Oliver Chaffee through The Downtown Gallery, New York, February 1938

EXHIBITIONS

"Contemporary American Paintings from the Downtown Gallery, New York City," High Museum, Atlanta, Ga., October 20–November 10, 1937. "Charles Demuth Memorial Exhibition," Whitney Museum of American Art, New York, December 15, 1937–January 16, 1938 (cat. no. 11). "Exhibition of Watercolors and Pastels by Eleven American Moderns from a Distinguished Private Collection," Munson-Williams-Proctor Institute, Utica, N.Y., fall 1938.

"Charles Demuth," The Museum of Modern Art, New York, March 8–June 11, 1950 (cat. no. 79). "The Edward Root Collection," The Metropolitan Museum of Art, New York, February 12–April 12, 1953 (catalog, 1). "Five Decades of American Painting," Union College, Schenectady, N.Y., September 27–October 23, 1959. "Edward Wales Root Bequest," MWPI, November 5, 1961–February 24, 1962 (catalog, illus.). "American 20th-Century Watercolors from MWPI," Albany Institute of History and Art, Albany, N.Y., September 10–October 4, 1967. "Paintings and Drawings from the Edward W. Root Bequest," Root Art Center, Hamilton College, Clinton, N.Y., April 7–May 5, 1968.

"The Root Bequest," Root Art Center, May 11–June 8, 1969. "Exhibition of American Paintings," Schenectady Museum & Planetarium, Schenectady, N.Y., March 20–April 30, 1970. "Charles Demuth: The Mechanical Encrusted on the Living," The Art Galleries, University of California, Santa Barbara, October 5–November 7, 1971 (traveling exhibition, cat. no. 52). "American Drawings and Watercolors from the Munson-Williams-Proctor Institute," E. B. Crocker Art Gallery, Sacramento, Calif., October 25–November 24, 1974 (cat. no. 22, illus.). "Watercolors: Historic and Contemporary," Hathorn Gallery, Skidmore College, Saratoga Springs, N.Y., February 4–20, 1977 (cat. no. 16).

"American Watercolors: 1855–1955," Herbert F. Johnson Museum of Art, Cornell University, Ithaca, N.Y., May 17–July 3, 1977 (catalog). "Five Decades of Collecting: Edward W. Root," MWPI, April 2–May 28, 1978.

"Flowers in Painting, Prints and Drawings," MWPI, April 20–May 28, 1980. "Painters of the Humble Truth," Philbrook Art Center, Tulsa, Okla., September 27–November 7, 1981 (traveling exhibition, catalog). "Nature in Art," MWPI, January 17–February 15 and June 2–September 1, 1987. "American Twentieth-Century Watercolors at the Munson-Williams-Proctor Institute," MWPAI, April 30–July 10, 2000 (traveling exhibition, cat. no. 10, illus.). "American Masterworks from the MWPAI, Celebrating an Educational Alliance with Pratt Institute," Hirschl & Adler Galleries, New York, November 16–December 29, 2006 (catalog).

PUBLICATIONS

Hale, Robert Beverly. "The Growth of a Collection," *The Metropolitan Museum of Art Bulletin* XI (February 1953): 154, illus., 160.
"Private Collections in Public," *Art News Annual* 52 (1954): 25, illus. Farnham, Emily. "Charles Demuth: His Life, Psychology, and Works," Ph.D. diss., Ohio State University,

1959. *Paintings, Drawings & Sculptures in the Museum of Art* (Utica, N.Y.: Munson-Williams-Proctor Institute, 1961), 15. *American Art in Upstate New York* (Buffalo, N.Y.: Buffalo Fine Arts Academy, 1974), 17.

70. *Purple Iris*, 1921

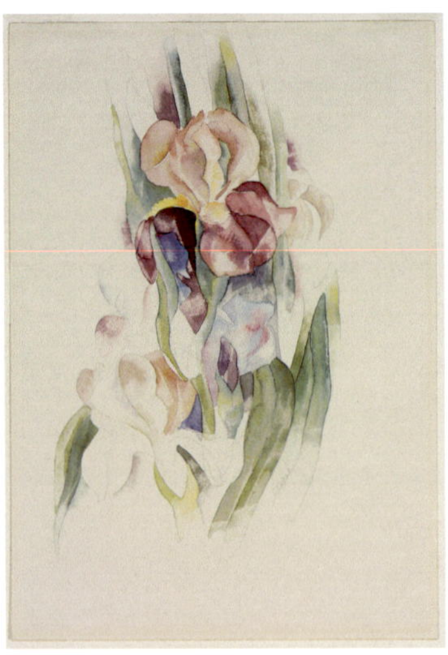

Watercolor and graphite on heavy white wove paper
14 x 10 in.
57.131
Signed and dated lower right center on iris leaf (graphite): C. D. 1921
Purchased from The Downtown Gallery, New York, March 1931

EXHIBITIONS

"7 Masters of Watercolor," The Downtown Gallery, New York, March 16–30, 1931 (cat. no. 3 [titled erroneously as *Yellow Iris*]). "10th Annual International Watercolor Exhibition," Art Institute of Chicago, March 20–April 20, 1931. "Selections from the 10th Annual International Watercolor Exhibition of the Art Institute of Chicago," Carnegie Institute, Pittsburgh, Pa., April 30–May 31, 1931. "Exhibition of Watercolors and Pastels by Eleven American Moderns from a Distinguished Private Collection," Munson-Williams-Proctor Institute, Utica, N.Y., fall 1938. "Edward Wales Root Bequest," MWPI, November 5, 1961–February 24, 1962 (catalog). "On Paper," American Federation of Arts, September 1966–September 1967 (traveling exhibition). "Flowers in Painting, Prints and Drawings," MWPI, April 20–May 25, 1980. "Nature in Art," MWPI, January 17–February 15 and June 2–September 1, 1987.

PUBLICATIONS

Paintings, Drawings & Sculptures in the Museum of Art (Utica, N.Y.: Munson-Williams-Proctor Institute, 1961), 15. *American Art in Upstate New York* (Buffalo, N.Y.: Buffalo Fine Arts Academy, 1974), 17.

PRESTON DICKINSON

(New York, N.Y., 1891–Irun, Spain, 1930)

71. *Fort George Hill*, 1915

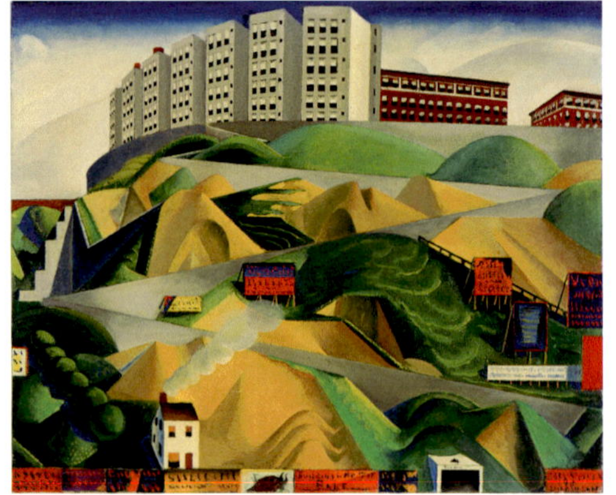

Oil on linen
14 x 17 in.
57.132
Signed and dated lower right (black paint): Preston / 1915 / Dickinson
Purchased from Charles Daniel Gallery, New York, May 1915

EXHIBITIONS

"Paintings from the Collection of Edward W. Root," Munson-Williams-Proctor Institute, Utica, N.Y., September 29–October 20, 1946. "The Edward Root Collection," The Metropolitan Museum of Art, New York, February 12–April 12, 1953 (catalog, 2). "20th-Century American Painting from the Edward W. Root Collection," Smithsonian Institution, Washington, D.C., July 1959–July 1960 (traveling exhibition). "Edward Wales Root Bequest," MWPI, November 5, 1961–February 24, 1962 (catalog). "Cubism: Its Impact in the USA 1910–1930," University of New Mexico Art Museum, Albuquerque, January 20–September 15, 1967 (traveling exhibition, catalog, illus. color pl. 23). "Paintings and Drawings from the Edward W. Root Bequest," Root Art Center, Hamilton College, Clinton, N.Y., April 7–May 5, 1968. "The Root Bequest," Root Art Center, May 11–June 8, 1969. "American Scene 1900–1970," Indiana University Art Museum, Bloomington, Ind., April 6–May 17, 1970 (cat. no. 40, illus.). "Five Decades of Collecting: Edward W. Root," MWPI, April 2–May 28, 1978. "Preston Dickinson," Sheldon Memorial Art Gallery, University of Nebraska, Lincoln, September 4–October 7, 1979 (traveling exhibition, cat. no. 4, illus., 71). "Nature Framed," MWPI, March 15–May 20 and July 16–August 15, 1985. "Insights," MWPI, January 7–April 13 and June 10–October 15, 1986. "Two Hundred Years of American Art," The Art Museum Association of America, November 15, 1986–May 8, 1988 (traveling exhibition, cat. no. 42, illus., 56). "Circa 1900: From the Genteel Tradition to the Jazz Age," Albright-Knox Art Gallery, Buffalo, N.Y., May 3–August 21, 2001 (traveling exhibition, cat. no. 87, illus., 92).

PUBLICATIONS

Paintings, Drawings & Sculptures in the Museum of Art (Utica, N.Y.: Munson-Williams-Proctor Institute, 1961), 15. Schweizer, Paul D., et al. *Masterworks of American Art from the Munson-Williams-Proctor Institute* (New York: Harry N. Abrams, Inc., 1989), cat. no. 53, illus., 118.

ARTHUR G. DOVE

(Canandaigua, N.Y., 1880–Centerport, N.Y., 1946)

72. *Frosty Moon*, 1940

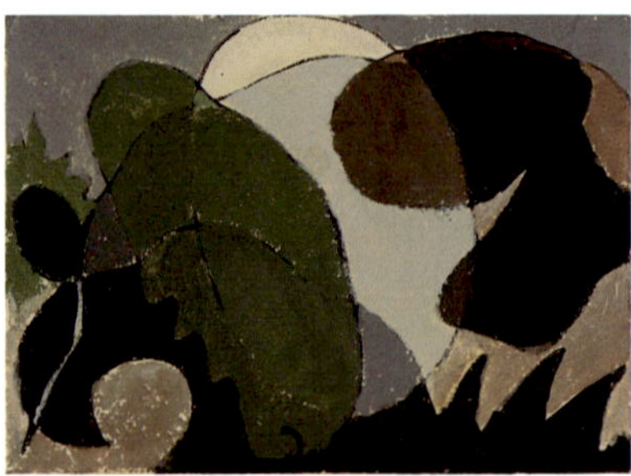

Opaque oil on heavy textured watercolor paper
5 x 7 in.
57.133
Signed bottom center (black paint): Dove
[Purchased from The Downtown Gallery, New York]

EXHIBITIONS

"American Watercolors and Drawings," Root Art Center, Hamilton College, Clinton, N.Y., April 4–May 7, 1961. "Edward Wales Root Bequest," Munson-Williams-Proctor Institute, Utica, N.Y., November 5, 1961–February 24, 1962 (catalog). "American 20th-Century Watercolors from MWPI," Albany Institute of History and Art, Albany, N.Y., September 10–October 4, 1967. "Arthur G. Dove: Paintings, Drawings, Memorabilia," The Historical Society Museum, under the auspices of the Historical Society of Geneva and Hobart and William Smith Colleges, Geneva, N.Y., October 15–30, 1967.

PUBLICATIONS

Paintings, Drawings & Sculptures in the Museum of Art (Utica, N.Y.: Munson-Williams-Proctor Institute, 1961), 16. *American Art in Upstate New York* (Buffalo, N.Y.: Buffalo Fine Arts Academy, 1974), 19. [Note: as a work on paper, *Frosty Moon* is not included in Ann Lee Morgan, *Arthur Dove: Life and Work, With a Catalogue Raisonné* (Newark, Del.: University of Delaware Press, 1984), but the oil for which it is a study is catalogue number 41.16, titled *Through a Frosty Moon*.]

73. *No Feather Pillow*, 1940

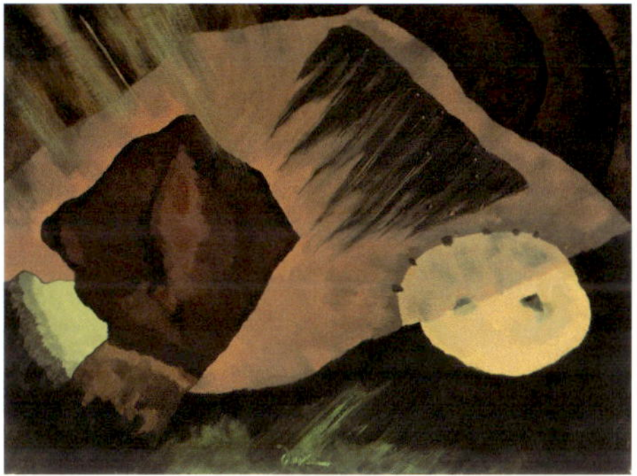

Oil and wax emulsion on linen
16 x 22 in.
57.134
Signed bottom center (green paint): Dove
Purchased from The Downtown Gallery, New York, March 1947

EXHIBITIONS

"Arthur G. Dove: Exhibition of New Oils and Water Colors," An American Place, New York, March 30–May 14, 1940 (cat. no. 10). "Paintings from New York Private Collections," The Museum of Modern Art, New York, July 2–September 22, 1946. "New York Private Collections," MoMA, July 20–September 12, 1948. "Current Trends in British and American Painting from the Collection of Edward W. Root," Munson-Williams-Proctor Institute, Utica, N.Y., December 3–31, 1950 (traveling exhibition, cat. no. 7). "The Edward Root Collection," The Metropolitan Museum of Art, New York, February 12–April 12, 1953 (catalog, 2). "Arthur G. Dove," Whitney Museum of American Art, New York, September 30–November 16, 1958 (traveling exhibition, cat. no. 75, illus., 82). [Union Carbide Corporation, March 27, 1961.] "Edward Wales Root Bequest," MWPI, November 5, 1961–February 24, 1962 (catalog). "European Sources of Contemporary American Art: Kandinsky," Root Art Center, Hamilton College, Clinton, N.Y., September 15–October 6, 1963 (cat. no. 13). "Abstract Paintings and Drawings from the Root Bequest," Root Art Center, September 11–October 9, 1966. "Arthur G. Dove: Paintings, Drawings, Memorabilia," The Historical Society Museum, under the auspices of the Historical Society of Geneva and Hobart and William Smith Colleges, Geneva, N.Y., October 15–30, 1967. "Arthur Dove," organized by MoMA, March 1968–April 1969 (traveling exhibition, cat. no. 28). "Arthur Dove," San Francisco Museum of Art, November 20, 1974–January 5, 1975 (traveling exhibition, catalog, illus., 99). "Five Decades of Collecting: Edward W. Root," MWPI, April 2–May 28, 1978. "Two Hundred Years of American Art," The Art Museum Association of America, November 15, 1986–May 8, 1988 (traveling exhibition, cat. no. 57, illus., 71).

PUBLICATIONS

Goldwater, Robert. "Arthur Dove: A Pioneer of Abstract Expressionism in American Art," *Perspective USA* II (Winter 1953), illus. *Paintings, Drawings & Sculptures in the Museum of Art* (Utica, N.Y.: Munson-Williams-Proctor Institute, 1961), 16. *American Art in Upstate New York* (Buffalo, N.Y.: Buffalo Fine Arts Academy, 1974), 17. Meador, Shirley. "Arthur G. Dove, Ahead of His Time," *American Artist* (November 1975): 53, illus. Morgan, Ann Lee. *Arthur Dove: Life and Work, With a Catalogue Raisonné* (Newark, Del.: University of Delaware Press, 1984), cat. no. 40.11, illus., 266.

74. *Summer Orchard*, 1937

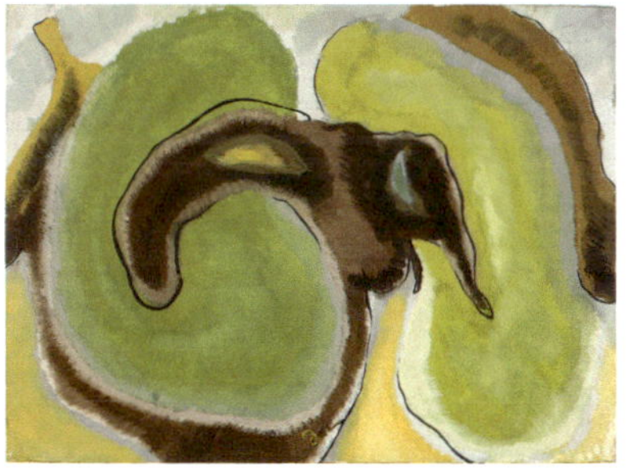

Wax emulsion, tempera, and gesso on linen
15 x 21 in.
57.135
Signed bottom center (green paint): dove
[Purchased from The Downtown Gallery, New York]

EXHIBITIONS

"Arthur G. Dove: New Oils and Watercolors," An American Place, New York, March 23–April 16, 1937 (cat. no. 6). "The Edward Root Collection," The Metropolitan Museum of Art, New York, February 12–April 12, 1953 (catalog, 2). "Five Decades of American Painting," Union College, Schenectady, N.Y., September 27–October 23, 1959. "New Trends in 20th-Century American Painting," Union College, March 5–26, 1961. "Edward Wales Root Bequest," Munson-Williams-Proctor Institute, Utica, N.Y., November 5, 1961–February 24, 1962 (catalog, illus.). "European Sources of Contemporary American Art: Kandinsky," Root Art Center, Hamilton College, Clinton, N.Y., September 15–October 6, 1963 (cat. no. 15). "Arthur G. Dove: Paintings, Drawings, Memorabilia," The Historical Society Museum, under the auspices of the Historical Society of Geneva and Hobart and William Smith Colleges, Geneva, N.Y., October 15–30, 1967. "American Art of the Depression Era," Amherst College, Amherst, Mass., February 25–March 19, 1969 (catalog, 5, illus., 7). "The Root Bequest," Root Art Center, May 11–June 8, 1969. "Arthur Dove," San Francisco Museum of Art, November 20, 1974–January 5, 1975 (traveling exhibition, catalog, illus., 86). "Five Decades of Collecting: Edward W. Root," MWPI, April 2–May 28, 1978. "Edward W. Root: Collector and Teacher," Fred L. Emerson Gallery, Hamilton College, October 2–November 14, 1982 (catalog, illus., 48). "Arthur Dove," The Katonah Gallery, Katonah, N.Y., September 25–November 6, 1983 (cat. no. 17, illus.). "Nature in Art," MWPI, January 17–February 15, 1987. "Modernist Idylls: Nature and the Avant-Garde, 1905–1930," Allentown Art Museum, Allentown, Pa., February 8–May 30, 1987 (catalog, illus. fig. 18). "Landscape of America: The Hudson River School to Abstract Expressionism," Nassau City Museum of Art, Roslyn Harbor, N.Y., November 10, 1991–February 9, 1992 (catalog, illus., 53). "Masterworks of American Art from the Munson-Williams-Proctor Institute Museum of Art," Knoxville Museum of Art, Knoxville, Tenn., February 26–August 23, 1998. "The Great American Thing," Figge Arts Center, Davenport, Ia., September 17, 2005–January 1, 2006 (traveling exhibition, catalog). "American Masterworks from the MWPAI, Celebrating an Educational Alliance with Pratt Institute," Hirschl & Adler Galleries, New York, November 16–December 29, 2006 (catalog).

ARTHUR G. DOVE

PUBLICATIONS

Paintings, Drawings & Sculptures in the Museum of Art (Utica, N.Y.: Munson-Williams-Proctor Institute, 1961), 16. Morgan, Ann Lee. *Arthur Dove: Life and Work, With a Catalogue Raisonné* (Newark, Del.: University of Delaware Press, 1984), cat. no. 37.12, illus., 244. Harrison, Helen A. "Arthur G. Dove and the Origins of Abstract Expressionism," *American Art* 12 (Spring 1998): 66–83, illus. fig. 6.

75. *Tree Composition*, 1937

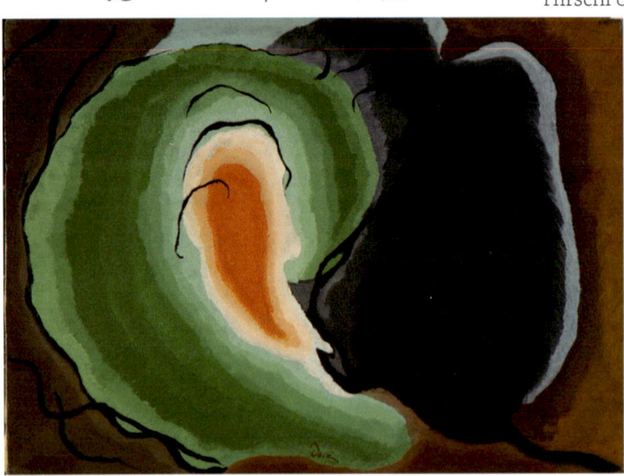

Wax emulsion on linen
15 1/16 x 21 in.
57.136
Signed bottom center (brown paint): Dove
[Purchased from The Downtown Gallery, New York]

EXHIBITIONS

"Arthur G. Dove: New Oils and Watercolors," An American Place, New York, March 23–April 16, 1937 (cat. no. 17). "Arthur Dove: Exhibition of Oils and Temperas," An American Place, April 10–May 7, 1939 (cat. no. 17). "Arthur G. Dove, Paintings: 1922–1944," An American Place, May 3–June 15, 1945 (cat. no. 10). "Retrospective Exhibition," The Downtown Gallery, New York, January 7–February 1, 1947 (traveling exhibition). "The Edward Root Collection," The Metropolitan Museum of Art, New York, February 12–April 12, 1953 (catalog, 2). Museum of Art Building inaugural exhibition, Munson-Williams-Proctor Institute, Utica, N.Y., October 15–December 31, 1960. "Edward Wales Root Bequest," MWPI, November 5, 1961–February 24, 1962 (catalog). "European Sources of Contemporary American Art: Kandinsky," Root Art Center, Hamilton College, Clinton, N.Y., September 15–October 6, 1963 (cat. no. 16). "Paintings and Drawings from the Edward W. Root Bequest," Root Art Center, April 7–May 5, 1968. "An American Place," The Parrish Art Museum, Southampton, N.Y., May 24–July 19, 1981 (cat. no. 6). "Nature Framed," MWPI, March 15–May 20 and July 16–August 15, 1985. "Insights," MWPI, January 7–April 13, 1986. "Nature in Art," MWPI, January 17–February 15, 1987. "The Expressionist Landscape," Birmingham Museum of Art, November 24, 1987–January 30, 1988 (traveling exhibition, cat. no. 39, illus. fig. 76). "American Masterworks from the MWPAI, Celebrating an Educational Alliance with Pratt Institute," Hirschl & Adler Galleries, New York, November 16–December 29, 2006 (catalog).

PUBLICATIONS

Paintings, Drawings & Sculptures in the Museum of Art (Utica, N.Y.: Munson-Williams-Proctor Institute, 1961), 16. Morgan, Ann Lee. *Arthur Dove: Life and Work, With a Catalogue Raisonné* (Newark, Del.: University of Delaware Press, 1984), cat. no. 37.14, illus., 245.

ELSIE DRIGGS

(Hartford, Conn., 1898–New York, N.Y., 1992)

76. *Cineraria*, 1928

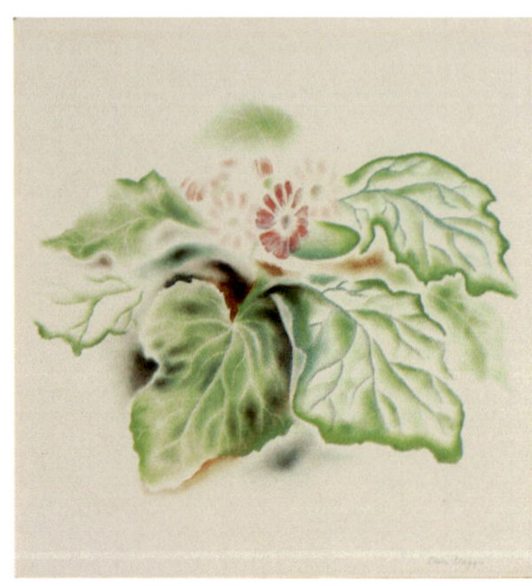

Pastel on smooth white wove paper
15 5/8 x 15 1/16 in.
57.319
Signed lower right (graphite): Elsie Driggs
Purchased from Charles Daniel Gallery, New York, January 1928

EXHIBITIONS

"Edward W. Root Loan Exhibition," Utica Art Society, Utica, N.Y., May 1928. "Edward W. Root Loan Exhibition," Utica Art Society, Utica, N.Y. May 1928. "Exhibition of Watercolors and Pastels by Eleven American Moderns from a Distinguished Private Collection," Munson-Williams-Proctor Institute, Utica, N.Y., fall 1938. "Edward Wales Root Bequest," MWPI, November 5, 1961–February 24, 1962 (catalog).

PUBLICATION

Paintings, Drawings & Sculptures in the Museum of Art (Utica, N.Y.: Munson-Williams-Proctor Institute, 1961), 16.

77. *Hydrangeas*, 1928

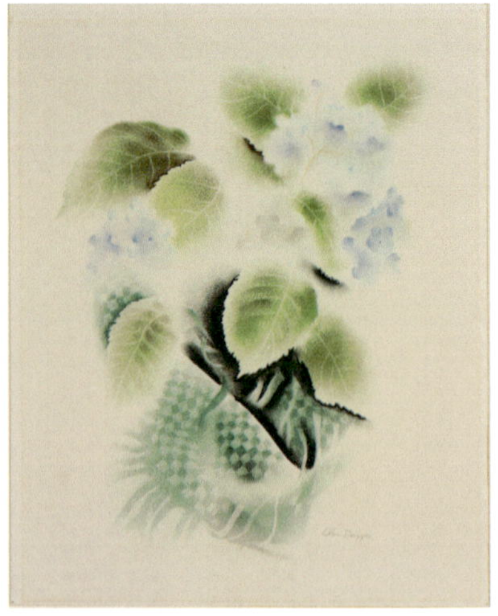

Pastel on smooth white paper
17 x 13 ¾ in.
57.137
Signed lower right (graphite): Elsie Driggs
Purchased from Charles Daniel Gallery, New York, November 1928

EXHIBITIONS

"Exhibition of Watercolors and Pastels by Eleven American Moderns from a Distinguished Private Collection," Munson-Williams-Proctor Institute, Utica, N.Y., fall 1938. "Paintings from the Collection of Edward W. Root," MWPI, September 29–October 20, 1946. "The Edward Root Collection," The Metropolitan Museum of Art, New York, February 12–April 12, 1953 (catalog, 2). The Strathmont Museum, Elmira, N.Y., June–September 1959. "Edward Wales Root Bequest," MWPI, November 5, 1961–February 24, 1962 (catalog). "Realism to Abstraction," State University College, Oneonta, N.Y., December 2–20, 1963.

PUBLICATION

Paintings, Drawings & Sculptures in the Museum of Art (Utica, N.Y.: Munson-Williams-Proctor Institute, 1961), 16.

LOUIS M. EILSHEMIUS

(Arlington, N.J., 1864–New York, N.Y., 1941)

78. *Black Hills, Delaware Water Gap (Back Country, Delaware Water Gap; Black Hills of Delaware Water Gap No. 2)*, 1896–97

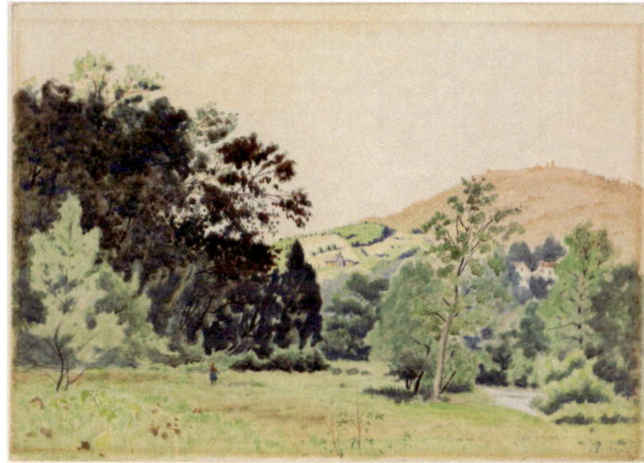

Watercolor on white wove watercolor paper
14 x 20 in.
57.138
Signed lower right (blue paint): Elshemus [artist used this simplified signature from 1890 to 1914]
Inscribed verso (graphite): Back Hills / Delaware
Purchased from Valentine Gallery, New York, March 1935

EXHIBITIONS

"Exhibition of Watercolors and Pastels by Eleven American Moderns from a Distinguished Private Collection," Munson-Williams-Proctor Institute, Utica, N.Y., fall 1938. "Paintings from the Collection of Edward W. Root," MWPI, September 29–October 20, 1946. "The Edward Root Collection," The Metropolitan Museum of Art, New York, February 12–April 12, 1953 (catalog, 2). "Edward Wales Root Bequest," MWPI, November 5, 1961–February 24, 1962 (catalog). "Watercolors: Historic and Contemporary," Hathorn Gallery, Skidmore College, Saratoga Springs, N.Y., February 4–20, 1977 (cat. no. 18). "American Art in Upstate New York," Albright-Knox Art Gallery, Buffalo, N.Y., July 12, 1974–April 27, 1975 (traveling exhibition, catalog, 19).

PUBLICATION

Paintings, Drawings & Sculptures in the Museum of Art (Utica, N.Y.: Munson-Williams-Proctor Institute, 1961), 16.

JIMMY ERNST

(Cologne, Germany, 1920–New York, N.Y., 1984)

79. *Calligraphics*, 1949

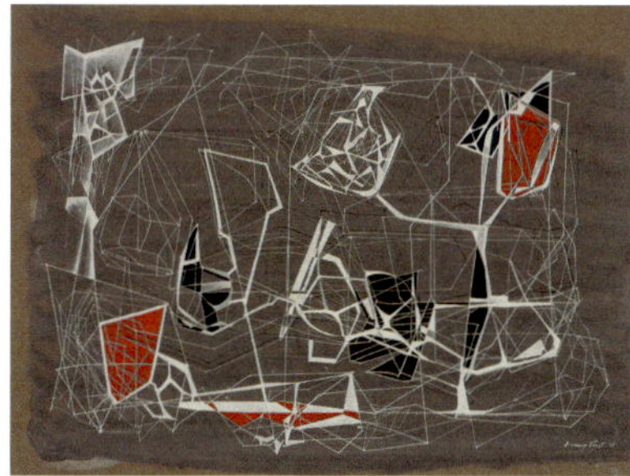

Gouache on brown paper
16 x 22 1/16 in.
57.139
Signed and dated lower right (white paint): Jimmy Ernst 49
Purchased from Laurel Gallery, New York

EXHIBITIONS

"Jimmy Ernst Gouaches," Laurel Gallery, New York, March 25–April 7, 1950. "Current Trends in British and American Painting from the Collection of Edward W. Root," Munson-Williams-Proctor Institute, Utica, N.Y., December 3–31, 1950 (traveling exhibition, cat. no. 8). "The Edward Root Collection," The Metropolitan Museum of Art, New York, February 12–April 12, 1953 (catalog, 2). "Trends in 20th-Century American Painting," Union College, Schenectady, N.Y., March 5–26, 1961. "American Watercolors and Drawings," Root Art Center, Hamilton College, Clinton, N.Y., April 4–May 7, 1961. "Edward Wales Root Bequest," MWPI, November 5, 1961–February 24, 1962 (catalog). "On Paper," American Federation of Arts, September 1966–September 1967 (traveling exhibition). "20th-Century Prints and Drawings," Schenectady Museum & Planetarium, Schenectady, N.Y., December 15, 1971–January 15, 1972.

PUBLICATION

Paintings, Drawings & Sculptures in the Museum of Art (Utica, N.Y.: Munson-Williams-Proctor Institute, 1961), 17.

80. *Honky Tonk*, 1951

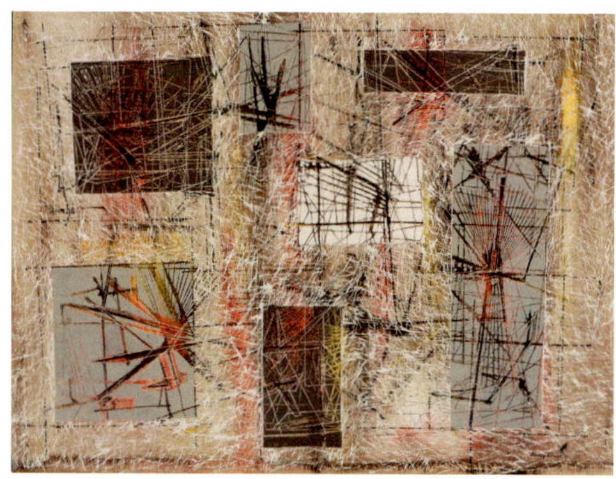

Gouache on heavy white paper
22 3/8 x 30 in.
57.140
Signed and dated lower right (black paint): Jimmy Ernst '51
Purchased from Grace Borgenicht Gallery, New York, February 1952

EXHIBITIONS

"The Edward Root Collection," The Metropolitan Museum of Art, New York, February 12–April 12, 1953 (catalog, 2). "20th-Century American Painting from the Edward W. Root Collection," Smithsonian Institution, Washington, D.C., July 1959–July 1960 (traveling exhibition). "Edward Wales Root Bequest," Munson-Williams-Proctor Institute, Utica, N.Y., November 5, 1961–February 24, 1962 (catalog). "American 20th-Century Watercolors from MWPI," Albany Institute of History and Art, Albany, N.Y., September 10–October 4, 1967. Rome Community Art Center, Rome, N.Y., September 14–November 9, 1975. "Insights," MWPI, June 10–October 15, 1986 and March 12–June 2, 1987.

PUBLICATION

Paintings, Drawings & Sculptures in the Museum of Art (Utica, N.Y.: Munson-Williams-Proctor Institute, 1961), 17.

JIMMY ERNST

81. *Improvisation*, 1949

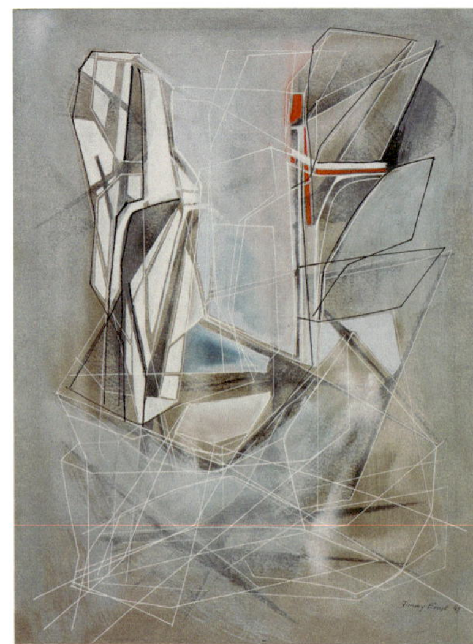

Tempera on gray paper
14 ¾ x 11 ¼ in.
57.141
Signed and dated lower right (black ink): Jimmy Ernst 49
Purchased from Laurel Gallery, New York

EXHIBITIONS

"Jimmy Ernst Gouaches," Laurel Gallery, New York, March 25–April 7, 1950.

"American Watercolors and Drawings," Root Art Center, Hamilton College, Clinton, N.Y., April 4–May 7, 1961. "Edward Wales Root Bequest," Munson-Williams-Proctor Institute, Utica, N.Y., November 5, 1961–February 24, 1962 (catalog). "European Sources of Contemporary American Art: Kandinsky," Root Art Center, September 15–October 6, 1963 (cat. no. 18). "20th-Century Prints and Drawings," Schenectady Museum & Planetarium, Schenectady, N.Y., December 15, 1971–January 15, 1972.

"Contemporary Artists: Early and Late Paintings," Root Art Center, April 4–May 2, 1973. "Watercolors: Historic and Contemporary," Hathorn Gallery, Skidmore College, Saratoga Springs, N.Y., February 4–20, 1977 (cat. no. 19).

PUBLICATIONS

Paintings, Drawings & Sculptures in the Museum of Art (Utica, N.Y.: Munson-Williams-Proctor Institute, 1961), 17. Prior, Harris K. "Edward Root–Talent Scout," *Art in America* L (1962): 71, illus. no. 6.

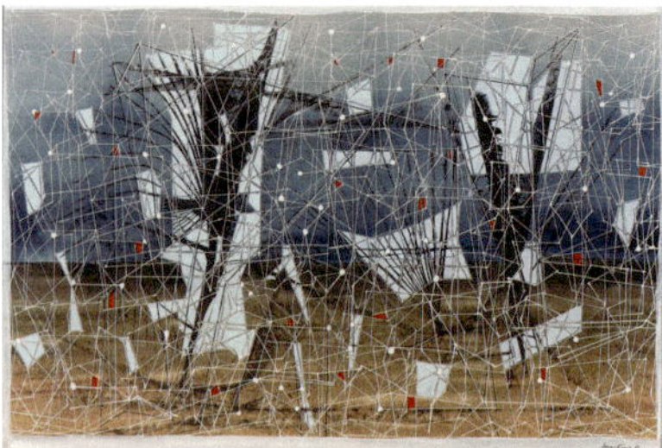

82. *Polar Space*, 1951

Gouache on paper
11 ¼ x 17 ½ in.
57.142
Signed and dated lower right (black ink): Jimmy Ernst 51
Purchased from Grace Borgenicht Gallery, New York, May 1951

EXHIBITIONS

"The Edward Root Collection," The Metropolitan Museum of Art, New York, February 12–April 12, 1953 (catalog, 2). "Five Decades of American Painting," Union College, Schenectady, N.Y., September 27–October 23, 1959. "Edward Wales Root Bequest," Munson-Williams-Proctor Institute, Utica, N.Y., November 5, 1961–February 24, 1962 (catalog, illus.). Root Art Center, Hamilton College, Clinton, N.Y., December 9–19, 1963. "Abstract Paintings and Drawings from the Root Bequest," Root Art Center, September 11–October 9, 1966.

"Paintings and Drawings from the Edward W. Root Bequest," Root Art Center, April 7–May 5, 1968. "The Root Bequest," Root Art Center, May 11–June 8, 1969. "Exhibition of American Paintings," Schenectady Museum & Planetarium, Schenectady, N.Y., March 20–April 30, 1970. "American Drawings and Watercolors from the Munson-Williams-Proctor Institute," E.B. Crocker Art Gallery, Sacramento, Calif., October 25–November 25, 1974 (cat. no. 23). "Five Decades of Collecting: Edward W. Root," MWPI, April 2–May 28, 1978. "Edward W. Root: Collector and Teacher," Fred L. Emerson Gallery, Hamilton College, October 2–November 14, 1982 (catalog, 58, illus., 58). "Influences of Klee," MWPI, December 19, 1987–May 13, 1988.

PUBLICATIONS

Hale, Robert Beverly, "The Growth of a Collection," *The Metropolitan Museum of Art Bulletin* XI (February 1953), illus., 159. Louchheim, Aline B. "A Collector with Personal Vision," *New York Times*, February 15, 1953, sect. X, 11, illus. *Paintings, Drawings & Sculptures in the Museum of Art* (Utica, N.Y.: Munson-Williams-Proctor Institute, 1961), 17.

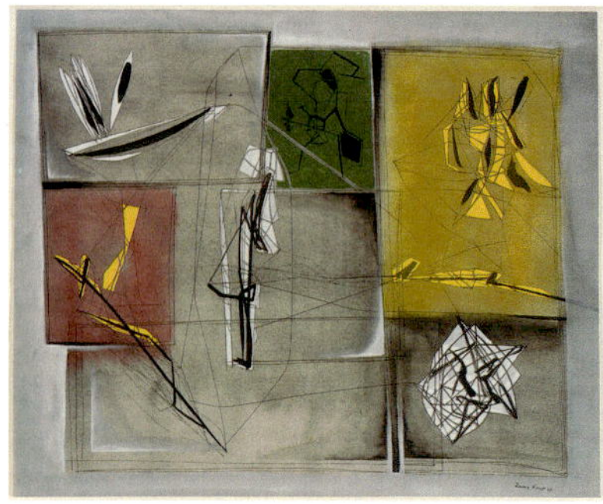

83. *Several Shadows*, 1949

Transparent and opaque watercolor and ink on light watercolor paper
17 ¼ x 21 $^{3}/_{16}$ in.
57.143
Signed and dated lower right (black ink): Jimmy Ernst 49
Purchased from the Laurel Gallery, New York

EXHIBITIONS

"Jimmy Ernst Gouaches," Laurel Gallery, New York, March 25–April 7, 1950. "Current Trends in British and American Painting from the Collection of Edward W. Root," Munson-Williams-Proctor Institute, Utica, N.Y., December 3–31, 1950 (traveling exhibition, cat. no. 9). "20th-Century American Painting from the Edward W. Root Collection," Smithsonian Institution, Washington, D.C., July 1959–July 1960 (traveling exhibition). "Edward Wales Root Bequest," MWPI, November 5, 1961–February 24, 1962 (catalog). "Abstract Paintings and Drawings from the Root Bequest," Root Art Center, Hamilton College, Clinton, N.Y., September 11–October 9, 1966. "American 20th-Century Watercolors from MWPI," Albany Institute of History and Art, Albany, N.Y., September 10–October 4, 1967. "Watercolors: Historic and Contemporary," Hathorn Gallery, Skidmore College, Saratoga Springs, N.Y., February 4–20, 1977 (cat. no. 20). "American Twentieth-Century Watercolors at the Munson-Williams-Proctor Arts Institute," MWPAI, April 30–July 10, 2000 (traveling exhibition, cat. no. 44, illus.).

PUBLICATIONS

"Jimmy Ernst," *Art News* XLIX (March 1950): 46. "Jimmy Ernst," *Magazine of Art* 43 (April 1950): 134, illus. *Paintings, Drawings & Sculptures in the Museum of Art* (Utica, N.Y.: Munson-Williams-Proctor Institute, 1961), 17.

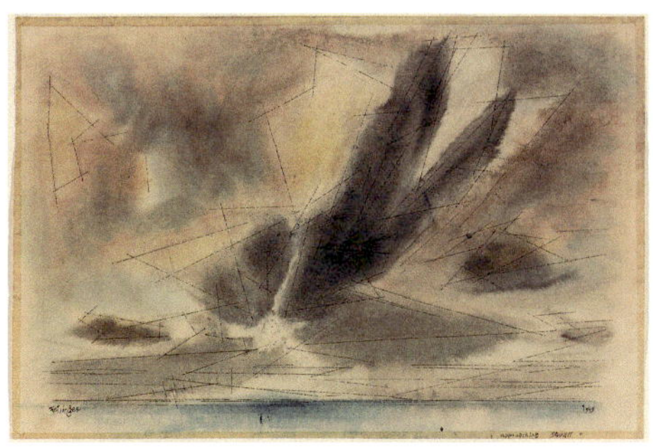

LYONEL FEININGER

(New York, N.Y., 1871–1956)

84. *Approaching Squall*, 1949

Watercolor and ink on pink-toned laid paper
12 ¼ x 18 ¾ in.
57.144
Signed lower left (black ink): Feininger; dated lower right (black ink): 949 / (graphite): "Approaching Squall"
Inscribed verso lower left (graphite): NY 1151
Purchased from Curt Valentin-Buchholz Gallery, New York, March 1950

EXHIBITIONS

"Lyonel Feininger," Curt Valentin-Buchholz Gallery, New York, April 11–29, 1950 (cat. no. 30). "Current Trends in British and American Painting from the Collection of Edward W. Root," Munson-Williams-Proctor Institute, Utica, N.Y., December 3–31, 1950 (traveling exhibition, cat. no. 10). "The Edward Root Collection," The Metropolitan Museum of Art, New York, February 12–April 12, 1953 (catalog, 2). "American Watercolors and Drawings," Root Art Center, Hamilton College, Clinton, N.Y., April 4–May 7, 1961. "Edward Wales Root Bequest," MWPI, November 5, 1961–February 24, 1962 (catalog). "On Paper," American Federation of Arts, September 1966–September 1967 (traveling exhibition). "The Root Bequest," Root Art Center, May 11–June 8, 1969. "American Art in Upstate New York," Albright-Knox Art Gallery, Buffalo, N.Y., July 12, 1974–April 27, 1975 (traveling exhibition, catalog, 19). "Watercolors: Historic and Contemporary," Hathorn Gallery, Skidmore College, Saratoga Springs, N.Y., February 4–20, 1977 (cat. no. 21). "Five Decades of Collecting: Edward W. Root," MWPI, April 2–May 28, 1978.

PUBLICATION

Paintings, Drawings & Sculptures in the Museum of Art (Utica, N.Y.: Munson-Williams-Proctor Institute, 1961), 17.

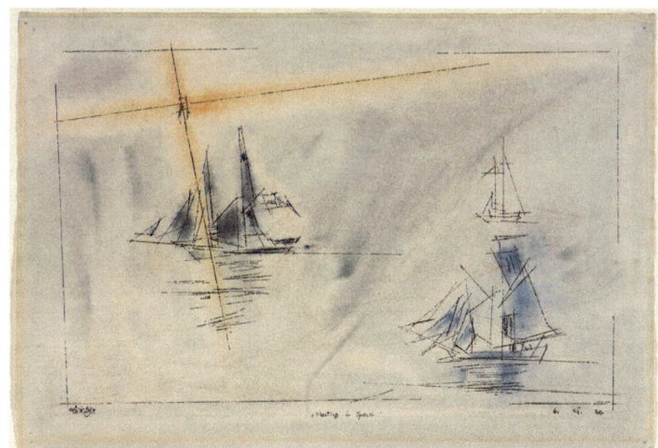

85. *Floating in Space*
December 6, 1944

Watercolor and ink on thin white paper
Watermark (lower left): Ingres
12 ⅜ x 18 ¼ in.
57.145
Signed lower left (black ink): Feininger
Inscribed lower center (black ink): "Floating in Space"
Inscribed lower right (black ink): 6. XII. 44
Inscribed verso lower right (graphite): $300
Purchased from Curt Valentin-Buchholz Gallery, February 1946

EXHIBITIONS

"Lyonel Feininger: Recent Paintings, Watercolors," Curt Valentin-Buchholz Gallery, New York, January 29–February 23, 1946 (cat. no. 33). "Paintings from the Collection of Edward W. Root," Munson-Williams-Proctor Institute, Utica, N.Y., September 29–October 20, 1946. "Lyonel Feininger Exhibition Arranged in Celebration of the Artist's Birthday," Curt Valentin Gallery, New York, March 18– April 12, 1952 (cat. no. 44). "In Memoriam," American Federation of Arts, November 1957–November 1958 (traveling exhibition). "20th-Century American Painting from the Edward W. Root Collection," Smithsonian Institution, Washington, D.C., May 1959–May 1960 (traveling exhibition). "Edward Wales Root Bequest," MWPI, November 5, 1961–February 24, 1962 (catalog). "American 20th-Century Watercolors from MWPI," Albany Institute of History and Art, Albany, N.Y., September 10–October 4, 1967. "Paintings and Drawings from the Edward W. Root Bequest," Root Art Center, Hamilton College, Clinton, N.Y., April 7–May 5, 1968. "Exhibition of American Paintings," Schenectady Museum & Planetarium, Schenectady, N.Y., March 20– April 30, 1970. "American Drawings and Watercolors from the Munson-Williams-Proctor Institute," E. B. Crocker Art Gallery, Sacramento, Calif., October 25–November 24, 1974 (cat. no. 24). "Watercolors: Historic and Contemporary," Hathorn Gallery, Skidmore College, Saratoga Springs, N.Y., February 4–20, 1977 (cat. no. 22). "American Twentieth-Century Watercolors at the Munson-Williams-Proctor Arts Institute," MWPAI, April 30–July 10, 2000 (traveling exhibition, cat. no. 32, illus.).

PUBLICATIONS

Paintings, Drawings & Sculptures in the Museum of Art (Utica, N.Y.: Munson-Williams-Proctor Institute, 1961), 17.
American Art in Upstate New York (Buffalo, N.Y.: Buffalo Fine Arts Academy, 1974), 19.

PERLE FINE

(Boston, Mass., 1908–East Hampton, N.Y., 1988)

86. *Taurus*, 1946

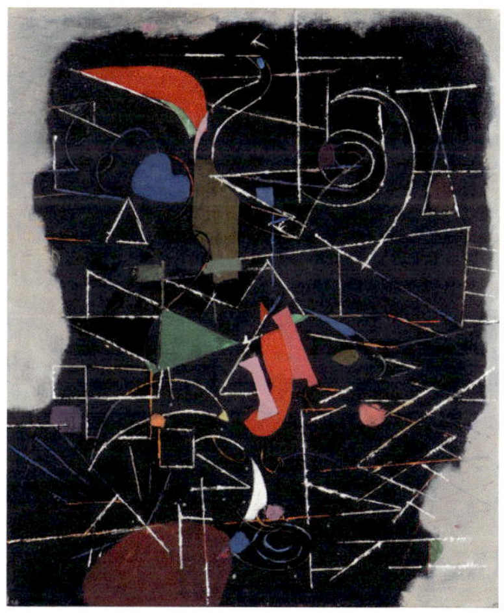

Oil on canvas
28 x 24 in.
57.311
Signed and dated lower left center (black paint): P. Fine '46
Inscribed verso on frame at top: Perle Fine Taurus / 51 W. 8th St. NY
Purchased from the Nierendorf Gallery, New York, April 1946

EXHIBITIONS

"Recent Paintings by Perle Fine," Nierendorf Gallery, New York, April 1–20, 1946 (checklist no. 7). "Edward Wales Root Bequest," Munson-Williams-Proctor Institute, Utica, N.Y., November 5, 1961–February 24, 1962 (catalog).

PUBLICATION

Paintings, Drawings & Sculptures in the Museum of Art (Utica, N.Y.: Munson-Williams-Proctor Institute, 1961), 17.

DAVID FREDENTHAL

(Detroit, Mich., 1914–Rome, Italy, 1958)

87. *Rocky Mountains*, 1946

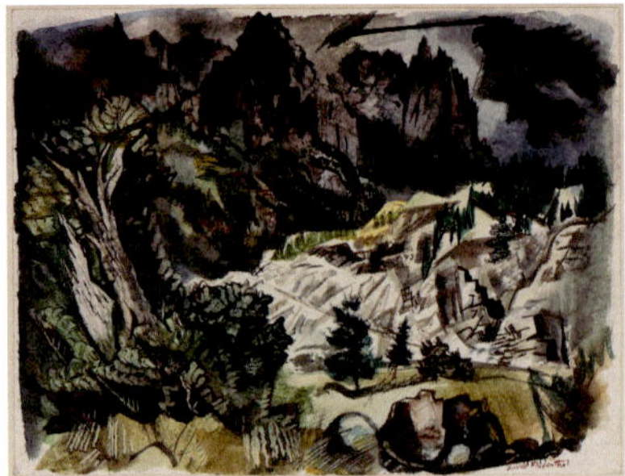

Watercolor on thick white paper
11 15/16 x 16 in.
57.322
Signed lower right (red ink): David Fredenthal
Purchased from The Downtown Gallery, New York

EXHIBITION

"Edward Wales Root Bequest," Munson-Williams-Proctor Institute, Utica, N.Y., November 5, 1961–February 24, 1962 (catalog).

PUBLICATION

Paintings, Drawings & Sculptures in the Museum of Art (Utica, N.Y.: Munson-Williams-Proctor Institute, 1961), 17.

88. *Two Wounded Soldiers*

Not dated

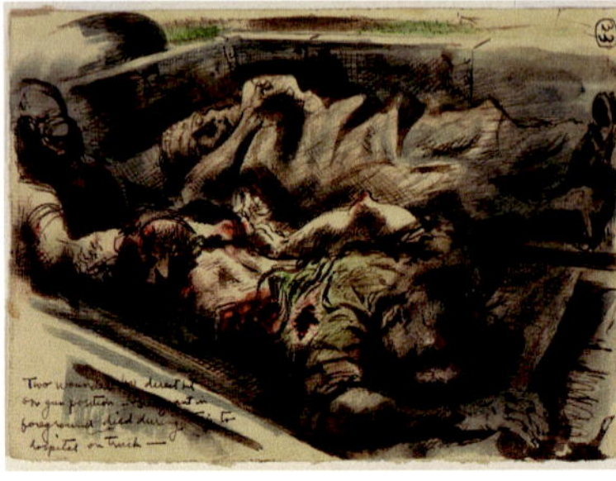

Watercolor and ink on laid paper
5 ½ x 7 ¾ in.
57.290
Inscribed lower left (brown ink): Two wounded by direct hit / on gun position–Sargeant in / foreground died during trip to / hospital on truck– ; upper right (brown ink): 33 [encircled]
Purchased from The Downtown Gallery, New York

EXHIBITIONS

"Edward Wales Root Bequest," Munson-Williams-Proctor Institute, Utica, N.Y., November 5, 1961–February 24, 1962 (catalog). "The Figure in 20th-Century Paintings and Drawings," Root Art Center, Hamilton College, Clinton, N.Y., April 15–May 6, 1962. "American 20th-Century Watercolors from MWPI," Albany Institute of History and Art, Albany, N.Y., September 10–October 4, 1967. "American Drawings and Watercolors from the Munson-Williams-Proctor Institute," E. B. Crocker Art Gallery, Sacramento, Calif., October 25–November 24, 1974 (cat. no. 25).

PUBLICATION

Paintings, Drawings & Sculptures in the Museum of Art (Utica, N.Y.: Munson-Williams-Proctor Institute, 1961), 17.

LEE GATCH

(Baltimore, Md., 1902–Trenton, N.J., 1968)

89. *The Eye of Silence*, 1951

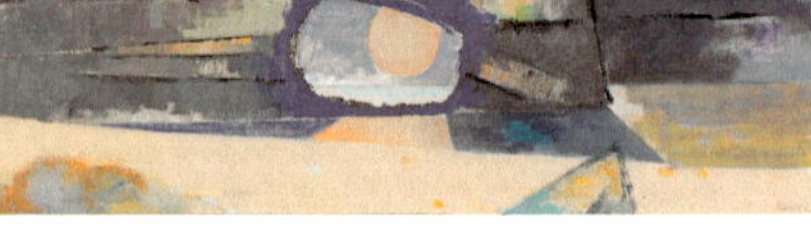

Oil on canvas mounted on wood
7 x 32 ⅛ in.
57.146
Signed lower right (brown paint): GATCH
Purchased from J. B. Neumann–New Art Circle, New York, fall 1951
[Letter from artist Max Kahn to Joseph S. Trovato, February 3, 1975: "When Gatch first showed me this panel he told me that he was well aware of the fact that the title was one that Paul Klee had already used. He searched unsucessfully for a title of his own but could discover none that conveyed so exactly the content of his painting."]

EXHIBITIONS

"The Edward Root Collection," The Metropolitan Museum of Art, New York, February 12–April 12, 1953 (catalog, 2). "A Retrospective Exhibition of Paintings by Lee Gatch," Grace Borgenicht Gallery, New York, March 8–27, 1954 (traveling exhibition, cat. no. 16). "New Trends in 20th-Century American Painting," Root Art Center, Hamilton College, Clinton, N.Y., October 26–November 30, 1958. "20th-Century American Painting from the Edward W. Root Collection," Smithsonian Institution, Washington, D.C., July 1959–July 1960 (traveling exhibition). Museum of Art Building inaugural exhibition, Munson-Williams-Proctor Institute, Utica, N.Y., October 15–December 31, 1960. "New Trends in 20th-Century American Paintings," Union College, Schenectady, N.Y., March 5–26, 1961. "Edward Wales Root Bequest," MWPI, November 5, 1961–February 24, 1962 (catalog). "Abstract Paintings and Drawings from the Root Bequest," Root Art Center, September 11–October 9, 1966.

PUBLICATION

Paintings, Drawings & Sculptures in the Museum of Art (Utica, N.Y.: Munson-Williams-Proctor Institute, 1961), 18.

90. *High Tension Tower (Green Landscapes; Garden Landscapes)*

Ca. 1942

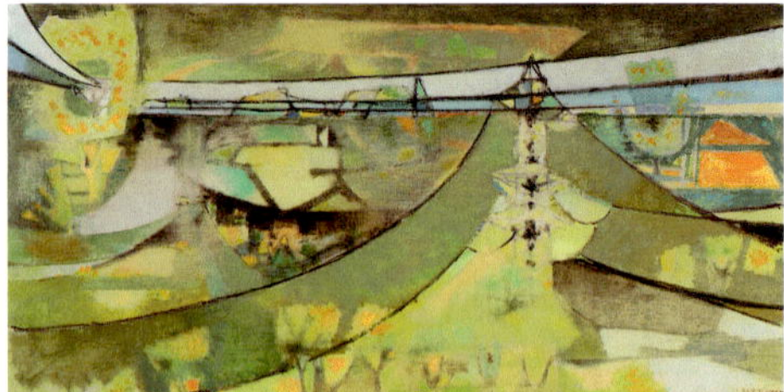

Oil on linen
20 ⅛ x 40 ⅛ in.
57.147
Signed lower right (brown paint): LEE GATCH
Purchased from J. B. Neumann–New Art Circle, New York, 1949 or 1950
[Undated letter from Gatch to J. B. Neumann: "The title got changed somehow when it was at the Willard Gallery. Would you agree that *High Tension Tower* would explain the composition a little better?"]

EXHIBITIONS

"Lee Gatch," Willard Gallery, New York, February 15–March 6, 1943. "Painting in the United States, 1945," Carnegie Institute, Pittsburgh, Pa., October 11–December 9, 1945 (cat. no. 134). "Lee Gatch," J. B. Neumann–New Art Circle, New York, March 18–April 20, 1946 (cat. no. 12, as *Green Landscape*). "Current Trends in British and American Painting from the Collection of Edward W. Root," Munson-Williams-Proctor Institute, Utica, N.Y., December 3–31, 1950 (traveling exhibition, cat. no. 11). "The Edward Root Collection," The Metropolitan Museum of Art, New York, February 12–April 12, 1953 (catalog, 2). "Some Contemporary Works of Art," The Cleveland Museum of Art, Cleveland, Ohio, November 11, 1958–January 1, 1959 (cat. no. 14, illus. no. 14). "Lee Gatch Retrospective Exhibition," American Federation of Arts, February 2, 1960–February 26, 1961 (traveling exhibition, cat. no. 21, illus.). "Edward Wales Root Bequest," MWPI, November 5, 1961–February 24, 1962 (catalog, illus.). "Paintings and Drawings from the Edward W. Root Bequest," Root Art Center, Hamilton College, Clinton, N.Y., April 7–May 5, 1968. "Five Decades of Collecting: Edward W. Root," MWPI, April 2–May 28, 1978. "Edward W. Root: Collector and Teacher," Fred L. Emerson Gallery, Hamilton College, October 2–November 14, 1982 (catalog, 57). "Influences of Klee," MWPI, December 19, 1987–May 13, 1988.

PUBLICATIONS

Tannenbaum, Libby. "Notes at Mid-Century," *Magazine of Art* XLIII (December 1950): 291, illus. Hale, Robert Beverly. "The Growth of a Collection," *The Metropolitan Museum of Art Bulletin* XI (February 1953): 155, illus., 162. Hayes, Jr., Bartlett H. "The Root of American Painting, " *Art News* LVI (January 1958): 61, illus. fig. 7. *Paintings, Drawings & Sculptures in the Museum of Art* (Utica, N.Y.: Munson-Williams-Proctor Institute, 1961), 18. Berryman, Florence S. "Art News of the D.C. Area: Gatch Retrospective at Phillips Gallery," *Star* (Washington D.C.), February 19, 1961. Gerdts, Jr., William H. *Painting and Sculpture in New Jersey*, The New Jersey Historical Series, vol. 21 (Princeton, N.J.: D. Van Nostrand Co., Inc., 1964), 242, illus. Michener, James. *Lee Gatch* (New York: Staempfli Gallery, 1967).

91. *Winter Garden No. 3 (Winter Garden)*, 1951

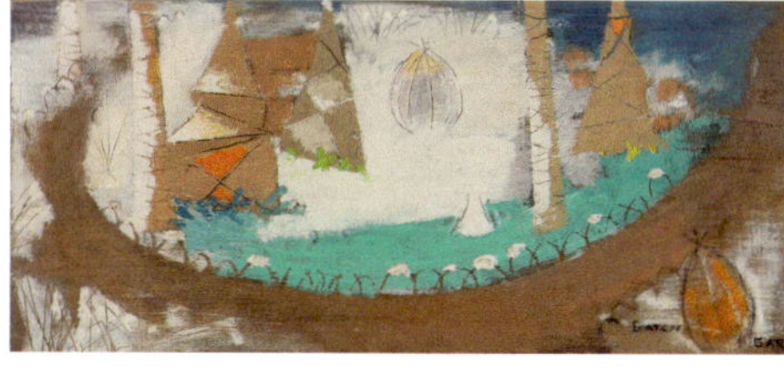

Oil on hardwood panel
7 3/16 x 16 3/8 in.
57.148
Signed lower right (black paint): GATCH
Purchased from J. B. Neumann–New Art Circle, 1951

EXHIBITIONS

"The Edward Root Collection," The Metropolitan Museum of Art, New York, February 12–April 12, 1953 (catalog, 2). Museum of Art Building inaugural exhibition, Munson-Williams-Proctor Institute, Utica, N.Y., October 15–December 31, 1960. "Edward Wales Root Bequest," MWPI, November 5, 1961–February 24, 1962 (catalog, as *Winter Garden*).

PUBLICATION

Paintings, Drawings & Sculptures in the Museum of Art (Utica, N.Y.: Munson-Williams-Proctor Institute, 1961), 18 [as *Winter Garden*].

92. *Winter Garden No. 5*, 1952

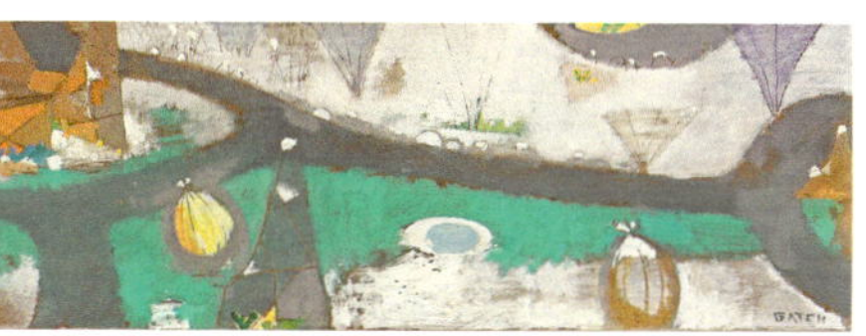

Oil on hardwood panel
7 7/16 x 25 1/4 in.
57.149
Signed lower right (black paint): GATCH
Purchased from J. B. Neumann–New Art Circle, New York, 1952

EXHIBITIONS

"Five Decades of American Painting," Union College, Schenectady, N.Y., September 27–October 23, 1959. Museum of Art Building inaugural exhibition, Munson-Williams-Proctor Institute, Utica, N.Y., October 15–December 31, 1960. "Edward Wales Root Bequest," MWPI, November 5, 1961–February 24, 1962 (catalog, as *Winter Garden No. 2*). "Five Decades of Collecting: Edward W. Root," MWPI, April 2–May 28, 1978.

PUBLICATION

Paintings, Drawings & Sculptures in the Museum of Art (Utica, N.Y.: Munson-Williams-Proctor Institute, 1961), 18 [as *Winter Garden No. 2*].

[Note on Lee Gatch's "Winter Garden" series: Letter from Jenny N. Strauss to Joseph S. Trovato [MWPI Curator], April 12, 1975, with information from her Master's thesis on Gatch, Washington University, St. Louis, 1973: "There are six of the *Winter Garden* series on my list of works, including your two. We know there are more because the one owned by Elizabeth Driggs (Mrs. Gatch's [artist Elsie Driggs] sister) is numbered 7, though it was painted in 1946, and hence predates the one that is numbered 2! *Winter Garden #1* is not panel shaped, and so can't be considered as an integral part of the series. *W [inter] G [arden] #2* is (or was) owned by Geo. Fitch of N.Y. dated 1948, no measurements. *Winter Garden #3*, dated 1951 is yours. Three *Winter Gardens* are dated 1952. *W [inter] G [arden] #4* is owned by Margaret Oschman of Glen More, Pennsylvania. Oil on panel, dimensions 5 ½ x 13 ½. *W [inter] G [arden] #5* is yours. *W [inter] G [arden] #6* belongs to the Heller Foundation, Dickerson, Md.; no dimensions. The only other Winter Garden on my list is the above mentioned #7, owned by Miss Driggs, painted in 1946, dimensions given by Miss Driggs as follows: painting 6 ½ x 13 ½; panel 8 ½ x 18 5/8 (oil on wood panel)."]

JOSEPH GLASCO

(Paul's Valley, Okla., 1925–Galveston, Tex., 1996)

93. *Boy*, 1952

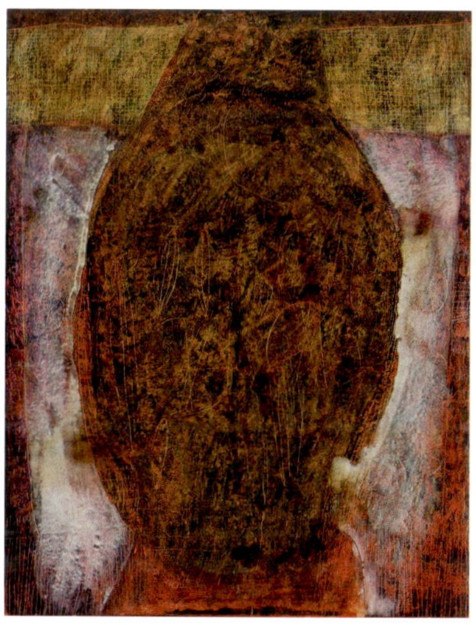

Gouache with incised lines on scratchboard
13 7/8 x 11 in.
57.150
Purchased from Catherine Viviano Gallery, New York

EXHIBITIONS

"The Edward Root Collection," The Metropolitan Museum of Art, New York, February 12–April 12, 1953 (catalog, 2). "Edward Wales Root Bequest," Munson-Williams-Proctor Institute, Utica, N.Y., November 5, 1961–February 24, 1962 (catalog). "The Figure in 20th-Century Paintings and Drawings," Root Art Center, Hamilton College, Clinton, N.Y., April 10–May 6, 1962. "European Sources of Contemporary American Art: Kandinsky," Root Art Center, September 15–October 6, 1963 (cat. no. 19). "Learning about Pictures from Mr. Root," Root Art Center, January 5–31, 1965 (catalog). "On Paper," American Federation of Arts, September 1966–September 1967 (traveling exhibition). Kirkland Art Center, Clinton, N.Y., October 16–November 16, 1974. Rome Art and Community Center, Rome, N.Y., September 14–November 9, 1975. "Figuratively Speaking," MWPI, April 11–November 10, 1985. "Life Lines: American Master Drawings (1788–1962) from the Munson-Williams-Proctor Institute," MWPI, September 17–November 13, 1994 (traveling exhibition, cat. no. 56, illus., 128, color pl. 23).

PUBLICATION

Paintings, Drawings & Sculptures in the Museum of Art (Utica, N.Y.: Munson-Williams-Proctor Institute, 1961), 18.

94. *Male Head*, 1953

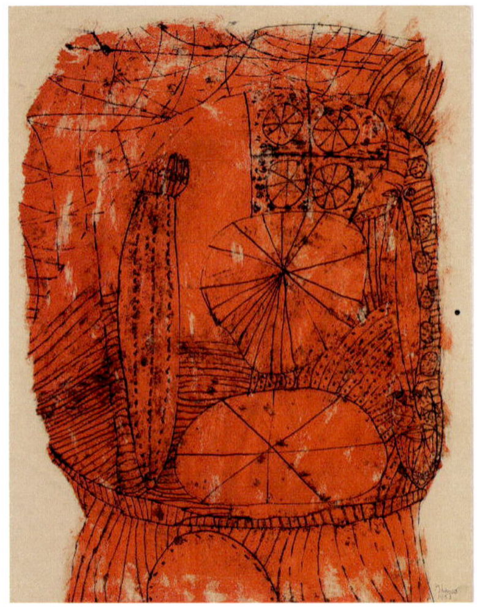

Oil and ink on heavy wove paper
19 ⅞ x 15 ¾ in.
57.151
Signed and dated lower right (black ink): Glasco / 1953
Purchased from Catherine Viviano Gallery, New York

EXHIBITIONS

"New Trends in 20th-Century American Painting," Root Art Center, Hamilton College, Clinton, N.Y., October 26–November 30, 1958. Museum of Art Building inaugural exhibition, Munson-Williams-Proctor Institute, Utica, N.Y., October 15–December 31, 1960. "New Trends in 20th-Century American Painting," Union College, Schenectady, N.Y., March 5–26, 1961. "American Watercolors and Drawings," Root Art Center, April 4–May 7, 1961. "Edward Wales Root Bequest," MWPI, November 5, 1961–February 24, 1962 (catalog). Kirkland Art Center, Clinton, N.Y., October 16–November 16, 1974.

PUBLICATION

Paintings, Drawings & Sculptures in the Museum of Art (Utica, N.Y.: Munson-Williams-Proctor Institute, 1961), 18.

95. *Marvello*, 1953

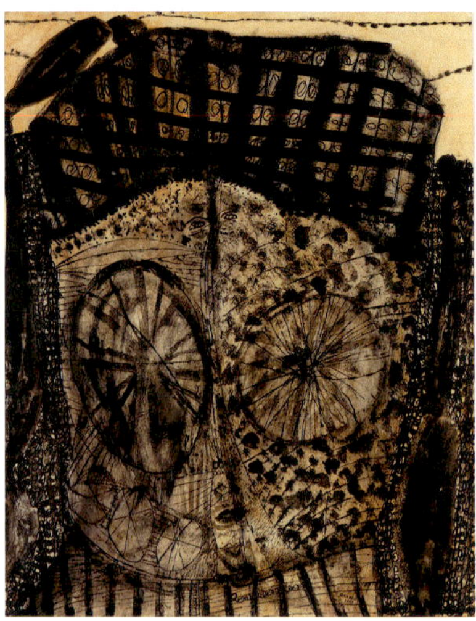

Watercolor with India ink on textured wove paper
19 ⅞ x 15 ⅞ in.
57.152
Signed and dated lower right (black ink): Glasco / 1953
Inscribed bottom center (black ink): M A R V E L L O [each letter encircled]
Purchased from Catherine Viviano Gallery, New York

EXHIBITIONS

"The People of Joseph Glasco, An Exhibition of Paintings, Sculpture and Drawings," Catherine Viviano Gallery, New York, March 24–April 18, 1953 (cat. no. 1). "Edward Wales Root Bequest," Munson-Williams-Proctor Institute, Utica, N.Y., November 5, 1961–February 24, 1962 (catalog). "Abstract Paintings and Drawings from the Root Bequest," Root Art Center, Hamilton College, Clinton, N.Y., September 11–October 9, 1966. "American 20th-Century Watercolors from MWPI," Albany Institute of History and Art, Albany, N.Y., September 10–October 4, 1967.

PUBLICATION

Paintings, Drawings & Sculptures in the Museum of Art (Utica, N.Y.: Munson-Williams-Proctor Institute, 1961), 18.

ARSHILE GORKY

(Khorkom Vari Haiyotz Dzor, Armenia, 1904–Sherman, Conn., 1948)

96. *Making the Calendar*, 1947

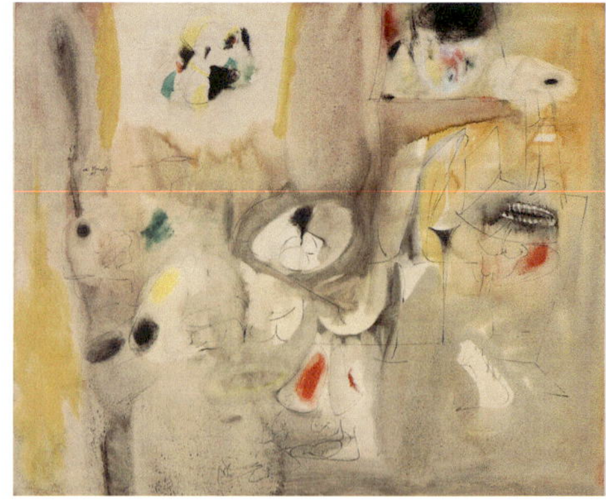

Oil on canvas
34 x 41 in.
57.153
Signed and dated left center (black ink): A. Gorky / '47
[Purchased from Kootz Gallery, New York]

EXHIBITIONS

"Arshile Gorky," Julien Levy Gallery, New York, March 23–April 10, 1948. "Selected Paintings by the Late Arshile Gorky," Kootz Gallery, New York, March 28–April 24, 1950. "Current Trends in British and American Painting from the Collection of Edward W. Root," Munson-Williams-Proctor Institute, Utica, N.Y., December 3–31, 1950 (traveling exhibition, cat. no. 12). "The Edward Root Collection," The Metropolitan Museum of Art, New York, February 12–April 12, 1953 (catalog, 2). "New Trends in 20th-Century American Painting," Root Art Center, Hamilton College, Clinton, N.Y., October 26–November 30, 1958. "20th-Century American Painting from the Edward W. Root Collection," Smithsonian Institution, Washington, D.C., July 1959–July 1960 (traveling exhibition). Museum of Art Building inaugural exhibition, MWPI, October 15–December 31, 1960. "New Trends in 20th-Century American Painting," Union College, Schenectady, N.Y., March 5– 26, 1961. "Edward Wales Root Bequest," MWPI, November 5, 1961–February 24, 1962 (catalog). "XXXI Esposizione Biennale Internazionale d'Arte," Venice, Italy, June 17–October 7, 1962 (cat.

no. 27). "Arshile Gorky: Paintings, Drawings, Studies," The Museum of Modern Art, New York, December 19, 1962–February 12, 1963 (traveling exhibition, cat. no. 94). "European Sources of Contemporary American Art: Kandinsky," Root Art Center, September 15–October 6, 1963 (cat. no. 20). "American Painting 1910 to 1960: A Special Exhibition Celebrating the 50th Anniversary of the Association of College Unions," Fine Art Gallery, Indiana University, Bloomington, Ind., April 19–May 10, 1964 (cat. no. 26, illus.). "Arshile Gorky, Paintings and Drawings," The Arts Council of Great Britain, Tate Gallery, London, April 2–May 2, 1965 (traveling exhibition, illus. no. 78). "Abstract Paintings and Drawings from the Root Bequest," Root Art Center, September 11–October 9, 1966. "Twentieth-Century American Painting," Grand Rapids Art Museum, Grand Rapids, Mich., April 1–30, 1967. "From El Greco to Pollock: Early and Late Works by European and American Artists," The Baltimore Museum of Art, Baltimore, Md., October 22–December 8, 1968 (cat. no. 106, illus., 129). "The Disappearance and Reappearance of the Image: American Painting Since 1945," International Art Program, National Collection of Fine Arts, Smithsonian Institution, Washington, D.C., January–November 1969 (traveling exhibition, catalog, 80, illus., 19). "In Search of the Present: The American Prophets," Lowe Art Museum, University of Miami, Coral Gables, Fla., February 22–March 25, 1973 (cat. no. 120). "Arshile Gorky: Drawings to Paintings," University Art Museum, Austin, Tex., October 12–November 23, 1975 (traveling exhibition, catalog, 62, illus. fig. 1). "Themes in American Painting," Grand Rapids Art Museum, October 1–November 30, 1977 (catalog, illus. no. 100). "Five Decades of Collecting: Edward W. Root," MWPI, April 2–May 28, 1978. "Two Hundred Years of American Art," The Art Museum Association of America, November 15, 1986–May 8, 1988 (traveling exhibition, cat. no. 66, illus., 80). "Abstract Expressionism: Other Dimensions," The Jane Vorhees Zimmerli Art Museum, Rutgers University, March 25–June 13, 1990 (traveling exhibition, cat. no. 31, illus. fig. 12). "American Art in the Twentieth Century," Royal Academy of Arts, London, September 9–December 12, 1993 (traveling exhibition, cat. no. 85, illus.). "Arshile Gorky: The Breakthrough Years," Modern Art Museum of Fort Worth, Fort Worth, Tex., May 14–September 17, 1995 (traveling exhibition, cat. no. 19, illus.). "Masterworks of American Art from the Munson-Williams-Proctor Institute Museum of Art," Knoxville Museum of Art, Knoxville, Tenn., February 26–August 23, 1998. "Vital Forms: American Art in the Atomic Age, 1940–1960," Brooklyn Museum of Art, Brooklyn, N.Y., October 12, 2001–January 6, 2002 (traveling exhibition, catalog) "American Masterworks from the MWPAI, Celebrating an Educational Alliance with Pratt Institute," Hirschl & Adler Galleries, New York, November 16–December 29, 2006 (catalog).

PUBLICATIONS

"Root's U.S. Pictures at Met," *New York Herald Tribune*, February 15, 1953, sect. 4, 47. Hayes, Bartlett H., Jr. "The Root of American Painting," *Art News* LVI (January 1958): 61, illus. fig. 6. *Paintings, Drawings & Sculptures in the Museum of Art* (Utica, N.Y.: Munson-Williams-Proctor Institute, 1961), 18. Rosenberg, Harold. *Arshile Gorky, The Man, The Time, The Idea* (New York: Grove Press, Inc., 1962), illus., 115. Levy, Julien. *Arshile Gorky* (New York: Harry N. Abrams, 1966), 21, illus. pl. 188. Joyner, Brooks. *The Drawings of Arshile Gorky* (College Park, Md.: University of Maryland Art Gallery, 1969), 11–12. Rand, Harry. "The Calendars of Arshile Gorky," *Arts* 50 (March 1976): 70–80, illus., 71 [incorrectly dated 1941]. Rand, Harry. *Arshile Gorky: The Implications of Symbols* (Montclair, N.J.: Allanheld & Schram, 1980), 131–32, illus. fig. 8–19. Jordon, Jim M. and Goldwater, Robert. *The Paintings of Arshile Gorky: A Critical Catalogue* (New York and London: New York University Press, 1982), cat. no. 319, illus. Lader, Melvin. *Arshile Gorky* (New York: Abbeville Press, 1985). Schweizer, Paul D., et al. *Masterworks of American Art from the Munson-Williams-Proctor Institute* (New York: Harry N. Abrams, Inc., 1989), cat. no. 80, illus., 173. Schweizer, Paul D. "Masterworks from the Munson-Williams-Proctor Institute," *American Art Review* X (May–June 1998): 180–89, 191, illus., 186. Herrera, Hayden. *Arshile Gorky: His Life and Work* (New York: Farrar, Straus and Giroux, 2003), 529, 567, 707 n. 563, 708 n. 567.

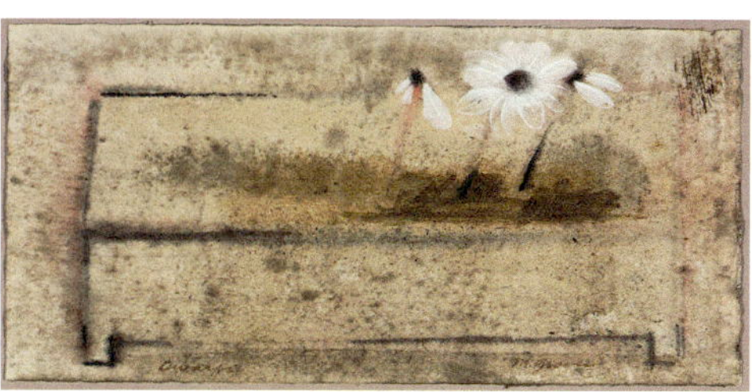

MORRIS GRAVES

(Fox Valley, Ore., 1910–Loleta, Calif., 2001)

97. *Dwarf Flowers (Dwarfs)*, 1950

Tempera on laminated paper
5 ¼ x 11 ⅛ in.
57.154
Signed lower right center (brown ink): M. Graves
Inscribed lower left (brown ink): Dwarfs
Purchased from Willard Gallery, New York, February 1950

EXHIBITIONS

"American Watercolors and Drawings," Root Art Center, Hamilton College, Clinton, N.Y., April 4–May 7, 1961. "Edward Wales Root Bequest," Munson-Williams-Proctor Institute, Utica, N.Y., November 5, 1961–February 24, 1962 (catalog). Root Art Center, December 9–19, 1963. "Paintings and Drawings by Morris Graves," St. Paul Art Center, St. Paul, Minn., October 10–November 3, 1963 (cat. no. 21). "American 20th-Century Watercolors from MWPI," Albany Institute of History and Art, Albany, N.Y., September 10–October 4, 1967. "Edward W. Root: Collector and Teacher," Fred L. Emerson Gallery, Hamilton College, October 2–November 14, 1982 (catalog, 57).

PUBLICATIONS

Paintings, Drawings & Sculptures in the Museum of Art (Utica, N.Y.: Munson-Williams-Proctor Institute, 1961), 18. *American Art in Upstate New York* (Buffalo, N.Y.: Buffalo Fine Arts Academy, 1974), 25.

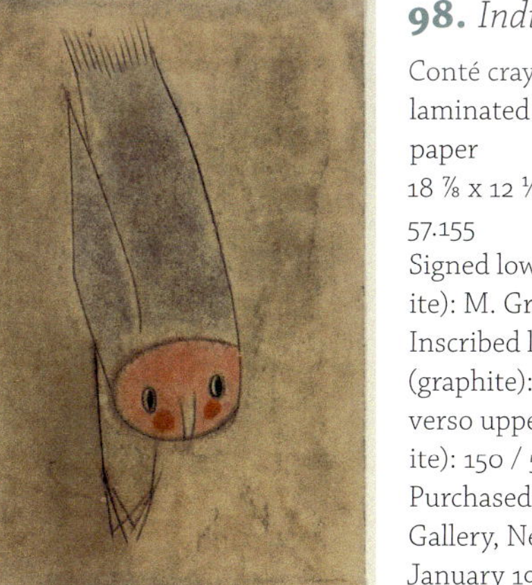

98. *Indian Bird*, 1950

Conté crayon and wash on laminated watercolor paper
18 ⅞ x 12 ½ in.
57.155
Signed lower right (graphite): M. Graves
Inscribed lower left (graphite): Indian Bird; verso upper left (graphite): 150 / 5 [encircled]
Purchased from Willard Gallery, New York, January 1951

MORRIS GRAVES

EXHIBITIONS

"The Edward Root Collection," The Metropolitan Museum of Art, New York, February 12–April 12, 1953 (catalog, 2). "Five Decades of American Painting," Union College, Schenectady, N.Y., September 27–October 23, 1959. "Edward Wales Root Bequest," Munson-Williams-Proctor Institute, Utica, N.Y., November 5, 1961–February 24, 1962 (catalog). "American 20th-Century Watercolors from MWPI," Albany Institute of History and Art, Albany, N.Y., September 10–October 4, 1967. "Carnival of the Animals," MWPI, December 10–31, 1972.

PUBLICATIONS

Paintings, Drawings & Sculptures in the Museum of Art (Utica, N.Y.: Munson-Williams-Proctor Institute, 1961), 18. *American Art in Upstate New York* (Buffalo, N.Y.: Buffalo Fine Arts Academy, 1974), 24.

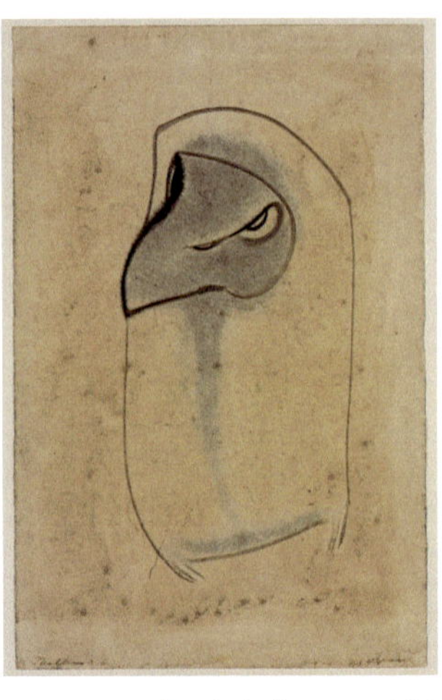

99. *Nestling (Fledgling)*, 1950

Watercolor and pastel on laid watercolor paper

18 ⅞ x 12 ½ in.

57.156

Signed lower right (brown ink): M. Graves

Inscribed lower left (brown ink): nestling; verso lower left (brown ink): no. 9 [encircled]; verso right center (graphite): 1 [encircled]

Purchased from Willard Gallery, New York January 1951

EXHIBITIONS

"The Edward Root Collection," The Metropolitan Museum of Art, New York, February 12–April 12, 1953 (catalog, 2). "Edward Wales Root Bequest," Munson-Williams-Proctor Institute, Utica, N.Y., November 5, 1961–February 24, 1962 (catalog). "American 20th-Century Watercolors from MWPI," Albany Institute of History and Art, Albany, N.Y., September 10–October 4, 1967.

PUBLICATIONS

Paintings, Drawings & Sculptures in the Museum of Art (Utica, N.Y.: Munson-Williams-Proctor Institute, 1961), 19. *American Art in Upstate New York* (Buffalo, N.Y.: Buffalo Fine Arts Academy, 1974), 24.

100. *Surf Reflected Upon Higher Space*, 1943

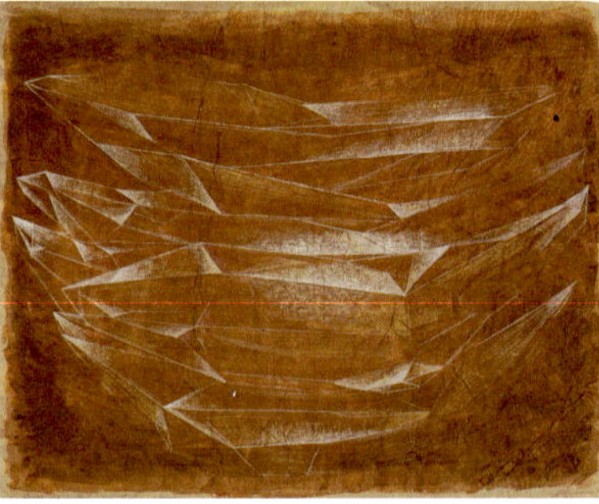

Transparent and opaque watercolor on thin light brown paper

23 ⅜ x 29 ½ in.

57.157

Signed and dated lower right (graphite): M. Graves '43

Purchased from Willard Gallery, New York, February 1945

EXHIBITIONS

"Morris Graves," Willard Gallery, New York, January 30–February 24, 1945 (cat. no. 12). "Edward Wales Root Bequest," Munson-Williams-Proctor Institute, Utica, N.Y., November 5, 1961–February 24, 1962 (catalog, illus.). "Masters of Landscape: East and West," MWPI, September 15–October 13, 1963 (traveling exhibition, cat. no. 76, illus., 80). "Morris Graves, A Retrospective," Museum of Art, University of Oregon, Eugene, February 8–March 13, 1966 (cat. no. 51, illus., 44). "American Art in Upstate New York," Albright-Knox Art Gallery, Buffalo, N.Y., July 12, 1974–April 27, 1975 (traveling exhibition, catalog, 23). "Watercolors: Historic and Contemporary," Hathorn Gallery, Skidmore College, Saratoga Springs, N.Y., February 4–20, 1977 (cat. no. 27). "Morris Graves: Vision of the Inner Eye," The Phillips Collection, Washington, D.C., April 9–May 29, 1983 (traveling exhibition, catalog, illus.). "Northwest Mythologies: The Interactions of Mark Tobey, Morris Graves, Kenneth Callahan and Guy Anderson," Tacoma Art Museum, Tacoma, Wash., May 3–August 10, 2003 (catalog, 165, illus.).

PUBLICATIONS

Paintings, Drawings & Sculptures in the Museum of Art (Utica, N.Y.: Munson-Williams-Proctor Institute, 1961), 19. Prior, Harris K. "Edward Root–Talent Scout," *Art in America* L (1962): 71, illus. fig. 7. Schweizer, Paul D., et al. *Masterworks of American Art from the Munson-Williams-Proctor Institute* (New York: Harry N. Abrams, Inc., 1989), cat. no. 74, illus., 160. Wolff, Theodore. *Morris Graves: Flower Paintings* (Seattle, Wash.: University of Washington Press, 1994), illus.

STEPHEN GREENE

(New York, N.Y. 1918–Valley Cottage, N.Y., 1999)

101. *Romaine and Radishes*

Ca. 1949

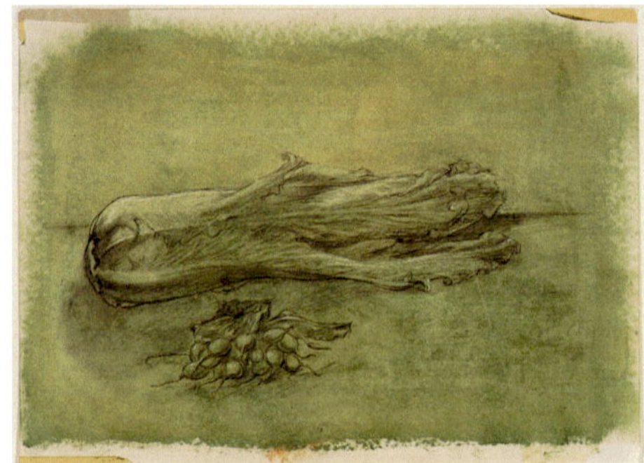

Green wash with graphite on paper

10 ⅞ x 13 ⅞ in.

57.167

Signed lower right (graphite): greene

Purchased from Durlacher Bros., New York March 1949

EXHIBITIONS

"Edith Gregor Halpert Collection," Root Art Center, Hamilton College, Clinton, N.Y., November 1960–January 15, 1961. "Edward Wales Root Bequest," Munson-Williams-Proctor Institute, Utica, N.Y., November 5, 1961–February 24, 1962 (catalog). "On Paper," American Federation of Arts, September 1966–September 1967 (traveling exhibition). "American Drawings and Watercolors from the Munson-Williams-Proctor Institute," E. B. Crocker Art Gallery, Sacramento, Calif., October 25–November 24, 1974 (cat. no. 28). Rome Community Art Center, Rome, N.Y., September 14–November 9, 1975.

PUBLICATION

Paintings, Drawings & Sculptures in the Museum of Art (Utica, N.Y.: Munson-Williams-Proctor Institute, 1961), 19.

THOMAS HANDFORTH

(Tacoma, Wash., 1897–Los Angeles, Calif., 1948)

102. *The Blue Ox*, ca. 1928

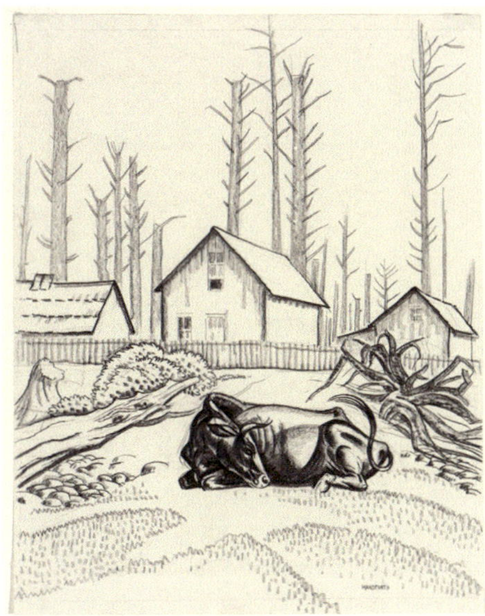

Graphite on paper
12 ¾ x 10 ⅛ in.
57.283
Signed lower right (graphite): HANDFORTH
Inscribed verso lower left (graphite): Bébé / The Blue Ox 40.00
Purchased from Weyhe Gallery, New York, November 1930

EXHIBITIONS

"Etchings and Drawings by Thomas Handforth," Weyhe Gallery, New York, January 2–19, 1929 (cat. no. 46). "Edward Wales Root Bequest," Munson-Williams-Proctor Institute, Utica, N.Y., November 5, 1961–February 24, 1962 (catalog). "Paintings and Drawings from the Edward W. Root Bequest," Root Art Center, Hamilton College, Clinton, N.Y., April 7–May 5, 1968. "Carnival of the Animals," MWPI, December 10–31, 1972.

PUBLICATION

Paintings, Drawings & Sculptures in the Museum of Art (Utica, N.Y.: Munson-Williams-Proctor Institute, 1961), 19.

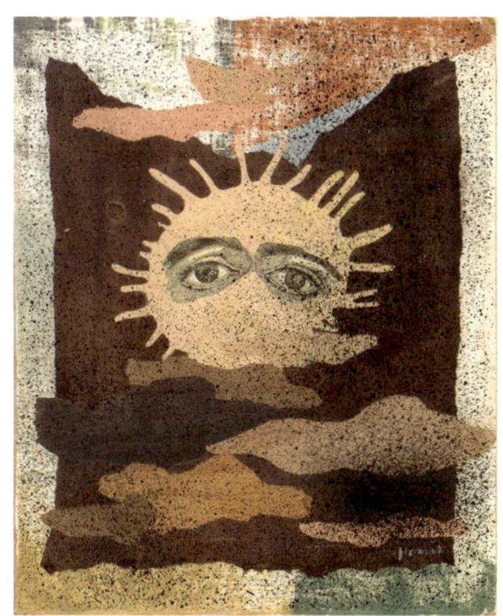

WILLIAM HARRIS

(active 1940s)

103. *Noonday Sun*, 1948

Collage with oil, ink, and paper on Masonite
12 x 9 ⅞ in.
57.158
Signed lower right (white paint): Harris
Purchased from American British Art Center, New York, December 1948

EXHIBITION

["William Harris Collages," American British Art Center, New York, December 6–24, 1948]. "Edward Wales Root Bequest," Munson-Williams-Proctor Institute, Utica, N.Y., November 5, 1961–February 24, 1962 (catalog).

PUBLICATION

Paintings, Drawings & Sculptures in the Museum of Art (Utica, N.Y.: Munson-Williams-Proctor Institute, 1961), 19.

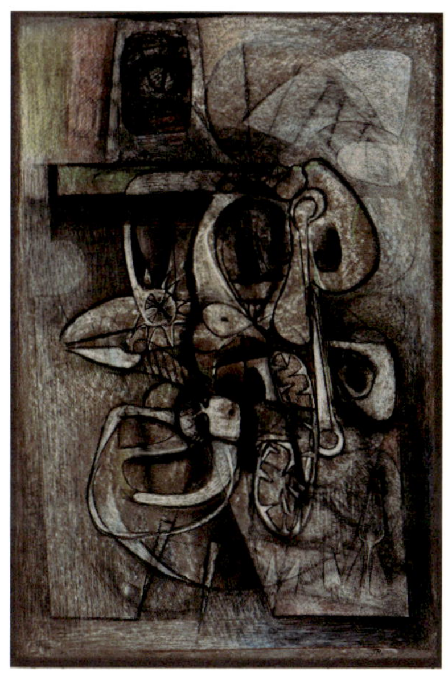

JOHN EDWARD HELIKER

(Yonkers, N.Y., 1909–Bar Harbor, Me., 2000)

104. *Deposition*, ca. 1947–48

Pastel and ink on dark gray paper
19 ¾ x 13 ½ in.
57.159
Signed lower right (charcoal): J.H.
Purchased from Kraushaar Galleries, New York, March 1949

EXHIBITIONS

"Annual Exhibition of Contemporary American Sculpture, Watercolors, and Drawings," Whitney Museum of American Art, New York, April 2–May 8, 1949 (cat. no. 171). "Current Trends in British and American Painting from the Collection of Edward W. Root," Munson-Williams-Proctor Institute, Utica, N.Y., December 3–31, 1950 (traveling exhibition, cat. no. 13). "The Edward Root Collection," The Metropolitan Museum of Art, New York, February 12–April 12, 1953 (catalog, 2). "New Trends in 20th-Century American Painting," Root Art Center, Hamilton College, Clinton, N.Y., October 26–November 30, 1958. "New Trends in 20th-Century American Painting," Union College, Schenectady, N.Y., March 5–26, 1961. "Edward Wales Root Bequest," MWPI, November 5, 1961–February 24, 1962 (catalog). "The Figure in 20th-Century Paintings and Drawings," Root Art Center, April 15–May 6, 1962. "On Paper," American Federation of Arts, September 1966–September 1967 (traveling exhibition). "Contemporary Artists: Early and Late Paintings," Root Art Center, April 4–May 2, 1973. "American Drawings and Watercolors from the Munson-Williams-Proctor Institute," E. B. Crocker Art Gallery, Sacramento, Calif., October 25–November 24, 1974 (cat. no. 31, illus.). Rome Community Art Center, Rome,

N.Y., September 14–November 9, 1975. "Five Decades of Collecting: Edward W. Root," MWPI, April 2–May 28, 1978. "Edward W. Root: Collector and Teacher," Fred L. Emerson Gallery, Hamilton College, October 2–November 14, 1982 (catalog, 54). "Influences of Klee," MWPI, December 19, 1987–May 13, 1988.

PUBLICATION

Paintings, Drawings & Sculptures in the Museum of Art (Utica, N.Y.: Munson-Williams-Proctor Institute, 1961), 19.

EDWARD HOPPER

(Nyack, N.Y., 1882–New York, N.Y., 1967)

105. *The Camel's Hump*, 1931

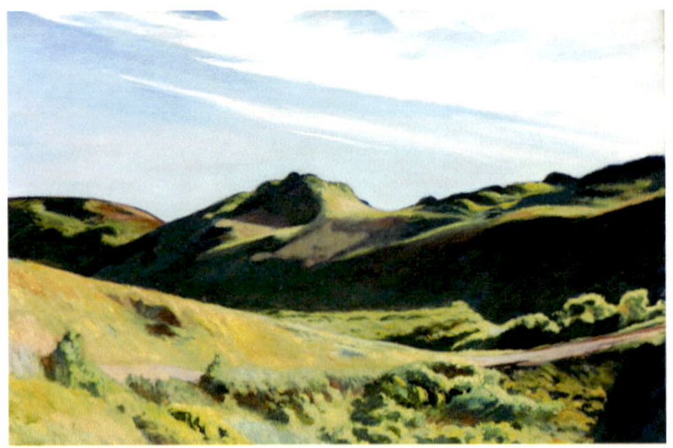

Oil on canvas
32 ¼ x 50 ⅛ in.
57.160
Signed lower right (light green paint): EDWARD HOPPER
Purchased by Mrs. Arthur N. Pack, Princeton, N.J., 1931; to Edward W. Root through Frank K. M. Rehn Galleries, New York, February 1936

EXHIBITIONS

"A Chapter in American Art," Frank K. M. Rehn Galleries, New York, January 4–30, 1932 (cat. no. 16). "Exhibition of The American Society of Painters, Sculptors and Gravers," Whitney Museum of American Art, New York, February 6–28, 1932 (cat. no. 65). "Edward Hopper Retrospective Exhibition," The Museum of Modern Art, New York, November 1–December 7, 1933 (cat. no. 22, illus.). "The Thirty-First Annual Exhibition of Contemporary American Paintings," Rhode Island School of Design, Providence, R.I., October 2–November 3, 1935 (cat. no. 23). "Paintings from the Collection of Edward W. Root," Munson-Williams-Proctor Institute, Utica, N.Y., September 29–October 20, 1946. "New York Private Collections," MoMA, July 20–September 12, 1948. "Edward Hopper Retrospective Exhibition," Whitney Museum, February 11–March 26, 1950 (traveling exhibition, cat. no. 38, illus. color pl. 13). "The Edward Root Collection," The Metropolitan Museum of Art, New York, February 12–April 12, 1953 (catalog, 2). "Boston Arts Festival," Institute of Contemporary Arts, Boston, Mass., June 5–21, 1959. Museum of Art Building inaugural exhibition, MWPI, October 15–December 31, 1960. "Edward Wales Root Bequest," MWPI, November 5, 1961–February 24, 1962 (catalog, illus.). "Edward Hopper, Oils, Watercolors, and Prints," Root Art Center, Hamilton College, Clinton, N.Y., May 10–June 7, 1964. "Edward Hopper: Retrospective Exhibition," Whitney Museum, September 29–November 29, 1964 (traveling exhibition, catalog, illus., 28). "IX Bienal de São Paulo, United States of America: Edward Hopper / Environment USA: 1956–1967," São Paulo, Brazil, 1967 (cat. no. 14, illus., 20). "Landscapes," MWPI, April 7–May 4, 1969. "Provincetown, A Painter's Place," Everson Museum of Art, Syracuse, N.Y., April 1–June 26, 1977. "Five Decades of Collecting: Edward W. Root," MWPI, April 2–May 28, 1978. "Edward Hopper: The Art and The Artist," Whitney Museum, September 9, 1980–January 25, 1981 (traveling exhibition, catalog, illus. pl. 413). "Edward W. Root: Collector and Teacher," Fred L. Emerson Gallery, Hamilton College, October 2–November 14, 1982 (catalog, illus., 36). "Nature Framed," MWPI, March 15–May 20, 1985. "Two Hundred Years of American Art," The Art Museum Association of America, November 15, 1986–May 8, 1988 (traveling exhibition, cat. no. 50, illus., 64). "Reckoning with Winslow Homer: His Late Paintings and Their Influence," The Cleveland Museum of Art, Cleveland, Ohio, September 19–November 18, 1990 (traveling exhibition, catalog, 125–26, illus. fig. 101). "Masterworks of American Art from the Munson-Williams-Proctor Institute Museum of Art," Knoxville Museum of Art, Knoxville, Tenn., February 26–August 23, 1998. "Edward Hopper," Museum of Fine Arts, Boston, May 6–August 19, 2007 (cat. no. 72, illus., 146).

PUBLICATIONS

Cortissoz, Royal. "The New Generation of American Painters," *New York Herald Tribune*, January 10, 1932, section VII, 9, illus. Crownshield, Frank. "Edward Hopper," *Vanity Fair* XXXVIII (June 1932): 31, illus. *Edward Hopper, Illustrated Monograph*, no. 8 (New York: American Artists Group, Inc., 1945), illus. Burchfield, Charles. "Hopper: Career of Silent Poetry," *Art News* XLIX (March 1950): 62, illus., 16. *Paintings, Drawings & Sculptures in the Museum of Art* (Utica, N.Y.: Munson-Williams-Proctor Institute, 1961), 20. Goodrich, Lloyd. *Edward Hopper* (Middlesex, England: Harmondsworth, 1950), illus. Goodrich, Lloyd. *Edward Hopper* (New York: Harry N. Abrams, Inc. 1971), illus., 215. Schweizer, Paul D., et al. *Masterworks of American Art from the Munson-Williams-Proctor Institute* (New York: Harry N. Abrams, Inc., 1989), cat. no. 64, illus., 140. Arthur, John. *Spirit of Place: Contemporary Landscape Painting and the American Tradition* (Boston: Little, Brown, Co., 1989), illus., 26. Marker, Sherry. *Edward Hopper* (New York: Crescent, Brompton Books, 1990), illus., 32. Beck, Huber. *Edward Hopper* ([Hamburg]: Ellert RichterVerlag, [1992]), illus, 27. Levin, Gail. *Edward Hopper: A Catalogue Raisonné* (New York: Whitney Museum of American Art, in association with W.W. Norton & Co., 1995), cat. no. O–281, illus. Schmied, Wieland. *Edward Hopper: Portraits of America* (Munich: Prestel-Verlag, 1995), 84, illus., 86. Mecklenberg, Virginia. *Edward Hopper: The Watercolors* (Washington, D.C.: National Museum of American Art, Smithsonian Institution, in association with W.W. Norton & Co., 1999), 110–11, illus. fig. 115.

106. *Skyline Near Washington Square (Self Portrait)*, 1925

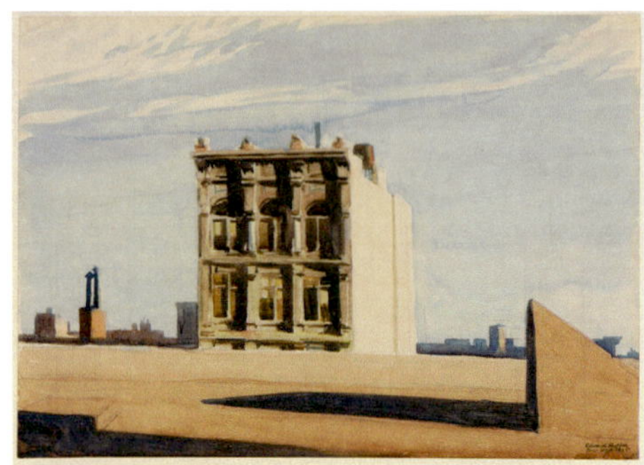

Watercolor and graphite on wove paper
15 x 21 ½ in.
57.161
Signed and dated lower right (black paint): Edward Hopper / New York 1925
Purchased from Frank K. M. Rehn Galleries, April 1927

EXHIBITIONS

"4th Exhibition of Watercolors and Pastels," The Cleveland Museum of Art, Cleveland, Ohio, February 17–March 13, 1927. "Exhibition of Watercolors and Pastels from a Distinguished Private Collection," Munson-Williams-Proctor Institute, Utica, N.Y., fall 1938. "The Edward Root Collection," The Metropolitan Museum of Art, New York, February 12–April 12, 1953 (catalog, 2). The Strathmont Museum, Elmira, N.Y., June–September 1959. "Five Decades of American Painting," Union College, Schenectady, N.Y., September 27–October 23, 1959. "American Watercolors and Drawings," Root Art Center, Hamilton College, Clinton, N.Y., April 4–May 7, 1961. "Centennial Exhibition," State University of New York College of Education, Oswego, N.Y., October 1–31, 1961 (catalog). "Edward Wales Root Bequest," MWPI, November 5, 1961–February 24, 1962 (catalog). "Edward Hopper, Oils, Watercolors, Prints," Root Art Center, May 10–June 7, 1964. "Learning About Pictures from Mr. Root," Root Art Center, January 4–31, 1965 (catalog, illus.). "The Twenties Revisited," The Gallery of Modern Art, New York, June 29–September 5, 1965. "Prints by American Artists," Root Art Center, January 9–February 12, 1967. "American 20th-Century Watercolors from MWPI," Albany Institute of History and Art, Albany, N.Y., September 10–October 4, 1967. "Paintings and Drawings from the Edward W. Root Bequest," MWPI, April 7–May 5, 1968. "The Root Bequest," Root Art Center, May 11–June 8, 1969. "Hopper-Burchfield Exhibition," The Katonah Gallery, Katonah, N.Y., September 7–30, 1969. "Edward Hopper 1882–1967," William A. Farnsworth Library and Art Museum, Rockland, Me., July 9–September 5, 1971 (traveling exhibition, cat. no. 17, illus.). "American Drawings and Watercolors from the Munson-Williams-Proctor Institute," E. B. Crocker Art Gallery, Sacramento, Calif., October 25–November 24, 1974 (cat. no. 32, illus.). "Watercolors: Historic and Contemporary," Hathorn Gallery, Skidmore College, Saratoga Springs, N.Y., February 4–20, 1977 (cat. no. 30, illus.). "American Works of Art on Paper 1850–1925," Schenectady Museum & Planetarium, Schenectady, N.Y., January 12–April 6, 1980 (cat. no. 53). "Edward Hopper: The Art and the Artist," Whitney Museum of American Art, New York, September 9, 1980–January 25, 1981 (traveling exhibition, catalog, illus. pl. 238). "Insights," MWPI, January 7–April 13 and June 10–October 15, 1986. "The Art Triangle: Artist, Dealer, Collector," Burchfield Art Center, Buffalo, N.Y., May 13–June 25, 1989 (traveling exhibition, cat. no. 40, illus., 60). "City of Ambition: Artists & New York," Whitney Museum, July 3–October 27, 1996 (catalog, 137, illus., 87). "American Twentieth-Century Watercolors at the Munson-Williams-Proctor Arts Institute," MWPAI, April 30–July 10, 2000 (traveling exhibition, cat. no. 16, illus.). "American Masterworks from the MWPAI, Celebrating an Educational Alliance with Pratt Institute," Hirschl & Adler Galleries, New York, November 16–December 29, 2006 (catalog).

PUBLICATIONS

Hale, Robert Beverly. "The Growth of a Collection," *The Metropolitan Museum of Art Bulletin* XI (February 1953): 158, illus. *Paintings, Drawings & Sculptures in the Museum of Art* (Utica, N.Y.: Munson-Williams-Proctor Institute, 1961), 20. Prior, Harris K. "Edward Root–Talent Scout," *Art in America* L, (1962): 71, illus. fig. 5. Goodrich, Lloyd. *Edward Hopper* (New York: Henry N. Abrams, Inc., 1971), illus., 182. *American Art in Upstate New York* (Buffalo, N.Y.: Buffalo Fine Arts Academy, 1974), 27. Finch, Christopher. *American Watercolors* (New York: Abbeville Press, 1986), illus. pl. 329. Finch, Christopher. *Twentieth-Century Watercolors* (New York: Abbeville Press, 1988), 209, illus. pl. 253. Costantino, Maria. *Edward Hopper* (New York: Barnes and Noble Books, 1995), illus., 29. Levin, Gail. *Edward Hopper: A Catalogue Raisonné* (New York: Whitney Museum of American Art, in association with W.W. Norton & Co., 1995), cat. no. W-129, illus. Levin, Gail. *Hopper's Places*, second ed. (Berkeley, Calif.: University of California Press, 1998), vii, illus., viii. Mecklenberg, Virginia. *Edward Hopper: The Watercolors* (Washington, D.C.: National Museum of American Art, Smithsonian Institution, in association with W.W. Norton & Co., 1999), 45–47, illus. fig. 50. Gillespie, Evan, "Watercolors Fertile Possibilities Surveyed," *South Bend Tribune*, January 20, 2006, D6, illus.

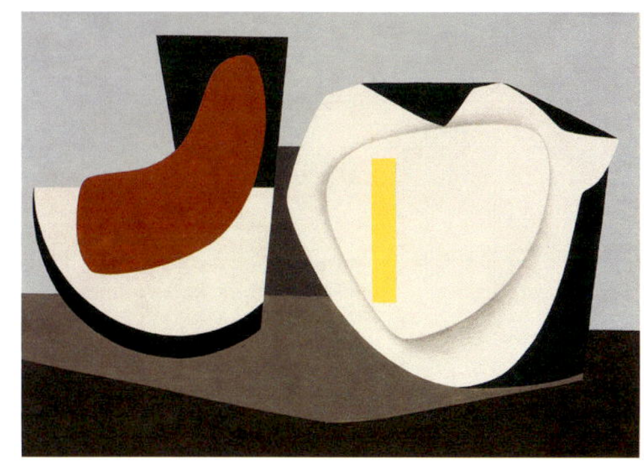

CHARLES HOWARD

(Montclair, N.J., 1899–Bagni di Lucca, Italy, 1978)

107. *Concretion*, 1937
Tempera and graphite on white watercolor paper
10 x 14 in.
57.162
Signed and dated right lower center (white paint): Chh. '37
Purchased from Nierendorf Gallery, New York, March 1946

EXHIBITIONS

"Charles Howard: Retrospective Exhibition, 1925–1946," California Palace of the Legion of Honor, San Francisco, Calif., May 10–June 9, 1946 (catalog, 121). "Paintings from the Collection of Edward W. Root," Munson-Williams-Proctor Institute, Utica, N.Y., September 29–October 20, 1946. "The Edward Root Collection," The Metropolitan Museum of Art, New York, February 12–April 12, 1953 (catalog, 2). "New Trends in 20th-Century American Painting," Root Art Center, Hamilton College, Clinton, N.Y., October 26–November 30, 1958. "New Trends in 20th-Century American Painting," Union College, Schenectady, N.Y., March 5–26, 1961. "Edward Wales Root Bequest," MWPI, November 5, 1961–February 24, 1962 (catalog). "Realism to Abstraction," State University College, Oneonta, N.Y., December 2–20, 1963. "On Paper," American Federation of Arts, September 1966–September 1967 (traveling exhibition). "20th-Century Prints and Drawings," Schenectady Museum & Planetarium, Schenectady, N.Y., December 15, 1971–January 15, 1972. "American Drawings and Watercolors from the Munson-Williams-Proctor Institute," E. B. Crocker Art Gallery, Sacramento, Calif., October 25–November 24, 1974 (cat. no. 33). Rome Community Art Center, Rome, N.Y., September 14–November 9, 1975. "Five Decades of Collecting: Edward W. Root," MWPI, April 2–May 28, 1978. "American Twentieth-Century Watercolors at the Munson-Williams-Proctor Arts Institute," MWPAI, April 30–July 10, 2000 (traveling exhibition, cat. no. 30, illus.).

CHARLES HOWARD

PUBLICATION

Paintings, Drawings & Sculptures in the Museum of Art (Utica, N.Y.: Munson-Williams-Proctor Institute, 1961), 20.

108. *Wild Park*, August 13, 1944

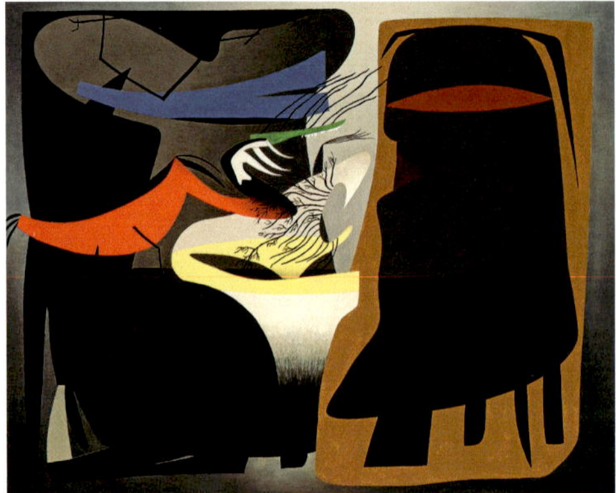

Oil on canvas board
13 ⅞ x 17 ⅞ in.
57.163
Signed and dated lower right (black paint): C.H. 13 VIII '44
Inscribed on back of canvas board, upper left: "Wild Park" / Charles Howard / 91 Water St. / San Francisco II / California / 14" x 18"—oil—13 August 1944
Purchased from Nierendorf Gallery, New York, January 1946

EXHIBITIONS

"Annual Exhibition of Contemporary American Painting," Whitney Museum of American Art, New York, November 14–December 12, 1944 (cat. no. 61). "Charles Howard: Retrospective Exhibition, 1925–1946," California Palace of the Legion of Honor, San Francisco, Calif., May 10–June 9, 1946 (catalog, 119). "Paintings from the Collection of Edward W. Root," Munson-Williams-Proctor Institute, Utica, N.Y., September 29–October 20, 1946. "20th-Century American Paintings from the Edward W. Root Collection," Smithsonian Institution, Washington, D.C., July 1959–July 1960 (traveling exhibition). "Edward Wales Root Bequest," MWPI, November 5, 1961–February 24, 1962 (catalog). "Abstract Paintings and Drawings from the Root Bequest," Root Art Center, Hamilton College, Clinton, N.Y., September 11–October 9, 1966.

PUBLICATIONS

Frost, Rosamund. "The Whitney Does It Again," *Art News* XLIII (November 15–30, 1944): 10. *Paintings, Drawings & Sculptures in the Museum of Art* (Utica, N.Y.: Munson-Williams-Proctor Institute, 1961), 20.

MORRIS KANTOR

(Minsk, Russia, 1896–New York, N.Y., 1974)

109. *Nocturne, Marblehead*, 1930

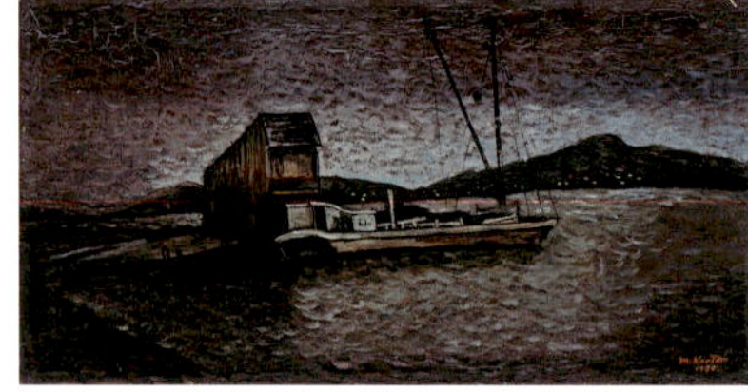

Oil on linen
11 ¾ x 22 ⅝ in.
57.164
Signed and dated lower right (red paint): M. Kantor / 1930
Purchased from Frank K. M. Rehn Galleries, New York, January 1931

EXHIBITIONS

"Edward Wales Root Bequest," Munson-Williams-Proctor Institute, Utica, N.Y., November 5, 1961–February 24, 1962 (catalog). "The Art Triangle: Artist, Dealer, Collector," Burchfield Art Center, Buffalo, N.Y., May 13–June 25, 1989 (traveling exhibition, cat. no. 45).

PUBLICATION

Paintings, Drawings & Sculptures in the Museum of Art (Utica, N.Y.: Munson-Williams-Proctor Institute, 1961), 21.

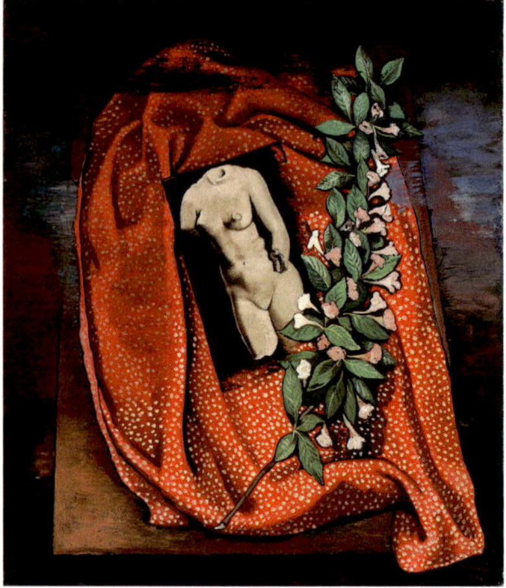

110. *Ode to the Antique*, 1929

Oil on linen
30 x 26 in.
57.165
Signed and dated lower right (red paint): M. Kantor / 1929
Purchased from Frank K. M. Rehn Galleries, New York, December 1930

EXHIBITIONS

"Paintings and Sculpture by Living Americans," The Museum of Modern Art, New York, December 2, 1930–January 20, 1931 (cat. no. 51). "Paintings from the Collection of Edward W. Root," Munson-Williams-Proctor Institute, Utica, N.Y., September 29–October 20, 1946. "Five Decades of American Painting," Union College, Schenectady, N.Y., September 27–October 23, 1959. "Edward Wales Root Bequest," MWPI, November 5, 1961–February 24, 1962 (catalog). "Learning About Pictures from Mr. Root," Root Art Center, Hamilton College, Clinton, N.Y., January 4–31, 1965 (catalog, illus.). "Order and Enigma: American Art Between the Wars," MWPI, October 13–December 16, 1984 (traveling exhibition, catalog, illus. fig. 37, 57). "Insights," MWPI, June 10–October 15, 1986. "The Art Triangle: Artist, Dealer, Collector," Burchfield Art Center, Buffalo, N.Y., May 13–June 25, 1989 (traveling exhibition, cat. no. 44, illus., 54).

PUBLICATIONS

"Ends and Means," *Magazine of Art* XXXIII (March 1940): 138–47. *Paintings, Drawings & Sculptures in the Museum of Art* (Utica, N.Y.: Munson-Williams-Proctor Institute, 1961), 21.

LEON KELLY

(Perpignan, France, 1901–Loveladies Harbor, N.J., 1982)

111. *Ancient Priest Counseling Artistic Weavers*, 1947

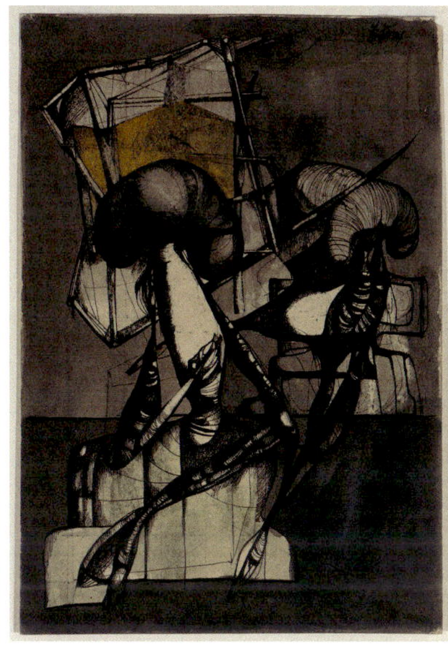

Ink and watercolor with graphite on buff paper
9 ⅝ x 6 ¾ in.
57.166
Signed and dated upper right (black ink): Leon Kelly 1947
Inscribed verso upper center (graphite): Paracos / Pacha Camac / Cuges / Paracas / (black ink): 1947 Leon Kelly / inv. no. 182; verso, bottom edge (black ink): Trellis of wisdom supernatural. (graphite): ancient priest counseling / artistic weavers / paracas
Purchased from Hugo Gallery, New York

EXHIBITIONS

"The Edward Root Collection," The Metropolitan Museum of Art, New York, February 12–April 12, 1953 (catalog, 2, as *Priest and Weaver*). Museum of Art Building inaugural exhibition, Munson-Williams-Proctor Institute, Utica, N.Y., October 15–December 31, 1960. "Edward Wales Root Bequest," MWPI, November 5, 1961–February 24, 1962 (catalog).

PUBLICATION

Paintings, Drawings & Sculptures in the Museum of Art (Utica, N.Y.: Munson-Williams-Proctor Institute, 1961), 22.

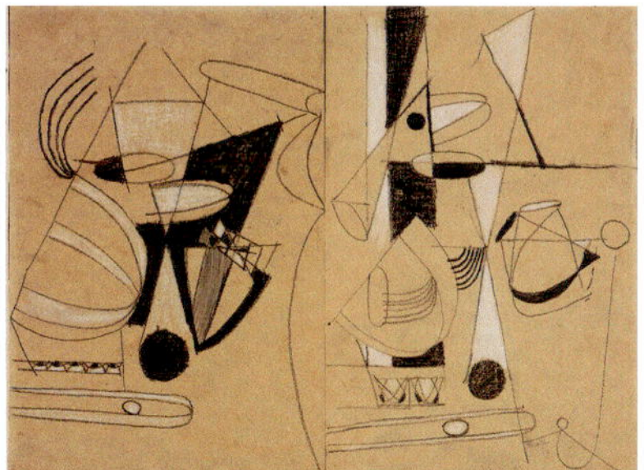

(OTTO) KARL KNATHS

(Eau Claire, Wis., 1891–Hyannis, Mass., 1971)

112. *Abstract Drawing*, not dated

Black and white chalk on buff paper mounted on Masonite
18 ¼ x 24 ½ in.
57.168
Signed lower right (graphite): Knaths
Purchased from Paul Rosenberg & Co., New York

EXHIBITIONS

"Paintings from the Collection of Edward W. Root," Munson-Williams-Proctor Institute, Utica, N.Y., September 29–October 20, 1946. "The Edward Root Collection," The Metropolitan Museum of Art, New York, February 12–April 12, 1953 (catalog, 2, as *Untitled*). "New Trends in 20th-Century American Painting," Union College, Schenectady, N.Y., March 5–26, 1961. "American Watercolors and Drawings," Root Art Center, Hamilton College, Clinton, N.Y., April 4–May 7, 1961. "Edward Wales Root Bequest," MWPI, November 5, 1961–February 24, 1962 (catalog). "European Sources of Contemporary American Art: Kandinsky," Root Art Center, September 15–October 6, 1963 (cat. no. 23). "On Paper," American Federation of Arts, September 1966–September 1967 (traveling exhibition). "Paintings and Drawings from the Edward W. Root Bequest," Root Art Center, April 7–May 5, 1968. Kirkland Art Center, Clinton, N.Y., February 6–March 6, 1972. "American Drawings and Watercolors from the Munson-Williams-Proctor Institute," E. B. Crocker Art Gallery, Sacramento, Calif., October 25–November 24, 1974 (cat. no. 35, illus.). Rome Community Art Center, Rome, N.Y., September 14–November 9, 1975. "Five Decades of Collecting: Edward W. Root," MWPI, April 2–May 28, 1978.

PUBLICATION

Paintings, Drawings & Sculptures in the Museum of Art (Utica, N.Y.: Munson-Williams-Proctor Institute, 1961), 22.

YASUO KUNIYOSHI

(Okayanas, Japan, 1889–New York, N.Y., 1953)

113. *By the Sea*, 1942

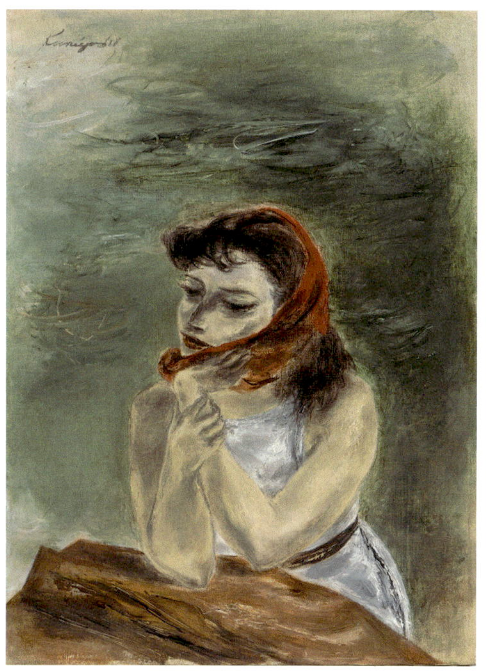

Oil on linen
16 x 12 in.
57.169
Signed upper left (black paint): Kuniyoshi
Inscribed at top of frame: Yasuo Kuniyoshi / "By the Sea" / 12 x 16 / oil
Purchased from The Downtown Gallery, New York, February 1943

EXHIBITIONS

"New Paintings by Kuniyoshi," The Downtown Gallery, New York, April 3–28, 1945 (cat. no. 3). "Five Decades of American Painting," Union College, Schenectady, N.Y., September 27–October 23, 1959. "Centennial Exhibition," State University of New York College of Education, Oswego, N.Y., October 1–31, 1961 (catalog, illus.). "Edward Wales Root Bequest," Munson-Williams-Proctor Institute, Utica, N.Y., November 5, 1961–February 24, 1962 (catalog). Root Art Center, Hamilton College, Clinton, N.Y., December 9–19, 1963. "The Seashore: Paintings of the 19th and 20th Centuries," Carnegie Institute, Museum of Art, Pittsburgh, Pa., October 22–December 5, 1965 (cat. no. 105, illus.). "Prints by American Artists," Root Art Center, January 9–February 12, 1967. "The Root Bequest," Root Art Center, May 11–June 8, 1969. "Five Decades of Collecting: Edward W. Root," MWPI, April 2–May 28, 1978. "Edward W. Root: Collector and Teacher," Fred L. Emerson Gallery, Hamilton College,

October 2–November 14, 1982 (catalog, 45). "Figuratively Speaking," MWPI, April 11–November 10, 1985.

PUBLICATIONS

Yasuo Kuniyoshi, Illustrated Monograph no. 11 (New York: American Artists Group, Inc., 1945), illus. *Paintings, Drawings & Sculptures in the Museum of Art* (Utica, N.Y.: Munson-Williams-Proctor Institute, 1961), 23. Faison, S. Lane, Jr. *Art Tours and Detours in New York State* (New York: Random House, 1964), 100, illus. no. 171. *Yasuo Kuniyoshi* (Okayama, Japan: Fukutake Publishing Co., 1991), 135.

114. *Empty Town in Desert*, 1943

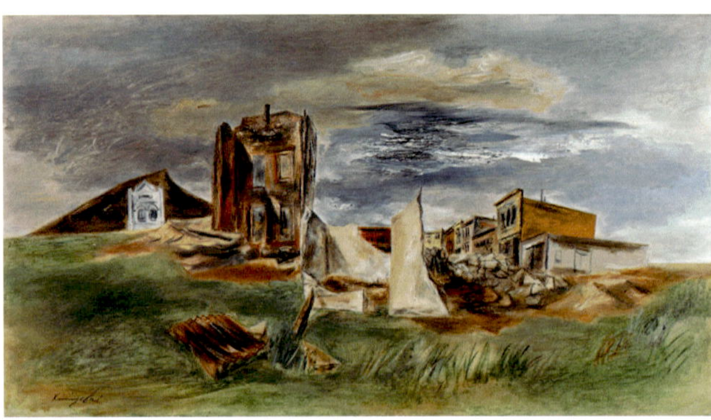

Oil on linen
20 x 36 ¼ in.
57.170
Signed lower left (black paint): Kuniyoshi
Printed across top of canvas stretcher: Empty Town in Desert 1943 Kuniyoshi
Purchased from The Downtown Gallery, New York

EXHIBITIONS

"18th Annual Exhibition," The Downtown Gallery, New York, October 5–30, 1943 (cat. no. 7). New School for Social Research, New York, January 1944. "Portrait of America (Artists for Victory, Inc.)," The Metropolitan Museum of Art, New York, October 4–December 3, 1944. "Paintings from the Collection of Edward W. Root," Munson-Williams-Proctor Institute, Utica, N.Y., September 29–October 20, 1946. "Yasuo Kunyoshi Retrospective Exhibition," Whitney Museum of American Art, New York, March 27–May 9, 1948 (cat. no. 55, illus. 25). "The Edward Root Collection," Metropolitan Museum of Art, February 12–April 12, 1953 (catalog, 2). "Edward Wales Root Bequest," MWPI, November 5, 1961–February 24, 1962 (catalog). "Paintings and Drawings from the Edward W. Root Bequest," Root Art Center, Hamilton College, Clinton, N.Y., April 7–May 5, 1968. "Landscapes," MWPI, April 7–May 4, 1969. "Nature Framed," MWPI, March 15–May 20, 1985. "Two Hundred Years of American Art," The Art Museum Association of America, November 15, 1986–May 8, 1988 (traveling exhibition, cat. no. 59, illus., 73).

PUBLICATIONS

Yasuo Kuniyoshi, Illustrated Monograph, no. 11 (New York: American Artists Group, Inc., 1945), illus. *Paintings, Drawings & Sculptures in the Museum of Art* (Utica, N.Y.: Munson-Williams-Proctor Institute, 1961), 23. Broder, Patricia Janis. *The American West, The Modern Vision* (New York Graphic Society Books and Boston: Little, Brown and Company, 1984), illus., 82. Schweizer, Paul D., et al. *Masterworks of American Art from the Munson-Williams-Proctor Institute* (New York: Harry N. Abrams, Inc., 1989), cat. no. 75, illus., 162. *Yasuo Kuniyoshi* (Okayama, Japan: Fukutake Publishing Co., 1991), 139.

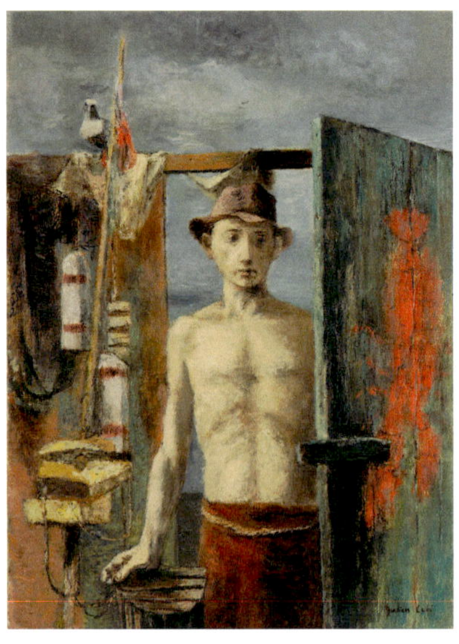

JULIAN LEVI

(New York, N.Y., 1900–82)

115. *Lobsterman*, 1945

Oil on linen
26 x 19 in.
57.171
Signed lower right (black paint): Julian Levi
Inscribed verso lower right: 1945
Purchased from The Downtown Gallery, New York

EXHIBITIONS

"Paintings from the Collection of Edward W. Root," Munson-Williams-Proctor Institute, Utica, N.Y., September 29–October 20, 1946. "The Edward Root Collection," The Metropolitan Museum of Art, New York, February 12–April 12, 1953 (catalog, 2). "Edward Wales Root Bequest," MWPI, November 5, 1961–February 24, 1962 (catalog). "The Figure in 20th-Century Paintings and Drawings," Root Art Center, Hamilton College, Clinton, N.Y., April 15–May 6, 1962. "Julian Levi: Retrospective Exhibition," Boston University Art Gallery, Boston, Mass., November 1–December 31, 1962 (traveling exhibition, cat. no. 18, illus.). "Prints by American Artists," Root Art Center, January 9–February 12, 1967. "Figuratively Speaking," MWPI, April 11–November 10, 1985.

PUBLICATION

Paintings, Drawings & Sculptures in the Museum of Art (Utica, N.Y.: Munson-Williams-Proctor Institute, 1961), 24.

NORMAN LEWIS

(New York, N.Y., 1909–79)

116. *Cadenza*, 1951

Watercolor and chalk on white paper
19 x 24 in.
57.172
Signed and dated lower right (black ink): 6–21–51 / NORMAN LEWIS
Purchased from Willard Gallery, New York, March 1952

EXHIBITION

"The Edward Root Collection," The Metropolitan Museum of Art, New York, February 12–April 12, 1953 (catalog, 2). "New Trends in Twentieth-Century Art," Union College, Schenectady, N.Y., March 5–26, 1961. "Edward Wales Root Bequest," Munson-Williams-Proctor Institute, Utica, N.Y., November 5, 1961–February 24, 1962 (catalog). "American 20th-Century Watercolors from the MWPI," Albany Institute of History and Art, September 10–October 4, 1967. "20th-Century Prints and Drawings," Schenectady Museum & Planetarium, Schenectady, N.Y., December 15, 1971–January 15, 1972. "Contemporary Artists, Early and Late," Root Art Center, Hamilton College, Clinton, N.Y., April 4–May 2, 1973.

PUBLICATIONS

Hayes, Bartlett H., Jr. "The Root of American Painting," *Art News* LVI (January 1958): 61, illus. fig. 5. *Paintings, Drawings & Sculptures in the Museum of Art* (Utica, N.Y.: Munson-Williams-Proctor Institute, 1961), 24.

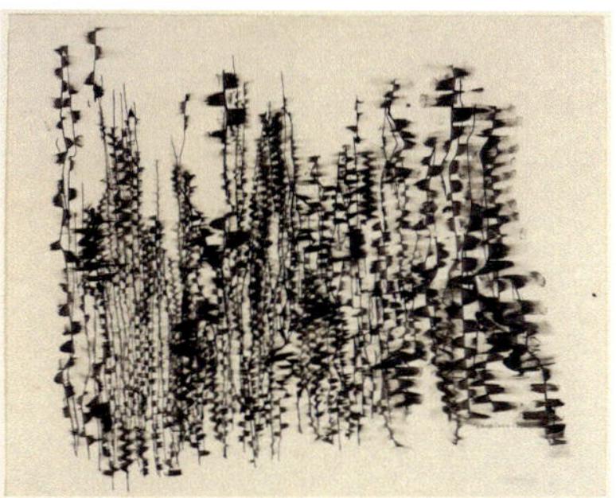

117. *Echoes*, 1950

Ink on white wove paper
19 x 24 in.
57.173
Signed and dated lower right (graphite): Norman Lewis – '50; lower left: erased inscription
Purchased from Willard Gallery, New York, April 1951

EXHIBITIONS

"Edward Wales Root Bequest," Munson-Williams-Proctor Institute, Utica, N.Y., November 5, 1961–February 24, 1962 (catalog). Kirkland Art Center, Clinton, N.Y., February 6–March 6, 1972.

PUBLICATION

Paintings, Drawings & Sculptures in the Museum of Art (Utica, N.Y.: Munson-Williams-Proctor Institute, 1961), 24.

118. *Mirage*, 1951

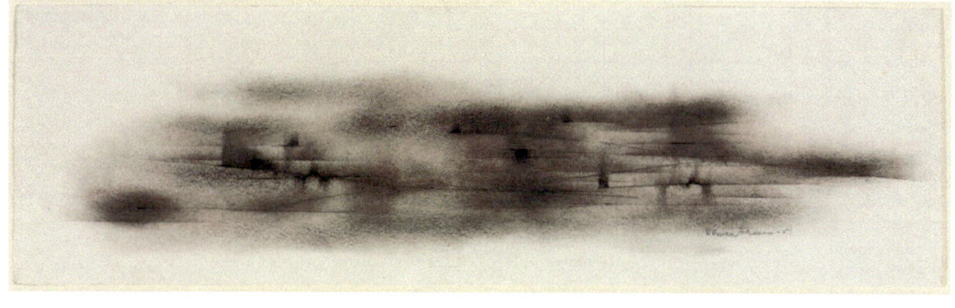

Watercolor on white wove watercolor paper
6 ⅝ x 23 in.
57.174
Signed and dated lower right (graphite): Norman Lewis–51
Purchased from Willard Gallery, New York, March 1952

EXHIBITIONS

"The Edward Root Collection," The Metropolitan Museum of Art, New York, February 12–April 12, 1953 (catalog, 2). "American Watercolors and Drawings," Root Art Center, Hamilton College, Clinton, N.Y., April 4–May 7, 1961. "Edward Wales Root Bequest," Munson-Williams-Proctor Institute, Utica, N.Y., November 5, 1961–February 24, 1962 (catalog). "American 20th-Century Watercolors from MWPI," Albany Institute of History and Art, Albany, N.Y., September 10–October 4, 1967. "The Root Bequest," Root Art Center, May 11–June 8, 1969. "Five Decades of Collecting: Edward W. Root," MWPI, April 2–May 28, 1978.

PUBLICATION

*Paintings, Drawings & Sculptures in the Museum of Art (Utica, N.Y.: Munson-Williams-Proc*tor Institute, 1961), 24.

GEORGE B. LUKS

(Williamsport, Pa., 1866–New York, N.Y., 1933)

Ten Oil Sketches of Paris and Environs, 1902

Root's handwritten inventory of his collection contains the following information about cat. nos. 119–28 (R.G. 13, F. 90):

"Oil Sketches of Paris & Environs by G. B. Luks, 1902. Bought—1922 at $250 a picture. [Root noted on a later page of the same inventory that he purchased these works from Luks in "December 1921."] Each picture is painted on a wooden panel 8 ⅝" x 6 ⅛". To my knowledge, there were altogether 21 panels of this size. One panel of no particular value was given to me in 1910 by the painter. It represents a Red Barge being unloaded into wagon on one of the Paris quays with a bridge in the background [*Docks and Bridge (Paris Quayside)*, MWPAI, 58.153]. The other 20 panels remained with the painter during his residence in West 56th St. and Jumel Place & Edgecomb Road. In 1921 Luks removed the entire 20 from the latter address and took them with him to 55 East 59th St. Soon after bringing them here he painted the title and his signature on the back of each panel and also a serial number in a circle. During the same year he framed 18 of the 20. One, no. 2, he gave to Miss Elizabeth Olds of Minneapolis, a favorite pupil. Another, no. 10, he did not frame, as he did not think it up to standard. Of the 18 remaining, I was given my choice of 10 at $250, each. The 10 pictures bought by me are listed herewith in the order of their serial number as follows:

1 Nurses Luxembourg Gardens Paris
2 [Given by Luks to Elizabeth Olds (1896–1991)]
3 The Fountain Luxembourg Gardens Paris (Group beneath Lion)
4 Café Neuilly Paris (Nocturne)
5 Push Cart Market Rue de Rennes Paris [cat. no. 128]
6 The Screen Café de Versailles Paris
7 Gardens at St. Maurice on the Marne France (Branching Tree)
8 The Lower Road Robinson, France (Pleached alley)
9 Luxembourg Gardens Paris (2 Black dresses in 2 values)
10 [No title listed by Root]
11 The Louvre Evening Paris [cat. no. 120]
12 Luxembourg Garden Paris [cat. no. 121]
13 On the Marne France [cat. no. 125]
14 Luxembourg Gardens Paris (The Red Skirt) [cat. no. 123]
15 Garden Café Serennes France [cat. no. 119]
16 Picnic in the Woods Robinson France [cat. no. 126]
17 Luxembourg Gardens Paris [cat. no. 122]
18 Main Entrance Luxembourg Gardens Paris [Flower Beds]
19 Picnic in the Woods Robinson France [cat. no. 127]
20 The Marne at Charenton Paris [cat. no. 124]

NOTE on the foregoing. There were besides these 21 oil sketches of Paris of 8 ⅝ x 6 ⅛ size, 3 smaller and much less definite sketches of 6 ¾ x 3 ¾ inches. Two of these small sketches [*Café (Paris Café)*, MWPAI, 58.155 and *Gardens (Statue, Luxembourg Gardens)*, MWPAI, 58.156] were given to me years ago by the painter and are inventoried along with the other oil pictures. There were besides several larger oil panels of Parisian subjects. One, called "Paul Verlaine" is still (1922) in the painter's possession and was exhibited at Kraushaar's during Jan. 1922. Another of 2 twin sisters in light blue bodices & straw sailor hats seen passing a café from inside the café."

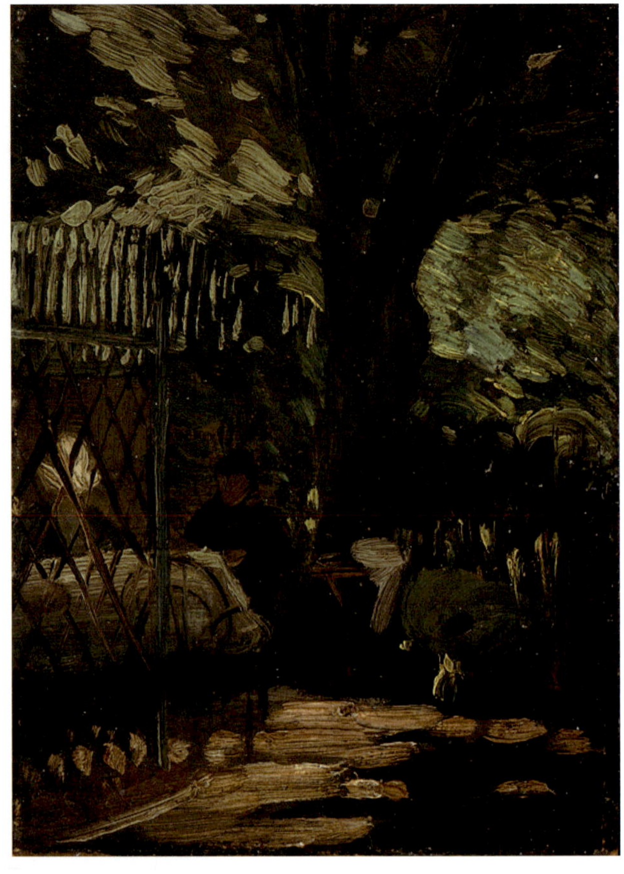

119. *Garden Café, Serennes, France*, 1902

Oil on hardwood panel
8 ⅝ x 6 ⅛ in.
57.177
Signed verso (black paint): Garden Café / Serennes / France / 15 / George Luks

EXHIBITIONS

"Retrospective Exhibition of Paintings by George Luks," C.W. Kraushaar Galleries, New York, January 8–27, 1923 (cat. no. 15).
"Five American Artists of the 20th Century: Davies, Luks, Burchfield, Tobey, Stamos," Root Art Center, Hamilton College, Clinton, N.Y., December 7, 1958–March 28, 1959.
Museum of Art Building inaugural exhibtion, Munson-Williams-Proctor Institute, Utica, N.Y., October 15–December 31, 1960.
"Edward Wales Root Bequest," MWPI, November 5, 1961–February 24, 1962 (catalog). "George Luks (1866–1933): An Exhibition of Paintings and Drawings Dating from 1889 to 1931," MWPI, April 1–May 20, 1973 (cat. no. 3, illus., 20). "Five Decades of Collecting: Edward W. Root," MWPI, April 2–May 28, 1978.

PUBLICATION

Paintings, Drawings & Sculptures in the Museum of Art (Utica, N.Y.: Munson-Williams-Proctor Institute, 1961), 25.

120. *The Louvre, Evening, Paris*

1902

Oil on hardwood panel
6 ⅛ x 8 ⅝ in.
57.178
Signed verso (black paint): The Louvre / Evening / Paris / 11 George Luks

EXHIBITIONS

"Retrospective Exhibition of Paintings by George Luks," C.W. Kraushaar Galleries, New York, January 8–27, 1923 (cat. no. 15). "Edward Wales Root Bequest," Munson-Williams-Proctor Institute, Utica, N.Y., November 5, 1961–February 24, 1962 (catalog). "Five Decades of Collecting: Edward W. Root," MWPI, April 2–May 28, 1978. "George Luks: An American Artist," Sordoni Art Gallery, Wilkes College, Wilkes-Barre, Pa., May 3–June 14, 1987 (traveling exhibition, cat. no. 3)

PUBLICATIONS

Paintings, Drawings & Sculptures in the Museum of Art (Utica, N.Y.: Munson-Williams-Proctor Institute, 1961), 25. *George Luks (1866–1933): An Exhibition of Paintings and Drawings Dating from 1889 to 1931* (Utica, N.Y.: MWPI, 1973), cat. no. 4.

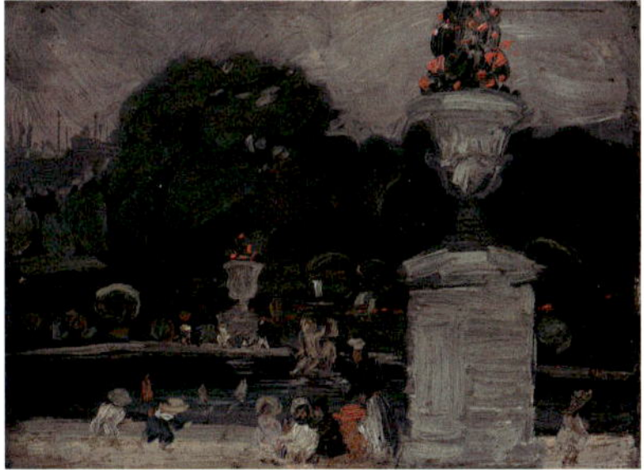

121. *Luxembourg Gardens, Paris, No. 1*, 1902

Oil on hardwood panel
6 x 8 ⅝ in.
57.179
Signed verso (black paint): Luxembourg / Gardens / Paris / 12 / George Luks

EXHIBITIONS

"Retrospective Exhibition of Paintings by George Luks," C.W. Kraushaar Galleries, New York, January 8–27, 1923 (cat. no. 15). "Edward Wales Root Bequest," Munson-Williams-Proctor Institute, Utica, N.Y., November 5, 1961–February 24, 1962 (catalog). "George Luks (1866–1933): An Exhibition of Paintings and Drawings Dating from 1889 to 1931," MWPI, April 1–May 20, 1973 (cat. no. 5). "Five Decades of Collecting: Edward W. Root," MWPI, April 2–May 28, 1978.

PUBLICATION

Paintings, Drawings & Sculptures in the Museum of Art (Utica, N.Y.: Munson-Williams-Proctor Institute, 1961), 25.

122. *Luxembourg Gardens, Paris, No. 2*, 1902

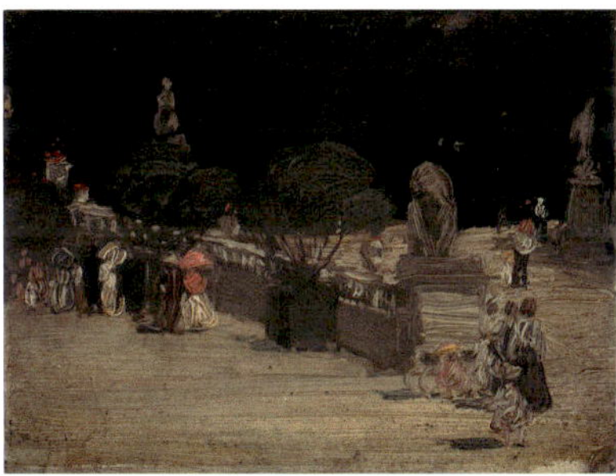

Oil on hardwood panel
6 x 8 ⅝ in.
57.180
Signed verso (black paint): Luxembourg / Gardens / Paris / 17 / George Luks

EXHIBITIONS

"Retrospective Exhibition of Paintings by George Luks," C.W. Kraushaar Galleries, New York, January 8–27, 1923 (cat. no. 15). Museum of Art Building inaugural exhibition, Munson-Williams-Proctor Institute, Utica, N.Y., October 15–December 31, 1960. "Edward Wales Root Bequest," MWPI, November 5, 1961–February 24, 1962 (catalog). "George Luks (1866–1933): An Exhibition of Paintings and Drawings Dating from 1889 to 1931," MWPI, April 1–May 20, 1973 (cat. no. 6). "Five Decades of Collecting: Edward W. Root," MWPI, April 2–May 28, 1978. "George Luks: An American Artist," Sordoni Art Gallery, Wilkes College, Wilkes-Barre, Pa., May 3–June 14, 1987 (traveling exhibition, cat. no. 4).

PUBLICATION

Paintings, Drawings & Sculptures in the Museum of Art (Utica, N.Y.: Munson-Williams-Proctor Institute, 1961), 25.

123. *Luxembourg Gardens, Paris, No. 3*, 1902

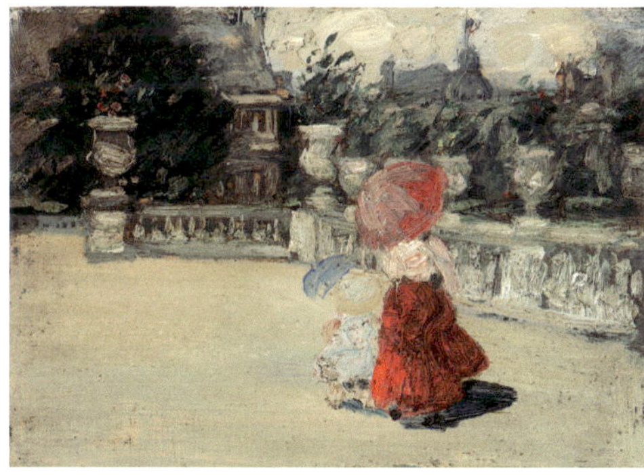

Oil on hardwood panel
6 ⅛ x 8 ⅝ in.
57.181
Signed verso (black paint): Luxembourg / Gardens / Paris / 14 / George Luks; inscribed verso (black ink, in another hand, possibly Mrs. Luks): In the Luxembourg Gardens / Paris–France / by Geo B. Luks

EXHIBITIONS

"Retrospective Exhibition of Paintings by George Luks," C.W. Kraushaar Galleries, New York, January 8–27, 1923 (cat. no. 15). "Edward Wales Root Bequest," Munson-Williams-Proctor Institute, Utica, N.Y., November 5, 1961–February 24, 1962 (catalog). "George Luks (1866–1933): An Exhibition of Paintings and Drawings Dating from 1889 to 1931," MWPI, April 1–May 20, 1973 (cat. no. 7, illus., 21). "Five Decades of Collecting: Edward W. Root," MWPI, April 2–May 28, 1978.

PUBLICATION

Paintings, Drawings & Sculptures in the Museum of Art (Utica, N.Y.: Munson-Williams-Proctor Institute, 1961), 25.

GEORGE B. LUKS

124. *The Marne at Charenton, Paris*, 1902

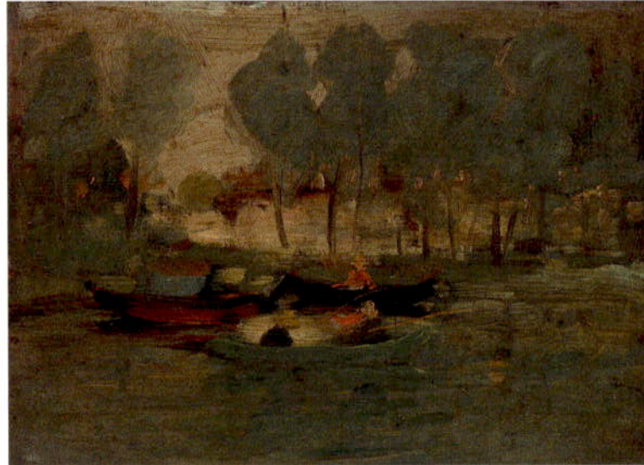

Oil on hardwood panel
6 ⅛ x 8 ⅝ in.
57.182
Signed verso (black paint): The Marne at / Charenton / Paris / 20 / George Luks

EXHIBITIONS

"Retrospective Exhibition of Paintings by George Luks," C.W. Kraushaar Galleries, New York, January 8–27, 1923 (cat. no. 15). "Edward Wales Root Bequest," Munson-Williams-Proctor Institute, Utica, N.Y., November 5, 1961–February 24, 1962 (catalog). "George Luks (1866–1933): An Exhibition of Paintings and Drawings Dating from 1889 to 1931," MWPI, April 1–May 20, 1973 (cat. no. 8, illus., 21). "Five Decades of Collecting: Edward W. Root," MWPI, April 2–May 28, 1978.

PUBLICATION

Paintings, Drawings & Sculptures in the Museum of Art (Utica, N.Y.: Munson-Williams-Proctor Institute, 1961), 25.

125. *On the Marne, France*, 1902

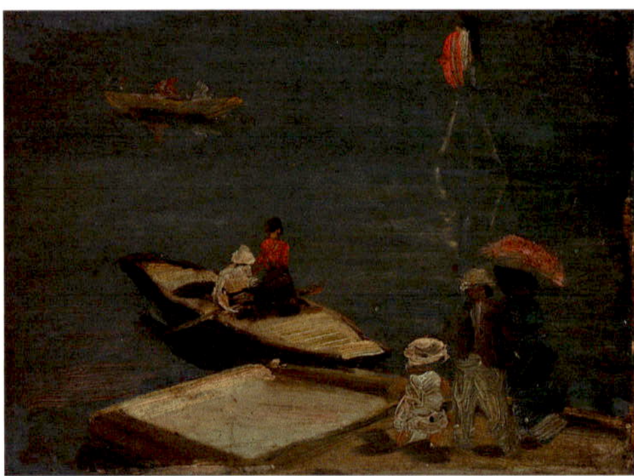

Oil on hardwood panel
6 ⅛ x 8 ⅝ in.
57.185
Signed verso (black paint): On the Marne / France / 13 / George Luks; inscribed verso (black ink, in another hand, possibly Mrs. Luks): On the Marne—France / by Geo. B. Luks
[Note: There is a watercolor of this subject, *On the Marne*, 6 x 8 ½ in.]

EXHIBITIONS

"Retrospective Exhibition of Paintings by George Luks," C.W. Kraushaar Galleries, New York, January 8–27, 1923 (cat. no. 15). "Five American Artists of the 20th Century: Davies, Luks, Burchfield, Tobey, Stamos," Root Art Center, Hamilton College, Clinton, N.Y., December 7, 1958–March 28, 1959. "Edward Wales Root Bequest," Munson-Williams-Proctor Institute, Utica, N.Y., November 5, 1961–February 24, 1962 (catalog). "George Luks (1866–1933): An Exhibition of Paintings and Drawings Dating from 1889 to 1931," MWPI, April 1–May 20, 1973 (cat. no. 9, illus., 21). "Five Decades of Collecting: Edward W. Root," MWPI, April 2–May 28, 1978.

PUBLICATION

Paintings, Drawings & Sculptures in the Museum of Art (Utica, N.Y.: Munson-Williams-Proctor Institute, 1961), 25.

126. *Picnic in the Woods, Robinson, France, No. 1*, 1902

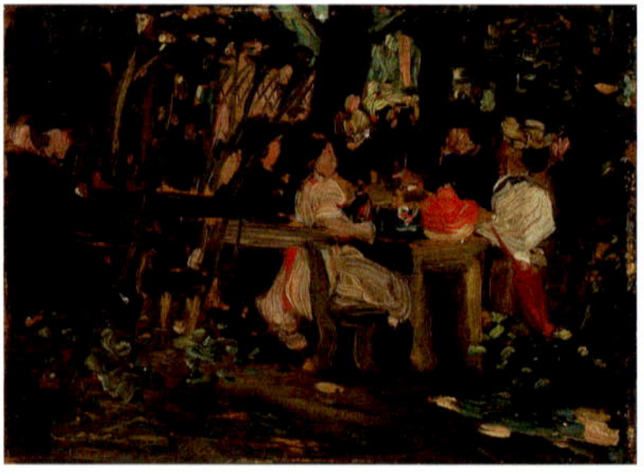

Oil on hardwood panel
6 ⅛ x 8 ⅝ in.
57.186
Signed verso (black paint): Picnic in the / 16 / Woods Robinson / France / George B. Luks; inscribed verso (black ink, in another hand): Robinson / France [there are some comic figures of men drawn on the back by the artist]

EXHIBITIONS

"Retrospective Exhibition of Paintings by George Luks," C.W. Kraushaar Galleries, New York, January 8–27, 1923 (cat. no. 15). "Edward Wales Root Bequest," Munson-Williams-Proctor Institute, Utica, N.Y., November 5, 1961–February 24, 1962 (catalog). "George Luks (1866–1933): An Exhibition of Paintings and Drawings Dating from 1889 to 1931," MWPI, April 1–May 20, 1973 (cat. no. 10, illus., 21). "Five Decades of Collecting: Edward W. Root," MWPI, April 2–May 28, 1978.

PUBLICATION

Paintings, Drawings & Sculptures in the Museum of Art (Utica, N.Y.: Munson-Williams-Proctor Institute, 1961), 25.

127. *Picnic in the Woods, Robinson, France, No. 2*, 1902

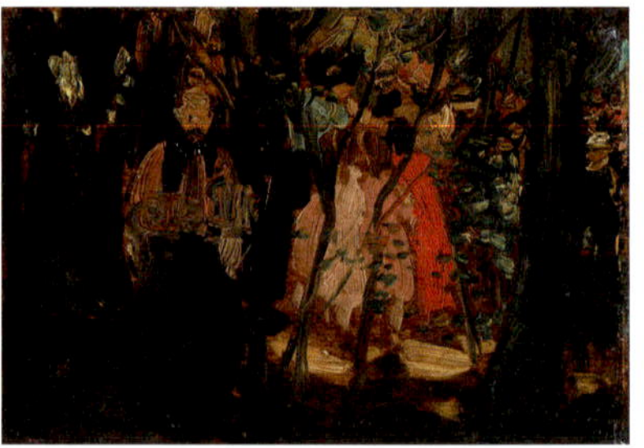

Oil on hardwood panel
6 ⅛ x 8 ⅝ in.
57.187
Signed verso (black paint): Picnic in the Wood / Robinson—France / George B. Luks / 19
Inscribed verso (black ink, in another hand, possibly Mrs. Luks): Picnic—Robinson—France / by Geo. B. Luks

EXHIBITIONS

"Retrospective Exhibition of Paintings by George Luks," C.W. Kraushaar Galleries, New York, January 8–27, 1923 (cat. no. 15). "Five American Artists of the 20th Century: Davies, Luks, Burchfield, Tobey, Stamos," Root Art Center, Hamilton College, Clinton, N.Y., December 7, 1958–March 28, 1959. "Edward Wales Root Bequest," Munson-Williams-Proctor Institute, Utica, N.Y., November 5, 1961–February 24, 1962 (catalog). "George Luks (1866–1933): An Exhibition of Paintings and Drawings Dating from 1889 to 1931," MWPI, April 1–May 20, 1973 (cat. no. 11). "Five Decades of Collecting: Edward W. Root," MWPI, April 2–May 28, 1978.

PUBLICATION

Paintings, Drawings & Sculptures in the Museum of Art (Utica, N.Y.: Munson-Williams-Proctor Institute, 1961), 25.

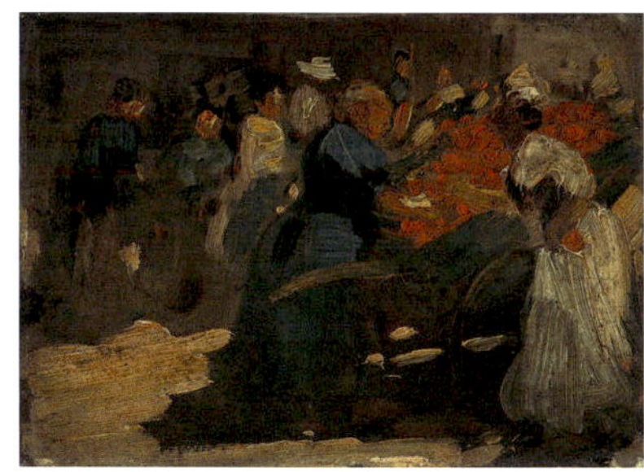

128. *Push Cart Market, Rue de Rennes, Paris*, 1902

Oil on hardwood panel
6 ⅛ x 8 ⅝ in.
57.188
Signed verso (black paint): Push Cart Market / Rue de Rennes / Paris 5 / George Luks

EXHIBITIONS

"Retrospective Exhibition of Paintings by George Luks," C.W. Kraushaar Galleries, New York, January 8–27, 1923 (cat. no. 15). "Edward Wales Root Bequest," Munson-Williams-Proctor Institute, Utica, N.Y., November 5, 1961–February 24, 1962 (catalog). "George Luks (1866–1933): An Exhibition of Paintings and Drawings Dating from 1889 to 1931," MWPI, April 1–May 20, 1973 (cat. no. 12). "Five Decades of Collecting: Edward W. Root," MWPI, April 2–May 28, 1978.

PUBLICATION

Paintings, Drawings & Sculptures in the Museum of Art (Utica, N.Y.: Munson-Williams-Proctor Institute, 1961), 25.

129. *Closing the Café*, 1904

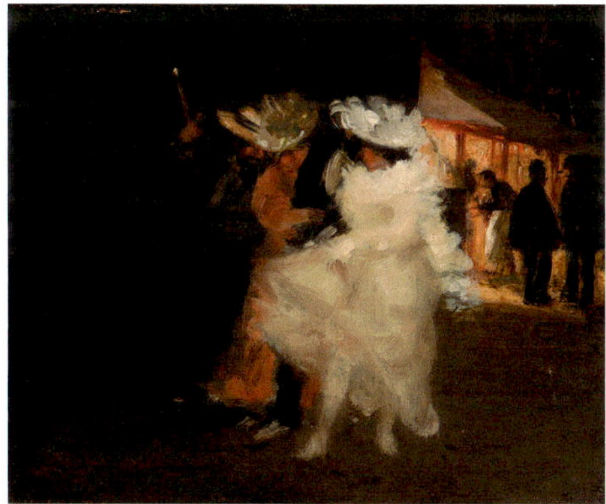

Oil on hardwood panel
8 ½ x 10 ⅝ in.
57.175
Signed and dated lower left (light brown paint): George Luks PARIS 1904

EXHIBITIONS

"Retrospective Exhibition of Paintings by George Luks," C. W. Kraushaar Galleries, New York, January 8–27, 1923 (cat. no. 14). "The Edward Root Collection," The Metropolitan Museum of Art, New York, February 12–April 12, 1953 (catalog, 2). "Five Decades of American Painting," Union College, Schenectady, N.Y., September 27–October 23, 1959. Museum of Art Building inaugural exhibition, Munson-Williams-Proctor Institute, Utica, N.Y., October 15–December 31, 1960. "Edward Wales Root Bequest," MWPI, November 5, 1961–February 24, 1962 (catalog). Root Art Center, Hamilton College, Clinton, N.Y., December 1963. "George Luks (1866–1933): An Exhibition of Paintings and Drawings Dating from 1889 to 1931," MWPI, April 1–May 20, 1973 (cat. no. 15, illus., 22). "Five Decades of Collecting: Edward W. Root," MWPI, April 2–May 28, 1978. "The Shock of Modernism in America: The Eight and Artists of the Armory Show," Nassau County Museum of Fine Art, Roslyn Harbor, N.Y., April 29–July 29, 1984 (cat. no. 31, illus., 23).

PUBLICATIONS

Du Bois, Guy Pène. "George B. Luks and Flamboyance," *The Arts* III (February 1923): 115, illus. The Gilder, "Palette and Brush," *Town Topics*, 1923, 15. *Paintings, Drawings & Sculptures in the Museum of Art* (Utica, N.Y.: Munson-Williams-Proctor Institute, 1961), 24. Young, Mahonri Sharp. "Luks Under The Elms," *Apollo* (July 1973): illus., 55.

130. *A Daughter of the Mines*
1923

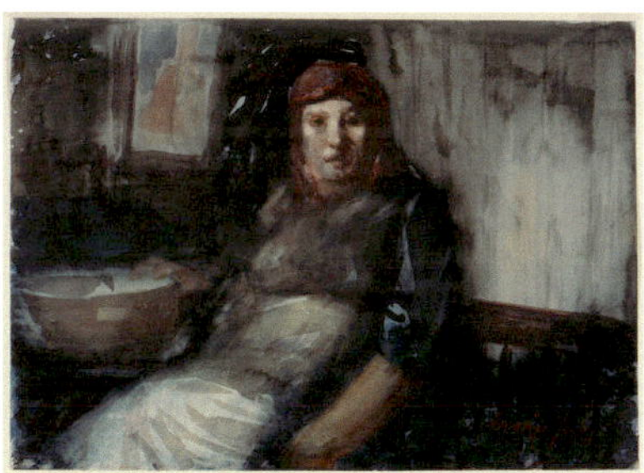

Watercolor on white wove paper
13 ⅞ x 20 in.
57.176
Signed lower right (red paint): George Luks; inscribed verso (charcoal): no. 4 / a daughter of the mines
Purchased from Frank K. M. Rehn Galleries, New York, November 1931

EXHIBITIONS

"Exhibition of Watercolors by Gifford Beal, William Zorach, Maurice Prendergast, Reynolds Beal and George Luks," C.W. Kraushaar Galleries, New York, October 15–November 3, 1923 (cat. no. 4). "Exhibition of Watercolors and Pastels by Eleven American Moderns from a Distinguished Private Collection," Munson-Williams-Proctor Institute, Utica, N.Y., fall 1938. "The Edward Root Collection," The Metropolitan Museum of Art, New York, February 12–April 12, 1953 (catalog, 2). "American Watercolors and Drawings," Root Art Center, Hamilton College, Clinton, N.Y., April 4–May 7, 1961. "Edward Wales Root Bequest," MWPI, November 5, 1961–February 24, 1962 (catalog, illus.). "The Figure in 20th-Century Paintings and Drawings," Root Art Center, April 15–May 6, 1962. "American Traditionalists of the 20th Century," Columbus Museum of Arts and Crafts, Columbus, Ga., February 16–March 17, 1963 (catalog, illus. no. 109). "American 20th-Century Watercolors from MWPI," Albany Institute of History and Art, Albany, N.Y., September 10–October 4, 1967. "Paintings and Drawings from Edward W. Root Bequest," Root Art Center, April 7–May 5, 1968. "The Root Bequest," Root Art Center, May 11–June 8, 1969. "George Luks (1866–1933): An Exhibition of Paintings and Drawings Dating from 1889 to 1931," MWPI, April 1–May 20, 1973 (cat. no. 58, illus., 11). "American Drawings and Watercolors from the Munson-Williams-Proctor Institute," E. B. Crocker Art Gallery, Sacramento, Calif., October 25–November 24, 1974 (cat. no. 37). "Graphic Styles of the American Eight," University of Utah, Salt Lake City, February 29–April 11, 1976 (cat. no. 68, illus., 47). "The Machine Image in 20th-Century Art," MWPI, November 5, 1983–February 5, 1984. "Woman," Terra Museum of American Art, Evanston, Ill., February 21–April 22, 1984 (cat. no. 39, illus., 34). "George Luks: An American Artist," Sordoni Art Gallery, Wilkes College, Wilkes-Barre, Pa., May 3–June 14, 1987 (traveling exhibition, cat. no. 48, illus., 103). "George Luks, Expressionist Master of Color, The Watercolors Rediscovered," The Canton Museum of Art, Canton, Ohio, November 25, 1994–January 29, 1995 (traveling exhibition, catalog, illus., 39). "American Twentieth-Century Watercolors at the Munson-Williams-Proctor Institute," MWPAI, April 30–July 10, 2000 (traveling exhibition, cat. no. 13, illus.).

GEORGE B.LUKS

PUBLICATIONS

"The World of Art: Comments of Some Current Exhibitions," *New York Times Magazine*, October 28, 1923, 10. *Paintings, Drawings & Sculptures in the Museum of Art* (Utica, N.Y.: Munson-Williams-Proctor Institute, 1961), 25. "The Edward W. Root Art Center, Hamilton College," MWPI *Bulletin* (April-May 1961), illus. [medium incorrectly listed as "oil"]. Talcott, Ralph C. "Watercolors of George Luks," Unpublished masters thesis, Pennsylvania State University, 1970, no. 47. *American Art in Upstate New York* (Buffalo, N.Y.: Buffalo Fine Arts Academy, 1974), 33. Coughery, John. "The Mysterious George Luks," *Arts Magazine* 62 (December 1987): 34–35, illus.

131. *Mexican Boy*, not dated

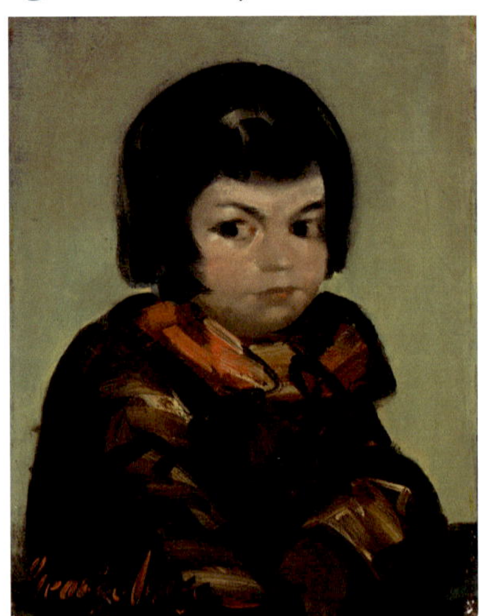

Oil on canvas
18 ¼ x 14 ¼ in.
57.183
Signed lower left (red paint): George Luks; inscribed verso on canvas (black paint): Mexican Boy / George Luks; stamped verso on canvas: George Luks Sale / [illegible]
Artist's Estate; Parke-Bernet Galleries, Inc., *Paintings, Watercolors and Drawings by George Luks*, no. 24, April 5, 1950; to Frank K. M. Rehn Galleries, New York; to Edward W. Root, May 1950

EXHIBITIONS

"Five American Artists of the 20th Century: Davies, Luks, Burchfield, Tobey, Stamos," Root Art Center, Hamilton College, Clinton, N.Y., December 7, 1958–March 28, 1959. Museum of Art Building inaugural exhibition, Munson-Williams-Proctor Institute, Utica, N.Y., October 15–December 31, 1960. "Edward Wales Root Bequest," MWPI, November 5, 1961–February 24, 1962 (catalog). "The Ash Can School," American Federation of Arts, September 1966–September 1967 (traveling exhibition, cat. no. 13). "George Luks (1866–1933): An Exhibition of Paintings and Drawings Dating from 1889 to 1931," MWPI, April 1–May 20, 1973 (cat. no. 86).

PUBLICATION

Paintings, Drawings & Sculptures in the Museum of Art (Utica, N.Y.: Munson-Williams-Proctor Institute, 1961), 25.

132. *Miners' Shacks, Pottsville*

1927

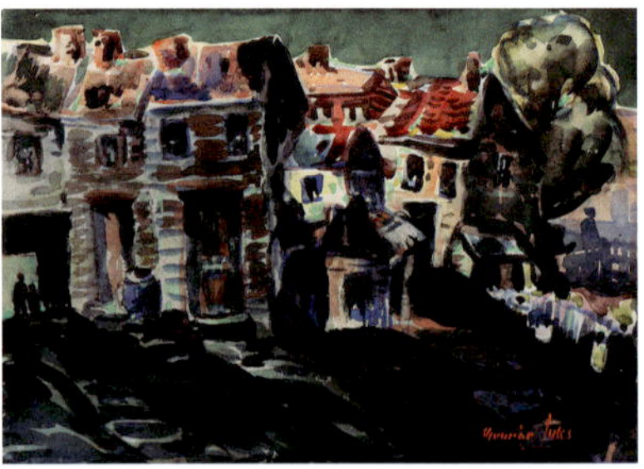

Watercolor on white wove watercolor paper
14 x 20 in.
57.184
Signed lower right (red paint): George Luks
Purchased from Frank K. M. Rehn Galleries, New York, December 1927

EXHIBITIONS

[Frank K. M. Galleries, New York, November 1927.] "Paintings from the Collection of Edward W. Root," Munson-Williams-Proctor Institute, Utica, N.Y., September 29–October 20, 1946. "Five American Artists of the 20th Century: Davies, Luks, Burchfield, Tobey, Stamos," Root Art Center, Hamilton College, Clinton, N.Y., December 7, 1958–March 28, 1959. "20th-Century American Painting from the Edward W. Root Collection," Smithsonian Institution, Washington, D.C., July 1959–July 1960 (traveling exhibition). "Edward Wales Root Bequest," MWPI, November 5, 1961–February 24, 1962 (catalog). "The Twenties Revisited," The Gallery of Modern Art, New York, June 29–September 6, 1965. "The Ashcan School," Root Art Center, September 10–October 12, 1967. "George Luks (1866–1933): An Exhibition of Paintings and Drawings Dating from 1889 to 1931," MWPI, April 1–May 20, 1973 (cat. no. 64, illus., 12). "George Luks, Expressionist Master of Color, The Watercolors Rediscovered," The Canton Museum of Art, Canton, Ohio, November 25, 1994–January 29, 1995 (traveling exhibition, catalog, illus., 42). "American Twentieth-Century Watercolors at the Munson-Williams-Proctor Arts Institute," MWPAI, April 30–July 10, 2000 (traveling exhibition, cat. no. 18, illus.).

PUBLICATIONS

Paintings, Drawings & Sculptures in the Museum of Art (Utica, N.Y.: Munson-Williams-Proctor Institute, 1961), 25. Talcott, Ralph C. "Watercolors of George Luks," Unpublished masters thesis, Pennsylvania State University, 1970, no. 145. "Etcetera: Exhibitions 'Chicago Whitey'," *The Art Gallery Magazine* (May 1973), illus., 21. *American Art in Upstate New York* (Buffalo, N.Y.: Buffalo Fine Arts Academy, 1974), 33.

133. *Sculptor*, before 1911

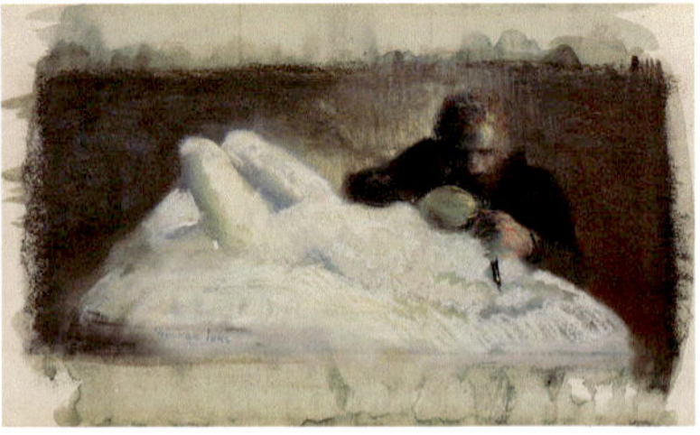

Pastel on heavy paper
10 ⅞ x 15 ¾ in.
57.189
Signed and dated lower left (blue pastel): George Luks
Purchased from the artist before 1911

EXHIBITIONS

"Five American Artists of the 20th Century: Davies, Luks, Burchfield, Tobey, Stamos," Root Art Center, Hamilton College, Clinton, N.Y., December 7, 1958–March 28, 1959. "Edward Wales Root Bequest," Munson-Williams-Proctor Institute, Utica, N.Y., November 5, 1961–February 24, 1962 (catalog). "George Luks (1866–1933): An Exhibition of Paintings and Drawings Dating from 1889 to 1931," MWPI, April 1–May 20, 1973 (cat. no. 89). "American Drawings and Watercolors from the Munson-Williams-Proctor Institute," E. B. Crocker Art Gallery, Sacramento, Calif., October 25–November 24, 1974 (cat. no. 39). "American Works of Art on Paper, 1850–1925," Schenectady Museum & Planetarium, Schenectady, N.Y., January 11–April 6, 1980 (cat. no. 62). "Figuratively Speaking," MWPI, April 11–November 10, 1985. "George Luks: An American Artist," Sordoni Art Gallery, Wilkes College, Wilkes-Barre, Pa., May 3–June 14, 1987 (traveling exhibition, cat. no. 53, illus., 106).

PUBLICATIONS

*Paintings, Drawings & Sculptures in the Museum of Art (Utica, N.Y.: Munson-Williams-*Proctor Institute, 1961), 25. *American Art in Upstate New York* (Buffalo, N.Y.: Buffalo Fine Arts Academy, 1974), 33.

DON MANFREDI

(b. Queens, N.Y., 1930)

134. *Evolution*, not dated

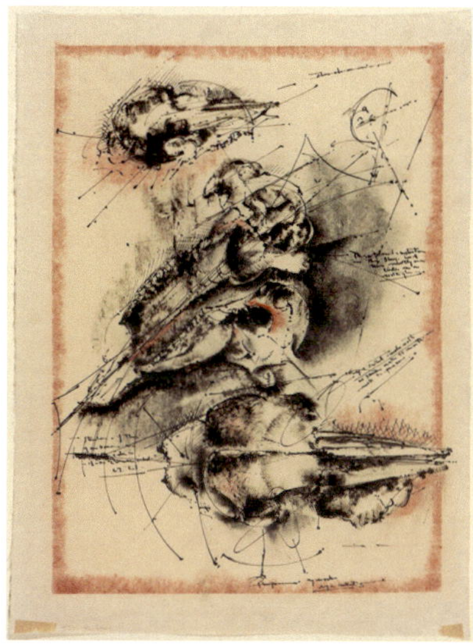

Ink and chalk on paper
22 1/16 x 16 3/4 in.
57.190
Purchased from the Weyhe Gallery, New York

EXHIBITIONS

"Don Manfredi," Weyhe Gallery, New York, December 6–22, 1948. "Contemporary American Watercolors and Drawings," Smithsonian Institution, Washington, D.C., May 1959–May 1960 (traveling exhibition). "American Watercolors and Drawings," Root Art Center, Hamilton College, Clinton, N.Y., April 4–May 7, 1961. "Edward Wales Root Bequest," Munson-Williams-Proctor Institute, Utica, N.Y., November 5, 1961–February 24, 1962 (catalog). "20th-Century Prints and Drawings," Schenectady Museum & Planetarium, Schenectady, N.Y., December 15, 1971–January 15, 1972.

PUBLICATION

Paintings, Drawings & Sculptures in the Museum of Art (Utica, N.Y.: Munson-Williams-Proctor Institute, 1961), 26.

PEPPINO MANGRAVITE

(Lipari, Italy, 1896–Westport, Conn., 1978)

135. *New England Bacchanal*

Ca.1940

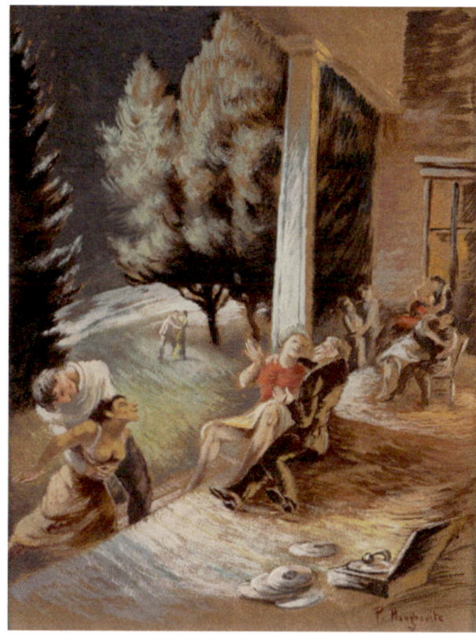

Tempera and metallic gold paint on coarse brown paper
15 ½ x 11 ½ in.
57.192
Signed lower right (brown paint): P. Mangravite
Purchased from Frank K. M. Rehn Galleries, New York, April 1943

EXHIBITIONS

"Paintings from the Collection of Edward W. Root," Munson-Williams-Proctor Institute, Utica, N.Y., September 29–October 20, 1946. "American Watercolors and Drawings," Root Art Center, Hamilton College, Clinton, N.Y., April 4–May 7, 1961. "Edward Wales Root Bequest," MWPI, November 5, 1961–February 24, 1962 (catalog). "American 20th-Century Watercolors from MWPI," Albany Institute of History and Art, Albany, N.Y., September 10–October 4, 1967. "Works by Peppino Mangravite," Burchfield Art Center, Buffalo, N.Y., July 19–September 26, 1982 (cat. no. 8).

PUBLICATION

Paintings, Drawings & Sculptures in the Museum of Art (Utica, N.Y.: Munson-Williams-Proctor Institute, 1961), 26.

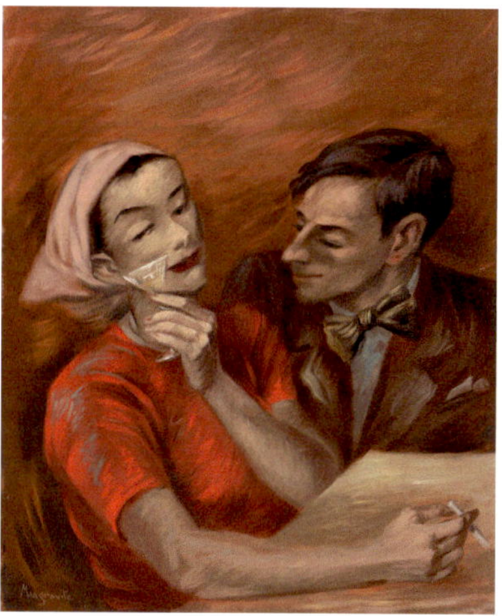

136. *Young Couple Drinking*, 1937

Oil on linen
24 x 20 in.
57.193
Signed lower left (scratched into paint): Mangravite; signed and dated verso upper left: Peppino Mangravite / 1937; top of frame, artist's handwriting: "Young Couple Drinking"
Purchased from Frank K. M. Rehn Galleries, New York, April 1938

EXHIBITIONS

"Paintings by Peppino Mangravite," Frank K. M. Rehn Galleries, New York, November 15–December 4, 1937 (cat. no. 9). "Paintings by Peppino Mangravite," Columbia University, New York, October 7–21, 1958. "Edward Wales Root Bequest," Munson-Williams-Proctor Institute, Utica, N.Y., November 5, 1961–February 24, 1962 (catalog, illus.). "The Figure in 20th-Century Paintings and Drawings," Root Art Center, Hamilton College, Clinton, N.Y., April 2–May 6, 1962. "Edward W. Root: Collector and Teacher," Fred L. Emerson Gallery, Hamilton College, October 2–November 14, 1982 (catalog, 38). "The Art Triangle: Artist, Dealer, Collector," Burchfield Art Center, Buffalo, N.Y., May 13–June 25, 1989 (traveling exhibition, cat. no. 53).

PUBLICATIONS

Salpeter, Harry. "Mangravite: Music in Art," *Esquire* (September 1939): 61, illus. *Paintings, Drawings & Sculptures in the Museum of Art* (Utica, N.Y.: Munson-Williams-Proctor Institute, 1961), 26.

PEPPINO MANGRAVITE

Peppino Mangravite was born in 1896 on the island of Lipari north of Sicily. He studied art under various teachers in the town of Carrara on the Italian mainland. His classes included fresco technique and anatomy. In 1914, he and his father moved to the United States. In New York Mangravite continued his studies at the Cooper Union Art School and, by 1917, at the Art Students League under the guidance of Robert Henri (1865–1929).

Mangravite was an art instructor for the majority of his life. He began his teaching career in 1919 at the Hansen School of Fine Arts in New York City and for the next two decades held positions in Washington, D.C., Colorado Springs, Chicago, and New York. Between 1942 and 1964, he taught at Columbia University. In addition to his wide-ranging teaching career, Mangravite contributed to the field of art pedagogy: he served as chairman of the College Art Association's Committee for the Study of Practice of Art Courses and wrote numerous articles on art education.

Mangravite received considerable public recognition. He was commissioned by the United States Treasury Department to paint murals for three post offices: Hempstead, New York (1936), Atlantic City, New Jersey (1939), and Jackson Heights in Queens, New York (1940). He exhibited and received a prize at the 1939 New York "Building the World of Tomorrow" World's Fair, and received a Gold Medal Purchase Prize from the 1939 Golden Gate Exposition held in San Francisco. In 1955, Mangravite traveled to Europe on behalf of United States Information Agency and Columbia University to interview renowned artists of the day such as Georges Braque (1882–1963), Marc Chagall (1887–1985), and Henry Moore (1898–1986). He also met with several art department heads of various European institutions to discuss Columbia University's plans for a future art center.

Edward Wales Root (1884–1956) met Mangravite through the Frank K. M. Rehn Gallery, where Mangravite first exhibited in 1934. Correspondence between Root and Mangravite in the Munson-Williams-Proctor Arts Institute archives suggests that they became friends early in 1936. Mangravite's involvement in art education was a potent catalyst for his friendship with Root. Both men shared a passion for teaching and creating art, and these qualities cemented an enduring simpatico. Root often addressed Mangravite as "Gino" and they corresponded until Root's death in 1956. The letters are filled with heartfelt advice, playful sketches, and lively discussions. The exchanges focus on various topics such as comparing teaching schedules and the importance for artists, like Root and Mangravite, to have time off for the sole purpose of painting. Root was also friendly and kind to Mangravite's wife Frances, who is the subject of Mangravite's 1941 painting, *Young Girl with Yellow Kerchief (Portrait of Frances Mangravite)* (cat. no. 137). Peppino Mangravite died in Westport, Connecticut in 1978.

—Michael D. Somple

PEPPINO MANGRAVITE

137. *Young Girl with Yellow Kerchief (Portrait of Frances Mangravite),* 1941

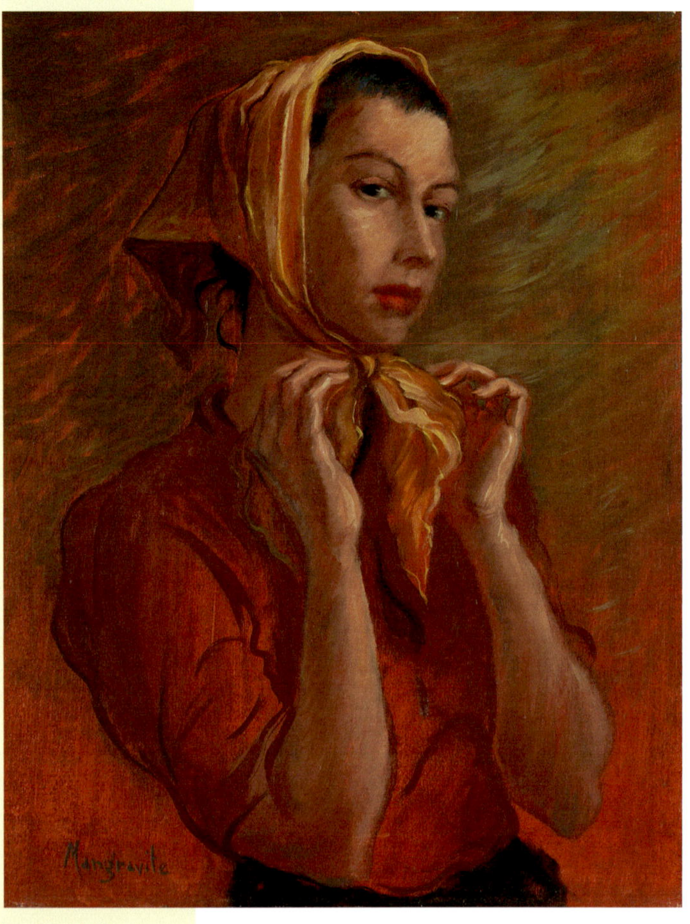

Oil on linen
20 x 16 in.
57.191
Signed lower left (black paint): Mangravite
Purchased from Frank K. M. Rehn Galleries, April 1943

EXHIBITIONS

"Edward Wales Root Bequest," Munson-Williams-Proctor Institute, Utica, N.Y., November 5, 1961–February 24, 1962 (catalog). "Picture of the Month," Stroebel Student Center, Utica College, May 1967.

PUBLICATION

Paintings, Drawings & Sculptures in the Museum of Art (Utica, N.Y.: Munson-Williams-Proctor Institute, 1961), 26.

JOHN MARIN

(Rutherford, N.J., 1870–Addison, Me., 1953)

138. *White Mountain Country, The Rapids (The Rapids, New Hampshire)*, 1927

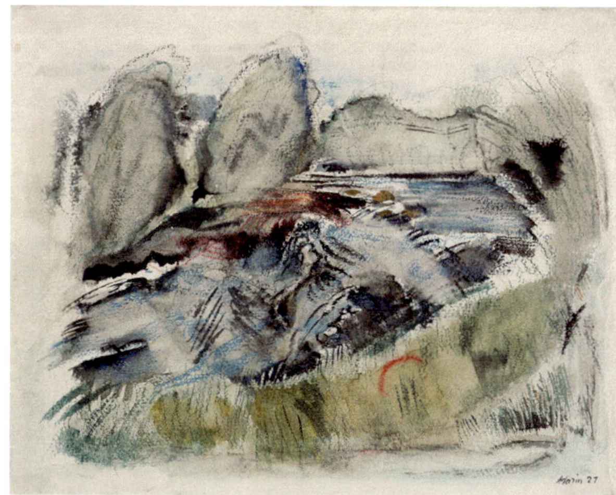

Watercolor, graphite, crayon and colored pencil on heavy watercolor paper
13 7/16 x 17 1/8 in.
57.194
Signed and dated lower right (black paint): Marin 27; inscribed on mount, verso, in Marin's handwriting (graphite): White Mountain Country / (31) The Rapids 1927 / Marin.
The Intimate Gallery, New York; An American Place, New York; The Downtown Gallery, New York; Purchased from The Downtown Gallery, January 1937

EXHIBITIONS

"John Marin," The Intimate Gallery, New York, November–December 1928 (cat. no. 31). "Exhibition of Watercolors and Pastels by Eleven American Moderns from a Distinguished Private Collection," Munson-Williams-Proctor Institute, Utica, N.Y., fall 1938. "John Marin Watercolors, Oils, Prints and Drawings," MWPI, December 2–30, 1951 (cat. no. 12). "The Edward Root Collection," The Metropolitan Museum of Art, New York, February 12–April 12, 1953 (catalog, 3). Museum of Art Building inaugural exhibition, MWPI, October 15–December 31, 1960. "Edward Wales Root Bequest," MWPI, November 5, 1961–February 24, 1962 (catalog). "John Marin 1870–1953," The University of Arizona Art Gallery, Tucson, February 9–March 10, 1963 (cat. no. 42). Root Art Center, Hamilton College, Clinton, N.Y., December 1963. "On Paper," American Federation of Arts, September 1966–September 1967 (traveling exhibition, cat. no. 24). "Paintings and Drawings from the Edward W. Root Bequest," Root Art Center, April 7–May 5, 1968. "The Root Bequest," Root Art Center, May 11–June 8, 1969. "20th-Century American Painting," Executive Mansion, Albany, N.Y., September–November 1974. "Five Decades of Collecting: Edward W. Root," MWPI, April 2–May 28, 1978. "Selections and Transformations: The Art of John Marin," National Gallery of Art, Washington, D.C., January 28–April 15, 1990 (catalog, 216, illus. pl. 209).

PUBLICATIONS

Paintings, Drawings & Sculptures in the Museum of Art (Utica, N.Y.: Munson-Williams-Proctor Institute, 1961), 26. Reich, Sheldon. *John Marin: A Stylistic Analysis and Catalogue Raisonné* (Tucson, Ariz.: The University of Arizona Press, 1970), no. 27.51, illus. 586. *American Art in Upstate New York* (Buffalo, N.Y.: Buffalo Fine Arts Academy, 1974), 33.

REGINALD MARSH

(Paris, France, 1898–Dorset, Vt., 1954)

139. *Lower Manhattan (New York Skyline)*, 1930

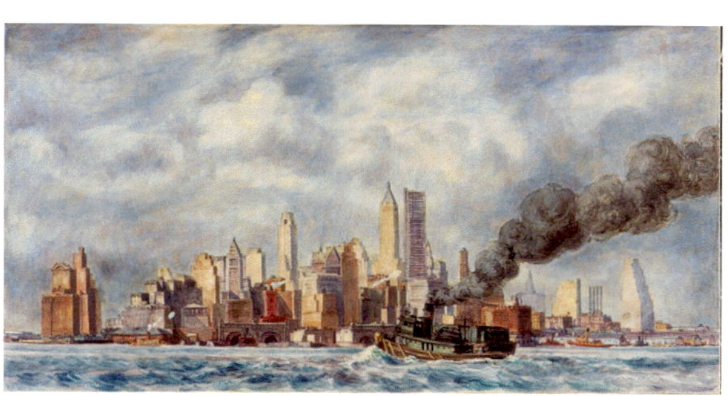

Tempera on linen mounted on Masonite
24 x 48 in.
57.195
Signed and dated lower right (blue paint): REGINALD MARSH 1930
Purchased from Frank K. M. Rehn Galleries, New York, January 1931
[Note: There is a later version of the same subject, *New York Skyline*, 1936, tempera, 24 x 40 in., and a print, *New York Skyline*, 1936, etching and engraving, 5 15/16 x 14 7/8.]

EXHIBITIONS

[Frank K. M. Rehn Galleries, New York, March 2–28, 1931.] "A Chapter in American Art," Rehn Galleries, January 4–30, 1932 (cat. no. 34). "20th-Century American Painting from the Edward W. Root Collection," Smithsonian Institution, Washington, D.C., July 1959–July 1960 (traveling exhibition). "Edward Wales Root Bequest," Munson-Williams-Proctor Institute, Utica, N.Y., November 5, 1961–February 24, 1962 (catalog). "Prints by American Artists," Root Art Center, Hamilton College, Clinton, N.Y., January 9–February 12, 1967. "Edward W. Root: Collector and Teacher," Fred L. Emerson Gallery, Hamilton College, October 2–November 14, 1982 (catalog, illus., 30). "Two Hundred Years of American Art," The Art Museum Association of America, November 15, 1986–May 8, 1988 (traveling exhibition, cat. no. 49, illus., 63). "Masterworks of American Art from the Munson-Williams-Proctor Institute Museum of Art," Knoxville Museum of Art, Knoxville, Tenn., February 26–August 23, 1998. "American Masterworks from the MWPAI, Celebrating an Educational Alliance with Pratt Institute," Hirschl & Adler Galleries, New York, November 16–December 29, 2006 (catalog).

PUBLICATIONS

Paintings, Drawings & Sculptures in the Museum of Art (Utica, N.Y.: Munson-Williams-Proctor Institute, 1961), 27. Schweizer, Paul D., et al. *Masterworks of American Art from the Munson-Williams-Proctor Institute* (New York: Harry N. Abrams, Inc., 1989) cat. no. 63, illus., 138. Schweizer, Paul D. "Masterworks from the Munson-Williams-Proctor Institute," *American Art Review* X (May–June 1998): 180–89, 191, illus., 186. Klein, Milton, M., ed. *The Empire State: A History of New York* (Ithaca, N.Y. and London: Cornell University Press, 2001), illus.

REGINALD MARSH

140. *Texas Guinan and Her Gang*

1931

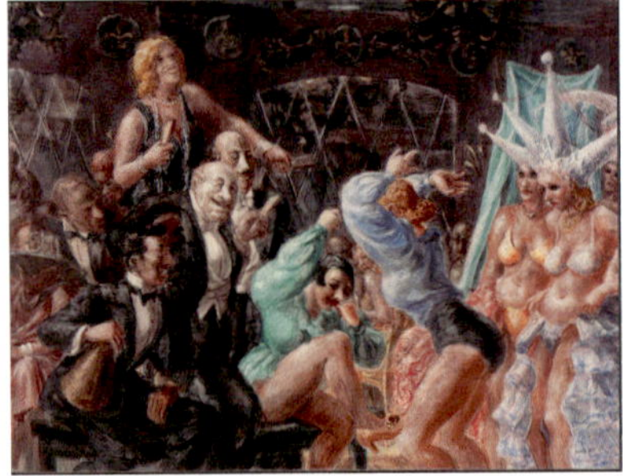

Tempera on linen
36 ¼ x 48 ¼ in.
57.196
Signed and dated lower right (black paint): REGINALD MARSH 1931
Purchased from Frank K. M. Rehn Galleries, New York, August 1933, in exchange for Marsh's *Burlesque*

EXHIBITIONS

1933 Annual Exhibition, Pennsylvania Academy of Fine Arts, Philadelphia (cat. no. 142). "American Scenes and Subjects," Frank K. M. Rehn Gallery, New York, organized by the College Art Association Traveling Exhibitions (cat. no. 22) [ca. 1930s]. "20th-Century American Painting from the Edward W. Root Collection," Smithsonian Institution, Washington, D.C., July 1959–July 1960 (traveling exhibition). "Edward Wales Root Bequest," Munson-Williams-Proctor Institute, Utica, N.Y., November 5, 1961–February 24, 1962 (catalog, illus.). "The Figure in 20th-Century Paintings and Drawings," Root Art Center, Hamilton College, Clinton, N.Y., April 15–May 6, 1962. "American Traditionalists of the 20th Century," Columbus Museum of Arts and Crafts, Columbus, Ga., February 16–March, 17, 1963 (catalog, 16). "Reginald Marsh," The Gallery of Modern Art, New York, November 25, 1964–January 29, 1965. "Paintings and Drawings from the Edward W. Root Bequest," Root Art Center, April 7–May 5, 1968. "American Art of the Depression Era," Amherst College, Amherst, Mass., February 25–March 19, 1969 (cat. no. 5, illus., 3). "The Root Bequest," Root Art Center, May 11–June 8, 1969. "The Thirties: Reaction to Crisis," Lowe Art Center, Syracuse University, Syracuse, N.Y., March 31–April 17, 1974 (catalog). "Figuratively Speaking," MWPI, April 11–November 10, 1985. "Insights," MWPI, January 7–April 13 and June 10–October 15, 1986.

PUBLICATIONS

Survey 67 (February 1, 1932): 470. Craven, Thomas. *Modern Art: The Men, The Movements, The Meaning* (New York: Simon & Schuster, 1934), illus. opp. 331. *Paintings, Drawings & Sculptures in the Museum of Art* (Utica, N.Y.: Munson-Williams-Proctor Institute, 1961), 27. Prior, Harris K. "Edward Root–Talent Scout," *Art in America* L (1962): 70, illus. fig. 1.

141. *Zeke Youngblood's Dance Marathon*, 1932

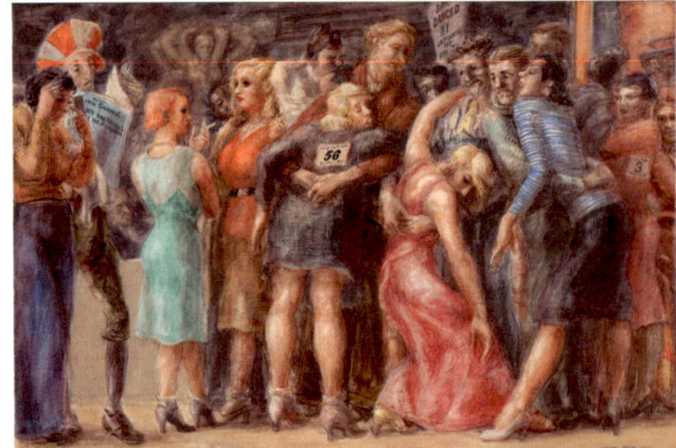

Tempera on wood
24 x 36 in.
57.197
Signed and dated lower right (black paint): REGINALD MARSH 1932
Purchased from Frank K. M. Rehn Galleries, New York, April 1932

EXHIBITIONS

"Recent Paintings by Reginald Marsh," Frank K. M. Rehn Galleries, New York, February 22–March 12, 1932 (cat. no. 9). "Reginald Marsh," Whitney Museum of American Art, New York, September 21–November 6, 1955 (traveling exhibition, cat. no. 11). "Five Decades of American Painting," Union College, Schenectady, N.Y., September 27–October 23, 1959. "Edward Wales Root Bequest," Munson-Williams-Proctor Institute, Utica, N.Y., November 5, 1961–February 24, 1962 (catalog). "The Figure in 20th-Century Paintings and Drawings," Root Art Center, Hamilton College, Clinton, N.Y., April 15–May 6, 1962. "Learning About Pictures from Mr. Root," Root Art Center, January 4–31, 1965 (catalog, illus.). "East Side West Side All Around the Town: A Retrospective Exhibition of Paintings, Watercolors and Drawings by Reginald Marsh," The University of Arizona Museum of Art, Tucson, March 9–April 6, 1969 (cat. no. 63, illus., 77). "Reginald Marsh, A Retrospective Exhibition," Newport Harbor Art Museum, Newport Beach, Calif., October 31–December 10, 1972 (traveling exhibition, catalog, illus. fig. 15). "Reginald Marsh, Fiftieth Anniversary Exhibition," Kalamazoo Institute of Arts, Kalamazoo, Mich., November 4–28, 1973 (cat. no. 6, illus., 6). "American Series: America Between the Wars," San Jose Museum of Art, fall 1976 (catalog, illus.). "The Thirties: Reaction to Crisis," Lowe Art Center, Syracuse University, Syracuse, N.Y., March 31–April 17, 1974 (catalog, illus.). "Five Decades of Collecting: Edward W. Root," MWPI, April 2–May 28, 1978. "The American Scene 1920–1940," Neue Gesellschaft für bildende Kunst, Berlin, West Germany, November 9–December 28, 1980 (catalog). "1931 America–The Artist's View," Sierra Nevada Museum of Art, Reno, Nev., September 1–October 31, 1982 (traveling exhibition, catalog, 20). "American Realism Between the Wars, 1914–1941," Nassau County Museum of Art, Roslyn Harbor, N.Y., March 27–June 5, 1994 (catalog, illus. fig. 1).

PUBLICATION

"Major Show at Art Center," *Kalamazoo Gazette*, November 4, 1973, illus.

HENRY MATTSON

(Gothenburg, Sweden, 1887–Woodstock, N.Y., 1971)

142. *Sumac*, 1930

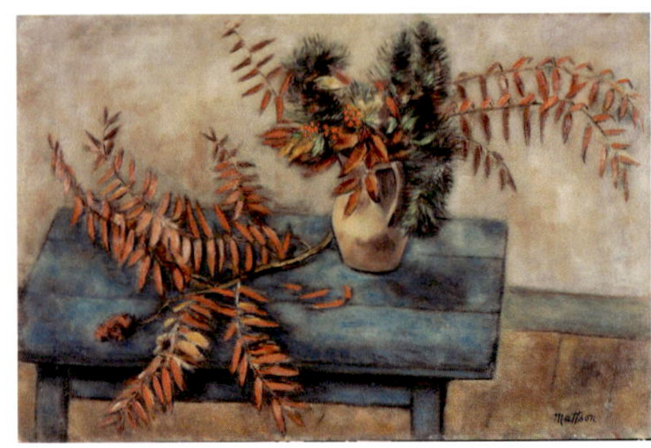

Oil on linen
30 ⅛ x 46 ⅛ in.
57.198
Signed lower right (black paint): Mattson
Purchased from Frank K. M. Rehn Galleries, New York, February 1931

EXHIBITIONS

"First Municipal Art Exhibition: Paintings, Sculpture, Drawings, and Prints by Living American Artists Identified with the New York Art World," Rockefeller Center, R.C.A. Building, New York, February 28–March 31, 1934 (cat. no. 601). "Paintings from the Collection of Edward W. Root," Munson-Williams-Proctor Institute, Utica, N.Y., September 29–October 20, 1946. "Edward Wales Root Art Bequest," MWPI, November 5, 1961–February 24, 1962 (catalog). "Learning About Pictures from Mr. Root," Root Art Center, Hamilton College, Clinton, N.Y., January 4–31, 1965 (catalog, illus.). "The Root Bequest," Root Art Center, May 11–June 8, 1969. "The Art Triangle: Artist, Dealer, Collector," Burchfield Art Center, Buffalo, N.Y., May 13–June 25, 1989 (traveling exhibition, cat. no. 65).

PUBLICATION

Paintings, Drawings & Sculptures in the Museum of Art (Utica, N.Y.: Munson-Williams-Proctor Institute, 1961), 27.

HENRY LEE MCFEE

(St. Louis, Mo., 1886–Los Angeles, Calif., 1953)

143. *Boy*, 1932

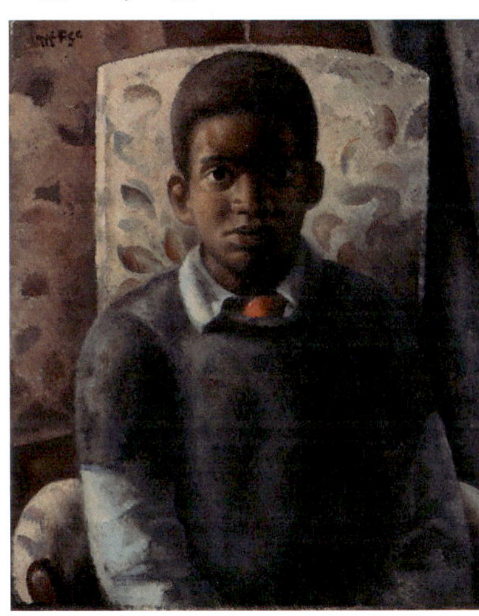

Oil on canvas
24 x 20 ⅛ in.
57.199
Signed upper left (black paint): McFee
Purchased from Frank K. M. Rehn Galleries, New York, November 1932

EXHIBITIONS

"Paintings and Drawings by Henry Lee McFee," Frank K. M. Rehn Galleries, New York, January 7–28, 1933 (cat. no. 8). "The Edward Root Collection," The Metropolitan Museum of Art, New York, February 12–April 12, 1953 (catalog, 3). "Edward Wales Root Bequest," Munson-Williams-Proctor Institute, Utica, N.Y., November 5, 1961–February 24, 1962 (catalog).

PUBLICATION

Paintings, Drawings & Sculptures in the Museum of Art (Utica, N.Y.: Munson-Williams-Proctor Institute, 1961), 27.

144. *Still Life–Knife*, ca. 1941

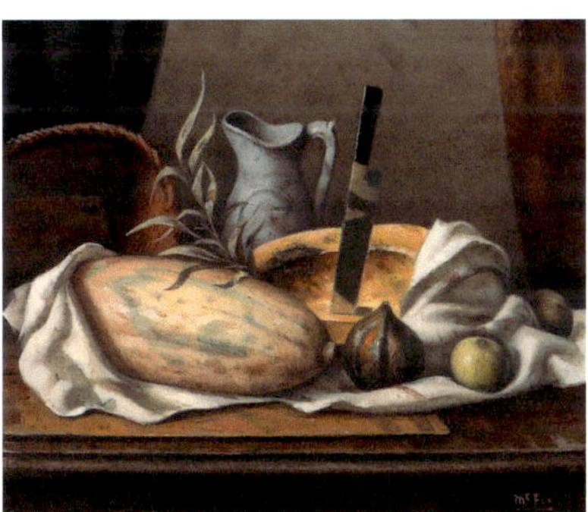

Oil on linen
25 x 30 ⅛ in.
57.200
Signed lower right (light brown paint): McFee
Purchased from exhibition, "Artists for Victory," New York, February 1943

EXHIBITIONS

"Artists for Victory," The Metropolitan Museum of Art, New York, December 7, 1942–February 22, 1943 (as *Still Life*). "The Edward Root Collection," Metropolitan Museum of Art, February 12–April 12, 1953 (catalog, 3). "20th-Century American Painting from the Edward W. Root Collection," Smithsonian Institution, Washington, D.C., July 1959–July 1960 (traveling exhibition). "Edward Wales Root Bequest," Munson-Williams-Proctor Institute, Utica, N.Y., November 5, 1961–February 24, 1962 (catalog).

PUBLICATION

Paintings, Drawings & Sculptures in the Museum of Art (Utica, N.Y.: Munson-Williams-Proctor Institute, 1961), 27.

BARSE MILLER

(New York, N.Y., 1904–Mazatlán, Mexico, 1973)

145. *Bombed Out*, before 1946

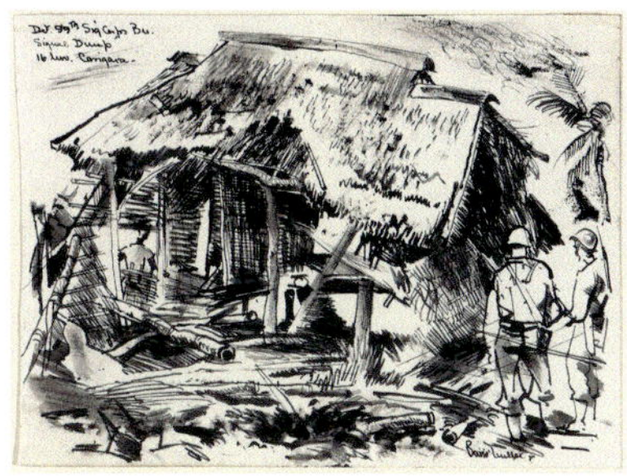

Ink on paper
4 15/16 x 6 ⅞ in.
57.320
Signed lower right (black ink): Barse Miller
[Purchased from Ferargil Galleries, New York, 1946]

EXHIBITIONS

"Barse Miller," Ferargil Galleries, New York, February 25–March 10, 1946 (cat. no. 27). "Edward Wales Root Bequest,"Munson-Williams-Proctor Institute, Utica, N.Y., November 5, 1961–February 24, 1962 (catalog).

PUBLICATION

Paintings, Drawings & Sculptures in the Museum of Art (Utica, N.Y.: Munson-Williams-Proctor Institute, 1961), 28.

BRUCE HANDISIDE MITCHELL

(Tayport, Scotland, 1908–Langhorne, Pa., 1963)

146. *Hudson River Nocturne*, 1937

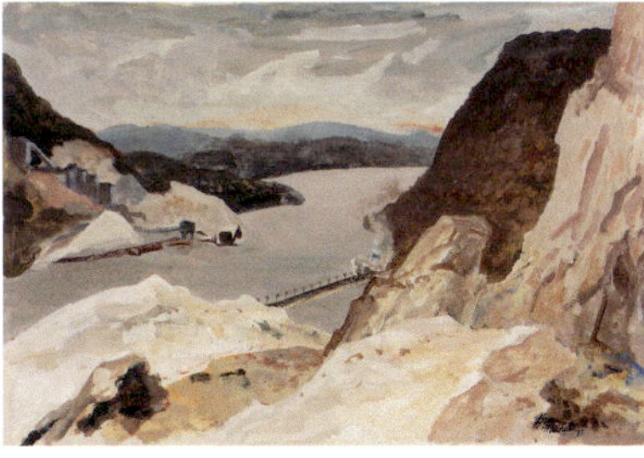

Gouache on cardboard
19 11/16 x 30 in.
57.312
Signed and dated lower right (black paint): Bruce / Miller / 37

BRUCE HANDISIDE MITCHELL

EXHIBITIONS

"The Edward Root Collection," The Metropolitan Museum of Art, New York, N.Y., February 12–April 12, 1953 (catalog, 3). "Edward Wales Root Bequest," Munson-Williams-Proctor Institute, Utica, N.Y., November 5, 1961–February 24, 1962 (catalog).

PUBLICATION

Paintings, Drawings & Sculptures in the Museum of Art (Utica, N.Y.: Munson-Williams-Proctor Institute, 1961), 28.

ROBERT MOTHERWELL

(Aberdeen, Wash., 1915–Provincetown, Mass., 1991)

147. *Nude*, 1952

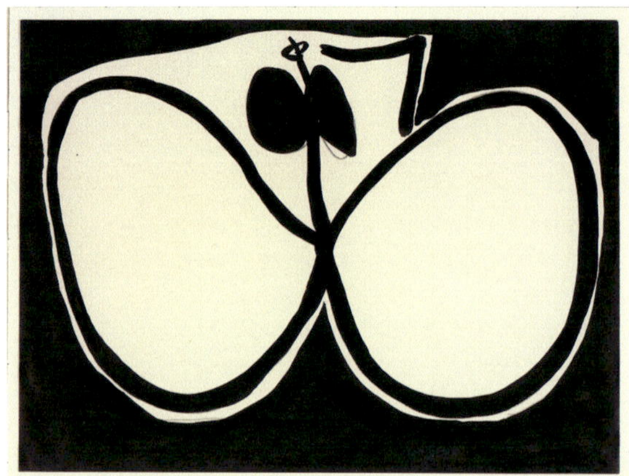

Brush-applied black ink over graphite on wove paper, mounted on illustration board
21 ⅞ x 29 ¾ in.
57.201
Signed verso upper left (graphite): Robert Motherwell / 1952
Purchased from Kootz Gallery, New York

EXHIBITIONS

"Robert Motherwell: Paintings, Drawings and Collages," Kootz Gallery, New York, April 1–19, 1952 (cat. no. 22, illus.). "The Edward Root Collection," The Metropolitan Museum of Art, New York, February 12–April 12, 1953 (catalog, 3). "New Trends in 20th-Century American Painting," Root Art Center, Hamilton College, Clinton, N.Y., October 26–November 30, 1958. "Contemporary American Watercolors and Drawings from the Edward W. Root Collection," Smithsonian Institution, Washington, D.C., June 1, 1959–May 31, 1960 (traveling exhibition). "New Trends in Twentieth-Century Art," Union College, Schenectady, N.Y., March 5–26, 1961. "Edward Wales Root Bequest," Munson-Williams-Proctor Institute, Utica, N.Y., November 5, 1961–February 24, 1962 (catalog). "The Figure in 20th-Century Paintings and Drawings," Root Art Center, April 10–May 6, 1962. "European Sources of Contemporary American Art: Kandinsky," Root Art Center, September 15–October 6, 1963 (cat. no. 29). "Abstract Paintings and Drawings and Prints from the Edward W. Root Bequest," Root Art Center, September 11–October 9, 1966. "Selections From the Edward W. Root Collection," Root Art Center, May 11–June 8, 1969. "Exhibition of American Paintings," Schenectady Museum & Planetarium, Schenectady, N.Y. March 20–April 30, 1970. "American Art in Upstate New York," Albright-Knox Art Gallery, Buffalo, N.Y., July 12, 1974–April 27, 1975 (traveling exhibition, catalog). "Edward W. Root: Collector and Teacher," Fred L. Emerson Gallery, Hamilton College, October 1–November 14, 1982 (catalog, illus., upside-down, 61.). "Life Lines: American Master Drawings (1788–1962) from the Munson-Williams-Proctor Institute," MWPI, September 17–November 13, 1994 (traveling exhibition, cat. no. 57, illus. color pl. 24).

PUBLICATION

Paintings, Drawings & Sculptures in the Museum of Art (Utica, N.Y.: Munson-Williams-Proctor Institute, 1961), 29.

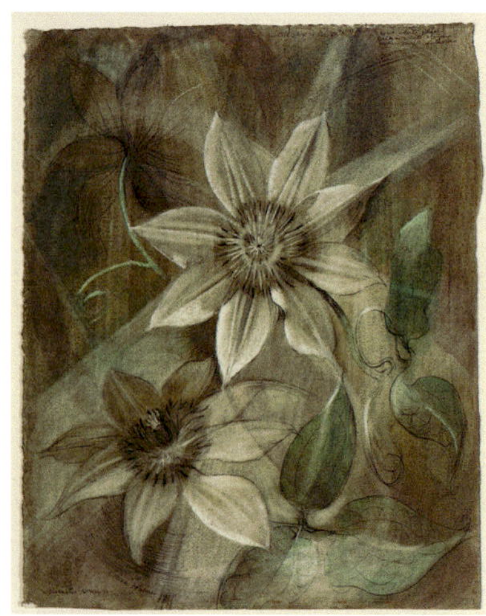

WILLIAM C. PALMER

(Des Moines, Ia., 1906–Clinton, N.Y., 1987)

148. *Clematis Henryi (Clematis)*
1950

Casein and ink on Whatman watercolor paper
14 ¼ x 11 ½ in., irregular
57.202
Signed and dated lower left (black ink): William C Palmer 1950 / Clematis Henryi; inscribed upper right (black ink): convex + concave violet white petals / cream and white stigma / brown purple antheras
Purchased from Midtown Galleries, New York, 1951

EXHIBITION

"William Palmer," Midtown Galleries, New York, October 31–November 25, 1950. "The Edward Root Collection," The Metropolitan Museum of Art, New York, February 12–April 12, 1953 (catalog, 3). Governor Rockefeller's suite, Hotel Utica, Museum of Art building inaugural, Munson-Williams-Proctor Institute, Utica, N.Y., October 13–17, 1960. "American Watercolors and Drawings," Root Art Center, Hamilton College, Clinton, N.Y., April 4–May 7, 1961. "Edward Wales Root Bequest," MWPI, November 5, 1961–February 24, 1962 (catalog, illus.). "Paintings and Drawings from the Edward W. Root Bequest," Root Art Center, April 7–May 5, 1968. "Five Decades of Collecting: Edward W. Root," MWPI, April 2–May 28, 1978. "Flowers in Painting, Prints and Drawings," MWPI, April 20–May 25, 1980. "Edward W. Root: Collector and Teacher," Fred L. Emerson Gallery, Hamilton College, October 2–November 14, 1982 (catalog, 57).

PUBLICATION

Paintings, Drawings & Sculptures in the Museum of Art (Utica, N.Y.: Munson-Williams-Proctor Institute, 1961), 29.

149. *Columbine*, 1950

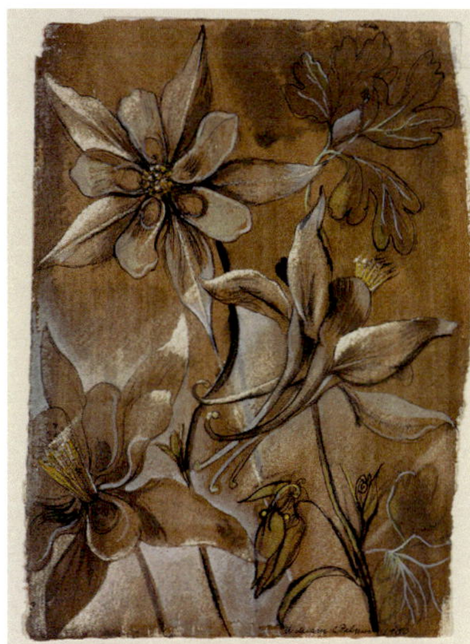

Casein and ink on heavy textured white paper
9 ½ x 6 ¾ in., irregular
57.203
Signed and dated lower right (black ink): William C. Palmer 1950
Purchased from the artist, 1950

EXHIBITIONS
"Edward Wales Root Bequest," Munson-Williams-Proctor Institute, Utica, N.Y., November 5, 1961–February 24, 1962 (catalog). "The Root Bequest," Root Art Center, Hamilton College, Clinton, N.Y., May 11–June 8, 1969. "Flowers in Painting, Prints and Drawings," MWPI, April 20–May 25, 1980. "William C. Palmer," MWPI, April 12–May 12, 1986.

PUBLICATION
Paintings, Drawings & Sculptures in the Museum of Art (Utica, N.Y.: Munson-Williams-Proctor Institute, 1961), 29.

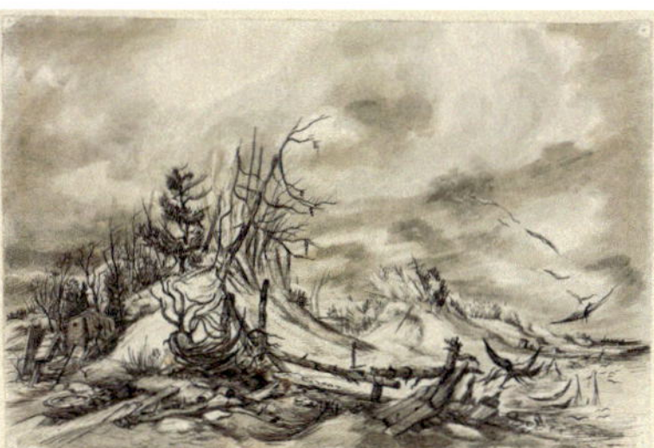

150. *Landscape with Birds*, 1939

Black and brown ink with watercolor wash on heavy watercolor paper
15 x 22 in.
57.204
Purchased from Midtown Galleries, May 1941

EXHIBITION
[Art Institute of Chicago]. "Edward Wales Root Bequest," Munson-Williams-Proctor Institute, Utica, N.Y., November 5, 1961–February 24, 1962 (catalog).

PUBLICATION
Paintings, Drawings & Sculptures in the Museum of Art (Utica, N.Y.: Munson-Williams-Proctor Institute, 1961), 29.

JACKSON POLLOCK

(Cody, Wyo., 1912–East Hampton, N.Y., 1956)

151. *Number 20, 1948*, 1948

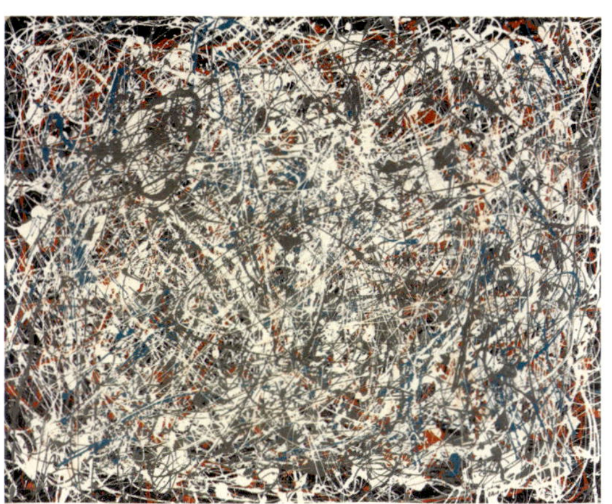

Oil and enamel paint on paper mounted on board
20 ⅜ x 26 in.
57.205
Signed and dated lower right (black paint): Jackson / Pollock 48
Purchased from Betty Parsons Gallery, January 1949

EXHIBITIONS
"Jackson Pollock," Betty Parsons Gallery, New York, January 24–February 12, 1949 (cat. no. 20). "Current Trends in British and American Painting from the Collection of Edward W. Root," Munson-Williams-Proctor Institute, Utica, N.Y., December 3–31, 1950 (traveling exhibition, cat. no. 20). "The Edward Root Collection," The Metropolitan Museum of Art, New York, February 12–April 12, 1953 (catalog, 3). "In Memoriam," American Federation of Arts, November 1957–November 1958 (traveling exhibition). "20th-Century American Painting from the Edward W. Root Collection," Smithsonian Institution, Washington, D.C., July 1959–July 1960 (traveling exhibition). "Edward Wales Root Bequest," MWPI, November 5, 1961–February 24, 1962 (catalog). "European Sources of Contemporary American Art: Kandinsky," Root Art Center, Hamilton College, Clinton, N.Y., September 15–October 6, 1963 (cat. no. 30). "Paintings and Drawings: Selections from the Edward W. Root Bequest," Root Art Center, April 7–May 5, 1968. "Jackson Pollock," Betty Parsons Gallery, April 9–27, 1983. "Abstract Expressionism," MWPI, July 19–August 18, 1985. "Insights," MWPI, January 7–April 13 and June 10–October 15, 1986. "Influences of Klee," MWPI, December 19, 1987–May 13, 1988. "Abstract Expressionism: Other Dimensions," The Jane Voorhees Zimmerli Art Museum, Rutgers University, March 25–June 13, 1990 (traveling exhibition [Whitney Museum of American Art at Philip Morris venue only, not listed in catalog]). "Life Lines: American Master Drawings (1788–1962) from the Munson-Williams-Proctor Institute," MWPI, September 17–November 13, 1994 (traveling exhibition, cat. no. 54, illus. color pl. 21). "Jackson Pollock," The Museum of Modern Art, New York, November 1, 1998–February 2, 1999 (traveling exhibition, catalog, illus. fig. 134).

PUBLICATIONS
Hale, Robert Beverly. "The Growth of a Collection," *The Metropolitan Museum of Art Bulletin* XI (February 1953): 154–55. *Paintings, Drawings & Sculptures in the Museum of Art* (Utica, N.Y.: Munson-Williams-Proctor Institute, 1961), 30. O'Connor, Francis and Thaw, Eugene, eds. *Jackson Pollock: A Catalogue Raisonné of Paintings, Drawings, and Other Works* (New Haven and London: Yale University Press, 1978), cat. no. 191, illus. Varnadoe, Kirk and Karmel, Pepe, eds. *Jackson Pollock: New Approaches* (New York: MoMA, 1999), illus. fig. 37.

JACKSON POLLOCK

152. *Number 34, 1949*, 1949

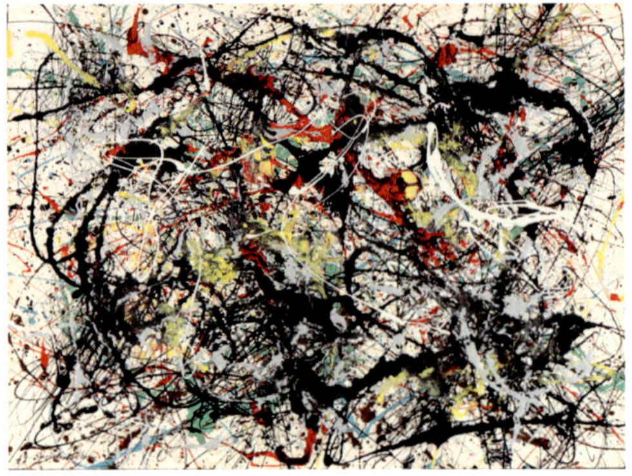

Oil and enamel paint on white paperboard mounted on Masonite
22 x 30 ½ in.
57.206
Signed and dated lower left (black paint): 49 Jackson Pollock
Purchased from Betty Parsons Gallery, December 1949

EXHIBITIONS

"Jackson Pollock," Betty Parsons Gallery, New York, November 21–December 10, 1949 (catalog). "Current Trends in British and American Painting from the Collection of Edward W. Root," Munson-Williams-Proctor Institute, Utica, N.Y., December 3–31, 1950 (traveling exhibition, cat. no. 21). "The Edward Root Collection," The Metropolitan Museum of Art, New York, February 12–April 12, 1953 (catalog, 3). "A Rationale for Modern Art," American Federation of Arts, October 1959–October 1960 (traveling exhibition). "New Trends in 20th-Century American Painting," Union College, Schenectady, N.Y., March 5–26, 1961. [Union Carbide Corporation, New York, 1961]. "Edward Wales Root Bequest," MWPI, November 5, 1961–February 24, 1962 (catalog, illus.). "European Sources of Contemporary American Art: Kandinsky," Root Art Center, Hamilton College, Clinton, N.Y., September 15–October 6, 1963 (cat. no. 31). "Jackson Pollock," Marlborough-Gerson Galleries, New York, January–February 1964 (catalog, illus. fig. 106). "American Painting 1910 to 1960," Indiana University, Bloomington, Ind., April 19–May 10, 1964 (cat. no. 53, illus.). "125 Years of New York State Painting and Sculpture," New York State Exposition, Syracuse, organized by the New York State Council on the Arts, August 30–September 5, 1966 (cat. no. 45). "20th-Century American Painting," Grand Rapids Art Museum, Grand Rapids, Mich., April 1–30, 1967 (cat. no. 46, illus., 30). "Jackson Pollock: Works on Paper," circulated by The Museum of Modern Art, New York, February 1968–February 1969 (traveling exhibition, cat. no. 42, illus., 74). "The Root Bequest," Root Art Center, May 11–June 8, 1969. "Exhibition of American Painting," Schenectady Museum & Planetarium, Schenectady, N.Y., March 20–April 30, 1970. "Drawings by Five Abstract Expressionist Painters," Hayden Gallery, Massachusetts Institute of Technology, Cambridge, Mass., February 21–March 26, 1975 (cat. no. 43, illus., 51). "20th-Century American Drawing: Three Avant-Garde Generations," Solomon R. Guggenheim Museum, New York, January 23–March 21, 1976 (cat. no. 93, illus., 67). "American Master Drawings and Watercolors," AFA, September 1, 1976–April 17, 1977 (traveling exhibition). "Five Decades of Collecting: Edward W. Root," MWPI, April 2–May 28, 1978. "The New York School 1940–1960," Sierra Nevada Museum of Art, Reno, Nev., February 2–March 4, 1979 (catalog, illus. pl. 1 [frontispiece]). "Edward W. Root: Collector and Teacher," Fred L. Emerson Gallery, Hamilton College, October 2–November 14, 1982 (catalog, 55). "Dorothy C. Miller: With an Eye to American Art," Smith College Museum of Art, Northampton, Mass., April 19–June 16, 1985. "Abstract Expressionism," MWPI, July 19–August 18, 1985. "Two Hundred Years of American Art," The Art Museum Association of America, November 15, 1986–May 8, 1988 (traveling exhibition, cat. no. 70, illus., 84). "Jackson Pollock: Drip Paintings on Paper, 1948–49," C & M Arts, New York, October 13–December 11, 1993 (catalog, illus.). "Affinities and Influences: Native American Art and American Modernism," Montclair Art Museum, July 16–October 1, 1995 (traveling exhibition, catalog). "Jackson Pollock in Venice: Pollock's America: The 'Irascibles' and The New York School," Museo Correr, Venice, Italy, March 23–June 30, 2002 (cat. no. 48, illus., 99). "American Masterworks from the MWPAI, Celebrating an Educational Alliance with Pratt Institute," Hirschl & Adler Galleries, New York, November 16–December 29, 2006 (catalog, illus.).

PUBLICATIONS

Hale, Robert Beverly. "The Growth of a Collection," *The Metropolitan Museum of Art Bulletin* XI (February 1953), illus., 161. Faulkner, Ray Nelson et al. *Art Today* Third Edition (New York: Hoer, Rinehart and Winston, 1956), 433, 437, 410, illus., 434. *Paintings, Drawings & Sculptures in the Museum of Art* (Utica, N.Y.: Munson-Williams-Proctor Institute, 1961), 30. Prior, Harris K. "Edward Root–Talent Scout," *Art in America* L (1962), 71, illus. fig. 4. "Tällalet för Att Sluta Mala," *Sydvenska Dagbladet*, May 21, 1963. O'Connor, Francis and Thaw, Eugene, eds. *Jackson Pollock: A Catalogue Raisonné of Paintings, Drawings, and Other Works* (New Haven and London: Yale University Press, 1978), cat. no. 235, illus. Davidson, Susan. "The Gesture of Intimate Scale," in *No Limits, Just Edges: Jackson Pollock Paintings on Paper* (Berlin and New York: Deutsche Bank and Solomon R. Guggenheim Foundation, 2005), 17, illus. pl. 59.

HENRY VARNUM POOR

(Chapman, Kans., 1888–New City, N.Y., 1970)

153. *Still Life–Apples*, 1933

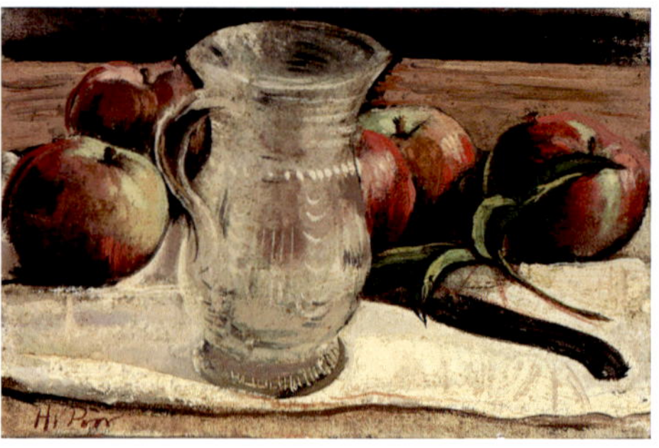

Oil on canvas mounted on plywood
7 ⅝ x 11 ¾ in.
57.207
Signed lower left (brown paint): HV Poor
Purchased from Frank K. M. Rehn Galleries, New York, November 1933

EXHIBITIONS

"Paintings by Henry Varnum Poor," Frank K. M. Rehn Galleries, New York, October 16–November 4, 1933 (cat. no. 17). "Paintings from the Collection of Edward W. Root," Munson-Williams-Proctor Institute, Utica, N.Y., September 29–October 20, 1946. "The Edward Root Collection," The Metropolitan Museum of Art, New York, February 12–April 12, 1953 (catalog, 3). "Edward Wales Root Bequest," MWPI, November 5, 1961–February 24, 1962 (catalog). "The Art Triangle: Artist, Dealer, Collector," Burchfield Art Center, Buffalo, N.Y., May 13–June 25, 1989 (traveling exhibition, cat. no. 75).

PUBLICATION

Paintings, Drawings & Sculptures in the Museum of Art (Utica, N.Y.: Munson-Williams-Proctor Institute, 1961), 30.

HENRY VARNUM POOR

Henry Varnum Poor was born on September 30, 1887 in Chapman, Kansas to Alfred James Poor and Josephine Graham Poor. His great-grandfather, the original Henry Varnum Poor (1821–1905), wrote *History of Railroads and Canals in the United States* (1860). This publication became the origin of Standard and Poor's, today's leading investment information source. The family moved to Kansas City, Missouri, in 1896 and then to Palo Alto, California in 1905. Poor attended Stanford University, graduated Phi Beta Kappa in 1910 and immediately departed for Europe. While in London, Poor studied at the Slade School with painter Walter Sickert (1860–1942) and, in Paris, took classes at the Académie Julien.

In 1911, Poor returned to the United States to teach at Stanford and had his first one-man show at Stanford's Old Studio in 1912. During this year, he married Lena Wiltz Emery (1885-1967) and moved to Bonner Springs, Kansas, to manage his father's farm. His first daughter, Josephine Lydia (died ca.1975), was born in 1913 and Poor returned to teaching at Stanford as an assistant professor of graphic arts. By 1916, Stanford dissolved its art department and Poor accepted a teaching position at the San Francisco Art Association. In 1917, he separated from his wife Lena, and began living with his former student Marion Dorn (1896–1964). Poor was drafted into the U.S. Army in 1918 and served in France with the 115th Regiment of Engineers as a regimental artist and company interpreter. In 1919 Poor was discharged from the army, married Dorn, moved to New York City and then New City in Rockland County, New York. Poor divorced Dorn in 1923 and spent the summer and fall of 1924 in Marlotte, France painting landscapes. In 1925, he married editor and novelist Bessie Freedman Breuer (1893–1975) and adopted her daughter Anne (1918–2002). Their son, Peter Varnum Poor, was born in May of 1926.

In New City, Poor purchased land on South Mountain Road where he designed and built by hand his home and studio, Crow House. Although never formally trained as an architect, Poor built houses and structural additions for his friends including textile designer Ruth Reeves (1892–1966) and Maxwell Anderson (1888–1959).

Poor joined the Frank K. M. Rehn Gallery in 1932. His first exhibition there was very successful. Many paintings were purchased by major museums such as The Metropolitan Museum of Art and the Addison Gallery of American Art. Edward Wales Root (1884–1956) acquired the painting *Still Life–Apples* (cat. no. 152) from this exhibition.

During the 1940s, Poor engaged in numerous professional activities. President Franklin Delano Roosevelt (1882–1945) appointed Poor to the United States Commission of Fine Arts. He was elected to the National Institute of Arts and Letters in 1942. Poor served in Alaska as a war correspondent in the War Artists Unit in 1943. His first book, *An Artist Sees Alaska* (1945), reflects on his time spent there. His most enduring legacy occurred in 1946 when Poor co-founded the Skowhegan School of Painting and Sculpture in Maine with the help of Willard W. Cummings (1915–75), Sidney Simon (1917–97), and Charles Cutler (1914–70). His second book, *A Book of Pottery: From Mud Into Immortality*, was published in 1958. Poor died on December 8, 1970 in New City, New York.

—Michael D. Somple

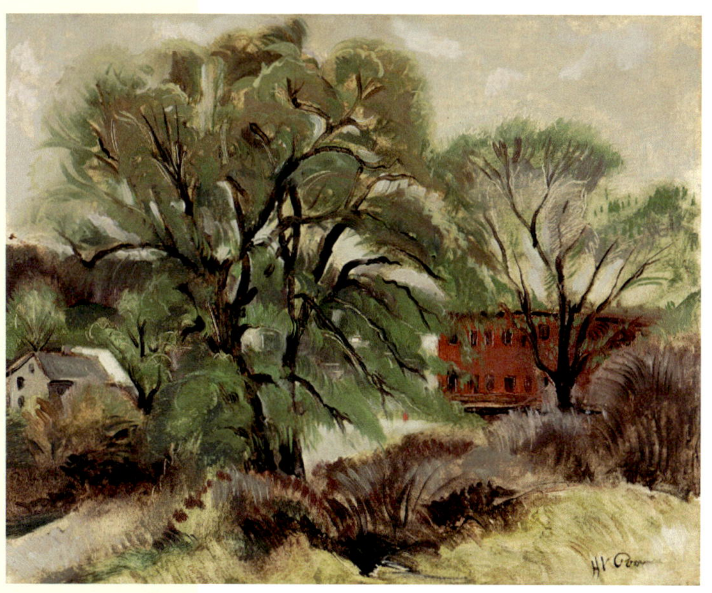

154. *Willow Tree*, 1934

Oil on canvas mounted on plywood
16 x 20 in.
57.208
Signed lower right (brown paint): HV Poor
Purchased from Frank K. M. Galleries, New York, January 1935

EXHIBITIONS

"The Edward Root Collection," The Metropolitan Museum of Art, New York, February 12–April 12, 1953 (catalog, 3). "Edward Wales Root Bequest," Munson-Williams-Proctor Institute, Utica, N.Y., November 5, 1961–February 24, 1962 (catalog). "Henry Varnum Poor: A Comprehensive Exhibition," Colby College Art Museum, Waterville, Me., October 1–28, 1961 (cat. no. 3 [as *The Willow*]). "The Art Triangle: Artist, Dealer, Collector," Burchfield Art Center, Buffalo, N.Y., May 13–June 25, 1989 (traveling exhibition, cat. no. 76).

PUBLICATION

Paintings, Drawings & Sculptures in the Museum of Art (Utica, N.Y.: Munson-Williams-Proctor Institute, 1961), 30.

RICHARD POUSETTE-DART

(St. Paul, Minn., 1916–New York, N.Y., 1992)

155. *Composition*, 1949

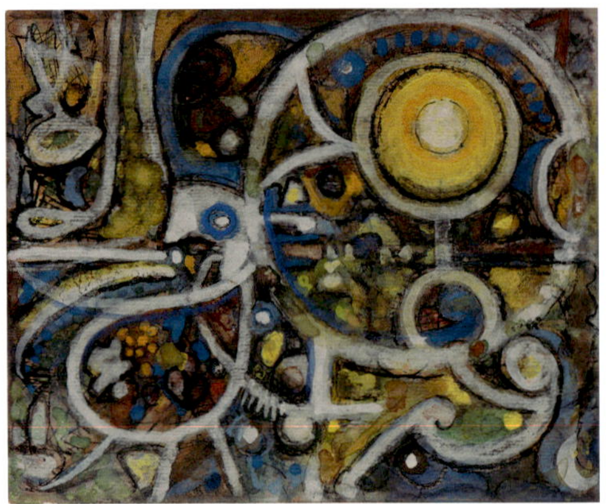

Gouache and watercolor on thin laid paper
6 ½ x 7 15/16 in.
57.209
Inscribed verso upper left (black ink): 49; upper center (graphite): Top / top
Purchased from Betty Parsons Gallery, New York

EXHIBITIONS

"New Trends in 20th-Century American Painting," Union College, Schenectady, N.Y., March 5–26, 1961. "Edward Wales Root Bequest," Munson-Williams-Proctor Institute, Utica, N.Y., November 5, 1961–February 24, 1962 (catalog). "European Sources of Contemporary American Art: Kandinsky," Root Art Center, Hamilton College, Clinton, N.Y., September 15–October 6, 1963 (cat. no. 32). "Abstract Paintings and Drawings from the Root Bequest," Root Art Center, September 11–October 9, 1966. "American Drawings and Watercolors from the Munson-Williams-Proctor Institute," E. B. Crocker Art Gallery, Sacramento, Calif., October 25–November 24, 1974 (cat. no. 51). "Watercolors: Historic and Contemporary," Hathorn Gallery, Skidmore College, Saratoga Springs, N.Y., February 4–20, 1977 (cat. no. 42). "American Twentieth-Century Watercolors at the Munson-Williams-Proctor Arts Institute," MWPAI, April 30–July 10, 2000 (traveling exhibition, cat. no. 45, illus.).

PUBLICATION

Paintings, Drawings & Sculptures in the Museum of Art (Utica, N.Y.: Munson-Williams-Proctor Institute, 1961), 30.

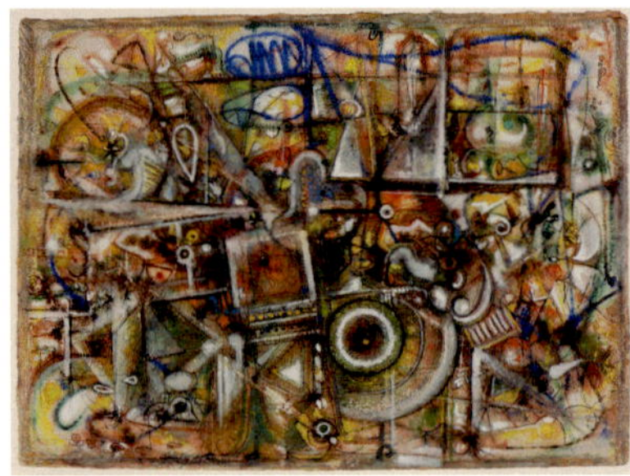

156. *Composition (Transfiguring)*
1946
Opaque and transparent watercolor with ink and chalk on heavy rag paper
22 ½ x 31 in.
57.210
Inscribed lower left of center: [illegible]; verso left (graphite): "Transfiguring"
Purchased from Willard Gallery, New York, December 1946

EXHIBITIONS

"20th-Century American Painting from the Edward W. Root Collection," Smithsonian Institution, Washington, D.C., July 1959–July 1960 (traveling exhibition). "American Watercolors and Drawings," Root Art Center, Hamilton College, Clinton, N.Y., April 4–May 7, 1961. "Edward Wales Root Bequest," Munson-Williams-Proctor Institute, Utica, N.Y., November 5, 1961–February 24, 1962 (catalog). "Abstract Paintings and Drawings from The Root Bequest," Root Art Center, September 11–October 9, 1966. "American 20th-Century Watercolors from MWPI," Albany Institute of History and Art, Albany, N.Y., September 10–October 4, 1967. "Richard Pousette-Dart: Presences," traveling exhibition organized by the Museum of Modern Art, 1969–70. Kirkland Art Center, Clinton, N.Y., October 16–November 16, 1974. "Watercolors: Historic and Contemporary," Hathorn Gallery, Skidmore College, Saratoga Springs, N.Y., February 4–20, 1977 (cat. no. 43 [as *Composition (no. 2)*]). "Five Decades of Collecting: Edward W. Root," MWPI, April 2–May 28, 1978. "Abstract Expressionism," MWPI, July 14–August 18, 1985.

PUBLICATION

Paintings, Drawings & Sculptures in the Museum of Art (Utica, N.Y.: Munson-Williams-Proctor Institute, 1961), 30.

MAURICE B. PRENDERGAST

(St. John's, Newfoundland, Canada, 1858–New York, N.Y., 1924)

157. *Beach Road No. 2*, 1910

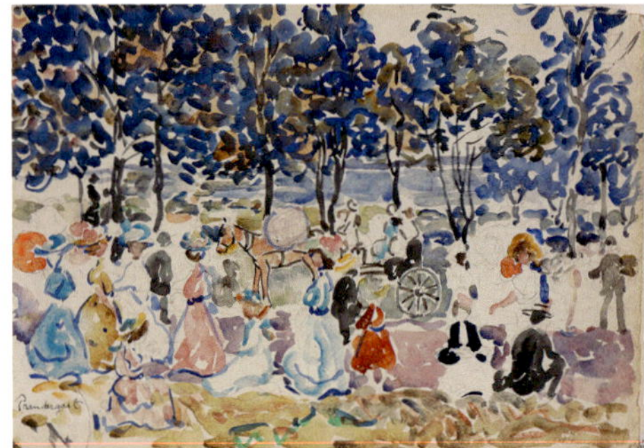

Watercolor and graphite on white watercolor paper
12 ⅜ x 17 ¾ in.
57.211
Signed lower left (black ink): Prendergast; inscribed verso upper center (graphite, in Edward Root's handwriting): Maurice B. Prendergast / "Beach Road" no. 2. (1910)
Purchased from Carroll Galleries, New York, March 1915

EXHIBITIONS

"Maurice B. Prendergast Paintings in Oil and Watercolors," Carroll Galleries, New York, February 15–March 6, 1915 (cat. no. 37). "Exhibition of Watercolors and Pastels by Eleven American Moderns from a Distinguished Private Collection," Munson-Williams-Proctor Institute, Utica, N.Y., fall 1938. "Paintings from the Collection of Edward W. Root," MWPI, September 29–October 20, 1946. "The Edward Root Collection," The Metropolitan Museum of Art, New York, February 12–April 12, 1953 (catalog, 3). "20th-Century American Painting from the Edward W. Root Collection," Smithsonian Institution, Washington, D.C., July 1959–July 1960 (traveling exhibition). Museum of Art Building inaugural exhibition, MWPI, October 15–December 31, 1960. "Edward Wales Root Bequest," MWPI, November 5, 1961–February 24, 1962 (catalog). "The Figure in 20th-Century Paintings and Drawings," Root Art Center, Hamilton College, Clinton, N.Y., April 15–May 6, 1962. "American Painting from 1830," Everson Museum of Art, Syracuse, N.Y., December 3, 1965–January 16, 1966 (cat. no. 61). "The Ashcan School," Root Art Center, September 10–October 12, 1967. "Paintings and Drawings from the Edward W. Root Bequest," Root Art Center, April 7–May 5, 1968. "Exhibition of American Paintings,"

Schenectady Museum & Planetarium, Schenectady, N.Y., March 20–April 30, 1970. "20th-Century Prints and Drawings," Schenectady Museum & Planetarium, December 15, 1971–January 15, 1972. "Watercolors: Historic and Contemporary," Hathorn Gallery, Skidmore College, Saratoga Springs, N.Y., February 4–20, 1977 (cat. no. 44).

PUBLICATIONS

Paintings, Drawings & Sculptures in the Museum of Art (Utica, N.Y.: Munson-Williams-Proctor Institute, 1961), 30. *American Art in Upstate New York* (Buffalo, N.Y.: Buffalo Fine Arts Academy, 1974), 43. Clark, Carol, Mathews, Nancy Mowll and Owens, Gwendolyn. *Maurice Brazil Prendergast and Charles Prendergast: A Catalogue Raisonné* (Williamstown, Mass.: Williams College in association with Prestel, 1989), cat. no. 974, illus.

158. *Canal*, 1912

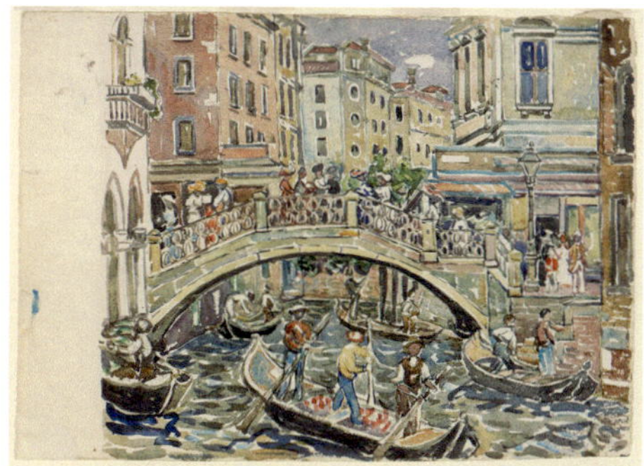

Transparent watercolor and graphite on heavy textured paper
15 ½ x 18 ⅞ in.
57.213
Signed and dated lower right (brown ink): Maurice B. Prendergast / Venice 1912; verso: *Rialto Bridge, Venice* (unfinished watercolor)
Purchased from the artist, May 1912, for $100.00 plus two Prendergast watercolors purchased from 1911 Independent exhibition

EXHIBITIONS

"45th Annual Exhibition," American Watercolor Society, New York, April 25–May 12, 1912 (cat. no. 215). "Maurice B. Prendergast: Paintings in Oil and Watercolors," Carroll Galleries, New York, February 15–March 6, 1915 (cat. no. 34). "Exhibition of Works by Maurice B. Prendergast and Charles E. Prendergast," Joseph Brummer Galleries, New York, April 4–23, 1921. "Edward W. Root Loan Exhibition," Utica Art Society, Utica, N.Y., May 1928, as *Venice*. "Maurice Prendergast Memorial Exhibition," Whitney Museum of American Art, New York, February 21–March 22, 1934 (cat. no. 101). "The Prendergasts: Retrospective Exhibition of the Work of Maurice and Charles Prendergast," Addison Gallery of American Art, Andover, Mass., September 24–November 6, 1938 (cat. no. 45, as *Canal, Venice*). "The Edward Root Collection," The Metropolitan Museum of Art, New York, February 12–April 12, 1953 (catalog, 3, as *Canal, Venice*). "Five Decades of American Painting," Union College, Schenectady, N.Y., September 27–October 23, 1959. Museum of Art Building inaugural exhibition, Munson-Williams-Proctor Institute, Utica, N.Y., October 15–December 31, 1960. "Edward Wales Root Bequest," MWPI, November 5, 1961–February 24, 1962 (catalog). "The Figure in 20th-Century Paintings and Drawings," Root Art Center, Hamilton College, Clinton, N.Y., April 15–May 6, 1962. "The Ashcan School," Arnot Art Gallery, Elmira, N.Y., February 1965. "American 20th-Century Watercolors from MWPI," Albany Institute of History and Art, Albany, N.Y., September 10–October 4, 1967. "The Root Bequest," Root Art Center, May 11–June 8, 1969. "American Drawings and Watercolors from the Munson-Williams-Proctor Institute," E. B. Crocker Art Gallery, Sacramento, Calif., October 25–November 24, 1974 (cat. no. 52). "Watercolors: Historic and Contemporary," Hathorn Gallery, Skidmore College, Saratoga Springs, N.Y., February 4–20, 1977 (cat. no. 45). "Five Decades of Collecting: Edward W. Root," MWPI, April 2–May 28, 1978. "American Works of Art on Paper, 1850–1925," Schenectady Museum & Planetarium, Schenectady, N.Y., January 11–April 6, 1980 (cat. no. 78). "Maurice Prendergast," Williams College Museum of Art, Williamstown, Mass., May 31–August 25, 1991 (cat. no. 71, 186, illus. color pl., 116). "American Twentieth-Century Watercolors at the Munson-Williams-Proctor Arts Institute," MWPAI, April 30–July 10, 2000 (traveling exhibition, cat. no. 2, illus.).

PUBLICATIONS

Paintings, Drawings & Sculptures in the Museum of Art (Utica, N.Y.: Munson-Williams-Proctor Institute, 1961), 31. *American Art in Upstate New York* (Buffalo, N.Y.: Buffalo Fine Arts Academy, 1974), 43. Wattenmaker, Richard J. *Maurice Prendergast* (New York: Harry N. Abrams, Inc., in association with the National Museum of American Art, Smithsonian Institution, 1994), illus. fig. 80. Clark, Carol, Mathews, Nancy Mowll and Owens, Gwendolyn. *Maurice Brazil Prendergast and Charles Prendergast: A Catalogue Raisonné* (Williamstown, Mass.: Williams College in association with Prestel, 1989), cat. no. 1018. Glavin, Ellen. "Maurice Prendergast's Second Visit to Venice: Disaster or New Impulse?" *Archives of American Art Journal* 42 (2002): 17–25, illus., 20.

159. *Landscape with Figures*
Ca. 1912

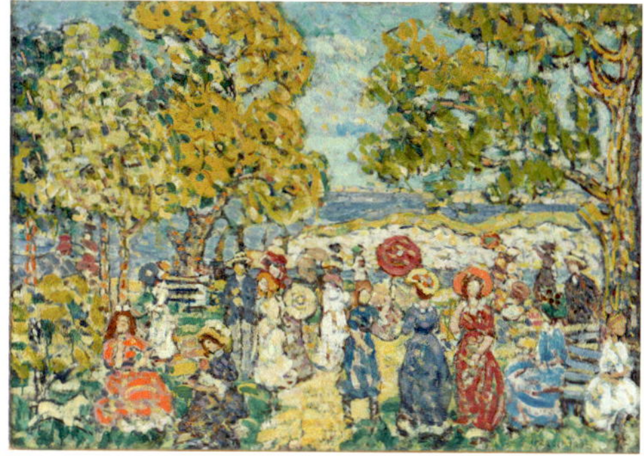

Oil on canvas
29 ⅝ x 42 ⅞ in.
57.212
Signed and dated lower right (faint black paint): Prendergast
Purchased from International Exhibition of Modern Art (Armory Show), New York, February 1913 [The Edward Root papers in the MWPAI Archives indicate ca. 1912 is the more correct date for this painting, which had been dated 1913 at the Armory Show. The Prendergast catalogue raisonné (see Publications below) dates the painting ca. 1910–13. Mr. Root's inventory gives the purchase date as February 1913. However, according to Milton Brown, *The Story of the Armory Show* (New York: Abbeville Press, 1988), 277, Root purchased this painting March 15, 1913, the date from the official ledger entry in the Elmer MacRae Papers, Archives of American Art, Smithsonian Institution, microfilm reels 4131–4132. MacRae was Treasurer of the Association of American Painters and Sculptors, the organizers of the Armory Show. See also Brown, 103: "Edward Root, whose commitment was, and remained, to American art, had lent some Luks drawings (now Addison Gallery of American Art, Phillips Academy, Andover, Mass., Gifts of Mrs. Edward Root) to the Armory Show and during the first week bought a large oil, *Landscape with Figures*, by Maurice Prendergast, an American artist who was among the closest in affinity to the modern movement abroad."]

MAURICE B. PRENDERGAST

EXHIBITIONS

"International Exhibition of Modern Art," Armory of the Sixty-ninth Infantry Regiment, New York, February 17–March 15, 1913 (traveling exhibition, cat. no. 895).

"Maurice B. Prendergast: Paintings in Oil and Watercolor," Carroll Galleries, Inc., New York, February 15–March 6, 1915. On extended loan, The Metropolitan Museum of Art, New York, ca. January 1920–ca. January 1927. "Maurice Prendergast Memorial Exhibition," Whitney Museum of American Art, New York, February 21–March 22, 1934 (cat. no. 34). "The Edward Root Collection," Metropolitan Museum of Art, February 12–April 12, 1953 (catalog, 3). "20th-Century American Painting from the Edward W. Root Collection," Smithsonian Institution, Washington, D.C., July 1959–July 1960 (traveling exhibition). Museum of Art Building inaugural exhibition, Munson-Williams-Proctor Institute, Utica, N.Y., October 15–December 31, 1960. "Edward Wales Root Bequest," MWPI, November 5, 1961–February 24, 1962 (catalog, illus.).

"Modern American Painting: 1915," Fine Art Gallery of San Diego, San Diego, Calif., December 6, 1962–January 7, 1963 (cat. no. 32). "The Armory Show: 50th Anniversary Exhibition," MWPI, February 17–March 31, 1963 (traveling exhibition, cat. no. 895, color pl.25). "Maurice Prendergast: Art of Impulse and Color," University of Maryland, College Park, Md., September 1–October 6 1976 (traveling exhibition, cat. no. 72, illus., 121). "Five Decades of Collecting: Edward W. Root," MWPI, April 2–May 28, 1978.

"Edward W. Root: Collector and Teacher," Fred L. Emerson Gallery, Hamilton College, Clinton, N.Y., October 2–November 14, 1982 (catalog, illus., 31). "Nature Framed," MWPI, March 15–May 20, 1985. "Insights," MWPI, January 7–March 24, 1986. "Two Hundred Years of American Art," The Art Museum Association of America, November 15, 1986–May 8, 1988 (traveling exhibition, cat. no. 39, illus., 53). "Maurice Prendergast," Williams College Museum of Art, Williamstown, Mass., May 31–August 25, 1991 (cat. no. 76, illus. color pl., 121). "Circa 1900: From the Genteel Tradition to the Jazz Age," Albright-Knox Art Gallery, Buffalo, N.Y., May 6–August 19, 2001 (traveling exhibition, cat. no. 90, illus., 79). "American Masterworks from the MWPAI, Celebrating an Educational Alliance with Pratt Institute," Hirschl & Adler Galleries, New York, November 16–December 29, 2006 (catalog, illus.).

PUBLICATIONS

Burroughs, Bryson. *The Metropolitan Museum of Art: Catalogue of Paintings* (New York: Metropolitan Museum, 1924), 259. Pach, Walter. *Queer Thing, Painting* (New York and London: Harper & Brothers, 1938), 228. "Paintings from the Collection of Edward W. Root," *Munson-Williams-Proctor Institute Bulletin* (April 1948), illus. Hale, Robert Beverly. "The Growth of a Collection," *The Metropolitan Museum of Art Bulletin* XI (February 1953): 154, illus. 158. Louchheim, Aline B. "Root's Collection of Art Displayed," *New York Times*, February 12, 1953. Geist, Sidney. "One Man's Collection," *Art Digest* XXXVII (March 1, 1953): 13. Hayes, Barlett H., Jr. "The Root of American Painting," *Art News* LVI (January 1958): 61, illus. fig. 2.

"Twentieth-Century Paintings from the Root Bequest," *MWPI Bulletin* (February 1958). *Paintings, Drawings & Sculptures in the Museum of Art* (Utica, N.Y.: Munson-Williams-Proctor Institute, 1961), 31. Prior, Harris K. "Edward Root–Talent Scout," *Art in America* L (1962): 72, illus. fig. 8. Perlman, Bennard. "The Story behind a Great Art Event," *American Artist* 27 (February 1963): 29, illus. Faison, Jr., S. Lane. *Art Tours & Detours in New York State* (New York: Random House, 1964), 97, illus. no. 164. Tomkins, Calvin. *The World of Marcel Duchamp* (New York: Time-Life Books, 1966), illus., 53. Owens, Gwendolyn. *Watercolors by Maurice Prendergast from New England Collections* (Williamstown, Mass.: Clark Art Institute, 1978), 11, as *The Park*. Langdale, Cecily. "Maurice Prendergast, An American Post-Impressionist," *Connoisseur* 202 (December 1979): 253. Langdale, Cecily. *Monotypes by Maurice Prendergast in the Terra Museum of American Art* (Chicago: Terra Museum, 1984), 17. Gerdts, William. *American Impressionism* (New York: Abbeville Press, 1984), 289, illus. fig. 382. Langdale, Cecily. "The Late Watercolors/Pastels of Maurice Prendergast," *The Magazine Antiques* 132 (November 1987): 1090. Brown, Milton W. *The Story of the Armory Show* (New York: Abbeville Press, 1988), cat. no. 895, illus. color pl. 19. Durham, Michael S. *The Smithsonian Guide to Historic America: The Mid-Atlantic States* (New York: Stewart Faburi and Chang, 1989). Schweizer, Paul D., et al. *Masterworks of American Art from the Munson-Williams-Proctor Institute* (New York: Harry N. Abrams, Inc., 1989), cat. no. 49, illus., 111. Clark, Carol, Mathews, Nancy Mowll and Owens, Gwendolyn. *Maurice Brazil Prendergast and Charles Prendergast: A Catalogue Raisonné* (Williamstown, Mass.: Williams College in association with Prestel, 1989), cat. no. 269, illus. color pl. 57. Wattenmaker, Richard J. *Maurice Prendergast* (New York: Harry N. Abrams, Inc., in association with the National Museum of American Art, Smithsonian Institution, 1994), illus. fig. 87. Bailey, W.H. *Defining Edges* (New York: Harry N. Abrams, Inc., 2002), 100–01, illus.

CLAYTON S. PRICE

(Bedford, Ia., 1874–Portland, Ore., 1950)

160. *Head*, 1949

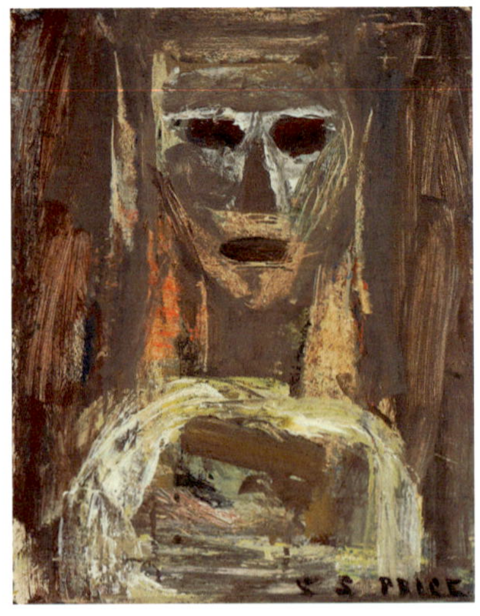

Oil on Masonite
20 x 16 in.
57.214
Signed lower right (black paint): C S Price
Purchased from Willard Gallery, January 1950

EXHIBITIONS

"C. S. Price," Willard Gallery, New York, November 20–December 23, 1949 (cat. no. 10). "Edward Wales Root Bequest," Munson-Williams-Proctor Institute, Utica, N.Y., November 5, 1961–February 24, 1962 (catalog). "C.S. Price: The Man and His Works," The Pavilion Gallery, Newport Harbor, Balboa, Calif., February 8–March 19, 1967 (catalog, illus., 47).

PUBLICATION

Paintings, Drawings & Sculptures in the Museum of Art (Utica, N.Y.: Munson-Williams-Proctor Institute, 1961), 31.

BOARDMAN ROBINSON

(Somerset, Nova Scotia, Canada, 1876– Stamford, Conn., 1952)

161. *Bathers Wrestling*, before 1928

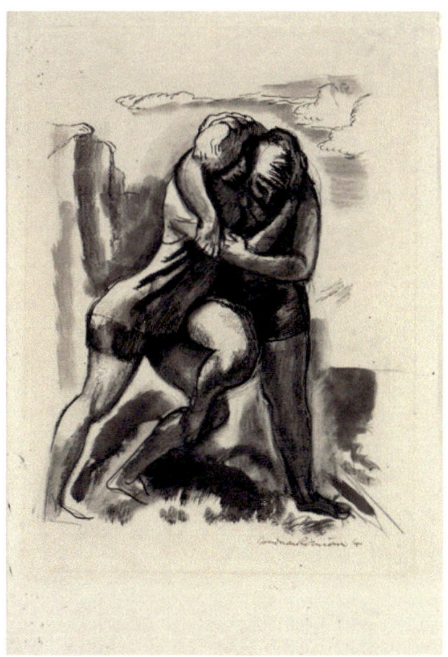

Ink and wash with crayon on white paper
19 x 13 in., irregular
57. 215
Signed lower right (black ink): Boardman Robinson; verso: drawing in black ink wash of a circus, scribbled over with black crayon
Purchased from the Utica Art Society, January 1928

EXHIBITIONS

Utica Art Society, Utica, N.Y., January 1928. "The Edward Root Collection," The Metropolitan Museum of Art, New York, N.Y., February 12–April 12, 1953 (catalog, 3). "20th-Century American Painting from the Edward W. Root Collection," Smithsonian Institution, Washington, D.C., May 1959–May 1960 (traveling exhibition). "American Watercolors and Drawings," Root Art Center, Hamilton College, Clinton, N.Y., April 4–May 7, 1961. "Edward Wales Root Bequest," Munson-Williams-Proctor Institute, Utica, N.Y., November 5, 1961–February 24, 1962 (catalog). "Paintings and Drawings from the Edward W. Root Bequest," Root Art Center, April 7–May 5, 1968. "The Root Bequest," Root Art Center, May 11–June 8, 1969. Kirkland Art Center, Clinton, N.Y., February 6–March 6, 1972. "American Drawings and Watercolors from the Munson-Williams-Proctor Institute," E.B. Crocker Art Gallery, Sacramento, Calif., October 25–November 24, 1974 (cat. no. 53). "Five Decades of Collecting: Edward W. Root," MWPI, April 2–May 28, 1978.

PUBLICATION

Paintings, Drawings & Sculptures in the Museum of Art (Utica, N.Y.: Munson-Williams-Proctor Institute, 1961), 32.

MARK ROTHKO

(Dvinsk, Russia, 1903–New York, N.Y., 1970)

162. *Number 11 (Untitled: Abstraction)*, 1947

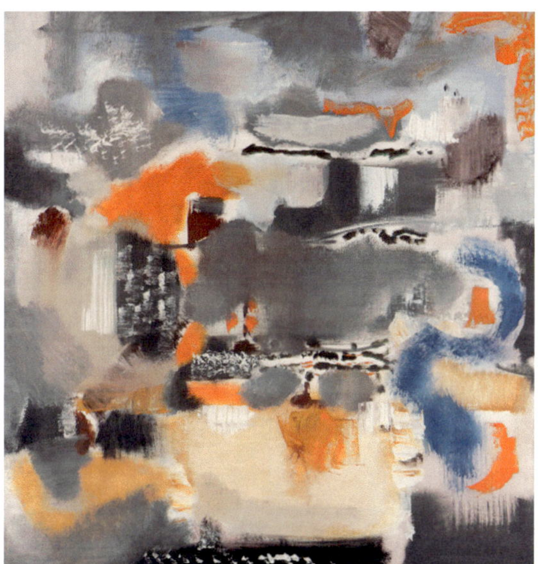

Oil on linen
39 ⅜ x 38 ⅝ in.
57.216
Purchased from Betty Parsons Gallery, New York, April 1949

EXHIBITIONS

"Mark Rothko," Betty Parsons Gallery, New York, March 28–April 16, 1949. "Current Trends in British and American Painting from the Collection of Edward W. Root," Munson-Williams-Proctor Institute, Utica, N.Y., December 3–31, 1950 (traveling exhibition, cat. no. 22, as *No Title*). "The Edward Root Collection," The Metropolitan Museum of Art, New York, February 12–April 12, 1953 (catalog, 3). "New Trends in 20th-Century American Painting," Root Art Center, Hamilton College, Clinton, N.Y., October 26–November 30, 1958. "20th-Century American Painting from the Edward W. Root Collection," Smithsonian Institution, Washington, D.C., July 1959–July 1960 (traveling exhibition). Museum of Art Building inaugural exhibition, MWPI, October 15–December 31, 1960. "New Trends in 20th-Century American Painting," Union College, Schenectady, N.Y., March 5–26, 1961. "Edward Wales Root Bequest," MWPI, November 5, 1961–February 24, 1962 (catalog). "European Sources of Contemporary American Art: Kandinsky," Root Art Center, September 15–October 6, 1963 (cat. no. 33). "125 Years of New York State Painting and Sculpture," New York State Exposition, Syracuse, organized by the New York State Council on the Arts, August 30–September 5, 1966 (cat. no. 51). "Abstract Paintings and Drawings from the Root Bequest," Root Art Center, September 11–October 9, 1966. "Contemporary Artists: Early and Late Paintings," Root Art Center, April 4–May 2, 1973. "Five Decades of Collecting: Edward W. Root," MWPI, April 2–May 28, 1978. "Abstract Expressionism," MWPI, July 19–August 18, 1985. "Two Hundred Years of American Art," The Art Museum Association of America, November 15, 1986–May 8, 1988 (traveling exhibition, cat no. 68, illus., 82, as *Untitled: Abstract Number 11*). "Masterworks of American Art from the Munson-Williams-Proctor Institute Museum of Art," Knoxville Museum of Art, Knoxville, Tenn., February 26–August 23, 1998. "Hamilton Collects: American Art," Emerson Gallery, Hamilton College, April 19–June 9, 2002 (catalog, illus., 83 and frontispiece).

PUBLICATIONS

Paintings, Drawings & Sculptures in the Museum of Art (Utica, N.Y.: Munson-Williams-Proctor Institute, 1961), 32. Prior, Harris K. "Edward Root–Talent Scout." *Art in America* L (1962): 72, illus. fig. 12. Anfam, David. *Mark Rothko: The Works on Canvas: Catalogue Raisonné* (New Haven, Conn.: Yale University Press and Washington, D.C.: National Gallery of Art, 1998), cat. no. 334, illus.

ANDRÉE RUELLAN

(New York, N.Y., 1905–Kingston, N.Y., 2006)

163. *Elijah*, 1936

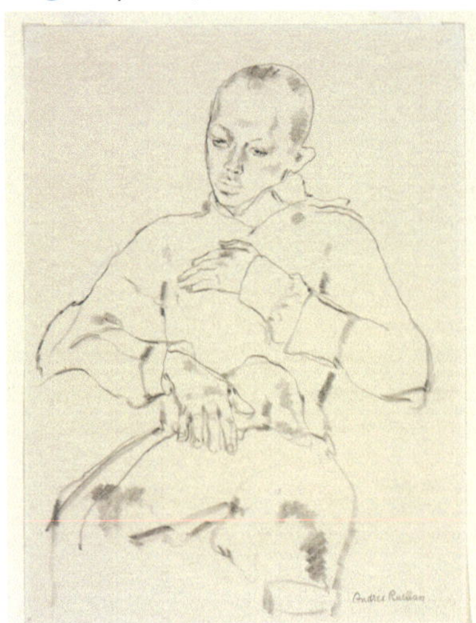

Graphite on smooth white wove paper
12 x 9 ⅛ in.
57.217
Signed lower right (graphite): Andree Ruellan; verso lower left (graphite): Elijah no. 2
Purchased from Maynard Walker Gallery, New York, January 1937

EXHIBITIONS

"The Edward Root Collection," The Metropolitan Museum of Art, New York, February 12–April 12, 1953 (catalog, 3). "American Watercolors and Drawings," Root Art Center, Hamilton College, Clinton, N.Y., April 4–May 7, 1961. "Edward Wales Root Bequest," Munson-Williams-Proctor Institute, Utica, N.Y., November 5, 1961–February 24, 1962 (catalog). "American Drawings and Watercolors from the Munson-Williams-Proctor Institute," E. B. Crocker Art Gallery, Sacramento, Calif., October 25–November 24, 1974 (cat. no. 54).

PUBLICATION

Paintings, Drawings & Sculptures in the Museum of Art (Utica, N.Y.: Munson-Williams-Proctor Institute, 1961), 32.

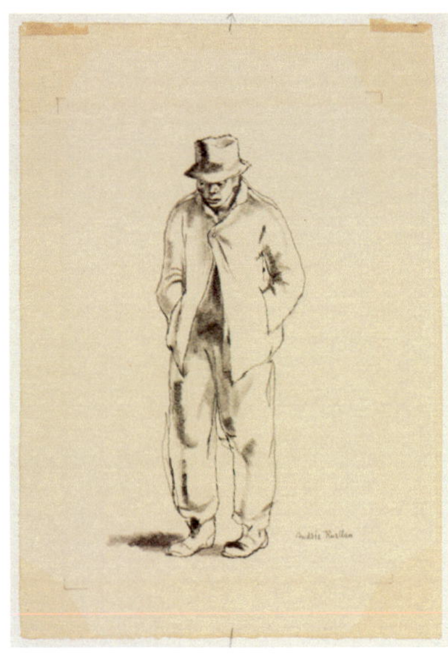

164. *Old Man*, not dated

Charcoal and graphite on wove paper mounted on mat board
12 ¹⁵⁄₁₆ x 9 ⅛ in.
57.218
Signed lower right (graphite): Andree Ruellan
Purchased from Kraushaar Gallery, New York

EXHIBITIONS

"Edward Wales Root Bequest," Munson-Williams-Proctor Institute, Utica, N.Y., November 5, 1961–February 24, 1962 (catalog). "The Figure in 20th-Century Paintings and Drawings," Root Art Center, Hamilton College, Clinton, N.Y., April 5–May 6, 1962.

PUBLICATION

Paintings, Drawings & Sculptures in the Museum of Art (Utica, N.Y.: Munson-Williams-Proctor Institute, 1961), 32.

ATTILIO SALEMME

(Boston, Mass., 1911–New York, N.Y., 1955)

165. *In the Realm of Fancy*, 1944

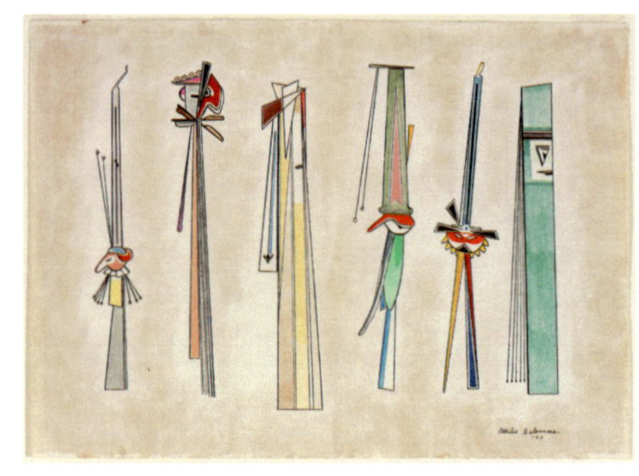

Black ink with opaque and transparent watercolor on medium-weight wove paper
9 ⅞ x 13 ¾ in.
57.220
Signed and dated lower right (black ink): Attilo Salemme / '44
Inscription verso upper left (graphite): 21 [circled]
Purchased from 67 Gallery, New York

EXHIBITIONS

"Attilio Salemme," 67 Gallery, New York, January 2–15, 1945 (cat. no. 34). "Paintings from the Collection of Edward W. Root," Munson-Williams-Proctor Institute, Utica, N.Y., September 29–October 20, 1946. "Contemporary Watercolors and Drawings from the Edward W. Root Collection," Smithsonian Institution, Washington, D.C., June 1, 1959–May 31, 1960 (traveling exhibition). "New Trends in 20th-Century American Painting," Union College, Schenectady, N.Y., March 5–26, 1961. "American Watercolors and Drawings from the Root Bequest," Root Art Center, Hamilton College, Clinton, N.Y., April 9–May 7, 1961. "Edward Wales Root Bequest," MWPI, November 5, 1961–February 24, 1962 (catalog). "The Figure in 20th-Century Paintings and Drawings," Root Art Center, April 5–May 6, 1962. "Abstract Drawings from the Root Bequest," Root Art Center, September 11–October 9, 1966. "Paintings and Drawings from the Edward W. Root Bequest," Root Art Center, April 7–May 5, 1968. "The Root Bequest," Root Art Center, May 11–June 8, 1969. "Edward W. Root: Collector and Teacher," Fred L. Emerson Gallery, Hamilton College, October 2–November 14, 1982 (catalog, 46). "American Twentieth-Century Watercolors at the Munson-Williams-Proctor Arts Institute," MWPAI, April 30–July 10, 2000 (traveling exhibition, cat. no. 35, illus.).

PUBLICATION
*Paintings, Drawings & Sculptures in the Museum of Art (Utica, N.Y.: Munson-Williams-Proc*tor Institute, 1961), 32.

166. *The Pathos of a Common Affinity*, 1944

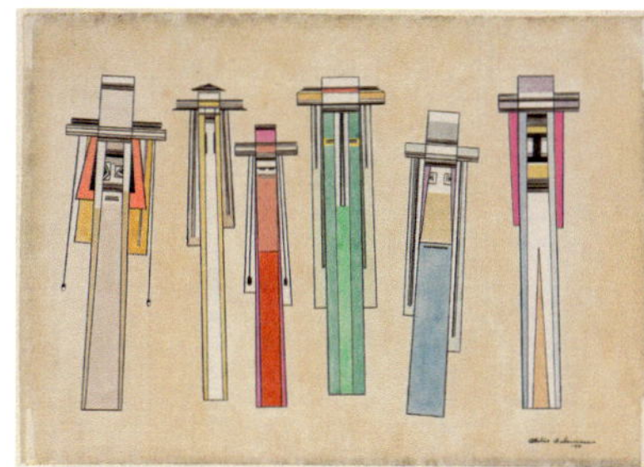

Watercolor on paper
9 ⅝ x 13 ¾ in.
57.219
Signed and dated lower right (black ink): Attilo Salemme / 44
Purchased from 67 Gallery, New York

EXHIBITIONS
"Attilio Salemme," 67 Gallery, New York, N.Y., January 2–15, 1945 (cat. no. 33). "The Edward Root Collection," The Metropolitan Museum of Art, New York, February 12–April 12, 1953 (catalog, 3). "Edward Wales Root Bequest," Munson-Williams-Proctor Institute, Utica, N.Y., November 5, 1961–February 24, 1962 (catalog).

PUBLICATION
Paintings, Drawings & Sculptures in the Museum of Art (Utica, N.Y.: Munson-Williams-Proctor Institute, 1961), 32.

167. *Portrait of an Enigma*
Ca. 1944

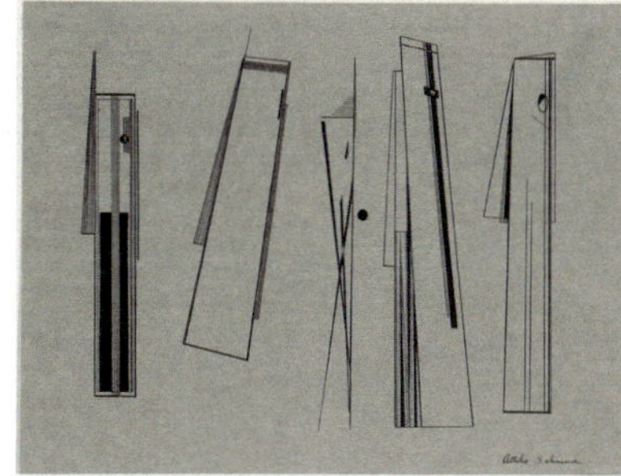

Pen and black ink on green-gray laid paper
9 ⅛ x 12 ⅜ in.
57.221
Signed lower right (black ink): Attilio Salemme
Purchased from 67 Gallery, New York

EXHIBITIONS
"Attilio Salemme," 67 Gallery, New York, January 2–15, 1945 (cat. no. 26). "The Edward Root Collection," The Metropolitan Museum of Art, New York, February 12–April 12, 1953 (catalog, 3). "Edward Wales Root Bequest," Munson-Williams-Proctor Institute, Utica, N.Y., November 5, 1961–February 24, 1962 (catalog). "The Figure in 20th-Century Drawings and Paintings," Root Art Center, Hamilton College, Clinton, N.Y., April 15–May 6, 1962. "Selections from the Edward W. Root Collection," Root Art Center, February 22–March 21, 1970. "20th-Century Prints and Drawings," Schenectady Museum & Planetarium, Schenectady, N.Y., December 15, 1971–January 15, 1972. "Life Lines: American Master Drawings (1788–1962) from the Munson-Williams-Proctor Institute," MWPI, September 17–November 13, 1994 (traveling exhibition, cat. no. 52, illus. color pl. 20).

PUBLICATION
Paintings, Drawings & Sculptures in the Museum of Art (Utica, N.Y.: Munson-Williams-Proctor Institute, 1961), 32.

LOUIS SCHANKER
(New York, N.Y., 1903–81)

168. *Composition No. 1*, 1944

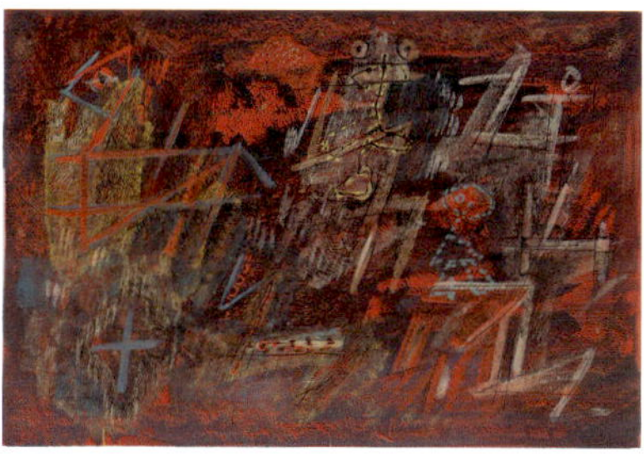

Tempera and black ink on wove watercolor paper
14 ⅞ x 21 ⅞ in.
57.222
Signed and dated lower right (black paint): Schanker 44
Purchased from Willard Gallery, New York

EXHIBITIONS
"Schanker: New Tempera Paintings," Mortimer Brandt Gallery, New York, January 13–February 3, 1945. "Schanker," Willard Gallery, New York, February 26–March 23, 1946 (cat. no. 17, as *Composition I*). "Paintings from the Collection of Edward W. Root," Munson-Williams-Proctor Institute, Utica, N.Y., September 29–October 20, 1946. "The Edward Root Collection," The Metropolitan Museum of Art, New York, February 12–April 12, 1953 (catalog, 3). "New Trends in 20th-Century American Painting," Union College, Schenectady, N.Y., March 5–26, 1961. "American Watercolors and Drawings," Root Art Center, Hamilton College, Clinton, N.Y., April 4–May 7, 1961. "Edward Wales Root Bequest," MWPI, November 5, 1961–February 24, 1962 (catalog, as *Untitled: Composition No. 1*). "Abstract Paintings and Drawings from the Root Bequest," Root Art Center, September 11–October 9, 1966. Kirkland Art Center, Clinton, N.Y., October 16–November 16, 1974. "Watercolors: Historic and Contemporary," Hathorn Gallery, Skidmore College, Saratoga Springs, N.Y., February 4–20, 1977 (cat. no. 46).

PUBLICATION
Paintings, Drawings & Sculptures in the Museum of Art (Utica, N.Y.: Munson-Williams-Proctor Institute, 1961), 33.

169. *Composition No. 2*, 1945

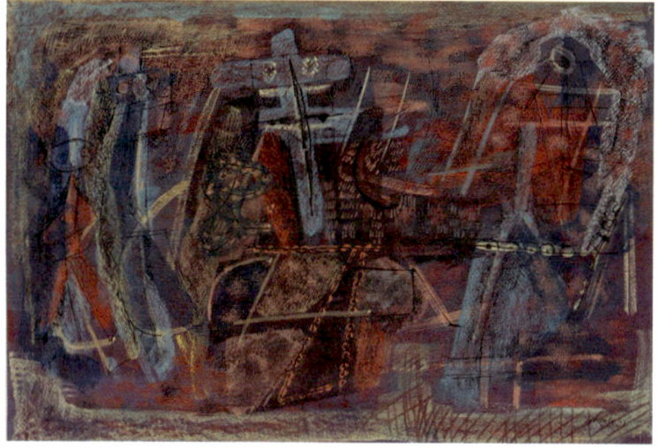

Tempera and black ink on laid watercolor paper
14 ⅞ x 21 ¹⁵⁄₁₆ in.
57.223
Signed and dated lower right (black ink): Schanker 45
Purchased from Willard Gallery, New York

EXHIBITIONS
"Schanker: New Tempera Paintings," Mortimer Brandt Gallery, New York, January 13–February 3, 1945. "Schanker," Willard Gallery, New York, February 26–March 23, 1946 (cat. no. 18, as *Composition II*). "The Edward Root Collection," The Metropolitan Museum of Art, New York, February 12–April 12, 1953 (catalog, 3). "Five Decades of American

LOUIS SCHANKER

Painting," Union College, Schenectady, N.Y., September 27–October 23, 1959. "American Watercolors and Drawings," Root Art Center, Hamilton College, Clinton, N.Y., April 4–May 7, 1961. "Edward Wales Root Bequest," Munson-Williams-Proctor Institute, Utica, N.Y., November 5, 1961–February 24, 1962 (catalog). "European Sources of Contemporary American Art: Kandinsky," Root Art Center, September 15–October 6, 1963 (cat. no. 34). "Realism to Abstraction," State University College, Oneonta, N.Y., December 2–20, 1963.

PUBLICATION

Paintings, Drawings & Sculptures in the Museum of Art (Utica, N.Y.: Munson-Williams-Proctor Institute, 1961), 33.

170. *Number 9*, 1951

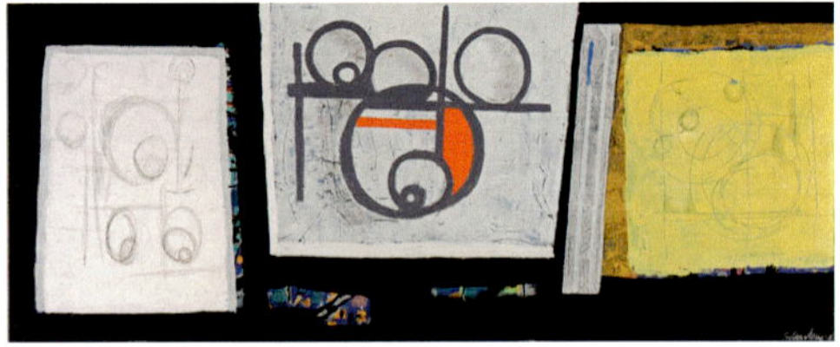

Oil and graphite on linen
30 x 75 in.
57.224
Signed and dated lower right (gray paint): Schanker 51
Inscribed verso upper right: Schanker 1951
Purchased from Grace Borgenicht Gallery, New York, February 1952

EXHIBITIONS

"The Edward Root Collection," The Metropolitan Museum of Art, New York, February 12–April 12, 1953 (catalog, 3). "The New Landscape in Art and Science," American Federation of Arts, October 1958–May 1960 (traveling exhibition). Museum of Art Building inaugural exhibition, Munson-Williams-Proctor Institute, Utica, N.Y., October 15–December 31, 1960. "Edward Wales Root Bequest," MWPI, November 5, 1961–February 24, 1962 (catalog). "European Sources of Contemporary American Art: Kandinsky," Root Art Center, Hamilton College, Clinton, N.Y., September 15–October 6, 1963 (cat. no. 35). "Abstract Painting and Drawing from the Root Bequest," Root Art Center, September 11–October 9, 1966. "Paintings and Drawings from the Edward W. Root Bequest," Root Art Center, April 7–May 5, 1968. "Five Decades of Collecting: Edward W. Root," MWPI, April 2–May 28, 1978. "Abstract Expressionism," MWPI, July 19–August 18, 1985. "Insights," MWPI, June 10–October 15, 1986.

PUBLICATION

Paintings, Drawings & Sculptures in the Museum of Art (Utica, N.Y.: Munson-Williams-Proctor Institute, 1961), 33.

SONJA SEKULA

(Lucerne, Switzerland, 1918–Zurich, Switzerland, 1963)

171. *When the People Had Left the Town*, 1948

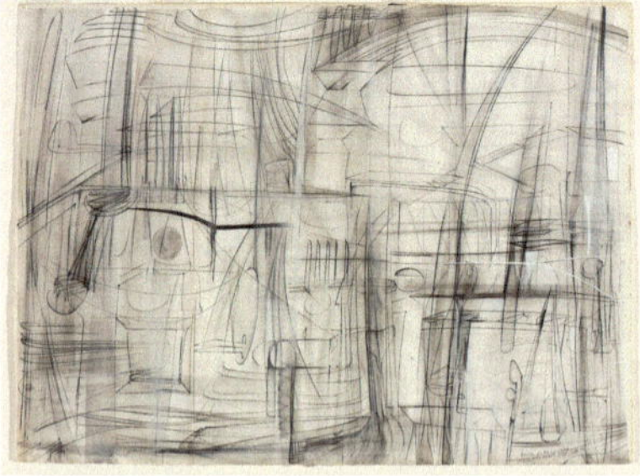

Black ink and opaque wash on heavy wove paper
22 ¼ x 30 ⅜ in.
57.313
Signed and inscribed lower right (black ink): Sonja Sekula 1948 / When the people had left the / town
Inscribed verso top center (graphite): 75
Purchased from Betty Parsons Gallery, New York

EXHIBITIONS

"Sekula: Drawings–Gouaches," Betty Parsons Gallery, New York, February 21–March 3, 1949. "Edward Wales Root Bequest," Munson-Williams-Proctor Institute, Utica, N.Y., November 5, 1961–February 24, 1962 (catalog). "Figuratively Speaking," MWPI, April 11–November 10, 1985. "Sonja Sekula (1918–1963): A Retrospective," Swiss Institute, New York, September 12–October 26, 1996. "American Twentieth-Century Watercolors at the Munson-Williams-Proctor Arts Institute," MWPAI, April 30–July 10, 2000 (traveling exhibition, cat. no. 43, illus.).

PUBLICATIONS

Paintings, Drawings & Sculptures in the Museum of Art (Utica, N.Y.: Munson-Williams-Proctor Institute, 1961), 34.
Schwarz, Dieter. *Sonja Sekula, 1918–1963* (Winterthur, Switzerland: Kunstmuseum, 1996), illus. pl. 29.

CHARLES SELIGER

(b. New York, N.Y., 1926, lives in Mount Vernon, N.Y.)

172. *Beetle No. 1*, 1949

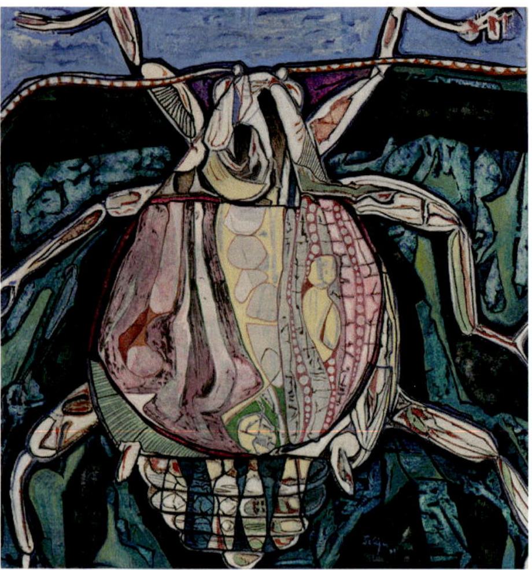

Tempera, oil, and ink on paperboard
7 $^{7}/_{16}$ x 7 ⅛ in.
57.225
Signed and dated lower right (white paint): Seliger / 49
Purchased from Carlebach Gallery, New York

EXHIBITIONS

["Charles Seliger," Carlebach Gallery, New York, April 18–May 7, 1949.] "Edward Wales Root Bequest," Munson-Williams-Proctor Institute, Utica, N.Y., November 5, 1961–February 24, 1962 (catalog). "Abstract Paintings and Drawings from the Root Bequest," Root Art Center, Hamilton College, Clinton, N.Y., September 11–October 9, 1966. "Carnival of the Animals," MWPI, December 10–31, 1972. "Nature in Art," MWPI, January 17–February 15 and June 2–September 1, 1987.

PUBLICATION

Paintings, Drawings & Sculptures in the Museum of Art (Utica, N.Y.: Munson-Williams-Proctor Institute, 1961), 34.

CHARLES SELIGER

Charles Seliger was born Charles Marvin Zekowski in New York City on June 3, 1926 to Hortense Seliger (1906–82) and George Zekowski (1899–81). At the age of fourteen, Seliger changed his last name from his father's to his mother's maiden name. Seliger's art education was chiefly from gallery and museum visits, art books, and hours of sketching. In 1943, when he was just 17, he had his first solo exhibition in New York at Jimmy Ernst's (1920–84) Norlyst Gallery. In 1945, Peggy Guggenheim (1898–1975) gave Seliger two one-man shows at Art of This Century Gallery. The gallery was a haven for young American artists who were influenced by Surrealism such as William Baziotes (1912–63) and Jackson Pollock (1912–56). Like many of his contemporaries, Seliger uses automatism, where the artist attempts to let the hand draw or paint without conscious control or aesthetic concern. When Guggenheim returned to Venice to live after World War II, Seliger moved to the Carlebach Gallery in New York City where he had exhibitions in 1948 and 1949. In 1950, Seliger began exhibiting at the Willard Gallery in New York City. There he had numerous shows from 1953 to 1968. Also in 1950, Seliger moved to the suburb of Mount Vernon, New York and took a job at the Commercial Decal Corporation. He began as Director of Design, making decorative patterns for Eva Zeisel Hallcraft China, and retired in 1993 as Senior Vice-President. After 1968, Seliger exhibited in New York at the Andrew Crispo Gallery (1976–83), the Gallery Schlesinger-Boisante (1986–87), the Saidenberg Gallery (1990), and, since 1991, the Michael Rosenfeld Gallery.

Seliger met Edward Wales Root (1884–1956) through Theodoros Stamos (1922–97) in the spring of 1949 at Root's home in Clinton, New York. Root had attended Seliger's 1949 exhibition at the Carlebach Gallery. Seliger, inspired by the writings of entomologist Jean-Henri Fabre (1823–1910), used insects as the subject of his work. Root appreciated Seliger's fascination and love of nature. Root's own affinity for nature led him to acquire a number of paintings by Seliger, including *Beetle No. 1* (cat. no. 172), *Horned Beetle: Claws and Head* (cat. no. 176), and *Caterpillar With Sky* (cat. no. 173).

Being an amateur artist himself, Edward Root seemed to grasp the plight of creative individuals, a concept not lost on Seliger. Seliger addressed these qualities in Root's understanding of the creative journey in 1957 by writing: "I had always the feeling that, although vitally interested in all art movements and isms, he [Edward Root] remained open and free. He was above all concerned with the individual's concept and performance: it wasn't the direction but the painting that counted."[1]

Seliger also gave Root one of his intricate hand-painted rocks sometime in the late 1940s. Seliger recalled visiting Grace Root (1891–1975) at her home in Clinton, New York on November 5, 1961 after Edward's death. He recounts seeing the stone displayed in the house. He wrote about the trip in his journal: "Inside, two [Ben] Nicholsons and a [Graham] Sutherland hung—room full of books and loads of odd natural forms: plants, rocks, minerals, fossils, etc.—pottery and the small painted stone I gave him." [2]

—Michael D. Somple

1. *Edward Wales Root, 1884–1956: An American Collector* (Utica, NY: Munson-Williams-Proctor Institute, 1957), 35.
2. Francis V. O'Connor, *Charles Seliger: Redefining Abstract Expressionism* (Manchester, Vt.: Hudson Hill Press, 2002), 55.

173. *Caterpillar With Sky*, 1949

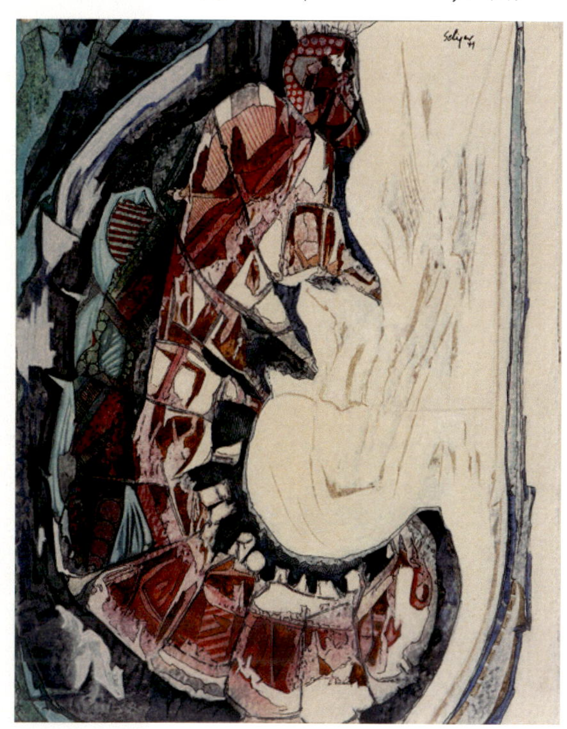

Oil, tempera, watercolor, and ink on heavy paper
7 15/16 x 6 3/8 in.
57.226
Signed and dated upper right (black ink): Seliger / 49
Inscribed on frame verso top: Caterpillar with Sky April–August 1949 / Oil, Tempera, Watercolor, ink on paper; verso on mount upper right: CATERPILLAR WITH SKY / oil, tempera / watercolor–ink / on paper– / Charles Seliger / Apr–Aug. '49
Purchased from Carlebach Gallery, New York

EXHIBITIONS

"New Trends in 20th-Century American Painting," Union College, Schenectady, N.Y., March 5–26, 1961. "Edward Wales Root Bequest," Munson-Williams-Proctor Institute, Utica, N.Y., November 5, 1961–February 24, 1962 (catalog). "Selections from the Edward W. Root Collection," Root Art Center, Hamilton College, Clinton, N.Y., February 22–March 21, 1970. "Carnival of the Animals," MWPI, December 10–31, 1972. "Nature in Art," MWPI, January 17–February 15 and June 2–September 1, 1987.

PUBLICATION

Paintings, Drawings & Sculptures in the Museum of Art (Utica, N.Y.: Munson-Williams-Proctor Institute, 1961), 34.

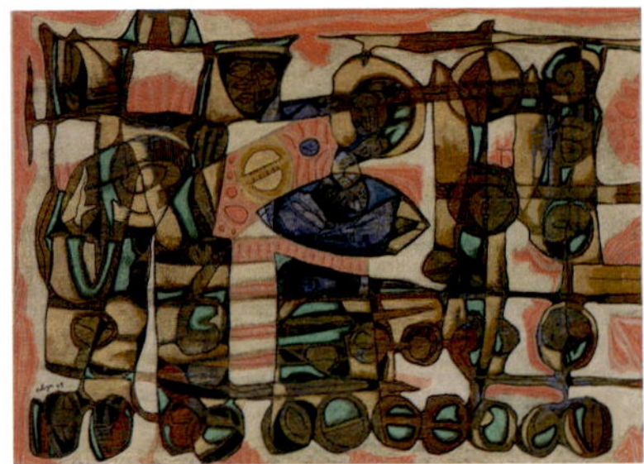

174. *Cross-Section: Plant Life*
1949

Oil, tempera, and ink on thin cardboard
7 ⅞ x 11 ¼ in.
57.227
Signed and dated lower left (black ink): Seliger 49
Inscribed verso upper right (black ink): "Cross Section: Plant Life" / oil, tempera, ink / Dec. 48–Jan. 49 / Charles Seliger; verso top center (graphite): #10; verso, center (black ink): #9
Purchased from Carlebach Gallery, New York

EXHIBITIONS

["Charles Seliger," Carlebach Gallery, New York, April 18–May 7, 1949.] "The New Landscape in Art and Science," American Federation of Arts, October 1958–May 1960 (traveling exhibition). "Edward Wales Root Bequest," Munson-Williams-Proctor Institute, Utica, N.Y., November 5, 1961–February 24, 1962 (catalog, illus.). "Paintings and Drawings from the Edward W. Root Bequest," Root Art Center, Hamilton College, Clinton, N.Y., April 7–May 5, 1968. "Selections from the Edward W. Root Collection," Root Art Center, February 22–March 21, 1970. "Five Decades of Collecting: Edward W. Root," MWPI, April 2–May 28, 1978. "Edward W. Root: Collector and Teacher," Fred L. Emerson Gallery, Hamilton College, October 2–November 14, 1982 (catalog, illus., 56). "Nature in Art," MWPI, January 17–February 15 and June 2–September 1, 1987.

PUBLICATION

Paintings, Drawings & Sculptures in the Museum of Art (Utica, N.Y.: Munson-Williams-Proctor Institute, 1961), 34.

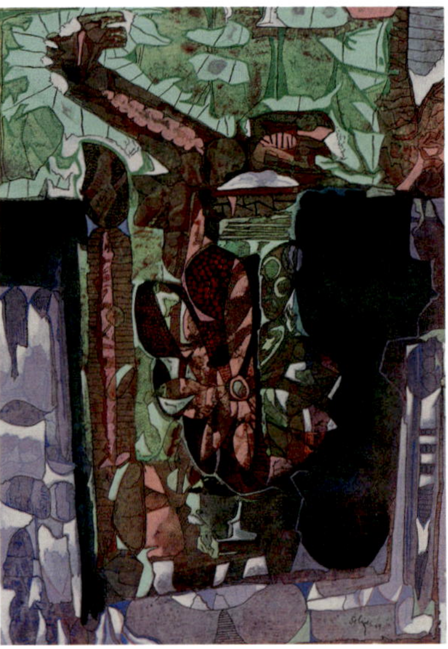

175. *Hidden Flower Under Earth*
1949

Oil, tempera, and ink mounted on cardboard
14 ⅜ x 10 ⅛ in.
57.228
Signed and dated lower right (black ink): Seliger 49
Inscribed verso upper right (black ink): #18 Hidden Flower Under Earth / tempera, oil, ink / Charles Seliger / Jan–Feb–49
Purchased from Carlebach Gallery, New York

EXHIBITIONS

["Charles Seliger," Carlebach Gallery, New York, April 18–May 7, 1949.] "The New Landscape in Art and Science," American Federation of Arts, October 1958–May 1960 (traveling exhibition). "Edward Wales Root Bequest," Munson-Williams-Proctor Institute, Utica, N.Y., November 5, 1961–February 24, 1962 (catalog). "Abstract Paintings and Drawings from the Root Bequest," Root Art Center, Hamilton College, Clinton, N.Y., September 11–October 9, 1966. "The Root Bequest," Root Art Center, May 11–June 8, 1969. "Selections from the Edward W. Root Collection," Root Art Center, February 22–March 21, 1970. "Nature in Art," MWPI, January 17–February 15 and June 2–September 1, 1987.

PUBLICATIONS

Paintings, Drawings & Sculptures in the Museum of Art (Utica, N.Y.: Munson-Williams-Proctor Institute, 1961), 34.
O'Connor, Francis. *Charles Seliger: Redefining Abstract Expressionism* (Manchester, Vt.: Hudson Hills Press, 2002), illus. pl. 14.

176. *Horned Beetle: Claws and Head*, 1949

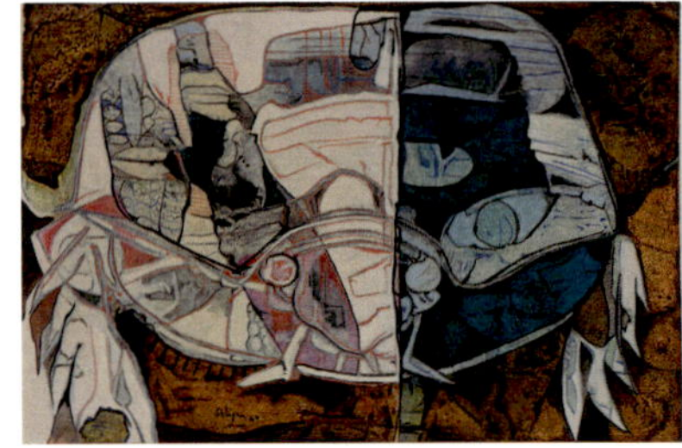

Oil, tempera, varnished glazes, watercolor and ink on paperboard mounted in fabric-covered cardboard
3 ⅞ x 5 ⅞ in.
57.291
Signed and dated lower left center (black ink): Seliger 49
Inscribed verso: "Horned Beetle: Claws & Head" April–May 1949; verso top center (graphite): "TOP"
Purchased from Carlebach Gallery, New York

EXHIBITIONS

"Edward Wales Root Bequest," Munson-Williams-Proctor Institute, Utica, N.Y., November 5, 1961–February 24, 1962 (catalog). "Selections from the Edward W. Root Collection," Root Art Center, Hamilton College, Clinton, N.Y., February 22–March 21, 1970. "Carnival of the Animals," MWPI, December 10–31, 1972. "Nature in Art," MWPI, January 17–February 15 and June 2–September 1, 1987.

PUBLICATION

Paintings, Drawings & Sculptures in the Museum of Art (Utica, N.Y.: Munson-Williams-Proctor Institute, 1961), 34.

177. *Organic Form: Air, Sea, Land Enveloped*, 1948

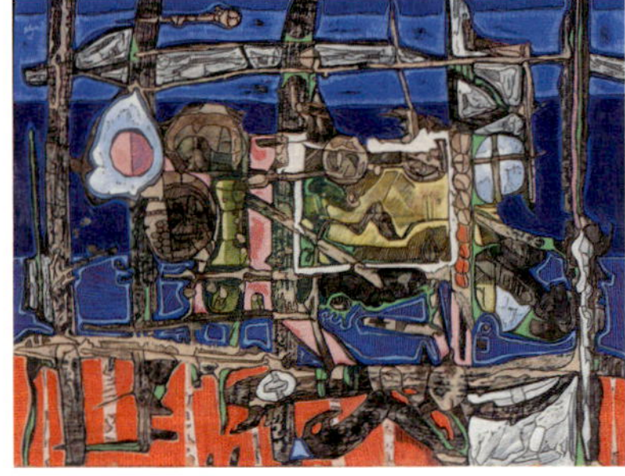

Tempera on Masonite
9 x 11 ⅞ in.
57.229
Signed and dated upper left (white paint):

Seliger / 48
Inscribed on tape verso: "Organic Form: Air, Sea, Land Enveloped" / Tempera on Masonite / #13 Nov '48 C. Seliger; inscribed verso top left edge: #7
Purchased from Carlebach Gallery, New York

EXHIBITIONS
["Charles Seliger," Carlebach Gallery, April 18–May 7, 1949.] "American Watercolors and Drawings," Root Art Center, Hamilton College, Clinton, N.Y., April 4–May 7, 1961. "Edward Wales Root Bequest," Munson-Williams-Proctor Institute, Utica, N.Y., November 5, 1961–February 24, 1962 (catalog). "Selections from the Edward W. Root Collection," Root Art Center, February 22–March 21, 1970.

PUBLICATIONS
Paintings, Drawings & Sculptures in the Museum of Art (Utica, N.Y.: Munson-Williams-Proctor Institute, 1961), 34.
O'Connor, Francis. *Charles Seliger: Redefining Abstract Expressionism* (Manchester, Vt.: Hudson Hills Press, 2002), illus. pl. 12.

178. *Untitled No. 1*, 1948

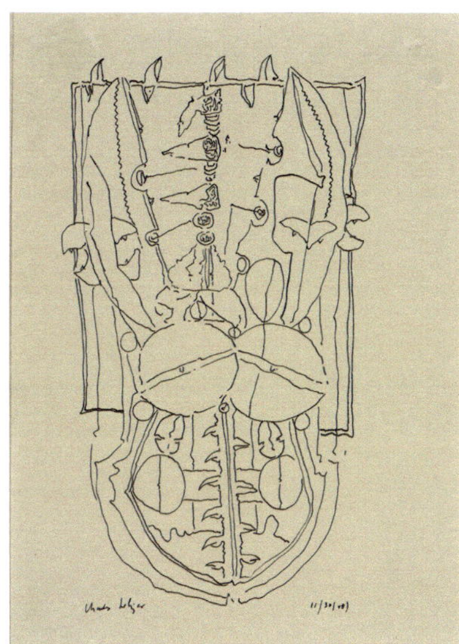

Ink on Japanese paper
6 ⅞ x 4 15⁄16 in.
57.230
Signed lower left (black ink): Charles Seliger; lower right (black ink): 11 / 30 / 48
Purchased from Carlebach Gallery, New York

EXHIBITIONS
["Charles Seliger," Carlebach Gallery, April 18–May 7, 1949.] "Edward Wales Root Bequest," Munson-Williams-Proctor Institute, Utica, N.Y., November 5, 1961–February 24, 1962 (catalog). "Abstract Paintings and Drawings from the Root Bequest," Root Art Center, Hamilton College, Clinton, N.Y., September 11–October 9, 1966.

PUBLICATION
Paintings, Drawings & Sculptures in the Museum of Art (Utica, N.Y.: Munson-Williams-Proctor Institute, 1961), 34.

179. *Untitled No. 2*, 1948

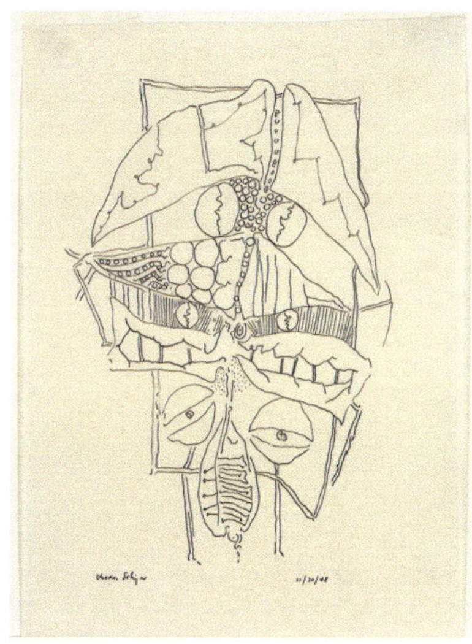

Ink on Japanese paper
6 ⅞ x 4 15⁄16 in.
57.231
Signed lower left (black ink): Charles Seliger; lower right (black ink): 11 / 30 / 48
Purchased from Carlebach Gallery, New York

EXHIBITIONS
["Charles Seliger," Carlebach Gallery, April 18–May 7, 1949.] "American Watercolors and Drawings," Root Art Center, Hamilton College, Clinton, N.Y., April 4–May 7, 1961. "Edward Wales Root Bequest," Munson-Williams-Proctor Institute, Utica, N.Y., November 5, 1961–February 24, 1962 (catalog).

PUBLICATION
Paintings, Drawings & Sculptures in the Museum of Art (Utica, N.Y.: Munson-Williams-Proctor Institute, 1961), 34.

CHARLES SHEELER
(Philadelphia, Pa., 1883–Dobbs Ferry, N.Y., 1965)

180. *Bucks County Barns*, 1924

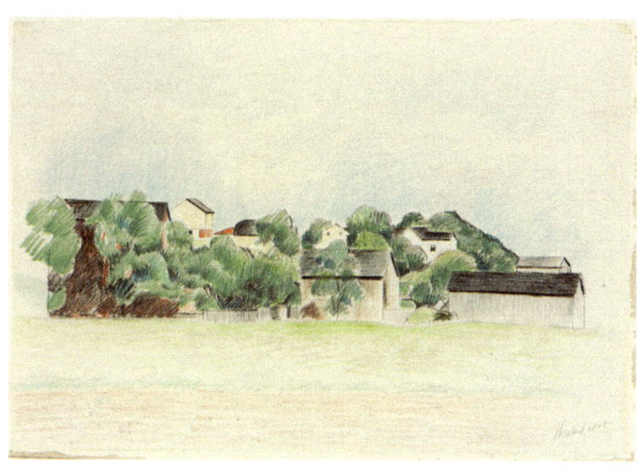

Colored pencil and graphite on white wove paper
8 ¾ x 12 15⁄16 in.
57.232
Signed and dated lower right (graphite): Sheeler 1924
Purchased from Charles Daniel Gallery, New York, January 1928

EXHIBITIONS
"Edward Wales Root Bequest," Munson-Williams-Proctor Institute, Utica, N.Y., November 5, 1961–February 24, 1962 (catalog). "The Quest of Charles Sheeler," The University of Iowa, Iowa City, Ia., March 17–April 14, 1963 (cat. no. 23, illus. fig. 5). "Landscapes," MWPI, April 7–May 4, 1969. "Charles Sheeler: The Works on Paper," The Pennsylvania State University Museum of Art, University Park, Pa., February 10–March 24, 1974 (cat. no. 28). "American Drawings and Watercolors from the Munson-Williams-Proctor Institute," E. B. Crocker Art Gallery, Sacramento, Calif., October 25–November 24, 1974 (cat. no. 56). Rome Community Art Center, Rome, N.Y., September 14–November 9, 1975. "American Modernism: Precisionist Works on Paper," Herbert F. Johnson Museum, Cornell University, Ithaca, N.Y., November 8–December 21, 1986 (traveling exhibition, cat. no. 24). "Life Lines: American Master Drawings (1788–1962) from the Munson-Williams-Proctor Institute," MWPI, September 17–November 13, 1994 (traveling exhibition, cat. no. 44, illus., 104 and color pl. 16).

PUBLICATIONS
Paintings, Drawings & Sculptures in the Museum of Art (Utica, N.Y.: Munson-Williams-Proctor Institute, 1961), 34.
American Art in Upstate New York (Buffalo, N.Y.: Buffalo Fine Arts Academy, 1974), 49.

CHARLES SHEELER

181. *Siphon*, 1923

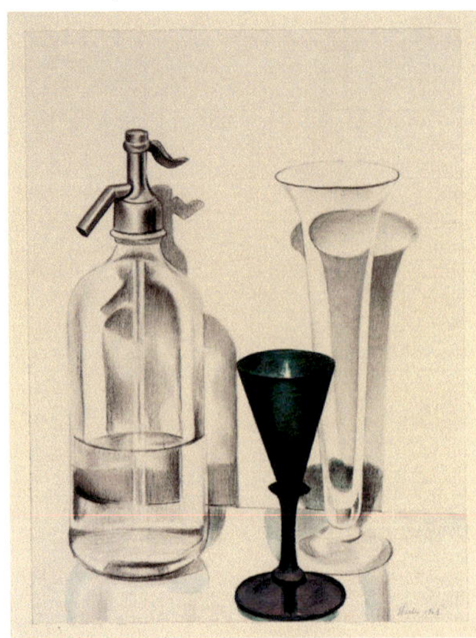

Charcoal and watercolor on white paper
16 7/16 x 12 ½ in.
57.233
Signed and dated lower right (graphite): Sheeler 1923
Purchased from Charles Daniel Gallery, New York, January 1928

EXHIBITIONS

"Exhibition of Watercolors and Pastels by Eleven American Moderns from a Distinguished Private Collection," Munson-Williams-Proctor Institute, Utica, N.Y., fall 1938. "The Edward Root Collection," The Metropolitan Museum of Art, New York, February 12–April 12, 1953 (catalog, 3). "Five Decades of American Painting," Root Art Center, Hamilton College, Clinton, N.Y., September 21–October 19, 1958 (traveling exhibition). The Strathmont Museum, Elmira, N.Y., June–September 1959. "Five Decades of American Painting," Union College, Schenectady, N.Y., September 27–October 23, 1959. "American Watercolors and Drawings," Root Art Center, April 4–May 7, 1961. "Edward Wales Root Bequest," MWPI, November 5, 1961–February 24, 1962 (catalog). "On Paper," New York State Council on the Arts / American Federation of Arts, September 1966–September 1967 (traveling exhibition, cat. no. 28). "The Quest of Charles Sheeler," The University of Iowa, Iowa City, Ia., March 17–April 14, 1963 (cat. no. 23). "The Root Bequest," Root Art Center, May 11–June 8, 1969. "Charles Sheeler: The Works on Paper," The Pennsylvania State University Museum of Art, University Park, Pa., February 10–March 24, 1974 (cat. no. 21). "American Drawings and Watercolors from the Munson-Williams-Proctor Institute," E. B. Crocker Art Gallery, Sacramento, Calif., October 25–November 24, 1974 (cat. no. 55, illus.). "Watercolors: Historic and Contemporary," Hathorn Gallery, Skidmore College, Saratoga Springs, N.Y., February 4–20, 1977 (cat. no. 48). "Charles Sheeler (1883–1965) Classic Themes: Paintings, Drawings and Photographs," Terry Dintenfass Gallery, New York, May 10–30, 1980 (cat. no. 10). "Edward W. Root: Collector and Teacher," Fred L. Emerson Gallery, Hamilton College, October 2–November 14, 1982 (catalog, illus., 26). "Life Lines: American Master Drawings (1788–1962) from the Munson-Williams-Proctor Institute," MWPI, September 17–November 13, 1994 (traveling exhibition, cat. no. 43, illus., 102 and color pl. 15).

PUBLICATIONS

Paintings, Drawings & Sculptures in the Museum of Art (Utica, N.Y.: Munson-Williams-Proctor Institute, 1961), 34. *American Art in Upstate New York* (Buffalo, N.Y.: Buffalo Fine Arts Academy, 1974), 49.

EVERETT SHINN

(Woodstown, N.J., 1876–New York, N.Y., 1953)

182. *Paris Cabaret*, 1917
Watercolor and pastel on paper

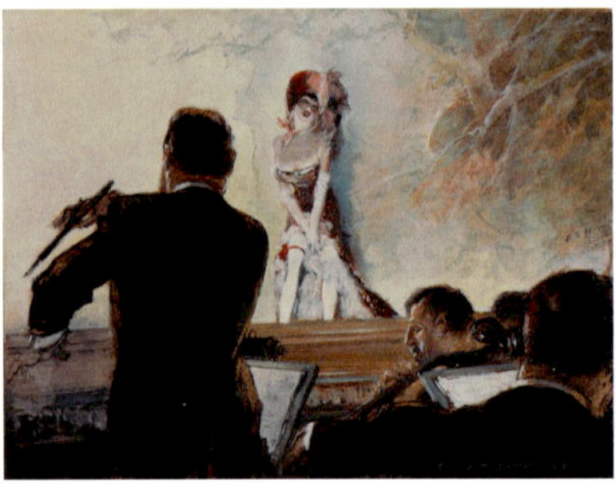

11 7/8 x 15 13/16 in.
57.234
Signed and dated lower right (white pastel): EVERETT SHINN / 1917
Purchased from The American British Art Center, New York, ca. March 1945

EXHIBITIONS

"Paintings and Drawings by Everett Shinn of Paris and New York 1900 to 1945," The American British Art Center, New York, February 13–March 3, 1945 (cat. no. 24). "Edward Wales Root Bequest," Munson-Williams-Proctor Institute, Utica, N.Y., November 5, 1961–February 24, 1962 (catalog). "The Figure in 20th-Century Paintings and Drawings," Root Art Center, Hamilton College, Clinton, N.Y., April 15–May 6, 1962. Root Art Center, December 1963. "The Ash Can School," Arnot Art Gallery, Elmira, N.Y., February 1965 (catalog, illus. cover). "New Jersey and the Artist," New Jersey State Museum, Trenton, N.J., October 16–November 28, 1965 (cat. no. 46). "American 20th-Century Watercolors from MWPI," Albany Institute of History and Art, Albany, N.Y., September 10–October 4, 1967. "Everett Shinn, 1873–1953," New Jersey State Museum, 1973 (traveling exhibition, cat. no. 50, illus., 43). "American Drawings and Watercolors from the Munson-Williams-Proctor Institute," E. B. Crocker Art Gallery, Sacramento, Calif., October 25–November 24, 1974 (cat. no. 57, illus.). "In This Academy," Pennsylvania Academy of the Fine Arts, Philadelphia, Pa., April 22–December 31, 1976 (cat. no. 261). "Figuratively Speaking," MWPI, April 11–November 10, 1985.

PUBLICATIONS

Paintings, Drawings & Sculptures in the Museum of Art (Utica, N.Y.: Munson-Williams-Proctor Institute, 1961), 35. De Shazo, Edith. *Everett Shinn, 1876–1953. A Figure In His Time* (New York: Clarkson N. Potter, Inc., 1974) 210, illus. *American Art in Upstate New York* (Buffalo, N.Y.: Buffalo Fine Arts Academy, 1974), 50.

183. *Paris Music Hall (Ventriloquist)*, 1902

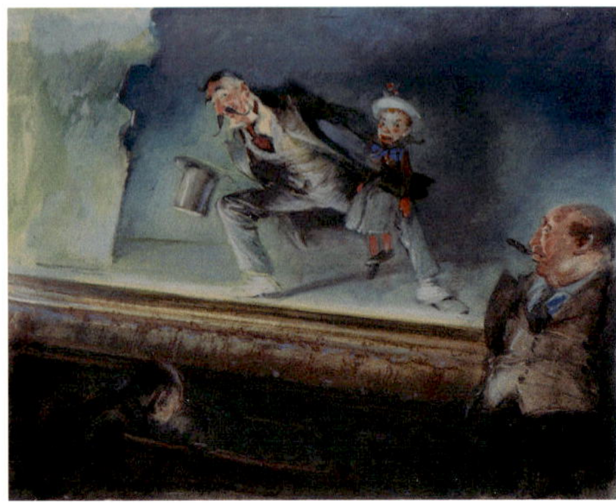

Opaque and transparent watercolor and pastel on wove paper
8 x 10 in.
57.235
Signed lower edge left center (black charcoal): EVERETT SHINN
Inscribed verso: no. 17 / Ventriloquist
Purchased from The American British Art Center, New York, ca. March 1945

EXHIBITIONS

"Everett Shinn," M. Knoedler & Co., New York, March 1903. "Paris-New York Personal by Everett Shinn," Ferargil Galleries, New York, January 18–February 1, 1943. "Everett Shinn," Ferargil Galleries, November 8–28, 1943 (cat. no. 26). "Paintings and Drawings by Everett Shinn of Paris and New York 1900 to 1945," The American British Art Center, New York, February 13–March 3, 1945 (cat. no. 17). "Paintings from 1904–1946 of Circus, Stage, and Streets by Everett Shinn," American British Art Center, November 19–December 7, 1946 (cat. no. 5, dated 1907). "The Edward Root Collection," The Metropolitan Museum of Art, New York, February 12–April 12, 1953 (catalog, 3). "Edward Wales Root Bequest," Munson-Williams-Proctor Institute, Utica, N.Y., November 5, 1961–February 24, 1962 (catalog). "Everett Shinn: Painter of City Life," Museum of Fine Arts, St. Petersburg, Fla., January 7–26, 1969. "20th-Century American Painting," Executive Mansion, Albany, N.Y., September–November 1974. "Graphic Styles of the American Eight," Utah Museum of Fine Arts, University of Utah, Salt Lake City, February 29–April 11, 1976 (cat. no. 101, illus., 56.). "American Works of Art on Paper 1850–1925," Schenectady Museum & Planetarium, Schenectady, N.Y., January 12–April 6, 1980 (cat. no. 83); "Edward W. Root: Collector and Teacher," Fred L. Emerson Gallery, Hamilton College, Clinton, N.Y., October 2–November 14, 1982 (catalog, illus., 46). "American Twentieth-Century Watercolors at the Munson-Williams-Proctor Arts Institute," MWPAI, April 30–July 10, 2000 (traveling exhibition, cat. no. 1, illus.).

PUBLICATION

Paintings, Drawings & Sculptures in the Museum of Art (Utica, N.Y.: Munson-Williams-Proctor Institute, 1961), 35.

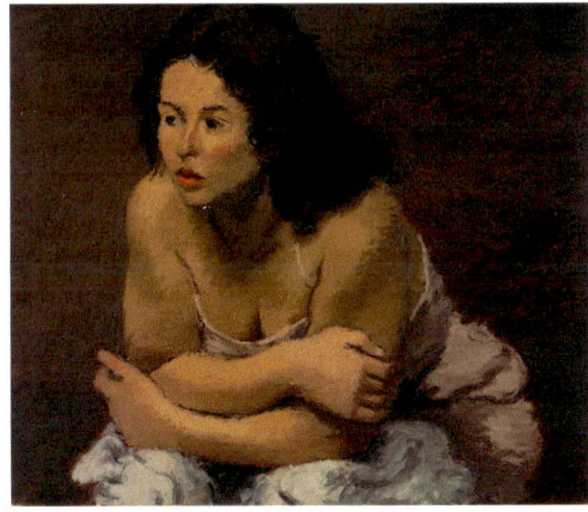

RAPHAEL SOYER

(Borisoglebsk, Russia, 1899–New York, N.Y., 1987)

184. *Study for "Sentimental Girl"*

1934

Oil on linen

20 x 24 in.

57.236

Signed upper right (black paint): Raphael Soyer

Purchased from Valentine Gallery, New York, February 1935

[Letter from the artist to MWPI Curator Joseph S. Trovato, March 29, 1975: "*Study for 'Sentimental Girl'* is not a title chosen by me, but by my dealer at the time Valentine Dudensing. The model who posed for it was a vivacious young dancer. I still remember her name—Silvia. The painting has no connection with the one called *Sentimental Girl* which is now in the collection of Mrs. Bella Fishko—my present dealer. Both were painted about the same time and exhibited at Dudensing's Gallery."]

EXHIBITIONS

"Second Biennial Exhibition of Contemporary American Painting, 1934–1935," Whitney Museum of American Art, New York, November 27, 1934–January 10, 1935 (cat. no. 146). "Recent Paintings by Raphael Soyer," Valentine Gallery, New York, February 18–March 7, 1935 (cat. no. 8). "Edward Wales Root Bequest," Munson-Williams-Proctor Institute, Utica, N.Y., November 5, 1961–February 24, 1962 (catalog). "Five Distinguished American Artists: Dickinson, Hofmann, Hopper, Shahn, Soyer," New York State Exposition, Syracuse, N.Y., August 31–September 6, 1965 (cat. no. 52). "Prints by American Artists," Root Art Center, Hamilton College, Clinton, N.Y., January 9–February 12, 1967. "The Root Bequest," Root Art Center, May 11–June 8, 1969. "Edward W. Root: Collector and Teacher," Fred L. Emerson Gallery, Hamilton College, October 2–November 14, 1982 (catalog, as *Figure*, illus., 34). "Figuratively Speaking," MWPI, July 16–November 10, 1985. "Two Hundred Years of American Art," The Art Museum Association of America, November 15, 1986–May 8, 1988 (traveling exhibition, cat. no. 53, illus., 67).

PUBLICATIONS

Paintings, Drawings & Sculptures in the Museum of Art (Utica, N.Y.: Munson-Williams-Proctor Institute, 1961), 35.
Schweizer, Paul D., et al. *Masterworks of American Art from the Munson-Williams-Proctor Institute* (New York: Harry N. Abrams, Inc., 1989) cat. no. 68, illus., 149.

EUGENE SPEICHER

(Buffalo, N.Y., 1883–Woodstock, N.Y., 1962)

185. *Brigham's Yard, Kingston*

1928

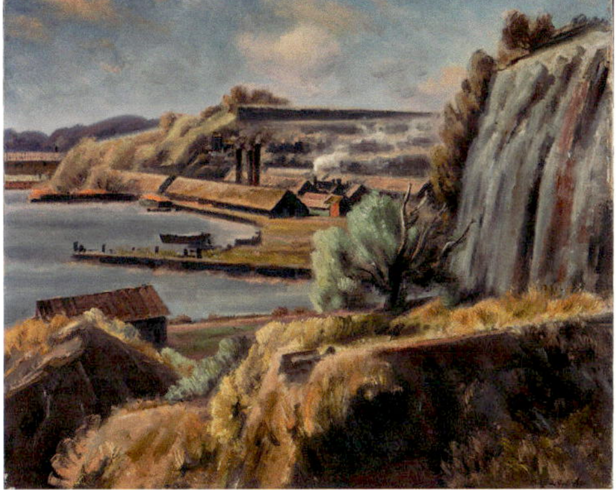

Oil on linen

27 ¼ x 34 ⅜ in.

57.237

Signed lower right (brown paint): Eugene Speicher

Inscribed verso (red paint): "Brigham's Yard, Kingston" / Eugene Speicher

Purchased from Frank K. M. Rehn Galleries, New York, January 1929

EXHIBITIONS

"Eugene Speicher," Frank K. M. Rehn Galleries, New York, January 2–19, 1929 (cat. no. 13). "Twenty-Eighth International Exhibition of Paintings," Carnegie Institute, Pittsburgh, Pa., October 17–December 8, 1929 (cat. no. 17). "Paintings by Nineteen Living Americans," The Museum of Modern Art, New York, December 13, 1929–January 13, 1930 (cat. no. 89). "22 Important Contemporary Paintings, Comparative Exhibition of European and American Paintings," Reinhardt Galleries, New York, January 23–February 20, 1932 (cat. no. 10). "Paintings and Drawings 1908–1951 by Eugene Speicher," The Century Association, New York, December 5, 1951–January 6, 1952 (cat. no. 7), as *Brigham's Yard, East Kingston.*

EUGENE SPEICHER

Eugene Speicher was born in Buffalo, New York, on April 5, 1883. At the age of twenty-three, he enrolled in night classes at the Buffalo Fine Arts Academy to study with Lucius Hitchcock (1868–1942), and Urquhart Wilcox (1876–1941). At the end of his first year, the Academy awarded Speicher an Albright Scholarship to the Art Students League in New York where his teachers included Frank Vincent Dumond (1865–1951) and William Merritt Chase (1849–1916). Always the passionate overachiever, Speicher supplemented his daily studies at the League by taking evening classes with Robert Henri (1865–1929) at the Henri School of Art. George Wesley Bellows (1882–1925) took Speicher to his first class at Henri's school and the two men remained friends until Bellows's death. In 1907, Speicher's industry paid off when he was awarded a Kelly Prize of one hundred dollars. He used the money to travel abroad for the first time, visiting galleries and museums in England, France, Italy, Germany, and Holland, accompanied by his bride Elsie Wilson (d.1959). Upon their return, they moved to Woodstock, next door to Bellows, and Speicher became an active member of the Woodstock Art Colony.

From 1911 until 1945, Speicher was honored with many awards for his work. In 1911, he won the Thomas R. Proctor Portrait Prize from the National Academy of Design in New York, thus furthering his career as a portrait painter.[1] In 1945 he received a degree of Doctor of Fine Arts from Syracuse University and became director of the American Academy of Arts and Letters. In his will, Speicher left all of his unsold work to the Academy with the stipulation that they periodically be sold off to buy new works by living artists, which, in turn, would be donated to museums. In November 2003, three hundred works were sold by the Academy for this purpose.

Speicher joined the Frank K. M. Rehn Gallery in 1925. Edward Wales Root (1884–1956) purchased his first Speicher painting, *Brigham's Yard, Kingston* (cat. no.184), from Speicher's 1929 Rehn Gallery exhibition. This work is one of Speicher's best landscapes and is unique in subject, compared to the portraits for which he is best known.

Critically acclaimed during his lifetime, Speicher gradually fell out of public favor and today is relatively unknown. His work is found in many private and public collections including The Metropolitan Museum of Art, the Cleveland Museum of Art, the Pennsylvania Academy of the Fine Arts, and the Whitney Museum of American Art. Root's commitment to education through his passion for teaching at Hamilton College and his many gifts to the Munson-Williams-Proctor Arts Institute parallels Eugene Speicher's commitment to the American Academy of Arts and Letters. He died in Woodstock, New York in 1962, three years after his wife, Elsie.

—Michael D. Somple

1. Thomas R. Proctor (1884–1920) was one of the founders of the Munson-Williams-Proctor Arts Institute.

186. *Landscape, East Kingston* Ca. 1926

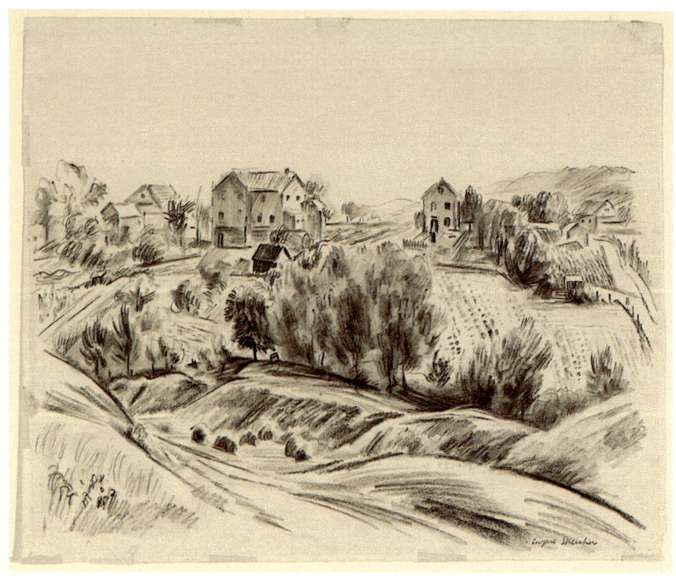

EUGENE SPEICHER

"The Edward Root Collection," The Metropolitan Museum of Art, February 12–April 12, 1953 [second checklist printing]. "20th-Century American Painting from the Edward W. Root Collection," Smithsonian Institution, Washington, D.C., July 1959–July 1960 (traveling exhibition). "Edward Wales Root Bequest," Munson-Williams-Proctor Arts Institute, Utica, N.Y., November 5, 1961–February 24, 1962 (catalog, illus.). "Learning About Pictures from Mr. Root," Root Art Center, Hamilton College, Clinton, N.Y., January 4–31, 1965 (catalog, illus.). "Paintings and Drawings from the Edward W. Root Bequest," Root Art Center, April 7–May 5, 1968. "The Root Bequest," Root Art Center, May 11–June 8, 1969. "The Art Triangle: Artist, Dealer, Collector," Burchfield Art Center, Buffalo, N.Y., May 13–June 25, 1989 (traveling exhibition, cat. no. 81, illus., 58). "Masterworks of American Art from the Munson-Williams-Proctor Institute Museum of Art," Knoxville Museum of Art, Knoxville, Tenn., February 26–August 23, 1998.

PUBLICATIONS

Watson, Forbes. "Exhibitions Coming and Going," *The Arts* XV (January 1929): 47, illus., 48. Palmer, Mildred. *Eugene Speicher* Arts Portfolio Series (New York: Arts Publishing Corporation, 1930), illus. Mather, Frank Jewett. *Eugene Speicher* (New York: Whitney Museum of American Art, 1931), illus., 27. *Eugene Speicher* **Illustrated Monograph** no. 7 (New York: American Artists Group, Inc. 1945), illus. *Paintings, Drawings & Sculptures in the Museum of Art* (Utica, N.Y.: Munson-Williams-Proctor Institute, 1961), 35.

186. *Landscape, East Kingston*

Ca. 1926

French crayon on Cameo paper
10 ⅞ x 13 ⅜ in. sheet
57.314
Signed lower right (graphite): Eugene Speicher
Purchased from Frank K. M. Rehn Galleries, New York, February 1928

EXHIBITIONS

"Edward W. Root Loan Exhibition," Utica Art Society, Utica, N.Y., May 1928. "Nature in Art," Root Art Center, Hamilton College, Clinton, N.Y., April 8–June 7, 1959.
"American Watercolors and Drawings from the Edward W. Root Bequest," Root Art Center, April 9–May 7, 1961. "Edward Wales Root Bequest," Munson-Williams-Proctor Institute, Utica, N.Y., November 5, 1961–February 24, 1962 (catalog). "Landscapes," MWPI, April 7–May 4, 1969. "Selections from the Edward W. Root Collection," Root Art Center, February 22–March 21, 1970. Kirkland Art Center, Clinton, N.Y., February 6–March 6, 1972. "Life Lines: American Master Drawings (1788–1962) from the Munson-Williams-Proctor Institute," MWPI, September 17–November 13, 1994 (traveling exhibition, cat. no. 45, illus., 106).

PUBLICATION

Paintings, Drawings & Sculptures in the Museum of Art (Utica, N.Y.: Munson-Williams-Proctor Institute, 1961), 35.

187. *Spring Bouquet–Brown Table*

1943

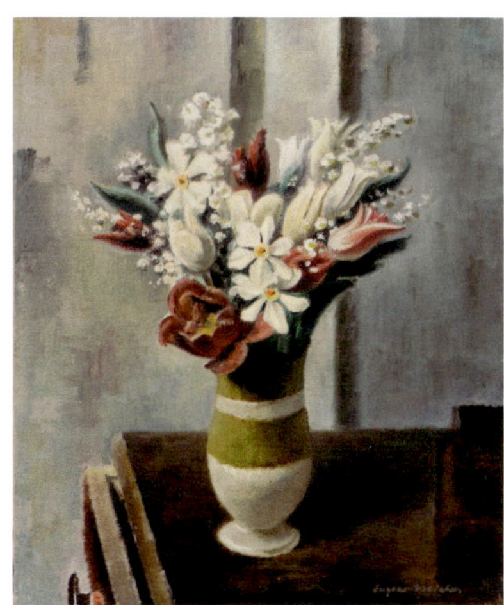

Oil on linen
23 x 19 ¼ in.
57.238
Signed lower right (light brown paint): Eugene Speicher
Inscribed verso on stretcher, top: Spring Bouquet–Brown Table
Purchased from Frank K. M. Rehn Galleries, New York, December 1943

EXHIBITIONS

"The Edward Root Collection," The Metropolitan Museum of Art, New York, February 12–April 12, 1953 (catalog, 3).
"Edward Wales Root Bequest," Munson-Williams-Proctor Arts Institute, Utica, N.Y., November 5, 1961–February 24, 1962 (catalog). "20th-Century American Painting," Executive Mansion, Albany, N.Y., September–November 1974. "Flowers in Painting, Prints and Drawings," MWPI, April 20–May 25, 1980. "Nature in Art," MWPI, June 2–September 1, 1987. "The Art Triangle: Artist, Dealer, Collector," Burchfield Art Center, Buffalo, N.Y., May 13–June 25, 1989 (traveling exhibition, cat. no. 87).

PUBLICATIONS

Eugene Speicher Illustrated Monograph no. 7 (New York: American Artists Group, Inc. 1945), illus. *Paintings, Drawings & Sculptures in the Museum of Art* (Utica, N.Y.: Munson-Williams-Proctor Institute, 1961), 35.

THEODOROS STAMOS

(New York, N.Y., 1922–Yiannia, Greece, 1997)

188. *Ancestral Construction*, 1946

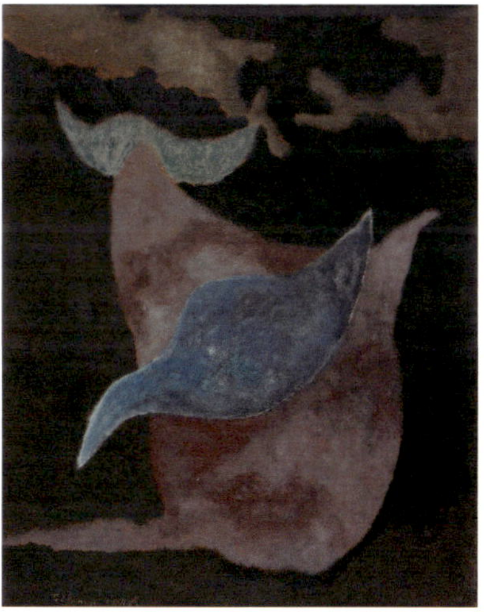

Oil on Masonite
30 x 24 in.
57.239
Signed and dated lower left (white paint): T. Σtamos '46 NYC
Inscribed verso top of Masonite: "Ancestral Construction" / Theodoros Stamos / 1946 NYC
Purchased from Betty Parsons Gallery, New York, February 1947

EXHIBITIONS

"Stamos," Betty Parsons Gallery, New York, February 10–March 1, 1947 (cat. no. 16).
"Current Trends in British and American Painting," Munson-Williams-Proctor Institute, Utica, N.Y., December 3–31, 1950 (traveling exhibition, cat. no. 25). "The Edward Root Collection," The Metropolitan Museum of Art, New York, February 12–April 12, 1953 (catalog, 3). "Five American Artists of the 20th Century: Davies, Luks, Burchfield, Tobey, Stamos," Root Art Center, Hamilton College, Clinton, N.Y., December 7, 1958–March 28, 1959.
"20th-Century American Painting from the Edward W. Root Collection," Smithsonian Institution, Washington, D.C., July 1959–July 1960 (traveling exhibition).
"Edward Wales Root Bequest," MWPI, November 5, 1961–February 24, 1962 (catalog). "European Sources of Contemporary American Art: Kandinsky," Root Art Center, September 15–October 6, 1963 (cat. no. 39).
"Abstract Paintings and Drawings from the Root Bequest," Root Art Center, September 11–October 9, 1966. "Abstract Expressionism," MWPI, July 19–August 18, 1985. "Insights," MWPI, January 7–April 13, 1986. "Nature in Art," MWPI, June 2–September 1, 1987. "Theodoros Stamos (1922–1997): A Retrospective," National Gallery and Alexandros Soutzos Museum, Athens, Greece, September 30–November 30, 1997 (cat. no. 17, illus., 103). "The Tiger's Eye: The Art of a Magazine," Yale University Art Gallery, New Haven, Conn., January 29–March 30, 2002 (catalog, illus.).

PUBLICATIONS

[*The Tiger's Eye* 2 (December 1947): 77, illus.]
Paintings, Drawings & Sculptures in the Museum of Art (Utica, N.Y.: Munson-Williams-Proctor Institute, 1961), 36.

THEODOROS STAMOS

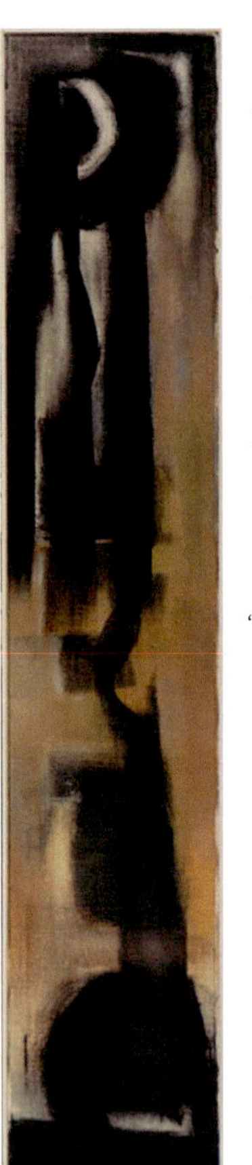

189. *Berkshire Morning No. 3*

Ca. 1949–50

Oil on canvas
60 x 11 in.
57.240
Signed lower left (blue paint): Σtamos
Inscribed verso: Oct / Berkshire / Morning
Purchased from Betty Parsons Gallery, New York, April 1952

EXHIBITIONS

"Edward Wales Root Bequest," Munson-Williams-Proctor Institute, Utica, N.Y., November 5, 1961–February 24, 1962. "Nature in Art," MWPI, June 2–September 1, 1987. "Influences of Klee," MWPI, December 19, 1987–May 13, 1988. "Theodoros Stamos (1922–1997): A Retrospective," National Gallery and Alexandros Soutzos Museum, Athens, Greece, September 30–November 30, 1997 (cat. no. 51, dated 1951–52, illus., 175).

PUBLICATIONS

Paintings, Drawings & Sculptures in the Museum of Art (Utica, N.Y.: Munson-Williams-Proctor Institute, 1961), 36 [as *Berkshire Morning*]. Pomeroy, Ralph. *Stamos* (New York: Harry N. Abrams, Inc., 1974), illus. pl. 101.

190. *Blue Fish*, 1944

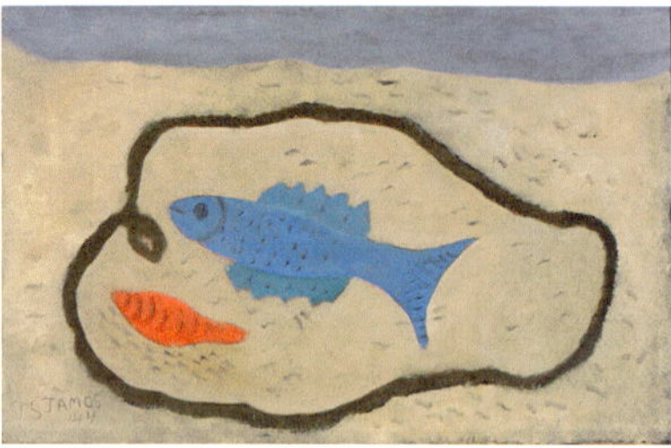

Oil on Masonite
10 3/16 x 16 1/8 in.
57.241
Signed and dated lower left (inscribed in paint): T Stamos / '44
Mortimer Brandt Gallery, New York; Purchased from Betty Parsons Gallery, New York, 1946

EXHIBITIONS

"New Trends in 20th-Century American Painting," Union College, Schenectady, N.Y., March 5–26, 1961. "Edward Wales Root Bequest," Munson-Williams-Proctor Institute, Utica, N.Y., November 5, 1961–February 24, 1962 (catalog). "Selections from the Edward W. Root Collection," Root Art Center, Hamilton College, Clinton, N.Y., February 22–March 21, 1970. "Carnival of the Animals," MWPI, December 10–31, 1972. "Contemporary Artists: Early and Late Paintings," Root Art Center, April 4–May 2, 1973. "Nature in Art," MWPI, June 2–September 1, 1987. "Influences of Klee," MWPI, December 19, 1987–May, 12, 1988.

PUBLICATIONS

Paintings, Drawings & Sculptures in the Museum of Art (Utica, N.Y.: Munson-Williams-Proctor Institute, 1961), 36. Murray, Mary E. "Theodoros Stamos and Edward Wales Root: A Friendship in Art and Nature," in *Theodoros Stamos (1922–1997): A Retrospective* (Athens, Greece: National Gallery and Alexandros Soutzos Museum, 1997), 55.

191. *Bone*, 1945

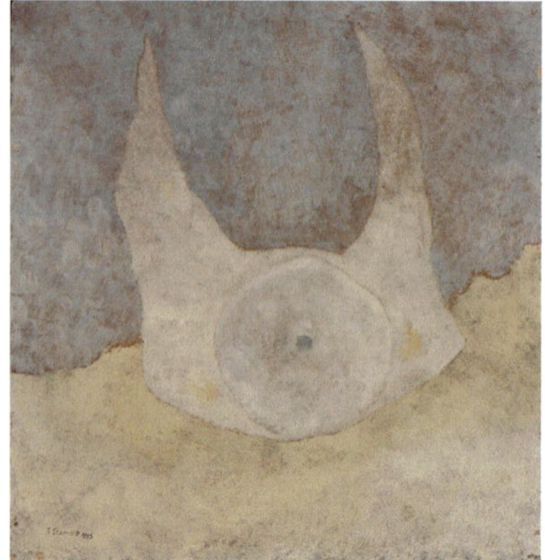

Oil on paper mounted on panel
18 ½ x 18 in.
57.242
Signed and dated lower left (scratched in paint): T. Σtamos '45
Inscribed verso (chalk): Theodore Stamos / 146 5 Ave. NYC; verso lower center the sketch "Fish Vertebra"; verso, lower right: "To capture the / mystery to cast surroun / ding a lonely Vertebra / on the beach."
Mortimer Brandt Gallery, New York; Purchased from Betty Parsons Gallery, New York, 1946

EXHIBITIONS

"Paintings by John Graham, David Hill, Theodoros Stamos, Hedda Sterne," Mortimer Brandt Gallery, New York, May 5–29, 1945 (cat. no. 9). "Five American Artists of the 20th Century: Davies, Luks, Burchfield, Tobey, Stamos," Root Art Center, Hamilton College, Clinton, N.Y., December 7, 1958–March 28, 1959. "20th-Century American Painting from the Edward W. Root Collection," Smithsonian Institution, Washington, D.C., July 1959–July 1960 (traveling exhibition). "Edward Wales Root Bequest," Munson-Williams-Proctor Institute, Utica, N.Y., November 5, 1961–February 24, 1962 (catalog). "Selections from the Edward W. Root Collection," Root Art Center, February 22–March 21, 1970. "20th-Century Prints and Drawings," Schenectady Museum & Planetarium, Schenectady, N.Y., December 15, 1971–January 15, 1972. "Nature in Art," MWPI, June 2–September 1, 1987.

PUBLICATIONS

Paintings, Drawings & Sculptures in the Museum of Art (Utica, N.Y.: Munson-Williams-Proctor Institute, 1961), 36. Murray, Mary E. "Theodoros Stamos and Edward Wales Root: A Friendship in Art and Nature," in *Theodoros Stamos (1922–1997): A Retrospective* (Athens, Greece: National Gallery and Alexandros Soutzos Museum, 1997), 55.

192. *Conversation Piece*

January 1948

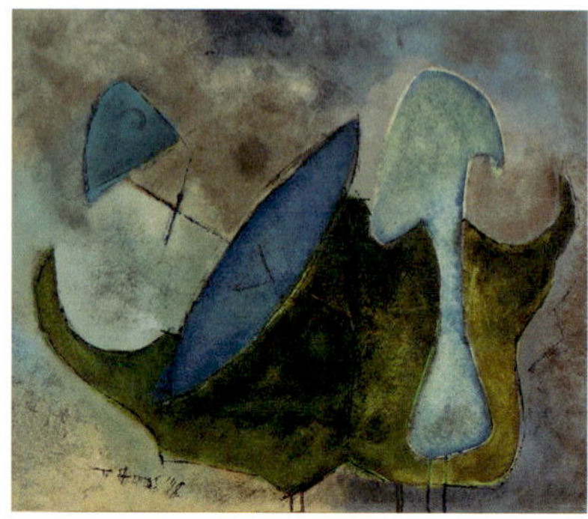

Oil on Masonite
20 x 24 in.
57.243
Signed and dated lower left (black paint): T. Σtamos '48
Inscribed verso (chalk): Jan / 48 Conversation Piece / 40 E 22nd St
Purchased from Betty Parsons Gallery, New York, 1949

EXHIBITIONS

"Five American Artists of the 20th Century: Davies, Luks, Burchfield, Tobey, Stamos," Root Art Center, Hamilton College, Clinton, N.Y., December 7, 1958–March 28, 1959. "20th-Century American Painting from the Edward W. Root Collection," Smithsonian Institution, Washington, D.C., July 1959–July 1960 (traveling exhibition). "Edward Wales Root Bequest," Munson-Williams-Proctor Institute, Utica, N.Y., November 5, 1961–February 24, 1962 (catalog). "European Sources of Contemporary American Art: Kandinsky," Root Art Center, September 15–October 6, 1963 (cat. no. 40). "Nature in Art," MWPI, June 2–September 1, 1987.

PUBLICATIONS

Paintings, Drawings & Sculptures in the Museum of Art (Utica, N.Y.: Munson-Williams-Proctor Institute, 1961), 36. Pomeroy, Ralph. *Stamos* (New York: Harry N. Abrams, Inc., 1974), illus. pl. 63. Cavaliere, Barbara. "Theodoros Stamos in Perspective," *Arts* 51 (December 1977): 112.

193. *Cosmological Battle (Formlings)*, 1945

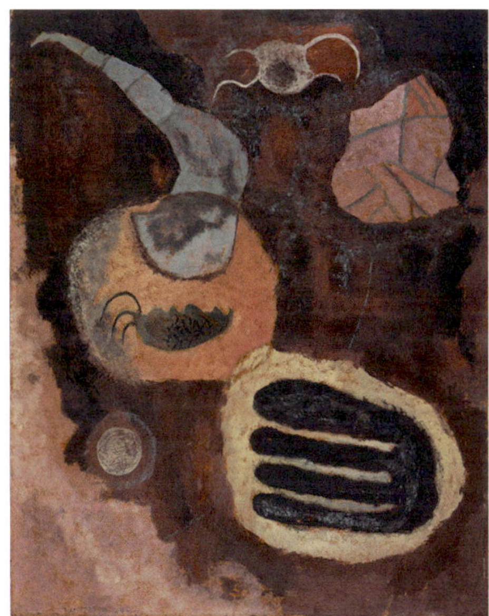

Oil on Masonite
30 x 23 ⅞ in.
57.244
Signed and dated lower left (black paint): T. Σtamos '45 NYC
Inscribed verso: Formlings / Theodoros Stamos / 146 5 Ave. / NYC / 1945
Purchased from Betty Parsons Gallery, New York, 1946

EXHIBITIONS

"Current Trends in British and American Painting," Munson-Williams-Proctor Institute, Utica, N.Y., December 3–31, 1950 (traveling exhibition, cat. no. 24). "Five American Artists of the 20th Century: Davies, Luks, Burchfield, Tobey, Stamos," Root Art Center, Hamilton College, Clinton, N.Y., December 7, 1959–March 28, 1959. "20th-Century American Painting from the Edward W. Root Collection," Smithsonian Institution, Washington, D.C., July 1959–July 1960 (traveling exhibition). "Edward Wales Root Bequest," MWPI, November 5, 1961–February 24, 1962 (catalog). "Abstract Expressionism," MWPI, July 19–August 18, 1985. "Two Hundred Years of American Art," The Art Museum Association of America, November 15, 1986–May 8, 1988 (traveling exhibition, cat. no. 63, illus., 77). "From Omaha to Abstract Expressionism: American Artists' Responses to World War II," Roland Gibson Gallery, Potsdam College, State University of New York, March 6–April 5, 1992 (catalog, 19, illus. fig. 13). "Theodoros Stamos (1922–1997): A Retrospective," National Gallery and Alexandros Soutzos Museum, Athens, Greece, September 30–November 30, 1997 (cat. no. 11, illus., 91). "Masterworks of American Art from the Munson-Williams-Proctor Institute Museum of Art," Knoxville Museum of Art, Knoxville, Tenn., February 26–August 23, 1998.

PUBLICATIONS

Paintings, Drawings & Sculptures in the Museum of Art (Utica, N.Y.: Munson-Williams-Proctor Institute, 1961), 36. Pomeroy, Ralph. *Stamos* (New York: Harry N. Abrams, Inc., 1974), illus. pl. 31. Cavaliere, Barbara. "Theodoros Stamos in Perspective," *Arts* 52 (December 1977): 106, illus., 105. Weiss, Jeffrey. "Science and Primitivism: A Fearful Symmetry in the Early New York School," *Arts* 57 (March 1983): 84, illus. fig. 9. Cavaliere, Barbara. "Theodoros Stamos: On the Horizon of Mind and Coast," in *Theodoros Stamos: Work from 1945 to 1984* (Zurich, Switzerland: M. Knoedler, 1984), 27. Schweizer, Paul D., et al. *Masterworks of American Art from the Munson-Williams-Proctor Institute* (New York: Harry N. Abrams, Inc., 1989), cat. no. 78, illus. Polcari, Stephen. *Abstract Expressionism and the Modern Experience* (Cambridge, England.: Cambridge University Press, 1991), 333.

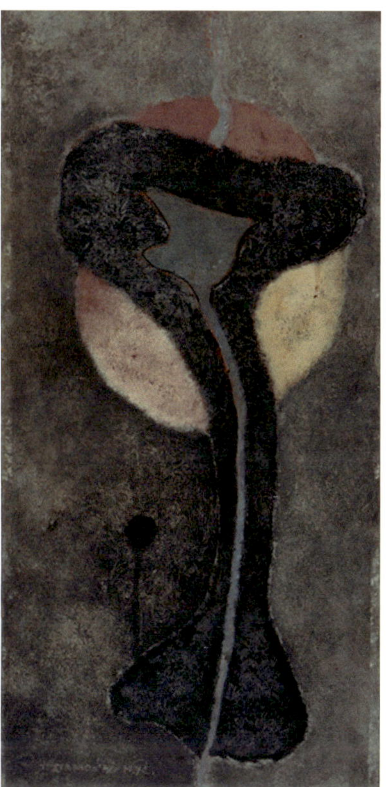

194. *The Heartbeat*, 1946

Oil on Masonite
24 x 12 in.
57.246
Signed and dated lower left (white paint): T. Σtamos '46 NYC
Inscribed verso frame at top: Theodoros Stamos / 237 West 26th St. / NYC / "The Heart Beat"
Purchased from Betty Parsons Gallery, New York, January 1947

EXHIBITIONS

"Five American Artists of the 20th Century: Davies, Luks, Burchfield, Tobey, Stamos," Root Art Center, Hamilton College, Clinton, N.Y., December 7, 1958–March 28, 1959. "Edward Wales Root Bequest," Munson-Williams-Proctor Institute, Utica, N.Y., November 5, 1961–February 24, 1962 (catalog). "Selections from the Edward W. Root Collection," Root Art Center, February 22–March 21, 1970. "Nature in Art," MWPI, June 2–September 1, 1987.

PUBLICATIONS

Paintings, Drawings & Sculptures in the Museum of Art (Utica, N.Y.: Munson-Williams-Proctor Institute, 1961), 36. Pomeroy, Ralph. *Stamos* (New York: Harry N. Abrams, Inc., 1974), illus. pl. 31.

THEODOROS STAMOS

195. *In Browns*, 1951

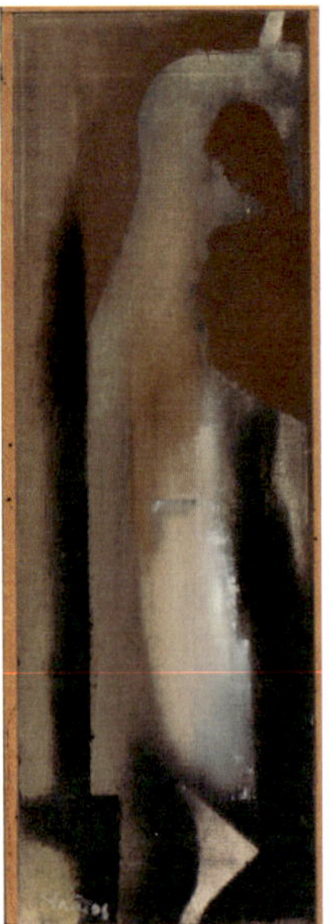

Oil on canvas
23 15⁄16 x 8 1⁄16 in.
57.247
Signed upper left (white paint): Σtamos
Purchased from Betty Parsons Gallery, New York, December 1951

EXHIBITIONS
"Theodoros Stamos," Betty Parsons Gallery, New York, February 18–March 8, 1952 (cat. no. 23). "Edward Wales Root Bequest," Munson-Williams-Proctor Institute, Utica, N.Y., November 5, 1961–February 24, 1962 (catalog). "Selections from the Edward W. Root Collection," Root Art Center, Hamilton College, Clinton, N.Y., February 22–March 21, 1970.

PUBLICATION
Paintings, Drawings & Sculptures in the Museum of Art (Utica, N.Y.: Munson-Williams-Proctor Institute, 1961), 36.

196. *Landscape*, 1949–50

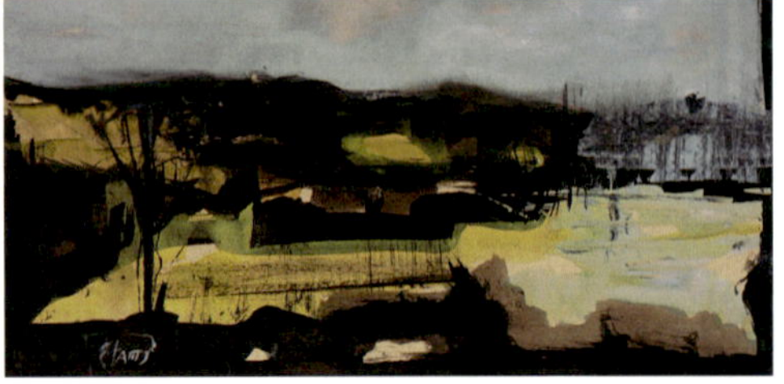

Tempera on laid watercolor paper mounted on pulp board
7 ½ x 15 ⅝ in.
57.248
Signed lower left (white paint): Σtamos
Purchased from Betty Parsons Gallery, New York

EXHIBITION
"Five American Artists of the 20th Century: Davies, Luks, Burchfield, Tobey, Stamos," Root Art Center, Hamilton College, Clinton, N.Y., December 7, 1958–March 28, 1959. "Edward Wales Root Bequest," Munson-Williams-Proctor Institute, Utica, N.Y., November 5, 1961–February 24, 1962 (catalog).

PUBLICATIONS
Paintings, Drawings & Sculptures in the Museum of Art (Utica, N.Y.: Munson-Williams-Proctor Institute, 1961), 36. Pomeroy, Ralph. *Stamos* (New York: Harry N. Abrams, Inc., 1974), illus. pl. 102.

197. *Mandrake Root*, 1949–50

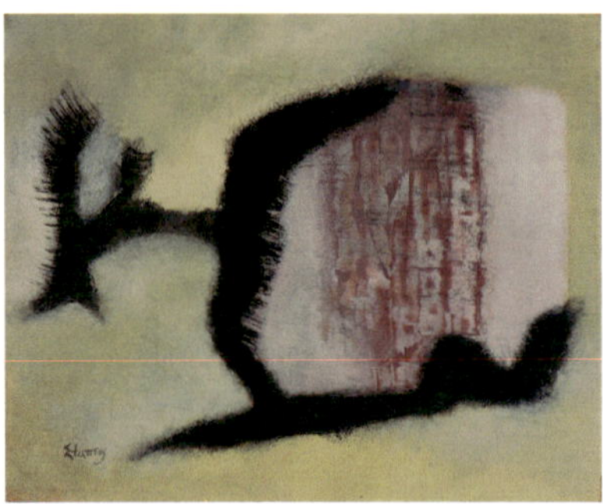

Oil on Masonite
15 ¼ x 19 ⅛ in.
57.249
Signed lower left (black ink): Σtamos
Inscribed verso top: "Mandrake Root"; verso bottom: Stamos / 45 E. 22 St. / NYC
Purchased from Betty Parsons Gallery, New York, January 1951

EXHIBITIONS
"Stamos," Betty Parsons Gallery, New York, January 8–27, 1951 (cat. no. 38). "Five American Artists of the 20th Century: Davies, Luks, Burchfield, Tobey, Stamos," Root Art Center, Hamilton College, Clinton, N.Y., December 7, 1958–March 28, 1959. "Edward Wales Root Bequest," Munson-Williams-Proctor Institute, Utica, N.Y., November 5, 1961–February 24, 1962 (catalog). "Selections from the Edward W. Root Collection," Root Art Center, February 22–March 21, 1970. "20th-Century Prints and Drawings," Schenectady Museum & Planetarium, Schenectady, N.Y., December 15, 1971–January 15, 1972. "Nature in Art," MWPI, June 2–September 1, 1987. "Influences of Klee," MWPI, December 19, 1987–May 13, 1988. "Theodoros Stamos (1922–1997): A Retrospective," National Gallery and Alexandros Soutzos Museum, Athens, Greece, September 30–November 30, 1997 (cat. no. 34, illus., 137).

PUBLICATIONS
Paintings, Drawings & Sculptures in the Museum of Art (Utica, N.Y.: Munson-Williams-Proctor Institute, 1961), 36. Pomeroy, Ralph. *Stamos* (New York: Harry N. Abrams, Inc., 1974), illus. pl. 103. Cavaliere, Barbara, "Theodoros Stamos in Perspective," *Arts Magazine* 52 (December 1977): 107, illus., 111.

198. *Monolith*, 1947

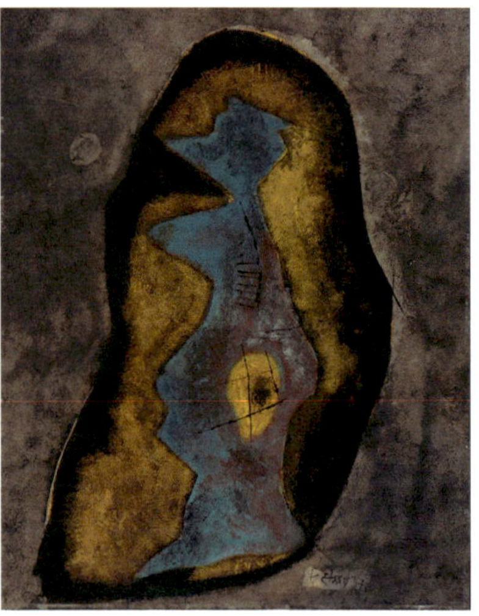

Oil on Masonite
30 x 23 ⅞ in.
57.250
Signed and dated lower right center (black paint): T. Σtamos '47
Inscribed verso (yellow crayon): Monolith / T. Stamos / 237 W. 26 St. / NYC. / $400 B.P. cat
Purchased from Betty Parsons Gallery, New York, February 1948

EXHIBITIONS
"Theodoros Stamos Paintings," Betty Parsons Gallery, New York, January 26–February 14, 1948 (cat. no. 8). "Current Trends in British and American Painting," Munson-Williams-Proctor Institute, Utica, N.Y., December 3–31, 1950 (traveling exhibition, cat. no. 26). "The Edward Root Collection," The Metropolitan Museum of Art, New York, February 12–April 12, 1953 (catalog, 3). "10th Anniversary Celebration," Des Moines Art Center, Des Moines, Ia., June 1–July 20, 1958. "Five Decades of American Painting," Union College, Schenectady, N.Y., September 27–October 23, 1959. "Edward Wales Root Bequest," MWPI, November 5, 1961–February 24, 1962 (catalog). "European Sources of Contemporary American Art: Kandinsky," Root Art Center, Hamilton College, Clinton, N.Y., September 15–October 6, 1963 (cat. no. 42). "125 Years of New York State Painting and Sculpture," New York State Exposition, organized by the New York State Council on the Arts, Syracuse, N.Y., August 30–September 5, 1966 (cat. no. 54). "Selections from the

Edward W. Root Collection," Root Art Center, February 22–March 21, 1970. "Contemporary Artists: Early and Late Paintings," Root Art Center, April 4–May 2, 1973. "Nature in Art," MWPI, June 2–September 1, 1987.

PUBLICATIONS

Paintings, Drawings & Sculptures in the Museum of Art (Utica, N.Y.: Munson-Williams-Proctor Institute, 1961),, 36. Prior, Harris K. "Edward Root–Talent Scout," *Art in America* L (1962): 72, illus. no. 9. Pomeroy, Ralph. *Stamos* (New York: Harry N. Abrams, Inc., 1974), illus. no. 103.

199. *Movement of Plants*, 1945

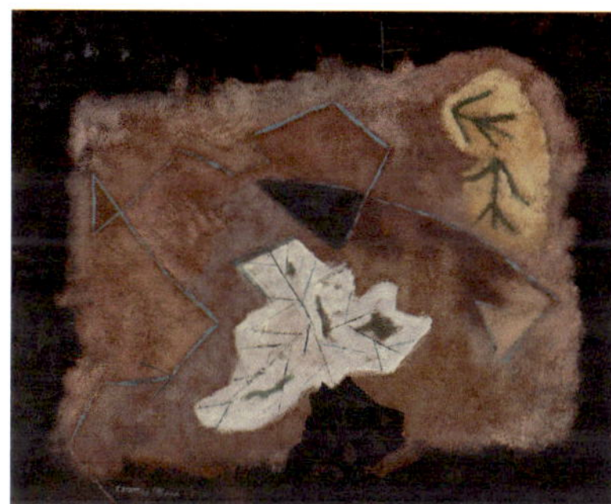

Oil on Masonite
16 x 20 in.
57.251
Signed and dated lower left (white paint): T. ΣTAMOS '45 NYC
Inscribed verso: "Movement of Plants" / $100 / Theodoros Stamos / 146 5 Ave. NYC / U.S.A; lower left: September / 1945
Purchased from "Annual Exhibition of Contemporary American Painting," Whitney Museum of American Art, through Mortimer Brandt Gallery, New York, 1946

EXHIBITIONS

"1945 Annual Exhibition of Contemporary American Painting," Whitney Museum of American Art, New York, November 27, 1945–January 10, 1946 (cat. no. 144). "Paintings from the Collection of Edward W. Root," Munson-Williams-Proctor Institute, Utica, N.Y., September 29–October 20, 1946. "Edward Wales Root Bequest," MWPI, November 5, 1961–February 24, 1962 (catalog). "The Root Bequest," Root Art Center, Hamilton College, Clinton, N.Y., May 11–June 8, 1969. "Abstract Expressionism: The Formative Years," Herbert F. Johnson Museum of Art, Cornell University, Ithaca, N.Y., March 30–May 14, 1978 (traveling exhibition, cat. no. 39, illus.). "Theodoros Stamos: Selected Paintings, 1945–1979," State University of New York, New Paltz, N.Y., January 27–February 17, 1980. "American Flower Genre," Whitney Museum of American Art, February 29–May 20, 1984. "Nature Framed" MWPI, March 15–May 20 and July 16–August 15, 1985. "Nature in Art," MWPI, June 2–September 1, 1987. "Theodoros Stamos (1922–1997): A Retrospective," National Gallery and Alexandros Soutzos Museum, Athens, Greece, September 30–November 30, 1997 (cat. no. 10, illus., 89).

PUBLICATIONS:

Paintings, Drawings & Sculptures in the Museum of Art (Utica, N.Y.: Munson-Williams-Proctor Institute, 1961), 36. Pomeroy, Ralph. *Stamos* (New York: Harry N. Abrams, Inc., 1974), 21, illus. color pl. 30. Cavaliere, Barbara. "Theodoros Stamos in Perspective," *Arts* 51 (December 1977): 106, 110. Weiss, Jeffrey. "Science and Primitivism: A Fearful Symmetry in the Early New York School," *Arts* 57 (March 1983): 84, illus. fig. 8. Cavaliere, Barbara. "Theodoros Stamos: On the Horizon of Mind and Coast," in *Theodoros Stamos: Work from 1945 to 1984* (Zurich, Switzerland: M. Knoedler, 1984), 27.

200. *The Reward*, 1948

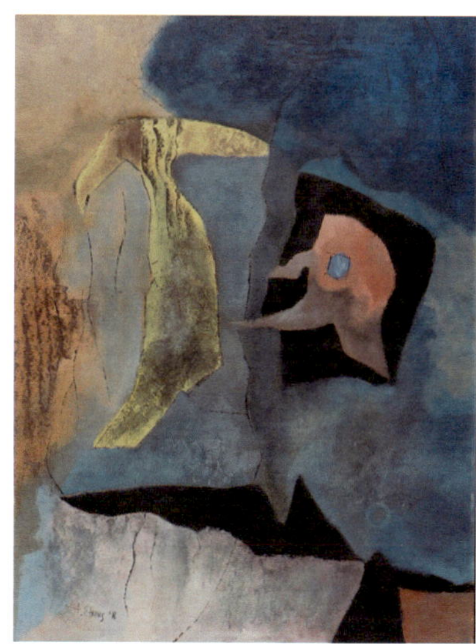

Oil on Masonite
48 x 36 in.
57.252
Signed and dated lower left (black paint): T. Σtamos '48
Inscribed verso: T. Stamos / April 1948 NYC
Purchased from Betty Parsons Gallery, New York, 1948

EXHIBITIONS

"Current Trends in British and American Painting from the Collection of Edward W. Root," Munson-Williams-Proctor Institute, Utica, N.Y., December 3–31, 1950 (traveling exhibition, cat. no. 28). "The Edward Root Collection," The Metropolitan Museum of Art, New York, February 12–April 12, 1953 (catalog, 3). "20th-Century American Paintings from the Edward W. Root Collection," Smithsonian Institution, Washington, D.C., July 1959–July 1960 (traveling exhibition). "Edward Wales Root Bequest," MWPI, November 5, 1961–February 24, 1962 (catalog, illus.). "European Sources of Contemporary American Art: Kandinsky," Root Art Center, Hamilton College, Clinton, N.Y., September 15–October 6, 1963 (cat. no. 43). "Abstract Paintings and Drawings from the Root Bequest," Root Art Center, September 11–October 9, 1966. "Paintings and Drawings from the Edward W. Root Bequest," Root Art Center, April 7–May 5, 1968. "Exhibition of American Paintings," Schenectady Museum & Planetarium, Schenectady, N.Y., March 20–April 30, 1970. "Contemporary Artists: Early and Late Paintings," Root Art Center, April 4–May 2, 1973. "Five Decades of Collecting: Edward W. Root," MWPI, April 2–May 28, 1978. "Theodoros Stamos: Selected Paintings, 1945–1979," State University of New York, New Paltz, N.Y., January 27–February 17, 1980. "Edward W. Root: Collector and Teacher," Fred L. Emerson Gallery, Hamilton College, October 2–November 14, 1982 (catalog, 52, illus., 53).

PUBLICATIONS

Paintings, Drawings & Sculptures in the Museum of Art (Utica, N.Y.: Munson-Williams-Proctor Institute, 1961), 36. Pomeroy, Ralph. *Stamos* (New York: Harry N. Abrams, Inc., 1974), 23, illus. pl. no. 61.

THEODOROS STAMOS

201. *Seedling (The Embryo; Vortex and Spiral)*, 1945

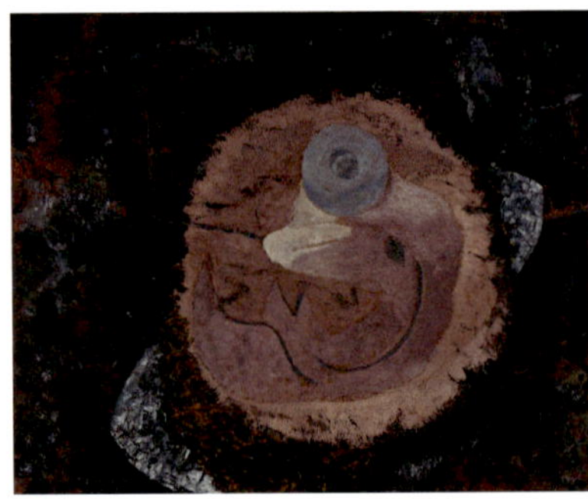

57.245
Oil on Masonite
24 x 30 in.
Signed and dated lower left (white paint): T. Stamos '45 / NYC
Inscribed verso: "Seedling" / Theodoros Stamos / 146 5 Ave. / N. Y. C.
Mortimer Brandt Gallery, New York; Purchased from Betty Parsons Gallery, New York, 1949

EXHIBITIONS

"Current Trends in British and American Painting from the Collection of Edward W. Root," Munson-Williams-Proctor Institute, Utica, N.Y., December 3–31, 1950 (traveling exhibition, cat. no. 23). "The Edward Root Collection," The Metropolitan Museum of Art, New York, February 12–April 12, 1953 (catalog, 3). "20th-Century American Paintings from the Edward W. Root Collection," Smithsonian Institution, Washington, D.C., July 1959–July 1960 (traveling exhibition).

"Edward Wales Root Bequest," MWPI, November 5, 1961–February 24, 1962 (catalog). "Selections from the Edward W. Root Collection," Root Art Center, Hamilton College, Clinton, N.Y., February 22–March 21, 1970. "Abstract Expressionism," MWPI, July 19–August 18, 1985. "Nature in Art," MWPI, June 2–September 1, 1987. "Influences of Klee," MWPI, December 19, 1987–May 13, 1988.

PUBLICATIONS

Paintings, Drawings & Sculptures in the Museum of Art (Utica, N.Y.: Munson-Williams-Proctor Institute, 1961), 36. Pomeroy, Ralph *Stamos* (New York: Harry N. Abrams, Inc., 1974), 22, illus. pl. 8. Cavaliere, Barbara. "Theodoros Stamos in Perspective," *Arts* 52 (December 1977): 106, illus., 104. Cavaliere, Barbara. "Theodoros Stamos: On the Horizon of Mind and Coast," in *Theodoros Stamos: Work from 1945 to 1984* (Zurich, Switzerland: M. Knoedler, 1984), 27. Murray, Mary E. "Theodoros Stamos and Edward Wales Root: A Friendship in Art and Nature," in *Theodoros Stamos (1922–1997): A Retrospective* (Athens, Greece: National Gallery and Alexandros Soutzos Museum, 1997), 55. *Expressionisme en primitivisme in de beeldendekunst van de twintigste eeuw* (Heerlen, Netherlands: Open Universiteit, 1998), 143, illus. fig. 139.

202. *(Spartan Way) Road to Sparta*, 1949

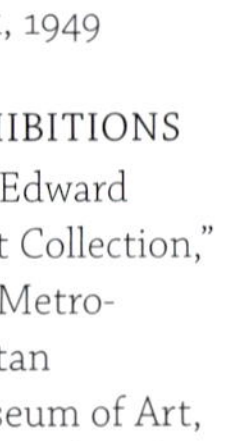

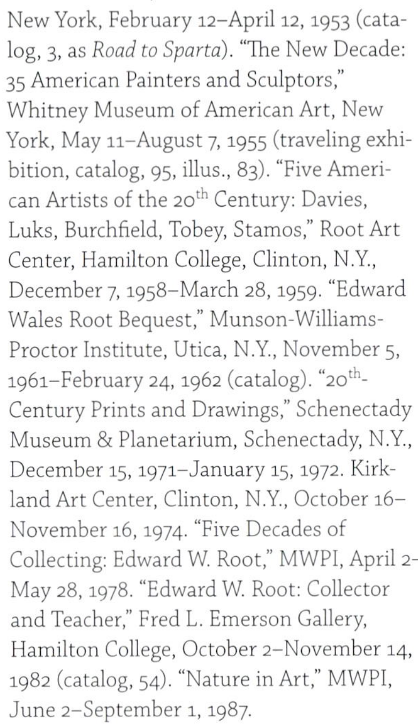

Oil on Masonite stippled with sand
54 x 18 in.
57.253
Signed and dated lower left (gray paint): Σtamos '49
Inscribed verso (chalk): Stamos / 1949 / "Spartan Way"
Purchased from Betty Parsons Gallery, New York, 1949

EXHIBITIONS

"The Edward Root Collection," The Metropolitan Museum of Art, New York, February 12–April 12, 1953 (catalog, 3, as *Road to Sparta*). "The New Decade: 35 American Painters and Sculptors," Whitney Museum of American Art, New York, May 11–August 7, 1955 (traveling exhibition, catalog, 95, illus., 83). "Five American Artists of the 20th Century: Davies, Luks, Burchfield, Tobey, Stamos," Root Art Center, Hamilton College, Clinton, N.Y., December 7, 1958–March 28, 1959. "Edward Wales Root Bequest," Munson-Williams-Proctor Institute, Utica, N.Y., November 5, 1961–February 24, 1962 (catalog). "20th-Century Prints and Drawings," Schenectady Museum & Planetarium, Schenectady, N.Y., December 15, 1971–January 15, 1972. Kirkland Art Center, Clinton, N.Y., October 16–November 16, 1974. "Five Decades of Collecting: Edward W. Root," MWPI, April 2–May 28, 1978. "Edward W. Root: Collector and Teacher," Fred L. Emerson Gallery, Hamilton College, October 2–November 14, 1982 (catalog, 54). "Nature in Art," MWPI, June 2–September 1, 1987.

PUBLICATIONS

Hale, Robert Beverly. "The Growth of a Collection," *The Metropolitan Museum of Art Bulletin* XI (February 1953), 157, illus. Hayes, Bartlett H., Jr. "The Root of American Painting," *Art News* LVI (January 1958): 61, illus. fig. 4. *Paintings, Drawings & Sculptures in the Museum of Art* (Utica, N.Y.: Munson-Williams-Proctor Institute, 1961), 36. Cavaliere, Barbara. "Theodoros Stamos in Perspective," *Arts* 51 (December 1977): 113. Murray, Mary E. "Theodoros Stamos and Edward Wales Root: A Friendship in Art and Nature," in *Theodoros Stamos (1922–1997): A Retrospective* (Athens, Greece: National Gallery and Alexandros Soutzos Museum, 1997), 55.

203. *Winter Harbor*, 1952

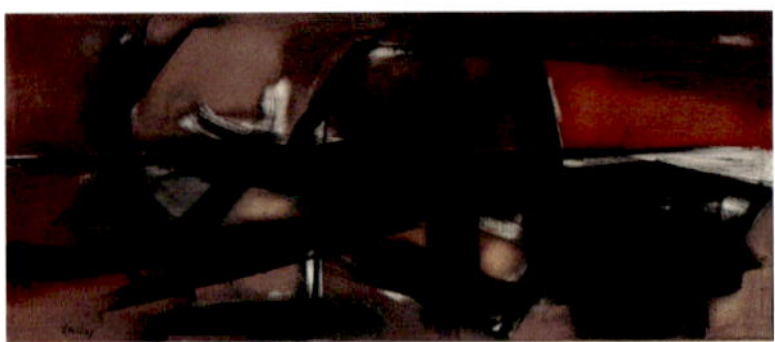

Oil on canvas
22 ¼ x 49 in.
57.254
Signed lower left (black paint): Σtamos
Inscribed verso: *("Winter Harbor")* 49 x 22 ¼ Stamos 80 W. 82 St
Purchased from Betty Parsons Gallery, New York, April 1953

EXHIBITIONS

"Theodoros Stamos: Recent Painting," Betty Parsons Gallery, January 5–24, 1953 (cat. no. 5). "Five American Artists of the 20th Century: Davies, Luks, Burchfield, Tobey, Stamos," Root Art Center, Hamilton College, Clinton, N.Y., December 7, 1959–March 28, 1959. "20th-Century American Painting from the Edward W. Root Collection," Smithsonian Institution, Washington, D.C., July 1959–July 1960 (traveling exhibition). Museum of Art Building inaugural exhibition, Munson-Williams-Proctor Institute, Utica, N.Y., October 15–December 31, 1960.

"Edward Wales Root Bequest," MWPI, November 5, 1961–February 24, 1962 (catalog). "Abstract Paintings and Drawings from the Root Bequest," Root Art Center, September 11–October 9, 1966. "Selections from the Edward W. Root Collection," Root Art Center, February 22–March 21, 1970.

"Contemporary Artists: Early and Late Paintings," Root Art Center, April 4–May 2, 1973. Kirkland Art Center, Clinton, N.Y., October 16–November 16, 1974.

PUBLICATION
Paintings, Drawings & Sculptures in the Museum of Art (Utica, N.Y.: Munson-Williams-Proctor Institute, 1961), 36.

WILLIAM STEIG

(Brooklyn, N.Y., 1907–Boston, Mass., 2003)

204. *Fat Woman*, not dated

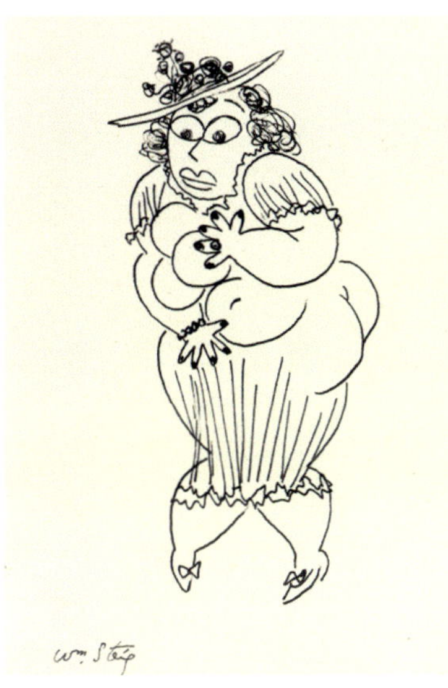

Ink on paper
4 ⅞ x 3 ⁹⁄₁₆ in.
57.289
Signed lower left (black ink): Wm. Steig

EXHIBITION
"Edward Wales Root Bequest," Munson-Williams-Proctor Institute, Utica, N.Y., November 5, 1961–February 24, 1962 (catalog).

PUBLICATION
Paintings, Drawings & Sculptures in the Museum of Art (Utica, N.Y.: Munson-Williams-Proctor Institute, 1961), 36.

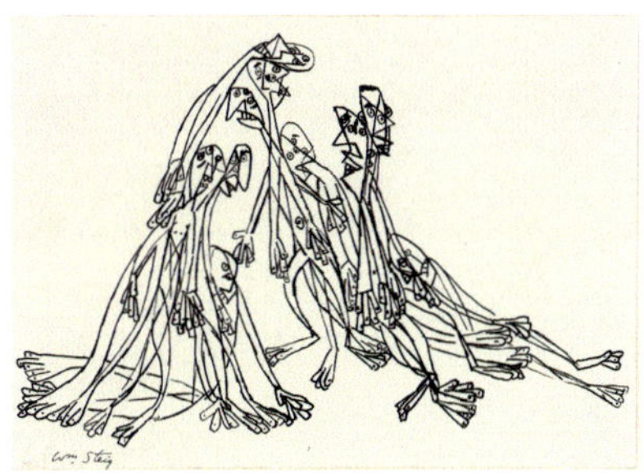

205. *Gregarious Creatures II*
Not dated
Ink on paper
4 ½ x 6 ½ in.
57.288
Signed lower left (black ink): Wm. Steig

EXHIBITION
"Edward Wales Root Bequest," Munson-Williams-Proctor Institute, Utica, N.Y., November 5, 1961–February 24, 1962 (catalog).

PUBLICATION
Paintings, Drawings & Sculptures in the Museum of Art (Utica, N.Y.: Munson-Williams-Proctor Institute, 1961), 36.

206. *Untitled*, ca. 1944

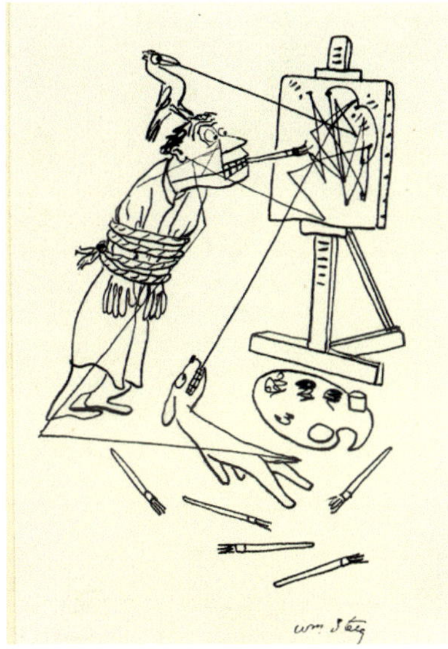

Ink on paper
5 ³⁄₁₆ x 3 ¹¹⁄₁₆ in.
57.324
Signed lower right (black ink): Wm. Steig

EXHIBITIONS
"The Edward Root Collection," The Metropolitan Museum of Art, New York, N.Y., February 12–April 12, 1953 (catalog, 3). "Edward Wales Root Bequest," Munson-Williams-Proctor Institute, Utica, N.Y., November 5, 1961–February 24, 1962 (catalog).

PUBLICATION
Paintings, Drawings & Sculptures in the Museum of Art (Utica, N.Y.: Munson-Williams-Proctor Institute, 1961), 36.

SAUL STEINBERG

(Râmnicu Sărat, Romania, 1914–New York, N.Y., 1999)

207. *At the Bar*, ca. 1955

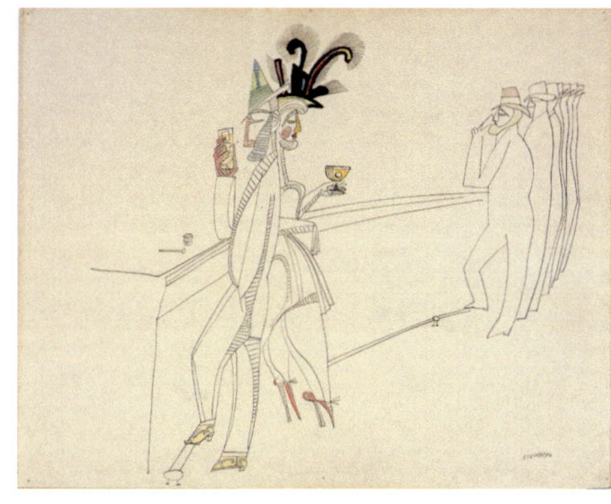

Ink and crayon on paper mounted on cardboard
18 ⅝ x 23 ¹¹⁄₁₆ in.
57.255
Signed lower right (black ink): STEINBERG

EXHIBITIONS
"Edward Wales Root Bequest," Munson-Williams-Proctor Institute, Utica, N.Y., November 5, 1961–February 24, 1962 (catalog). "Edward W. Root: Collector and Teacher," Fred L. Emerson Gallery, Hamilton College, Clinton, N.Y., October 2–November 14, 1982 (catalog, 60).

PUBLICATION:
Paintings, Drawings & Sculptures in the Museum of Art (Utica, N.Y.: Munson-Williams-Proctor Institute, 1961), 37.

SAUL STEINBERG

208. *Racing*, 1950–51

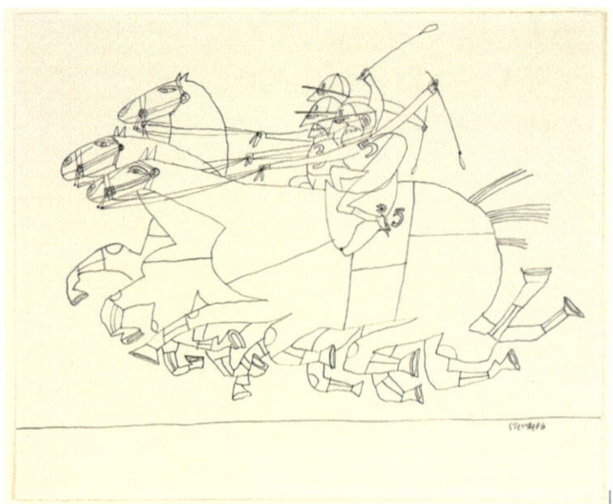

Ink on paper
11 ½ x 14 7/16 in.
57.256
Signed lower right (black ink): STEINBERG

EXHIBITIONS

"The Edward Root Collection," The Metropolitan Museum of Art, New York, N.Y., February 12–April 12, 1953 (catalog, 3).
"Edward Wales Root Bequest," Munson-Williams-Proctor Institute, Utica, N.Y., November 5, 1961–February 24, 1962 (catalog). "American Drawings and Watercolors from the Munson-Williams-Proctor Institute," E. B. Crocker Art Gallery, Sacramento, Calif., October 25–November 24, 1974 (cat. no. 57).

PUBLICATIONS

"Eight Drawings by Steinberg," *Wake* no. 10 (1951), illus., unpaginated. *Paintings, Drawings & Sculptures in the Museum of Art* (Utica, N.Y.: Munson-Williams-Proctor Institute, 1961), 37.

MAURICE STERNE

(Libau, Latvia, 1878–Mt. Kisco, N.Y.,, 1957)

209. *Three Figures, Bali*, 1912

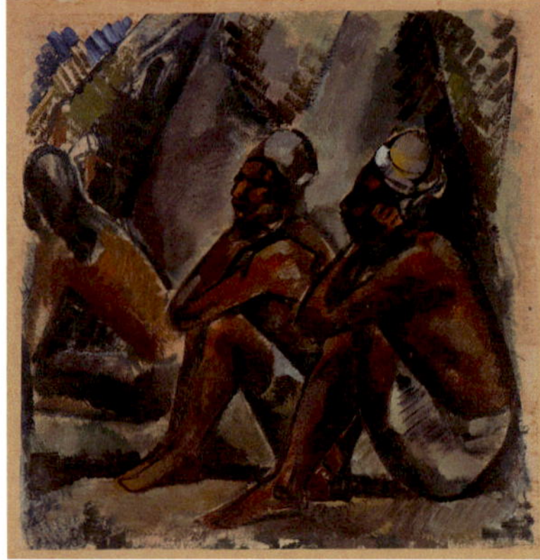

Oil on rice paper mounted on cardboard
16 ⅜ x 16 5/16 in.
57.257
Signed and dated lower left center (black paint): Maurice Sterne / Bali 1912
Purchased from the College Art Association "Exhibition of American Paintings," through Reinhardt Gallery, May 1931

EXHIBITIONS

"The Thirty-Seventh Annual Exhibition of American Art," Cincinnati Art Museum, Cincinnati, Ohio, June 1–29, 1930 (catalog).
"American Paintings," Hamilton College, Clinton, N.Y., May 1931, circulated by College Art Association. "The Edward Root Collection," The Metropolitan Museum of Art, New York, February 12–April 12, 1953 (catalog, 3). "Five Decades of American Painting," Union College, Schenectady, N.Y., September 27–October 23, 1959. "Edward Wales Root Bequest," Munson-Williams-Proctor Institute, Utica, N.Y., November 5, 1961–February 24, 1962 (catalog). "Edward W. Root: Collector and Teacher," Fred L. Emerson Gallery, Hamilton College, October 2–November 14, 1982 (catalog, 33).

PUBLICATION

Paintings, Drawings & Sculptures in the Museum of Art (Utica, N.Y.: Munson-Williams-Proctor Institute, 1961), 37.

EDWARD J. STEVENS, JR.

(Jersey City, N.J., 1923–88)

210. *The Legend: Return of the Victorious Chieftains*, 1944

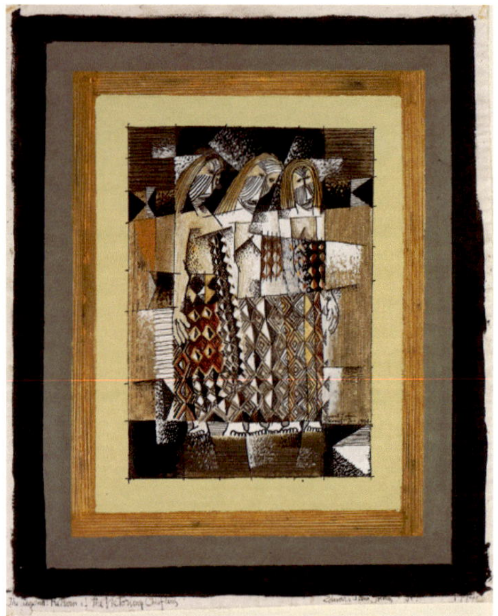

Gouache on paper
23 ½ x 19 ½ in.
57.258
Signed and dated lower right (black ink): Edward John / Stevens, Jr., 1944
Inscribed lower right (black ink): The Legend: Return of the Victorious Chieftens [sic]
Purchased from Weyhe Gallery, New York

EXHIBITIONS

["Stevens," Weyhe Gallery, New York, February 5–March 3, 1945]. "Edward Wales Root Bequest," Munson-Williams-Proctor Institute, Utica, N.Y., November 5, 1961–February 24, 1962 (catalog, as *Victorious Chieftains*).

PUBLICATIONS

"Jersey City Artist's Works Bequeathed by Collector," *Jersey City Journal*, October 2, 1957. *Paintings, Drawings & Sculptures in the Museum of Art* (Utica, N.Y.: Munson-Williams-Proctor Institute, 1961), 37.

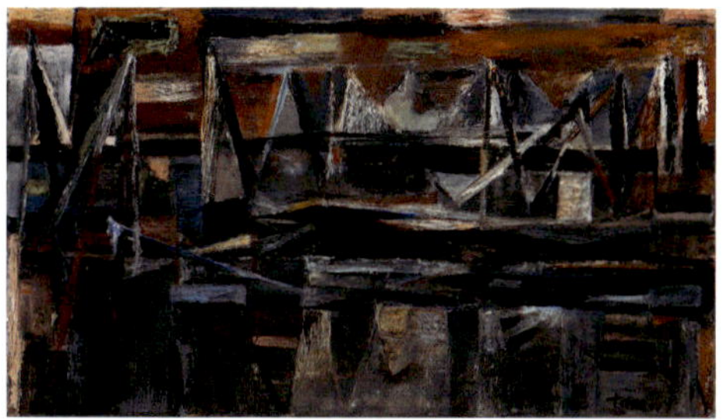

REUBEN TAM

(Kapaa, Kauai, Hawaii, 1916–91)

211. *Horizon Conditions*, 1944

Oil on linen
17 x 30 ⅛ in.
57.259
Signed and dated lower right (black paint): Tam '44
Inscribed verso on stretcher (graphite): Horizon Conditions R. Tam
Purchased from The Downtown Gallery, New York, February 1945

EXHIBITIONS

"Reuben Tam Paintings in Oil," The Downtown Gallery, New York, January 23–February 10, 1945 (cat. no. 18). "Paintings from the Collection of Edward W. Root," Munson-Williams-Proctor Institute, Utica, N.Y., September 29–October 20, 1946. "New Trends in 20th-Century American Painting," Root Art Center, Hamilton College, Clinton, N.Y., October 26–November 30, 1958. "New Trends in 20th-Century American Painting," Union College, Schenectady, N.Y., March 5–26, 1961. "Edward Wales Root Bequest," MWPI, November 5, 1961–February 24, 1962 (catalog, illus.). "Paintings and Drawings from the Edward W. Root Bequest," Root Art Center, April 7–May 5, 1968. "Selections from the Edward W. Root Collection," Root Art Center, February 22–March 21, 1970. "Influences of Klee," MWPI, December 19, 1987–May 12, 1988.

PUBLICATION

Paintings, Drawings & Sculptures in the Museum of Art (Utica, N.Y.: Munson-Williams-Proctor Institute, 1961), 37.

212. *Migration Images*, 1944

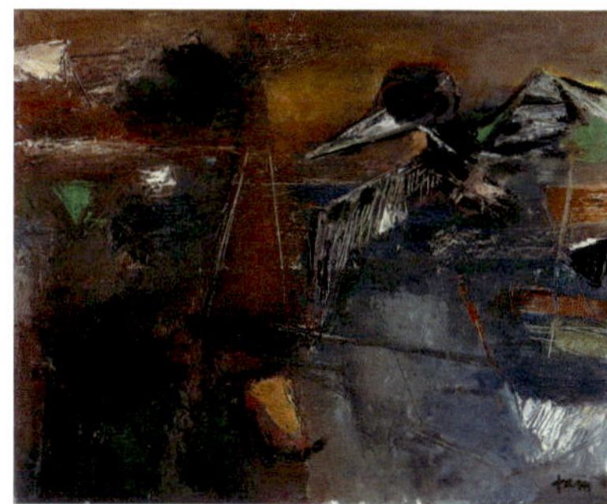

Oil on canvas board
16 x 20 in.
57.260
Signed lower right (black paint): Tam
Purchased from The Downtown Gallery, New York, February 1945

EXHIBITIONS

"Reuben Tam Paintings in Oil," The Downtown Gallery, New York, January 23–February 10, 1945 (cat. no. 17). "Five Decades of American Painting," Union College, Schenectady, N.Y., September 27–October 23, 1959. "Edward Wales Root Bequest," Munson-Williams-Proctor Institute, Utica, N.Y., November 5, 1961–February 24, 1962 (catalog).

PUBLICATION

Paintings, Drawings & Sculptures in the Museum of Art (Utica, N.Y.: Munson-Williams-Proctor Institute, 1961), 37.

213. *Waipahee Mountains*, 1949

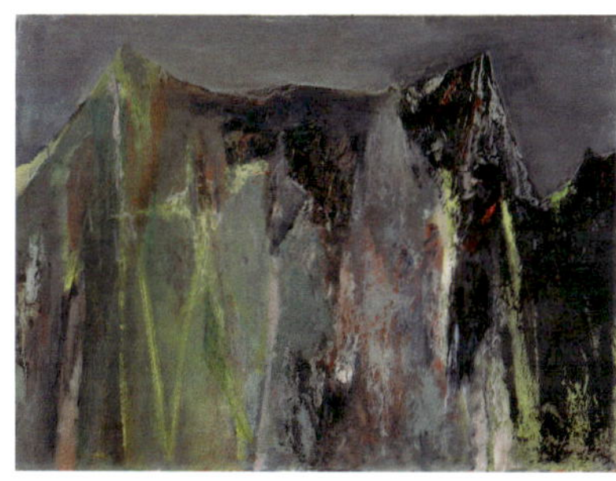

Oil on Masonite
21 ⅞ x 30 in.
57.261
Signed and dated lower right (light brown paint): Tam '49
Inscribed verso: Waipahee Mountains / oil on gesso board 30 x 22 Hawaii 1949 / by Reuben Tam / c / o Downtown Gallery
Purchased from The Downtown Gallery, New York

EXHIBITIONS

"Reuben Tam," The Downtown Gallery, New York, November 15–December 3, 1949 (cat. no. 15). "Edward Wales Root Bequest," Munson-Williams-Proctor Institute, Utica, N.Y., November 5, 1961–February 24, 1962 (catalog). Root Art Center, Hamilton College, Clinton, N.Y., March 1964. "Edward W. Root: Collector and Teacher," Fred L. Emerson Gallery, Hamilton College, October 2–November 14, 1982 (catalog, 56).

PUBLICATIONS

Hess, Thomas B, "Reviews and Previews: Reuben Tam," *Art News* XLVIII (1949): 42, illus. *Paintings, Drawings & Sculptures in the Museum of Art* (Utica, N.Y.: Munson-Williams-Proctor Institute, 1961), 37.

MARK TOBEY

(Centerville, Wis., 1890–Basel, Switzerland, 1976)

214. *Awakening Night*, 1949

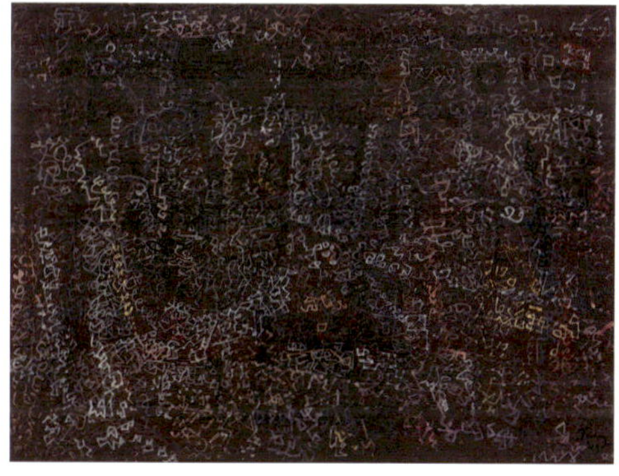

Tempera and opaque watercolor on Masonite
20 x 27 ⅛ in.
57.262
Signed and dated lower right (black paint): Tobey / '49
Purchased from Willard Gallery, New York, November 1949

EXHIBITIONS

"Mark Tobey," Willard Gallery, New York, November 1–26, 1949 (cat. no. 7, illus.). "Current Trends in British and American Painting from the Collection of Edward W. Root," Munson-Williams-Proctor Institute, Utica, N.Y., December 3–31, 1950 (traveling exhibition, cat. no. 32). "Mark Tobey Retrospective Exhibition," Whitney Museum of American Art, New York, October 4–November 4, 1951 (cat. no. 55). "The Edward Root Collection," The Metropolitan Museum of Art, New York, February 12–April 12, 1953 (catalog, 4). "Lipton, Rothko, Smith, Tobey," XXIX Esposizione Biennale Internazionale d'Arte, The United States Pavilion, Venice, Italy, June–October, 1958 (cat. no. 50). "Five American Artists of the 20th Century: Davies, Luks, Burchfield, Tobey, Stamos," Root Art Center, Hamilton College, Clinton, N.Y., December 7, 1958–March 28, 1959. "Five Decades of American Painting," Union College, Schenectady, N.Y., September 27–October 23, 1959. "American Watercolors and Drawings," Root Art Center, April 4–May 7, 1961. "Rétrospective Mark Tobey," Palais du Louvre, Musée des Arts Décoratifs, Paris, France, October 18–December 1, 1961 (traveling exhibition, cat. no. 73, illus. pl. 28; Whitechapel Gallery, cat. no. 47, illus. pl. XV). "Mark Tobey," The Phillips Collection, Washington D.C., May 6–July 6, 1962 (cat. no. 17, illus. on cover). "Mark Tobey," The Museum of Modern Art, New York, September 12–November 4, 1962 (traveling exhibition, cat. no. 61). "European Sources of Contemporary American Art: Kandinsky," Root Art Center, September 15–October 6, 1963 (cat. no. 44). "Mark Tobey, Werke 1933–1966," Stedelijk Museum, Amsterdam, The Netherlands, March 19–May 8, 1966 (traveling exhibition, cat. no. 26). "American 20th-Century Watercolors from MWPI," Albany Institute of History and Art, Albany, N.Y., September 10–October 4, 1967. "Mark Tobey Retrospective," Dallas Museum of Fine Arts, Dallas, Tex., March 20–April 21, 1968 (cat. no. 48). "American Paintings," Schenectady Museum & Planetarium, Schenectady, N.Y., March 20–April 30, 1970. "Tribute to Mark Tobey," National Collection of Fine Arts, Smithsonian Institution, Washington, D.C., June 7–September 8, 1974 (cat. no. 14, illus.). "American Painting 1900–1976: The American Scene and New Forms of Modernism, 1935–1954," Katonah Art Museum, Katonah, N.Y., January 17–March 1, 1976 (catalog, illus. no. 65). "Five Decades of Collecting: Edward W. Root," MWPI, April 2–May 28, 1978. "Northwest Visionaries: Mark Tobey, Kenneth Callahan, Morris Graves, Leo Kenney," Institute of Contemporary Art, Boston, Mass., July 7–September 6, 1981 (catalog). "Mark Tobey: City Paintings," National Gallery of Art, Washington, D.C., March 11–June 2, 1984 (cat. no. 34). "Night Lights: 19th- and 20th-Century American Nocturnes," Taft Museum, Cincinnati, Ohio, May 2–June 30, 1985 (catalog, illus., 16). "Influences of Klee," MWPI, December 19, 1987–May 12, 1988.

PUBLICATIONS

Coates, Robert M. "The Art Galleries: Mazes and Planes," *The New Yorker* (October 13, 1951): 98. "Painter Wins Top European Prize," *Life* (July 21, 1958): 50, illus. Roberts, Colette. *Mark Tobey* (New York: Grove Press, 1960), illus., 22. *Paintings, Drawings & Sculptures in the Museum of Art* (Utica, N.Y.: Munson-Williams-Proctor Institute, 1961), 37. *Edward Wales Root Bequest* (Utica, N.Y.: MWPI, 1961). [*America Illustrated* (U.S. Information Agency), illus.] Rathbone, Eliza. "The Role of Music in the Development of Mark Tobey's Abstract Style," *Arts* 58 (December 1983): 99, illus. fig. 7. Findsen, Owen. "Taft Exhibit 'Night Lights' Illuminative, Highly Seductive," *Cincinnati Enquirer*, May 5, 1985, F-6.

215. *New York Tablet*, 1946

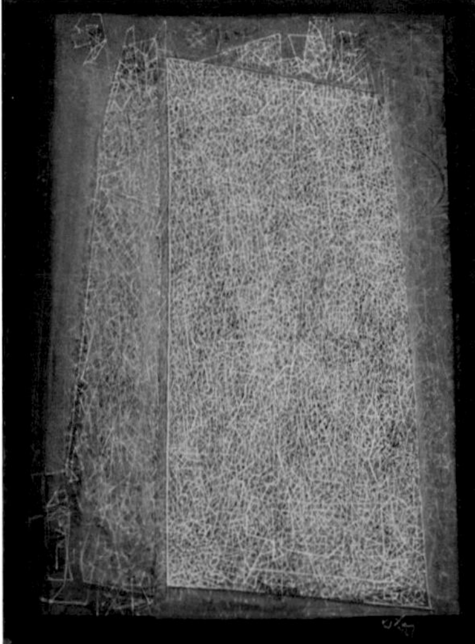

Tempera and chalk on laid paper mounted on wood panel
24 ⅞ x 19 in.
57.263
Signed and dated lower right (gray paint): Tobey / '46
Purchased from Willard Gallery, New York, January 1947

EXHIBITIONS

"Tobey," Willard Gallery, New York, November 4–29, 1947 (cat. no. 4). "Western Roundtable on Modern Art," San Francisco Museum of Art, April 8–10, 1949. "Current Trends in British and American Painting from the Collection of Edward W. Root," Munson-Williams-Proctor Institute, Utica, N.Y., December 3–31, 1950 (traveling exhibition, cat. no. 30). "Mark Tobey Retrospective," Whitney Museum of American Art, New York, October 4–November 4, 1951 (cat. no. 48). "The Edward Root Collection," The Metropolitan Museum of Art, New York, February 12–April 12, 1953 (catalog, 4). "Tendancies Actuelles," Kunsthalle Bern, Bern, Switzerland, January 29–March 6, 1955 (cat. no. 80). "Lipton, Rothko, Smith, Tobey," XXIX Esposizione Biennale Internazionale d'Arte, The United States Pavilion, Venice, Italy, June–October, 1958 (cat. no. 46). "Five American Artists of the 20th Century: Davies, Luks, Burchfield, Tobey, Stamos," Root Art Center, Hamilton College, Clinton, N.Y., December 7, 1958–March 28, 1959. "20th-Century American Painting from the Edward W. Root Collection," Smithsonian Institution, Washington, D.C., July 1959–July 1960 (traveling exhibition). "Rétrospective Mark Tobey," Palais du Louvre, Musée des Arts Décoratifs, October 18–December 1, 1961 (traveling exhibition, cat. no. 52; Whitechapel Gallery, cat. no. 33). "Mark Tobey," The Phillips Collection, Washington, D.C., May 6–July 6, 1962 (cat. no. 12). "Mark Tobey," The Museum of Modern Art, New York, September 12–November 4, 1962 (traveling exhibition, cat. no. 47, illus., 25). "About New York, Night and Day 1915–1965," Women's City Club of New York, Gallery of Modern Art, New York, October 19–November 15, 1965 (catalog, 25). "Mark Tobey, Werke 1933–1966," Stedelijk Museum, Amsterdam, The Netherlands, March 19–May 8, 1966 (traveling exhibition, cat. no. 22). "American 20th-Century Watercolors from MWPI," Albany Institute of History and Art, Albany, N.Y., September 10–October 4, 1967. "Mark Tobey Retrospective," Dallas Museum of Fine Arts, Dallas, Tex., March 20–April 21, 1968 (cat. no. 40). "The Disappearance and Reappearance of the Image: American Painting Since 1945," International Art Program, National Collection of Fine Arts, Smithsonian Institution, Washington, D.C., January–February, 1969 (traveling exhibition, catalog, 84). "Tribute to Mark Tobey," National Collection of Fine Arts, June 7–September 8, 1974 (traveling exhibition, cat. no. 12, illus.). "Five Decades of Collecting: Edward W. Root," MWPI, April 2–May 28, 1978. "Northwest Visionaries: Mark Tobey, Kenneth Callahan, Morris Graves, Leo Kenney," Institute of Contemporary Art, Boston, Mass., July 7–September 6, 1981 (catalog). "Mark Tobey: City Paintings," National Gallery of Art, Washington, D.C., March 11–June 3, 1984 (cat. no. 28, illus., 83). "Influences of Klee," MWPI, December 19, 1987–May 13, 1988. "The Tiger's Eye: The Art of a Magazine," Yale University Art Gallery, New Haven, Conn., January 29–March 30, 2002 (cat. no. 100, illus., 106). "Northwest Mythologies: The Interactions of Mark Tobey, Morris Graves, Kenneth Callahan and Guy Anderson," Tacoma Art Museum, Tacoma, Wash., May 3–August 10, 2003 (catalog, illus.).

PUBLICATIONS

Coates, Robert M. "The Art Galleries: Mazes and Planes," *The New Yorker* (October 13, 1951): 98. Hale, Robert Beverly. "The Growth of a Collection," *The Metropolitan Museum of Art Bulletin* XI (February 1953): 161, illus. *Munson-Williams-Proctor Institute Bulletin*, December 1957. *Paintings, Drawings & Sculptures in the Museum of Art* (Utica, N.Y.: Munson-Williams-Proctor Institute, 1961), 37. *Edward Wales Root Bequest* (Utica, N.Y.: MWPI, 1961), illus. *American Art in Upstate New York* (Buffalo, N.Y.: Buffalo Fine Arts Academy, 1974), 53.

216. *Partitions of the City*, 1945

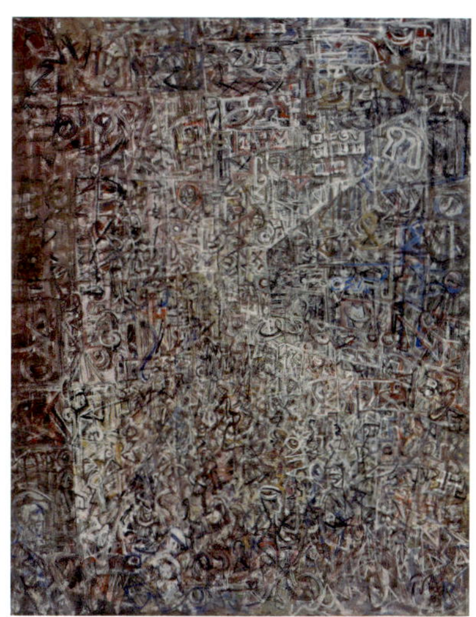

Tempera and opaque watercolor on Masonite
30 ½ x 23 ⅞ in.
57.264
Signed and dated lower right (black paint): Tobey / '45
Purchased from artist, 1951

EXHIBITIONS

"Mark Tobey Paintings 1944–45," Willard Gallery, New York, November 13–December 8, 1945 (cat. no. 10). "1946 Annual Exhibition of Contemporary American Painting," Whitney Museum of American Art, New York, December 10, 1946–January 16, 1947 (cat. no. 157). "Mark Tobey Retrospective," Henry Gallery, University of Washington, Seattle, May 20–June 27, 1951 (cat. no. 72). "The Edward Root Collection," The Metropolitan Museum of Art, New York, February 12–April 12, 1953 (catalog, 4). "New Trends in 20th-Century American Painting," Union College, Schenectady, N.Y., March 5–26, 1961. [Union Carbide Corporation, New York, 1961]. "Rétrospective Mark Tobey," Palais du Louvre, Musée des Arts Décoratifs, Paris, France, October 18–December 1, 1961 (traveling exhibition, cat. no. 43). "Abstract Paintings and Drawings from the Edward W. Root Bequest," Root Art Center, Hamilton College, Clinton, N.Y., April 7–May 5, 1968. "American Drawings and Watercolors from the Munson-Williams-Proctor Institute," E. B. Crocker Art Gallery, Sacramento, Calif., October 25–November 24, 1974 (cat. no. 61). Rome Community Art Center, Rome, N.Y., September 14–November 9, 1975. "Watercolors: Historic and Contemporary," Hathorn Gallery, Skidmore College, Saratoga Springs, N.Y., February 4–20, 1977 (cat. no. 50). "Mark Tobey: City Paintings," National Gallery of Art, Washington, D.C., March 11–June 3, 1984 (cat. no. 24). "Flying Tigers: Paintings and Sculpture in New York," Bell Gallery, Brown University, Providence, R.I., April 26–May 27, 1985. "Two Hundred Years of American Art," The Art Museum Association of America, November 15, 1986–May 8, 1988 (traveling exhibition, cat. no. 64, illus., 78). "Masterworks of American Art from the Munson-Williams-Proctor Institute Museum of Art," Knoxville Museum of Art, Knoxville, Tenn., February 26–August 23, 1998. "Pathways and Parallels: Roads to Abstract Expressionism," Hollis Taggart Galleries, New York, April 12–May 12, 2007 (cat. no. 44, illus., 105).

PUBLICATIONS

Paintings, Drawings & Sculptures in the Museum of Art (Utica, N.Y.: Munson-Williams-Proctor Institute, 1961), 37. *Edward Wales Root Bequest* (Utica, N.Y.: MWPI, 1961). *American Art in Upstate New York* (Buffalo, N.Y.: Buffalo Fine Arts Academy, 1974), 53. Schweizer, Paul D., et al. *Masterworks of American Art from the Munson-Williams-Proctor Institute* (New York: Harry N. Abrams, Inc., 1989) cat. no. 79, illus., 170.

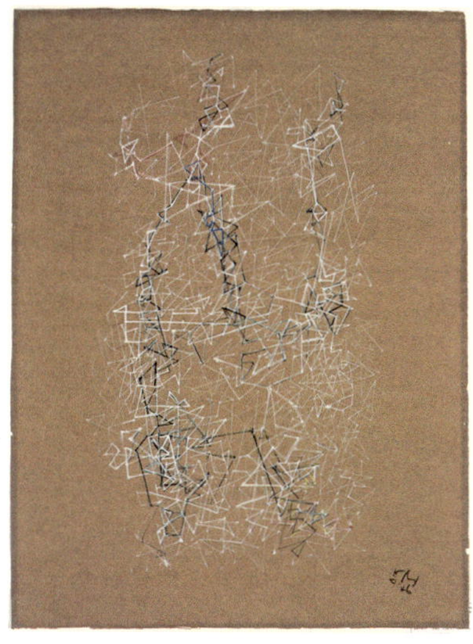

217. *Structures*, 1946

Tempera on brown tinted paper
Watermark, right center: MBM MADE IN FRANCE INGRES D'ARCHE [S]
24 ⅝ x 18 ⅞ in.
57.265
Signed and dated lower right (brown paint): Tobey / '46
Inscribed verso upper center (red paint): TOP; upper right (red paint): 3; upper left-center (graphite): 1 ¼ over the [illegible]
Purchased from Willard Gallery, New York, January 1947

EXHIBITIONS

"Tobey," Willard Gallery, New York, November 4–29, 1947 (cat. no. 8). "New York Private Collections," The Museum of Modern Art, New York, July 20–September 12, 1948. "Current Trends in British and American Painting from the Collection of Edward W. Root," Munson-Williams-Proctor Institute, Utica, N.Y., December 3–31, 1950 (traveling exhibition, cat. no. 31). "The Edward Root Collection," The Metropolitan Museum of Art, New York, February 12–April 12, 1953 (catalog, 4). "Lipton, Rothko, Smith, Tobey," XXIX Esposizione Biennale Internazionale d'Arte, The United States Pavilion, Venice, Italy, June–October, 1958 (cat. no. 47). "Five American Artists of the 20th Century: Davies, Luks, Burchfield, Tobey, Stamos," Root Art Center, Hamilton College, Clinton, N.Y., December 7, 1958–March 28, 1959. "20th-Century American Painting from the Edward W. Root Collection," Smithsonian Institution, Washington, D.C., July 1959–July 1960 (traveling exhibition). "Rétrospective Mark Tobey," Palais du Louvre, Musée des Arts Décoratifs, Paris, France, October 18–December 1, 1961 (traveling exhibition, cat. no. 54, illus. pl. 17). "Mark Tobey," The Phillips Collection, Washington D.C., May 6–July 6, 1962 (cat. no. 17, illus. on cover). "On Paper," American Federation of Arts, September 1966–September 1967 (traveling exhibition). "Mark Tobey Retrospective," Dallas Museum of Fine Arts, Dallas, Tex., March 20–April 21, 1968 (cat. no. 41). "The Root Bequest," Root Art Center, May 11–June 8, 1969. "20th-Century Prints and Drawings," Schenectady Museum & Planetarium, Schenectady, N.Y., December 15, 1971–January 15, 1972. "40's The Homefront," Lowe Art Gallery, Syracuse University, Syracuse, N.Y., May 7–June 4, 1972. "Five Decades of Collecting: Edward W. Root," MWPI, April 2–May 28, 1978.

PUBLICATIONS

Hess, Thomas B. *Abstract Painting: Background and American Phase* (New York: The Viking Press, 1951), 121, illus. pl. 74 [as *Structure*]. Hayes, Bartlett H., Jr. "The Root of American Painting," *Art News* LVI (January 1958): 31, 61, illus. fig. 8. *Paintings, Drawings & Sculptures in the Museum of Art* (Utica, N.Y.: Munson-Williams-Proctor Institute, 1961), 37. *Edward Wales Root Bequest* (Utica, N.Y.: MWPI, 1961). Prior, Harris K. "Edward Root–Talent Scout," *Art in America* L (1962): 73, illus. pl. 13. Seitz, William C. *Mark Tobey* (New York: MoMA, 1962), 87. *Tobey* (Stockholm, Sweden: Konstsalongen Samlaren, 1962), illus. *American Art in Upstate New York* (Buffalo, N.Y.: Buffalo Fine Arts Academy, 1974), 53.

218. *Vita Nova*, 1945

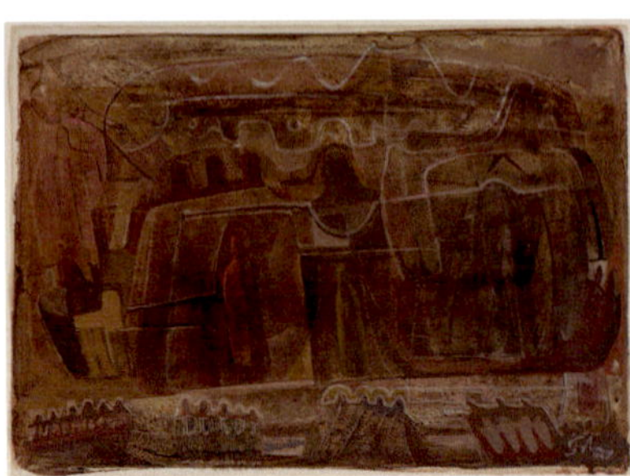

Tempera on wove paper
11 ⅞ x 16 3/16 in.
57.266
Signed and dated lower right (white paint): Tobey / 44
Purchased from Willard Gallery, New York, April 1946
[possible mural study]

EXHIBITIONS

"Mark Tobey Paintings 1944–45," Willard Gallery, New York, November 13–December 8, 1945 (cat. no. 15). "Paintings from the Collection of Edward W. Root," Munson-Williams-Proctor Institute, Utica, N.Y., September 29–October 20, 1946. "Mark Tobey Retrospective Exhibition," Whitney Museum of American Art, New York, October 4–November 4, 1951 (cat. no. 39. as *Vita Nuova*). "Five American Artists of the 20th Century: Davies, Luks, Burchfield, Tobey, Stamos," Root Art Center, Hamilton College, Clinton, N.Y., December 7, 1958–March 28, 1959. "Rétrospective Mark Tobey," Palais du Louvre, Musée des Arts Décoratifs, Paris, France, October 18–December 1, 1961 (traveling exhibition, cat. no. 45). "American 20th-Century Watercolors from MWPI," Albany Institute of History and Art, Albany, N.Y., September 10–October 4, 1967. "American Drawings and Watercolors from the Munson-Williams-Proctor Institute," E. B. Crocker Art Gallery, Sacramento, Calif., October 25–November 24, 1974 (cat. no. 62, illus.). "Figuratively Speaking," MWPI, April 11–November 10, 1985. "Mark Tobey," MWPI, August 1991–January 1992. "American Twentieth-Century Watercolors at the Munson-Williams-Proctor Arts Institute," MWPAI, April 30–July 10, 2000 (traveling exhibition, cat. no. 36, illus.).

PUBLICATIONS

"Tobey: A City's Magic in White Writing," *Art News* XLIV (December 1–14, 1945): 24–25, illus., 25. *Paintings, Drawings & Sculptures in the Museum of Art* (Utica, N.Y.: Munson-Williams-Proctor Institute, 1961), 37. *Edward Wales Root Bequest* (Utica, N.Y.: MWPI, 1961). *American Art in Upstate New York* (Buffalo, N.Y.: Buffalo Fine Arts Academy, 1974), 53.

219. *Voyage of the Saints*, 1952

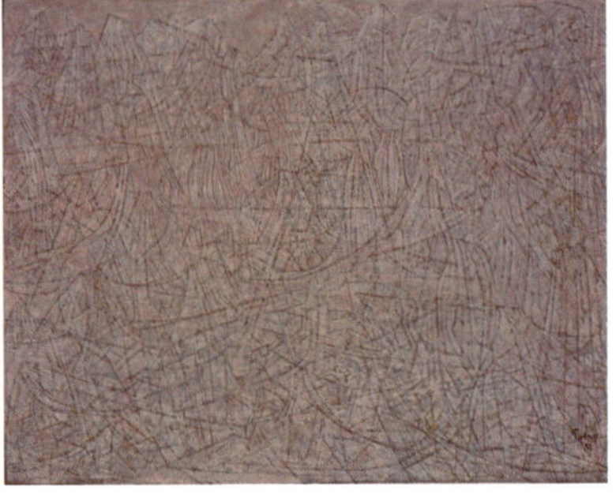

Tempera and crayon on paperboard
22 x 28 in.
57.267
Signed and dated lower right (red-brown paint): Tobey / '52
Purchased from Willard Gallery, New York, May 1953

EXHIBITIONS

"Tobey," Willard Gallery, New York, April 1–May 2, 1953 (cat. no. 1). "Five American Artists of the 20th Century: Davies, Luks, Burchfield, Tobey, Stamos," Root Art Center, Hamilton College, Clinton, N.Y., December 7, 1958–March 28, 1959. "20th-Century American Paintings from the Edward W. Root Collection," Smithsonian Institution, Washington, D.C., July 1959–July 1960 (traveling exhibition). Museum of Art Building inaugural exhibition, Munson-Williams-Proctor Institute, Utica, N.Y., October 15–December 31, 1960. "Rétrospective Mark Tobey," Palais du Louvre, Musée des Arts Décoratifs, Paris, France, October 18–December 1, 1961 (traveling exhibition, cat. no. 87, illus. pl. 37; Whitechapel Gallery, cat. no. 55, illus. pl. XXIX). "Mark Tobey," The Phillips Collection, Washington, D.C., May 6–July 6, 1962 (cat. no. 19). "Mark Tobey," The Museum of Modern Art, New York, September 12–November 4, 1962 (traveling exhibition, cat. no. 72, illus., 72). "European Sources of Contemporary American Art: Kandinsky," Root Art Center, September 15–October 6, 1963 (cat. no. 45). "Mark Tobey, Werke 1933–1966," Stedelijk Museum, Amsterdam, The Netherlands, March 19–May 8, 1966 (traveling exhibition, catalog). "American 20th-Century Watercolors from MWPI," Albany Institute of History and Art, Albany, N.Y., September 10–October 4, 1967. "Mark Tobey Retrospective," Dallas Museum of Fine Arts, Dallas, Tex., March 20–April 21, 1968 (cat. no. 55). "American Art in Upstate New York," Albright-Knox Art Gallery, Buffalo, N.Y., July 12, 1974–April 27, 1975 (traveling exhibition, cat. 53). "Watercolors: Historic and Contemporary," Hathorn Gallery, Skidmore College, Saratoga Springs, N.Y., February 4–20, 1977 (cat. no. 51). "Five Decades of Collecting: Edward W. Root," MWPI, April 2–May 28, 1978. "Edward W. Root: Collector and Teacher," Fred L. Emerson Gallery, Hamilton College, October 2–November 14, 1982 (catalog, 62). "'Tis the Season," MWPI, December 18, 1985–January 20, 1986. "Influences of Klee," MWPI, December 19, 1987–May 13, 1988. "Northwest Mythologies: The Interactions of Mark Tobey, Morris Graves, Kenneth Callahan and Guy Anderson," Tacoma Art Museum, Tacoma, Wash., May 3–August 10, 2003 (catalog, 166, illus., 141).

PUBLICATIONS

Paintings, Drawings & Sculptures in the Museum of Art (Utica, N.Y.: Munson-Williams-Proctor Institute, 1961), 38. *Edward Wales Root Bequest* (Utica, N.Y.:

MWPI, 1961). Rathbone, Eliza. "The Role of Music in the Development of Mark Tobey's Abstract Style," *Arts* 58 (December 1983): 99, illus. fig. 8.

BRADLEY WALKER TOMLIN

(Syracuse, N.Y., 1899–New York N.Y., 1953)

220. *Number 1*, 1951

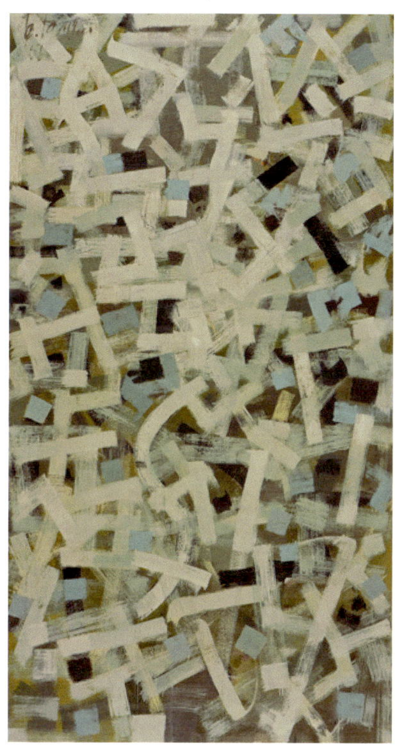

Oil on linen
78 x 42 in.
57.269
Signed and dated upper left (gray paint): B. Tomlin / '51
Purchased from Betty Parsons Gallery, New York, December 1951

EXHIBITIONS

"Fifteen Americans," The Museum of Modern Art, New York, April 9–July 27, 1952 (catalog, 47, illus., 26). "The Edward Root Collection," The Metropolitan Museum of Art, New York, February 12–April 12, 1953 (catalog, 4). "Bradley Walker Tomlin," Art Galleries of University of California, Los Angeles and Whitney Museum of American Art, New York (traveling exhibition, cat. no. 36). "20th-Century American Painting from the Edward W. Root Collection," Smithsonian Institution, Washington, D.C., July 1959–July 1960 (traveling exhibition). "Art Across America," Munson-Williams-Proctor Institute, Utica, N.Y., October 15–December 31, 1960 (cat. no. 107, illus.). "Edward Wales Root Bequest," MWPI, November 5, 1961–February 24, 1962 (catalog, illus., as *No. 1–1951*). "Bradley Walker Tomlin, Art Since 1950," World's Fair, Seattle, Wash., April 21–October 21, 1962 (traveling exhibition, cat. no. 71, illus., 56). "European Sources of Contemporary American Art: Kandinsky," Root Art Center, Hamilton College, Clinton, N.Y., September 15–October 6, 1963 (cat. no. 46). "American Painting: The 1950's," American Federation of Arts, November 1968–November 1969 (traveling exhibition, cat. no. 33, illus.). "Bradley Walker Tomlin, A Retrospective View," The Emily Lowe Gallery, Hofstra University, Hempstead, N.Y., April 17–May 25, 1975 (traveling exhibition, cat. no. 62, illus., 124). "Five Decades of Collecting: Edward W. Root," MWPI, April 2–May 28, 1978. "Abstract Expressionism," MWPI, July 19–August 18, 1985. "Influences of Klee" MWPI, December 19, 1987–May 12, 1988.

PUBLICATIONS

Paintings, Drawings & Sculptures in the Museum of Art (Utica, N.Y.: Munson-Williams-Proctor Institute, 1961), 38. Mendelowitz, Daniel M. *History of American Art* (New York: Holt, Rinehart and Winston, [1970]), 436, illus. no. 589.

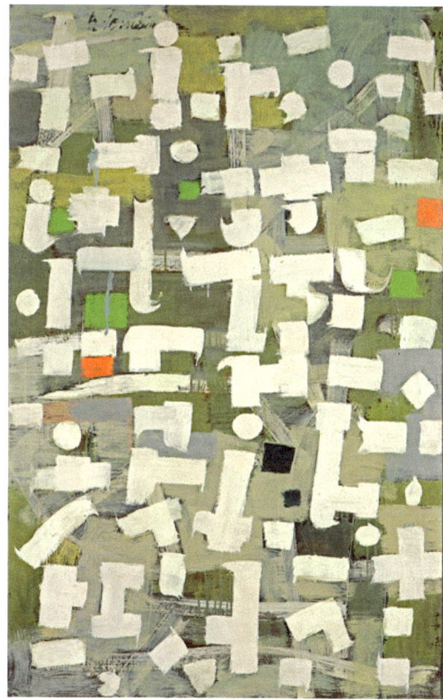

221. *Number 11*, ca. 1949

Oil on linen
44 ⅛ x 29 in.
57.268
Signed top left center (black paint): B. Tomlin
Purchased from Betty Parsons Gallery, New York, March 1951

EXHIBITIONS

"The Edward Root Collection," The Metropolitan Museum of Art, New York, February 12–April 12, 1953 (catalog, 4). Syracuse Museum of Fine Arts, June 1959–September 1959. "Five Decades of American Painting," Union College, Schenectady, N.Y., September 27–October 23, 1959. Museum of Art Building inaugural exhibition, Munson-Williams-Proctor Institute, Utica, N.Y., October 15–December 31, 1960. "Centennial Exhibition," State University of New York College of Education, Oswego, N.Y., October 1–31, 1961 (catalog). "Edward Wales Root Bequest," MWPI, November 5, 1961–February 24, 1962 (catalog). "European Sources of Contemporary American Art: Kandinsky," Root Art Center, Hamilton College, Clinton, N.Y., September 15–October 6, 1963 (cat. no. 47). "Yesterday and Today," Oswego Art Gallery, Inc., Oswego, N.Y., May 30–June 14, 1964. "Abstract Paintings and Drawings from the Root Bequest," Root Art Center, September 11–October 9, 1966. "Paintings and Drawings from the Edward W. Root Bequest," Root Art Center, April 7–May 5, 1968. "New York Painting and Sculpture: 1940–1970," Metropolitan Museum of Art (cat. no. 399, illus., 328). "Bradley Walker Tomlin, A Retrospective View," The Emily Lowe Gallery, Hofstra University, Hempstead, N.Y., April 17–May 25, 1975 (traveling exhibition, cat.

no. 50, illus., 62). "Five Decades of Collecting: Edward W. Root," MWPI, April 2–May 28, 1978. "Edward W. Root: Collector and Teacher," Fred L. Emerson Gallery, Hamilton College, October 2–November 14, 1982 (catalog, 57). "Two Hundred Years of American Art," The Art Museum Association of America, November 15, 1986–May 8, 1988 (traveling exhibition, cat. no. 71, illus., 85). "The Art Triangle: Artist, Dealer, Collector," Burchfield Art Center, Buffalo, N.Y., May 13–June 25, 1989 (traveling exhibition, cat. no. 92).

PUBLICATIONS

McBride, Henry. "Patriotism and Arts," *Art News* LII (March 1953): 40, illus. *Paintings, Drawings & Sculptures in the Museum of Art* (Utica, N.Y.: Munson-Williams-Proctor Institute, 1961), 38. Vars, Nancy. "He was Elegant and Outspoken," *Syracuse Post-Standard Magazine*, April 28, 1963, illus., 15.

222. *Watermelon*, 1942

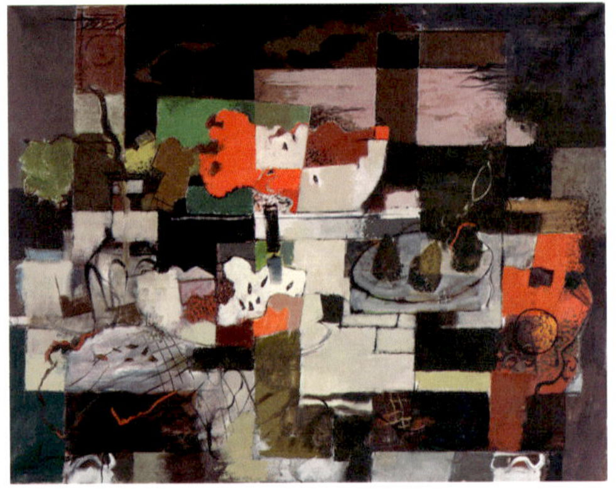

Oil on linen
37 x 48 ⅛ in.
57.270
Signed upper right (black paint): Tomlin
Purchased from Frank K. M. Rehn Galleries, New York, January 1945

EXHIBITIONS

"Artists For Victory," The Metropolitan Museum of Art, New York, December 7, 1942–February 22, 1943 (catalog, 12). "Paintings by Bradley Walker Tomlin," Frank K. M. Rehn Galleries, New York, January 10–29, 1944 (cat. no. 5). "42nd Annual Watercolor and Oil Painting Exhibition," Pennsylvania Academy of Fine Arts, Philadelphia, Pa., October 29–December 3, 1944. "140th Annual Exhibition of Painting and Sculpture," Pennsylvania Academy, January 19–February 25, 1945 (cat. no. 77). "The Edward Root Collection," Metropolitan Museum of Art, February 12–April 12, 1953 (catalog, 4). "In Memoriam," American Federation of Arts, November 1957–November 1958 (traveling exhibition). Museum of Art Building inaugural exhibition, Munson-Williams-Proctor Institute, Utica, N.Y., October 15–December 31, 1960. "Edward Wales Root Bequest," MWPI, November 5, 1961–February 24, 1962 (catalog). "Learning About Pictures from Mr. Root," Root Art Center, Hamilton College, Clinton, N.Y., January 4–31, 1965 (catalog, illus.). "Abstract Paintings and Drawings from the Root Bequest," Root Art Center, September 11–October 9, 1966. "The Root Bequest," Root Art Center, May 11–June 8, 1969. "Bradley Walker Tomlin, A Retrospective View," The Emily Lowe Gallery, Hofstra University, Hempstead, N.Y., April 17–May 25, 1975 (traveling exhibition, cat. no. 33, illus., 105). "Five Decades of Collecting: Edward W. Root," MWPI, April 2–May 28, 1978. "Abstract Expressionism," MWPI, July 19–August 18, 1985. "The Art Triangle: Artist, Dealer, Collector," Burchfield Art Center, Buffalo, N. Y., May 13–June 25, 1989 (traveling exhibition, cat. no. 91).

PUBLICATIONS

Goldwater, Robert. "The State of American Art," *Magazine of Art* XLII (March 1949): illus., 81. *Paintings, Drawings & Sculptures in the Museum of Art* (Utica, N.Y.: Munson-Williams-Proctor Institute, 1961), 38. Vars, Nancy. "He was Elegant and Outspoken," *Syracuse Post-Standard Magazine*, April 28, 1963, illus., 14.

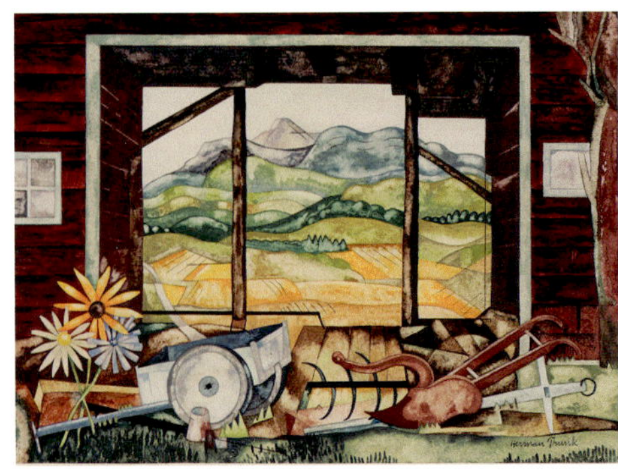

HERMAN TRUNK, JR.

(Brooklyn, N.Y., 1894–1963)

223. *Haying (Summer Fantasy)*

1930

Transparent watercolor over black ink and graphite on watercolor paper
16 x 22 in.
57.271
Inscribed lower right (black ink): Herman Trunk
Purchased from Dudensing Galleries, New York

EXHIBITIONS

"Herman Trunk," Dudensing Galleries, New York, January–February 1932. "40 Americans," Dudensing Galleries (ca. 1930–31, cat. no. 36). "Exhibition of Watercolors and Pastels by Eleven American Moderns from a Distinguished Private Collection," Munson-Williams-Proctor Institute, Utica, N.Y., fall 1938. "Paintings from the Collection of Edward W. Root," MWPI, September 29–October 20, 1946. "Edward Wales Root Bequest," MWPI, November 5, 1961–February 24, 1962 (catalog). "American Twentieth-Century Watercolors at the Munson-Williams-Proctor Arts Institute," MWPAI, April 30–July 10, 2000 (traveling exhibition, cat. no. 22, illus.).

PUBLICATIONS

"Presenting the Case Decoratively," *New York Sun*, January 27, 1932, A36. *Paintings, Drawings & Sculptures in the Museum of Art* (Utica, N.Y.: Munson-Williams-Proctor Institute, 1961), 38.

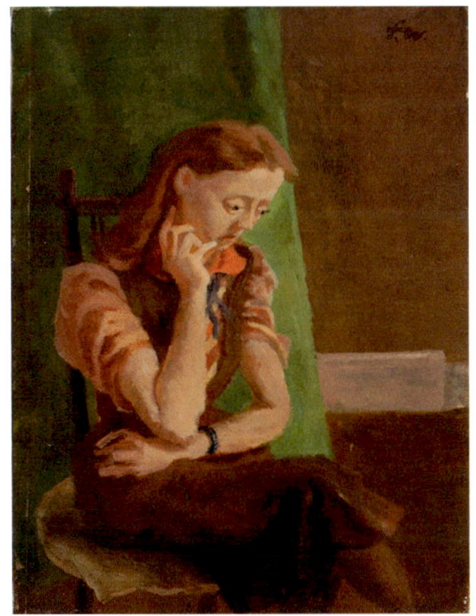

FRANKLIN C. WATKINS

(New York, N.Y., 1894–Bologna, Italy, 1972)

224. *Girl Thinking*, 1933

Oil on linen
12 1/16 x 9 1/8 in.
57.272
Signed upper right (black paint): F. W.
Inscribed verso: Watkins
Purchased from Frank K. M. Rehn Galleries, New York, April 1934

EXHIBITIONS

"Paintings by Franklin C. Watkins," Frank K. M. Rehn Galleries, New York, April 16–May 5, 1934 (cat. no.). "The Edward Root Collection," The Metropolitan Museum of Art, New York, February 12–April 12, 1953 (catalog, 4). "Edward Wales Root Bequest," Munson-Williams-Proctor Institute, Utica, N.Y., November 5, 1961–February 24, 1962 (catalog). "The Figure in 20th-Century Paintings and Drawings," Root Art Center, Hamilton College, Clinton, N.Y., April 15–May 6, 1962. Root Art Center, from December 30, 1963. "Selections from the Edward W. Root Collection," Root Art Center, February 22–March 21, 1970. "1933 Revisited," Sordoni Art Gallery, Wilkes College, Wilkes-Barre, Pa., March 19–April 24, 1983 (catalog, illus. no. 38). "The Art Triangle: Artist, Dealer, Collector," Burchfield Art Center, Buffalo, N.Y., May 13–June 25, 1989 (traveling exhibition, cat. no. 94 [note: illustration of a painting with same title, 65, is mislabled as MWPI painting]).

PUBLICATION

Paintings, Drawings & Sculptures in the Museum of Art (Utica, N.Y.: Munson-Williams-Proctor Institute, 1961), 39.

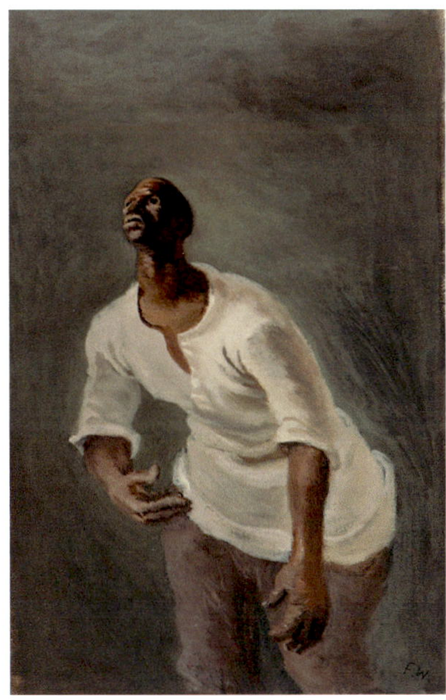

225. *Spiritual Singer*, 1931

Oil on linen
12 1/4 x 8 in.
57.273
Signed lower right (black paint): F. W.
Purchased from Frank K. M. Rehn Galleries, New York, January 1932

EXHIBITIONS

"Paintings by Franklin C. Watkins," Frank K. M. Rehn Galleries, New York, April 16–May 5, 1934. "Paintings from the Collection of Edward W. Root," Munson-Williams-Proctor Institute, Utica, N.Y., September 29–October 20, 1946. "The Edward Root Collection," The Metropolitan Museum of Art, New York, February 12–April 12, 1953 (catalog, 4). "Five Decades of American Painting," Union College, Schenectady, N.Y., September 27–October 23, 1959. "Edward Wales Root Bequest," MWPI, November 5, 1961–February 24, 1962 (catalog). "The Figure in 20th-Century Paintings and Drawings," Root Art Center, Hamilton College, Clinton, N.Y., April 15–May 6, 1962 (catalog). Root Art Center, from December 30, 1963. "The Root Bequest," Root Art Center, May 11–June 8, 1969. "Selections from the Edward W. Root Collection," Root Art Center, February 22–March 21, 1970. "Five Decades of Collecting: Edward W. Root," MWPI, April 2–May 28, 1978. "Edward W. Root: Collector and Teacher," Fred L. Emerson Gallery, Hamilton College, October 2–November 14, 1982 (catalog, 33).

PUBLICATIONS

Hale, Robert Beverly. "The Growth of a Collection," *The Metropolitan Museum of Art Bulletin* XI (February 1953): 157, illus.

Paintings, Drawings & Sculptures in the Museum of Art (Utica, N.Y.: Munson-Williams-Proctor Institute, 1961), 39.

[Study for *Negro Spiritual*, 1933, Maier Museum of Art. See *Franklin C. Watkins* (New York: MOMA, 1950), 8: "I heard a fine Negro choir at the Barnes Foundation.... It echoed in my head and the picture was the result."]

MAHONRI M. YOUNG

(Salt Lake City, Utah, 1877–Norwalk, Conn., 1957)

226. *Horse Round-Up*, ca. 1917–22

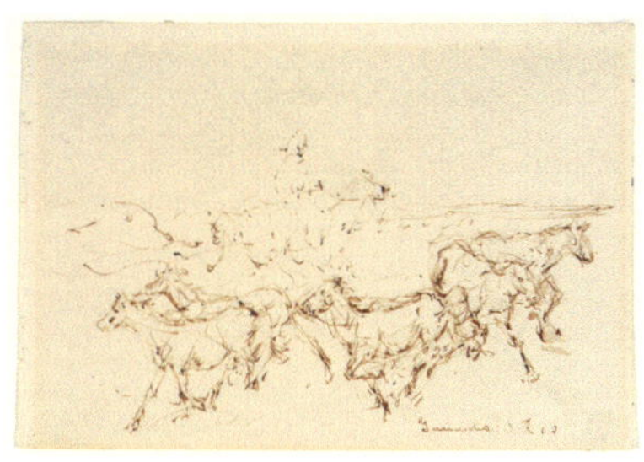

Bistre ink on white wove paper
5 1/4 x 7 7/8 in.
57.274
Inscribed lower right (brown ink): Ganado Oct 10
Purchased from Weyhe Gallery, New York, January 1945

EXHIBITIONS

["Drawings by Mahonri Young," Weyhe Gallery, New York, April 1–29, 1929.] "Paintings from the Collection of Edward W. Root," Munson-Williams-Proctor Institute, Utica, N.Y., September 29–October 20, 1946. "American Watercolors and Drawings," Root Art Center, Hamilton College, Clinton, N.Y., April 4–May 7, 1961. "Edward Wales Root Bequest," MWPI, November 5, 1961–February 24, 1962 (catalog). "Paintings and Drawings from the Edward W. Root Bequest," Root Art Center, April 7–May 5, 1968. "Carnival of the Animals," MWPI, December 10–31, 1972.

PUBLICATION

Paintings, Drawings & Sculptures in the Museum of Art (Utica, N.Y.: Munson-Williams-Proctor Institute, 1961), 40.

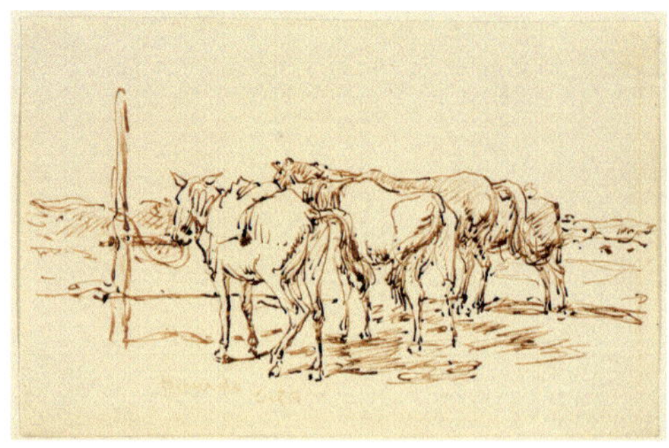

227. *Tied Horses*, ca. 1917–22

Bistre ink on white wove paper mounted on board
5 x 7 ¾ in.
57.275
Inscribed lower left (brown ink): Ganado / Oct 9
Inscribed on mount (graphite): From one of Mahroni Young's sketchbooks [in Edward Wales Root's handwriting]
Purchased from Weyhe Gallery, New York, January 1945

EXHIBITIONS

["Drawings by Mahonri Young," Weyhe Gallery, New York, April 1–29, 1929.]
"Edward Wales Root Bequest," Munson-Williams-Proctor Institute, Utica, N.Y., November 5, 1961–February 24, 1962 (catalog). "Carnival of the Animals," MWPI, December 10–31, 1972.

PUBLICATION

Paintings, Drawings & Sculptures in the Museum of Art (Utica, N.Y.: Munson-Williams-Proctor Institute, 1961), 40.

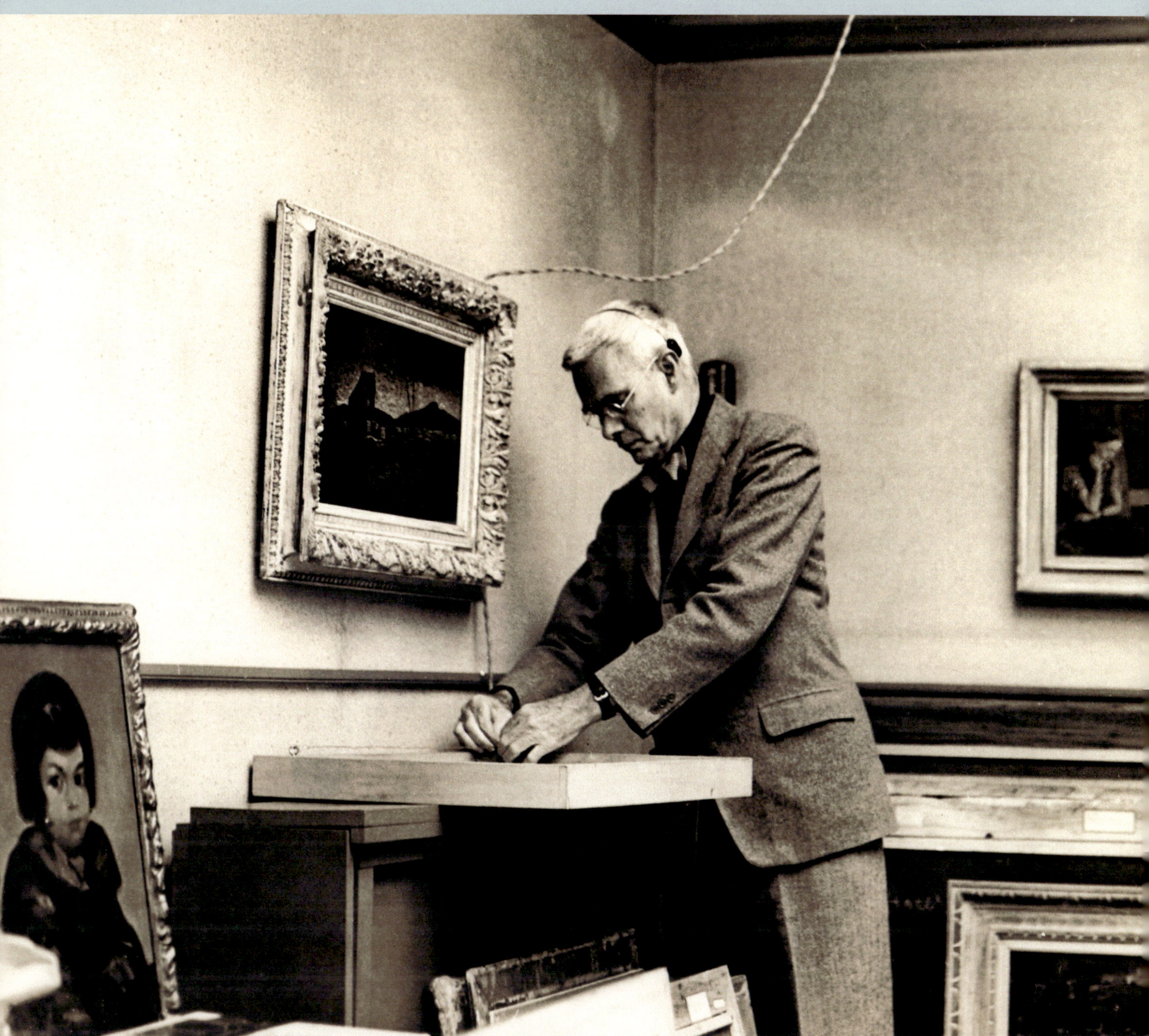

Edward W. Root in his private, fireproof "pocket gallery"
adjacent to the Homestead, Clinton, N.Y., ca. 1950

Appendix 1
Edward W. Root's Gifts to the Munson-Williams-Proctor Institute, 1949 to 1955

AMERICAN PAINTINGS AND DRAWINGS

(chronologically by accession number)

Luigi Lucioni (1900–88)
Vermont Landscape, ca. 1944
Oil on canvas
18 ½ x 26 ⅛ in.
49.32

Henry Billings (1901–85)
Hurricane Damage, 1945
Gouache on illustration board
22 ¼ x 15 in.
50.23

Byron Browne (1907–61)
Toto the Drummer, 1946
Oil on canvas
28 x 24 in.
50.24

Federico Castellón (1914–71)
Mystery of the Night, 1936
Watercolor and graphite on black paper
10 ⅛ x 12 3/16
50.25

Nicolai Cikovsky (1894–1984)
Bowl of Fruit, ca. 1932
Oil on canvas
24 x 30 ¼ in.
50.26

Dong Kingman (1911–2000)
Church Street, 1945
Watercolor on paper
20 x 27 ¼ in.
50.27

Wesley Lea (1896–1981)
Plateau Flowers, 1946
Oil on board
10 ¾ x 13 ⅞ in.
50.28

Peppino Mangravite (1896–1978)
Child Blowing Balloon, 1940
Oil on canvas
20 x 16 ¼ in.
50.29

Peppino Mangravite (1896–1978)
Mountain Bouquet, 1945
Oil on canvas
28 ¼ x 24 ⅛ in.
50.30

Reginald Marsh (1898–1954)
Reclining Nude, ca. 1935
Red Conté crayon on paper
13 15/16 x 17 ¾ in.
50.31

Henry Mattson (1887–1971)
Sand Pit, n.d.
Oil on canvas
16 x 20 in.
50.32

Randall Morgan (1920–94)
Romanum, 1949
Oil on wood panel
13 ¾ x 17 ¾
50.33

Andrée Ruellan (1905–2006)
Crabmen, Charleston, n.d.
Oil on canvas
10 ¾ x 18 ¼ in.
50.34

Eugene Speicher (1883–1962)
Tulips in a Brown Pitcher, n.d.
Oil on canvas
22 x 17 ¼ in.
50.35

Harold Weston (1894–1972)
Cabbage, 1928–33
Oil on canvas
15 x 18 ⅛ in.
50.36

Byron Browne (1907–61)
Rope and Branches, 1945
Oil on canvas
24 x 27 ⅞ in.
53.400

Federico Castellón (1914–71)
In the Blindness of the Night, 1936
Gouache on black paper
12 ¾ x 10 in.
53.401

Howard Norton Cook (1901–80)
Baptism of the Hard-Shelled Baptists, 1934
Crayon on paper
22 x 35 13/16 in.
53.402

Howard Norton Cook (1901–80)
Henry Willy's Log House, Penland, N.C., n.d.
Crayon on paper
22 x 16 ¼ in.
53.403

Howard Norton Cook (1901–80)
Snow Patterns, 1935
Watercolor on paper
13 15/16 x 20 in.
53.404

Howard Norton Cook (1901–80)
Spinster Sisters of Plumtree, N.C., n.d.
Crayon on paper
13 13/16 x 18 ⅝ in.
53.405

Stuart Davis (1894–1964)
Black Roofs, 1931
Watercolor on paper
24 x 17 15/16 in.
53.406

Adolf Dehn (1895–1968)
Garden of the Gods, 1940
Watercolor on paper
20 x 28 in.
53.407

Adolf Dehn (1895–1968)
Summer Landscape (Green Fields), 1938
Watercolor on paper
15 ⅛ x 22 ¼ in.
53.408

Adolf Dehn (1895–1968)
Victor, Colorado, 1940
Watercolor on paper
18 ¼ x 26 ⅜ in.
53.409

David Fredenthal (1914–58)
Dawn Mist Falls, 1946
Watercolor on paper
11 13/16 x 15 15/16 in.
53.410

Charles E. Heaney (1897–1981)
Shell Fossils, n.d.
Oil on board
17 ½ x 23 ⅜ in.
53.411

John Edward Heliker (1909–2000)
The White Cloud, n.d.
Oil on Masonite
18 x 23 ⅞ in.
53.412

Howard Mandel (1917–99)
Midnight, 1950
Gouache on board
19 1/16 x 26 in.
53.413

Reginald Marsh (1898–1954)
The Britannic Sails, 1939
Tempera on panel
20 x 30 in.
53.414

Reginald Marsh (1898–1954)
Standing Nude, n.d.
Red Conté crayon on paper
18 ⅜ x 13 ½ in.
53.415

Lily Michael (active 1950s)
Processional, 1951
Casein on board
53.416, deaccessioned October 6, 1953

Bruce Handiside Mitchell (1908–63)
Midday, Minnesota, 1938
Gouache on board
20 x 30 in.
53.417

John Sennhauser (1907–78)
Emotive No. 10, 1950
Watercolor on paper
19 ⅞ x 25 ¾ in.
53.418

John Sennhauser (1907–78)
Synchroformic No. 9—Duo Legato, 1950
Oil on canvas
17 x 23 in.
53.419

Edward J. Stevens, Jr. (1923–88)
A Tropical Still Life, 1946
Oil on Masonite
23 ⅞ x 20 in.
53.420

Richard Taylor (1902–70)
The Somnambulist, 1945
Watercolor on board
12 ⅜ x 20 in.
53.421

George B. Luks (1866–1933)
Jack and Russell Burke, 1911–23
Oil on canvas
45 ⅛ x 20 in.
54.157

Dwight Williams (1856–1932)
Landscape, 1929
Pastel on black paper
18 x 24 ⅛ in.
55.103

AMERICAN DECORATIVE ARTS

James Cunningham (active 1834–48)
Coverlet, 1842
Cotton, wool
92 x 36 in.
54.147

James Cunningham (active 1834–48)
Coverlet, 1843
Cotton, wool
75 x 37 in.
54.148

EUROPEAN PRINTS

When Root started teaching art appreciation at Hamilton College in 1920 he began assembling a collection of prints "to illustrate and support each assertion" he made in the classroom (Root to William H. Cowley, October 9, 1938, Edward Wales Root Papers, Munson-Williams-Proctor Arts Institute Archives, Record Group 13, Folder 156). He advocated using original prints instead of photographic reproductions to teach art appreciation in his 1922 article, "Pictures and the College" (See Appendix 5). Shortly thereafter Root asked his friend Louise B. Saunders (1870–1961), then in Paris, to purchase for him a collection of lithographs by Honoré Daumier (1808–79). Root noted that he considered Daumier a "very great artist" (Root to Saunders, March 28, 1923, Saunders Family Papers, Daniel Burke Library, Hamilton College Archives, Clinton, N.Y.). More than a decade later, in December 1938, Root wrote to the print expert Carl Zigrosser (1891–1975) to say he intended, the following month, to stop by at the Weyhe Gallery in New York where Zigrosser was Director. "I want to build up gradually a little collection of 15th- to 20th-century prints," Root noted. With what is likely a reference to the Daumier prints he probably owned by this time, Root continued: "I have made a good beginning already, but a lot remains to be done" (Root to Zigrosser, December 14, 1938, courtesy University of Pennsylvania, photocopy in the Edward Wales Root Papers, Munson-Williams-Proctor Arts Institute Archives, Record Group 13, Folder 106).

In 1952, Root gave the Museum 169 European prints dating from the late 15th through the early 20th centuries (accession nos. 53.1–53.167). One hundred and thirty-one of these prints were listed in a brochure the Museum published shortly thereafter: *European Prints, 15th Century—20th Century: Gift of Edward W. Root* (Utica, N.Y.: Munson-Williams-Proctor Institute, 1953). The Museum's acting director, Mahonri S. Young (1911–96), noted in the Foreword that this gift "is merely the latest in a long series of services and benefits" Root provided the Institute since its inception. He added that the collection "will form a solid base upon which the Institute's future print collection can be built. It is a happy gallery which has such a faithful friend and advisor."

In the fall of 1953 Museum director Harris K. Prior (1911–75) recommended to the Institute's Board of Trustees that Root be provided with a purchase fund. "It occurs to me that he could do us a real service in helping to fill in any gaps in his collection, which he knows better than anyone else" (Prior to Thomas B. Rudd [1898–1955], October 23, 1953, Board of Trustees: Acquisitions, Munson-Williams-Proctor Institute Archives, Record Group 1.2, Folder 4).

AMERICAN PRINTS AND DRAWINGS

In 1953 Root also gave the Museum 153 early-20th-century American prints (accession nos. 53.220–53.373), as well as four drawings and twenty-two production cells by Walt Disney Studios (accession nos. 53.374–53.399), whose imagery Root once described as "the great anthropomorphic menagerie" ("I Remember Quite Clearly How I Came to Buy My First Painting," ca. 1950, 3, Root Papers, Munson-Williams-Proctor Arts Institute Archives, Record Group 13, Folder 255). Disney's works appealed to Root's enthusiasm for cartooning, a lifelong interest that extended from his youthful acquaintance with the graphic work of George B. Luks (1866–1933), and other members of The Eight, through the cartoons he collected later in life by William Steig (1907–2003), and Saul Steinberg (1914–99).

JAPANESE PRINTS

In 1954 Root gave the Museum seventy-five Japanese color woodblock prints (accession nos. 54.89–54.146; 54.179–54.195). Most of these date from the 18th and first half of the 19th centuries. Approximately thirty different artists are represented, with multiple examples by a number of the most important. Root acquired most of these prints in New York City auctions before 1922, the year the Utica Public Library exhibited 59 of them (*Exhibition of Japanese Color Prints From Designs by the Late Eighteenth Century and Early Nineteenth Century Masters*, 1922, in the Edward Wales Root Papers, Munson-Williams-Proctor Arts Institute Archives, Record Group 13, Folder 79). There is some evidence that Root put together this collection for his mother, Clara F. Wales Root (d. 1928). Grace Root (1897–1975) told Aline B. Saarinen (1914–72) that Edward's mother "gave him money to buy them for her" (Aline and Eero Saarinen Papers, 1906–1977. Archives of American Art, Smithsonian Institution).

Appendix 2

Purchases and Gifts of Art from Grace Root between 1956 and 1964

(chronologically by accession number)

Peppino Mangravite
(1896–1978)
Head of a Woman, n.d.
Pastel and gouache on board
9 ¼ x 7 ½ in.
Gift, 56.62

Matta-Echaurren
(1912–2002)
Study for "The Heart Players"
1945
Graphite and watercolor on paper
9 3/16 x 11 5/16 in.
Purchase, 57.325

Matta-Echaurren
(1912–2002)
Two Stone Story of Their Metamorphose, 1941
Pencil and crayon on cardboard
16 ½ x 21 in.
Purchase, 57.326

Arthur B. Davies (1862–1928)
Refluent Season, before 1911
Oil on canvas
18 x 30 in.
Purchase, 58.39

Ernest Lawson (1873–1939)
The Dock, ca. 1909
Oil on canvas
25 x 30 in.
Purchase, 58.40

Ernest Lawson (1873–1939)
Winter, Spuyten Duyvil
Ca. 1907
Oil on canvas
25 ⅛ x 30 in.
Purchase, 58.41

Ernest Lawson (1873–1939)
Washington Bridge, ca. 1910
Oil on canvas
25 x 30 ¼ in.
Purchase, 58.42

George B. Luks (1866–1933)
The Pawnbroker's Daughter
1905
Oil on canvas
30 x 25 ⅛ in.
Purchase, 58.43

George B. Luks (1866–1933)
Group of Small Watercolors and Sketches, n.d.
Watercolor, graphite, ink, and crayon
Dimensions vary, largest: 10 3/16 x 14 ⅝ in.
Purchase, 58.157–213

Antonio Frasconi (b. 1919)
Fish in the Sky, 1952
Woodcut on paper
15 7/16 x 12 1/16 in.
Purchase, 58.288

Wanda Gág (1893–1946)
Backyard Corner, 1929
Watercolor on paper
10 ½ x 13 in.
Purchase, 58.289

Wanda Gág (1893–1946)
Snoopy Asleep, 1929
Watercolor on paper
10 7/16 x 13 in.
Purchase, 58.290

Charles D. Gibson
(1867–1944)
Cupid and Old Age, ca. 1956
Ink on paper
12 ⅜ x 18 ⅜ in.
Purchase, 58.291

George B. Luks (1866–1933)
Dyckman Street Cottage, n.d.
Oil on panel
8 ¼ x 10 9/16 in.
Purchase, 58.292

George B. Luks (1866–1933)
Dyckman Street Church
Ca. 1915
Watercolor on paper
15 ⅛ x 22 5/16 in.
Purchase, 58.293

George B. Luks (1866–1933)
The Lowing Heifer, n.d.
Oil on canvas
12 x 16 ⅛ in.
Purchase, 58.294

George B. Luks (1866–1933)
Paul Plaut, n.d.
Oil on canvas
30 x 25 in.
Purchase, 58.295

George B. Luks (1866–1933)
Pavlova's First Appearance in New York, 1910
Oil on canvas
16 ½ x 20 in.
Purchase, 58.296

George B. Luks (1866–1933)
Mountain Stream, 1931
Watercolor on wallpaper
14 x 20 ¼ in.
Purchase, 58.297

George B. Luks (1866–1933)
Sheet of Animal Subjects, n.d.
Crayon and watercolor on paper
14 ⅞ x 10 5/16 in.
Purchase, 58.298

Elizabeth Olds (1897–1991)
Man on a Bench, n.d.
Pastel on paper
10 13/16 x 9 ⅛ in.
Purchase, 58.299

Helen F. Price (1893–?)
Composition, 1950
Gouache on cardboard
5 15/16 x 15 ⅝ in.
Purchase, 58.300

Gene Charleton
(dates unknown)
Wind and Trees, n. d.
Watercolor on paper
Purchase, 59.10

Antonio Frasconi (b. 1919)
The Eagle, the Cat and the Sow, 1950
Woodcut on paper
12 x 14 ½ in.
Purchase, 59.11

Antonio Frasconi (b. 1919)
Corn, Cabbage, and Landscape
1951
Woodcut on paper
29 9/16 x 26 ⅛ in.
Purchase, 59.12

Morris Graves (1910–2001)
Resting Duck, 1953
Watercolor and sumi ink on laminated paper
19 ⅞ x 30 3/16 in.
Purchase, 59.13

Robert Motherwell (1915–91)
The Tomb of Captain Ahab
1953
Oil on canvas
8 x 10 3/16 in.
Purchase, 59.14

Native American
Rattle, 19th century?
Wood
Gift, 63.1

Native American
Basket, 19th century?
Reed
5 ¼ (h) x 4 ⅞ (w) in.
Gift, 64.129.1

Native American
Basket, 19th century
Reed
5 ¼ (h) x 4 ⅞ (w) in.
Gift, 64.129.2

Pre-Columbian
(Chimú culture?)
Pair of Ear Spools
Ca. 1000–1400 A.D.
Silver?
1 ⅜ in. diameter
Gift, 64.130.1–2

Appendix 3

Edward W. Root's Gifts of Art to the Addison Gallery of American Art, Everson Museum of Art, Museum of Modern Art, and Whitney Museum of American Art

ADDISON GALLERY OF AMERICAN ART, PHILLIPS ACADEMY, ANDOVER, MASS.

(Chronologically by accession number)

George Benjamin Luks (1866–1933)
Child Eating Apple, 1884
Pen, ink and graphite on wove paper
10 ½ x 8 ⅛ in.
Gift of Edward W. Root, Esq., 1941.4

Edward Hopper (1883–1967)
Freight Cars, Gloucester, 1928
Oil on canvas
29 x 40 ⅛ in.
Gift of Edward Wales Root in recognition of the 25th Anniversary of the Addison Gallery, 1956.7

William Brice (b. 1921)
Las Tunas, ca.1948
Oil on board
15 x 25 ½ in.
Bequest of Edward Wales Root, 1957.28

Arthur Dove (1880–1946)
Autumn, 1935
Tempera on canvas
14 x 23 in.
Bequest of Edward Wales Root, 1957.29

Theodoros Stamos (1922–97)
Gray Ungrounded, 1946
Oil on Masonite
20 x 20 $^{3}/_{16}$ in.
Bequest of Edward Wales Root, 1957.30

Theodoros Stamos (1922–97)
Hibernation, 1947
Oil on Masonite
24 x 30 in.
Bequest of Edward Wales Root, 1957.31

William Baziotes (1912–63)
Three Forms, 1946
Oil on canvas
28 ¼ x 36 ⅛ in.
Bequest of Edward Wales Root, 1957.32

John Wesley Carroll (1892–1959)
Night Pasture, ca.1944
Oil on canvas
12 ⅛ x 16 ⅛ in.
Bequest of Edward Wales Root, 1957.33

John Wesley Carroll (1892–1959)
Anita, ca. 1930
Oil on canvas
30 x 25 ⅛ in.
Bequest of Edward Wales Root, 1957.34

Charles Burchfield (1893–1967)
Cicada, 1944
Watercolor on paper mounted on board
39 x 24 $^{11}/_{16}$ in.
Bequest of Edward Wales Root, 1957.35

Mark Tobey (1890–1976)
Lines of the City, 1945
Tempera on paper mounted on board
117 ⅞ x 21 ¾ in.
Bequest of Edward Wales Root, 1957.36

Mark Tobey (1890–1976)
Eventuality, 1944
Tempera on paper mounted on board
10 x 14 $^{15}/_{16}$ in.
Bequest of Edward Wales Root, 1957.37

Eugene E. Speicher (1883–1962)
Plowed Field and Winter Rye 1942
Oil on canvas
10 x 18 in.
Bequest of Edward Wales Root, 1957.38

Walter Tandy Murch (1907–67)
Winter Palace, ca.1946
Oil on canvas
15 x 19 ¾ in.
Bequest of Edward Wales Root, 1957.39

Reuben Tam (1916–91)
Ominous Reef, 1945
Oil on canvas
20 x 40 in.
Bequest of Edward Wales Root, 1957.40

Edward J. Stevens (1923–88)
Triadic Bull, 1945
Oil on paper board
21 ¾ x 26 ¼ in.
Bequest of Edward Wales Root, 1957.41

Peppino Mangravite (1896–1978)
Ferns and Dead Bird, 1931
Oil on canvas
20 $^{3}/_{16}$ x 24 $^{1}/_{16}$ in.
Bequest of Edward Wales Root, 1957.42

Peppino Mangravite (1896–1978)
The Poet in Rye, n.d.
Gouache, graphite on wove paper
12 $^{11}/_{16}$ x 25 ⅝ in.
Bequest of Edward Wales Root, 1957.43

Morris Kantor (1896–1974)
The Poet and His Muse, 1938
Oil on canvas
21 x 26 in.
Bequest of Edward Wales Root, 1957.44

Morris Kantor (1896–1974)
Sailing, Marblehead, 1929
Oil on canvas
24 ⅛ x 26 $^{3}/_{16}$ in.
Bequest of Edward Wales Root, 1957.45

Henry Lee McFee (1886–1953)
Leaves, 1927
Oil on canvas
3 ¼ x 24 ¼ in.
Bequest of Edward Wales Root, 1957.46

Andrew Michael Dasburg (1887–1979)
The Reservoir, ca. 1927
Oil on canvas
16 ¼ x 20 $^{1}/_{16}$ in.
Bequest of Edward Wales Root, 1957.47

George Benjamin Luks (1866–1933)
Bear Cubs, 1904
Conté crayon
7 x 10 in.
Gift of Mrs. Edward Wales Root, 1958.5

George Benjamin Luks (1866–1933)
Bear Cubs, 1904
Conté crayon
7 x 10 in.
Gift of Mrs. Edward Wales Root, 1958.6

George Benjamin Luks (1866–1933)
Bears, 1904
Conté crayon
7 x 10 in.
Gift of Mrs. Edward Wales Root, 1958.7

George Benjamin Luks (1866–1933)
Bears, 1904
Conté crayon
7 x 10 in.
Gift of Mrs. Edward Wales Root, 1958.8

George Benjamin Luks (1866–1933)
Bears, 1904
Conté crayon
7 x 10 in.
Gift of Mrs. Edward Wales Root, 1958.9

George Benjamin Luks (1866–1933)
Bears, 1904
Conté crayon
7 x 10 in.
Gift of Mrs. Edward Wales Root, 1958.10

George Benjamin Luks (1866–1933)
Bears, 1904
Conté crayon
7 x 10 in.
Gift of Mrs. Edward Wales Root, 1958.11

George Benjamin Luks (1866–1933)
Bears, 1904
Conté crayon
7 x 10 in.
Gift of Mrs. Edward Wales Root, 1958.12

George Benjamin Luks (1866–1933)
Bears, 1904
Conté crayon
7 x 10 in.
Gift of Mrs. Edward Wales Root, 1958.13

Appendix 3

Edward W. Root's Gifts of Art to the Addison Gallery of American Art, Everson Museum of Art, Museum of Modern Art, and Whitney Museum of American Art

George Benjamin Luks (1866–1933)
Bears, 1904
Conté crayon
7 x 10 in.
Gift of Mrs. Edward Wales Root, 1958.14

George Benjamin Luks (1866–1933)
Bears, 1904
Conté crayon
7 x 10 in.
Gift of Mrs. Edward Wales Root, 1958.15

George Benjamin Luks (1866–1933)
Black Bear, 1904
Conté crayon
7 x 10 in.
Gift of Mrs. Edward Wales Root, 1958.16

George Benjamin Luks (1866–1933)
Bears, 1904
Conté crayon
7 x 10 in.
Gift of Mrs. Edward Wales Root, 1958.17

George Benjamin Luks (1866–1933)
Bear, 1904
Conté crayon
7 x 10 in.
Gift of Mrs. Edward Wales Root, 1958.18

George Benjamin Luks (1866–1933)
Bears, 1904
Conté crayon
10 x 7 in.
Gift of Mrs. Edward Wales Root, 1958.19

George Benjamin Luks (1866–1933)
Bear, Cub, Cubs, 1904
Conté crayon
9 15/16 x 7 in.
Gift of Mrs. Edward Wales Root, 1958.20

George Benjamin Luks (1866–1933)
Bear, 1904
Conté crayon
10 x 7 in.
Gift of Mrs. Edward Wales Root, 1958.21

George Benjamin Luks (1866–1933)
Bear and Cubs, 1904
Conté crayon
7 x 10 in.
Gift of Mrs. Edward Wales Root, 1958.22

George Benjamin Luks (1866–1933)
Brown Bear, 1904
Conté crayon
7 x 10 in.
Gift of Mrs. Edward Wales Root, 1958.23

George Benjamin Luks (1866–1933)
Deer, 1904
Conté crayon
7 x 10 in.
Gift of Mrs. Edward Wales Root, 1958.24

George Benjamin Luks (1866–1933)
Deer, 1904
Conté crayon
7 x 10 in
Gift of Mrs. Edward Wales Root, 1958.25

George Benjamin Luks (1866–1933)
Fawns, 1904
Conté crayon
7 x 9 15/16 in.
Gift of Mrs. Edward Wales Root, 1958.26

George Benjamin Luks (1866–1933)
Flamingos, 1904
Conté crayon
10 x 7 in.
Gift of Mrs. Edward Wales Root, 1958.27

George Benjamin Luks (1866–1933)
Cassowaries, 1904
Conté crayon
7 x 10 in.
Gift of Mrs. Edward Wales Root, 1958.28

George Benjamin Luks (1866–1933)
Emus, 1904
Conté crayon
10 x 7 in.
Gift of Mrs. Edward Wales Root, 1958.29

George Benjamin Luks (1866–1933)
Ducks, etc., 1904
Conté crayon
7 x 10 in
Gift of Mrs. Edward Wales Root, 1958.30

George Benjamin Luks (1866–1933)
Cranes, 1904
Conté crayon
10 x 7 in.
Gift of Mrs. Edward Wales Root, 1958.31

George Benjamin Luks (1866–1933)
Owls, 1904
Conté crayon
10 x 7 in.
Gift of Mrs. Edward Wales Root, 1958.32

George Benjamin Luks (1866–1933)
Tiger, 1904
Conté crayon
7 x 9 15/16 in.
Gift of Mrs. Edward Wales Root, 1958.33

George Benjamin Luks (1866–1933)
Lion (rear), 1904
Conté crayon
10 x 7 in.
Gift of Mrs. Edward Wales Root, 1958.34

George Benjamin Luks (1866–1933)
Lioness, 1904
Conté crayon
7 x 9 15/16 in.
Gift of Mrs. Edward Wales Root, 1958.35

George Benjamin Luks (1866–1933)
Lioness, 1904
Conté crayon
7 x 10 in.
Gift of Mrs. Edward Wales Root, 1958.36

George Benjamin Luks (1866–1933)
Boy, 1904
Conté crayon
10 x 7 in.
Gift of Mrs. Edward Wales Root, 1958.37

EVERSON MUSEUM OF ART, SYRACUSE, N.Y.

Clarence Carter (1904–2000)
Hewig Street Crossing, n.d.
Watercolor
21 x 14 ¼ in.
Gift of Mrs. Edward W. Root, Utica, N.Y.
60.3

Glenn Coleman (1887–1932)
Ferry, 1927–30
Oil on canvas
29 ½ x 34 ⅝ in.
Gift of Mrs. Edward W. Root, Utica, N.Y.
60.4

Jan Matulka (1890–1972)
Pastoral, 1927
Oil on canvas
36 x 36 in.
Gift of Mrs. Edward W. Root, Utica, N.Y.
60.5

Emil Hess (born 1913)
Woodshells No. 9, n.d.
Wood, glass
18 ¾ x 19 in
Gift of Mrs. Edward W. Root, Utica, N.Y.
60.6

William Meyerowitz (1887–1981)
Street Scene, n.d.
Oil on canvas
26 ⅝ x 28 ⅝ in.
Gift of Mrs. Edward W. Root, Utica, N.Y.
60.7

Carl Morris (1911–93)
Beach Riders, 1950
Oil and casein
12 x 8 in.
Gift of Mrs. Edward W. Root, Utica, N.Y.
60.8

MUSEUM OF MODERN ART, NEW YORK

Theodoros Stamos (1922–97)
Sounds in the Rock, 1946
Oil on composition board
48 ⅛ x 28 ⅜ in.
Gift of Edward W. Root, 27.1947

WHITNEY MUSEUM OF AMERICAN ART, NEW YORK

Robert Henri (1865–1929)
George Luks Playing Baseball
1904
Ink on paper
7 x 4 ⅜ in.
Gift of Mr. and Mrs. Edward W. Root, 42.37

George Luks (1866–1933)
Maurice Prendergast, ca. 1904
Graphite on paper
10 x 6 ¾ in.
Gift of Mr. and Mrs. Edward W. Root, 42.38

Appendix 4
Edward W. Root's Art Library

Within a year of his death, approximately seven hundred art-related books and periodicals were transferred from Edward Root's home in Clinton, N.Y. to the Munson-Williams-Proctor Institute's Art Reference Library. These volumes were part of a much larger book collection Edward and Grace Root assembled during their lives. In 1919, the Institute's founding charter called for the establishment of an "auxiliary library" to complement its museum, art school, and music programs, but around 1956 when Root died the book collection numbered fewer than two thousand volumes. Root's titles increased the size of the Institute's library by approximately one third. This gift was mentioned in the Institute's 1956–1957 year book and the Museum's 1961 exhibition catalog, the *Edward Wales Root Bequest*. While not the largest donation the Institute's library has ever received, Root's book collection is certainly one of the most valuable because it reflects the art-historical interests of an individual who played a key role in shaping the scope and character of the Museum's permanent collection, as well as reinforcing the library's role as a scholarly resource for research on the permanent collection.

At the time of the bequest, no record was prepared of the titles Root gave the Institute. However, the following subject categories that were listed on a checklist of the thirty-eight packing cartons that were shipped from Clinton to the Institute provide an overview of Root's wide-ranging interests: European painting and architecture; American art and architecture; European and American sculpture; prints and printmaking; "minor" arts; photography and film; "exotic" art; mixed media; art history, theory, and criticism; and periodicals. Some titles were returned to Mrs. Root because copies were already in the Institute's library. These duplicates may have become part of the collection of books she later donated to Hamilton College's Edward W. Root Art Center (see the October 21, 1957 Minutes of Munson-Williams-Proctor Institute's Board of Trustees).

Because the notes that Root made in the margins of some of his books and periodicals provide potentially valuable insights about his taste and aesthetic point of view, an ambitious effort was begun in 2005 to identity each of the Root volumes now in the Institute's library collection. Using the database of the library's current thirty-thousand-volume collection, a list of approximately three thousand titles was prepared of all the volumes published through 1957. Library staff, interns, and student assistants checked each of these volumes for Root's bookplate. The provenance of some books was determined by the presence of Root's signature or initials. In other cases a small label that had been placed in the volume when it was cataloged in 1957 identified it as being part of Root's collection. If no bookplate, inscription, or label was found, each page of a prospective volume was examined for handwritten notations that matched samples of Root's handwriting. The titles of all Root's books, exhibition catalogs, serials, brochures, and pamphlets that were identified by this means are now listed as such on the Art Reference Library's web site: http://www.mwpai.org/museum/library/. Any additional Root volumes that are identified in the future will be added to this list.

Kathryn L. Corcoran
Library Services Director

Kathleen Salsbury
Library Assistant

Ellen B. Damsky
Editor

Appendix 5

Edward W. Root Bibliography: Unpublished and Published Sources

This bibliography, the first ever to be compiled about Edward Root, lists as many of the unpublished and published sources written by or about him, and as many of the secondary sources, that it has been possible to identify within the time constraints of this project. A more comprehensive bibliography of Root's pioneering roles as a collector, teacher, and champion of modernism would include all his letters, diaries, notebooks, literary efforts, poems, and "philosophic notes," as well as his classroom lectures, research notes, commentaries on pictures he owned, and the diagrams of installations of his collection that are preserved in Root's archives at the Munson-Williams-Proctor Arts Institute and at Hamilton College, his alma mater. Such a bibliography would also list whatever editorials Root wrote around 1908–09 for the *New York Evening Sun* and *Harper's Weekly* that can be identified as having been written by him, as well as any letters, not yet discovered, that he may have written to the editor of the *Utica Daily Press* in the late 1920s in support of the series of contemporary art exhibitions which the Utica Art Society undertook at that time to promote a "permanent and growing interest in art" in the decade before the Munson-Williams-Proctor Institute opened to the public in 1935. It would also include all the course descriptions, notices, and articles written by or about Root that appeared in Hamilton College's academic catalogs, campus newspaper, and alumni magazine, and any of Root's surviving correspondence with contemporary collectors such as Duncan Phillips (1886–1966), or with relatives such as Henry Francis du Pont (1880–1969), as well as whatever letters there are in the archives of the artists whose works he owned, the art dealers from whom he purchased pictures, and the staff members of the museums with which he had either a brief or extended relationship, such as the Addison Gallery of American Art, the Everson Museum of Art, The Metropolitan Museum of Art, The Museum of Modern Art, and the Whitney Museum of American Art.

The authors wish to express their thanks and profound gratitude to Susanna White, Associate Director and Curator, Emerson Gallery, for the substantial assistance she graciously provided in the preparation of this bibliography.

M.E.M., P.D.S., M.D.S.

UNPUBLISHED MATERIAL

Aline and Eero Saarinen Papers, 1906–1977. Archives of American Art, Smithsonian Institution.

Alumni Center / Edward Root House / Root Art Center Folder. Photograph Collection (0000.92). Hamilton College Library Archives, Clinton, N.Y.

Burchfield, Charles. Hamilton College Letters and Memorabilia (0000.187). Hamilton College Library Archives, Clinton, N.Y.

Correspondence Relating to Members of the Root Family. William H. Welch Papers. The Alan Mason Chesney Medical Archives, The Johns Hopkins University, Baltimore, Md.

Department of Art Folder. Hamilton College Miscellaneous (0000.93). Hamilton College Library Archives, Clinton, N.Y.

Edward Wales Root Papers, 1896–1968. Archives of American Art, Smithsonian Institution.

Edward Wales Root Papers. Munson-Williams-Proctor Arts Institute Archives, Record Group 13, Folders 1–295.

Edward W. Root Philip Hooker Book Research Material Collection (0000.163). Hamilton College Library Archives, Clinton, N.Y.

Edward W. Root '05 Folder. Photograph Collection (0000.92). Hamilton College Library Archives, Clinton, N.Y.

Edward W. Root '05 Folders. Hamilton College Alumni Biographical Materials (0000.182). Hamilton College Library Archives, Clinton, N.Y.

Elihu Root, Jr. Collection (2005.14). Hamilton College Library Archives, Clinton, N.Y.

Elihu Root House, Homestead, Root Glen, and Root Art Center Folders. Hamilton College Miscellaneous (0000.93). Hamilton College Library Archives, Clinton, N.Y.

Elihu Root Papers, 1904–37 (0000.14). Hamilton College Library Archives, Clinton, N.Y.

Frederick C. Ferry, Hon. '17 Folders. Hamilton College Presidents' Files (0000.95). Hamilton College Library Archives, Clinton, N.Y.

Grant House / Elihu Root House Folder. Photograph Collection (0000.92). Hamilton College Library Archives, Clinton, N.Y.

Harry D. Yates '25 Folders. Hamilton College Alumni Biographical Materials (0000.182). Hamilton College Library Archives, Clinton, N.Y.

Hayes, Jr., Bartlett H. "Address at Opening of Exhibition to Honor the Memory of Edward Wales Root," Munson-Williams-Proctor Institute, Utica, New York, April 28, 1957. Record Group 4,21, Folder 164, Joseph S. Trovato Papers, Munson-Williams-Proctor Arts Institute Archives.

Interview with Charles Alan conducted by Paul Cummings, August 20, 1970. Archives of American Art, Smithsonian Institution.

Interview with Charles Seliger conducted by Paul Cummings, May 8, 1968. Archives of American Art, Smithsonian Institution.

Interview with Grace Cogswell Root conducted by Donald S. Sade, May 1, 1961. Hamilton College Library Archives, Clinton, N.Y.

Interview with Louise Sheffield Brownell Saunders conducted by C. Woodruff Starkweather, April 24, 1960. Hamilton College Library Archives, Clinton, N.Y.

Minutes of the Meetings. Board of Trustees, Hamilton College. Hamilton College Library Archives, Clinton, N.Y.

Minutes of the Meetings: 1944–57. Board of Trustees, Munson-Williams-Proctor Arts Institute Archives.

Murray, Mary E. "American and Modern: Edward W. Root and the Munson-Williams-Proctor Arts Institute." Paper read at the College Art Association, New York, February 17, 2007. Curatorial Files, Museum of Art, Munson-Williams-Proctor Arts Institute.

Picture Rental Collection Folder. Hamilton College Letters and Memorabilia (0000.187). Hamilton College Library Archives, Clinton, N.Y.

Root, Edward W. "Art Club Paper" [The Study of Italian Renaissance Art]. Typescript of Root's November 2, 1930 lecture to Hamilton College's Art Club. Edward W. Root '05 Folders. Hamilton College Alumni Biographical Materials (0000.182). Hamilton College Library Archives, Clinton, N.Y.

___. "College Teaching and Contemporary Pictures." Paper read at the College Art Association, New York, March 30, 1932. Edward Wales Root Papers, Munson-Williams-Proctor Arts Institute Archives, Record Group 13, Folder 260.

___. "An Essay in Aesthetics (1909)." Edward Wales Root Papers, Munson-Williams-Proctor Arts Institute Archives, Record Group 13, Folder 249.

___. "The 'Expert and Downright' Criticism of 1913" (Winter 1929). Edward Wales Root Papers, Munson-Williams-Proctor Arts Institute Archives, Record Group 13, Folder 260.

___. "Factors Improving Interest in Art," June 15, 1955. Edward Wales Root Papers, Munson-Williams-Proctor Arts Institute Archives, Record Group 13, Folder 241.

___. "Function of the Artist." Edward Wales Root Papers, Munson-Williams-Proctor Arts Institute Archives, Record Group 13, Folder 254.

___. "He Walked Across the Lawn Slowly," ca. 1949–50. Edward Wales Root Papers, Munson-Williams-Proctor Arts Institute Archives, Record Group 13, Folder 255.

___. "I Remember Quite Clearly How I Came to Buy My First Painting," ca. 1950. Edward Wales Root Papers, Munson-Williams-Proctor Arts Institute Archives, Record Group 13, Folder 255.

___. "If I Had My Life to Live Over Again" (November 25, 1914). Edward Wales Root Papers, Munson-Williams-Proctor Arts Institute Archives, Record Group 13, Folder 255.

___. Letter to the Editor of the Albany *Knickerbocker Press* Concerning the Proposed Partial Demolition of Philip Hooker's Second Presbyterian Church, August 1, 1919. Edward Wales Root Papers, Munson-Williams-Proctor Arts Institute Archives, Record Group 13, Folder 261.

___. Letter to William H. Cowley, President, Hamilton College, Clinton, N.Y., October 9, 1938. Edward Wales Root Papers, Munson-Williams-Proctor Arts Institute Archives, Record Group 13, Folder 156.

___. Letter to William H. Cowley, President, Hamilton College, Clinton, N.Y., December 27, 1940. Edward W. Root '05 Folders. Hamilton College Alumni Biographical Materials (0000.182). Hamilton College Library Archives, Clinton, N.Y.

___. "Modern Art Introduced to America at the Armory Show, N.Y., in 1913." Notes for a Lecture at the Munson-Williams-Proctor Institute, April 13, 1947. Edward Wales Root Papers, Munson-Williams-Proctor Arts Institute Archives, Record Group 13, Folder 242.

___. "Non-Objective, Ideographic, and Surrealist Pictures." Notes for a Lecture at the Munson-Williams-Proctor Institute, April 13, 1947. Edward Wales Root Papers, Munson-Williams-Proctor Arts Institute Archives, Record Group 13, Folder 254.

___. "Notes on Pictures /Notes on Paintings / Hanging Charts, Etc.," ca. 1944–49. Edward Wales Root Papers, Munson-Williams-Proctor Arts Institute Archives, Record Group 13, Folder 91.

___. "Notes on Vision and Design—Roger Fry: Art and Life (1917)." Edward Wales Root Papers, Munson-Williams-Proctor Arts Institute Archives, Record Group 13, Folder 249.

___. "Objective Realism; Objective Distortions; Objective Abstractions; Non-Objective Compositions; Mixed Combinations," undated. Edward Wales Root Papers, Munson-Williams-Proctor Arts Institute Archives, Record Group 13, Folder 241.

___. "Some Characteristics of Modern Art." Final draft of a Lecture at the Munson-Williams-Proctor Institute, April 13, 1947. Edward Wales Root Papers, Munson-Williams-Proctor Arts Institute Archives, Record Group 13, Folder 242.

___. "Some of the Characteristics of Contemporary Painting." Fourth draft of a gallery talk at the Munson-Williams-Proctor Institute, April 13, 1947. Edward Wales Root Papers, Munson-Williams-Proctor Arts Institute Archives, Record Group 13, Folder 242.

___. "A Statement Introductory to a Course in Appreciation of Painting," ca. 1935. Edward Wales Root Papers, Munson-Williams-Proctor Arts Institute Archives, Record Group 13, Folder 191.

___."To be Considered by the Critic of Painting," ca. 1944–45. Edward Wales Root Papers, Munson-Williams-Proctor Arts Institute Archives, Record Group 13, Folder 254.

___. "The Uneducated Public and Pictures." Edward Wales Root Papers, Munson-Williams-Proctor Arts Institute Archives, Record Group 13, Folder 254.

___. "Why Abstraction," July 4, 1946. Edward Wales Root Papers, Munson-Williams-Proctor Arts Institute Archives, Record Group 13, Folder 241.

Root, Grace C., comp. "Fathers and Sons, 1924–37" (1971). Hamilton College Library Archives, Clinton, N.Y.

Root Art Center Records and Scrapbooks (0000.30–31). Hamilton College Library Archives, Clinton, N.Y.

Root Family Papers (0000.188). Hamilton College Library Archives, Clinton, N.Y.

Root Glen Folder. Photograph Collection (0000.92). Hamilton College Library Archives, Clinton, N.Y.

Saunders Family Papers (0000.61). Hamilton College Library Archives, Clinton, N.Y.

William C. Palmer Papers (0000.196). Hamilton College Library Archives, Clinton, N.Y.

ARTICLES AND BOOKS PUBLISHED BY EDWARD W. ROOT DURING HIS LIFETIME

"An Appreciation." *Arthur B. Davies: Essays on the Man and His Art*, Phillips Collection. Cambridge, Mass.: Riverside, 1924, 59–66.

"Bradley Walker Tomlin." *15 Americans*, ed. by Dorothy C. Miller. New York: The Museum of Modern Art, 1952, 24.

"Charles E. Burchfield." *American Art Portfolios (Series One)*. New York: Raymond and Raymond, 1936, 65–68.

"Clinton Man Comments on Art Exhibit." *Utica Daily Press*, January 21, 1928, 9.

"Foreword." *Current Trends in British and American Painting From the Collection of Mr. Edward W. Root, Clinton, New York*. Utica, N.Y.: Munson-Williams-Proctor Institute, 1950, unpaginated.

"The Function of the Small College in the Development of Artistic Appreciation." Unlocated paper read at the College Art Association, Ithaca, N.Y., December 30, 1925, as cited in *The Art Bulletin* 8, no. 3 (March 1926): 183.

"George Benjamin Luks." *The One Hundred and Fiftieth Anniversary Exhibition of the Pennsylvania Academy of the Fine Arts*. Philadelphia, Pa.: The Pennsylvania Academy of the Fine Arts, 1955, 120–23.

"Hamilton's Portrait Collection." *Hamilton Alumni Review* 4, no. 3 (March 1939): 129–33.

"Hopper's Works Now on Exhibition Here." *Utica Daily Press*, March 3, 1928, 9.

"Local Pens Abroad." *Clinton Courier*, August 19, 1948, 4.

"Local Pens Abroad." *Clinton Courier*, September 2, 1948, 4.

"Local Pens Abroad." *Clinton Courier*, September 16, 1948, 4.

"Local Pens Abroad." *Clinton Courier*, September 23, 1948, 4.

"Mexican Market Scene: One of Maurice Becker's Paintings Now Displayed by Utica Art Society." *Utica Daily Press*, April 14, 1928, 12.

"New York Instructor Guest of Art Society." *Utica Daily Press*, December 19, 1927, 17.

[Untitled Introduction.] *The Paintings of Charles Burchfield*. Utica, N.Y.: Munson-Williams-Proctor Institute, 1945, unpaginated.

Philip Hooker: A Contribution to the Study of the Renaissance in America. New York: Charles Scribner's Sons, 1929.

"Pictures and the College." *American Magazine of Art* 13, no. 5 (May 1922): 144–48.

Review of *The American Renaissance*, by R. L. Duffus (New York: Alfred A. Knopf, 1928). *Association of American Colleges Bulletin* 14, no. 6 (December 1928): 501–3. [Root's typescript of this review is in the Edward W. Root '05 Folders. Hamilton College Alumni Biographical Materials (0000.182). Hamilton College Library Archives, Clinton, N.Y.]

"Some Unprinted Minutes of the Albany Common Council." *Proceedings of the New York State Historical Association with the Quarterly Journal* 18 (1923): 43–47.

[Untitled Introduction.] *Thurloe Conolly*. New York: Willard Gallery, 1951, unpaginated.

"Works of William Simmons Exhibited by Art Society." *Utica Daily Press*, November 2, 1927, 11.

SECONDARY SOURCES

Adams, Henry. "A Heartland Artist Who Broke the Old Regionalist Mold." *Smithsonian Magazine*, May 1997, 67.

"Allan Donn [*sic*] Puts to Sea." *Utica Daily Press*, May 12, 1928, 4.

"Alumni Department." *Hamilton Literary Magazine* 52, no. 1 (October 1917): 37–38.

"Alumniana." *The Hamilton Literary Magazine* 40, no. 2 (October 1905): 71.

"American Collector." *Time*, March 2, 1953, 62.

"Another Root Gift." *Munson-Williams-Proctor Institute Bulletin*, January 1954, unpaginated.

"Another Talk Given by Edward W. Root: Utica Art Society Members Go to Clinton." *Utica Daily Press*, February 13, 1928, 17.

"The Appreciation of Art." *Hamilton Alumni Review* 2, no. 1 (October 1936): 10.

"Art Expert Passes at 72." *Rochester Democratic and Chronicle*, December 6, 1956, 8.

"Art World Appointments." *Art Digest* 24 (January 1, 1950): 29.

Baur, John I. H. *Inlander: The Life and Work of Charles Burchfield 1893–1967*. New York: Cornwall, 1982, 128, 149–50, 188, 190–92.

Berman, Avis. "Creating a Tradition: The Addison and the Artist," in *Addison Gallery of American Art, 65 Years: A Selective Catalogue*. Andover, Mass.: Addison Gallery of American Art, 1996, 148, 168, 170, 177.

Bottino, Betsy M. "The Root Glen." *Hamilton Alumni Review* 53, no. 1 (Spring / Summer 1988): 10–13.

Breslin, James. *Mark Rothko: A Biography*. Chicago: University of Chicago Press, 1993, 252.

Brown, Milton W. *The Story of the Armory Show*. New York: Abbeville, 1988, 127, 129.

Burchfield, Charles E. [Memoir of Edward Root] Reprinted from *Edward Wales Root, 1884–1956: An American Collector*. Utica, N.Y.: Munson-Williams-Proctor Institute, 1957, in Joseph S. Trovato, *Paintings by Charles E. Burchfield*. Clinton, N.Y.: Edward W. Root Art Center, Hamilton College, 1962, unpaginated.

Cashen, Jon. "Edward W. Root: Into the Next Generation." *Hamilton Alumni Review* 48, no. 3 (December 1982): 21–23.

Cavaliere, Barbara. "Theodoros Stamos in Perspective." *Arts* 51 (December 1977): 110.

Collecting on a Shoestring: William Roehrick '34. Clinton, N.Y.: Root Art Center, Hamilton College, 1964, unpaginated.

Committee of the College Art Association. "A Statement on the Practice of Art Courses," *College Art Journal* 4, no. 1 (November 1944): 33–38.

Constable, W. G. "The Return of the Native." *Art Collecting in the United States of America*. London: Thomas Nelson and Sons, 1964, 141–54.

"Current Trends in British and American Painting from the Collection of Edward W. Root." *Munson-Williams-Proctor Institute Bulletin*, December 1950, unpaginated.

Current Trends in British and American Painting from the Collection of Mr. Edward W. Root, Clinton, New York. Utica, N.Y.: Munson-Williams-Proctor Institute, 1950.

"Death Claims E. W. Root, Noted Author, Art Critic." *Rome Sentinel*, December 6, 1956, 7.

"Edward Root, Noted Author, Critic, Dies." *Utica Observer-Dispatch*, December 6, 1956, 16A.

The Edward Root Collection: Exhibited at The Metropolitan Museum. New York: The Metropolitan Museum of Art, February 12–April 12, 1953. [Root's annotated copy of this brochure is filed in the Edward Wales Root Papers, Munson-Williams-Proctor Arts Institute Archives, Record Group 13, Folder 77.]

"Edward W. Root." *Munson-Williams-Proctor Institute Bulletin*, January 1957, unpaginated.

"Edward W. Root." *Year Book 1956–1957: Munson-Williams-Proctor Institute*, 4, 5, 21–28.

Edward W. Root: Collector and Teacher. Introductory essay by Joseph S. Trovato. Clinton, N.Y.: Fred L. Emerson Gallery, Hamilton College, 1982.

"Edward W. Root: Consultant in Art." *Munson-Williams-Proctor Institute Bulletin*, January 1950, unpaginated.

"Edward W. Root, 72 Dies; Noted Author, Art Critic." *Utica Daily Press*, December 6, 1956, 4A.

The Edward W. Root Art Center. Clinton, N.Y.: Hamilton College, ca. 1962.

"The Edward W. Root Collection of Prints." *Munson-Williams-Proctor Institute Bulletin*, March 1953, unpaginated.

Edward Wales Root, 1884–1956: An American Collector. Prologue by Aline B. Saarinen. Utica, N.Y.: Munson-Williams-Proctor Institute, 1957.

"Edward Wales Root Bequest." *Munson-Williams-Proctor Institute Bulletin*, December 1961–January 1962: unpaginated.

"Edward Wales Root Bequest." *Munson-Williams-Proctor Institute Bulletin*, February–March 1962, unpaginated.

"Edward Wales Root Dies, Leading Authority on Art." *New York Herald Tribune*, December 6, 1956, 20.

European Prints, 15th Century–20th Century: Gift of Edward W. Root. Utica, N.Y.: Munson-Williams-Proctor Institute, 1953.

"Exhibit Opens Today at M-W-P." *Utica Observer-Dispatch*, November 5, 1961, 2B.

Exhibition of Japanese Color Prints From Designs by the Late Eighteenth Century and Early Nineteenth Century Masters, Loaned to the Utica Public Library by Edward W. Root of New York. [Utica, N.Y.?]: privately printed, 1922.

Fails, Sonia. "The Art of Edward W. Root." *Munson-Williams-Proctor Institute Bulletin*, March 1987, unpaginated.

Faxon, Susan C. "Portraits of Patronage: The History of the Addison Gallery's Collection and Its Donors," in *Addison Gallery of American Art, 65 Years: A Selective Catalogue*. Andover, Mass.: Addison Gallery of American Art, 1996, 55–56, 58, 62, 65, 66, 72, 76.

Geist, Sidney. "One Man's Collection." *Art Digest* 27, no. 11 (March 1, 1953): 13.

George B. Luks: Bronx Park, May 8, 1904. Thirty-three Drawings of Animals in the Bronx Zoo. Andover, Mass.: Addison Gallery of American Art, 1990.

Glackens, Ira. *William Glackens and the Ashcan Group: The Emergence of Realism in American Art*. New York: Crown, 1957, 101.

Hale, Robert B. "The Growth of a Collection." *The Metropolitan Museum of Art Bulletin* 11, no.6 (February 1953): 153–63.

"Hamilton Students Now Rent Old Masters; Sons of Elihu Root Foster Art Plan." *New York Times*, September 27, 1936, N9.

Hayes, Jr., Bartlett H. "The Root of American Painting." *ARTnews* 56, no. 9 (January 1958): 29–31, 61–62.

Jaeger, Roland, ed. *Karl With, Autobiography of Ideas: Memoirs of an Extraordinary Art Scholar*. Berlin: Mann, 1997, 231.

"Japanese Prints Exhibit at Utica Public Library." *Utica Daily Press*, April 22, 1922, 5.

Jessup, Philip C. *Elihu Root*. 2 vols. New York: Dodd, Mead, 1938, passim.

Kendall, M. Sue. "Serendipity at the Sunwise Turn: Mary Mowbray-Clark and the Early Patronage of Charles Burchfield," in Nannette V. Maciejunes and Michael D. Hall et al. *The Paintings of Charles Burchfield: North by Midwest*. New York: Harry N. Abrams, 1997, 89–90, 96.

Keno, Leigh R. *Early American Paintings and Furniture From the Hamilton College Collection*. Clinton, N.Y.: The Edward W. Root Art Center, Hamilton College, 1979, 10–16.

Knox, Sanka. "Two Art Centers Get Root Collection." *New York Times*, September 23, 1957, 27.

LeQuire, Louise. "Root Collection Watercolors to Go on View at Peabody." *Nashville Banner*, April 1, 1960, 14.

Levin, Gail. *Edward Hopper: An Intimate Biography*. Berkeley, Calif.: University of California Press, 1995, 215–16, 230, 254, 411, 462.

"Library Print Exhibit Ends on Saturday." *Utica Observer-Dispatch*, May 4, 1922, 8.

Lindemann, Edna M. "The Collector—Edward Wales Root." *The Art Triangle: Artist, Dealer, Collector*. Buffalo, N.Y.: Burchfield Art Center, 1989, 35–41.

"The Little League." *Time*, October 31, 1960, 64.

"Locals." *Hamilton Literary Magazine* 37, no. 1 (October 1902): 90.

Louchheim [Saarinen], Aline B. "A Collector with Personal Vision." *New York Times*, February 15, 1953, 12.

___. "Root's Collection of Art Displayed." *New York Times*, February 12, 1953, 21.

"Lovers of Art Enjoy College Hill Visit: Group Hears Edward Root Tell of His Paintings." *Utica Daily Press*, February 6, 1928, 7.

Maciejunes, Nannette V. "Burchfield on Burchfield: An Artist's Journal Reconsidered," in Nannette V. Maciejunes and Michael D. Hall et al. *The Paintings of Charles Burchfield: North by Midwest*. New York: Harry N. Abrams, 1997, 101, 107.

McBride, Henry. "Patriotism and Art." *ARTnews* 52, no. 1 (March 1953): 40.

Mecklenburg, Virginia M. *Edward Hopper: The Watercolors*. Washington. D.C.: National Museum of American Art, 1999, 75–76.

Murray, Mary E. *American Twentieth-Century Watercolors at the Munson-Williams-Proctor Arts Institute*. Utica, N.Y.: Munson-Williams-Proctor Arts Institute, 2000, 13–14.

___. *Collecting Modernism: European Masterworks from the Munson-Williams-Proctor Arts Institute*. Utica, N.Y.: Munson-Williams-Proctor Arts Institute, 2005, 6–11.

___. "Theodoros Stamos and Edward Wales Root: A Friendship in Art and Nature." *Theodoros Stamos 1922–1997: A Retrospective*, ed. by Anna Kafetsi. Athens, Greece: National Gallery and Alexandros Soutzos Museum, 1997, 53–57.

Murray, Mary E., Paul D. Schweizer, and Michael D. Somple. *Auspicious Vision: Edward Wales Root and American Modernism: Gallery Guide*. Utica, N.Y.: Munson-Williams-Proctor Arts Institute, 2007.

O'Connor, Francis V. *Charles Seliger: Redefining Abstract Expressionism*. Manchester, Vt.: Hudson Hill, 2002, 44, 49, 54.

Owens, Gwendolyn. *Watercolors by Maurice Prendergast from New England Collections*. Williamstown, Mass.: Sterling and Francine Clark Art Institute, 1978, 11.

Pach, Walter. *Queer Thing, Painting: Forty Years in the World of Art*. New York and London: Harper and Brothers, 1938, 228.

"A Painting by Sheeler." *Utica Daily Press*, February 4, 1928, 9.

Paintings, Drawings and Sculptures in the Munson-Williams-Proctor Institute Museum of Art. Utica, N.Y.: Munson-Williams-Proctor Institute, 1961.

"Paintings from the Collection of Edward W. Root." *Munson-Williams-Proctor Institute Bulletin*, April 1948, unpaginated.

Passantino, Erika D., ed. *The Eye of Duncan Phillips: A Collection in the Making*. Washington, D.C.: The Phillips Collection, 1999, 556, 794n6.

Patterson, Ferne K. *Pioneers of Vernon, Oneida County, New York*. Interlaken, N.Y.: I-T Publishing, 1985, 27 passim.

Penny, James. *Hamilton College Alumni Artists*. Clinton, N.Y.: The Edward W. Root Art Center, Hamilton College, 1972, unpaginated.

Perlman, Bennard B. *The Lives, Loves, and Art of Arthur B. Davies*. Albany, N.Y.: State University of New York Press, 1998, 195, 233, 330.

"Persons in the Foreground: Personal Characteristics of Elihu Root." *Current Literature* 39 (October 1905): 441–43.

"Pictures, Also Paintings, Are Now Available: Novel System Being Adopted for Hill Students, Also Faculty." *Utica Daily Press*, September 25, 1936, 10.

Pilkington, Walter. *Hamilton College, 1812–1962*. Clinton, N.Y.: Hamilton College, 1962, 233.

___. *The Homestead*. Clinton, N.Y.: Hamilton College, 1959.

"Pioneers of Modern Art in America." *Munson-Williams-Proctor Institute Bulletin*, April 1947, unpaginated.

Pokinski, Deborah, David Nathans, et al. "Elihu Root, Jr., Class of 1903: Lawyer–Painter." *Elihu Root, Jr., Class of 1903: Lawyer–Painter*. Clinton, N.Y.: Emerson Gallery, Hamilton College, 2004, 10.

Pollock, Lindsay. *The Girl with the Gallery: Edith Gregor Halpert and the Making of the Modern Art Market*. New York: PublicAffairs, 2006, 102.

Prior, Harris K. "Edward Root, Talent Scout." *Art in America* 50, no.1 (1962): 70–73.

Putala, Eugene C. "The Root Legacy: Homestead, Glade, and Glen." Video recording of a lecture presented at The Glen House (formerly "The Studio"), Hamilton College, sponsored by the Emerson Gallery, Hamilton College, Clinton, N.Y., September 29, 2007. Hamilton College Library Archives, Clinton, N.Y.

Reynolds, Jock. "The End Depends on the Beginning," in *Addison Gallery of American Art, 65 Years: A Selective Catalogue*. Andover, Mass.: Addison Gallery of American Art, 1996, 241.

Robson, Deirdre. "The Avant-Garde and the On-Guard: Some Influences on the Potential Market for the First Generation Abstract Expressionists in the 1940s and Early 1950s." *Art Journal* 47, no. 3 (Autumn 1988): 216, 218, 219, 220n16, 221n48.

Roehrick, Jr., William G. "Edward W. Root as a Teacher." *Hamilton Alumni Review* 22, no. 4 (May 1957): 195.

___. "Edward W. Root as a Teacher." *Munson-Williams-Proctor Institute Bulletin*, March 1957, unpaginated.

___. Video recording of a lecture about Edward Root presented at the Emerson Gallery, Hamilton College, Clinton, N.Y., October 23, 1982. Hamilton College Library Archives, Clinton, N.Y.

Root, Edward W. "Postscript, 1929: The 'Expert and Downright' Criticism of 1913." *1913, Armory Show, 50th Anniversary Exhibition, 1963*. Utica, N.Y.: Munson-Williams-Proctor Institute, 1963, 172–75.

[Root, Edward W.?] "Special Course in Art to be Conducted by Edward W. Root, '05." *Hamilton Life*, November 23, 1920, 8.

Root, John B. "Lenders Statement," in Michael E. Shapiro, *Hamilton Collects American Art*. Clinton, N.Y.: Emerson Gallery, 2002, 108–9.

"Root Appointed by Institute to be Honorary Consultant." *Utica Observer-Dispatch*, July 10, 1956, 7A.

"Root Art Collection on Exhibit." *Syracuse Herald-American*, November 5, 1961, 57.

"Root Bequest." *Museum News* 35, no. 9 (November 1, 1957): 2.

"Root Collections Feature Utica, New York Exhibits." *Utica Observer-Dispatch*, March 1, 1953, 2A.

"Root Gift of Japanese Prints." *Munson-Williams-Proctor Institute Bulletin*, January 1955, unpaginated.

"Root is Appointed as Art Consultant." *Utica Daily Press*, July 10, 1956, 3A.

"Root's U.S. Pictures at Met." *New York Herald Tribune*, February 15, 1953, 4:7.

[Saarinen, Aline B.?]. "Edward Root, 72, Art Patron Dies: Ex-Hamilton Professor Lent Collection Here, Wrote on Renaissance." *New York Times*, December 6, 1956, 37.

Saarinen, Aline B. [Prologue]. Reprinted from *Edward Wales Root, 1884–1956: An America Collector*. Utica, N.Y.: Munson-Williams-Proctor Institute, 1957, in *Edward Wales Root Bequest*. Utica, N.Y.: Munson-Williams-Proctor Institute, 1961.

__. "The Quiet World: Edward Wales Root." *The Proud Possessors: The Lives, Times and Tastes of Some Adventurous American Art Collectors*. New York: Random House, 1958, 250–68.

Salzillo, William, and Susanna White. "A Century of Curiosities: The Story of the Hamilton College Collection." *Hamilton Collects: A Century of Curiosities: The Story of the Hamilton College Collection*. Clinton, N.Y.: Emerson Gallery, Hamilton College, 2005, 21–26.

Sandler, Irving. "Roy R. Neuberger: Patron of American Art." *Roy R. Neuberger: Patron of the Arts*. Purchase, N.Y.: Neuberger Museum of Art, State University of New York at Purchase, 1993, 8–9.

Saunders, Silvia. "With Simplicity and Sophistication." *Hamilton Alumni Review* 40, no. 3–4 (Summer 1975): 22–26.

Schweizer, Paul D., and John R. Sawyer. "A History of the Collection." *Masterworks of American Art from the Munson-Williams-Proctor Institute*. New York: Harry N. Abrams, 1989, 9–10 passim.

Selections from the Edward Root Collection. Washington, D.C.: Smithsonian Institution, 1959–60.

"Son of Elihu Root Is Dead: Former Professor of Art Appreciation at Hamilton College." *Watertown Times*, December 6, 1956, 17.

"Special Course on Hill: Edward W. Root to Conduct 18 Exercises in Art." *Clinton Courier*, November 23, 1920, 4.

Tomkins, Calvin. "A Keeper of the Treasure." *The New Yorker*, June 9, 1975, 54.

Trapp, Frank A. "The Armory Show: A Review." *Art Journal* 23, no.1 (Autumn 1963): 3.

Trovato, Joseph S. *Charles Burchfield: Catalogue of Paintings in Public and Private Collections.* Utica, N.Y.: Munson-Williams-Proctor Institute, 1970, 10, 345.

__. "Foreword." *Edward Hopper: Oils, Watercolors, Prints.* Clinton, N.Y.: The Edward W. Root Art Center, Hamilton College, 1964, unpaginated.

___. "Foreword." *Selections from the Edith Gregor Halpert Collection.* Clinton, N.Y.: The Edward W. Root Art Center, Hamilton College, 1960, unpaginated.

___. ed. "Foreword." *Learning About Pictures from Mr. Root.* Clinton, N.Y.: The Edward W. Root Art Center, Hamilton College, 1965, unpaginated.

Troyen, Carol et al. *Edward Hopper.* Boston: Museum of FIne Arts, 2007, 124.

"Utica Art Society Buys Picture." *Utica Daily Press*, March 24, 1928, 9.

Vars, Nancy. "Utica Museum Receives International Renown." *Syracuse Post-Standard*, May 6, 1962, 19.

"Weds Miss Cogswell: Ex-Senator's Son Marries Daughter of Mr. and Mrs. Ledyard Cogswell of Albany." *New York Times*, September 9, 1917, 18.

White, Susanna, et al. *The Best Kind of Life: Edward W. Root as Teacher, Collector, and Naturalist.* Clinton, N.Y.: Emerson Gallery, Hamilton College, 2007.

Wilson, Edmund. *Upstate.* New York: Farrar, Straus and Giroux, 1971, 121–22.

Zilczer, Judith. *"The Noble Buyer": John Quinn, Patron of the Avant-Garde.* Washington, D.C.: Hirshhorn Museum and Sculpture Garden, 1978, 154.

Index

Pages on which illustrations appear are set in bold. EWR stands for Edward Wales Root. MWPAI stands for Munson-Williams-Proctor Arts Institute.

Index

A NOTE ON THE TYPE

Chaparral is the work of type designer Carol Twombly (b. 1959) and combines the legibility of slab serif designs popularized in the 19th century with the grace of 16th-century roman book lettering. The result is a versatile, hybrid slab serif design. Unlike "geometric" slab serif designs, Chaparral has varying letter proportions that give it an accessible and friendly appearance in all weights from light to bold. Chaparral is clear and legible in smaller text settings while remaining subtle and attractive at display sizes.

Chaparral bears a striking resemblance to the cover type used on the brochure for the 1913 International Exhibition of Modern Art, the renowned Armory Show with which Edward Root was personally involved.

Photograph Credits

John Bigelow Taylor and Dianne Dubler photographed all the works of art in the catalogue section of this book except numbers 74 & 78 (David Revette Photography, Syracuse, N.Y.); and 152 (Williamstown Art Conservation Laboratory). David Revette also made the cover details of catalogue number 6. At Munson-Williams-Proctor Arts Institute David McHarg and Kathleen Salsbury scanned material from the Institute's Art Reference Library and Archives. Root family photographs published in this book were made by Hamilton College, David Broda, Jamesville, N.Y., and the Munson-Williams-Proctor Arts Institute, and are published by permission of John B. Root. Richard Carver Wood's photograph of the Homestead is published courtesy of the Hamilton College Library Archives (Richard Carver Wood Photograph Collection, 0000.92.39).

Works of art by the following artists are reproduced with permission of the following institutions or individuals: William A. Baziotes © 2007 Estate of William Baziotes / Roebling Hall, Brooklyn, N.Y.; Harry Bertoia © 2007 Estate of Harry Bertoia / Artists Rights Society (ARS), New York; Charles E. Burchfield, reproduced with permission of the Charles E. Burchfield Foundation; Willem de Kooning © 2007 The Willem de Kooning Foundation / Artists Rights Society (ARS), New York; Jimmy Ernst © 2007 Artists Rights Society (ARS), New York / ADAGP, Paris; Lyonel Feininger © 2007 Artists Rights Society (ARS), New York / VG Bild-Kunst, Bonn; Arshile Gorky © 2007 Artists Rights Society (ARS), New York; John Marin © 2007 Estate of John Marin / Artists Rights Society (ARS), New York; Reginald Marsh © 2007 Estate of Reginald Marsh / Art Students League, New York / Artists Rights Society (ARS), New York; Jackson Pollock © 2007 Pollock-Krasner Foundation / Artists Rights Society (ARS), New York; Richard Pousette-Dart © 2007 Estate of Richard Pousette-Dart / Artists Rights Society (ARS), New York; Mark Rothko © 1998 Kate Rothko Prizel & Christopher Rothko / Artists Rights Society (ARS), New York; Saul Steinberg, The Saul Steinberg Foundation / Artists Rights Society (ARS), New York.

E. W. Root
Hamilton College
Clinton, New York

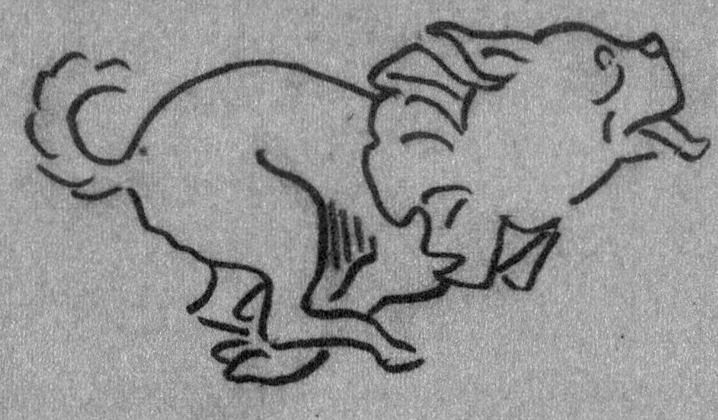

Toby going on the Rampage

Sept 1925

E. W. ROOT
HAMILTON COLLEGE
CLINTON NEW YORK

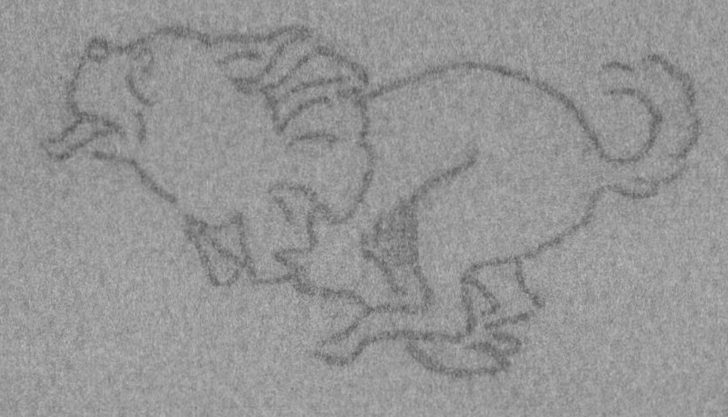

Toby going on the Rampage